Microsoft Power BI Cookbook

Creating Business Intelligence Solutions of Analytical Data Models, Reports, and Dashboards

Brett Powell

BIRMINGHAM - MUMBAI

Microsoft Power BI Cookbook

First published: September 2017

Production reference: 1220917

Published by Packt Publishing Ltd.
Livery Place
35 Livery Street
Birmingham
B3 2PB, UK.

ISBN 978-1-78829-014-2

www.packtpub.com

Credits

Author
Brett Powell

Copy Editor
Vikrant Phadkay

Reviewers
Gilbert Quevauvilliers
Ruben Oliva Ramos
Juan Tomas Oliva Ramos

Project Coordinator
Nidhi Joshi

Commissioning Editor
Amey Varangaonkar

Proofreader
Safis Editing

Acquisition Editor
Varsha Shetty

Indexer
Tejal Daruwale Soni

Content Development Editor
Mayur Pawanikar

Graphics
Tania Dutta

Technical Editor
Vivek Arora

Production Coordinator
Arvindkumar Gupta

Foreword

Microsoft Power BI Cookbook is a great example of how to leverage the multitude of features that are available in Power BI. You will find some great examples in this book that will first explain the issues and then give a solution on how to achieve the desired result. I, personally, learned something when going through this cookbook and all the recipes provided in it. This is a book that can be picked up and referenced when looking for solutions for particular challenges or issues. Likewise, it is a great read from cover to cover to expand your skills, which in turn will help build great Power BI Models for your clients/customers.

Gilbert Quevauvilliers,
Microsoft MVP - Power BI & Microsoft Power BI Consultant at Fourmoo

About the Author

Brett Powell is the owner of and business intelligence consultant at Frontline Analytics LLC, a data and analytics research and consulting firm and Microsoft Power BI partner. He has worked with Power BI technologies since they were first introduced as the SQL Server 2008R2 PowerPivot add-in for Excel 2010. He has contributed to the design and development of Microsoft and Power BI solutions of diverse scale and complexity across the retail, manufacturing, financial, and services industries. Brett regularly blogs and shares technical papers regarding the latest MSBI and Power BI features and development techniques and patterns at Insight Quest. He is also an organizer of the Boston BI User Group.

Erin Stellato, featured in *Developing Solutions for System Monitoring and Administration*, is a principal consultant at SQLskills and Microsoft Data Platform MVP.

I'd first like to thank Varsha Shetty, acquisition editor at Packt, for giving me the opportunity to author this book and her guidance throughout the planning process. I'd also like to thank the Packt board and team for approving the book outline and for their flexibility with page counts and topics. Like most Power BI projects, we followed an agile delivery model in creating this book and this allowed us to include essential details supporting the recipes and the latest Power BI features. Additionally, I'd like to thank Mayur Pawanikar, content editor at Packt, for his thorough reviews and guidance throughout the development process. His contributions were invaluable to the structure and overall quality of the book.

I'd also like to thank Gilbert Quevauvilliers and Juan Tomas Oliva Ramos for their technical reviews and suggestions.

Finally, I'd like to thank the Power BI team for creating such an amazing platform and for everyone around the Power BI community that contributes documentation, white papers, presentations, videos, blogs, and more.

About the Reviewers

Gilbert Quevauvilliers has been working in the BI space for the past 9 years. He started out learning the basics of business intelligence on the Microsoft stack, and as time went on, he became more experienced. Gilbert has since moved into the Power BI space, after starting out with Power Pivot in Excel 2010. He has used Power BI since its inception and works exclusively in it. He has been recognized with the Microsoft MVP award for his contributions to the community and helping other users.

Gilbert is currently consulting in his own company, called FourMoo (which represents the four family members). Fourmoo provides Microsoft Power BI solutions for business challenges by using customers' data and working with their business users. Gilbert also has an active blog at `http://www.fourmoo.com/blog/`. This is the first book that he has been asked to review.

> *I would like to say a big thanks to my wife, Sian, for her endless support and for helping me find the time to review this book.*

Ruben Oliva Ramos is a computer systems engineer from Tecnologico de Leon Institute, with a master's degree in computer and electronic systems engineering, teleinformatics, and networking specialization from the University of Salle Bajio in Leon, Guanajuato, Mexico. He has more than 5 years of experience in developing web applications to control and monitor devices connected with Arduino and Raspberry Pi using web frameworks and cloud services to build the Internet of Things applications.

He is a mechatronics teacher at the University of Salle Bajio and teaches students of the master's degree in design and engineering of mechatronics systems. Ruben also works at Centro de Bachillerato Tecnologico Industrial 225 in Leon, Guanajuato, Mexico, teaching subjects such as electronics, robotics and control, automation, and microcontrollers at Mechatronics Technician Career; he is a consultant and developer for projects in areas such as monitoring systems and datalogger data using technologies (such as Android, iOS, Windows Phone, HTML5, PHP, CSS, Ajax, JavaScript, Angular, and ASP.NET), databases (such as SQlite, MongoDB, and MySQL), web servers (such as Node.js and IIS), hardware programming (such as Arduino, Raspberry pi, Ethernet Shield, GPS, and GSM/GPRS, ESP8266), and control and monitor systems for data acquisition and programming.

He wrote *Internet of Things Programming with JavaScript* by Packt Publishing. He is also involved in the monitoring, controlling, and acquisition of data with Arduino and Visual Basic .NET for Alfaomega.

> *I would like to thank my savior and lord, Jesus Christ, for giving me the strength and courage to pursue this project; my dearest wife, Mayte; our two lovely sons, Ruben and Dario; my dear father, Ruben; my dearest mom, Rosalia; my brother, Juan Tomas; and my sister, Rosalia, whom I love, for all their support while reviewing this book, for allowing me to pursue my dream, and tolerating not being with them after my busy day job.*

Juan Tomás Oliva Ramos is an environmental engineer from the university of Guanajuato, with a master's degree in administrative engineering and quality. He has more than 5 years of experience in management and development of patents, technological innovation projects, and development of technological solutions through the statistical control of processes.

He is a teacher of statistics, entrepreneurship and technological development of projects since 2011. He became an entrepreneur mentor, and started a new department of technology management and entrepreneurship at Instituto Tecnologico Superior de Purisima del Rincon.

He is a Packt Publishing reviewer and he has worked on the book: *Wearable designs for Smart watches, Smart TV's and Android mobile devices.*

He has developed prototypes through programming and automation technologies for the improvement of operations, which have been registered to apply for his patent.

I want to thank God for giving me wisdom and humility to review this book.

I want to thank Packt for giving me the opportunity to review this amazing book and to collaborate with a group of committed people.

I want to thank my beautiful wife, Brenda, our two magic princesses, Regina and Renata, and our next member, Angel Tadeo, all of you, give me the strength, happiness and joy to start a new day. Thanks for being my family.

www.PacktPub.com

For support files and downloads related to your book, please visit `www.PacktPub.com`. Did you know that Packt offers eBook versions of every book published, with PDF and ePub files available? You can upgrade to the eBook version at `www.PacktPub.com`, and as a print book customer, you are entitled to a discount on the eBook copy.

Get in touch with us at `service@packtpub.com` for more details. At `www.PacktPub.com`, you can also read a collection of free technical articles, sign up for a range of free newsletters and receive exclusive discounts and offers on Packt books and eBooks.

`https://www.packtpub.com/mapt`

Get the most in-demand software skills with Mapt. Mapt gives you full access to all Packt books and video courses, as well as industry-leading tools to help you plan your personal development and advance your career.

Why subscribe?

- Fully searchable across every book published by Packt
- Copy and paste, print, and bookmark content
- On demand and accessible via a web browser

Customer Feedback

Thanks for purchasing this Packt book. At Packt, quality is at the heart of our editorial process. To help us improve, please leave us an honest review on this book's Amazon page at https://www.amazon.com/dp/1788290143.

If you'd like to join our team of regular reviewers, you can email us at customerreviews@packtpub.com. We award our regular reviewers with free eBooks and videos in exchange for their valuable feedback. Help us be relentless in improving our products!

Table of Contents

Preface

Microsoft Power BI is a business intelligence and analytics platform consisting of applications and services designed to provide coherent visual, and interactive insights into data.

This book will provide thorough, technical examples of using all primary Power BI tools and features as well as demonstrate high-impact end-to-end solutions that leverage and integrate these technologies and services. You'll get familiar with Power BI development tools and services; go deep into the data connectivity and transformation, modeling, visualization and analytical capabilities of Power BI; and see Power BI's functional programming languages of DAX and M come alive to deliver powerful solutions to address common, challenging scenarios in business intelligence.

This book will excite and empower you to get more out of Power BI via detailed recipes, advanced design and development tips, and guidance on enhancing existing Power BI projects.

What this book covers

Chapter 1, *Configuring Power BI Development Tools*, covers the installation and configuration of the primary tools and services that BI professionals utilize to design and develop Power BI content, including Power BI Desktop, the On-Premises Data Gateway, DAX Studio, and the Power BI Publisher for Excel.

Chapter 2, *Accessing and Retrieving Data*, dives into Power BI Desktop's Get Data experience and walks through the process of establishing and managing data source connections and queries.

Chapter 3, *Building a Power BI Data Model*, explores the primary processes of designing and developing robust data models.

Chapter 4, *Authoring Power BI Reports*, develops and describes the most fundamental report visualizations and design concepts. Additionally, guidance is provided to enhance and control the user experience when consuming and interacting with Power BI reports in the Power BI service and on mobile devices.

Chapter 5, *Creating Power BI Dashboards*, covers Power BI dashboards constructed to provide simple at-a-glance monitoring of critical measures and high-impact business activities.

Chapter 6, *Getting Serious with Date Intelligence*, contains three recipes for preparing a data model to support robust date intelligence and two recipes for authoring custom date intelligence measures.

Chapter 7, *Parameterizing Power BI Solutions*, covers both standard parameterization features and techniques in Power BI as well as more advanced custom implementations.

Chapter 8, *Implementing Dynamic User-Based Visibility in Power BI*, contains detailed examples of building and deploying dynamic, user-based security for both import and DirectQuery datasets, as well as developing dynamic filter context functionality to enhance the user experience.

Chapter 9, *Applying Advanced Analytics and Custom Visuals*, contains a broad mix of recipes highlighting many of the latest and most popular custom visualization and advanced analytics features of Power BI.

Chapter 10, *Developing Solutions for System Monitoring and Administration*, highlights the most common and impactful administration data sources, including Windows Performance Monitor, SQL Server Query Store, the Microsoft On-Premises Data Gateway, the MSDB system database, and Extended Events.

Chapter 11, *Enhancing and Optimizing Existing Power BI Solutions*, contains top data modeling, DAX measure, and M query patterns to enhance the performance, scalability, and reliability of Power BI datasets.

Chapter 12, *Deploying and Distributing Power BI Content*, contains detailed examples and considerations in deploying and distributing Power BI content via the Power BI service and Power BI mobile applications.

Chapter 13, *Integrating Power BI with Other Applications*, highlights new and powerful integration points between Power BI and SSAS, SSRS, Excel, PowerPoint, PowerApps, and Microsoft Flow.

What you need for this book

You will be guided through the chapters about the prerequisites. However, in order to work through the chapters, along with other components, you will primarily require the following:

- Power BI Desktop (Free download): Recommended four-core CPU and minimum 1 GB of RAM
- Windows 7-10+ or Windows Server 2008R2–2012R2

Who this book is for

This book is for BI professionals who wish to enhance their knowledge of Power BI design and development topics and to enhance the value of the Power BI solutions they deliver. Those interested in quick resolutions to common challenges and a reference guide to Power BI features and design patterns will also find this book to be a very useful resource. Some experience with Power BI will be helpful.

Conventions

In this book, you will find a number of text styles that distinguish between different kinds of information. Here are some examples of these styles and an explanation of their meaning. Code words in text, database table names, folder names, filenames, file extensions, pathnames, dummy URLs, user input, and Twitter handles are shown as follows: "Indicator columns, such as `Weekday Indicator`, `Holiday Indicator`, and `Working Day Indicator`."

A block of code is set as follows:

```
FALSE()
[Reseller Product Line] IN {"Mountain","Touring"}
[Sales Territory Group] = "Europe"
```

When we wish to draw your attention to a particular part of a code block, the relevant lines or items are set in bold:

```
Internet Net Sales (CY YTD) = CALCULATE([Internet Net Sales],
 FILTER(ALL('Date'),'Date'[Calendar Year Status] = "Current Calendar Year"
&& 'Date'[Date] <= MAX('Date'[Date])))
```

New terms and **important words** are shown in bold. Words that you see on the screen, for example, in menus or dialog boxes, appear in the text like this: "Click on **Save** and then choose the new role from **View as Roles** on the **Modeling** tab"

Warnings or important notes appear like this.

Tips and tricks appear like this.

Reader feedback

Feedback from our readers is always welcome. Let us know what you think about this book-what you liked or disliked. Reader feedback is important for us as it helps us develop titles that you will really get the most out of. To send us general feedback, simply email `feedback@packtpub.com`, and mention the book's title in the subject of your message. If there is a topic that you have expertise in and you are interested in either writing or contributing to a book, see our author guide at `www.packtpub.com/authors`.

Customer support

Now that you are the proud owner of a Packt book, we have a number of things to help you to get the most from your purchase.

Downloading the example code

You can download the example code files for this book from your account at `http://www.packtpub.com`. If you purchased this book elsewhere, you can visit `http://www.packtpub.com/support` and register to have the files emailed directly to you. You can download the code files by following these steps:

1. Log in or register to our website using your email address and password.
2. Hover the mouse pointer on the **SUPPORT** tab at the top.
3. Click on **Code Downloads & Errata**.
4. Enter the name of the book in the **Search** box.
5. Select the book for which you're looking to download the code files.
6. Choose from the drop-down menu where you purchased this book from.
7. Click on **Code Download**.

Once the file is downloaded, please make sure that you unzip or extract the folder using the latest version of:

* WinRAR / 7-Zip for Windows
* Zipeg / iZip / UnRarX for Mac
* 7-Zip / PeaZip for Linux

The code bundle for the book is also hosted on GitHub at `https://github.com/PacktPublishing/Microsoft-Power-BI-Cookbook`. We also have other code bundles from our rich catalog of books and videos available at `https://github.com/PacktPublishing/`. Check them out!

Downloading the color images of this book

We also provide you with a PDF file that has color images of the screenshots/diagrams used in this book. The color images will help you better understand the changes in the output. You can download this file from `https://www.packtpub.com/sites/default/files/downloads/MicrosoftPowerBICookbook_ColorImages.pdf`.

Errata

Although we have taken every care to ensure the accuracy of our content, mistakes do happen. If you find a mistake in one of our books-maybe a mistake in the text or the code-we would be grateful if you could report this to us. By doing so, you can save other readers from frustration and help us improve subsequent versions of this book. If you find any errata, please report them by visiting `http://www.packtpub.com/submit-errata`, selecting your book, clicking on the **Errata Submission Form** link, and entering the details of your errata. Once your errata are verified, your submission will be accepted and the errata will be uploaded to our website or added to any list of existing errata under the Errata section of that title. To view the previously submitted errata, go to `https://www.packtpub.com/books/content/support` and enter the name of the book in the search field. The required information will appear under the **Errata** section.

Piracy

Piracy of copyrighted material on the internet is an ongoing problem across all media. At Packt, we take the protection of our copyright and licenses very seriously. If you come across any illegal copies of our works in any form on the internet, please provide us with the location address or website name immediately so that we can pursue a remedy. Please contact us at `copyright@packtpub.com` with a link to the suspected pirated material. We appreciate your help in protecting our authors and our ability to bring you valuable content.

Questions

If you have a problem with any aspect of this book, you can contact us at `questions@packtpub.com`, and we will do our best to address the problem.

1
Configuring Power BI Development Tools

In this chapter, we will cover the following recipes:

- Configuring Power BI Desktop options and settings
- Installing the On-Premises Data Gateway
- Installing Power BI Publisher for Excel
- Installing and configuring DAX Studio

Introduction

Power BI is a suite of business analytics tools and services that work together to access data sources, shape, analyze and visualize data, and share insights. Although not all tools are required for all projects or deployments of Power BI, synergies are available by utilizing the unique features of multiple tools as part of integrated solutions encompassing diverse data sources and visualization types.

In this chapter, we walk through the installation and configuration of the primary tools and services BI professionals utilize to design and develop Power BI content including Power BI Desktop, the On-Premises Data Gateway, DAX Studio, and the Power BI Publisher for Excel. Additionally, as Power BI tools and services are regularly updated with new features and enhancements, resources are identified to stay up-to-date and to best take advantage of these tools for your projects.

It's assumed that the reader has access to a Power BI Pro license, rights to download and install (or allow installation) the development tools on their machine, and has the necessary access and rights to deploy and manage content in the Power BI Service and utilize the Power BI mobile applications. Power BI licensing options and assigning and managing these rights is outside the scope of this book.

Configuring Power BI Desktop options and settings

Power BI Desktop is the primary tool used to develop the visual and analytical content which can then be deployed and collaborated on in the Power BI Service and optionally embedded in other applications and portals or even shared on the public internet. Although Power BI Desktop runs as a single application, it includes three tightly integrated components with their own options and settings:

- The Get Data and Query Editor experience, with its underlying M language and data mashup engine
- The **SQL Server Analysis Services** (**SSAS**) tabular data modeling engine and its DAX analytical language
- The interactive reporting and visualization engine formerly known as Power View

Configuring and leveraging these capabilities, in addition to advanced analytics and customization features such as R, mobile layout, and natural language queries, makes it possible to build robust and elegant BI and analytics solutions.

Getting ready

Most organizations set policies restricting downloads of software from the internet and many choose to centrally distribute a specific version of Power BI Desktop. For example, the March 2017 version of Power BI Desktop would be available on a corporate IT portal and it would be the approved version for 1-2 months while the April 2017 version is internally evaluated. Additionally, BI organizations may define policies restricting the use of native queries, custom visualizations, and establishing source privacy level settings.

How to do it...

Power BI Desktop is a relatively large download at 110 MB but can be installed simply and provides an intuitive **Options** and **Settings** interface for configuration.

Installing and running Power BI Desktop

1. Download the Power BI Desktop installer package. The Windows installer package (`.msi`) can be downloaded from the Power BI Service or from the Power BI downloads page (`https://powerbi.microsoft.com/en-us/downloads/`).

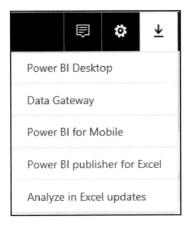

Figure 1: Download from the Power BI Service

The Download dropdown, along with Settings and Notifications, is available in the upper-right corner of the Power BI Service window. The On-Premises Data Gateway and Power BI Publisher for Excel described later this chapter are also available for download.

Figure 2: Downloaded Installer Package for 64-bit Power BI Desktop

The web service will determine whether the 64-bit (x64) or 32-bit version of Power BI Desktop is appropriate for your machine's operating system. If Power BI Desktop has already been installed on your machine and notifications of new versions are enabled, you will have the option to initiate the download of the latest Power BI Desktop version when it's available. Notifications of new versions are enabled by default and available under **Global Options | Updates**.

2. Install Power BI Desktop. Launch the installation wizard from the `.msi` package and complete the installation after accepting the license agreement and choosing the file directory.

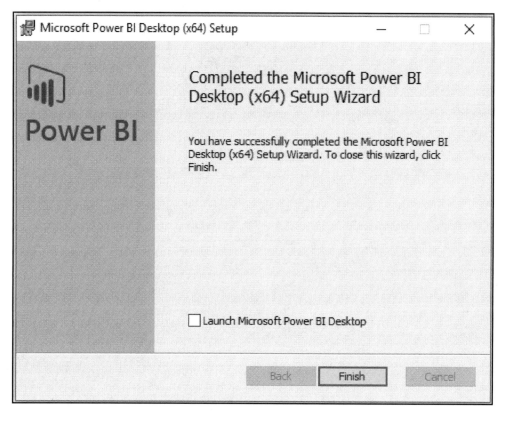

Figure 3: Successful Installation of Power BI Desktop

Configuring Power BI Desktop options

Developers of Power BI content should become familiar with the settings available in Power BI options and data source settings as these configurations determine available functionality, user interface options, default behaviors, performance, and the security of the data being accessed.

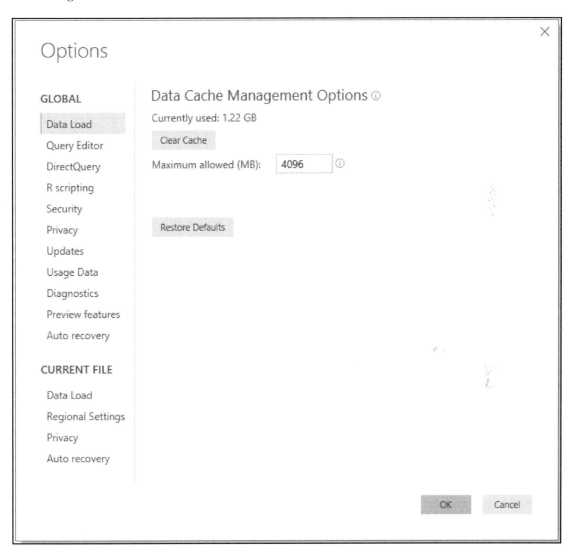

Figure 4: Power BI Desktop Options (July 2017)

GLOBAL options are applied to all Power BI Desktop files created or accessed by the user, while **CURRENT FILE** options must be defined for each Power BI Desktop file. The following steps are recommended for **GLOBAL** options.

1. On the **Data Load** tab, confirm that the currently used data cache is below the **Maximum allowed (MB)** setting. If it is near the limit and local disk space is available, increase the value of the **Maximum allowed (MB)**. Do not clear the cache unless local disk space is unavailable as this will require additional, often unnecessary, queries to be executed at design time.

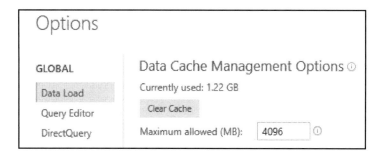

Figure 5: Global Data Load options

2. On the **Query Editor** tab, display both the query settings pane and the formula bar. This will allow for greater visibility to the structure and specific M functions utilized by individual queries.

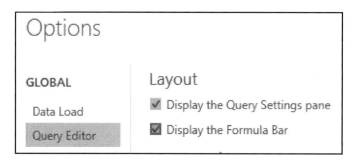

Figure 6: Global Query Editor options

3. On the **DirectQuery** tab, enable the **Allow unrestricted measures in DirectQuery mode** setting.

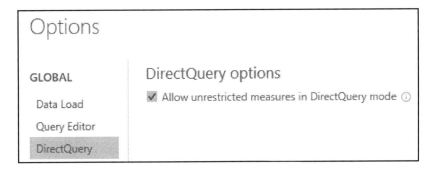

Figure 7: Global DirectQuery options

 This enables additional DAX functions to be used in metrics against DirectQuery data models that are necessary to meet many common requirements. Although all DAX functions are supported for DirectQuery models, certain functions are not optimized for DirectQuery; they may not generate an efficient SQL query and may require local, single-threaded resources to execute. For this reason, among others discussed in `Chapter 3`, *Building a Power BI Data Model*, the default Import mode is often a better option than DirectQuery for more complex data models.

4. On the **Security** tab, select the option to require user approval for new native database queries. Native queries are the user-specified SQL statements passed to data sources as opposed to the queries Power BI generates internally.

Figure 8: Security Option for Native Database Queries

- Optionally, set **Show security warning when adding a custom visual to a report** as well.

 From a security standpoint, custom visuals can be divided between those developed by Microsoft, those developed by third parties but available in the Office Store, and finally those developed by third parties but available exclusively from sources outside the Office Store. Custom visuals developed by Microsoft have been thoroughly tested for safety. Third-party custom visuals available in the Office Store have been through a validation process though there is no guarantee that all code paths have been tested. Third-party visuals not available in the Office Store should therefore be used with caution and it's recommended to establish a policy regarding the use of custom visuals.

5. On the privacy tab, configure the privacy levels for all data sources and enable the option to **Always combine data according to your Privacy Level settings for each source**. See *How it Works...* for details on these settings.

GLOBAL	Privacy Levels
Data Load	⦿ Always combine data according to your Privacy Level settings for each source
Query Editor	○ Combine data according to each file's Privacy Level settings
DirectQuery	○ Always ignore Privacy Level settings ⓘ
R scripting	
Security	Learn more about Privacy Levels
Privacy	

Figure 9: Global Privacy Level Options

6. From the **Data Source** settings, select an individual source and choose **Edit Permissions** to configure the privacy level:

Figure 10: Edit Permissions of a Data Source

 The **Edit Permissions** dialog is also required to update credentials as data source system credentials expire or password resets are required.

7. Enable **Preview features** for evaluation purposes:

GLOBAL	Preview features
Data Load	The following features are available for you to try in this release. Preview features might change or be removed in future releases.
Query Editor	
DirectQuery	☑ Amazon Redshift Learn more
R scripting	☑ Impala Learn more
Security	☑ Snowflake Learn more
Privacy	☑ Shape map visual Learn more
Updates	☑ Custom Report Themes Learn more
Usage Data	☑ Enable cross filtering in both directions for DirectQuery Learn more
Diagnostics	☑ ArcGIS Maps for Power BI Learn more
Preview features	☑ New matrix visual Learn more
Auto recovery	☑ Numeric range slicer Learn more

Figure 11: Preview Features available with the March 2017 Release of Power BI Desktop

8. On the **Data Load** tab for the **CURRENT FILE**, disable the automatic detection of column types and relationships. These model design decisions should be implemented explicitly by the Power BI developer with knowledge of the source data.

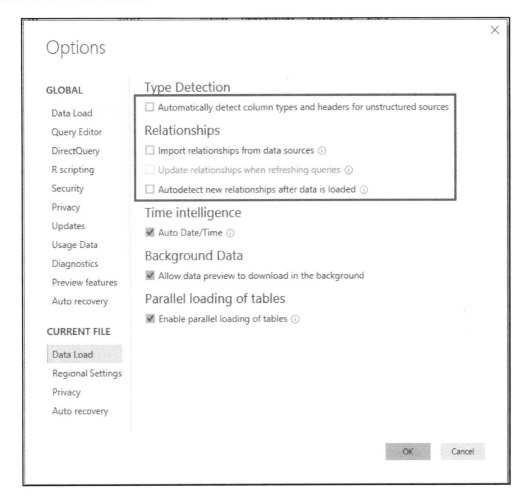

Figure 12: Disabled Relationships Options for the Current File

- As the current file options, it's necessary to apply these settings with each Power BI Desktop file to avoid default behaviors.

For example, the default detection of column types from unstructured sources such as text or Excel files will create a hardcoded dependency on the column names in the source file. Additionally, this default transformation will be applied prior to any filter expression and thus can require more time and resources to perform the refresh.

How it works...

Defining data source privacy levels such as **Organizational** or **Private** prevents the data from these sources being exposed to external or inappropriate data sources during data retrieval processes. For example, if a query calls for merging a **Private** data source with a **Public** data source, the join operation will be executed locally--the private data will not be sent to the public source. In the absence of **Privacy Level** settings set for data sources, the M query engine will look to optimize for performance by utilizing source system resources.

The options under **Preview features** change with new versions as some previous options become generally available and new preview features are introduced. The monthly Power BI Desktop update video and blog post provides details and examples of these new features. Usually a restart of the Power BI Desktop application is required once a new preview option has been activated, and tooltips and dialogs in Power BI Desktop will advise you if a preview feature is being used.

The enable tracing option in the **Diagnostic Options** section writes out detailed trace event data to the local hard drive and thus should only be activated for complex troubleshooting scenarios.

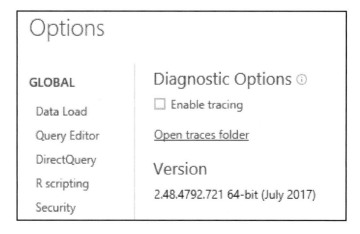

Figure 13: Global Diagnostics Options

There's more...

As a modern cloud and service-oriented analytics platform, Power BI delivers new and improved features across its toolset on a monthly cadence. These scheduled releases and updates for Power BI Desktop, the Power BI Service, the On-Premises Data Gateway, Power BI mobile applications, and more reflect customer feedback, industry trends, and the Power BI team's internal ideas and product roadmap.

BI professionals responsible for developing and managing Power BI content can both stay informed of these updates as well as review detailed documentation and guidance on implementing the features via the Microsoft Power BI Blog (`http://bit.ly/2ObcQb4`), Power BI Documentation (`http://bit.ly/2o22qi4`), and the Power BI Community (`http://bit.ly/2mqiuxP`).

Figure 14: Blog post and supporting video for the March 2017 update to Power BI Desktop

The Power BI Community portal provides a robust, searchable hub of information across common topics as well as an active, moderated forum of user experiences and troubleshooting. The community also maintains its own blog featuring examples and use cases from top community contributors, and links to local **Power BI User Groups** (**PUGs**) and relevant events such as Microsoft Data Insights Summit.

See also

Power BI's advantages over Excel

Although Power BI Desktop and Excel 2016 both contain the same data transformation and modeling BI engines (M and DAX, respectively), features exclusive to Power BI Desktop and the features in the Power BI Service exclusive to datasets created from Power BI Desktop create an incentive to migrate existing Excel data models and queries to Power BI Desktop. At the time of writing, those top incremental features and benefits are the following:

Row-level security roles	Custom third-party Visuals
DirectQuery Data models	Data-Driven Alerts
Max Size of 1 GB per dataset*	Quick Insights
Interactive reports*	Interactive Mobile Reports
Bidirectional relationships	Mobile report layouts
Natural language queries	Advanced analytics with R
Power BI report templates	Custom Report Themes

The maximum size of an Excel dataset that can be published to Power BI is 250 MB, compared to 1 GB for Power BI Desktop. With Power BI Premium, even larger Power BI datasets will be supported (ie 10GB, 100GB). Additionally, Excel reports created via connections to external data sources such as Analysis Services databases or published Power BI datasets are not interactive when published to Power BI (that is, slicers or drill down) and their data does not update with refreshes to the source dataset. Therefore, only Excel reports based on the more limited Excel data model can be published to include interactivity and the scheduled refresh. Additionally, new features added or improved in Power BI Desktop's monthly update cycle such as new M or DAX functions become available to Excel in Office 365 subscription updates. Thus, even with the latest Office 365 update, new features may not be available in Excel for months.

Power BI Security and Data Source Privacy

The documentation and the official Power BI Security white paper are available here: http://bit.ly/22NHzRS and detailed documentation on data source privacy levels is available here: http://bit.ly/2nC0Lmx

Installing the On-Premises Data Gateway

The On-Premises Data Gateway, originally referred to as the Power BI Enterprise Gateway, is a Windows service that runs in on-premises environments. The sole purpose of the gateway is to support secure (encrypted) and efficient data transfer between On-Premises data sources and MS Azure services such as Power BI, PowerApps, MS Flow, and Azure Logic Apps via an outbound connection to the Azure Service Bus. Once installed, a gateway can be used to schedule data refreshes of imported Power BI datasets and to support Power BI reports and dashboards built with DirectQuery Power BI datasets and those which use Live Connections to **SSAS** (**SQL Server Analysis Services**) databases.

A single On-Premises Data Gateway can support the refresh and query activity for multiple data sources, and permission to use the gateway can be shared with multiple users. Currently the gateway supports all common data sources via scheduled imports (including ODBC connections) and many of the most common sources via Live Connection and DirectQuery.

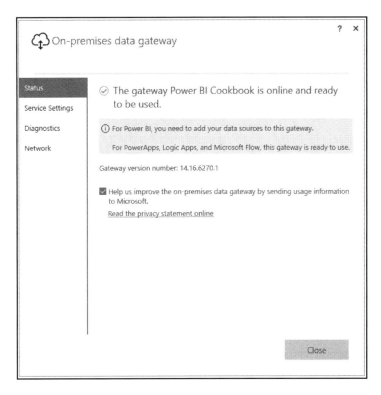

Figure 15: User interface of the On-Premises Data Gateway (March 2017)

Getting ready

Hardware and network configuration

The hardware resources required by the gateway vary based on the type of connection (import versus live connection), the usage of the reports and dashboards in the Power BI service, and the proportion of data volume handled by the gateway versus the on-premises source systems. It's recommended to start with eight-core CPUs with an 8 GB of RAM server. This machine cannot be a domain controller, and to maintain availability of Power BI content, the gateway server should be always on and connected to the internet.

Based on an analysis of current and projected workloads, the gateway resources can be scaled up or down and optionally additional gateways can be installed on separate servers to distribute the overall Power BI refresh and query deployment workload. For example, one gateway server can be dedicated to scheduled refresh/import workloads, thus isolating this activity from a separate gateway server responsible for DirectQuery and Live Connection queries.

The gateway does not require inbound ports to be opened and defaults to the outbound port of TCP 443, 5671, 5672 and 9350 through 9354. The gateway can be forced to use HTTPS communication exclusively and avoid the use of IP addresses via both the UI and the configuration files directly but this may impair performance. For the default communication mode, it's recommended to whitelist the IP addresses in your data region in your firewall. This list is updated weekly and is available via the Microsoft Azure Datacenter IP list (http://bit.ly/2oeAQyd).

How to do it...

Installation of on-premises gateway

1. Download the latest Microsoft On-Premises Data Gateway (http://bit.ly/2nNNveZ).
2. Save and run the install application on the machine to use as the gateway server.

Figure 16: The Gateway Installation Application

3. Choose the **On-premises data gateway (recommended)**.

Figure 17: Selection of On-Premises Data Gateway

4. Choose the file directory for the installation and accept the terms of use and privacy agreement.

5. Sign in to the Power BI Service to register the gateway:

Figure 18: Registering the Gateway

6. Enter a user-friendly name for the gateway and a recovery key. Click on **Configure**.

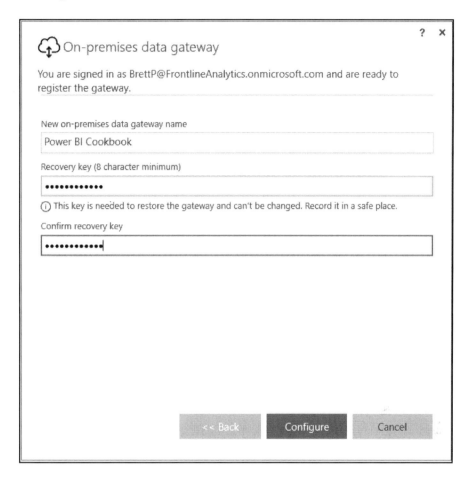

Figure 19: Creating the Gateway Recovery Key

 With the Gateway installed and registered, data sources, gateway admins, and authorized data source users can be added in the Power BI Service. A **Manage Gateways** option will be available under the Gear Icon in the Power BI Service. See the *Configuring Refresh Schedules and DirectQuery Connections with the On-Premises Data Gateway*recipe of `Chapter 12`, *Deploying and Distributing Power BI Content*, for details on this process.

How it works...

- As new versions of the gateway are available, a notification is made available in the Status tab of the On-Premises Data Gateway UI as per *Figure 1*. The Power BI Gateway team recommends that updates should be installed as they become available.
- The On-Premises Data Gateway, rather than the personal gateway, is required for the DirectQuery datasets created in this book and the use of other Azure services in the Microsoft Business Application Platform.
- The Power BI service uses read-only connections to on-premises sources but the other services (for example, PowerApps) can use the gateway to write, update, and delete these sources.

Gateway recovery key

The recovery key is used to generate a symmetric and asymmetric key which encrypts data source credentials and stores them in the cloud. The credentials area is only decrypted by the gateway machine in response to a refresh or query request. The recovery key will be needed in the following three scenarios:

- Migrating a gateway and its configured data sources to a different machine
- Restoring a gateway to run the service under a different domain account or restoring a gateway from a machine that has crashed
- Taking over ownership of an existing gateway from an existing gateway administrator

It's important that the recovery key is stored in a secure location accessible to the BI/IT organization. Additionally, more than one user should be assigned as a gateway administrator in the Power BI service.

There's more...

The Power BI Ideas Forum (`http://bit.ly/2n5bFPd`) is a valuable source for identifying requested features and enhancements and their status relative to future releases. For example, filtering on the Idea status of 'Started' implies that the feature has already been reviewed and planned and, with development activity taking place, will likely be released, at least in an initial or preview form, relatively soon. Filtering on **Planned** ideas, particularly those with higher community vote counts, provides a sense of impactful updates to be released over a longer time horizon.

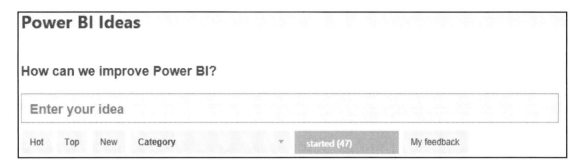

Figure 20: Power BI Ideas Forum filtered on the status of started

See also...

- Details of configuring and managing data sources through the On-Premises Gateway are covered in Chapter 12, *Deploying and Distributing Power BI Content*.
- Guidance on analyzing performance monitor counters associated with gateway activity is included in Chapter 10, *Developing Solutions for System Monitoring and Administration*.

Installing Power BI Publisher for Excel

Excel-based data analysis and reporting artifacts such as pivot tables, charts, and cell range formula expressions with custom formatting remain pervasive in organizations. Although a significant portion of this content and its supporting processes can be migrated to Power BI, and despite the many additional features and benefits this migration could provide, Power BI is not intended as a replacement for all Excel reporting or **SQL Server Reporting Services** (**SSRS**) reporting. Organizations and particularly departments which use Excel extensively, such as Finance and Accounting, may prefer to leverage these existing assets and quickly derive value from Power BI by both deploying Excel content to Power BI and analyzing Power BI-hosted data from within Excel.

The Microsoft Power BI Publisher for Excel supplements Excel's native Power BI publishing features of uploading Excel workbooks to the Power BI Service or exporting Excel workbook data to Power BI datasets, as individual Excel objects can be "pinned" to Power BI dashboards and managed from the local Excel file.

Figure 21: The Power BI Publisher Tab in Excel 2016

Additionally, the Power BI Publisher's data source providers support Excel-to-Power BI connection strings reflecting the local user's rights to the given Power BI hosted source.

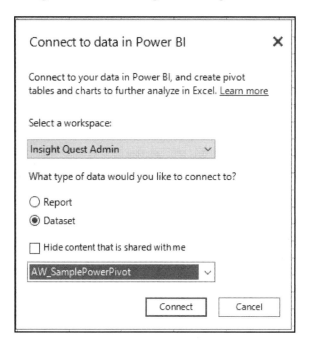

Figure 22: Connecting to Power BI sources via Power BI Publisher

How to do it...

Installation of Power BI Publisher for Excel

1. Download the Power BI Publisher (`http://bit.ly/2nCsWC0`).
2. Choose the version appropriate for the version of Microsoft Office installed: 32-bit or 64-bit.

Name	Date modified	Type	Size
PowerBIpublisher_[64bit][en-us].msi	3/22/2017 1:12 PM	Windows Installer Package	46,512 KB

Figure 23: Power BI Publisher for Excel Install Package

3. Install the publisher.
4. Accept the license agreement and choose the file directory.

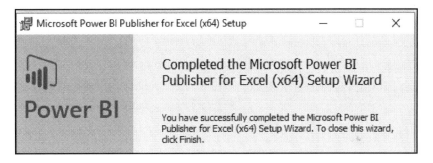

Figure 24: Successful installation of Power BI Publisher for Excel

The drivers required to connect to Power BI hosted sources from Excel, such as the Excel OLE DB driver for Analysis Services, are automatically updated with each release. Additionally, once Power BI Publisher is installed, it's not necessary to use the **Analyze in Excel** option from the Power BI Service, which downloads an ODC file referencing the given model. The necessary connection to Power BI is created when the data source is selected via the Publisher dialog.

5. Access the Power BI Publisher from Excel. Upon opening Excel following successful installation, you should get a message box advising of Power BI Publisher for Excel. It can be deactivated and the Power BI tab in the Excel ribbon should be visible. If it is not visible, you can check out the COM Add-ins dialog in Excel.

- Click on **File** and then **Options** in Excel to bring up the Excel Options menu
- Select **Add-Ins** and use the drop-down menu at the bottom to choose **COM Add-ins**
- Click on **Go...** to launch the following **COM Add-ins** window

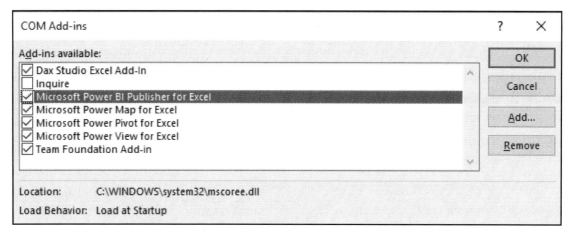

Figure 25: Excel COM-Add-ins

6. Use the Profile icon to sign into the Power BI Service. Sign in will be automatic with future instances of Excel.

Figure 26: The Profile command from Power BI Publisher for Excel

There's more...

The following is a list of 11 blogs that contain many articles and examples on Power BI's tools and features:

Blogger(s)	Blog	URL
Michael Carlo	Power BI Tips and Tricks	`http://powerbi.tips`
Chris Webb	Crossjoin	`https://blog.crossjoin.co.uk`
Rob Collie Avi Singh	PowerPivotPro	`https://powerpivotpro.com`
Alberto Ferrari Marco Russo	SQL BI	`http://www.sqlbi.com`
Kasper De Jonge	Kasper On BI	`https://www.kasperonbi.com`
Matt Allington	ExceleratorBI	`http://exceleratorbi.com.au/exceleratorblog`
Ruth Martinez	Curbal	`https://curbal.com/blog`
Dustin Ryan	SQL Dusty	`https://sqldusty.com`
Reza Rad	RADACAD	`http://radacad.com/blog`
Imke Feldman	The BIccountant	`http://www.thebiccountant.com`
Brett Powell	Insight Quest	`https://insightsquest.com`
Gilbert Quevauvilliers	Fourmoo	`https://www.fourmoo.com/blog`

With the exception of Kasper On BI, all of these blogs are from non-Microsoft employees and thus do not necessarily reflect the views of MS or recommended practices with its products. Additionally, several of these blogs are not exclusive to Power BI; they may also include coverage of other MSBI, Azure, SQL Server, and Office 365 tools and services.

Installing and Configuring DAX Studio

DAX (**Data Analysis Expressions**) is the "language of Power BI" as it's used to create the measures and queries visualized in Power BI reports and dashboards. Power BI generates and submits DAX queries to the source data model based on the structure of the visualization, user selections, and filters, just as other tools such as Excel generate MDX queries based on the selections and structure of pivot tables and slicers from workbooks. DAX expressions are also used to define security roles and can optionally be used to create columns and tables in data models based on other tables and columns in the model, which can be refreshed at processing time and used by measures and queries. Given that DAX serves the same function in **SQL Server Analysis Services** (**SSAS**) Tabular models and Power Pivot for Excel models, it's essential that BI professionals have a robust tool for developing and analyzing DAX code and the data models containing these expressions.

DAX Studio is a third-party tool used to query data models, edit and format code, browse the structure and metadata of data models, and analyze the performance and execution characteristics of DAX queries. For larger and more complex data models and expressions, as well as projects involving multiple models, DAX Studio becomes an essential supplement to the development and performance tuning processes.

How to do it...

Installation of DAX Studio

1. Download the latest version from CodePlex (`https://daxstudio.codeplex.com/`).

 CodePlex is in the process of shutting down and thus DAX Studio may be available on GitHub or another open source project repository in the future. The CodePlex archive may provide guidance to the new home for DAX Studio and the SQLBI.com blog's link to DAX Studio will likely be updated to the latest version as well.

2. Save the `.exe` application file to your local PC.

3. A notification is displayed as new versions are available.

Name	Date modified	Type	Size
DaxStudio_2_6_0a_setup.exe	3/22/2017 9:10 AM	Application	3,990 KB

Figure 27: Downloaded Setup Application from CodePlex

4. Initiate the installation and setup Process.
5. Accept the license agreement and choose a folder path to install the tool.
6. Choose whether the DAX Studio add-in for Excel will also be installed.
   - The Add-In for Excel is required to connect to Power Pivot for Excel data models
   - Additionally, when DAX Studio is opened from Excel, query results can be exported directly to Excel tables

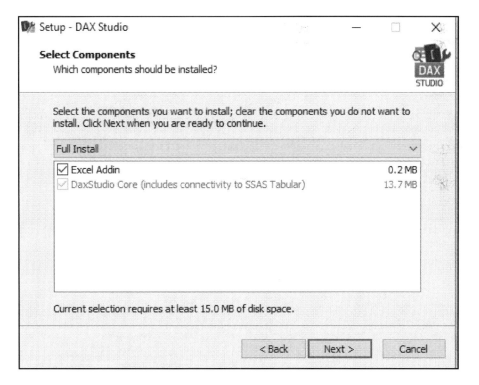

Figure 28: DAX Studio Setup

- Upon full installation including the Add-in for Excel, a DAX Studio icon will appear on the **Add-Ins** Tab in the Excel Ribbon; the DAX Studio Add-in can be deactivated via the manage **COM Add-ins** dialog available from Excel--**Options | Add-Ins** tab.

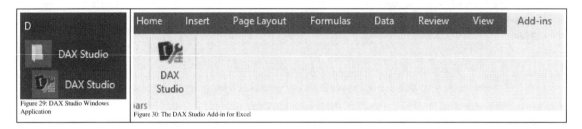

Figure 29: DAX Studio Windows Application

Figure 30: The DAX Studio Add-in for Excel

The full installation with the Excel add-in is recommended as this enables direct output of DAX query results to Excel workbook tables and is required for connecting to Power Pivot data models.

Configuration of DAX Studio

1. Open an Excel workbook.
2. Open a Power BI Desktop file.
3. From the **Add-Ins** tab of the toolbar, activate DAX Studio.

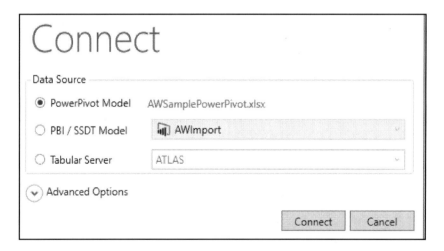

Figure 31: The DAX Studio Add-in for the Excel Connect Dialog

4. Close the Excel workbook.
5. Launch the DAX Studio standalone Windows application.
6. Connect to a Power BI Desktop file or SSAS Tabular instance.

> The **Advanced Options** settings of the **Connect** dialog establishes a connection in the context of the `Sales Territory-North America` security role defined in the model.

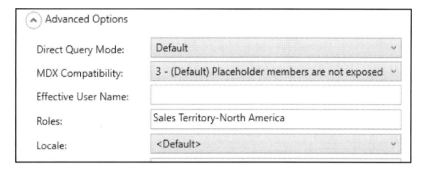

Figure 32: Advanced connect options

7. Enable the DirectQuery Trace setting from the Options menu (**File | Options**).
8. This provides visibility to the SQL queries passed from DirectQuery models.

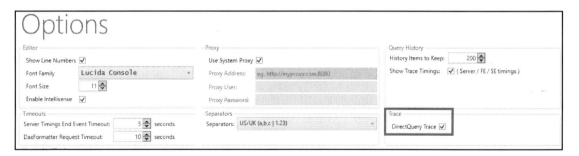

Figure 33: DirectQuery trace enabled

How it works...

- The standalone application provides the same functionality as the Excel add-in, excluding connectivity to Power Pivot for Excel data models and Excel output options
- Powerful configuration options include the ability to specify a security role, effective user name identity, and **Locale** when defining connections to data models and when analyzing trace events associated with DirectQuery data models (that is, the SQL statements generated and passed to sources)
- With DirectQuery Trace enabled, a connection to a DirectQuery model will expose the SQL statements passed to the source system in the **Server Timings** window

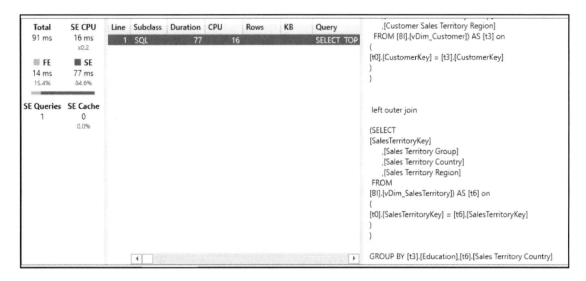

Figure 34: DAX Studio Trace of a DirectQuery Model

There's more...

Guy in a Cube video channel

An additional resource for learning and deploying Power BI is Adam Saxton's *Guy in a Cube* video channel (`http://bit.ly/2o2lRqU`). These videos, currently released every Tuesday and Thursday, feature concise, hands-on reviews and resolutions to common issues and scenarios. They also have high-level summaries of recent Power BI updates and releases. As a member of the MSBI content team, Adam can incorporate specific guidance from Microsoft product and technical teams, and regularly identifies recent blog posts from the wider Power BI community.

2
Accessing and Retrieving Data

In this chapter, we will cover the following recipes:

- Viewing and analyzing M functions in the Query Editor
- Establishing and managing connections to data sources
- Building source queries for DirectQuery models
- Importing data to Power BI Desktop models
- Applying multiple filtering conditions
- Choosing columns and column names
- Transforming and cleansing source data
- Creating custom and conditional columns
- Integrating multiple queries
- Choosing column data types
- Visualizing the M library

Introduction

Power BI Desktop contains a very rich set of data source connectors and transformation capabilities that support the integration and enhancement of source data. These features are all driven by a powerful functional language and query engine, **M**, which leverages source system resources when possible and can greatly extend the scope and robustness of the data retrieval process beyond what's possible via the standard query editor interface alone. As with almost all BI projects, the design and development of the data access and retrieval process has great implications for the analytical value, scalability, and sustainability of the overall Power BI solution.

In this chapter, we dive into Power BI Desktop's Get Data experience and walk through the process of establishing and managing data source connections and queries. Examples are provided of using the Query Editor interface and the M language directly to construct and refine queries to meet common data transformation and cleansing needs. In practice and as per the examples, a combination of both tools is recommended to aid the query development process.

A full explanation of the M language and its implementation in Power BI is outside the scope of this book, but additional resources and documentation are included in the *There's more...* and *See also* sections of each recipe.

Viewing and analyzing M functions

Every time you click on a button to connect to any of Power BI Desktop's supported data sources or apply any transformation to a data source object, such as changing a column's data type, one or multiple M expressions are created reflecting your choices. These M expressions are automatically written to dedicated M documents and, if saved, are stored within the Power BI Desktop file as Queries. M is a functional programming language like F#, and it's important that Power BI developers become familiar with analyzing and later writing and enhancing the M code that supports their queries.

Getting ready

1. Build a query through the user interface that connects to the
   `AdventureWorksDW2016CTP3` SQL Server database on the ATLAS server and
   retrieves the `DimGeography` table, filtered by United States for English.

2. Click on **Get Data** from the **Home** tab of the ribbon, select SQL Server from the
   list of database sources, and provide the server and database names.
   - For the **Data Connectivity mode**, select **Import**.

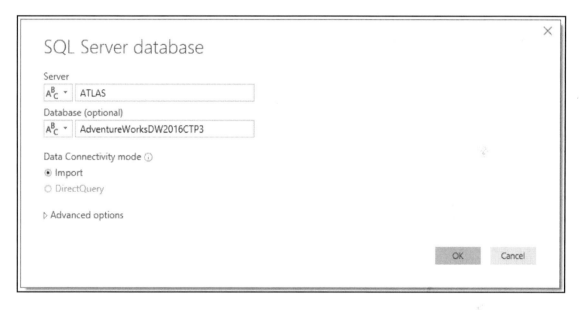

Figure 1: The SQL Server Get Data dialog

A navigation window will appear, with the different objects and schemas of
the database. Select the `DimGeography` table from the **Navigation** window
and click on **Edit**.

3. In the **Query Editor** window, select the **EnglishCountryRegionName** column and then filter on **United States** from its dropdown.

Figure 2: Filtering for United States only in the Query Editor

At this point, a preview of the filtered table is exposed in the Query Editor and the Query Settings pane displays the previous steps.

Figure 3: The Query Settings pane in the Query Editor

How to do it...

Formula Bar

1. With the Formula Bar visible in the Query Editor, click on the **Source step** under **Applied Steps** in the **Query Settings** pane.
   - You should see the following formula expression:

Figure 4: The SQL.Database() function created for the Source step

2. Click on the **Navigation step** to expose the following expression:

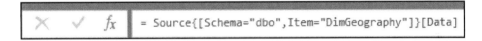

Figure 5: The metadata record created for the Navigation step

- The navigation expression (2) references the source expression (1)
- The Formula Bar in the Query Editor displays individual query steps, which are technically individual M expressions
- It's convenient and very often essential to view and edit all the expressions in a centralized window, and for this, there's the **Advanced Editor**

 M is a functional language, and it can be useful to think of query evaluation in M as similar to Excel spreadsheet formulas in which multiple formulas can reference each other. The M engine can determine which expressions are required by the final expression to return and evaluate only those expressions.

- Per the guidance in `Chapter 1`, *Configuring Power BI Development Tools*, the display setting for both the Query Settings pane and the Formula bar should be enabled as **GLOBAL** | **Query Editor** options.

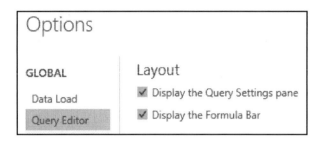

Figure 6: Global layout options for the Query Editor

- Alternatively, on a per file basis, you can control these settings and others from the **View** tab of the Query Editor toolbar.

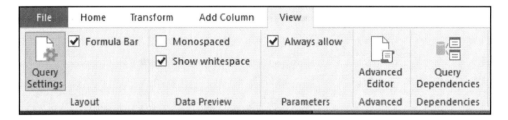

Figure 7: Property settings of the View tab in the Query Editor

Advanced Editor window

Given its importance to the query development process, the **Advanced Editor** dialog is exposed on both the **Home** and **View** tabs of the Query Editor.

It's recommended to use the Query Editor when getting started with a new query and when learning the M language. After several steps have been applied, use the Advanced Editor to review and optionally enhance or customize the M query. As a rich, functional programming language, there are many M functions and optional parameters not exposed via the Query Editor; going beyond the limits of the Query Editor enables more robust data retrieval and integration processes.

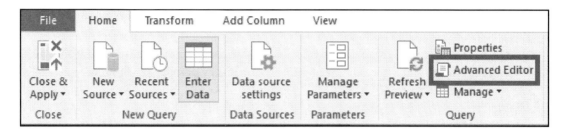

Figure 8: The Home tab of the Query Editor

1. Click on **Advanced Editor** from either the **View** or **Home** tabs (*Figure 8* and *Figure 9*, respectively).
   - All M function expressions and any comments are exposed

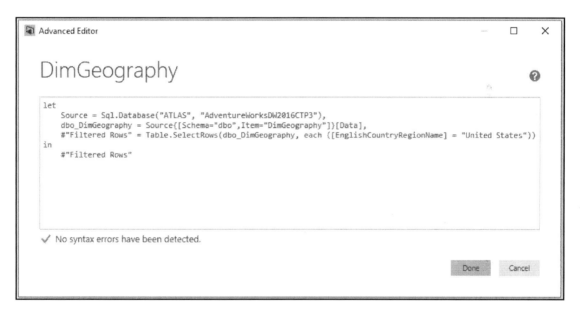

Figure 9: The Advanced Editor view of the DimGeography query

When developing retrieval processes for Power BI models, consider these common ETL questions:

- How are our queries impacting the source systems?
- Can we make our retrieval queries more resilient to changes in source data such that they avoid failure?

- Is our retrieval process efficient and simple to follow and support or are there unnecessary steps and queries?
- Are our retrieval queries delivering sufficient performance to the BI application?
- Is our process flexible such that we can quickly apply changes to data sources and logic?

M queries are not intended as a substitute for the workloads typically handled by enterprise ETL tools such as SSIS or Informatica. However, just as BI professionals would carefully review the logic and test the performance of SQL stored procedures and ETL packages supporting their various cubes and reports environment, they should also review the M queries created to support Power BI models and reports.

How it works...

Two of the top performance and scalability features of M's engine are Query Folding and Lazy Evaluation. If possible, the M queries developed in Power BI Desktop are converted (folded) into SQL statements and passed to source systems for processing. M can also reduce the required resources for a given query by ignoring any unnecessary or redundant steps (variables).

M is a case-sensitive language. This includes referencing variables in M expressions (`RenameColumns` versus `Renamecolumns`) as well as the values in M queries. For example, the values "Apple" and "apple" are considered unique values in an M query; the `Table.Distinct()` function will not remove rows for one of the values.

Variable names in M expressions cannot have spaces without a hash sign and double quotes. Per Figure 10, when the Query Editor graphical interface is used to create M queries this syntax is applied automatically, along with a name describing the M transformation applied. Applying short, descriptive variable names (with no spaces) improves the readability of M queries. See the *Strengthening Data Import and Integration Processes* recipe in `Chapter 11`, *Enhancing and Optimizing Existing Power BI Solutions* for additional details.

Query folding

The query from this recipe was "folded" into the following SQL statement and sent to the ATLAS server for processing.

Native Query

```
select [_].[GeographyKey],
    [_].[City],
    [_].[StateProvinceCode],
    [_].[StateProvinceName],
    [_].[CountryRegionCode],
    [_].[EnglishCountryRegionName],
    [_].[SpanishCountryRegionName],
    [_].[FrenchCountryRegionName],
    [_].[PostalCode],
    [_].[SalesTerritoryKey],
    [_].[IpAddressLocator]
from [dbo].[DimGeography] as [_]
where [_].[EnglishCountryRegionName] = 'United States' and [_].[EnglishCountryRegionName] is not null
```

Figure 10: The SQL statement generated from the DimGeography M query

Right-click on the **Filtered Rows** step and select **View Native Query** to access the **Native Query** window from *Figure 11*:

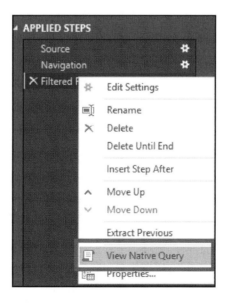

Figure 11: View Native Query in Query Settings

Finding and revising queries that are not being folded to source systems is a top technique for enhancing large Power BI datasets. See the *Pushing Query Processing Back to Source Systems* recipe of `Chapter 11`, *Enhancing and Optimizing Existing Power BI Solutions* for an example of this process.

M query structure

- The great majority of queries created for Power BI will follow the `let...in` structure as per this recipe, as they contain multiple steps with dependencies among them.
- Individual expressions are separated by commas.
- The expression referred to following the `in` keyword is the expression returned by the query.
- The individual step expressions are technically "variables", and if the identifiers for these variables (the names of the query steps) contain spaces then the step is placed in quotes, and prefixed with a # sign as per the **Filtered Rows** step in *Figure 10*.

Lazy evaluation

- The M engine also has powerful "lazy evaluation" logic for ignoring any redundant or unnecessary variables, as well as short-circuiting evaluation (computation) once a result is determinate, such as when one side (operand) of an OR logical operator is computed as True. The order of evaluation of the expressions is determined at runtime; it doesn't have to be sequential from top to bottom.
- In the following example, a step for retrieving `Canada` was added and the step for the `United States` was ignored. Since the `CanadaOnly` variable satisfies the overall let expression of the query, only the `Canada` query is issued to the server as if the `United States` row were commented out or didn't exist.

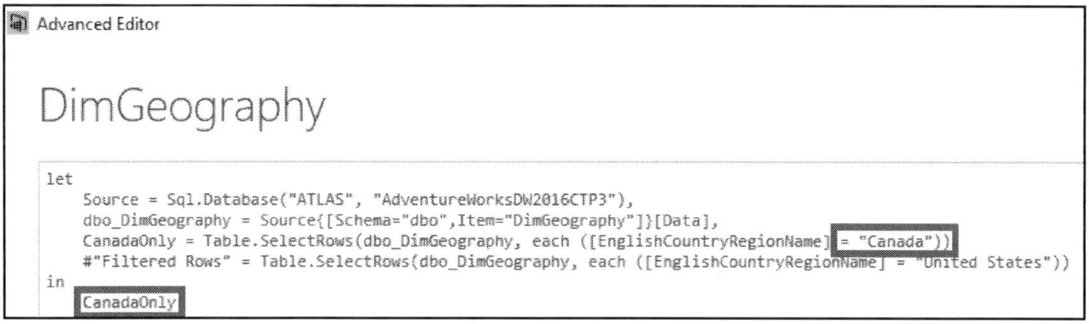

Figure 12: Revised query that ignores Filtered Rows step to evaluate Canada only

View Native Query (*Figure 12*) is not available given this revision, but a SQL Profiler trace against the source database server (and a refresh of the M query) confirms that `CanadaOnly` was the only SQL query passed to the source database.

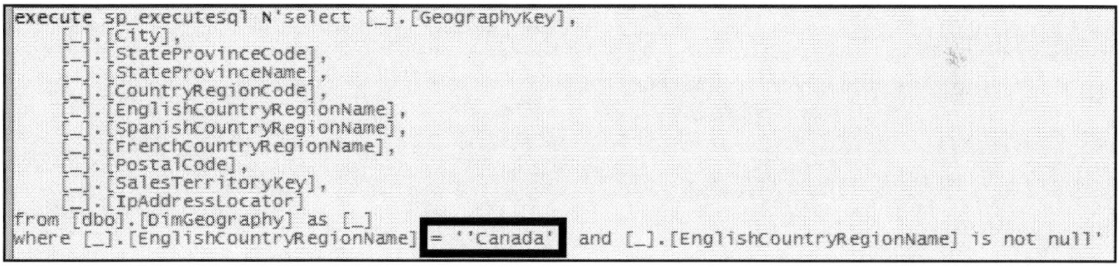

Figure 13: Capturing the SQL statement passed to the server via SQL Server Profiler trace

There's more...

Partial query folding

- A query can be "partially folded", in which a SQL statement is created resolving only part of an overall query
- The results of this SQL statement would be returned to Power BI Desktop (or the on-premises data gateway) and the remaining logic would be computed using M's in-memory engine with local resources
- M queries can be designed to maximize the use of the source system resources, by using standard expressions supported by query folding early in the query process

- Minimizing the use of local or on-premises data gateway resources is a top consideration

Limitations of query folding

- No folding will take place once a native SQL query has been passed to the source system. For example, passing a SQL query directly through the **Get Data** dialog. The following query, specified in the **Get Data** dialog, is included in the **Source** step:

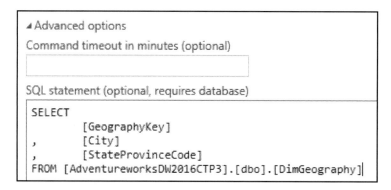

Figure 14: Providing a user defined native SQL query

- Any transformations applied after this native query will use local system resources. Therefore, the general implication for query development with native or user-defined SQL queries is that if they're used, try to include all required transformations (that is, joins and derived columns), or use them to utilize an important feature of the source database not being utilized by the folded query, such as an index.
- Not all data sources support query folding, such as text and Excel files.
- Not all transformations available in the Query Editor or via M functions directly are supported by some data sources.
- The privacy levels defined for the data sources will also impact whether folding is used or not.
- SQL statements are not parsed before they're sent to the source system.
- The `Table.Buffer()` function can be used to avoid query folding. The table output of this function is loaded into local memory and transformations against it will remain local.

See also...

M language references

- The two official resources for documentation on the M language are the Power Query M language specification (`http://bit.ly/2oaJWwv`) and the Power Query M Reference (`http://bit.ly/2noOzTX`).
- The following table introduces the main concepts of the M language utilized in this book.

Concept	Definition
Expression	Formulas evaluated to yield a single value. Expressions can reference other values such as functions and may include operators.
Value	The result of evaluation of an expression. Values can be categorized into kinds which are either primitive, such as text ("abc"), or structured kinds such as tables and lists.
Function	A value that produces a new value based on the mapping of input values to the parameters of the function. Functions can be invoked by passing parameter values.
Type	A value that classifies other values. The structure and behavior of values is restricted based on the classification of its type such as Record, List, or Table.
let	An expression that allows a set of unique expressions to be assigned names (variables) and evaluated (if necessary) when evaluating the expression following the in expression in a let . . . . in construct.
Variable	A unique, named expression within an environment to be conditionally evaluated. Variables are represented as **Applied Steps** in the Query Editor.
Environment	A set of variables to be evaluated. The global environment containing the M library is exposed to root expressions.
Evaluation	The computation of expressions. Lazy evaluation is applied to expressions defined within let expressions; evaluation occurs only if needed.

Operators	A set of symbols used in expressions to define the computation. The evaluation of operators depends on the values to be operated on.

Establishing and managing connections to data sources

There are two primary components of queries in Power BI: the data source and the query logic executed against this source. The data source includes the connection method (DirectQuery or Import), its privacy setting, and the authentication credentials. The query logic consists of the M expressions represented as queries in the Query Editor and stored internally as M documents.

In a typical corporate BI tool, such as **SQL Server Reporting Services** (**SSRS**), the properties of a data source such as the server and database name are defined separately from the queries that reference them. In Power BI Desktop, however, by default each individual query created explicitly references a given data source (for example, server A and database B). This creates an onerous, manual process of revising each query if necessary to change the source environment or database.

This issue is addressed in the following steps by using dedicated M queries to centralize and isolate the data source information from the individual queries. Additionally, detail and reference information is provided on managing source credentials and data source privacy levels.

Getting ready

1. Create a query from a database, which would serve as the source for other queries via the standard **Get Data** and Query Editor experience described earlier in this chapter.
   - Select **Get Data** from the ribbon, choose SQL Server, select a table or view, and click on **Edit**.
   - A preview of the data will appear in the Query Editor and the **Advanced Editor** window will expose the server and database name.

Advanced Editor

DimEmployee

```
let
    Source = Sql.Database("ATLAS", "AdventureWorksDW2016CTP3")
    dbo_DimEmployee = Source{[Schema="dbo",Item="DimEmployee"]}[Data]
in
    dbo_DimEmployee
```

Figure 15: Source Properties within Query

How to do it...

Isolate data sources from individual queries

In this example, a separate data source connection query is created and utilized by individual queries. By associating many individual queries to a single (or few) data source queries, it's easy to change the source system or environment such as when switching from a Development to a **User Acceptance Testing** (**UAT**) environment.

1. Create a new, blank query by selecting the **Blank Query** data source type from the Get Data icon. The **New Source** icon in the Query Editor can also be used.

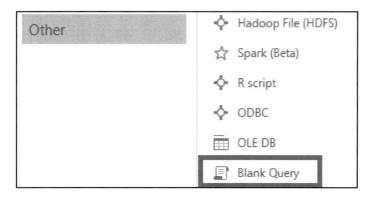

Figure 16: Creating a blank query

---

2. Enter the source information into the blank query. This should follow the syntax from the **Source** step of the first query.

3. Give the source query an intuitive name, such as AdWorksProd.

Figure 17: Data source expression used in a blank query

4. Replace the **Source** step expression of the DimEmployee query with the name of the new query.

```
let
    Source = AdWorksProd,
    dbo_DimEmployee = Source{[Schema="dbo",Item="DimEmployee"]}[Data]
in
    dbo_DimEmployee
```

Figure 18: Revised expression to reference a new query

5. Click on **Close and Save** and refresh the query to confirm that the change was successful.

6. To further validate the retrieval, revise the source query to point to a separate database containing the same table. Make note of one or two differences between the tables in the two source systems, and observe the query preview change based on the parameters used in the source query.

Now make a copy of the source query and revise the source information to point to the different environment, such that you always reference either source query without manual changes.

Query groups

You should also use query Groups to help isolate data source and staging queries from queries loaded to the dataset.

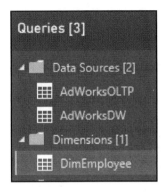

Figure 19: Data Source Queries

1. Duplicate a query or copy and paste via the right-click context menu for a query.
2. Create a new group by right-clicking in a blank area in the Queries window or an existing group.
   - With the `DimEmployee` table referencing the source query, you can simply duplicate this query and then revise the **Navigation** step (via Navigator or Formula Bar) to retrieve a different table from this source into the model, such as the `Account` dimension table.

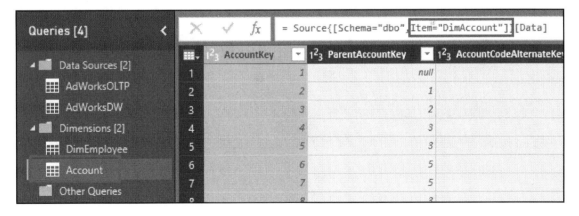

Figure 20: Account table retrieved and still referencing AdWorksDW for Source

3. Ensure that the Data Source queries are not loaded to the data model.
   - Right-click on the tables and disable the **Enable Load** option such that they only exist to support retrieval queries and are invisible to the model and report layers.

The **Query Dependencies** view in the Query Editor (**View** | **Query Dependencies**) provides a visual representation of the relationships similar to the Diagram view available for Power BI Desktop's data modelling component.

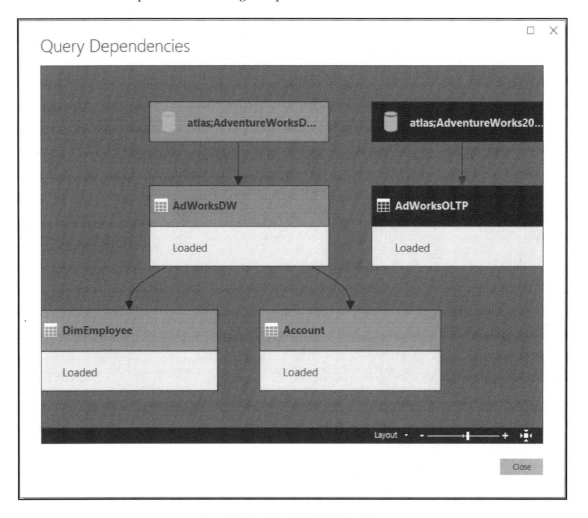

Figure 21: The Query Dependencies View in Query Editor

Manage source credentials and privacy levels

The purpose of this example is to demonstrate the process of managing data source settings, including authentication credentials and privacy levels:

1. Open the **Data Source** settings. Click on the **Global Permissions** radio button such that your settings are persisted in other Power BI Desktop reports.
2. Select a data source.
3. Click on **Edit Permissions**.

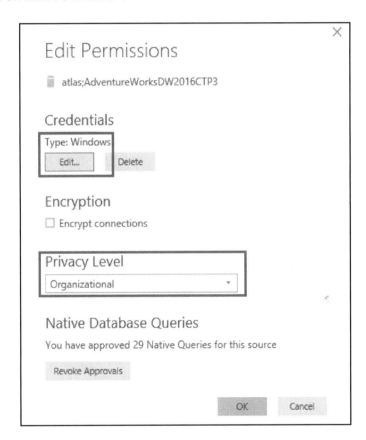

Figure 22: Edit Permissions for a Data Source

Definitions of the available **Privacy Level** settings are provided in the *How it works...* section.

How it works...

Data Source settings

- Power BI Desktop saves a data source credential for each data source defined and a privacy level for that source. It's necessary to modify these credentials as passwords change and to set privacy levels on data sources, to prevent confidential information from being exposed to external sources during the query folding process.
- Data source credentials and settings are not stored in the PBIX file but rather on the computer of the installed application. Privacy levels are described in the following table and a reference to additional documentation is provided in the See also section.

Data source privacy settings

Privacy Setting	Description
Private	A Private data source is completely isolated from other data sources during query retrieval. For example, marking a text file as private would prevent that data from being processed on an external server.
Organizational	An Organizational data source is isolated from all public data sources but is visible to other organizational data sources during retrieval.
Public	A Public data source is visible to other sources. Only files, Internet sources, and workbook data can be marked as public.

- Just as relational databases such as SQL Server consider many potential query plans, the M engine also searches for the most efficient methods of executing queries given the data sources and query logic defined.
- In the absence of data source privacy settings, the M engine is allowed to consider plans that merge disparate data sources. For example, a local text file of customer names can be merged with an external or third-party server given the better performance of the server.
- Defining privacy settings isolates data sources from these operations. Given the increased likelihood of local resource usage, query performance may be reduced.

There's more...

- In this example, a single query with only one expression was used by multiple queries, but more complex interdependencies can be designed to manage the behavior and functionality of the retrieval and analytical queries.
- This recipe illustrates the broader concept used in later recipes--"composability" of functions calling other functions--and this is one of the primary strengths of functional programming languages such as M, DAX, R, and F#.

See also

- Data source privacy levels documentation: `http://bit.ly/29blFBR`

Building source queries for DirectQuery models

One of the most valuable features of Power BI is its deep support for real-time and streaming datasets--the ability to provide immediate visibility to business processes and events as this data is created or updated. As Power BI Desktop's data modeling engine reflects the latest **SQL Server Analysis Services** (**SSAS**) features, including the enhanced DirectQuery mode for SSAS 2016, it becomes feasible to design DirectQuery models in Power BI Desktop and thus avoid the scalability limitations and scheduled refresh requirements of import-based models.

This recipe walks through the primary steps in designing the data access layer that supports a DirectQuery model in Power BI Desktop. As these models are not cached into memory and dynamically convert the DAX queries from report visualizations to SQL statements, guidance is provided to maintain performance. Additional details, resources, and documentation on DirectQuery's current limitations and comparisons with the default import mode are also included to aid your design decision.

Getting ready

1. Choose a database to serve as the source for the DirectQuery data model.
2. Create a logical and physical design of the fact and dimension tables of the model including the relationship keys and granularity of the facts.
3. Determine or confirm that each fact-to-dimension relationship has referential integrity.
   - Providing this information to the DirectQuery model allows for more performant inner join queries.
4. Create view objects in the source database to provide efficient access to the dimensions and facts defined in the physical design.

 Be aware that DirectQuery models are limited to a single source database and not all databases are supported for DirectQuery. If multiple data sources are needed, such as SQL Server and and Oracle or Teradata and Excel, then the default Import mode model, with scheduled refresh to the Power BI Service, will be the only option.

How to do it...

1. Create a new Power BI Desktop file (`.pbix`).
2. Create a Query using DirectQuery **Data Connectivity mode**.
   - Click on **Get Data** and choose **SQL Server database**.

3. Select a view to be used by the model via the navigator.

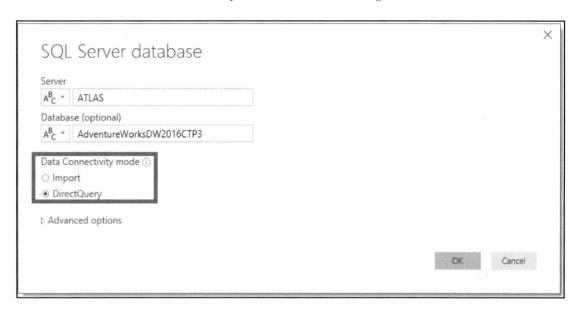

4. Duplicate the initial query and revise the Item value of the **Navigation** step to reference an additional view supporting the model:

5. Repeat step 3 until all the dimensions and facts are being accessed by their associated SQL view.

6. Create a data source query to store the server and database connection information. This is similar to the previous recipe (duplicate a query and use the **Source** step) but to maintain the DirectQuery connection, do not remove or alter the navigation step; simply point the `in` to the Source step.

AdWorksDW

```
let
    Source = Sql.Database("ATLAS", "AdventureWorksDW2016CTP3"),
    BI_vDim_SalesTerritory = Source{[Schema="BI",Item="vDim_Currency"]}[Data]
in
    Source
```

Figure 25: A DirectQuery Data Source Query

Note from this example that M queries do not have to follow a top-down order and do not have to return the final step or variable. In this case, the second variable expression is ignored and only the source database is referenced. The fact and dimension table queries used in the DirectQuery model can reference this query.

7. Disable the **Enable Load** setting of the source query and update the individual queries to reference this query.

Figure 26: DirectQuery Model Queries

- When complete, the data source query will be grayed out (*Figure 30*) and all queries will reference this source.
- The **Report Canvas** view will confirm that the model is in **DirectQuery** mode via the status bar at the bottom right (*Figure 27*) and the **Data** view, which is visible for import models, will not be visible.

Figure 27: DirectQuery Status in Power BI Desktop

Applying M transformations with DirectQuery models

- The M transformation functions supported in DirectQuery are limited by compatibility with the source system. The Query Editor will advise when a transformation is not supported in **DirectQuery** mode per *Figure 32*.

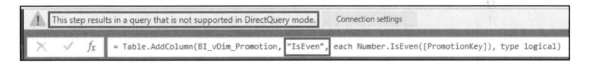

Figure 28: A warning in Query Editor that the IsEven M function is not supported in DirectQuery Mode

- Given this limitation and the additional complexity the M-based transforms would add to the solution, it's recommended to embed all the necessary logic and transforms in the source relational layer.
- Ideally, the base tables in the source database themselves would reflect these needs. As a secondary option, the layer of views used to support the DirectQuery Model can be modified as well to incorporate new or additional logic.

- If the database objects themselves cannot be revised, the `Value.Native()` M function can be used to directly pass the SQL statement from Power BI Desktop to the source database as per *Figure 29*.

```
ProductNativeQry

let
    Source = AdWorksDW,
    ProductNativeQuery = Value.NativeQuery(Source,
"SELECT
        P.ProductKey
,       P.Class AS 'Product Class'
,       p.Color as 'Product Color'
,       p.EnglishProductName as 'Product Name'
,       p.ListPrice as 'List Price'
,       p.ModelName as 'Product Model'
,       p.Weight as 'Product Weight'
,       p.Style as 'Product Style'
,       p.StandardCost as 'Standard Cost'
,       p.ProductLine as 'Product line'
,       p.Status as 'Product Status'
,       S.EnglishProductSubcategoryName AS 'Product Subcategory'
,       C.EnglishProductCategoryName AS 'Product Category'
FROM
DBO.DimProduct AS P
LEFT JOIN DBO.DimProductSubcategory AS S
ON P.ProductSubcategoryKey = S.ProductSubcategoryKey
LEFT JOIN DBO.DimProductCategory AS C
ON S.ProductCategoryKey = C.ProductCategoryKey")
in
    ProductNativeQuery
```

Figure 29: The Value.Native() function used to pass a SQL statement to a source system

How it works...

- As report visualizations are refreshed or interacted with in Power BI, the DAX queries from each visual or `tile` are translated into SQL statements and utilize the source SQL statements to return the results.
- Be aware that Power BI does cache query results with DirectQuery models. Therefore, when accessing a recently utilized visual, a local cache may be used rather than a new query sent to the source.

- DAX Studio can provide visibility to the specific queries sent to the source.

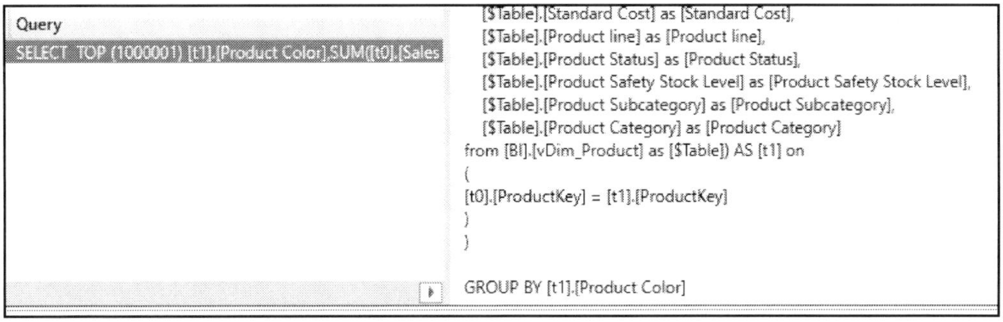

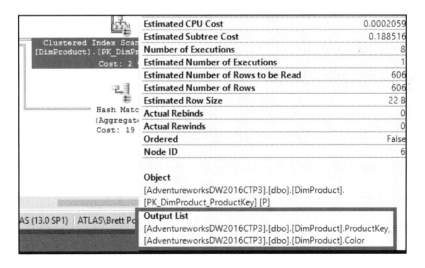

Figure 30: DAX Studio Trace of a DirectQuery Power BI Desktop Model

- The SQL statements passed from Power BI to the DirectQuery data source include all columns from the tables referenced by the visual.
- For example, a Power BI visual with total sales grouped by product category would result in a SQL statement that selects the columns from both tables (for example, `Product Color` or `Order Quantity`) and implements the join defined in the model.
- However, as the SQL statement passed embeds these source views as derived tables, the relational engine is able to generate a query plan that only scans the required columns to support the join and aggregation.

Figure 31: Execution Plan of a DirectQuery SQL Statement

There's more...

DirectQuery project candidates

Three common candidates for DirectQuery model projects are the following:

- The data model is larger than the current 1 GB file size limit or there's insufficient RAM for an in-memory SSAS model.
    - Power BI Premium is expected to raise this file size limit soon as well as support incremental data refresh
- Access to near real-time data is of actionable or required value to users or other applications such as with notifications.
    - For example, an updateable Nonclustered Columnstore index could be created on OLTP disk-based tables or memory optimized tables in SQL Server 2016 to provide near real-time access to database transactions
- A high performance and/or read-optimized system is available to service report queries such as a SQL Server or Azure SQL Database with the Clustered Columnstore index applied to fact tables.
    - Azure SQL Data Warehouse is not recommended for Power BI in DirectQuery mode

In summary, the performance and scalability of DirectQuery models is primarily driven by the relational data source. A de-normalized star schema with referential integrity and a system that's isolated from OLTP workloads is recommended if near real-time visibility is not required. Additionally, in-memory and columnar features available to supported DirectQuery sources are recommended for reporting and analytical queries.

DirectQuery performance

- DirectQuery models generate outer join SQL queries by default to ensure that measures return the correct value even if there's not a related dimension.
- However, you can configure DirectQuery models to send inner join queries via the modeling window's **Assume referential integrity** setting (see *Figure 32*).
- Along with source system resources, this is one of the top factors contributing to the DirectQuery model's performance.

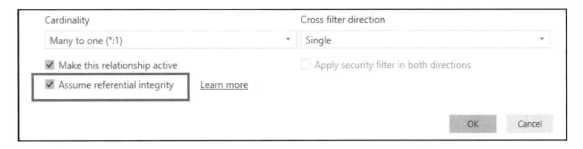

Figure 32: Activating the referential Integrity Assumption in Relationships

- Of course, you should ensure that there is referential integrity in the source before enabling this setting as incorrect results could be returned.
- The design of the source relational schema and the hardware resources of this system can, of course, greatly impact the performance of DirectQuery models.
- A classic star-schema design with denormalized tables is recommended to reduce the required join operations at query time.
- Optimizing relational fact tables with column store technologies such as the Clustered Columnstore Index for SQL Server 2016 and table partitions will also significantly benefit DirectQuery models.
- Not all DAX functions are optimized for DirectQuery. It's important to utilize the optimized functions when possible when defining DAX measures.

See also

- Power BI Desktop DirectQuery documentation: `http://bit.ly/2nUoLOG`
- Nine of the most common data sources are currently supported for DirectQuery datasets

SQL Server	Azure SQL Database	Azure SQL Data Warehouse
SAP HANA	Oracle Database (v12+)	Teradata Database
Amazon Redshift	Impala	Snowflake

Table 1: Supported DirectQuery Data Sources

- The on-premises data gateway documentation provides a detailed list of data sources broken down by the connectivity options supported: Scheduled Refresh or Live/DirectQuery (`http://bit.ly/2oKc7SP`)

The Power BI team have expressed their intent to expand the list of DirectQuery-supported sources to include other sources such as IBM DB2, SAP Business Warehouse, MySQL, Google BigQuery, and others. As of this writing, Spark (version .9 and above), SAP Business Warehouse, and IBM Netezza are available as Beta or Preview DirectQuery sources.

Importing data to Power BI Desktop models

Import is the default data connectivity mode for Power BI Desktop, and the import models created in Power BI Desktop use the same in-memory, columnar compressed storage engine (Vertipaq) featured in SSAS Tabular 2016+ import models. Import mode models support the integration of disparate data sources (for example, SQL Server and DB2) and allow more flexibility in developing metrics and row-level security roles given via full support for all DAX functions.

This recipe describes a process of using M and the Query Editor to develop the queries supporting a standard star-schema analytical model. A **staging query** approach is introduced as a means of efficiently enhancing the dimensions of a model, and tips are included to use less resources during refresh and to avoid refresh failures from revised source data. More details of these methods are included in other recipes in this chapter.

How to do it...

Denormalize a dimension

In this example, the `DimProduct`, `DimProductSubcategory`, and `DimProductCategory` tables are integrated into one query. This query will include all product rows, only the English language columns, and user-friendly names.

Figure 33: Source Tables for Product Dimension

Many-to-one relationships have been defined in the source database.

1. Create three queries for each source table and disable their loads.
2. Use query group folders in the Query Editor to isolate these queries.

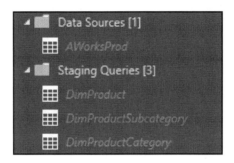

Figure 34: Staging Queries

- The gray font indicates that the queries will not be loaded into the model.

```
let
    Source = AWorksProd,
    DimProduct = Source{[Schema = "dbo",Item = "DimProductSubcategory"]}[Data]
in
    DimProduct
```

Figure 35: Subcategory Table referenced via DimProduct Variable

- Each staging query references the dedicated data source query (`AWorksProd`) that specifies the server and database.
- In this example, the `AWorksProd` query has the following syntax:
  `Sql.Database("ATLAS","AdventureWorksDW2016CTP3")`

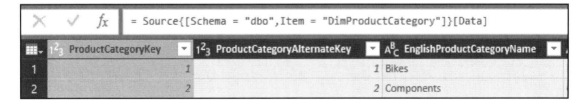

Figure 36: Query Preview of DimProductCategory

3. Create a new (blank) query and name it Product.

4. In the Product query, use the `Table.NestedJoin()` function to join the `DimProduct` and `DimProductSubcategory` queries created in step 1.

- A left outer join is required to preserve all `DimProduct` rows since the foreign key column to `DimProductCategory` allows null values.

5. Add a `Table.ExpandColumns()` expression to retrieve the necessary columns from the `DimProductSubcategory` table.

```
let
    ProductSubCatJoin =
        Table.NestedJoin(DimProduct,"ProductSubcategoryKey",DimProductSubcategory,"ProductSubcategoryKey",
            "SubCatColumn",JoinKind.LeftOuter),

    ProductSubCatColumns =
        Table.ExpandTableColumn(ProductSubCatJoin,"SubCatColumn",
            {"EnglishProductSubcategoryName","ProductCategoryKey"},  {"Product Subcategory", "ProductCategoryKey"})
in
    ProductSubCatColumns
```

Figure 37: Product Subcategory Join

- The `join` function inserts the results of the join into a column (`SubCatColumn`) as table values.
- The second expression converts these table values into the necessary columns from the `Subcategory` query and provides the simple `Product Subcategory` column name.

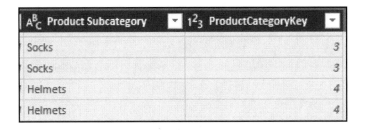

A^B_C Product Subcategory	1²₃ ProductCategoryKey
Socks	3
Socks	3
Helmets	4
Helmets	4

Figure 38: Product Subcategory Columns Added

- The query preview in the Query Editor will expose the new columns.

6. Add another expression with a `Table.NestedJoin()` function that joins the previous expression (the Product to Subcategory join) with the `DimProductCategory` query.

7. Just like step 4, use a `Table.ExpandTableColumn()` function in a new expression to expose the required Product Category columns.

```
ProductCatJoin =
    Table.NestedJoin(ProductSubCatColumns,"ProductCategoryKey",DimProductCategory,"ProductCategoryKey",
        "ProdCatColumn",JoinKind.LeftOuter),

ProductCatColumns =
    Table.ExpandTableColumn(ProductCatJoin, "ProdCatColumn",
        {"EnglishProductCategoryName"}, {"Product Category"})

in ProductCatColumns
```

Figure 39: Joining to Dim Product Category

- The first expression adds the results of the join to `DimProductCategory` (the right table) to the new column (`ProdCatColumn`).
- The second expression adds the `Product Category` columns required and revises the `EnglishProductCategoryName` column to `Product Category`.
- A left outer join was necessary with this join operation as well since the product category foreign key column on `DimProductSubcategory` allows null values.

8. Write an expression that selects the columns needed for the load to the data model with a `Table.SelectColumns()` function.

9. Add a final expression to rename these columns via `Table.RenameColumns()` to eliminate references to the English language and provide spaces between words.

```
SelectProductColumns =
    Table.SelectColumns(ProductCatColumns,
        {"ProductKey", "EnglishDescription","EnglishProductName",
        "Product Subcategory", "Product Category"
        })

RenameProductColumns =
    Table.RenameColumns(SelectProductColumns,
        {
        {"EnglishDescription", "Product Description"},
        {"EnglishProductName", "Product Name"}
        })

in
    RenameProductColumns
```

Figure 40: Selected Columns and Renamed

- The preview in the Query Editor will present the results of steps 1 through 8:

ProductKey	Product Description	Product Name	Product Subcategory	Product Category
212	Universal fit, well-vented, light...	Sport-100 Helmet, Red	Helmets	Accessories
213	Universal fit, well-vented, light...	Sport-100 Helmet, Red	Helmets	Accessories
214	Universal fit, well-vented, light...	Sport-100 Helmet, Red	Helmets	Accessories
215	Universal fit, well-vented, light...	Sport-100 Helmet, Black	Helmets	Accessories
216	Universal fit, well-vented, light...	Sport-100 Helmet, Black	Helmets	Accessories
217	Universal fit, well-vented, light...	Sport-100 Helmet, Black	Helmets	Accessories

Figure 41: Product Query Results

- It's not necessary to rename `ProductKey` since this column will be hidden from the reporting layer.
- In practice, the product dimension would include many more columns.
- The denormalized `Product` query can now support a three-level hierarchy in the Power BI Desktop model to significantly benefit reporting and analysis.

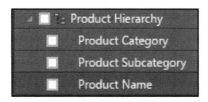

Figure 42: Product Hierarchy

Provide automatic sorting

The goal of this example is to provide automatic sorting of an attribute in report visuals. Specifically, the United States regional organizations should appear next to one another by default in visuals. By default, the Central Division (a part of the USA), appears between Canada and France given the alphabetical sorting of text columns:

1. Add a `Table.Sort()` expression to the import query for the Organization dimension.
    - The columns for the sort should be at the parent or higher level of the hierarchy.

2. Add an expression with the `Table.AddIndexColumn()` function that will add a sequential integer based on the table sort applied in step 1.

```
OrgSorted = Table.Sort(Source,
        {
            {"Parent Organization", Order.Ascending},
            {"Organization Currency", Order.Ascending}
        }),
    OrgSortIndex = Table.AddIndexColumn(OrgSorted, "OrgSortIndex", 1, 1)
in
    OrgSortIndex
```

Figure 43: Sort Order and Index Column Expressions

- With this expression, the `Source` dimension is first sorted by the `Parent Organization` column and then by `Organization Currency`. The new index column starts at the first row of this sorted table with an incremental growth of 1 per row.

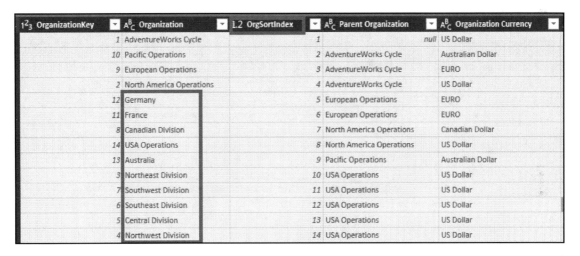

1²₃ OrganizationKey	Aᴮc Organization	1.2 OrgSortIndex	Aᴮc Parent Organization	Aᴮc Organization Currency
1	AdventureWorks Cycle	1		null US Dollar
10	Pacific Operations	2	AdventureWorks Cycle	Australian Dollar
9	European Operations	3	AdventureWorks Cycle	EURO
2	North America Operations	4	AdventureWorks Cycle	US Dollar
12	Germany	5	European Operations	EURO
11	France	6	European Operations	EURO
8	Canadian Division	7	North America Operations	Canadian Dollar
14	USA Operations	8	North America Operations	US Dollar
13	Australia	9	Pacific Operations	Australian Dollar
3	Northeast Division	10	USA Operations	US Dollar
7	Southwest Division	11	USA Operations	US Dollar
6	Southeast Division	12	USA Operations	US Dollar
5	Central Division	13	USA Operations	US Dollar
4	Northwest Division	14	USA Operations	US Dollar

Figure 44: Modified Organization Dimension Query

3. In the **Data View**, select the `Organization` column.

4. From the **Modeling** tab, set the **Sort by Column** dropdown to the index column created in step 2.

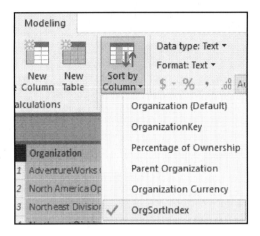

Figure 45: **Sort By in Data View**

5. Finally, right-click on the **OrgSortIndex** option and select **Hide** in **Report View**.

- Visuals using the Organization column will now sort the values by their parent organization such that the USA organizations appear together (not alphabetically).

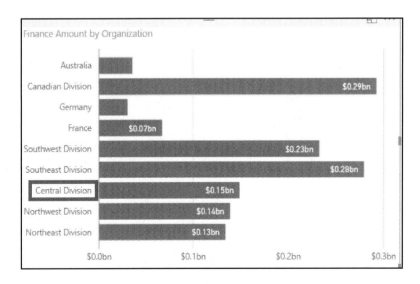

Figure 46: Organization Automatically Sorted

How it works...

- The default join kind for `Table.NestedJoin()` is left outer join. However, as other join kinds are supported (for example, inner, anti, and full outer), explicitly specifying this parameter in expressions is recommended.
- Left outer joins were required in the product table example as the foreign key columns on `DimProduct` and `DimProductSubcategory` both allowed null values.
- Inner joins implemented either via `Table.NestedJoin()` or `Table.Join()` functions would be recommended for performance purposes otherwise.
- Additional details on the joining functions as well as tips on designing inline queries as an alternative to staging queries are covered in the *Integrating and working with multiple queries* recipe.

There's more...

One GB dataset limit and Power BI Premium

- Power BI Desktop files (`.pbix`) larger than 1 GB in size cannot be published to shared capacity in the Power BI service. However, with a Power BI Premium capacity provisioned (dedicated, isolated hardware), datasets up to 10GB in size are expected to be supported by October of 2017. Moreover, an incremental data refresh feature identified on the Power BI Premium whitepaper will likely make it possible to support much larger datasets in the future.
  - See Chapter 12 (*Deploying and Distributing Power BI Content*) for additional details on Power BI Premium.
- Scalability is one of the main drivers of migrating a Power BI model to a **SQL Server Analysis Services** (SSAS) instance. The model can be migrated to an on-premises SSAS tabular server or to Azure Analysis Services.
- In the absence of SSAS migration and any new partitioning or incremental data refresh feature available to Power BI models, it's important to design data models that compress well and only include essential columns and grains.

See also

- Power BI Desktop Dataset Limits: `http://bit.ly/2od5gDX`
- Azure Analysis Services: `http://bit.ly/2g7C4KB`

Applying multiple filtering conditions

The application of precise and often complex filter conditions has always been at the heart of business intelligence, and Power BI Desktop supports rich filtering capabilities across its query, data model, and visualization components. In many scenarios, filtering at the query level via the Query Editor and M functions is the optimal choice, as this reduces the workload of both import and DirectQuery data models and eliminates the need for re-applying the same filter logic across multiple reports.

Although the Query Editor graphical interface can be used to configure filtering conditions, this recipe demonstrates M's core filtering functions and the use of M in common multi-condition filter scenarios.

Getting ready

1. Retrieve a dimension table and your date dimension into a new PBIX file. The pattern of splitting data sources from queries described earlier applies here as well.

Figure 47: Data Source and Base Query Groups

```
CustomersDim

let
    Source = AdWorksProd,
    ProductDim = Source{[Schema = "BI",Item = "vDim_Customer"]}[Data]
in
    ProductDim
```

Figure 48: CustomersDim M Query Expression

2. As per *Figure 47* (gray font), disable the **Enable Load** settings of these queries.

How to do it...

The M expression queries constructed in this recipe are intended to highlight some of the most common filtering use cases.

The following eight filtering queries will be developed in this recipe:

- United States customers only
- Customers with 3+ children
- Customers with null values for either the middle name or title columns
- The customers with first purchase dates between 2012 and 2013
- Customers in management with female gender or bachelors education
- Top 100 customers based on income
- List of distinct sales territory countries

- Dates less than or equal to the current date and more than 3 years prior

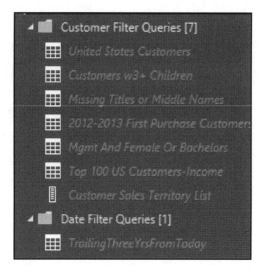

Figure 49: Queries developed in this recipe

Query filter example steps

1. Create a new blank query and open the **Advanced Editor** window.
2. Use the `Table.SelectRows()` function to apply the `US` query predicate.
3. From a new blank query, filter on the `Children` column with a `>=` operator.

```
let
    Customers = CustomersDim,
    USCustomers = Table.SelectRows(Customers, each [Country Code] = "US")
in
    USCustomers
```

Figure 50: M expression for the United States Customers query

```
let
    Customers = CustomersDim,
    ThreePlusChildFamilies = Table.SelectRows(Customers, each [Children] >= 3)
in
    ThreePlusChildFamilies
```

Figure 51: M expression for the Customers w3+ Children query

- `Table.SelectRows()` is the primary table-filtering function in the M language.
- It's functionally aligned with the `FROM` and `WHERE` clauses of SQL.
- Observe that variable names are used as inputs to M functions.

4. From a new blank query, use the conditional logic operator `or` to define the filter condition for the `Middle Name` and `Title` columns.

```
let
    Customers = CustomersDim,
    MissingTitleOrMiddleName = Table.SelectRows(Customers, each [Middle Name] = null or [Title] = null)
in
    MissingTitleOrMiddleName
```

Figure 52: M expression for the Missing Titles or Middle Names query

- Use the lowercase literal `null` to represent the absence of values.

5. From a new blank query, use the #date literal to apply the 2012-2013 filter.

```
let
    Customers = CustomersDim,
    BetweenDates = Table.SelectRows
        (
            Customers,
            each [First Purchase Date] >= #date(2012,01,01) and [First Purchase Date] <= #date(2013,12,31)
        )
in
    BetweenDates
```

Figure 53: M expression for the 2012-2013 First Purchase Customers query

- Literals are also available for `DateTime`, `Duration`, `Time`, and `DateTimeZone`.

6. From a new blank query, use parentheses to define the filter conditions: management occupation and either female gender or bachelors education.

```
let
    Customers = CustomersDim,
    MgmtAndFemaleOrBachelors = Table.SelectRows(Customers, each
        [Occupation] = "Management" and ([Gender] = "F" or [Education] = "Bachelors"))
in
    MgmtAndFemaleOrBachelors
```

Figure 54: M expression for the Mgmt and Female or Bachelors query

- The parentheses ensure that the `or` condition filters are isolated from the filter on `Occupation`.

7. From a new blank query, reference the `United States Customers` query and use the `Table.Sort()` function to order this table by the `Annual Income` column. Finally, use the `Table.FirstN()` function to retrieve the top 100 rows.

```
let
    Source = #"United States Customers",
    SortedByIncome = Table.Sort(Source,{{"Annual Income", Order.Descending}}),
    TopUSIncomeCustomers = Table.FirstN(SortedByIncome,100)
in
    TopUSIncomeCustomers
```

Figure 55: M expression for the Top 100 US Customers-Income query

- `Table.Sort()` supports multiple columns as per the *Importing data to Power BI Desktop models* recipe.
- 100 Rows are returned by the query starting from the very top of the sorted table. In this example, the set returned is not deterministic due to ties in income.

8. From a new query, use the `List.Distinct()` and `List.Sort()` functions to retrieve a distinct list of values from the `Customer Sales Territory Country` column.

```
let
    SalesTerritoryCountryList = List.Distinct(CustomersDim[Customer Sales Territory Country]),
    OrderedList = List.Sort(SalesTerritoryCountryList,Order.Ascending)
in
    OrderedList
```

Figure 56: M expression for the Customer Sales Territory List query

	List
1	Australia
2	Canada
3	France
4	Germany
5	United Kingdom
6	United States

Figure 57: List Preview from the Customer Sales Territory List query

- A list of distinct values can be used in multiple ways, such as a dynamic source of available input values to parameters.

9. From a new query, use the `DateTime.LocalNow()`, `DateTime.Date()`, and `Date.Year()` functions to retrieve the trailing 3 years from the current date.

```
let
    Dates = DateDim,
    TrailingThreeFromToday = Table.SelectRows(Dates, each
    [Date] <= DateTime.Date(DateTime.LocalNow()) and
    [Calendar Year] >= Date.Year(DateTime.LocalNow()) - 3 )
in
    TrailingThreeFromToday
```

Figure 58: M expression for the Trailing Three Years query

- The current date and year are retrieved from the `DateTime.LocalNow()` function and then compared to columns from the date dimension with these values.

How it works...

Readers should not be concerned with the `each` syntax of `Table.SelectRows()`.

In many languages, this would suggest row-by-row iteration, but when possible, the M engine *folds* the function into the WHERE clause of the SQL query submitted to the source system.

There's more...

Filtering via the Query Editor interface

With simple filtering conditions and in proof-of-concept projects, using the UI to develop filter conditions may be helpful to expedite query development.

However, the developer should review the M expressions generated by these interfaces as they're only based on the previews of data available at design time, and logical filter assumptions can be made under certain conditions.

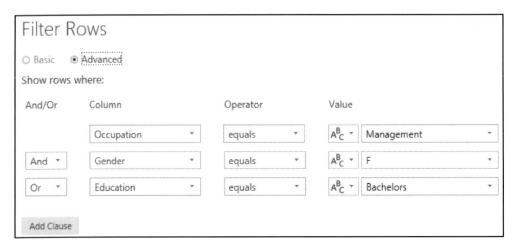

Figure 59: Advanced Filter Rows Dialog in the Query Editor

See also

- The following blog post from Gil Raviv at Data Chant provides an example of the Query Editor's construction of M filter logic and the potential for unintended query results: `http://bit.ly/2nLX6QW`.

Choosing columns and column names

The columns selected in data retrieval queries impact the performance and scalability of both import and DirectQuery data models. For import models, the resources required by the refresh process and the size of the compressed data model are directly impacted by column selection. Specifically, the cardinality of columns drives their individual memory footprint and memory (per column) correlates closely to query duration when these columns are referenced in measures and report visuals. For DirectQuery models, the performance of report queries is directly affected.

Regardless of the model type, how this selection is implemented also impacts the robustness of the retrieval process. Additionally, the names assigned to columns (or accepted from the source) directly impact the Q & A or natural language query experience. This recipe provides examples of choosing columns for a data model and applying user-friendly names.

How to do it...

The following three examples walk through a process of identifying columns to include or exclude in a data retrieval process and then accessing and renaming those columns.

Identify expensive columns

1. Analyze the largest fact table(s) of your model to identify columns that could be excluded to improve performance.
2. For import models, search for high-cardinality columns that aren't required by the model for relationships or measures.

   - In this example, the following three fact table columns are identified as candidates for exclusion from the data model

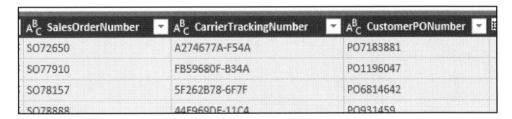

Figure 60: High-cardinality columns

   - All three columns have over 1.5M distinct values and thus don't compress well, resulting in greater data storage

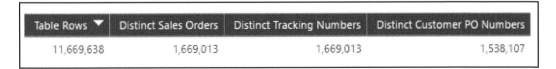

Table Rows ▼	Distinct Sales Orders	Distinct Tracking Numbers	Distinct Customer PO Numbers
11,669,638	1,669,013	1,669,013	1,538,107

Figure 61: Row and Distinct Count Profile

3. Use the `Table.RemoveColumns()` function against these columns

```
let
    ResellerSales = AdWorksProd{[Schema="BI",Item="vFact_ResellerSalesXL_CCI_AllColumns"]}[Data],

    RemovedCols =
Table.RemoveColumns(ResellerSales, {"SalesOrderNumber", "CarrierTrackingNumber", "CustomerPONumber"})
in
    RemovedCols
```

Figure 62: Removing three high-cardinality columns

- The size of the Power BI Desktop file is reduced from 394 MB to 227 MB
- The file is also faster to open refresh, and could support more data, while remaining below the 1 GB limit for published Power BI datasets

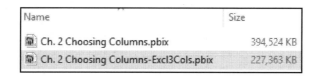

Name	Size
Ch. 2 Choosing Columns.pbix	394,524 KB
Ch. 2 Choosing Columns-Excl3Cols.pbix	227,363 KB

Figure 63: File Size Difference

- The two fact tables have 27 and 24 columns, respectively, indicating that the three columns removed were among the most resource-intensive columns
- See the *There's More...* section for an additional method of eliminating columns

Select columns

1. Use the `Table.SelectColumns()` function to accomplish the following:
   - Explicitly define the only columns retrieved
   - Set the presentation order of the columns in the Query Editor
   - Avoid query failure if one of the source columns changes or is missing

- In this example, 29 columns are available from the `AdventureWorks Customer Dimension` table, but only 11 are selected

```
    SelectCustCols =
        Table.SelectColumns(Customer,
            {
            "CustomerKey","FirstName","LastName", "YearlyIncome", "Gender", "EnglishEducation",
            "MaritalStatus", "Phone","CommuteDistance","AddressLine1", "TotalChildren"
            }, MissingField.UseNull)
    in
        SelectCustCols
```

Figure 64: The Expression for Selecting Columns

- The `MissingField.UseNull` parameter is optional but recommended
- If a column selected isn't available or is renamed in the source database, the query will still succeed (see *Figure 65*):

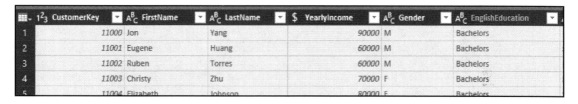

Figure 65: Columns from the expression in Figure 64 viewed in the Query Editor interface

- The columns are presented in the Query Editor in the order specified
- This can be helpful for the query design process, and avoids the need for an additional expression with a `Table.ReorderColumns()` function

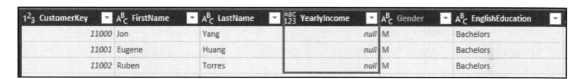

Figure 66: Missing Field Null Values

- In this example, the source system column was renamed to `AnnualIncome`. Rather than the query failing, null values were passed into this column.

2. Create a name column from the first and last names via `Table.AddColumn()`.

- Add a final `Table.SelectColumns()` expression that excludes the `FirstName` and `LastName` columns.

```
CustomerNameAdd = Table.AddColumn(SelectCustCols, "Customer Name", each
    [FirstName] & " " & [LastName]),

CustomerTable =   Table.SelectColumns(CustomerNameAdd,
        {
        "CustomerKey","Customer Name","YearlyIncome", "Gender", "EnglishEducation",
        "MaritalStatus", "Phone","CommuteDistance","AddressLine1", "TotalChildren"
        })
in
    CustomerTable
```

Figure 67: Customer Name Expression

- The `MissingField.UseNull` parameter isn't needed for this expression since it was already used in the `Table.SelectColumns()` function against the source.

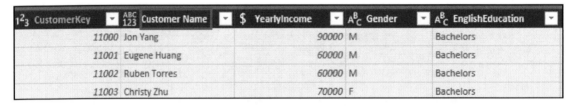

1²₃ CustomerKey	ABC 123 Customer Name	$ YearlyIncome	AᵇC Gender	AᵇC EnglishEducation
11000	Jon Yang	90000	M	Bachelors
11001	Eugene Huang	60000	M	Bachelors
11002	Ruben Torres	60000	M	Bachelors
11003	Christy Zhu	70000	F	Bachelors

Figure 68: Revised Customer Name Column

- Columns representing an attribute in other languages such as `SpanishEducation` and `FrenchOccupation` are excluded.
- The type of the `Customer Name` column should be set to text (type text) in the `Table.AddColumn()` function.

Rename columns

1. Use the `Table.RenameColumns()` to apply intuitive names for users and to benefit the Q & A engine for natural language queries.

```
RenamedColumns = Table.RenameColumns(CustomerTable,
        {
            {"YearlyIncome", "Customer Annual Income"},
            {"Gender", "Customer Gender"},
            {"EnglishEducation", "Customer Education"},
            {"Phone", "Customer Phone Number"}
        }
    )
```

Figure 69: Column Aliases Applied

2. Use renaming to remove any source system indicators, add a space between words for non-key columns, and apply dimension-specific names such as `Customer Gender` rather than `Gender`.
3. Key columns will be hidden from the **Report View**.
4. `Table.RenameColumns()` also offers the `MissingField.UseNull` option.

How it works...

Column memory usage

Import models are internally stored in a columnar compressed format. The compressed data for each column contributes to the total disk size of the file.

The primary factor of data size is a columns' cardinality. Columns with many unique values do not compress well and thus consume more space.

The example in this recipe reduced the size of the overall file, but it's the size of the individual columns being accessed by queries that, among other factors, drives query performance for import models.

There's more...

Fact table column eliminations

For import data models, you can remove a column that represents a simple expression of other columns from the same table. For example, if the Extended Amount column is equal to the multiplication of the Unit Price and Order Quantity columns, you can choose to only import these two columns.

```
Extended Amount Metric = SUMX('Reseller Sales',
        'Reseller Sales'[UnitPrice]*'Reseller Sales'[OrderQuantity])
```

Figure 70: DAX Measure Replacement for Column

The DAX SUMX() function computes the same result as a sum of the column and can be parallelized by the storage engine. This approach is not recommended for DirectQuery models.

Column orders

The initial column order of a query loaded to the data model is respected in the Data view, but later changes to the column ordering are only local to the query.

The field list exposed to both the Report and Data views of Power BI Desktop is automatically alphabetized.

See also

- Power BI Documentation on preparing data for Q & A: (http://bit.ly/2nBLAGc)

Transforming and cleansing source data

The transformations applied within Power BI's M queries serve to protect the integrity of the data model and to support enhanced analysis and visualization. The specific transformations to implement varies based on data quality, integration needs, and the goals of the overall solution. However, at a minimum, developers should look to protect the integrity of the model's relationships and to simplify the user experience via denormalization and standardization.

This recipe includes examples of protecting a data model from duplicate values and enhancing the quality of a dimension column via a relationship to a separate data source.

Getting ready

To best follow the duplicate removal example, you may identify any data models that source directly from an unstructured source such as an Excel or text file.

How to do it...

Remove duplicates

The objective of this example is to prevent refresh failures due to duplicate source values in the relationship column of a dimension table. Additionally, the duplicates are to be isolated for further inspection and troubleshooting:

1. Access a dimension table query from an unstructured data source such as an Excel Workbook.

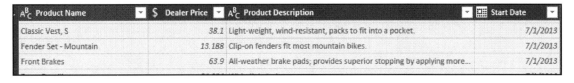

AᴮC Product Name	$ Dealer Price	AᴮC Product Description	Start Date
Classic Vest, S	38.1	Light-weight, wind-resistant, packs to fit into a pocket.	7/1/2013
Fender Set - Mountain	13.188	Clip-on fenders fit most mountain bikes.	7/1/2013
Front Brakes	63.9	All-weather brake pads; provides superior stopping by applying more...	7/1/2013

Figure 71: Product Query Preview

- The source is an Excel table maintained by business users.

Product Name	Dealer Price	Product Description	Start Date
Chain	12.144	Superior shifting perfo	7/1/2013
Classic Vest, L	38.1	Light-weight, wind-res	7/1/2013
Classic Vest, M	38.1	Light-weight, wind-res	7/1/2013
Classic Vest, S	38.1	Light-weight, wind-res	7/1/2013
Fender Set - Mountain	13.188	Clip-on fenders fit mos	7/1/2013

Figure 72: Excel Data Source

- The `Product Name` column is used for the relationship to the `Sales fact` table; therefore it must uniquely identify each row.

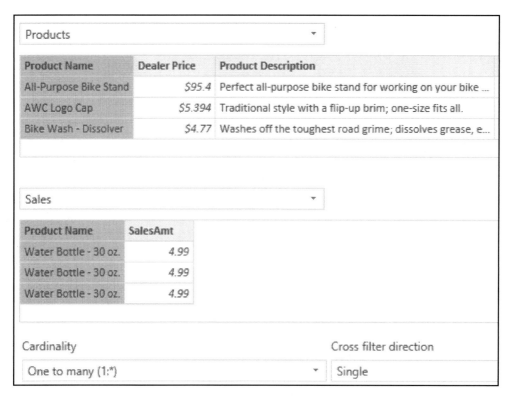

Figure 73: Product to Sales Relationship

- Given the one-to-many relationship, any duplicate values in the `Product Name` column of the `Products` table will result in refresh failures.

Products
Column 'Product Name' in Table 'Products' contains a duplicate value 'Fender Set - Mountain' and this is not allowed for columns on the one side of a many-to-one relationship or for columns that are used as the primary key of a table.

Figure 74: Duplicate Refresh Failure

2. Add the following four M expressions to the Products query per *Figure 75*:
   - Remove any leading and trailing empty spaces in the `Product Name` column with a `Text.Trim()` function
   - Create a duplicate column of the `Product Name` key column with the `Table.DuplicateColumn()` function
   - Add an expression to the Products query with the `Table.Distinct()` function to remove duplicate rows
   - Add another `Table.Distinct()` expression to specifically remove duplicate values from the `Product Name` column

- As an unstructured source, the column types were defined explicitly in the query via `Table.TransformColumnTypes()`.

```
let
    ProductsTbl = Table.TransformColumnTypes(ProductListExcel,
     {
        {"Product Name", type text},
        {"Dealer Price",    Currency.Type},
        {"Product Description", type text},
        {"Start Date", type date}
        }
    ),
    TrimText = Table.TransformColumns(ProductsTbl,{"Product Name",Text.Trim}),
    DuplicateKey = Table.DuplicateColumn(TrimText,"Product Name", "Product Name-Copy"),
    DistinctProductRows = Table.Distinct(UpperCase),
    DistinctProductNames = Table.Distinct(DistinctProductRows, {"Product Name"})
in
    DistinctProductNames
```

Figure 75: Duplicated key and distinct expressions

- The query is still vulnerable to mixed cases such as `Fender Set` and `Fender set`.

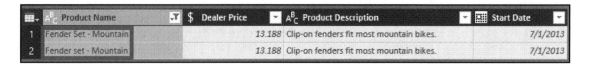

	Product Name	Dealer Price	Product Description	Start Date
1	Fender Set - Mountain	13.188	Clip-on fenders fit most mountain bikes.	7/1/2013
2	Fender set - Mountain	13.188	Clip-on fenders fit most mountain bikes.	7/1/2013

Figure 76: Distinct cases in key values

- The M engine considers the values unique but the data model engine doesn't.

3. Add an expression to force uppercase on the `Product Name` column via the `Table.TransformColumns()` function. This new expression must be applied before the duplicate removal expressions are applied.

```
    TrimText = Table.TransformColumns(ProductsTbl,{"Product Name",Text.Trim}),
    DuplicateKey = Table.DuplicateColumn(TrimText,"Product Name", "Product Name-Copy"),

    UpperCase = Table.TransformColumns(DuplicateKey,{{"Product Name", Text.Upper}}),

    DistinctProductRows = Table.Distinct(UpperCase),
    DistinctProductNames = Table.Distinct(DistinctProductRows, {"Product Name"})
in
    DistintProductNames
```

Figure 77: Uppercase expression inserted into the query

- The query is now resilient to duplicate values and rows, mixed cases, and spaces. However, the `Product Name` column is now in the uppercase format.

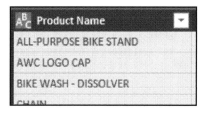

Product Name
ALL-PURPOSE BIKE STAND
AWC LOGO CAP
BIKE WASH - DISSOLVER
CHAIN

Figure 78: All caps after duplicate removal

4. Add two final expressions to replace the `Product Name` column with the duplicate column created in step 2.

```
RemoveProductName = Table.RemoveColumns(DistinctProductNames,"Product Name"),
ReplaceProductName = Table.RenameColumns(RemoveProductName,{"Product Name-Copy","Product Name"})
in
    ReplaceProductName
```

Figure 79: Product Name Column Replacement

- The capitalized `Product Name` column is dropped via `Table.RemoveColumns()`, and `Table.RenameColumns()` is used convert the duplicate column into the column loaded to the data model for the Product-to-Sales relationship.

5. To support troubleshooting, create a query that accesses the same source table and retrieves the values from the `Product Name` column with more than one row.

```
UpperCase = Table.TransformColumns(ProductSourceRows,{{"Product Name", Text.Upper}}),
ProductName = Table.SelectColumns(UpperCase,"Product Name"),
GroupedRows = Table.Group(ProductName, {"Product Name"}, {{"Rows", each Table.RowCount(_), Int64.Type}}),
Duplicates = Table.SelectRows(GroupedRows, each [Rows] > 1)
in
    Duplicates
```

Figure 80: 'Duplicate Products' query expression retrieves the Product Names with more than one row

- The `Product Name` column is selected, grouped, and then filtered to always retrieve any duplicate key values. It also accounts for mixed casing of values.

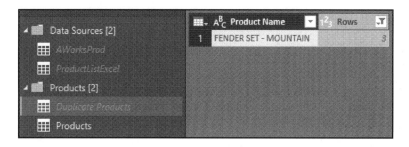

Figure 81: The **Duplicates Query**

6. Disable the load of the query retrieving duplicate product names--`Duplicate Products` in this example.

Update a column through a join

The objective of this example is to update the values of a column (DealerPrice) based on the values of a separate column stored in a separate data source.

The Products dimension table is retrieved from a SQL Server database, but over 200 rows do not have dealer price values.

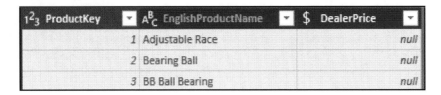

1²₃ ProductKey	AᴮC EnglishProductName	$ DealerPrice
1	Adjustable Race	null
2	Bearing Ball	null
3	BB Ball Bearing	null

Figure 82: Null Values for Dealer Prices

The dealer prices for new, unsold products that are not yet available to the SQL Server database are stored in an Microsoft Access database.

ProductKey	Product Name	Dealer Price
1	Adjustable Race	$48.25
2	Bearing Ball	$37.50
3	BB Ball Bearing	$29.50

Figure 83: MS Access Price List

1. Create dedicated data source queries to the SQL Server and Microsoft Access sources.
2. Disable the load for both.

Figure 84: Data Source Queries

- The `Sql.Database()` function is used for the SQL Server database
- The `Access.Database()` function is used for the MS Access database:
  `Access.Database(File.Contents("C:\Finance\Data\DealerPrices.acc db"), [CreateNavigationProperties=true])`

- The retrieval queries will reference these sources such that changes in the data sources (for example, different server or file location) can be implemented quickly

3. Create a query that retrieves the product price list from the Microsoft Access table.
4. Give it a distinctive name and disable the load.

```
let
    Source = DealerPricesMSAccess,
    DealerPriceList = Source{[Schema="",Item="DealerPrices"]}[Data]
in
    DealerPriceList
```

Figure 85: Dealer Price List Query

Like other examples in this chapter, the `Source` variable calls the dedicated data source query.

5. Create the `Products` query from the SQL Server database (products).
   - This query represents the primary source for the `Products` dimension in the data model.

Figure 86: Product Queries

- Only the `Products` query is enabled for load to the data model.
- In scenarios with more source inputs and transformations to perform, it may be beneficial to further isolate the inputs into staging queries.

```
let
    Source = AWorksProd,
    Products = Source{[Schema = "dbo",Item = "DimProduct"]}[Data],
    ProductSelect = Table.SelectColumns(Products, {"ProductKey", "EnglishProductName", "DealerPrice"}),
    ProductRename = Table.RenameColumns(ProductSelect,
        {
            {"EnglishProductName", "Product Name"},
            {"DealerPrice", "Dealer Price"}
        }
    )
in
    ProductRename
```

Figure 87: Product SQL Query

- `Table.SelectColumns()` retrieves the required columns from the `DimProduct` table and `Table.RenameColumns()` adds spaces between column headers.

6. Add an expression that performs a left outer join from the SQL Server-based `Products` query to the `DealerPriceList` query on the `ProductKey` column.

7. Expose the `Dealer Price` column from the `Dealer Price List` query to the `Products` query with a distinct column name.

1²₃ ProductKey	Aᴮ𝒸 Product Name	$ Dealer Price	$ Dealer List Price
209	Rear Derailleur Cage	null	116.885
210	HL Road Frame - Black, 58	null	117.385
211	HL Road Frame - Red, 58	null	117.885
212	Sport-100 Helmet, Red	20.1865	null
213	Sport-100 Helmet, Red	20.1865	null
214	Sport-100 Helmet, Red	20.994	null

Figure 88: Dealer List Price Added to Query

- `Table.NestedJoin()` is used to perform the Left Outer Join from the `Products` query to the `DealerPriceList` query
- `Table.ExpandTableColumn()` is used to add the `Dealer List Price` column from the result of the join

```
DealerPriceJoin = Table.NestedJoin(ProductRename,"ProductKey",DealerPriceList,"ProductKey","PriceListColumns",JoinKind.LeftOuter),

    DealerPriceListCols = Table.ExpandTableColumn(DealerPriceJoin, "PriceListColumns",{"Dealer Price"},{"Dealer List Price"})
in
    DealerPriceListCols
```

Figure 89: Left Outer Join and Column Expansion

8. Add a conditional column to the query that uses the `Dealer List Price` column added in step 7 if the `Dealer Price` column is null.

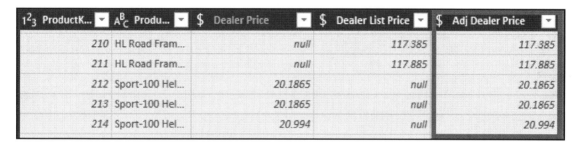

1²₃ ProductK...	Aᴮ_C Produ...	$ Dealer Price	$ Dealer List Price	$ Adj Dealer Price
210	HL Road Fram...	*null*	*117.385*	*117.385*
211	HL Road Fram...	*null*	*117.885*	*117.885*
212	Sport-100 Hel...	*20.1865*	*null*	*20.1865*
213	Sport-100 Hel...	*20.1865*	*null*	*20.1865*
214	Sport-100 Hel...	*20.994*	*null*	*20.994*

Figure 90: Conditional Dealer Price Column Added

- `Table.AddColumns()` is used with a simple `if...then`
- `Currency.Type` is specified to avoid an `Any` type from being loaded to the model as a text value

```
AdjDealerPriceCol = Table.AddColumn(DealerPriceListCols, "Adj Dealer Price", each
    if [Dealer Price] = null then [Dealer List Price] else [Dealer Price]
    , Currency.Type)

in
    AdjDealerPriceCol
```

Figure 91: Conditional Dealer Price Column Added to the Query

9. Add two final expressions to exclusively select the conditional price column added in step 6 and rename this column to `Dealer List Price`.

1²₃ ProductKey	ABC Product Name	$ Dealer Price
1	Adjustable Race	48.25
2	Bearing Ball	37.5
3	BB Ball Bearing	29.5
4	Headset Ball Bearings	27.5

Figure 92: Products Query with an updated Dealer Price Column

- `Table.SelectColumns()` and `Table.RenameColumns()` are used in step 7.

```
ProductAdjSelect = Table.SelectColumns(AdjDealerPriceCol,{"ProductKey", "Product Name", "Adj Dealer Price"}),
ProductAdjRename = Table.RenameColumns(ProductAdjSelect,
    {
        {"Adj Dealer Price", "Dealer Price"}
    })
in
    ProductAdjRename
```

Figure 93: Column Selection and Renaming Expressions

There's more...

- The most common text functions include `Text.Length()`, `Text.Start()`, `Text.End()`, and `Text.Range()`. These provide equivalent functionality to the `LEN`, `LEFT`, `RIGHT`, and `MID` functions in SQL, respectively.
- Text functions start at a 0 base; the second character of the string is `1`.
- The `Table.Unpivot()` and `Table.UnpivotOtherColumns()` functions are commonly used to transpose data structures in a report layout with financial periods across the columns.

See also

- M Functions Reference for Text: `http://bit.ly/2nUYjnw`

Creating custom and conditional columns

Business users often extend the outputs of existing reports and data models with additional columns to help them analyze and present data. The logic of these columns is generally implemented through Excel formulas or as calculated DAX columns. A superior solution, particularly if the logic cannot quickly be migrated to a data warehouse or IT resource, is to create the columns via the Query Editor and M language.

Developing custom columns can also significantly enhance the ease-of-use and analytical power of data models and the visualizations they support. In the examples of this recipe, columns are created to simplify the analysis of a customer dimension via existing columns and to apply a custom naming format.

How to do it...

Create a dynamic banding attribute

The goal of this example is to create an attribute on the `Customer` dimension table that groups the customer into age ranges to support demographic analysis:

1. Retrieve the current dimension table with the date column to be used for segmentation. The Date of Birth column is the source for this example.

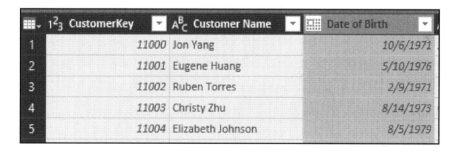

Figure 94: Customer Dimension

2. Add variables to the let expression to support the comparison between the current system date and the dimension date (Date of Birth).

```
let
    CurrentDate = DateTime.Date(DateTime.LocalNow()),
    CurrentYear =   Date.Year(CurrentDate),
    CurrentMonth = Date.Month(CurrentDate),
    CurrentDay = Date.Day(CurrentDate),

    Source = AdWorksProd,
    BI_vDim_Customer = Source{[Schema="BI",Item="vDim_Customer"]}[Data],
    CustomerTbl = Table.SelectColumns(BI_vDim_Customer,{"CustomerKey", "Customer Name", "Date of Birth"}),
```

Figure 95: Current Date Variables

- DateTime.LocalNow() is used as the source for current date.
- The result of this variable is used for year, month, and day.

3. Use the Table.AddColumn() function to create Year, Month, and Day columns for the customer dimension (see *Figure 95* and *Figure 96*).

CustomerKey	Customer Name	Date of Birth	Customer Year	Customer Month	Customer Day
1	11000	Jon Yang	10/6/1971	1971	10	6
2	11001	Eugene Huang	5/10/1976	1976	5	10
3	11002	Ruben Torres	2/9/1971	1971	2	9
4	11003	Christy Zhu	8/14/1973	1973	8	14
5	11004	Elizabeth Johnson	8/5/1979	1979	8	5
6	11005	Julio Ruiz	8/1/1976	1976	8	1

Figure 96: Customer Columns Added

- Currently, the equivalent of a DATEDIFF() function with date intervals (Year, Month, Week, and so on), like the ones in T-SQL and DAX languages, is not available in M.
- A Duration.Days() function can be used for day intervals and additional duration functions are available for hour, minute, and second intervals.

```
    Source = AdWorksProd,
    BI_vDim_Customer = Source{[Schema="BI",Item="vDim_Customer"]}[Data],
    CustomerTbl = Table.SelectColumns(BI_vDim_Customer,{"CustomerKey", "Customer Name", "Date of Birth"}),

    CustomerYr = Table.AddColumn(CustomerTbl, "Customer Year", each Date.Year([Date of Birth]), Int64.Type),
    CustomerMonth = Table.AddColumn(CustomerYr, "Customer Month", each Date.Month([Date of Birth]), Int64.Type),
    CustomerDay = Table.AddColumn(CustomerMonth, "Customer Day", each Date.Day([Date of Birth]), Int64.Type)
in
    CustomerDay
```

Figure 97: Customer Columns Added Syntax

- The `Int64.Type` value is passed to the optional type parameter of `Table.AddColumn()` to set the new columns as whole numbers.

4. Add an `Age` column via an `if...then` expression.

```
CustomerAge = Table.AddColumn(CustomerDay, "Customer Age", each
if  [Customer Month] < CurrentMonth then CurrentYear - [Customer Year]
else if [Customer Month] > CurrentMonth then CurrentYear - [Customer Year]  - 1
else if [Customer Day] < CurrentDay then CurrentYear - [Customer Year]
else CurrentYear - [Customer Year]  - 1
)
```

Figure 98: Customer Age Expression

1²₃ CustomerKey	Aᴮ𝒸 Customer Na...	Date of Birth	ABC 123 Customer Age
11000	Jon Yang	10/6/1971	45
11001	Eugene Huang	5/10/1976	40
11002	Ruben Torres	2/9/1971	46
11003	Christy Zhu	8/14/1973	43
11004	Elizabeth Johnson	8/5/1979	37

Figure 99: Customer Age Column

- The `Customer Age` expression compares the Current Year, Month, and Day variables against the values of the customer columns created in step 3.
- The `Age` column can then be used to derive the age segmentation column.

5. Add a `Segment` column via the column computed in step 4.

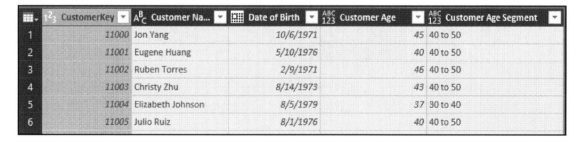

	1²₃ CustomerKey	Aᴮ𝒸 Customer Na...	Date of Birth	ABC 123 Customer Age	ABC 123 Customer Age Segment
1	11000	Jon Yang	10/6/1971	45	40 to 50
2	11001	Eugene Huang	5/10/1976	40	40 to 50
3	11002	Ruben Torres	2/9/1971	46	40 to 50
4	11003	Christy Zhu	8/14/1973	43	40 to 50
5	11004	Elizabeth Johnson	8/5/1979	37	30 to 40
6	11005	Julio Ruiz	8/1/1976	40	40 to 50

Figure 100: Customer Age Segment Column

- The Customer Age Segment expression simply references the Customer Age column created in step 4.

```
CustomerSegment = Table.AddColumn(CustomerAgeOnly, "Customer Age Segment", each
if [Customer Age] < 30 then "Less Than 30"
else if [Customer Age] < 40 then "30 to 40"
else if [Customer Age] < 50 then "40 to 50"
else if [Customer Age] < 60 then "50 to 60"
else                          "Over 60"
)
in
    CustomerSegment
```

Figure 101: Customer Segment Expression

- The new custom columns can be used to support various visualizations.

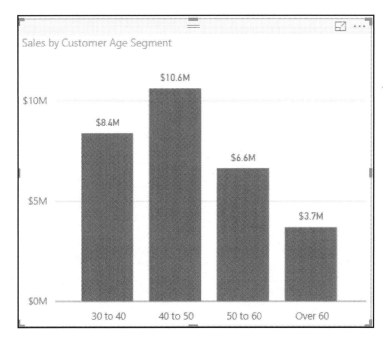

Figure 102: Customer Age Segment Visualized

- The Age Segment and Age columns can be used in a model hierarchy.

Create a formatted name column

- The goal of this example is to implement a formatted name using the existing name (first, middle, and last) and Title columns of a customer dimension
- The target format is `Mr. John A. Doe`
- The query must account for nulls in the `Middle Name` and `Title` columns as well as different values in the `Middle Name` column:

1. Use `Table.SelectColumns()` to retrieve the required source columns.

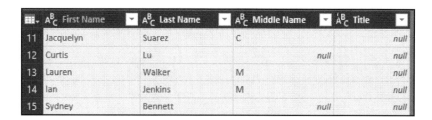

Figure 103: Name Columns

2. Write a `Table.AddColumns()` function with an `if...then` expression that accounts for the different scenarios:

```
NameFormatTbl = Table.AddColumn(NameTbl,"Formatted Name", each
if      [Title] = null and [Middle Name] = null then [First Name] & " " & [Last Name]
else if    [Title] = null then [First Name] & " " & Text.Range([Middle Name],0,1) & ". " & [Last Name]
else [Title] & " " & [First Name] & " " & Text.Range([Middle Name],0,1) & ". " & [Last Name]
)
```

Figure 104: Formatted Name Column Expression

- `Text.Range()` is used to extract the first character of the middle name.

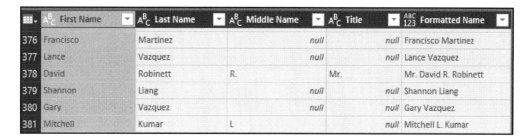

Figure 105: Formatted Name Column

- The three `if...then` conditions account for all scenarios to return the formatted name as per the requirements defined in step 1.

Comparing the current and previous rows

The goal of this example is to compare the values of one row with the next or previous row to compute a value for a variance or status column. In this example, the output of a factory for a given date needs to be compared to its previous days' output:

1. Retrieve the essential columns into a query.
   - In this case, there are four factories, with each row representing the quantity output of a factory by date.

1^2_3 Factory ID	A^B_C Factory	Date	1^2_3 Qty
18	Atchula	3/12/2017	20
15	Jasper	3/12/2017	24
11	Crandall	3/12/2017	25
14	Jenkins	3/12/2017	27
15	Jasper	3/13/2017	17
11	Crandall	3/13/2017	20
18	Atchula	3/13/2017	22

Figure 106: Source Data - Factory Qty by Day

2. Use the `Table.Sort()` function to sort the table by `Factory ID` and then by `Date`.

```
SortedTbl = Table.Sort(SourceTbl,
    {{"Factory ID", Order.Ascending},{"Date",Order.Ascending}})
in
    SortedTbl
```

Figure 107: Sorting Expression Applied Source

- The order of columns specified from left to right drives the sorting precedence.

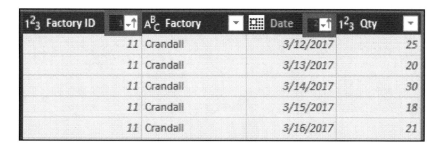

Figure 108: Sorted Table

- Observe the **1** and **2** indicators added to the sort by columns in the Query Editor.

3. Use the `Table.AddIndexColumn()` function to add two different index columns to the table.
    - `Row Index` and `PrevRow Index` have seed values of 1 and 0, respectively.

```
RowIndex = Table.TransformColumnTypes
    (Table.AddIndexColumn(SortedTbl, "Row Index", 1, 1),
    {{ "Row Index",Int64.Type}}),

PrevRowIndex =
    Table.TransformColumnTypes{
    Table.AddIndexColumn(RowIndex, "PrevRow Index",0,1),{{"PrevRow Index",Int64.Type}}
```

Figure 109: Two Index Columns Added

- The index function is wrapped inside `Table.TransformColumnTypes()` to convert the column to a whole number data type.

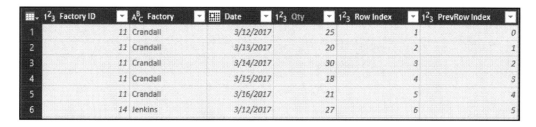

Figure 110: Index Columns in Query Editor

- The new index columns provide an ability to self-join the table.

4. Use a `Table.NestedJoin()` function to join the table to itself based on the index columns created in step 3.

5. Use a `Table.ExpandTableColumn()` function to add `Prev Factory ID` and `Prev Qty` columns to the table.

```
SelfJoin = Table.NestedJoin(PrevRowIndex,{"PrevRow Index"},PrevRowIndex,{"Row Index"},
    "NewColumn",JoinKind.LeftOuter),

AddPreviousColumns = Table.ExpandTableColumn(SelfJoin, "NewColumn", {"Factory ID", "Qty"},
    {"Prev Factory ID", "Prev Qty"}),
```

Figure 111: Join and Expand Expressions

- See "Integrating and Working with Multiple Queries" for details on joining queries.

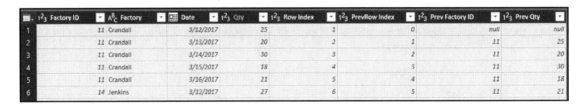

	1²₃ Factory ID	Aᴮ꜀ Factory	Date	1²₃ Qty	1²₃ Row Index	1²₃ PrevRow Index	1²₃ Prev Factory ID	1²₃ Prev Qty
1	11	Crandall	3/12/2017	25	1	0	null	null
2	11	Crandall	3/13/2017	20	2	1	11	25
3	11	Crandall	3/14/2017	30	3	2	11	20
4	11	Crandall	3/15/2017	18	4	3	11	30
5	11	Crandall	3/16/2017	21	5	4	11	18
6	14	Jenkins	3/12/2017	27	6	5	11	21

Figure 112: Previous Row Columns Added

6. Add a column with an `if...then` expression that compares `Qty` and `Prev Qty`.

```
VarianceColumn = Table.AddColumn(RemovedCols, "Daily Qty Var", each

    if [Factory ID] = [Prev Factory ID] then [Qty] - [Prev Qty]
    else null,
        Int64.Type)
```

Figure 113: Variance Column Expression

- The expression checks whether the `Factory ID` matches with the `Prev Factory ID` and sets the new column as a whole number.

7. Finally, use `Table.SelectColumns()` to retrieve only the columns needed.

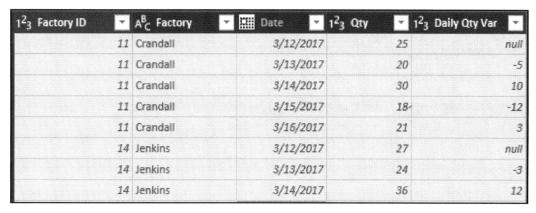

1²₃ Factory ID	A^BC Factory	Date	1²₃ Qty	1²₃ Daily Qty Var
11	Crandall	3/12/2017	25	null
11	Crandall	3/13/2017	20	-5
11	Crandall	3/14/2017	30	10
11	Crandall	3/15/2017	18	-12
11	Crandall	3/16/2017	21	3
14	Jenkins	3/12/2017	27	null
14	Jenkins	3/13/2017	24	-3
14	Jenkins	3/14/2017	36	12

Figure 114: Final Table with Daily Qty Var

- The source data starts at `3/12/2017`; this causes the nulls in *Figure 114*.

How it works...

Conditional expression syntax

`if...then` expressions follow the following structure:

```
if <condition1> then <result1> else <result2>
```

All three inputs (condition1, result1, and result2) accept M expressions.

`if` expressions can be nested together with the following structure:

```
if <condition1> then <result1> else if <condition2> then <result2> else
<result3>
```

The equivalent of a SQL CASE expression is not available in M.

Case sensitivity

- M is a case-sensitive language, as seen in the "remove duplicates" example
- So, writing `IF` instead of `if` or `Table.Addcolumn` instead of `Table.AddColumn` will return an error

Conditional expression evaluation

- The order of conditions specified in 'if...then' expressions drives the evaluation process. Multiple conditions could be true but the second and later conditions will be discarded and not evaluated.
- If the value produced by the 'if' condition is not a logical value, an error is raised.

Query folding of custom columns

- Although there were several M expressions involved in creating the additional columns in the customer age segmentation example, the source system (SQL Server 2016 in this case) executed the entire query.
- Clicking on **View Native Query** from the Query Editor reveals that both `if...then` M expressions were *folded* into T-SQL CASE Expressions.
- Additionally, the T-SQL `DATEPART()` function was used to implement the customer year, month, and day columns.

There's more...

Add column from example

- The **Column From Examples** feature allows users to simply type an example of a desired column rather than apply the necessary transformations
- The engine determines which M functions and series of steps to add to the query that return results consistent with the examples provided

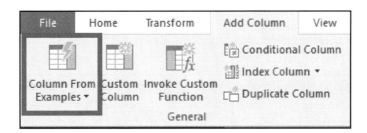

Figure 115: Column from Examples UI

- In the following example, the sample value of `Jon` is provided and only the `Customer Name` column is evaluated for possible transformations

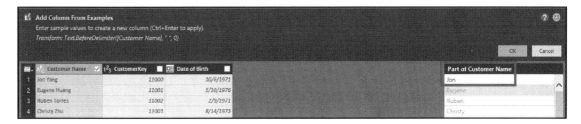

Figure 116: Sample Value Entry for Add Column From Example

- The engine determined, based on the example, that the `Text.BeforeDelimiter()` function was appropriate

Conditional columns interface

The Query Editor provides a basic and advanced conditional column interface as an alternative to writing out the `if...then` expressions.

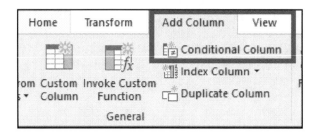

Figure 117: Conditional Column in Query Editor

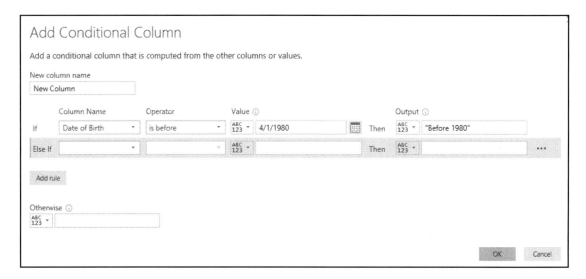

Figure 118: Conditional Column Dialog

Any column from the table can be referenced and multiple steps created can be moved up or down the order of evaluation.

DAX calculated columns

- For both import and DirectQuery data models, it's possible to create additional model columns via DAX functions.
- In almost every scenario, a superior alternative to DAX calculated columns is available such as via M expressions or the SQL database views that the model accesses. DAX calculated columns are not compressed like normal columns of import mode datasets and can lead to inefficient queries for DirectQuery models. Additionally, the presence of DAX calculated columns (and DAX calculated tables for import models) adds complexity to Power BI datasets.
- Greater analysis of DAX calculated columns is included in `Chapter 11`, *Enhancing and Optimizing Existing Power BI Solutions*.

Error handling and comments

The M query examples in this chapter do not address error handling or comments. These items and related elements for strengthening queries are also covered in `Chapter 11`, *Enhancing and Optimizing Existing Power BI Solutions*.

Integrating multiple queries

The full power of Power BI's querying capabilities is in the integration of multiple queries via it's merge and append operations. Retrieval processes which consolidate files from multiple network locations or which integrate data from multiple data sources can be developed efficiently and securely. Additionally, the same join types and data transformation patterns SQL and ETL developers are familiar with can be achieved with the M language.

This recipe provides examples of combining sources into a single query and leveraging the table join functions of M to support common transformation scenarios.

Getting ready

- To follow along with this recipe, you can use the Merge Queries and Append Queries icons on the **Home** tab of the Query Editor to generate the join expressions used in this recipe
- As joining queries is fundamental to the retrieval process, it's recommended to learn the `Table.Join()`, `Table.NestedJoin()`, and `Table.Combine()` functions

How to do it...

Consolidate files

The goal of this example is to produce an integrated table based on three text files stored in separate network paths:

1. Create a query to one of multiple text files that need to be integrated.
2. Click on **Get Data** and choose **Text/CSV** from the list of file sources.
3. Navigate to the folder and select the file to query.

Name	Date modified	Type	Size
2015Sales.txt	4/7/2017 4:59 PM	Text Document	16 KB

Figure 119: Tab-delimited text file

- In this example, the three text files are tab delimited but the same process applies to other delimiters and file sources.

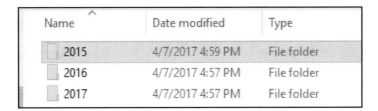

Figure 120: Source Folders

- If the files are stored in a single folder, a combine binaries transformation could be used. See the *There's more...* section for additional details.

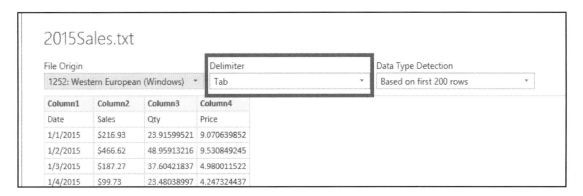

Figure 121: Text File Connection

4. Apply **Transformations to Prepare for the Consolidation**.
   - Promote the header row and set the data types.

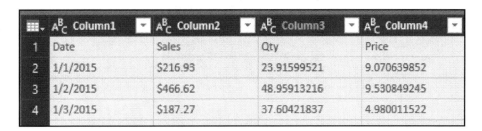

Figure 122: Source File Imported

- Use `Table.PromoteHeaders()` and `Table.TransformColumnTypes()` to prepare the table for integration with the other two files.

```
    HeaderPromote = Table.PromoteHeaders(Source),
    ColumnTypes = Table.TransformColumnTypes(HeaderPromote,
    {{"Date", type date}, {"Sales", Currency.Type}, {"Qty", Int64.Type}, {"Price", Currency.Type}})
in
    ColumnTypes
```

Figure 123: M Expressions to Promote Headers and Revise Data Types

- When connecting to an individual file such as this scenario, using the built-in data connectivity options via the interface is more convenient.

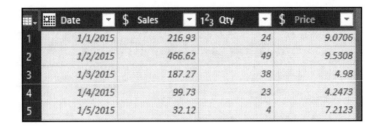

Figure 124: Transformed Header and Types

5. Give the query a name such as Sales-2015 and duplicate the query.
6. In each duplicated query, modify the file source connection to reference the given file directory path.
7. Disable the load for these queries and add them to a query group.

Figure 125: Three Text File Queries

10. Create a new, blank query for integrating the text file queries.
11. Use the `Table.Combine()` function to return a single table based on the rows of the three other queries.

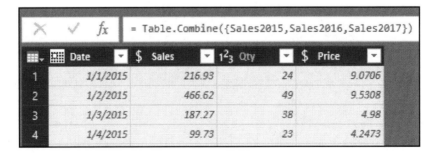

Figure 126: Consolidated Text File Query

- No other expressions are necessary in this example given the transformations applied against the source queries in step 2.
- Depending on the scenario, the developer could apply `Table.Distinct()` functions to avoid any duplicate rows from reaching the data model.
- Selecting the `Sales` table in **Query Dependencies View** highlights all input queries and their source files.
- Hovering over the data sources provides additional details (network path, server, and database).

Self-joining querying

The goal of this example is to add `Manager Name` and `Manager Title` columns to an existing Employee dimension table:

- The `EmployeeKey` and `ParentEmployeeKey` columns of the table are used in expressions to self-join the table.

1. Create a query that retrieves the key columns of the hierarchy and the attribute columns to be added.
    - The existing table has the key columns, `Employee Name`, and `Title`.

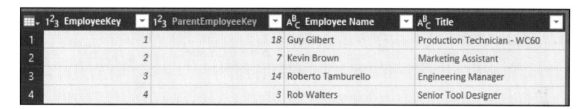

	1^2_3 EmployeeKey	1^2_3 ParentEmployeeKey	A^B_C Employee Name	A^B_C Title
1	1	18	Guy Gilbert	Production Technician - WC60
2	2	7	Kevin Brown	Marketing Assistant
3	3	14	Roberto Tamburello	Engineering Manager
4	4	3	Rob Walters	Senior Tool Designer

Figure 127: Existing Employee Dimension

- The new staging query references the existing dimension table and selects the required columns.

```
let

    Source = AdWorksProd,
    Employee = Source{[Schema = "dbo",Item = "DimEmployee"]}[Data],
    SelectCols = Table.SelectColumns(Employee,
        {"EmployeeKey","FirstName", "LastName", "Title"}),
    EmployeeName = Table.AddColumn(SelectCols, "Employee Name", each
            [FirstName] & " " & [LastName]
            , type text),
    SelectCols2 = Table.SelectColumns(EmployeeName,
        {"EmployeeKey","Employee Name","Title"}),
    EmployeeStage = Table.RenameColumns(SelectCols2,
        {"Title","Employee Title"})
in
    EmployeeStage
```

Figure 128: Manager Staging Expression

- The `ParentEmployeeKey` from *Figure 128* can be joined to the `EmployeeKey` of *Figure 129* to provide access to the Manager columns.
- The `Manager Name` and `Manager Title` columns could optionally be applied in the staging query via `Table.RenameColumns()`, but in this example the alias is applied within the merge operation.

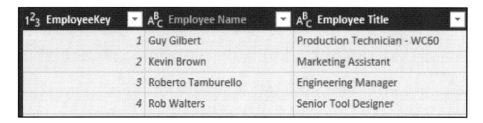

1²₃ EmployeeKey	AᴮC Employee Name	AᴮC Employee Title
1	Guy Gilbert	Production Technician - WC60
2	Kevin Brown	Marketing Assistant
3	Roberto Tamburello	Engineering Manager
4	Rob Walters	Senior Tool Designer

Figure 129: Manager Staging Query

- The query is named `Managers` and load is disabled.

2. Join the `Manager` staging query created in step 1 with the existing `Employee` table and add the `Manager Name` and `Manager Title` columns.

```
EmployeeManagerJoin = Table.NestedJoin(Employees,
    "ParentEmployeeKey",Managers,"EmployeeKey","ManagerColumn", JoinKind.LeftOuter),

ManagerColumns = Table.ExpandTableColumn(EmployeeManagerJoin,"ManagerColumn",
    {"Employee Name", "Employee Title"},{"Manager Name", "Manager Title"}),

EmployeeManager = Table.SelectColumns
        (ManagerColumns,
        {"EmployeeKey","Employee Name", "Employee Title", "Manager Name", "Manager Title"})
in
    EmployeeManager
```

Figure 130: Self Join Syntax

- The `Employees` query is referenced as the Left table in a `Table.NestedJoin()` function and joined to the `Managers` query via a left outer join.
- The left join is required to retain all employee rows in this scenario, as the `Employee` table includes one employee that doesn't have a parent employee key: `Chief Executive Officer`.
- Given the join on `Parent Employee Key` to `Employee Key`, the Manager columns are renamed in the `Table.ExpandTableColumn()` expression.

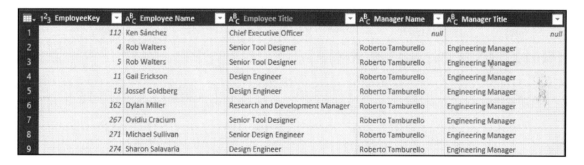

Figure 140: Employee Table with Manager Columns

- The two rows for Rob Walters are due to a **Slowly Changing Dimension (SCD)** Type 2 process applied in the source database.

- With the revised table loaded, it's simple to create a manager-employee hierarchy or use the columns separately in visuals with drill up/down capabilities.

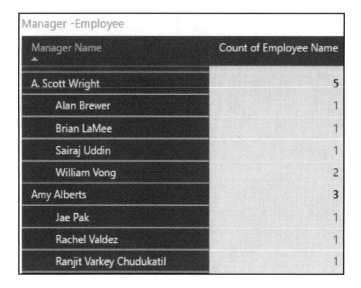

Manager -Employee	
Manager Name	Count of Employee Name
A. Scott Wright	5
Alan Brewer	1
Brian LaMee	1
Sairaj Uddin	1
William Vong	2
Amy Alberts	3
Jae Pak	1
Rachel Valdez	1
Ranjit Varkey Chudukatil	1

Figure 141: Employee Dimension in Matrix Visual

How it works...

Nested join versus flat join

- In implementing the table joins, you can choose to use the `Table.Join()` and `Table.NestedJoin()` functions
- All six join types are supported by both functions: inner, left outer, right outer, full outer, left anti, right anti
- `Table.NestedJoin()` enters the results of the join (the right or second table) into a new column of table values and will use local resources to execute the join operation, unless the `Table.ExpandTableColumn()` function is used to replace this new column with columns from the right table

- A left outer join type is the default if the `JoinKind` parameter is not specified.
- `Table.Join()` automatically expands the left table with the columns from the right table input (a flat join) and defaults to an inner join if the `JoinKind` parameter is not specified
- This function will get folded to the source without any additional functions but requires that there are no matching column names between the joined tables for JoinKinds other than inner join
- For inner joins, the matching column names from both tables must be specified in the join key parameters
- An additional `Table.SelectColumns()` functions is required to exclude any columns from the right table added with the join
- For performance reasons, `Table.NestedJoin()` should not be used without a `Table.ExpandTableColumn()` function removing the column of tables
- Whether implemented via `Table.NestedJoin()` or `Table.Join()`, developers should look to use inner joins if the source tables have referential integrity such as with foreign key constraints and this meets requirements
- For joins against larger tables, developers should confirm that query folding is occurring and can evaluate different query plans generated and performance by alternative retrieval designs

Append multiple files

- The `Table.Combine()` function performs an append operation and does not remove duplicate rows
- Any columns which are unique to one of the input tables in a `Table.Combine()` function will be added to the result set with null values for the rows from the other tables
- The `Table.Distinct()` function can be applied at the table level to remove duplicate rows
- It can also be applied against a single column or a group of columns

There's more...

Combine binaries

- If data source files with the same structure are stored in a network directory folder, Power BI offers the **Combine Binaries** transformation that can be used with text, CSV, Excel, JSON and other file formats
- This feature automatically creates an example query and a function linked to this query, such that any required modification to the source files can be applied to all files, and the source location of the files can be easily revised

Staging queries versus inline queries

- Rather than creating separate lookup/join staging queries, it's possible to consolidate these expressions into a single let ... in M expression
- For example, the following Employee expression returns the same table as the staging approach described in this recipe

```
    { EmployeeKey , ParentEmployeeKey , Employee Name , Title }),
    Employees = Table.RenameColumns(SelectCols2,{"Title", "Employee Title"}),
    ManagerInLine = Employees,

    EmployeeManagerJoin = Table.NestedJoin(Employees,
        "ParentEmployeeKey" ManagerInLine, EmployeeKey","ManagerColumn", JoinKind.LeftOuter),

    ManagerColumns = Table.ExpandTableColumn(EmployeeManagerJoin,"ManagerColumn",
        {"Employee Name", "Employee Title"},{"Manager Name", "Manager Title"}),

    EmployeeManager = Table.SelectColumns
            (ManagerColumns,
            {"EmployeeKey","Employee Name", "Employee Title", "Manager Name", "Manager Title"})
in
    EmployeeManager
```

Figure 142: In-Line Query of Employees and Managers

- The expression in *Figure 142* defines a variable expression of ManagerInLine as equivalent to the Employees expression and then joins to this expression

- Inline query approaches are helpful in limiting the volume of queries but you lose the management benefits provided by group folders and the query dependencies view
- The graphical support makes it easier to explain and quickly troubleshoot a data retrieval process than a single but complex M expression
- Staging queries are recommended for projects and retrieval processes of medium or greater complexity
- These queries should never be loaded to the data model as they could both confuse the user and would require additional resources to process and store by the data model

See also

- Combine Binaries in Power BI Desktop (`http://bit.ly/2oL2nM4`)
- The following table breaks outs the six different join types that can be specified in both the `Table.NestedJoin()` and `Table.Join()` functions

Join type	Parameter	Parameter value
Inner	JoinKind.Inner	0
Left Outer	JoinKind.LeftOuter	1
Right Outer	JoinKind.RightOuter	2
Full Outer	JoinKind.FullOuter	3
Left Anti	JoinKind.LeftAnti	4
Right Anti	JoinKind.RightAnti	5

- Both the Parameter and Parameter Value can be used, though the recipes in this book use Parameter as this makes the expressions easier to follow
- See the M Table Function Reference (`http://bit.ly/2oj0k0I`)

Choosing column data types

Setting the data types of columns in Power BI Desktop is usually the final step of queries and has great implications for all layers of the solution including data refresh, modeling, and visualization. Choosing appropriate data types reduces the risk of refresh failures, ensures consistent report results, and provides analytical flexibility to the data model and visualization layers.

This recipe includes four common examples of choosing and defining data types to load to Power BI Desktop. Additional details on data types and the implications of data types for Power BI development are contained in the sections following these examples.

How to do it...

Remove automatic type detection steps

1. Remove any **Changed Type** steps that were applied automatically to your queries.
2. This step will be applied to unstructured sources such as data tables from Excel workbooks and can be found immediately following selection of the source item.

Figure 143: Automatic Data Type Selection Step

3. View the expression of the step to observe that every column was referenced by its specific column name.

```
Table.TransformColumnTypes(DimProductTbl_Table,{{"ProductKey", Int64.Type}, {"Product Class", type text}, {"Product Color", type text}, {"Days to
Manufacture", Int64.Type}, {"Dealer Price", type any}, {"Product Start Date", type date}, {"Product End Date", type any}, {"Product Description",
type any}, {"Product Name", type text}, {"Finished Goods Flag", type text}, {"List Price", type any}, {"Product Model", type any}, {"Product
Weight", Int64.Type}, {"Product Style", type any}, {"Standard Cost", type any}, {"Product line", type any}, {"Product Status", type text},
{"Product Safety Stock Level", Int64.Type}, {"Product Subcategory", type any}, {"Product Category", type any}})
```

Figure 144: M Expression generated by automatic data type detection

- If even one of the source columns is removed or revised in the future, the query will fail due to the dependency on all original source columns.

Align relationship column data types

1. Identify the data types of the columns used to define relationships.
2. If there are any mismatches, such as a text joined with whole number, implement revisions to the data types.
3. In this example, `Account` is a dimension table with a one-to-many relationship to the `Finance` fact table on the `AccountKey` column per *Figure 145*.

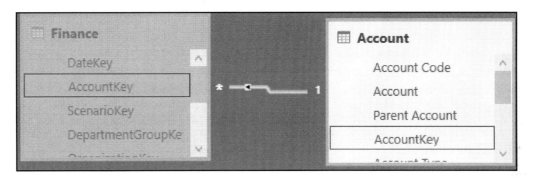

Figure 145: Relationships Window

- Both columns store whole number values but in this case the `AccountKey` column from `Account` is defined as a text data type.
- `AccountKey` is stored in the model as a text data type reflecting the type of the query.

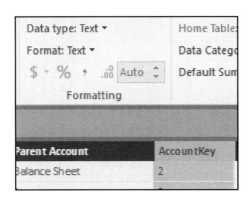

Figure 146: Data View

4. Use the `Table.TransformColumnTypes()` function to revise the type.

```
AccountKeyToWholeNumber = Table.TransformColumnTypes(Source,{{"AccountKey", Int64.Type}})
```

Figure 147: M expression to revise AccountKey to Whole Number data type

5. Close and apply the revised query and the data type in the model will also be revised to whole number.

- With the possible exception of the `Date` dimension, the relationship columns will generally be whole numbers, as this type supports both precision and slowly changing dimensions for historical tracking.
- If it is necessary to use text data types for relationship columns, either ensure the data will conform to a defined format for both fact and dimension columns, or pro-actively apply transformations to these columns to enforce a single standard.

Add numeric columns from text columns

1. Add a numeric column from a source column stored as text.
2. Use the `Number.FromText()` function within `Table.AddColumn()`.

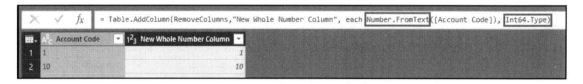

Figure 148: New Whole Number Column from Text Column

- The type parameter to `Table.AddColumn()` is optional.
- Leaving it blank results in a `Any` data type which would be loaded to the data model as a text data type.

- By specifying `Int64.Type` (*Figure 148*), as the optional type parameter to `Table.AddColumn()`, the new column is a whole number:
  - `Currency.Type` sets the column as a Fixed Decimal Number
  - `type number` sets the new column as a Decimal Number
  - `type text` sets the column to a Text data type
  - `type date` sets the column to a Date data type
  - `type time` sets the column to a Time data type
- Like all M expressions, data type declarations are case sensitive.

Use fixed decimal number for precision

1. Convert **Decimal Number** to **Fixed Decimal Number** data types if consistent rounding results are required and the Fixed Decimal type provides sufficient size.
   - A **Decimal** data type is an approximate and can produce inconsistent reporting results due to rounding. Converting to a **Fixed Decimal** type provides 4 decimal places and ensures consistent results.
2. Confirm that the scale of the **Fixed Decimal** type (19,4) will be sufficient before implementing this change.

- In this example, the `Measurement` column is stored as a decimal number, but precise rounding (consistent results) is required:

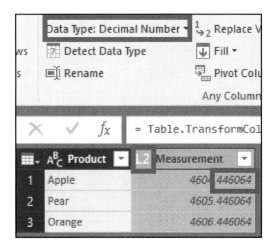

Figure 149: Decimal Number data type

- The query editor provides multiple indications of a decimal data type including the header icon and the **Data Type** dropdown in the toolbar.

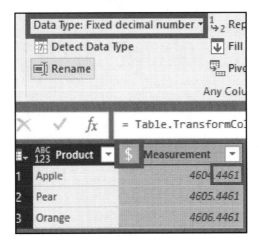

Figure 150: Fixed decimal number type

- The **Fixed decimal number** data type is equivalent to **Currency** in the M language as per *Figure 151*.

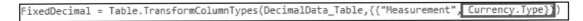

Figure 151: Conversion to Fixed decimal number data type

How it works...

Automatic data type detection

- The automatic data type detection step uses a sampling or preview of each source column to determine the appropriate type. If this sample doesn't reflect the full or future set of values for the column the data type selected may be incorrect.
- Automatic type detection is not used with structured relational database systems such as SQL Server.

- If enabled, this step only applies to unstructured data sources such as flat files and Excel workbooks.
- As per the *Choosing columns and column names* recipe, it's important to avoid dependencies on columns not required by the query.
- As per configuration guidance in Chapter 1 (*Configuring Power BI Development Tools*) you can avoid automatic type detection via the **Data Load** options. As this is a **Current File** option only and since the setting is enabled by default you currently need to disable this automatic type detection for each new file.

Numeric data types

- Decimal number data types are floating-point (approximate) data types with 15 digits of precision
- Fixed decimal number data types store 19 digits of precision and four significant digits to the right of the decimal (19,4)
- Whole number data types store up to 19 digits of precision

Power BI Desktop automatic time intelligence

- Power BI Desktop automatically creates internal date tables for columns stored as dates and relates these tables to the data model
- Connecting a Power BI Desktop model from DAX Studio exposes these additional tables as `LocalDateTables` with GUIDs
- This Time Intelligence feature is enabled by default in the **Data Load** options for the **CURRENT FILE**

There's more...

Data type impacts

- Converting from decimal number to fixed decimal number can also marginally improve data compression and query performance.
- Power BI Desktop provides rich analysis capabilities for columns of the date data type including drill down hierarchies, visual calendar pickers for chart axis, custom date filtering logic in slicers, and calculations such as first and last date.

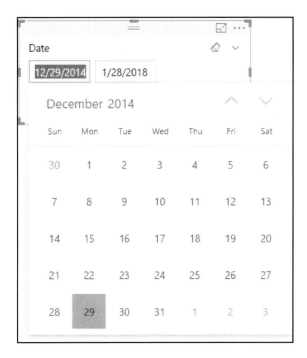

Figure 152: Date data type column used as a slicer

- Given these capabilities, as well as DAX functionality with Date data types, converting text and numeric types to date data types can provide significantly more options to develop Power BI content.

- Revising text data types to numeric data types per the example also impacts the DAX metrics that can be written. For example, if the `Calendar Year` column is stored as a text data type, the following DAX metric will fail due to type incompatibility:

```
Sales in 2016 and Later = CALCULATE([Internet Sales], 'Date'[Calendar Year] >= 2016)
```

Figure 153: DAX Measure Expression

- Revising calendar year to a whole number type avoids the need to use `VALUE` or `FORMAT` functions in each DAX measure.

Date with locale

- If there's any potential for date data types to be sourced from a region with a different date standard than your local system, you should apply the **Locale** option to the **Type Transform** expression
- In the following example, the `Original Date` column stores date values in the format `dd/mm/yyyy` whereas the local system uses `mm/dd/yyyy`
- Trying to convert from **Original Date** to **Date** directly causes the error in Date Transform Only as the first two digits are greater than 12
- Specifying the source locale in the transform expression allows for successful conversion to the `Date` with `Locale` column in *Figure 154*:

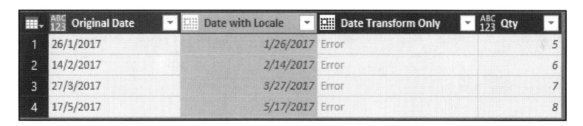

	Original Date	Date with Locale	Date Transform Only	Qty
1	26/1/2017	1/26/2017	Error	5
2	14/2/2017	2/14/2017	Error	6
3	27/3/2017	3/27/2017	Error	7
4	17/5/2017	5/17/2017	Error	8

Figure 154: Converting a Date from a Different Standard

- The Query Editor provides a simple interface for the source locale:
- Right-click on the column and select **Using Locale** from the **Change Type** dropdown

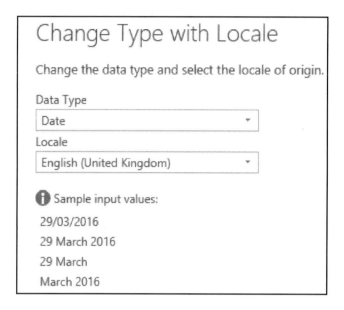

Figure 155: Change Type with Locale Interface

- Alternatively, you can add the locale to the expression itself directly

```
#"Changed Type" = Table.TransformColumnTypes(#"Renamed Columns",{{"Date Transform Only", type date}}),
#"Changed Type with Locale" = Table.TransformColumnTypes(#"Changed Type", {{"Date with Locale", type date}}, "en-GB")
```

Figure 156: M syntax for Date Source Locale

Percentage data type

Percentage was added as fourth numeric data type to the Query Editor/M in November of 2016. Unlike whole number, fixed decimal number, and decimal number, this type does not have a corresponding type in the data model.

When loaded to the data model, the percentage data type is represented as a decimal number type.

See also

- The following blog post from Gil Raviv at DataChant describes the issues caused by automatic detection of column data types (`http://bit.ly/2otDbcU`)
- The following blog post from Marco Russo at SQLBI details the numeric data types of DAX including the rounding of decimal data types and performance considerations (`http://bit.ly/2nOWYAm`)

Visualizing the M library

To implement complex and less common data transformation requirements, it's often necessary to browse the M library to find a specific function or review the parameters of a specific function. This short recipe provides a pre-built M query expression you can use to retrieve the M library into a table for analysis in Power BI Desktop. Additionally, an example is provided of visualizing and cross-filtering this table of functions on the Power BI report canvas.

How to do it...

1. Open a new Power BI Desktop file (PBIX) and create a blank Query.
2. Enter the following M code in the Advanced Editor:

```
M Functions

let
    SharedToTable = Record.ToTable(#shared),
    RenamedToFunction = Table.RenameColumns(SharedToTable,{{"Name", "function"}}),
    SortedFunctionTable = Table.Sort(RenamedToFunction,{{"Function", Order.Ascending}}),
    DuplicatedColumn = Table.DuplicateColumn(SortedFunctionTable, "Function", "FunctionColumnDuplicate"),
    SplitFunctionColumn = Table.SplitColumn(DuplicatedColumn,"FunctionColumnDuplicate",Splitter.SplitTextByDelimiter(
    ".", QuoteStyle.Csv),{"Function Group", " Function Detail"}),
    MLibraryTable = Table.TransformColumnTypes(SplitFunctionColumn,{{"Function Group", type text}, {" Function Detail", type text}})
in
    MLibraryTable
```

Figure 157: M Expression to Retrieve a Table of the M Library

- The Query Editor should look like the following screenshot:

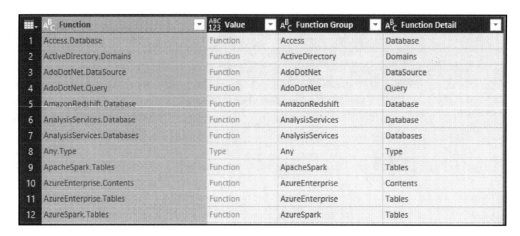

Figure 158: Query Editor View of Library Table Function

3. Click on **Close and Apply** from the Query Editor.
4. The 785+ rows from the M library are now loaded to the data model.
5. Create a **Report Page Visual** that uses the `Function Group` column for filtering.

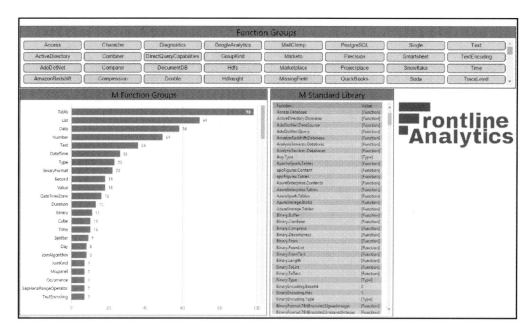

Figure 159: Report Page of M Standard Library

How it works...

The M expression leverages the `#shared` variable, which returns a record of the names and values currently in scope. The record is converted to a table value and then the `Function` column, originally `Name` in the context of the library, is split based on the period delimiter to allow for the `Function Group` column.

There's more...

M library details for every function are made available by entering the function without any parameters.

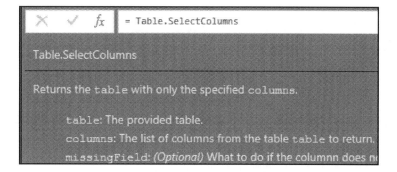

Figure 160: Library Function Details

Building a Power BI Data Model

3

In this chapter, we will cover the following recipes:

- Designing a multi fact data model
- Implementing a multi fact data model
- Handling one-to-many and many-to-many relationships
- Assigning data formatting and categories
- Configuring Default Summarization and sorting
- Setting the visibility of columns and tables
- Embedding business definitions into DAX measures
- Enriching a model with analysis expressions
- Building analytics into data models with DAX
- Integrating math and statistical analysis via DAX
- Supporting virtual table relationships
- Creating browsable model hierarchies and groups

Introduction

The data models developed in Power BI Desktop are at the center of Power BI projects, as they expose the interface in support of data exploration and drive the analytical queries visualized in reports and dashboards. Well-designed data models leverage the data connectivity and transformation capabilities described in Chapter 2, *Accessing and Retrieving Data* to provide an integrated view of distinct business processes and entities. Additionally, data models contain predefined calculations, hierarchies and groupings, and metadata to greatly enhance both the analytical power of the dataset and its ease of use. The combination of Chapter 2, *Accessing and Retrieving Data* and Chapter 3, *Building a Power BI Data Model*, querying and modeling, serves as the foundation for the BI and analytical capabilities of Power BI.

> *"The data model is what feeds and what powers Power BI."*
>
> *- Kasper de Jonge, Senior Program Manager, Microsoft*

In this chapter, we explore the primary processes of designing and developing robust data models. Common challenges in dimensional modeling are mapped to corresponding features and approaches in Power BI Desktop, including multiple grains and many-to-many relationships. Examples are also provided to embed business logic and definitions, develop analytical calculations with the DAX language, and configure metadata settings to increase the value and sustainability of models.

Additional modeling topics, including row-level security, performance tuning, and migration of Power BI models to SSAS are covered in Chapter 8, *Implementing Dynamic User-Based Visibility in Power BI*, Chapter 11, *Enhancing and Optimizing Existing Power BI Solutions*, and Chapter 13, *Integrating Power BI with other Applications*, respectively.

Designing a multi fact data model

Power BI Desktop lends itself to rapid, agile development in which significant value can be obtained quickly despite both imperfect data sources and an incomplete understanding of business requirements and use cases. However, rushing through the design phase can undermine the sustainability of the solution as future needs cannot be met without structural revisions to the model or complex workarounds. A balanced design phase in which fundamental decisions such as DirectQuery versus in-memory are analyzed while a limited prototype model is used to generate visualizations and business feedback can address both short- and long-term needs.

This recipe describes a process for designing a multiple fact table data model and identifies some of the primary questions and factors to consider.

Getting ready

Setting business expectations

Everyone has seen impressive Power BI demonstrations and many business analysts have effectively used Power BI Desktop independently. These experiences may create an impression that integration, rich analytics, and collaboration can be delivered across many distinct systems and stakeholders very quickly or easily.

It's important to reign in any unrealistic expectations and confirm feasibility. For example, Power BI Desktop is not an enterprise BI tool like SSIS or SSAS in terms of scalability, version control, features, and configurations. Power BI datasets cannot be incrementally refreshed like partitions in SSAS, and the current 1 GB file limit (after compression) places a hard limit on the amount of data a single model can store. Additionally, if multiple data sources are needed within the model, then DirectQuery models are not an option. Finally, it's critical to distinguish the data model as a platform supporting robust analysis of business processes, not an individual report or dashboard itself.

Identify the top pain points and unanswered business questions in the current state. Contrast this input with an assessment of feasibility and complexity (for example, data quality and analytical needs) and target realistic and sustainable deliverables.

How to do it...

Dimensional modeling best practices and star schema designs are directly applicable to Power BI data models. Short, collaborative modeling sessions can be scheduled with subject matter experts and main stakeholders. With the design of the model in place, an informed decision of the model's data mode (Import or DirectQuery) can be made prior to development.

Four-step dimensional design process

1. **Choose the business process**
    - The number and nature of processes to include depends on the scale of the sources and scope of the project
    - In this example, the chosen processes are Internet Sales, Reseller Sales, and General Ledger

2. **Declare the granularity**
    - For each business process (or fact) to be modeled from *step 1*, define the meaning of each row:
        - These should be clear, concise business definitions--each fact table should only contain one grain
        - Consider scalability limitations with Power BI Desktop and balance the needs between detail and history (for example, greater history but lower granularity)
        - Example: One Row per Sales Order Line, One Row per GL Account Balance per fiscal period

 Separate business processes, such as plan and sales should never be integrated into the same table. Likewise, a single fact table should not contain distinct processes such as shipping and receiving. Fact tables can be related to common dimensions but should never be related to each other in the data model (for example, PO Header and Line level).

3. **Identify the dimensions**
    - These entities should have a natural relationship with the business process or event at the given granularity
    - Compare the dimension with any existing dimensions and hierarchies in the organization (for example, Store)
        - If so, determine if there's a conflict or if additional columns are required

Be aware of the query performance implications with large, high-cardinality dimensions such as customer tables with over 2 million rows. It may be necessary to optimize this relationship in the model or the measures and queries that use this relationship. See `Chapter 11`, *Enhancing and Optimizing Existing Power BI Solutions*, for more details.

4. **Identify the facts**
   - These should align with the business processes being modeled:
     - For example, the sum of a quantity or a unique count of a dimension
   - Document the business and technical definition of the primary facts and compare this with any existing reports or metadata repository (for example, *Net Sales = Extended Amount - Discounts*).
   - Given steps 1-3, you should be able to walk through top business questions and check whether the planned data model will support it. Example: "What was the variance between Sales and Plan for last month in Bikes?"
     - Any clear gaps require modifying the earlier steps, removing the question from the scope of the data model, or a plan to address the issue with additional logic in the model (M or DAX).

Focus only on the primary facts at this stage such as the individual source columns that comprise the cost facts. If the business definition or logic for core fact has multiple steps and conditions, check if the data model will naturally simplify it or if the logic can be developed in the data retrieval to avoid complex measures.

Data warehouse and implementation bus matrix

The Power BI model should preferably align with a corporate data architecture framework of standard facts and dimensions that can be shared across models. Though consumed into Power BI Desktop, existing data definitions and governance should be observed. Any new facts, dimensions, and measures developed with Power BI should supplement this architecture.

1. **Create a data warehouse bus matrix:**
   - A matrix of business processes (facts) and standard dimensions is a primary tool for designing and managing data models and communicating the overall BI architecture.

BUSINESS PROCESSES	Date	Customer	Product	Vendor	Promotion	Reseller	Sales Territory	Employee	Account	Organization
Internet Sales	✓	✓	✓	✓	✓		✓			
Reseller Sales	✓		✓		✓	✓	✓	✓		
General Ledger	✓								✓	✓
Sales Plan	✓		✓				✓			
Inventory	✓		✓	✓					✓	
Customer Surveys	✓	✓								
Customer Service Calls	✓	✓	✓					✓		

Data Warehouse Bus Matrix

   - In this example, the business processes selected for the model are **Internet Sales**, **Reseller Sales**, and **General Ledger**.

2. **Create an implementation bus matrix:**
   - An outcome of the model design process should include a more detailed implementation bus matrix.

BUSINESS PROCESSES	Row Granularity	Measures	Date	Customer	Product	Promotion	Reseller	Sales Territory	Employee	Account	Organization	Department
Internet Sales	Sales Order Line (SKU)	Internet Sales Dollars and Units, Count of Customers and Products	✓	✓	✓	✓		✓				
Reseller Sales	Sales Order Line (SKU)	Gross and Net Sales, Discounts, Margin Amount and %	✓		✓	✓	✓	✓	✓			
General Ledger	GL Account Entry	Account Balance Amount	✓							✓	✓	✓

Implementation Bus Matrix: Internet Sales, Reseller Sales, and General Ledger

- Clarity and approval of the grain of the fact tables, the definitions of the primary measures, and all dimensions gives confidence when entering the development phase.

 Power BI queries (M) and analysis logic (DAX) should not be considered a long-term substitute for issues with data quality, master data management, and the data warehouse. If it is necessary to move forward, document the "technical debts" incurred and consider long-term solutions such as **Master Data Services** (**MDS**).

Choose the dataset storage mode - Import or DirectQuery

With the logical design of a model in place, one of the top design questions is whether to implement this model with DirectQuery mode or with the default imported In-Memory mode.

In-Memory mode

The default in-memory mode is highly optimized for query performance and supports additional modeling and development flexibility with DAX functions. With compression, columnar storage, parallel query plans, and other techniques an import mode model is able to support a large amount of data (for example, 50M rows) and still perform well with complex analysis expressions. Multiple data sources can be accessed and integrated in a single data model and all DAX functions are supported for measures, columns, and role security.

However, the import or refresh process must be scheduled and this is currently limited to eight refreshes per day for datasets in shared capacity (48X per day in premium capacity). As an alternative to scheduled refreshes in the Power BI service, REST APIs can be used to trigger a data refresh of a published dataset. For example, an HTTP request to a Power BI REST API calling for the refresh of a dataset can be added to the end of a nightly update or ETL process script such that published Power BI content remains aligned with the source systems. More importantly, it's not currently possible to perform an incremental refresh such as the Current Year rows of a table (for example, a table partition) or only the source rows that have changed. In-Memory mode models must maintain a file size smaller than the current limits (1 GB compressed currently, 10GB expected for Premium capacities by October 2017) and must also manage refresh schedules in the Power BI Service. Both incremental data refresh and larger dataset sizes are identified as planned capabilities of the Microsoft Power BI Premium Whitepaper (May 2017).

DirectQuery mode

A DirectQuery mode model provides the same semantic layer interface for users and contains the same metadata that drives model behaviors as In-Memory models. The performance of DirectQuery models, however, is dependent on the source system and how this data is presented to the model. By eliminating the import or refresh process, DirectQuery provides a means to expose reports and dashboards to source data as it changes. This also avoids the file size limit of import mode models. However, there are several limitations and restrictions to be aware of with DirectQuery:

- Only a single database from a single, supported data source can be used in a DirectQuery model.
- When deployed for widespread use, a high level of network traffic can be generated thus impacting performance.
    - Power BI visualizations will need to query the source system, potentially via an on-premises data gateway.
- Some DAX functions cannot be used in calculated columns or with role security.
    - Additionally, several common DAX functions are not optimized for DirectQuery performance.
- Many M query transformation functions cannot be used with DirectQuery.
- MDX client applications such as Excel are supported but less metadata (for example, hierarchies) is exposed.

Given these limitations and the importance of a "speed of thought" user experience with Power BI, DirectQuery should generally only be used on centralized and smaller projects in which visibility to updates of the source data is essential. If a supported DirectQuery system (for example, Teradata or Oracle) is available, the performance of core measures and queries should be tested.

 Confirm referential integrity in the source database and use the **Assume Referential Integrity** relationship setting in DirectQuery mode models. This will generate more efficient inner join SQL queries against the source database.

How it works...

DAX formula and storage engine

Power BI Datasets and **SQL Server Analysis Services** (**SSAS**) share the same database engine and architecture. Both tools support both Import and DirectQuery data models and both DAX and MDX client applications such as Power BI (DAX) and Excel (MDX). The DAX Query Engine is comprised of a formula and a storage engine for both Import and DirectQuery models. The formula engine produces query plans, requests data from the storage engine, and performs any remaining complex logic not supported by the storage engine against this data such as IF and SWITCH functions

In DirectQuery models, the data source database is the storage engine--it receives SQL queries from the formula engine and returns the results to the formula engine. For In-Memory models, the imported and compressed columnar memory cache is the storage engine. See `Chapter 11`, *Enhancing and Optimizing Existing Power BI Solutions*, for more details.

There's more...

Project ingestion questions

Several topics and specific questions are so common that a standard "project ingestion" form or document can be created to support design and planning meetings. These topics and questions include the following:

Data Sources: Is all the data required in system X? What other sources are required or currently used?

Security: Will the data model contain PCII or sensitive data? Does any data need to be secured from certain users?

Version Control: Are there existing reports or models with the same measures?

Complexity: Can the source data be used directly or are transformations required?

Analytics: Are any custom or advanced analytics required (for example, exception measures, statistical analyses)?

Data Refresh: Is there a need for real-time access? If not, how frequently does the data need to be refreshed?

Model Scale: How much historical data is required? How many rows per week/month/year are in the largest fact table?

Distribution: Approximately how many users will need to access the reports and dashboards this model will support?

Power BI delivery approaches

Power BI can be fully delivered and managed by corporate BI professionals from data retrieval through visualization and content distribution. Some BI and analytics organizations also adopt hybrid approaches in which different components of Power BI are developed and owned by different teams such as the BI/IT teams providing an optimized data source, its supporting ETL process, and the analytical data model, including its measure definitions, relationships, and data refresh process. Business teams can then leverage these assets in developing Power BI reports and dashboards and optionally Excel reports as well.

As Power BI projects can have widely varying and often overlapping needs (for example, security, data refresh, and scalability) it's important to adopt a process for allocating the appropriate resources and planning for the longer term deployment such as migrating important, relatively mature Power BI datasets to SSAS Tabular.

 The Planning a Power BI Enterprise Deployment Whitepaper identifies the fundamental decisions and factors that guide Power BI deployments including licensing, scalability and performance, data sources (cloud and on-premises), report visualization options, administration and more.

See also

- Planning a Power BI Enterprise Deployment: https://powerbi.microsoft.com/en-us/documentation/powerbi-whitepapers
- Microsoft Power BI Premium: https://powerbi.microsoft.com/en-us/documentation/powerbi-whitepapers
- The Ten Essential Rules of Dimensional Modeling: http://bit.ly/1QijUwM
- Using DirectQuery in Power BI Desktop: http://bit.ly/2nUoLOG
- DirectQuery in SSAS Tabular 2016 Whitepaper: http://bit.ly/2oe4Xcn
- DAX Formula Compatibility in DirectQuery: http://bit.ly/2oK8QXB
- Announcing Data Refresh APIs: http://bit.ly/2rOUd3a

Implementing a multi fact data model

The implementation of a data model proceeds from the design phase described in the previous recipe. The design process and its supporting documentation clarify which entities to model, their granularity, the fact-to-dimension relationships, and the fact measures that must be developed. Additionally, the model mode (Import or DirectQuery) has already been determined and any additional business logic to be implemented via M or DAX functions is also known. The different components of the model can now be developed including data source connectivity, queries, relationships, measures, and metadata.

In this recipe we walk through all primary steps in the physical implementation of a model design. Three fact tables and their related dimensions are retrieved, relationships are created, and the core measures and metadata are added. When complete, the multi-fact data model can be exposed to business users for initial testing and feedback.

How to do it...

The following steps align with the logical flow of model development and can be implemented in discrete phases across teams or by an individual Power BI developer. Given different lead times associated with components of the model, it can be advantageous to move forward with a more mature or simple component such that business teams can engage and provide feedback as enhancements and other components are deployed.

SQL view layer

1. Create a SQL View for each fact and dimension table to be represented in the data model
   - The views should only select the columns required of the model and apply the model's column names

The layer of views protects the model from changes in the source system and provides visibility to administrators of the model's dependency. Additionally, the views can denormalize source tables via joins to conform to the structure of the model tables and potentially include derived columns not available in the source.

- In the following SQL example, the product dimension view joins three tables and applies model column names:

```
, C.EnglishProductCategoryName AS 'Product Category'
, P.ProductAlternateKey AS 'Product Alternate Key'
FROM
DBO.DimProduct AS P
 LEFT JOIN DBO.DimProductSubcategory AS S ON
P.ProductSubcategoryKey = S.ProductSubcategoryKey
 LEFT JOIN DBO.DimProductCategory AS C ON S.ProductCategoryKey =
C.ProductCategoryKey
```

Defining the SQL views is especially important if supporting a DirectQuery model. For DirectQuery model views, evaluate the efficiency of the query plans and the referential integrity between the views to support inner join DirectQuery queries.

M queries in Power BI Desktop

1. Create M queries containing the data source connection information (for example, server name, or database name).
   - For example, an M query with the `Sql.Database()` function could serve as a data source for other tables
2. Build an M query for each dimension and fact table that accesses the SQL views defined in step 1.
   - In this example, the `AWProd` query contains the data source information and a fact table view is accessed:

```
let
 Source = AWProd,
 InternetSales = Source{[Schema = "BI_Sales", Item =
"vFact_InternetSales"]}[Data]
in
 InternetSales
```

- Each new query references the data source query and is given the name to be surfaced in the model

3. Duplicate a query and replace the `Item` parameter with the source view. Disable the load of the data source query.

Query groups in Query Editor

4. Confirm that the column data types align with the design (for example, a fixed decimal number to avoid rounding issues).
5. Close the Query Editor and load the tables into the Power BI model.

Create model relationships

1. From the **Modeling** tab of the Report or Data view, select **Manage Relationships** and click on **New**.
2. Create many-to-one, single direction relationships from each fact table to its corresponding dimension table.
   - Date data type columns should be used for the `Date` table relationships.

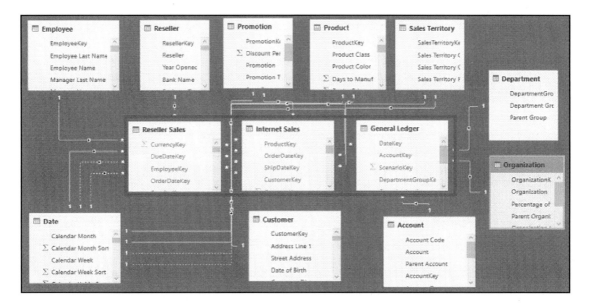

Relationships view of a multi fact data model

- Bidirectional relationships should only be implemented with clear guidance and evaluation.

Author DAX measures

1. Write the core measures for each fact table identified in the planning phase and validate for accuracy.
2. If complex DAX expressions are needed for the core measures the source and retrieval should be reviewed.
3. Give each measure an intuitive name and a standard format (for example, two decimal places, thousands separator).

The most relevant examples for this step of the implementation are covered in the *Embedding business definitions into DAX measures* recipe later in this chapter. Other more advanced examples of DAX expressions are included in recipes of `Chapter 8`, *Implementing Dynamic User-Based Visibility in Power BI*, `Chapter 9`, *Applying Advanced Analytics and Custom Visuals*, `Chapter 10`, *Developing Solutions for System Monitoring and Administration*, and in later chapters.

Configure model metadata

1. Add hierarchies such as `Product Category`, `Product Subcategory`, and `Product Name` and a `Date` hierarchy.
2. Set the **Default Summarization** and **Sorting of Columns** such as **Month Name** sorted by **Month Number**.
3. Assign **Data Categories** to columns such as **Address** or **Postal Code** to support geographical visualization.
4. Hide columns from the fact tables such that only measure groups are visible
    * If it's necessary to expose a column from the fact table, consider a dedicated measure table and associate the `Home` table of related measures to this table.

 Details on all primary metadata settings are included in this chapter in recipes, *Assigning data formatting and categories, Configuring default summarization and sorting, Setting the visibility of columns and tables*, and *Creating browseable model hierarchies and groups*. All of these settings impact the usability and functionality of the data model and should not be neglected.

* The **Field List** in Power BI Desktop and the data exploration and visualization process should all reflect and benefit from the detailed implementation of steps 1-5.

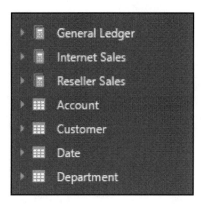

Power BI Field List

- Validation and user testing of the new model should follow implementation.
- Model documentation can be developed via **Dynamic Management Views (DMVs)** to provide users of definitions and relationships. See the *Importing and visualizing dynamic management view data of SSAS and Power BI data models* recipe of `Chapter 10`, *Developing Solutions for System Monitoring and Administration* for a detailed example of this pattern.

There's more...

Shared views

If a model's source view is shared with other applications and may change or include columns not needed by the model, the `Table.SelectColumns()` M function can be used:

```
let
  Source = AWProd,
  InternetSales = Source{[Schema = "BI_Sales", Item =
"vFact_InternetSales"]}[Data],
  InternetSalesColumns =
Table.SelectColumns(InternetSales,{"ProductKey","OrderDateKey"},MissingFiel
d.UseNull)
in
  InternetSalesColumns
```

- Each column required by the table in the model is explicitly selected
- The `MissingField.UseNull` parameter allows the query to refresh successfully despite a specified column being missing such as when a column's name has changed

Handling one-to-many and many-to-many relationships

One of the most important data modeling features of Power BI, which is shared with SQL Server Analysis Services Tabular 2016 and later versions, is the control the modeler has over defining the filtering behavior through relationships. In addition to one-to-many single direction relationships, Power BI models can contain bidirectional relationships as well as DAX measures that contain their own relationship filtering logic via the new `CROSSFILTER()` function. These relationship tools, along with modifying the filter context of measures through DAX, can be used to support many-to-many modeling scenarios and provide alternative model behaviors for multiple business requirements.

In this recipe, we look at the primary use cases for bidirectional relationships and DAX-based cross filtering. The first example uses a bidirectional relationship and the `CROSSFILTER()` function to support analytical needs at different scopes--the data model and specific measures. The second example model uses a bidirectional relationship with a bridge table to enable a filter through a many-to-many relationship. Examples of related DAX filter context approaches are also included for reference.

Getting ready

To follow along and test the examples with your own data, you may consider the following:

- Create simple `COUNTROWS()` measures for each table in your model and add them to a blank report canvas
- The numbers will adjust (or not) as different techniques and filter selections are applied

How to do it...

Single, bidirectional, and CROSSFILTER()

Single direction relationships

1. Access a simple star schema data model with row count measures for each table.

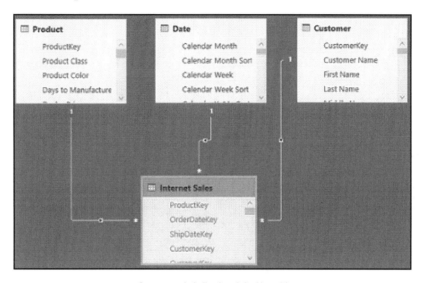

One-to-many single direction relationship model

- The relationships are all single-direction from the dimension to the fact table.

2. Add the row count measures to the report canvas and create slicer visuals from the dimension tables.

| 60,398 | 18,484 | 1,127 | 606 |
| Sales Table Rows | Customer Table Rows | Date Table Rows | Product Table Rows |

Calendar Year	Product Category	Customer Gender
☐ 2018	☐ (Blank)	☐ F
☐ 2017	☐ Accessories	☐ M
☐ 2016	☐ Bikes	
☐ 2015	☐ Clothing	
☐ 2014	☐ Components	

Relationship and cross filter testing visualization

- With single-direction relationships, a selection on any of the slicers will only impact its own table and the sales table.

Bidirectional relationship

1. Open the **Manage Relationships** window from the **Modeling** tab and select the **Sales to Product** relationship.
2. Modify the relationship between Product and Sales to **Both** for the **Cross filter direction**.

Cardinality	Cross filter direction
Many to one (*:1) ▾	Both ▾
✅ Make this relationship active	☐ Apply security filter in both directions

Bi-Directional Relationship Configuration (Both) from Edit Relationships Dialog

- Filter selections on one of the other dimension tables (`Customer` or `Date`) now also filter the `Product` table:
  - Filtering on the male gender reduces the `Product` table to only the rows associated with a sale to the male gender.

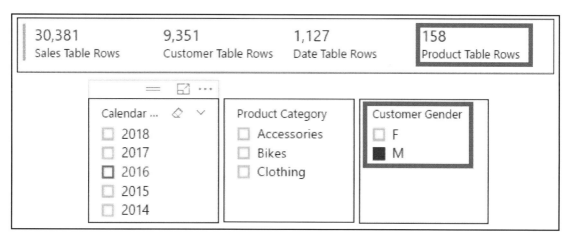

Bi-Directional Cross Filter Impact on Product Table via Customer Table Filter

- Only the Date table is not impacted by the slicer selection given its single-direction relationship to the Sales fact table.
- The customer table filters the Product table via the Sales table and its bidirectional relationship with product.

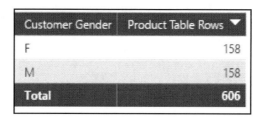

Bidirectional Cross Filter Impact in Report Visual

- With a single-direction cross filter, the Product table measure would show 606 for male and female (all products).
  - Unsold products (products without rows in the Sales table) account for the difference in all product rows.

Bidirectional relationships between fact and dimension tables should generally be avoided when the given dimension table is also related to other fact tables. This can cause over filtering or unintended filter contexts. For similar reasons, the bidirectional cross-filtering white paper recommends single-direction relationships between date and fact tables. However, bidirectional relationships are an integral part of efficient solutions to common (and otherwise complex) modeling scenarios such as Actual versus Budget and classical Many-to-Many scenarios.

CROSSFILTER() Measure

1. Create a DAX measure that applies an alternative cross filter behavior to the relationship in the model:

```
Product Table Rows (CF) = CALCULATE([Product Table Rows],
CROSSFILTER('Internet
Sales'[ProductKey],'Product'[ProductKey],OneWay) )
```

- The measure (**Product Table Rows (CF)**) overrides the bi-directional relationship to apply single-direction cross filtering.

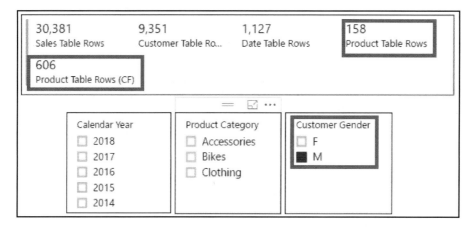

Single direction CROSSFILTER() measure relative to standard measure with bi-directional model relationship

- Though limited to specific measures, `CROSSFILTER()` can provide a simple and powerful supplement to the relationship cross filtering defined in the model.

The cross filter direction should be set to Single for the large majority of relationships and particularly dimension-to-fact-table relationships. Bidirectional relationships are very useful with bridge tables and many-to-many relationships. See the Building Analytics into data models with DAX recipe later in this chapter for an example of using bridge tables and bidirectional relationships to support Budget versus Actual reporting. Additionally, bidirectional relationships can be used for dynamic (user specific) Row-level security models - see `Chapter 8`, *Implementing Dynamic User-Based Visibility in Power BI* for examples of these implementations.

2. Write a DAX measure to propagate filter context.
    - The following measure respects the filters applied to the `Internet Sales` table, such as `Customer Gender = "M"`:

Product Rows (Sales) = CALCULATE(COUNTROWS('Product'),'Internet Sales')

- The `Product Rows (Sales)` measure returns the same 158 row count as the bidirectional relationship example.

Many-to-many relationships

In the following many-to-many model, multiple customers are associated with a given account and some customers have multiple accounts:

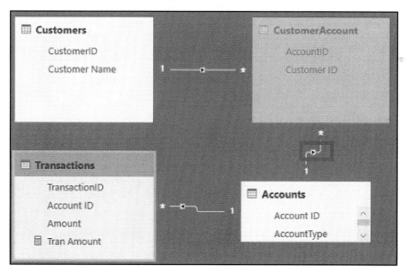

Many-to-many model with single direction cross-filtering relationships

Given the highlighted single direction relationship from `Accounts` to the `CustomerAccount` bridge table, a filter selection on the `Customer` dimension does not filter the `Transactions` table.

Bidirectional cross-filtering for many-to-many

1. Modify the cross filter direction of the relationship between `Accounts` and `CustomerAccount` to **Both**.
2. Create a simple testing visual by customer to validate the impact of the bi-directional cross-filtering behavior.

Customer Name ▼	Tran Amount
Terry Hatcher	$300
Rick Stevens	$300
Larry Michaels	$500
James Langford	$600
Gary Reynolds	$500
Bob Johnson	$300
Total	**$1,400**

Report Results with Bidirectional Cross-Filtering

- A report visual by customer will now correctly display both the total amount from the fact table ($1,400) and the amounts associated with each customer.
- A DAX alternative to the bidirectional relationship is the following:

```
M2M Tran Amount = CALCULATE([Tran
Amount],SUMMARIZE(CustomerAccount,Accounts[Account ID]))
```

- `SUMMARIZE()` leverages the one-to-many relationships of `Customers` and `Accounts` to the bridge table and, via `CALCULATE()`, passes the filter context of `Customers` to the `Accounts` table, which filters transactions.

For similar many-to-many scenarios, bidirectional relationship is recommended over the DAX approach for manageability and performance reasons.

How it works...

Ambiguous relationships

- Power BI data models will reject ambiguous relationships, in which there are multiple possible cross filtering paths
- For example, a bridge table cannot have two many-to-one bidirectional relationships to tables (A and B), both of which have one-to-many, single-direction cross filtering relationships to table C
    - The model would not know (or try to guess) whether table A or B should be filtered prior to filtering table C
- Inactive relationships, cross filter direction, and the CROSSFILTER() function provide additional modeling flexibility

CROSSFILTER()

- The CROSSFILTER() function requires an existing relationship (active or inactive) column with fully qualified syntax
    - The third parameter accepts the following values: OneWay, Both, and None
- CROSSFILTER() always overrides the relationship settings of the model

There's more...

DirectQuery supported

- Both bi-directional relationships and the CROSSFILTER() function can be used with DirectQuery models
    - The **Global DirectQuery** setting **Allow unrestricted measures** needs to be enabled to use CROSSFILTER()
- The additional SQL queries generated may negatively impact the performance depending on the model and source system

See also

- The Bidirectional Cross-Filtering Whitepaper: `http://bit.ly/2oWdwbG`

Assigning data formatting and categories

Two important metadata properties to configure for any column that will be visible on the Power BI report canvas are the data format and data category. The data formats should be consistent across data types and efficiently convey the appropriate level of detail. Data categories serve to enhance the data exploration experience by providing Power BI with information to guide its visualizations.

In this recipe, we set the data formats for dimension columns and measures. Additionally, geographical data category values are assigned to location columns to aid the visualization of this data.

How to do it...

Data formats

1. Select the **Data** view--the icon between the **Report** and **Relationships** views
   - If the model is in the DirectQuery mode, these settings are available on the **Modeling** tab of the **Report** view
2. Use the **Fields** list on the right to navigate the tables and select the column to format
3. When selected, the **Modeling** tab will expose a **Format** dropdown that is contextually based on the data type:

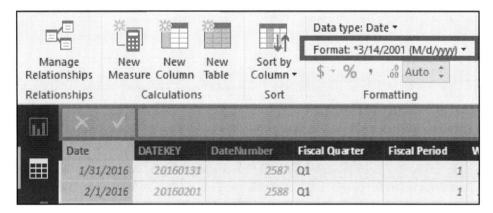

Column Formatting

4. Repeat this process by selecting the measures in the **Fields** list and setting the appropriate format:

Measure Formatting

- These settings can also be accessed from the **Modeling** tab of the **Report** view

Formatting decisions should consider the impact of precision on visualizations. Fewer decimal places and more abbreviated date formats consume less space in reports and are easier to visually comprehend in dashboards.

Data category

1. From the **Data** view, select a dimension table containing geographical attributes such as City or Zip Code.

2. With a column selected, use the **Data Category** dropdown on the **Modeling** tab to choose the most accurate category.

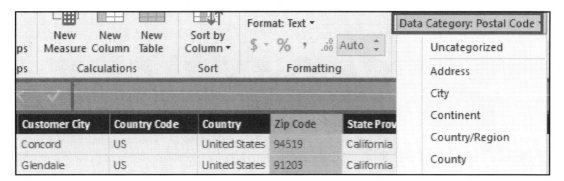

Data Category Selection

3. A globe icon will appear next to the geographical data category columns in the field list.

How it works...

- With the zip code column assigned a **Postal Code** category, Power BI chooses a bubble map visual by default

Default Visual of Geographical Data Category

- The **Web URL Data** category is important for mailto email address links and any URL links exposed in reports
  - When the column is used in Table visuals, email and link icons are displayed, respecively

There's more...

Model level settings

- These metadata settings cannot be modified in the Power BI Service once the model is published
  - Reports can be created and edited in the service but data types, names, and other metadata are not available

See also

- Power BI Documentation on Data Categorization: `http://bit.ly/2peNqPm`

Configuring Default Summarization and sorting

Two important metadata properties that directly impact the user experience and report visualization of Power BI models include Default Summarization and Sort By Column. Both column-scoped properties, Default Summarization determines the aggregation, if any, to apply to the column when added to the report canvas. Sort By Column provides the ability to display the values of a column based on the order of a separate column.

Although relatively simple to configure, careful attention to both properties helps to deliver higher quality Power BI visualizations and a more user friendly platform for self-service. This recipe includes two examples of configuring the Sort By Column property as well as guidance on Default Summarization.

How to do it...

Sort By Column

1. Identify columns requiring custom sort:
    - Calendar text columns such as `Month` and `Weekday` are the most common candidates
    - Other columns may represent an organizational structure or entity hierarchy such as general ledger accounts

2. Create the **Sort By Column** sort:
    - The **Sort By Column** sort must contain only one distinct value for each value in the column to be sorted

It's recommended to embed the sorting logic as deep into the BI architecture as possible. For example, the sorting column could be added to a dimension table in a data warehouse or the SQL view used to load the data model. If these options aren't available, M query transformations are recommended over DAX calculated columns.

3. Set the **Sort By Column** sort:
    - Select the column to be sorted from either the Data View or the Report View

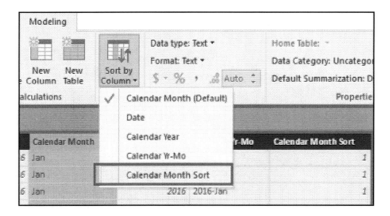

Implementing Sort By Column on Calendar Month

- Use the dropdown of the **Sort by Column button** to select the column to use for sorting

- With Sort By Column configured, the values of the column will display based on the proper sort (January, February, or March)

DAX Year-Month sorting

In this example, a DAX calculated column is created to support sorting of the `Calendar Yr-Mo` column.

1. Access the `Date` table in Data view and click on **New Column** from the **Modeling** tab.
2. Enter the following DAX expression to create sorting column at the grain of calendar months across years:

Date	Calendar Month	Calendar Year	Calendar Yr-Mo	Calendar Month Sort	CalYr-Mo Sort
1/1/2016	Jan	2016	2016-Jan	1	201601
1/2/2016	Jan	2016	2016-Jan	1	201601

DAX Sorting Calculated Column

- The `YEAR()` function is applied against the Date column and multiplied by 100 to add two digits:
  - `MONTH()` returns a value of 1 to 12 and this is added to the six digit number

Although this approach is simple to implement and inexpensive in resource usage, the values of the new column are not sequential thus limiting the use of the column in Time Intelligence measures (for example, trailing 3 months). Sequential surrogate key columns for each grain of the date dimension, including fiscal calendars, is an essential component to robust Date Intelligence logic. See `Chapter 6`, *Getting Serious with Date Intelligence* for examples of implementing these columns via both SQL and M expressions.

DAX Ranking Sort

1. Create a Sort By Column sort based on a measure.
   - In some scenarios, values from the RANKX() DAX function can provide a custom sorting column
     - Per the sorting requirements, a unique rank value is required for each value sorted
   - Create the DAX calculated column with the RANK(X) function:

DepartmentGroupKey	Department Group	Parent Group	DeptGroupRank
1	Corporate		5
2	Executive General and Administration	Corporate	4
3	Inventory Management	Corporate	3
4	Manufacturing	Corporate	6
5	Quality Assurance	Corporate	7
6	Research and Development	Corporate	2
7	Sales and Marketing	Corporate	1

RankX () Calculated Column

- Sort the Department Group column by the new ranking column and hide the ranking column

 The calculated column is re-evaluated during each refresh and thus sort order could change to reflect the source data.

Department Group	Finance Row Count
Sales and Marketing	9,057
Research and Development	12,003
Inventory Management	1,908
Executive General and Administration	4,088
Corporate	8,843
Total	**39,409**

Sort By Rank Effect

- The `Department Group` column now defaults to the order of the rank column with `Sales and Marketing` first
    - In the report visual, revising the order displays the values in descending order with quality assurance first

Default Summarization

1. Set **Dimensions** to **Don't summarize**.
    - By default, whole number, decimal number, and fixed decimal number are set to **Sum**

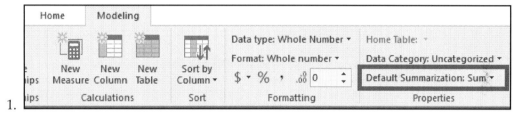

1.

Default Summarization Modeling Option

2. Select each dimension table column and revise **Default Summarization** to **Don't Summarize**:
    - The **Fields** list applies a summation symbol and sums the column's values when selected for a report visual

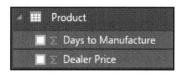

Default Summarization in Fields List

- The same symbol is applied regardless of the Default Summarization configured (for example, **Average** and **Count**)

In this example, `Days to Manufacture` and `Dealer Price` would be summed as though they're measures. In most scenarios, the user intent is to group the data by these columns rather than sum.

- Default Summarization can be accessed from either the Data View or the Report View

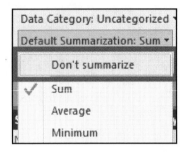

Default Summarization

Simple DAX measures can deliver all **Default Summarization** options (**Sum**, **Min**, **Max**, **Average**, **Count**, and **Count Distinct**). Additionally, measure names such as **Count of Products** eliminate confusion of the Default Summarization icon.

3. Replace fact columns with measures:
    - Develop DAX measures with aggregation functions and formatting such that fact columns can be hidden
    - When all fact columns are hidden, associated measures will display at the top of the **Field** list
    - Measures with names such as `Count of Products` avoid the confusion of which summarization is applied
    - Additionally, measures allow for business logic to be applied, such as including or excluding certain values

The quick measures feature can be used as an alternative to Default Summarization as well.

    - The end result should be the elimination of **Default Summarization** settings from all columns exposed in the **Field** List

How it works...

Default Summarization

- Text and date data type columns are set to **Don't summarize** by default when first loaded to Power BI models
- These data types also have calculations that can be defined as a secondary option on the report canvas
  - **Text**: **First**, **Last**, **Count (Distinct)**, or **Count**
  - **Date**: **Earliest**, **Latest**, **Count (Distinct)**, or **Count**

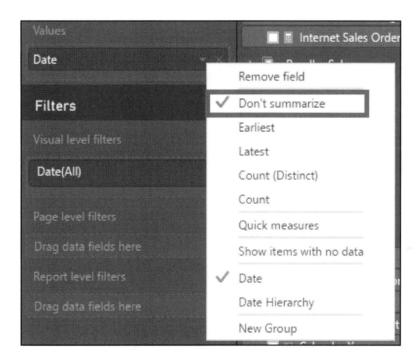

Summarization options of Date data type column set to Don't Summarize

There's more...

Quick measures

- **Quick measures** provide a graphical interface for developing DAX measures against Power BI models
- The logic defined in the interface is transformed into DAX expressions and persisted in the Power BI data model
- Per the **Fields** list, **Quick measures** can be based on both columns and existing measures (like DAX measures)

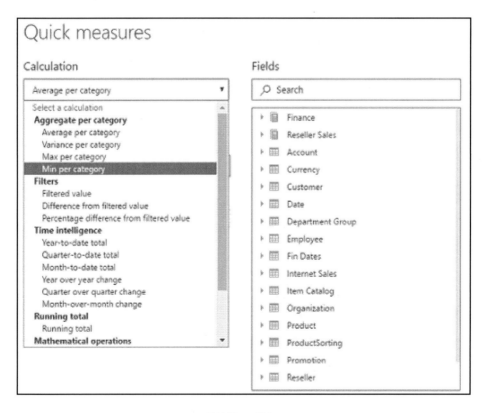

Quick Measure Dialog

- It's expected that Quick Measures will be expanded to support increasingly complex DAX expressions and patterns

See also

- Quick Measures Preview Feature Introduction: `http://bit.ly/2r4HVmt`
- Sort By Documentation: `http://bit.ly/2pFXhgh`

Setting the visibility of columns and tables

Data models must balance the competing demands of functionality, scope, and usability. As additional tables, columns, measures, and other structures are added to meet various analytical needs, a model can quickly become confusing to end users. Given that Power BI Desktop does not currently support perspectives or display folders, both SSAS Tabular 2016 usability features, it's important to minimize the visibility of columns and tables to provide an intuitive interface.

In this recipe an example data model is presented with guidance on configuring its display in the Power BI **Field** list. Additionally, a list of data model objects identifies candidates for hiding from the Report View.

How to do it...

Isolate measures from tables

The objective of this example is to provide an intuitive **Fields** list to support self-service analysis and report development. The following Power BI data model contains three fact tables and 12 dimension tables:

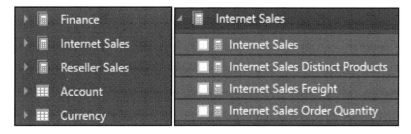

Field List with Hidden Columns

The `Finance`, `Internet Sales`, and `Reseller Sales` fact tables have all of their columns hidden. This results in only the measures associated with each table being displayed at the top of the `Fields` list.

1. Hide columns:
    - Select a column from the **Fields** list in Report view and right-click. Select **Hide in Report View**
    - Repeat this process for all columns that should be hidden in the model

Hiding a Column

- For import models, the same visibility setting is available from the Data View

2. Refresh the **Fields** list:
    - With all necessary columns hidden, click the Field List's 'Show/hide pane' arrow twice to refresh the Field List

Field List

- Following the refresh, tables with only visible measures (all columns hidden) will appear at the top of the **Fields** list

 In general, hide any column which isn't directly required in Power BI reports. Relationship key columns, fact table columns represented via measures, custom **Sort by** columns, and any degenerate dimensions can be hidden. As this is only a visibility metadata setting, the columns can still be used in measures and accessed from other tools via DAX queries.

3. Hide measures:
    - Hide any measure which exclusively supports other measures and isn't used directly in reports
    - The same process of hiding columns via right-click from the Report view applies to measures

How it works...

Measure home tables

- Dedicated measure group tables can be created to organize and group similar measures:
    - These are empty tables created with queries that don't return rows or other sources that don't require refresh
    - Their names indicate the measure group, such as `Marketing Analytics`
- Measures can be associated with any table of the model via the **Home Table** property

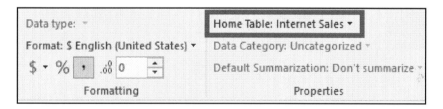

Measure Home Table

- One option to simplify the **Fields** List is to consolidate measures into fewer home tables and hide unused tables

There's more...

Hiding hierarchy columns

- Columns which are visible within hierarchies can sometimes be hidden as individual columns

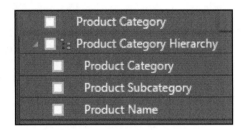

Column Visible with Hierarchy

- Exposing both an individual column and a hierarchy which includes it can confuse users and lengthen the **Fields** list
- However, not hiding the hierarchy column provides more flexibility such as viewing the columns on separate axes

Group visibility

- The grouping of column values described in the Hierarchies and Grouping recipe is still possible with hidden columns
    - For example, the Product Name column could be hidden but a group based on the Product Name column could be visible and usable from the **Fields** list.
- Groups and Hierarchies can both be hidden from the **Fields** List as well
    - Generally, however, these structures wouldn't have been created if their visibility wasn't needed

Row level security visibility

- Users mapped to security roles which forbid them from accessing all the rows of a table are still able to see related metadata such as the table name, its column names, and any metric names not hidden
- New object-level security features of SSAS 2017 can eliminate this visibility

Visibility features from SSAS

- Perspectives are essentially view definitions of models such that only a defined set of tables, columns, and metrics of a model are exposed to a given view
- Display folders are used to consolidate similar measures and columns and simplify the interface
    - For example, a `Sales` measure folder may have multiple subfolders, each with a group of similar measures
- It's currently unclear if either of these SSAS features will be made available to Power BI Desktop models

Embedding business definitions into DAX measures

In order to drive user adoption and to provide a foundation to support more advanced analytics it's essential that DAX measures reflect business definitions. These fundamental measures deliver version control across the many reports built off of the model and avoid the need for additional logic to be applied at the report layer. Clear business definitions should be documented and the corresponding measures should be validated for accuracy before report visualizations and analytical measures are developed.

In this recipe measures are created representing business definitions such as sales only for transactions that have shipped. Additionally, role playing measures are created to allow visibility to secondary relationships to a date dimension table.

Getting ready

1. Identify the set of base measures to create, the data source to validate against, and the subject matter experts
    - Reconcile differences in definitions between source systems and any custom logic applied in reports
2. Request a project sponsor from a business organization to review and approve the definitions and validation
3. Identify any conflicts with existing business definitions and advise of complexity in implementing the measures

How to do it...

Sales and cost metrics

The measure definitions to implement in this example are the following:

- Gross Sales is equal to Unit Price multiplied by Order Quantity with no discounts applied
- Net Sales are Gross Sales reduced by Discounts and must have been shipped
- Product Cost is equal to Product Standard Cost * Order Quantity

1. Create Sales and Cost DAX Measures

```
Reseller Gross Sales = SUMX('Reseller Sales',
'Reseller Sales'[Unit Price] *'Reseller Sales'[Order Quantity])
Reseller Discount Amount = SUM('Reseller Sales'[Discount Amount])
Reseller Net Sales = CALCULATE([Reseller Gross Sales] - [Reseller
Discount Amount],
'Reseller Sales'[Ship Date] <> DATEVALUE("12/31/2099"))
Reseller Product Cost = SUMX('Reseller Sales',
'Reseller Sales'[Order Quantity]*'Reseller Sales'[Product Standard
Cost])
```

Two columns exist in the source database reflecting Reseller Gross Sales and Reseller Product Cost. Performance and memory usage can be improved by only importing the price and quantity columns and multiplying within the measure.

- The net sales measure deducts discounts from gross sales and only includes shipped products
    - The existing ETL process assigns a date value of `12/31/2099` for any sales orders that haven't shipped

Margin and count metrics

Margin percentage measures reflecting both gross and net sales (with discounts) are required. Additionally, the distinct count of sales orders and products sold are also core measures used in many reports and referenced by other measures.

1. Create margin and distinct count measures

```
Reseller Gross Margin % = DIVIDE([Reseller Gross Sales] - [Reseller
Product Cost],[Reseller Gross Sales])
Reseller Margin % = DIVIDE([Reseller Net Sales] - [Reseller Product
Cost],[Reseller Net Sales])
Reseller Count of Sales Orders = DISTINCTCOUNT('Reseller
Sales'[Sales Order Number])
Reseller Count of Products Sold =
CALCULATE(DISTINCTCOUNT('Product'[Product Alternate Key]),
'Reseller Sales')
```

- Margin Amount measures might also be created and could replace the numerator of the Margin % measures
- `DISTINCTCOUNT()` can be used directly against foreign key relationship columns and any degenerate dimension columns on the fact table such as `Sales Order Number`
    - See the *How it works...* section for details on the `Reseller Count of Products Sold` measure

Optionally, Margin Amount measures could be created and replace the numerator of the Margin % measures. The Count of Products Sold measure uses the natural key of the product in the filter context of the fact table to count unique products. Using the product key on the fact table would count multiple versions of a product given slowly changing dimensions.

Secondary relationships

1. Create role playing relationships:
    *   Create additional relationships to the date dimension with other date data type columns on the fact table

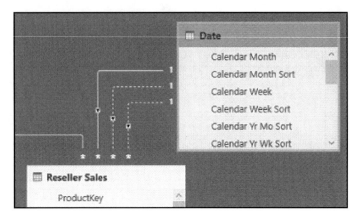

Active and Inactive Relationships Defined

*   Only one relationship between two tables can be active at once. In this example, Order Date is the active relationship.

2. Create role playing measures:
    *   Measures which invoke the `Due Date` and `Ship Date` relationships would be created for core business measures

```
Reseller Net Sales by Ship Date = CALCULATE([Reseller Net Sales],
USERELATIONSHIP('Reseller Sales'[Ship Date],'Date'[Date]) )
Reseller Sales Order Count by Due Date = CALCULATE([Reseller Sales
Order Count],
USERELATIONSHIP('Reseller Sales'[Due Date],'Date'[Date]))
```

Do not confuse the `USERELATIONSHIP()` function with the `CROSSFILTER()` function. `CROSSFILTER()` is used for controlling relationship filter propagation (Single, Bidirectional, or None) and is not a replacement for `USERELATIONSHIP()`.

Reseller Net Sales: Q1 Order to Ship

Calendar Yr-Mo ▲	Reseller Net Sales	Reseller Net Sales by Due Date	Reseller Net Sales by Ship Date
2017-Jan	$131,651,752	$118,238,803	$116,693,960
2017-Feb	$147,208,806	$149,143,063	$159,811,869
2017-Mar	$164,929,146	$169,099,064	$170,129,081
Total	**$443,789,703**	**$436,480,931**	**$446,634,910**

Secondary Relationships Invoked via DAX Measures

Given the multiplication effect of role playing measures it may be appropriate to group the secondary relationship measures into dedicated measure group tables. See the *Setting visibility of columns and tables* recipe in this chapter for additional detail.

How it works...

Date relationships

- The `Time Intelligence` functions of DAX, such as `DATESYTD()`, `DATEADD()`, and `SAMEPERIODLASTYEAR()`, all require either a relationship based on a date data type or a **Mark as Date Table** setting

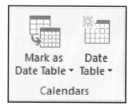

Mark as Date Table in Power Pivot for Excel 2016

- The **Mark as Date Table** setting is currently exclusive to Power Pivot for Excel and SSAS Tabular models
- Therefore, date relationships in Power BI should use date data type columns rather than surrogate keys (20170101)

There's more...

Measure definitions

- Measure definitions can be straight forward when the data is internally managed with processes and tools such as a data governance council, **Master Data Services (MDS)**, Data Quality Services, and Azure Data Catalog
    - Per the *Power BI Governance and Deployment Whitepaper*, Power BI projects and all BI projects greatly benefit from these data cleansing and information management tools
- The data warehouse bus matrix and stakeholder matrix referenced in this chapter and Chapter 4, *Authoring Power BI Reports*, respectively, can help to focus the measure definition process on version control and transparency

Measure names and additional measures

- The names used for measures should be intuitive and specific to the business process
- Preferably a naming standard is followed to balance the detail of the name with the impact of text on visualizations
- In a real project scenario several additional measures would likely be created following validation
    - These could include Net Sales as a % of Gross Sales, Sales and Quantity per Order, and Sales Not Shipped
    - These measures and more advanced measures would all leverage the validated measures

See also

- Power BI Governance and Deployment Approaches: http://bit.ly/1VLWdVg

Enriching a model with analysis expressions

Performance, usability, and version control are all fundamental characteristics of effective data models but often it's the additional analytical context that set models apart. Once fundamental measures have been implemented, additional DAX measures can be developed to support common and high priority business analysis. These measures can often replace ad hoc and manual data analysis for business users as well as dedicated custom reports maintained by the BI organization. As measures are stored within the data model, the logic can be re-used in various combinations and in future projects.

In this recipe DAX measures are created to support deeper pricing analysis. Additionally, an example of computing the geometric mean at day, month, and year grains is provided.

How to do it...

Pricing analysis

The objective of this example is to support deeper analysis of pricing trends. New measures should accomplish the following:

- Describe the central tendency and distribution of prices
- Account for the impact of product sales mix to support analysis of effective pricing versus product pricing

1. Create a `Pricing Measures` table:
    - The pricing table will be dedicated to measures and not store any data. Use a blank query that returns no data
    - Hide columns from the new table and associate pricing measures to it via the **Home Table** measure setting

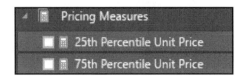

Pricing Measures Group Table

2. Create Pricing Measures.

```
Effective Unit Price = DIVIDE([Reseller Sales Extended
Amount],[Reseller Sales Order Quantity])
25th Percentile Unit Price = PERCENTILE.INC('Reseller Sales'[Unit
Price],.25)
75th Percentile Unit Price = PERCENTILE.INC('Reseller Sales'[Unit
Price],.75)
Maximum Unit Price = MAX('Reseller Sales'[Unit Price])
Median Unit Price = MEDIAN('Reseller Sales'[Unit Price])
Minimum Unit Price = MIN('Reseller Sales'[Unit Price])
Range of Unit Prices = [Maximum Unit Price] – [Minimum Unit Price]
```

- The `Effective Unit Price` metric accounts for the impact of quantity sold and uses the existing sales and quantity metrics
- The percentile and median metrics help better describe the distribution of prices
- The minimum, maximum, and range of unit prices provide additional context to the variability of the prices

3. Embed the pricing measures into Power BI visuals.
    - The new measures could be added to existing visuals directly or as supporting tooltip values

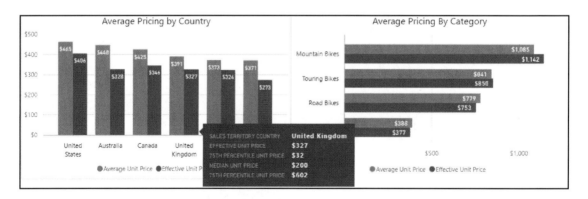

Example Power BI Pricing Reports

- The visuals compare the average unit price metric to the new effective unit price metric
- Pricing metrics are added to visual tooltips such that hovering over values in the charts provides additional context

Embedding hierarchies in visuals with supporting measures can allow users to investigate interesting values via drill up and down. Additionally, exception reports and notifications can be developed using the new measures as thresholds.

Geometric mean at all grains

The goal of this example is to compute the geometric mean of a security at the day, month, and year grains.

- A table of security prices for the security by day exists in the model with a relationship to the date table

IndexKey	Date	Adj Close	Security
1	4/18/2012	$25.96	Balanced Fund A
2	4/19/2012	$25.74	Balanced Fund A
3	4/20/2012	$26.01	Balanced Fund A

Daily Prices Fact Table

1. Create `Last Price` measures
   - The last price active in the filter context is used by each of the previous price measures (`Day`, `Month`, and `Year`)

```
Last Price = CALCULATE(VALUES(Daily Prices[Adj
Close]),LASTNONBLANK('Date'[Date],[Max Daily Price]))
Previous Daily Price = CALCULATE([Last Price],
FILTER(ALL(Daily Prices),Daily Prices[IndexKey] = MAX(Daily
Prices[Index Key]) - 1))
Previous Monthly Price = CALCULATE([Last Price],
FILTER(ALL('Date'),'Date'[Cal Year Month Index] = MAX('Date'[Cal
Year Month Index]) -1))
Previous Year Price = CALCULATE([Last Price],
FILTER(ALL('Date'),'Date'[Calendar Year] = MAX('Date'[Calendar
Year]) -1))
```

`LASTNONBLANK()` is needed for days in which the security wasn't traded. `Max Daily Price` is a simple `MAX()` measure of the `Adj Close` column and is used to simplify the syntax. See `Chapter 6`, *Getting Serious with Date Intelligence* for details on controlling date filter contexts.

2. Create `Percentage Change` measures
    - These are the source values for the geometric mean calculations and thus are expressed as positive numbers

```
Daily Return% = DIVIDE([Last Price],[Previous Daily Price])
Monthly Return% = DIVIDE([Last Price],[Previous Monthly Price])
Yearly Return% = DIVIDE([Last Price],[Previous Year Price])
```

- As only inputs to the geometric mean calculation, these measures should be hidden from the Report view

3. Create daily, monthly, and yearly geometric mean % measures:

```
Daily Geometric Return = GEOMEANX(Daily Prices,[Daily Return%])-1
Monthly Geometric Return = GEOMEANX(VALUES('Date'[Calendar Yr-
Mo]),[Monthly Return%])-1
Yearly Geometric Return = GEOMEANX(VALUES('Date'[Calendar
Year]),[Yearly Return%])-1
```

- The `GEOMEANX()` function iterates over tables at the different grains and computes the `Return%` measure for each row
- The geometric mean (the product of values taken to the Nth root) is computed last against this list of values.
- Visualize geometric mean

6.27%	0.65%	0.03%
Yearly Geometric Return	Monthly Geometric Return	Daily Geometric Return

Geometric Mean Power BI Tiles

- Given the date table relationships the metrics would reflect date dimension filter selections

How it works...

Pricing analysis

- The `MEDIAN()` function returns the 50th percentile of values in a column
    - It's equivalent the `PERCENTILE.INC()` functions used for the 25th and 75th percentile.
- Performance is not negatively impacted when adding measures to visuals from the same table due to measure fusion
    - The `Tooltip` measures in the recipe were from the same table and did not create additional DAX queries

Building analytics into data models with DAX

Several table-valued functions were added to the DAX language in 2015 that simplify the development of relational and set logic based measures and queries. With functions such as `NATURALINNERJOIN()`, `EXCEPT()`, and `UNION()`, developers can create DAX measures to identify outliers and precise segments of dimensions to better support analysis such as cross-selling and customer retention. Additionally, as many business processes have a corresponding budget or plan, it's important to use Power BI modeling features to build support for actual versus budget reporting.

In this recipe new DAX functions are used to drive two analyses--inactive customers and cross-selling products. Additionally, a data model is modified to support the distinct grains of budget and sales fact tables.

How to do it...

Cross-selling opportunities

The objective of this example is to identify customer segments based on their purchase history across product categories. For example, the business wants to identify customers who've purchased a bike but not any bike accessories.

1. Assess the current state
   - 18,484 distinct customers have made purchases across three product categories

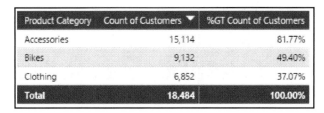

Product Category	Count of Customers ▼	%GT Count of Customers
Accessories	15,114	81.77%
Bikes	9,132	49.40%
Clothing	6,852	37.07%
Total	**18,484**	**100.00%**

Unique Customers by Product Category

- As expected, there's significant overlap among the categories with customers purchasing from multiple categories.

Accessories but not bike customers

1. Create a DAX measure which returns the count of customers who've purchased an accessory but not a bike:

```
Count of Accessory But Not Bike Customers =
 VAR BikeCustomers =
  SUMMARIZE(CALCULATETABLE('Internet Sales','Product'[Product
Category] = "Bikes"),
  Customer[Customer Alternate Key])
 VAR AccessoryCustomers =
  SUMMARIZE(CALCULATETABLE('Internet Sales','Product'[Product
Category] = "Accessories"),
  Customer[Customer Alternate Key])
RETURN
CALCULATE(DISTINCTCOUNT(Customer[Customer Alternate
Key]),EXCEPT(AccessoryCustomers,BikeCustomers))
```

- Variables are used to store the distinct customer keys associated with the two product categories.
- SUMMARIZE() groups the customer key values and EXCEPT() performs the set-based operation.

2. Create card and table visuals in a Power BI Report to visualize the new measure:

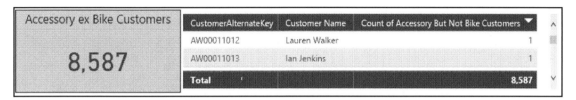

Visualization of EXCEPT() DAX Measure: Accessory Customers excluding Bike Customers

- The measure can be visualized across dimensions such as filtering for one or two calendar years

Bike only customers

1. Create a measure to compute the customers who've only make a bike purchase (not clothing or accessories)

```
Count of Bike Only Customers =
 VAR BikeCustomers =
  SUMMARIZE(CALCULATETABLE('Internet Sales','Product'[Product
Category] = "Bikes"),
  Customer[Customer Alternate Key])
 VAR ClothesAndAccessoryCustomers =
  SUMMARIZE(CALCULATETABLE('Internet Sales',
  'Product'[Product Category] IN {"Accessories","Clothing"}),
Customer[Customer Alternate Key])
RETURN
CALCULATE(DISTINCTCOUNT(Customer[Customer Alternate Key]),
 EXCEPT(BikeCustomers,ClothesAndAccessoryCustomers))
```

- The syntax aligns with the structure of the first measure except for the use of the IN DAX operator to include accessories and clothing in the same group of customer keys.

Given the power of these measures they could be candidates for sales and marketing dashboards and exception reports. For example sales teams could focus on cross-selling bike only customers and selling bikes to non-bike customers.

Active verus inactive customers

The following example identifies the customers who purchased last year but haven't yet purchased this year.

1. Create a measure for missing or inactive customers
   - Use DAX variables and time intelligence functions to produce two filtered sets of customer keys.

```
Count of Last Year Customers ex Current Year =
 VAR Today = TODAY() VAR CurrentYear = YEAR(Today) VAR LastYear =
YEAR(Today) - 1
 VAR LYCustomers =
  SUMMARIZE(CALCULATETABLE('Internet Sales',
   FILTER(ALL('Date'),'Date'[Calendar Year] =
LastYear)),Customer[Customer Alternate Key])
 VAR CYCustomers =
  SUMMARIZE(CALCULATETABLE('Internet Sales',
   FILTER(ALL('Date'),'Date'[Calendar Year] =
CurrentYear)),Customer[Customer Alternate Key])
RETURN
CALCULATE(DISTINCTCOUNT(Customer[Customer Alternate
Key]),EXCEPT(LYCustomers,CYCustomers))
```

- Pass the time variables to the CALCULATETABLE() function and then group the keys by SUMMARIZE()

2. Visualize the measure in Power BI Desktop

Visualization of Last Year Customer Count excluding Current Year Customers

- A visual level filter applied to the new measure exposes the specific 287 customers without a 2017 purchase yet

Actual versus budget model and measures

This example provides support for actual versus budget analysis in a model containing different grains.

1. Create the bridge tables
    - `Budget Product Categories` and `Budget Dates` bridge tables are added to the model at the grain of the budget
    - Each table contains the unique values of the dimension at the grain of the Budget table

These bridge tables can potentially leverage the existing M queries in the model used to load the dimension tables. For example, the following M expression references the Date table query as it's source and selects only the distinct values of the Calendar Yr-Mo column. If this is the grain of the budget table, this single column table could be used as the bridge table.

let Source = Date,
YearMonthColumn = Table.SelectColumns(Source,{"Calendar Yr-Mo"}),
RemoveDuplicates = Table.Distinct(YearMonthColumn)
in RemoveDuplicates

Alternatively, a simple SQL view could be created ('Select Distinct [Calendar Yr-Mo] From dbo.DimDate') that selects the distinct values of the column and this view could be accessed from a new bridge table M query.

2. Create the relationships
   - Create one-to-many relationships with single direction cross filtering from the bridge tables (Budget Dates, Budget Product Categories) to the Internet Sales Budget table
   - Create many-to-one relationships with bidirectional cross filtering between the dimension tables (Date, Product) to their respective bridge tables (Budget Dates, Budget Product Categories)

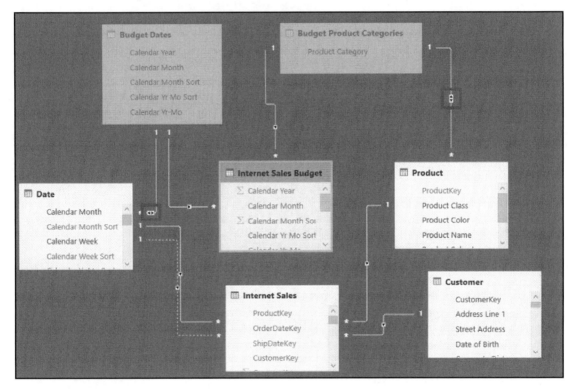

Internet Sales versus Budget Data Model

- The two bidirectional relationships highlighted in the image allow filters on the Date and Product tables to propagate to the Internet Sales Budget table in addition to the Internet Sales fact table
- The only remaining steps requiring some level of code is to avoid invalid filter contexts. For example, the Internet Sales fact table can of course be filtered by individual products and dates but this granularity isn't available for the Budget and thus a blank value should be returned.

3. Create a measure to test for filter context
   - The following measure checks whether filters have been applied at higher grains than the budget table

```
Budget Filter Test =
 VAR CustomerFilter = ISCROSSFILTERED(Customer)
 VAR ProductGrain =
  ISFILTERED('Product'[Product Class]) ||
ISFILTERED('Product'[Product Color]) ||
  ISFILTERED('Product'[Product Subcategory]) ||
ISFILTERED('Product'[Product Name])
 VAR DateGrain =
  ISFILTERED('Date'[Calendar Yr-Wk]) || ISFILTERED('Date'[Date]) ||
ISFILTERED('Date'[Wk End Date])
 RETURN
 IF(CustomerFilter = TRUE() || ProductGrain = TRUE() || DateGrain
=TRUE(),
  "Higher Grain", "Common Grain")
```

- The filter test is used to protect against invalid sales to budget reports with different filters applied to each fact table

4. Create the budget measures
   - Create a budget measure and an actual to budget variance measure

```
Internet Sales Budget =
 VAR BudgetSales = sum('Internet Sales Budget'[Online Sales
Budget])
 RETURN
 IF([Budget Filter Test] = "Common Grain", BudgetSales, BLANK())
```

```
Internet Sales Actual to Budget Variance =
 IF(ISBLANK([Internet Sales Budget]),BLANK(), [Internet Sales] -
[Internet Sales Budget])
```

- In this scenario, the requirement is to only test for a common grain and return a blank otherwise.

It's possible to build allocation logic into the DAX budget measure to account for higher grains. In general, these allocation rules are better implemented in the budget process itself or via ETL tools and query languages such as SQL and M.

5. Hide the bridge tables, budget columns, and the filter test metric from the Report View
6. Validate and visualize actual versus budget
   - Create sample visualizations which filter budget and sales by `Product` and `Date` dimensions

Product Category	2017-Jan	2017-Feb	2017-Mar	2017-Apr	2017-May	2017-Jun	2017-Jul
Accessories	($5,524)	($462)	$13,281	($3,103)	($16,784)	($1,876)	$8,120
Bikes	($66,393)	$98,532	($48,389)	$271,293	($336,043)	$465,368	$385,256
Clothing	($87)	$2,131	$2,679	$5,333	$266	($2,943)	($5,602)
Total	($72,005)	$100,200	($32,428)	$273,523	($352,562)	$460,549	$387,774

Internet Sales Actual versus Budget by Product Category and Year-Month

Matrix visuals provide functionality similar to Excel pivot tables and are therefore a good choice for Budget versus Actuals.

How it works...

Filter Context Functions

- `ISFILTERED()` and `ISCROSSFILTERED()` return Boolean values based on the filter context of the table or columns
- `ISFILTERED()` is limited to a single column in the model and is specific to the given column
- `ISCROSSFILTERED()` can check a single column or an entire table. Filters from other tables are included in evaluation.

There's more...

SUMMARIZECOLUMNS()

- `SUMMARIZECOLUMNS()` is more efficient than `SUMMARIZE()` but does not currently support a modified filter context.
  - Therefore, `SUMMARIZE()` is used in certain examples of measures in this recipe and others in this book.

Integrating math and statistical analysis via DAX

Power BI Desktop and the Power BI Service provide advanced analytics features such as Forecasting, Clustering, and Quick Insights that go far beyond traditional BI reporting of historical data. However, many valuable mathematical and statistical analyses such as Correlation Coefficients and Chi-Square Tests and are only possible by embedding the logic of these methodologies into DAX measures. Aligning these analyses to support specific business questions can generate new insights and provide a higher level of validation and confidence in business decisions.

In this recipe DAX measures are built into a Power BI model to calculate the correlation coefficient of two variables. Additionally, an example of computing the Goodness-of-Fit test statistic in validating a model is provided.

How to do it...

Correlation coefficient

The objective of this example is to create a DAX measure which executes the the Pearson correlation coefficient formula.

$$Correl(X,Y) = \frac{\sum (x - \bar{x})(y - \bar{y})}{\sqrt{\sum (x - \bar{x})^2 \sum (y - \bar{y})^2}}$$

Correlation Coefficient for Sample Formula

- A fact table is available at the grain of product category by month with both marketing expense and sales amount

Calendar Yr-Mo	Year	Month	Product Category	Marketing Amt	Sales
2016-Jul	2016	Jul	Bikes	$22,005.621	$444,558.2281
2016-Sep	2016	Sep	Bikes	$23,579.5845	$486,177.4502

Aggregate Fact Table: Marketing Expense and Sales Amount by Product Category

- The values in the active filter context for the `Marketing Amt` and `Sales` columns will provide the X and Y arrays

1. Create the correlation numerator measure

```
Correl Numerator Marketing-Sales =
 SUMX('Marketing Expense',
('Marketing Expense'[Marketing Amt]-AVERAGE('Marketing
Expense'[Marketing Amt]))*
('Marketing Expense'[Sales]-AVERAGE('Marketing Expense'[Sales])))
```

The numerator measure iterates over the active (unfiltered) rows of the aggregate fact table and multiplies the differences from the sample mean for each variable. The result of this product is then summed via `SUMX()`.

2. Create the correlation denominator measure.

```
Correl Denominator Marketing-Sales =
 VAR Marketing = SUMX('Marketing Expense',
   ('Marketing Expense'[Marketing Amt]-AVERAGE('Marketing
Expense'[Marketing Amt]))^2)
 VAR Sales = SUMX('Marketing Expense',
   ('Marketing Expense'[Sales]-AVERAGE('Marketing
Expense'[Sales]))^2)
 RETURN SQRT(Marketing*Sales)
```

- The sum of the squared differences from the mean for each variable's active row are multiplied prior to the square root.

3. Create the correlation coefficient measure
    - The correlation measure is a trivial `DIVIDE()` of the numerator and denominator measures
    - The measure name `Correlation Marketing-Sales` is used to avoid confusion with other correlation measures

4. Visualize the Correlation Measure

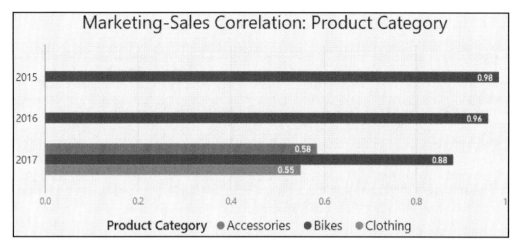

Correlation Coefficient Visualization

- The measure indicates a much stronger marketing-to-sales relationship for bikes than other other categories.
    - Additionally, the bikes correlation is weakening, potentially due to brand awareness and repeat customers.
    - `Accessories` and `Clothing` categories were not available for sale in 2015-2016

Goodness-of-Fit test statistic

The objective of this example is to create a Goodness-of Fit statistic measure to evaluate a customer distribution model.

$$\sum_{i=1}^{n} \frac{\left(O_i - E_i\right)^2}{E_i}$$

Goodness-of-Fit Statistic

- The existing model is based on the historical distribution of customers by country for the past three years

- The measure will use actual customer data from Q1 of 2017 to compare against the predicted value from the model
- Customers are historically split across the following six countries:

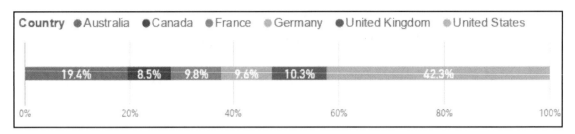

Historical Customer Distribution %

- The Goodness-of-Fit measure will help answer the question: "Are these percentages still valid in 2017?"

1. Create the base Measures
    - Measures compute all time customers, the 2017-Q1 customers, and the historical percentages by country

```
All Time Customers =
CALCULATE(CALCULATE(DISTINCTCOUNT('Customer'[Customer Alternate
Key]),'Internet Sales'),ALL('Date'))
Sample Customer Count =
CALCULATE(CALCULATE(DISTINCTCOUNT(Customer[Customer Alternate
Key]),'Internet Sales'),
FILTER(ALL('Date'),'Date'[Calendar Yr-Qtr] = "2017-Q1"))
USA All Time Customer % =
DIVIDE(CALCULATE([All Time Customers],'Sales Territory'[Sales
Territory Country] = "United States"),
[All Time Customers])
```

- The other five country metrics not displayed are defined exactly like the USA All Time Customer % metric
    - The Customer Alternate Key column is used to avoid double-counting due to slowly changing dimensions

2. Create the Goodness-of-Fit test statistic Measure

```
Goodness-of-Fit Stat (USA Only) =
VAR SampleCount =
CALCULATE(CALCULATE(DISTINCTCOUNT(Customer[CustomerAlternateKey]),'
Internet Sales'),
 FILTER(ALL('Date'),'Date'[Calendar Yr-Qtr] = "2017-Q1"))
VAR USAExpect = SampleCount * [USA All Time Customer %]
RETURN
SUMX(CALCULATETABLE(VALUES('Sales Territory'[Sales Territory
Country]),'Sales Territory'[Sales Territory Country] <> "NA"),
 SWITCH(TRUE(),
 'Sales Territory'[Sales Territory Country] = "United States",
 DIVIDE((([Sample Customer Count] - USAExpect)^2),USAExpect),0))
```

The actual Goodness-of-Fit Stat measure would include the same components for the five other countries - sample variables declaring the expected values and Goodness-of-Fit expressions within the `SWITCH()` for the given country. See the *'How it Works...'* section for details on the structure of the measure.

3. Interpret the Goodness-of-Fit measure

- A next step in the analysis would be to utilize the new Goodness-of-Fit measure in a Chi-Square Goodness-of-Fit test

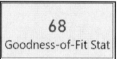

Return Value of Goodness-of-Fit Statistic Measure

- The measure result (68 in this example), would be compared to a Chi-Square distribution given the number of categories (countries in this example) to determine if the historical distribution model can be rejected or not.

Implementing additional logic to perform the Chi-Square test in the Power BI model is possible as the Chi-Square distribution data set is small. In most scenarios, however, this final evaluation is handled outside the data model.

How it works...

Correlation coefficient syntax

- It's necessary to use AVERAGE() expressions within the row iterating parameter to SUM(X) rather than measures.
- Measures are transformed into a filter context when inside a row operation resulting in a row being compared to itself
- Parentheses are used to control the order of operations to align with the Pearson formula definition

Goodness-of-Fit logic and syntax

- The logic implemented by the Goodness-of-Fit statistic measure can be described by the following table:

Country	Observe	Expected	O - E	Squared	Result
USA	1,281	1,490	-209	43,798	29
Canada	382	299	83	6,818	23
Australia	763	685	78	6,159	9
France	347	345	2	4	0
Germany	337	339	-2	5	0
UK	413	365	48	2,341	6
Total					68

Goodness-of-Fit Statistic Sample Data Logic

- The expected variables all reference and re-use the SampleCount variable, which is filtered for 2017-Q1.
- A SUMX() function is used to used to iterate over each of the six countries represented by a single row via VALUES()
  - This distinct list of countries is filtered to avoid any NA values
- The Sample Customer Count measure created in step 1 executes in a filter context to provide the observed customer count for the given country
- The observed and expected values are passed into the Goodness-of-Fit equation with the sum of each calculation (one for each country) being returned by the measure

Observe that the `SampleCount` variable is re-used by the expected variables but that the `Sample Customer Count` measure created in step 1 is used within the `SWITCH()`. This is because the measure executes in a filter context (the given country) whereas the `SampleCount` variable does not transition to a filter context when invoked in the expression.

Supporting virtual table relationships

Virtual table relationships are DAX expressions implemented to filter a table from another table when a relationship doesn't exist between these tables. Report visualizations can then be constructed using both tables (and their related tables) and the DAX measures will update as though a normal relationship is defined. Virtual relationships are often used to address disparate grains of tables and to leverage performance segmentation tables.

Although physical relationships are the preferred long term solution for both performance and manageability, virtual relationships provide an attractive alternative when physical relationships are not feasible. In this recipe we provide virtual relationship examples of using a custom performance segmentation table and an aggregated table.

How to do it...

Segmentation example

The goal of this example is to apply the following segmentation table to the measures of the data model:

GrowthTierKey	Growth Tier ▲	Min	Max
1	Problem	-100 %	-25 %
2	Underperform	-25 %	0 %
3	Average	0 %	25 %
4	Overperform	25 %	900 %

Sales Growth Segmentation Table

A sample Power BI report based on the virtual relationship expressions could appear as follows:

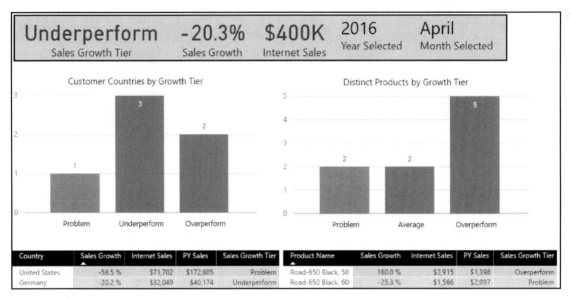

Power BI Report Utilizing Segmentation Table and Virtual Relationships

- Three separate DAX measures are utilized for this example report:
  - A distinct count of customer countries and one for products, both filtered by the segmentation table
  - A sales growth tier metric that returns the text value of the Growth Tier column (for example, Underperform)

1. Create the Sales Growth Tier measure

```
Sales Growth Tier =
VAR Growth = [Sales Growth]
VAR Level1 = CALCULATE(MIN('Sales Growth Tiers'[Max]),'Sales
Growth Tiers'[GrowthTierKey] = 1)
VAR Level2 = CALCULATE(MIN('Sales Growth Tiers'[Max]),'Sales
Growth Tiers'[GrowthTierKey] = 2)
VAR Level3 = CALCULATE(MIN('Sales Growth Tiers'[Max]),'Sales
Growth Tiers'[GrowthTierKey] = 3)
VAR Level4 = CALCULATE(MIN('Sales Growth Tiers'[Max]),'Sales
Growth Tiers'[GrowthTierKey] = 4)
RETURN
SWITCH(TRUE(),ISBLANK(Growth), BLANK(),
 Growth <= Level1,
  CALCULATE(VALUES('Sales Growth Tiers'[Growth Tier]),'Sales
```

```
Growth Tiers'[GrowthTierKey] = 1),
 Growth <= Level2,
 CALCULATE(VALUES('Sales Growth Tiers'[Growth Tier]), 'Sales
Growth Tiers'[GrowthTierKey] = 2),
 Growth <= Level3,
 CALCULATE(VALUES('Sales Growth Tiers'[Growth Tier]),'Sales
Growth Tiers'[GrowthTierKey] = 3),
 Growth <= Level4,
 CALCULATE(VALUES('Sales Growth Tiers'[Growth Tier]),'Sales
Growth Tiers'[GrowthTierKey] = 4),"Unknown")
```

- The existing `Sales Growth Tier` measure and the four segment threshold values are stored in DAX variables
- The `SWITCH()` function compares sales growth with the segment thresholds to assign the Growth Tier value

 Providing `TRUE()` as the first parameter to the `SWITCH()` function allows for independent logical conditions to be evaluated in order (from top to bottom). This is similar to the Searched form of the CASE expression in SQL.

2. Create the virtual relationship measures

```
Customer Countries =
CALCULATE(DISTINCTCOUNT(Customer[Country]),FILTER(ALL(Customer[Coun
try]),
[Sales Growth] > MIN('Sales Growth Tiers'[Min]) && [Sales Growth] <
MAX('Sales Growth Tiers'[Max])))
```

- The measures apply filters based on the segmentation table thresholds and the Sales Growth measure
- The virtual relationship measures can be used with the segmentation table in visuals per the example.

Summary to detail example

In this example, a summary table (Subcategory Plan) needs to be integrated into a Power BI data model. The business wants to filter plan data via the same Product and Date tables they use regularly and to create actual versus plan reports.

- The grain of the Plan table is Plan Subcategory by Calendar Year and Calendar Month

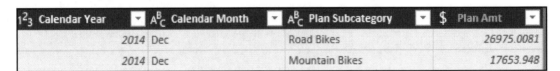

1²₃ Calendar Year	▼	Aᴮ꜀ Calendar Month	▼	Aᴮ꜀ Plan Subcategory	▼	$ Plan Amt	▼
2014		Dec		Road Bikes		26975.0081	
2014		Dec		Mountain Bikes		17653.948	

Plan Summary Table for Virtual Relationships

- Relationships from Plan to the Date and Product tables can't be created directly given the many-to-many relationship

 Each physical relationship in Power BI is based on a single column from each table with one of the relationship columns uniquely identifying all the rows of its host table. This is consistent with SSAS Tabular and Power Pivot for Excel models.

1. Create the subcategory plan measure

   The following DAX measure filters the subcategory plan measure by the Product table and the Date table:

   ```
   Subcat Plan Amt =
   VAR ProductSubCats = VALUES('Product'[Product Subcategory])
   VAR DateTbl = SUMMARIZE('Date','Date'[Calendar
   Year],'Date'[Calendar Month])
   RETURN
   CALCULATE([Subcategory PlanAmt],
   TREATAS(ProductSubCats,'Subcategory Plan'[Plan Subcategory]),
   TREATAS(DateTbl,'Subcategory Plan'[Calendar Year],'Subcategory
   Plan'[Calendar Month]))
   ```

- Variables are used to store tables representing the filtered values of the Product and Date dimension tables
- The TREATAS() function transfers the variables to the corresponding plan column(s), thus filtering Subcategory Plan

Actual versus plan

- Actual-to-Plan visuals can now be developed using columns from the `Date` and `Product` dimension tables

Calendar Month	Jan			Feb		
Product Subcategory	Subcat Plan Amt	Internet Sales	Internet Sales vs Plan	Subcat Plan Amt	Internet Sales	Internet Sales vs Plan
Bike Racks	$1,513	$1,560	$47	$2,444	$2,520	$76
Bike Stands	$1,361	$1,272	($89)	$2,722	$2,544	($178)

Subcategory Plan versus Actual Matrix Visual

- Any column with the same or lower grain than the product subcategory and calendar Year-Month can be used
    - Columns from other other tables or columns without a virtual relationship will not filter the `Plan` table

Bridge tables to support physical relationships to the `Product` and `Date` tables could be created in this scenario. The two bridge tables would contain the unique product subcategory and month values and one-to-many relationships would link the bridge tables to the `Plan`, `Product`, and `Date` tables. The `Plan` and bridge tables could be hidden from the Report view and bidirectional relationships would be configured between the bridge tables and the `Product` and `Date` tables. For better performance and manageability physical relationships are recommended over virtual relationships.

How it works...

Year and month selected

The `Year Selected` and `Month Selected` visuals are both supported by simple DAX measures returning text values

```
Year Selected = if(HASONEVALUE('Date'[Calendar Year]),
FORMAT(VALUES('Date'[Calendar Year]),"####"),"Multiple")
```

Virtual relationship functions

The TREATAS() DAX function was added in early 2017 and provides both simpler syntax and better performance than alternative virtual relationship methods involving INTERSECT() or FILTER() with a CONTAINS() function parameter.

There's more...

Multiple dimensions

The Sales Growth Tier measure can be used for analyzing other dimensions of the model and at different grains

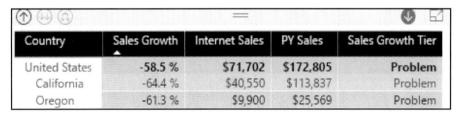

Country	Sales Growth	Internet Sales	PY Sales	Sales Growth Tier
United States	-58.5 %	$71,702	$172,805	Problem
California	-64.4 %	$40,550	$113,837	Problem
Oregon	-61.3 %	$9,900	$25,569	Problem

Drill Down into Problem Customer Country

In the example visual, a user could drill down with the matrix visual and see the growth tiers by state

Alternatives to virtual relationships

There are options to modify data models to support physical relationships and thus avoid the limitations with virtual relationships.

- A concatenated column such as Year-Month could be created for each table via SQL, M, or a DAX calculated column.
- Bridge tables with bidirectional cross filtering relationships provide simple solutions to many-to-many scenarios
- For small fact tables (for example, Plan), LOOKUPVALUE() could be used in a calculated column supporting the relationship

See also

- Physical and Virtual Relationships in DAX: `http://bit.ly/2oFpe8T`

Creating browsable model hierarchies and groups

Hierarchies and groups are data model structures that can be implemented to simplify the user and report authoring experience. Hierarchies provide single-click access to multiple columns of a table enabling users to navigate through pre-defined levels such as the weeks within a given month. Groups are comprised of individual values of a column that enable analysis and visualization of the combined total as though it's a single value. Hierarchies and groups have useful applications in almost all data models and it's important to understand the relationship of these structures to the data model and visualizations.

This recipe provides an example of utilizing DAX parent and child hierarchy functions to create columns of a hierarchy. The hierarchy is then implemented into the data model and a group is created to further benefit analysis.

How to do it...

Create hierarchy columns with DAX

The purpose of this example is to create columns in the Account dimension which will support a six-level hierarchy.

- The table is self-joined based on the `AccountKey` and `ParentAccountKey` parent account code

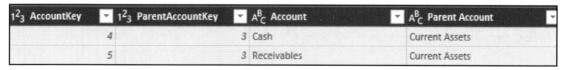

AccountKey	ParentAccountKey	Account	Parent Account
4	3	Cash	Current Assets
5	3	Receivables	Current Assets

Account Dimension Parent-Child Hierarchy

1. From the Data View, select the `Account` table and click on **New Column** from the **Modeling** tab.
2. Create a DAX calculated column to return the account name of the top most parent for the given account row

```
Account Level 1 =
VAR AccountPath = PATH(Account[AccountKey],Account[ParentAccountKey])
VAR AccountKey = PATHITEM(AccountPath,1,1)
RETURN
LOOKUPVALUE(Account[Account],Account[AccountKey],AccountKey)
```

count Type	Operator	Parent Account Code	ParentAccountKey	ValueType	Account Level 1
ets	+	1	1	Currency	Balance Sheet
ets	+	10	2	Currency	Balance Sheet
ets	+	110	3	Currency	Balance Sheet

Calculated Column for Account Hierarchy

3. Create five additional calculated columns to support the additional levels of the hierarchy.
   - In each calculation, revise the second parameter of the `PATHITEM()` function for the level of the hierarchy .
   - For example, the `Account Level 3` column's `PATHITEM()` function should use (AccountPath,3,1).

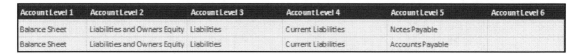

Account Level 1	Account Level 2	Account Level 3	Account Level 4	Account Level 5	Account Level 6
Balance Sheet	Liabilities and Owners Equity	Liabilities	Current Liabilities	Notes Payable	
Balance Sheet	Liabilities and Owners Equity	Liabilities	Current Liabilities	Accounts Payable	

Data View of Calculated Columns

Some rows will have blank values for a given column because it's higher in the structure. For example, the balance sheet account doesn't have values for the level 2 through 6 columns. The calculated columns will appear in the Fields list with formula icons.

Implement a hierarchy

With the necessary hierarchy columns created, a hierarchy structure can be implemented in the data model.

1. In the **Fields** list of the Report view select the `Account Level 2` field and drag it on top of the `Account Level 1` field
    * A hierarchy will be created. Right-click the hierarchy and give it a name such as `Account Level Hierarchy`
2. Drag the `Account Level 3` field on top of the name of the hierarchy. Repeat this for all other account level columns.

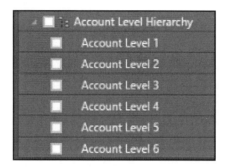

Hierarchy in Field List

* The hierarchy can now be added to visuals with a single click. Drill down is available to navigate all six columns.

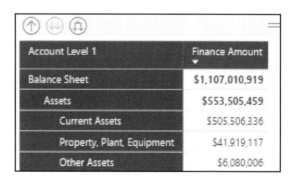

Matrix Visual of Account Hierarchy

With the hierarchy in the **Fields** list, usability may be improved by hiding the individual columns. However, individual columns are needed to view a different order of the columns or to view the columns of the hierarchy on opposing axes.

Create and manage a group

The objective of this example is to create a group consisting of four product subcategory values.

1. Identify similar or related values of a column to be grouped
   - These are generally less common dimension values which can clutter data visualizations
   - In this example, vests, gloves, caps, and socks are small and similar subcategories that can be grouped
2. From the Data View or the Report View, select the `Product Subcategory` column
   - On the **Modeling** tab, click on **New Group** to open the **Groups** dialog
   - You can also just right-click the column in the **Fields** list and select **New Group**
3. Select one of the four subcategories and click on **Group**. Also, give the group a short, descriptive name (for example, **Accessories**)
   - Add values to the group by selecting both the group name and the ungrouped value and clicking on **Group**

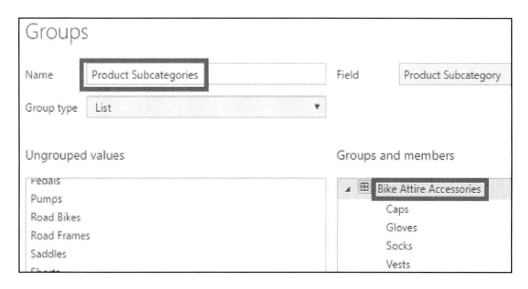

Groups Dialog

- The name for the new groups (that is, `Product Subcategories`) will be exposed in the **Fields** list with a shape icon.
- In this example, `Product Subcategory Groups` is the name assigned to this group

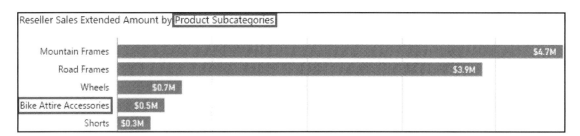

Product Subcategories Group

- The grouping can be make Power BI reports and dashboards more intuitive and help simplify analyses

If a particular grouping created in Power BI Desktop becomes pervasive throughout reports and dashboards it may be appropriate to build the equivalent into the data warehouse or the retrieval queries of the data model.

How it works...

DAX parent and child functions

- The PATH() function compares a child key column with the parent key column and returns a delimited text string containing all the parent members for the given row

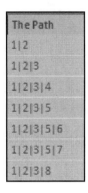

PATH() Function example

- The PATHITEM() function returns the key value from a path from highest to lowest based on the position parameter.
    - The third and final parameter to this function (1) indicates to return this value as an integer.
- The LOOKUPVALUE() function compares the account key with the key returned by the PATHITEM() function

Include other grouping option

- By default, the **Include Other group** option in the **Groups** dialog box is not enabled.
    - If enabled, all other distinct values or members of the column will be grouped into an **Other** group

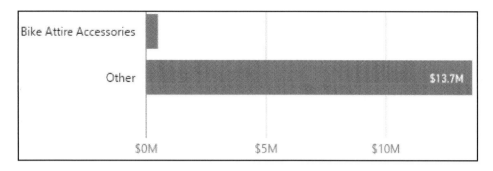

Other Group Enabled

Model scoped features

- Creating and editing groups and hierarchies is only available in Power BI Desktop with the data model loaded
- Users accessing the data model in Power BI are only able to use the existing groups and hierarchies

There's more...

DAX calculated columns as rare exceptions

- In almost all scenarios, the SQL source views or M queries are preferable alternatives to DAX calculated columns.
- The DAX parent-child functions used were developed for this scenario and the Account table only has 100 rows.

 Calculated columns and tables in DAX use the resources of the model during processing/refresh operations and are not compressed, thus increasing the memory footprint of the model. Avoid calculated columns on large fact tables.

Natural hierarchies versus unnatural hierarchies

- A natural hierarchy contains unique child values for each parent value and is the recommended structure of hierarchies.
  - For example, each unique value in the Fiscal Year column would have 12 unique child values, such as "2017-Mar". An unnatural hierarchy would have the same child value repeated across multiple parent values.

Grouping dates and numbers

- Grouping is also available for date and numerical data type columns.
- For example, a `List Price` column can be divided into equally sized bins for analysis across the ranges of prices.

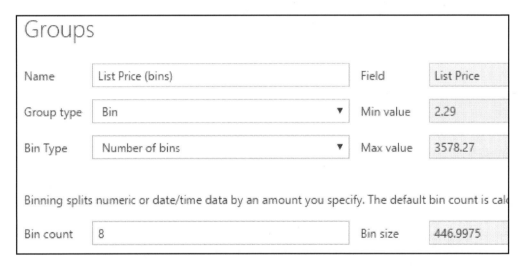

Grouping Bins for Numeric Data Type Column

- A specific size of bin or a set number of bins can be selected. A similar dialog is available for date data types.

DirectQuery models supported

- Groups and hierarchies can also be created in DirectQuery data models
- Calculated columns can be created in DirectQuery models too, though performance can be negatively impacted
- In this example, the `PATH()` function is not supported in DirectQuery models

See also

- Grouping and Binning Documentation: `http://bit.ly/2pALaBc`
- DAX Formula Compatibility in DirectQuery Mode: `http://bit.ly/2oK8QXB`

4
Authoring Power BI Reports

In this chapter, we will cover the following recipes:

- Building rich and intuitive Power BI reports
- Creating table and matrix visuals
- Utilizing graphical visualization types
- Enhancing exploration of reports
- Integrating card visualizations
- Controlling interactive filtering between visuals
- Associating slicers with report pages
- Applying filters at different scopes
- Formatting reports for publication
- Designing mobile report layouts

Introduction

Power BI reports serve as the basic building blocks for dashboards, data exploration, and content collaboration and distribution in Power BI. Power BI Desktop provides abundant data visualization features and options, enabling the construction of highly targeted and user-friendly reports across devices. As each Power BI Desktop report can contain multiple pages within each page, including multiple visuals, a single Power BI report can support multiple use cases, audiences, and business needs. For example, a KPI visual can be pinned to a dashboard, while a report page can support detailed and domain-specific analysis. These capabilities compete directly with visualization offerings from competitor analytics platforms and can be further extended with custom visuals and report themes.

The selection and configuration of Power BI visualization features in report design is essential to derive value from the data retrieval and modeling processes covered in Chapter 2, *Accessing and Retrieving Data* and Chapter 3, *Building a Power BI Data Model*, respectively. In this chapter, we develop and describe the most fundamental report visualizations and design concepts. Additionally, guidance is provided to enhance and control the user experience when interacting with Power BI reports and consuming them on Windows and mobile devices.

Building rich and intuitive Power BI reports

Power BI Desktop provides the means to design reports that are both highly customized to specific use cases and requirements as well as aligned with a corporate BI standard. The report design and development process should naturally flow from the data modeling process as the measures, relationships, and dimensions from the model are now utilized to visualize and analyze business questions. As the purpose and scope of Power BI reports can range widely from dashboard visualizations to interactive analytical experiences to role-specific detail reporting, it's essential that report authoring features are aligned closely to these distinct use cases.

In this recipe, a report design planning process is shared to bring clarity to the primary design elements of Power BI reports, such as visualization types. Two finished report pages are described with supporting details included in the How it Works section, and additional report design features and practices are discussed in *There's more*.

Getting ready

Stakeholder Matrix

1. Create a Stakeholder Matrix to help structure the report design planning process around the needs of the different parties accessing the model (Power BI Dataset).
   - The Stakeholders or business units such as **Merchandising** appear on the columns axis and replace the conformed dimensions (that is, Product or Vendor) that were used in the data warehouse bus matrix described in Chapter 3, *Building a Power BI Data Model*

BUSINESS PROCESSES	Stakeholders							
	Executive	Sales	Finance	Marketing	Merchandising	eCommerce	Customer Service	Supply Chain
Internet Sales	✓	✓	✓	✓	✓	✓		
Internet Sales Plan	✓	✓	✓	✓	✓	✓	✓	✓
Reseller Sales	✓	✓	✓		✓			
General Ledger	✓		✓					
Inventory			✓	✓	✓	✓		✓
Customer Surveys	✓	✓	✓	✓		✓	✓	
Customer Service Calls			✓				✓	
Shipping			✓		✓			✓

Stakeholder Matrix

- The stakeholders replace the dimension columns from the bus matrix. In this example, the data model contains the four highlighted fact tables: `Internet Sales`, `Internet Sales Plan`, `Reseller Sales`, and `General Ledger`.

 When there can be multiple stakeholders within a given business function with their own unique needs and use cases, these can be added as columns to the stakeholder matrix. In Power BI, there are many options for meeting the unique needs of different stakeholders with the same data model and underlying retrieval and data architecture.

How to do it...

Report planning and design process

1. Identify the user and use case:
    - Like a PowerPoint presentation, report pages should support a single theme and target a specific audience
    - Per the stakeholder matrix, there are often many disparate users and use cases for a given data model

A single report should not attempt to address unrelated business questions, or to meet the needs of highly diverse users such as a corporate financial analyst or a store manager. Multi-Scope reports can lead to convoluted user experiences and report-level customization that can be difficult to maintain and scale.

The report planning and design process should answer the following four questions:

1. Who will be accessing this report?
    - If identified users have highly disparate needs, choose one user role and plan to address the others separately
    - Page level filtering and optionally row-level security can provide a robust solution for a single team
    - Reports for different teams can be developed quickly if the model includes the necessary data and grain
    - If users are deeply familiar with the data, then report titles and descriptive text and labels are less necessary

It's recommended to involve the business users or a representative early in the report design process and potentially before all elements of the data model are complete. Any initial iterations of the report and feedback can contribute to the design of the final report to be published.

2. What are the top priorities of this report in terms of business questions?
    - Establish the starting point for the analysis process including measures and grain such as weekly sales
    - It's common for the stakeholder to have many related questions and a need to navigate the model quickly
        - Additional drilling and filtering features can be added to a report's starting point

The prioritized business questions directly drive visualization choices such as line/bar charts and tables. If the trend or fluctuations of measures is the top priority then line charts, with custom scales and supporting trend and reference lines, may be chosen. If precise individual data points are required, either as standalone numbers or related to one or two dimensions, then Cards, KPIs, and tables or matrices should be used. The choice of visuals and their size, color, and positioning on the canvas relative to other visuals should not be an arbitrary decision or guess.

Standard line, bar/column, and scatter charts have natural advantages in terms of visual perception and user comprehension. Other visuals should be utilized for their specific use cases and strengths, such as a Funnel for stages of a process and a Waterfall for the contributions of dimension values to an overall total.

3. How will the report be accessed and utilized?
   - Will users only view the updated report or will this often serve as the starting point for further analysis?
     - If there is no to limited interaction, plan to embed conditional logic and exceptions in the report
     - If there is high interaction, plan to use hierarchies, Tooltips, and slicers to enable data exploration
   - How does the report relate to existing dashboards?
     - Identify the components of the report that will contribute to an existing dashboard
     - If creating a new dashboard based on the report, identify the tiles and interaction of this dashboard
   - Will the report only be accessed via the web browser or will mobile devices be used regularly?
     - If mobile consumption is expected, reports can be designed to optimize this experience
     - Power BI dashboards can also be optimized for phone layout in the Power BI Service

4. Does the Data Model (Power BI Dataset) need to be revised?
   - If a report requirement is systemic to all reports for a given stakeholder group, consider revising the model
   - If complex report-level customization is required or if the performance is poor, consider revising the model
     - These revisions often include new logical attributes or new DAX measures

Power BI is not a full replacement for the reports from other BI tools such as **SQL Server Reporting Services** (**SSRS**) or Microsoft Excel. Existing Excel and SSRS reports can generally be migrated to Power BI but this might not always be beneficial given the different advantages of the tools. See `Chapter 13`, *Integrating Power BI with Other Applications* for additional details on these considerations and guidance on integrating Excel and SSRS with Power BI.

Report Design Example

In this example, the stakeholder is the European Sales Territory Group comprised of France, Germany, and the United Kingdom. The planning process revealed top priorities to be Internet Sales versus Plan, Reseller Sales, and sales margins at the monthly grain as well as product category breakdowns.

The report should allow each country manager to analyze their own data and for the group manager to analyze Europe.

European Sales and Margin Report Page

1. Develop a Power BI Report with four report pages: one page per country and one for the Europe Sales Group Manager

   - All the report pages include the same four priority measures in the top left and an **Internet Sales to Plan** chart
      - A KPI visual with a monthly trend and a `Goal` measure is used to provide greater context

- The Europe report is designed for a higher level view of the senior manager and for easy filter selections

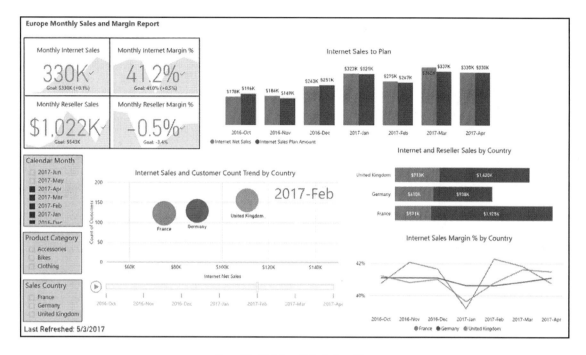

Europe Monthly Sales and Margin Report Page

- The slicer visuals as well as the **Play** axis on the scatter chart are organized on the left to support user filter selections.
    - The manager can further analyze a country-specific question on these report pages.

DAX queries are generated for report visuals, and the queries associated with dense visuals such as tables or matrices with many rows and columns are much slower than Cards and KPI visuals. Additionally, report pages with many visuals can appear crowded and complex to use. With the possible exception of Cards, Gauges, and KPIs, look to limit the number of visuals per page to 4-5 and to avoid dense "data extract or dump" visuals. Additionally, look to apply simple filters (`Current Year` or `Prior Year`) at the report and page levels to further aid performance.

European country sales and margin report page

The country level managers are also accountable for the sales plan, but are interested in greater self-service flexibility, and require some detailed reporting in tabular formats to expose specific values for several measures.

1. Develop country-specific report pages, including a map by state/region or city and a table visual with measures by product category.

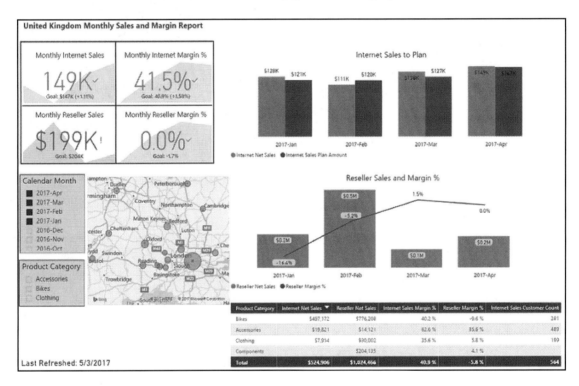

United Kingdom Report Page

- Each country report page also offers at a glance values with the KPIs visuals updating automatically
- By hovering over the bubbles in the map or the bars in the chart, additional measures are exposed as tooltips
- More details on the individual report components used in this example are contained in other recipes in this chapter.

A reliable predictor of a report's effectiveness is the ratio of business insights (measures, context, or analysis) to the user effort required to consume the information. Ideally a report should offer out-of-the-box analytics requiring nothing from the user beyond access and basic knowledge of the terminology and domain. The more a user is required to scroll, click, and avoid unnecessary colors or data elements, the less effective the report will be.

How it works...

European sales report design

- The report is filtered on Europe at the report level and on the individual countries at the page level for these pages.
- For the measures that don't have a target or goal (plan), a trailing 6-month average measure is used.
- A rectangle and two Line shape objects are used to group the KPI visuals.
- A textbox is used for the page titles and the last refreshed date footer is a card visual.
  - An M query with the `DateTime.LocalNow()` function is retrieved and passed to a DAX measure returning text.
- The chart titles are customized and the *y* axis is removed when possible.
- Standard visual types with advantages in visual perception and with additional analysis context were chosen.
  - For example, KPIs are used instead of card visuals. Gauges, treemaps, and pie charts are avoided.
  - A clustered column chart was chosen over a line chart for **Internet Sales to Plan** given the importance of the individual values for each month.

There's more...

Power BI report design checklist

Similar to the simple yet important details with data modeling shared in Chapter 3, *Building a Power BI Data Model,* a number of design practices significantly improve the value and user adoption of Power BI reports.

- **Minimalism**: Any report element which isn't strictly required for comprehension should be removed.
    - Examples include images, redundant chart axis, verbose text and unnecessary data legends.
- **Efficient visuals**: Leverage visuals and features that provide additional insights with the same amount of space.
    - Examples include KPI and combination chart visuals, tooltips, trend lines, and color saturation.
- **Meaningful colors**: Colors should be used to convey meaning such as high or low variances to a target or measure.
    - Use colors selectively and avoid overwhelming or distracting users with color variety or density.
- **Organized**: Report visuals should be aligned, distributed evenly, and situated near related visuals.
    - The most important visuals should be near the top-left corner of the canvas, and white space should separate visuals.
- **Consistent:** Layout and formatting choices such as visual placement, fonts, and text alignment should be consistent.
    - For example, slicer visuals should always be placed on the left or top of the visual.

Custom visuals

- Custom visuals available for download from the MS Office store extend the functionality and visualization options of Power BI reports beyond what's available in Power BI Desktop:

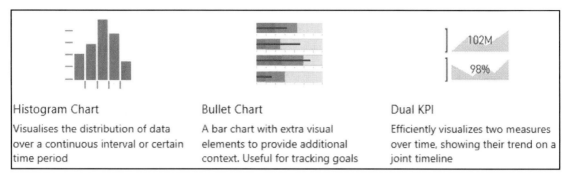

Histogram Chart

Visualises the distribution of data over a continuous interval or certain time period

Bullet Chart

A bar chart with extra visual elements to provide additional context. Useful for tracking goals

Dual KPI

Efficiently visualizes two measures over time, showing their trend on a joint timeline

A sample of custom visuals from Office Store Custom Visuals Gallery

- Each custom visual is a `.pbiviz` file that can be added to the **Visualizations** pane and used like any other visual
    - See `Chapter 9`, *Applying Advanced Analytics and Custom Visuals*, for additional details

Published Power BI datasets as data sources

- Reports can be developed against a Power BI data model (dataset) that has been published to the Power BI service
- The report developer would need to be a member of the App Workspace containing the dataset with Edit rights
    - The Power BI Service is available under the Online Services group in the Get Data dialog

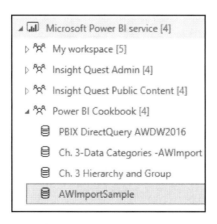

Published Datasets as sources for Live Connection Reports

- Only report authoring functionality will be available to Power BI Desktop, not data modeling or M queries
    - Report authoring of Live Connection reports (reports connected to Power BI datasets and SSAS data models) includes the ability to author DAX measures specific to the given Power BI report

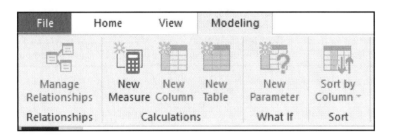

'New Measure' option available to a Live Connected Report

- Note that SSAS Multidimensional data models do not currently support report-scoped measures. This functionality is specific to Power BI Datasets and SSAS Tabular Datasets.

It can be beneficial to allow business analysts to create reports or evaluate the functionality and logic of published Power BI datasets while additional modeling, data retrieval queries, and other BI/IT activities take place. In this example, Power BI Desktop is used for report development but Power BI Publisher for Excel can also be used to quickly sample or validate datasets with Excel's familiar pivot tables and formatting properties.

Power BI reports can also be created and edited in the Power BI Service with published datasets as a source. However, reports created in the Power BI Service must always be edited in the Power BI Service, and currently no form of source control is available to store different versions of these reports. For this reason, Power BI Desktop is recommended for report development.

See also

- Power BI Report Design Practices: http://bit.ly/2poUeMv

Creating table and matrix visuals

Table and matrix visuals are appropriate when visibility to precise, individual measures is needed or when data is viewed at a detailed level, such as individual transactions. Table visuals in Power BI conform to the classic "list" report format of columns and rows but support powerful cross-highlighting and formatting options, including conditional formatting. Matrix visuals include table visual features and correspond to the layout and general functionality of pivot tables in Excel: two-dimensional representations of measures with the ability to drill up and down the row and column axes.

In this recipe, a table visual is used to identify exceptions based on conditional formatting rules. Additionally, an example matrix visual is created to support interactive drill down and cross-highlighting. Brief examples of table visuals support for URLs and email as well as clustering are included in the *There's more...* section.

How to do it...

Table visual exceptions

In this example, a report is designed to identify and analyze transactions that negatively impact the margin.

1. Identify the dimension columns and add them to the canvas as a table visual.
2. Add the measures to the table including `Sales Amount` and `Margin %`.
3. Apply a visual level filter to the `Sales Amount` such that each row represents a significant transaction or grouping.

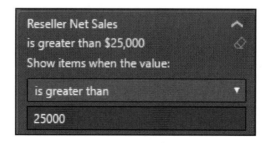

Visual Level Filter Applied to Measure

4. Turn the **Totals** off from the formatting pane given the filter condition applied to the visual.

5. Apply a **Table** style such as **Alternating Rows** or use the **Values and Column headers** options to apply a standard format.

6. From the field well of the **Visualizations** pane, click on the **Margin %** dropdown and choose **Conditional formatting**.

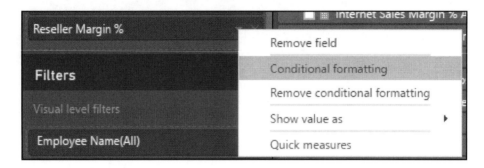

Applying Conditional Formatting to a Measure in a Table Visual

7. From the **Conditional formatting** dialog, choose **Diverging** colors based on min and max values.

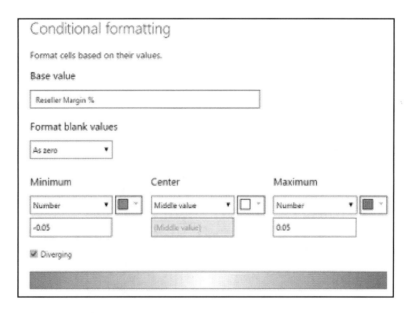

Diverging Conditional Formatting based on numbers

8. With these settings, margin % cells will be shaded red with increased intensity based on the value for the row .

Employee Name	Reseller	Promotion	Reseller Net Sales	Reseller Sales Order Quantity	Reseller Margin %
Ranjit Varkey Chudukatil	Metropolitan Equipment	No Discount	$561,291	1,596	-1.4 %
Ranjit Varkey Chudukatil	Registered Cycle Store	No Discount	$516,783	1,818	10.8 %
José Saraiva	Bulk Discount Store	No Discount	$423,881	984	-3.4 %
José Saraiva	Metropolitan Bicycle Supply	No Discount	$413,625	929	10.6 %
Ranjit Varkey Chudukatil	Roadway Bicycle Supply	No Discount	$404,119	657	-2.3 %

Conditionally Formatting table Visual

9. The table is sorted by Reseller Net Sales per the arrow and the third row is shaded dark red for the -3.4% value.
10. Clicking on any cell of this row will filter the other visuals by the Employee Name, Reseller, and Promotion associated with this specific row. Multiple rows can also be selected for cross-filtering via *Ctrl* + click.

Identifying blanks in tables

A similar conditional formatting technique can be used to identify blank values. In the following example, blank values are formatted as either red for one measure (Germany) or blue for a different measure (France) if these values are blank.

The goal is to visually identify dates in which no German customers purchased anything from the Accessories category.

1. Create a DAX measure with a filter on Germany, used in comparison with overall (all countries) measures.

Conditional Formatting of Blank Values

2. Create a table visual with both the overall measures and the Germany and France-specific measures.

Date ▼	Internet Net... ▼	Internet Sales Order Quantity	Internet Sales Germany Customer Count	Internet Sales France Customer Count
7/14/2017	$388	28	2	6
7/13/2017	$536	23	6	5
7/12/2017	$314	18		4
7/11/2017	$223	11	2	1
7/10/2017	$548	29	4	4

Table Visual with Blank Conditional Formatting

- Scrolling up or down the table visual will call out these days and the row

Alternatively you can select **Show Items with No Data** from the `Date` or `Dimension` column in the values field well. Dates without customer count measure values would appear the measure would be formatted as red.

Using **Show Items with No Data** avoids the need for other measures in the table such as overall sales and quantity. However, in most scenarios the other measures and the exceptions the blanks represent are useful. For example, a holiday in which there were no sales wouldn't appear, and in the first approach but would appear in **Show Items with No Data**.

Matrix visual hierarchies

1. Add the `Internet Sales` measure to the canvas and choose matrix as the visual from the **Visualizations** pane.
2. Add the `Sales Territory Hierarchy` to the **Rows** axis and `Product Category Hierarchy` to the **Columns** axis.

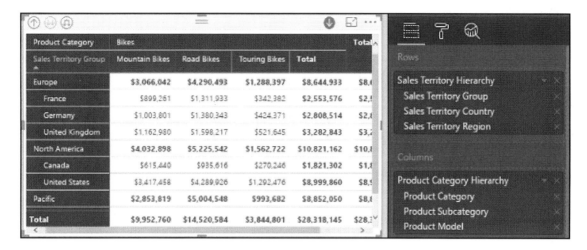

Matrix Visual with Two Hierarchies

- Both hierarchies contain three levels and the matrix automatically adjusts in size based on navigation

How it works...

Matrix visual navigation

- The rows hierarchy can be navigated via the three icons on the top left of the visual.
- The columns hierarchy can be navigated via the Drill Mode icon on the top right and the right click context menu available from the column headers.
- If Drill Mode (top right icon) is turned off, selecting a value in the matrix will cross-filter other visuals based on the dimensions the matrix value reflects. This cross-filtering also applies to table visuals as per the table example.

There's more...

URL and mail to email support

- Links can be added to Table visuals to launch email applications and websites

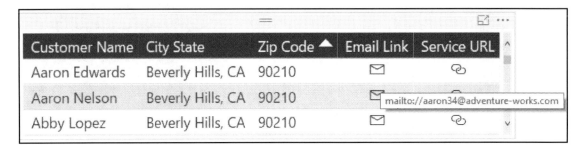

- Clicking on the icon in the `Email Link` column launches an email to the address specified following `mailto://`
- Clicking on the icon in the `Service URL` column launches the website for the given row

If you have an email address column, a `mailto` URL can be added in the Query Editor or M language. Set the **Data Category** in the **Modeling** tab to **Web URL** for both `Mailto` and `URL` columns. To get the email and URL icons to appear in the table, set the URL icon option in the **Formatting pane** of the visual under **Values** to **On**.

Percent of total formatting

- A **Show Values As** option is available for measures added to table and matrix visuals to display the measure value as a percentage of the row, column, or grand total. However, measures in table and matrix visuals cannot currently be formatted to display units and decimal places such as thousands or millions.

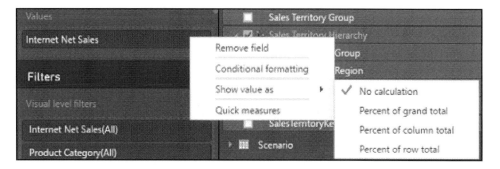

Show Value as Option for Table and Matrix Visuals

- For table visuals, only **Percent of grand total** is available given the single dimension of the visual.

Measures on matrix rows

- Multiple measures can be displayed on the rows of matrix visuals, a very common use case in financial reporting

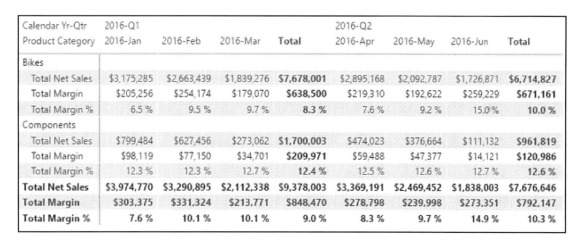

| Calendar Yr-Qtr | 2016-Q1 | | | | 2016-Q2 | | | |
Product Category	2016-Jan	2016-Feb	2016-Mar	Total	2016-Apr	2016-May	2016-Jun	Total
Bikes								
Total Net Sales	$3,175,285	$2,663,439	$1,839,276	$7,678,001	$2,895,168	$2,092,787	$1,726,871	$6,714,827
Total Margin	$205,256	$254,174	$179,070	$638,500	$219,310	$192,622	$259,229	$671,161
Total Margin %	6.5 %	9.5 %	9.7 %	8.3 %	7.6 %	9.2 %	15.0 %	10.0 %
Components								
Total Net Sales	$799,484	$627,456	$273,062	$1,700,003	$474,023	$376,664	$111,132	$961,819
Total Margin	$98,119	$77,150	$34,701	$209,971	$59,488	$47,377	$14,121	$120,986
Total Margin %	12.3 %	12.3 %	12.7 %	12.4 %	12.5 %	12.6 %	12.7 %	12.6 %
Total Net Sales	$3,974,770	$3,290,895	$2,112,338	$9,378,003	$3,369,191	$2,469,452	$1,838,003	$7,676,646
Total Margin	$303,375	$331,324	$213,771	$848,470	$278,798	$239,998	$273,351	$792,147
Total Margin %	7.6 %	10.1 %	10.1 %	9.0 %	8.3 %	9.7 %	14.9 %	10.3 %

Matrix Visual with Three Measures in the Values Field Well Displayed on Rows

- Enable the **Show on rows** option under the values formatting card for the matrix visual
- An attribute for the rows field well, such as `Product Category`, in this example is optional

Data bar conditional formatting

- In addition to color scale formatting, data bars can be used to apply conditional formatting to table and matrix visuals:

Product Subcategory	Internet Net Sales	Internet Sales Margin %
Road Bikes	$11,119,297	38.7 %
Mountain Bikes	$5,578,970	45.3 %
Touring Bikes	$1,039,045	37.8 %
Tires and Tubes	$83,895	62.6 %

Data Bars Conditional Formatting

- Data bars can be displayed with the measure values per this example or as stand-alone bars. Specific minimum and maximum threshold values can also be entered to drive the conditional formatting of the bars.

 Font color scales can also be conditionally formatted in addition to background color scales and data bar formatting. If the same formatting logic and colors are used for both font color scales and background color scales, only the color of the value will be displayed, such as in a heat map.

Utilizing graphical visualization types

Data visualization and exploration is central to Power BI, and the visualization types chosen in reports contribute greatly to user comprehension and adoption. Power BI Desktop includes an array of modern visuals such as the Treemap and the Funnel, but also includes rich formatting options for traditional line, bar/column, combination and scatter charts. Additionally, four map visuals are available to analyze geographical data, and many custom visuals are available for download and integration into Power BI Desktop reports.

This recipe provides three examples of utilizing graphical visualization types including the waterfall chart, the line chart, and a shape map. Additional report design guidance as well as a tip on conditional formatting in column/bar charts is included in the *There's more...* section.

Getting ready

Choosing visual types

- Choose column charts when individual values and their comparison is more important than the trend.
    - Select bar charts when the axis category labels are long.
- Use line charts when the trend or shape of data is more important than individual values and their comparison.
- Select scatter charts to demonstrate a correlation of a dimension to two measures.
- Choose special purpose visuals such as Treemaps and Waterfall Charts as supplements to standard visuals.

It's generally recommended to avoid pie charts, donut charts, gauges, and treemap visuals, given the advantages in visual perception and comprehension of other visuals. For example, the curved shapes of pie charts and gauges are more difficult to interpret than straight lines and the distance between points in column/bar and scatter charts, respectively. Note that the "Breakdown" feature of the waterfall chart may increase its use cases.

How to do it...

Waterfall chart for variance analysis

The waterfall chart visual is best used to show the contributions of individual values to an overall total. In this example, the variance between **Internet Sales (Actuals)** and the **Internet Sales Plan by Sales Territory Country** is visualized.

1. Select the measure and dimension:
    - Measures that can be positive or negative and dimensions with few distinct values are the best candidates.

2. Create the waterfall chart:
   - Add the measure and dimension to the canvas and switch the visualization type to waterfall chart.
     - The measure will be in the *y* axis, the dimension in the category of the field well.

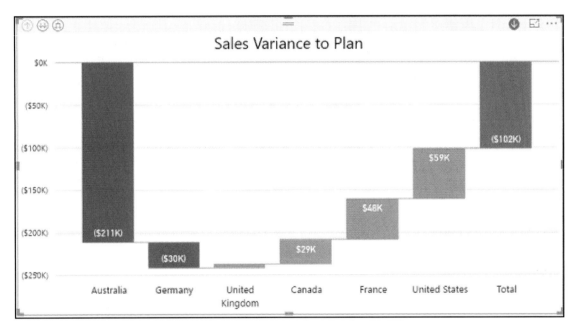

Waterfall Chart of Sales Variance to Plan

3. Sort the visualization by the measure to support an intuitive "walk" from the components to the `Total` column:
   - The default color formatting of red for negative and green for positive is usually appropriate

4. Add a drill-down dimension and tooltip measures:
   - Add another dimension column below the category dimension to support drill-down
     - With drill mode on, clicking on **Australia** breaks the ($211K) by calendar quarters
   - Add a measure or multiple measures to the tooltips field well such as `Sales Amount` and `Sales Plan`
     - Hovering over the waterfall bars exposes these values for additional context

5. Format the chart:
  - Remove the legend if the chart is self-explanatory and set the data labels to a position of **Inside End**.

The waterfall chart visual has been enhanced to include a **Breakdown** field well that calculates the variance and variance % of an individual dimension value between two category values. For example, a date attribute such as Fiscal Year-Quarter could be used as the **Category** field well and filtered to display only the current and prior Fiscal Year-Quarter. Adding a product category column to the Breakdown field well would display the product categories with the most significant variances between the two fiscal quarters, with details available in tooltips.

This increases the use cases for waterfall charts, particularly if dynamic date columns (that is, `Current Week` or `Prior Week`) are built into the dataset, such that the two date category values used for the comparison update automatically.

Line chart with conditional formatting

In this example, a DAX measure is used to highlight segments of a line chart that meet a certain condition.

1. Define the measure and conditional logic
  - The measure is `Internet Sales` and the logic is *Anything below an 8.5% miss to Plan.*
2. Create the conditional DAX measure:

```
Sales Below Plan 8.5% = IF([Internet Sales Var to Plan %] < -.085,
[Internet Net Sales],BLANK())
```

- The conditional measure will be included in the line chart but will have a value (not blank) only when the condition is met.

3. Create the line chart
   - Add the `Internet Sales` measure and the `Date` hierarchy to the canvas and select the **Line chart Visualization.**
   - Add the conditional DAX measure to the line chart and set its color **Data Color** to **Red.**

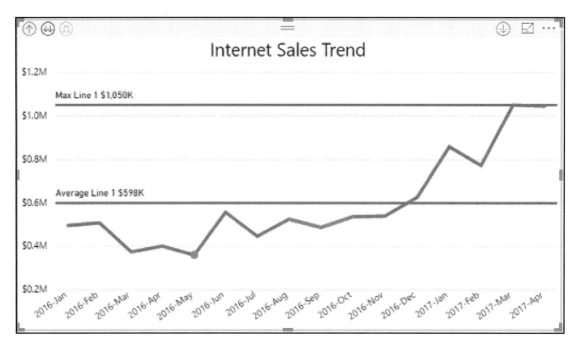

Line Chart with Conditional Formatting

- Only a single line appears on the chart and is highlighted in red for the four months which were below (-8.5%)

 This approach follows general report design goals in providing more analytical value in the same space without impacting usability. Drill-down via the data hierarchy in the axis and additional measures in the Tooltips provide further support in the same space on the report canvas.

4. Add the `Sales Amount`, `Variance to Plan`, and `Plan Amount` measures to the tooltips field well.
5. Click on the **Analytics** pane to the right of the **Formatting** pane and add a max and average Line.

6. In the **Formatting** pane increase the **Stroke** width of the line to 3 points.
7. Turn data labels and the legend off and provide a custom title.
8. With data labels off, expose the value and name of the **Reference Lines** in the **Analytics** pane.

Shape map visualization

For the Germany Monthly Sales and Margin report a shape map is used to expose the different German states:

1. Add the `State Province` column from the `Customer` table and the `Internet Sales` measure to the canvas.
2. Choose **Shape map** from the **Visualizations** pane.
3. In formatting options, select **Shape** and choose the map to display. See '*How it works...*' for details on map key values.
4. Choose the projection of the map, provide a title, and align the visual on the report page with other visuals.
    - Add related measures to the tooltips field well to provide additional context.

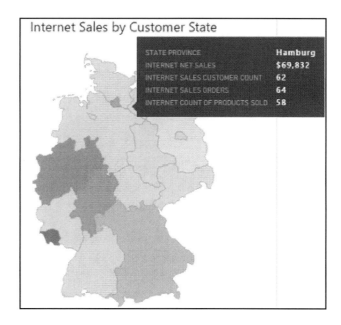

Shape Map

- States with higher sales have greater color saturation by default, and the tooltips display when hovering over states.

How it works...

Shape map

- The available shape maps include a Key dialog that is used to plot your location column

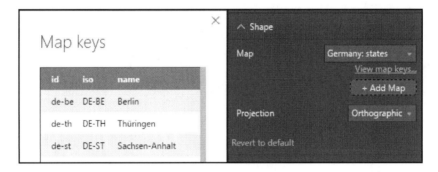

Map Keys for Germany States Shape Map

- With a shape map visual selected, click on **View map keys** from the **Shape** option in the **Formatting** pane
    - Ensure that your location data matches the keys before using the given shape map.
- The bubble map and filled map visuals can be used when a custom shape map either isn't available for the location data or isn't appropriate for the given use case.
    - Both visuals use Bing to plot location points. The filled map color-codes the individual countries

Enhancing exploration of reports

Power BI reports can be accessed and dynamically filtered via natural language queries in both Power BI Q&A as well as Windows Cortana. This can greatly extend the self-service experience as the user isn't required to navigate through reports or make slicer selections within a report page. To best take advantage of these features, report designers can create featured Q&A questions, expose report pages to common natural language terms, and create report pages specific to Cortana or Q&A queries. Report authors can also design drillthrough report pages to enable users to quickly and easily explore the details associated with a specific item of interest. Finally, report themes can be imported or created from scratch to apply custom formatting to new and existing reports, such as with a corporate report layout standard.

In this recipe, we walk through the essential setup and components of Power BI Q&A and Cortana natural language queries. Examples of Q&A suggestion questions as well as creating and accessing report pages from Q&A and Cortana are provided. Additionally, the process of configuring a drillthrough report page and applying a report theme template is described. Further details on mobile support, model synonyms for Q&A, and custom report themes are included in the *There's more...* section.

Getting ready

Drillthrough report page requirements

1. Obtain guidance from business users or teams on the most important dimensions to target with drillthrough pages such as products, customers, or stores. Note that these report pages will be filtered to a single item such as `Store #123`.

2. Also obtain guidance on the business questions the drillthrough page should answer for this specific item.

Drillthrough is a very powerful and popular feature in that it effectively serves as a custom generated report tailored to a user's question as the user views the report. Therefore, multiple drillthrough report pages across common dimensions may be included with popular reports which are actively interacted with. Consider utilizing the Power BI templates (`.pbit` files) described in the *Preserving Report Metadata with Power BI Templates* recipe of `Chapter 7`, *Parameterizing Power BI Solutions* to leverage existing drillthrough report pages in new reports.

Enable Cortana integration and Q&A

1. Enable Cortana in the Power BI Admin Portal:
   - Click on the Gear icon in the top-right corner of the Power BI service and select **Admin Portal.**

> ◢ Ask questions about data using Cortana
> *Enabled for the entire organization*
>
> Users in the organization can ask questions about their data using Cortana.
>
> ⬤◯ Enabled

Power BI Admin Portal: Cortana Option within Integration Settings

 The Power BI Admin Portal is restricted to global admin accounts within Office 365 or Azure Active Directory and to accounts assigned to the Power BI service administrator role.

2. Enable the dataset for Q&A and Cortana:
   - Click on the Gear Icon in the top-right corner of the Power BI service and select **Settings.**
   - Click on the **Datasets** tab at the top and with the dataset highlighted enable **Q&A and Cortana.**

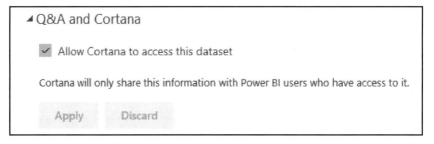

> ◢ Q&A and Cortana
>
> ☑ Allow Cortana to access this dataset
>
> Cortana will only share this information with Power BI users who have access to it.
>
> Apply   Discard

Enable Cortana and Q & A on a Dataset

3. Associate the Power BI credential with Windows:
    - In Windows, select **Settings** and click on **Accounts**. Click on **Connect** from the **Access work or school** tab

Set up a work or school account

You'll get access to resources like email, apps, and the network. Connecting means your work or school might control some things on this device, such as which settings you can change. For specific info about this, ask them.

someone@example.com

Connecting a Power BI Account through Windows

- If a Windows 10 version earlier than 1607 is running, both the work or school and Microsoft account are needed

4. Create a dashboard:
    - With a dataset published to Power BI, select one of its reports and click on a visual from one of its pages
    - Click on the pin icon in the top-right corner of the visual and select **New dashboard**

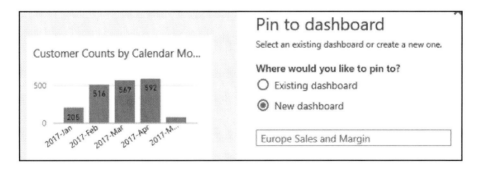

Pinning a Report Visual to a New Dashboard

- Q&A natural language queries are submitted from dashboards against the underlying datasets.

In order for Q&A queries to access a dataset and its dependent reports, at least one tile of the given Q&A dashboard must be dependent on this dataset.

How to do it...

Create featured Q&A questions

1. Open the Datasets Settings Window.
2. Click on the Gear icon in the top-right corner of the Power BI service and select **Settings**.
3. Select the **Datasets** tab and the specific dataset to be queried via Q& A and Cortana.
4. Scroll to the bottom to edit the **Featured Q&A questions** dialog.

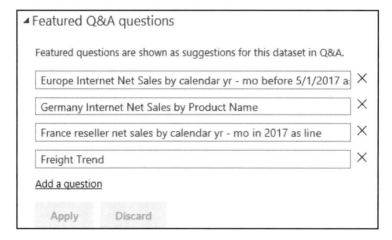

Featured Q & A questions option in Datasets Settings

5. Enter Q&A terms and phrases to feature:
   - Click on **Add a Question** and enter terms associated with specific report pages or queries of interest to users.
   - Click on **Apply** and access the dashboard connected to the dataset.

6. Test the featured questions:
   - From the dashboard, click on the underlined **Ask a question about your data** dialog.

EUROPE SALES AND MARGIN MONTHLY:

| Europe Internet Net Sales by calendar yr - mo before 5/1/2017 as line | | Germany Internet Net Sales by Product Name |
| France reseller net sales by calendar yr - mo in 2017 as line | Freight Trend | Internet Sales Freight | last re |

Featured Questions of the Dataset Displayed in Dashboard Q&A

7. Click on one of the featured Q&A questions at the top to confirm that the appropriate query or report page is rendered:

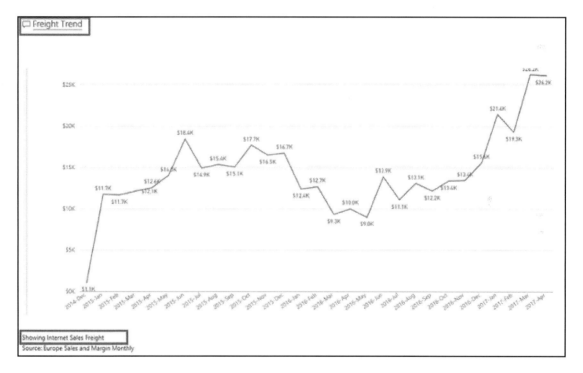

A page from the Internet Sales Freight Report is rendered via the Q&A alias of Freight Trend

- The featured term `Freight Trend` is associated with a page of the Internet Sales Freight report:

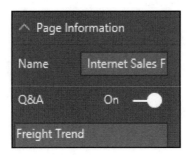

 The other featured questions in this example are not associated with specific report pages. Instead, the Q&A service creates visuals for their terms on the fly, and the user can optionally modify the terms or pin the result visual to a dashboard.

Parameterized Q&A report

1. Create a report from the dataset enabled for Q&A.
2. Design visuals for only one report page. This page should usually focus on a specific dimension.
3. In the **Page Information** options, enable Q&A and provide a simple Q&A alias or multiple terms.
4. Set a page level filter on a common dimension such as `Country` and click on **Require single selection**.
5. Save the report and return to the dashboard to test the Q&A experience for the parameter.

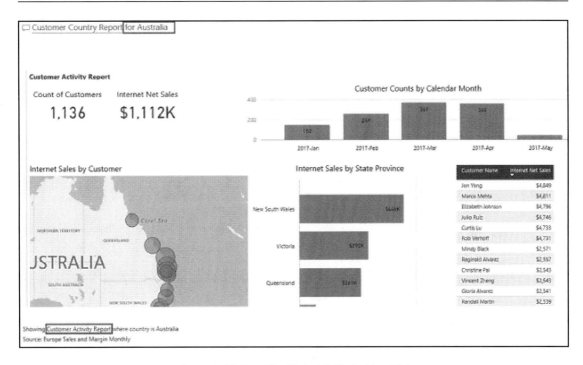

Customer Activity Report filtered by Australia Rendered from Q & A

- In this example, the alias Customer Country Report was associated with the Customer Activity Report.
  - The `for` keyword is used to pass in the parameter value to the page level filter column
- Auto complete is available in Q&A to assist in changing the country name and running the report again.

Cortana integration

1. Create a Cortana answer card:
   - Add a report page to an existing report or create a new report based on the Cortana-enabled dataset.
   - From the **Page Formatting** pane, enable **Q&A** and set the **Page Size Type** to **Cortana.**

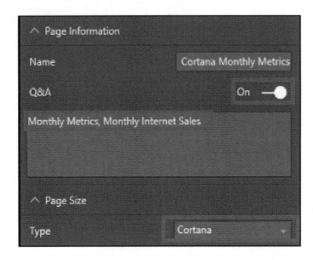

Page Formatting Options for a Cortana Answer Card

2. Provide aliases in the Q&A form that Cortana can associate with this answer card.

 Answer cards are sized specifically for Cortana and are the only way Cortana can find answers in Power BI Data. Similar to Phone Layout, Card, Gauge and KPI visuals are more easily viewed in Cortana Answer Cards than chart visuals.

3. Set a page level filter and configure **Require Single Selection** like the Q&A example earlier in this recipe.

4. Test Cortana Search for the answer card:

- From the search bar in Windows, enter the Q&A alias for the Cortana answer card.

Search terms 'Monthly Metrics for Germany' is matched with the Cortana Answer Card in Power BI

- The name of the dataset enabled for Cortana is identified below the answer card. Click on the highlighted best match

Cortana Answer Card Displayed in Windows

- The answer card will be displayed and filtered to the specific page filter you entered (Germany in this example)
    - If applicable, the visuals in the card can be interacted with like a Power BI report
- An option at the bottom to **Open in Power BI** propagates the search criteria to Power BI Q&A

Drillthrough Report Pages

In this example, the Sales team wants to drill into the details of individual products to understand the sales trend by channel.

1. Open a report in Power BI Desktop and add a report page with the name Product Details.
2. Drag the Product Name column from the Product dimension table to the **Drillthrough filters** field well.

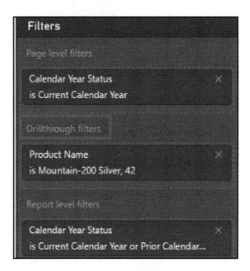

Drillthrough Filter Field Well with Product Name Column

3. Select an item from the list of values of the Drillthrough column such as Mountain-200 Silver, 42 in this example.
    - Choose an item that has transaction or fact table data associated with it and which you consider a representative sample of the items that will be drilled into.

4. Create report visualizations on this page that describe or analyze the given drillthrough item and which answer the top business questions of this item per the *Getting ready* section

5. Give the report page a clear title with a supporting visual that displays the name of the item drilled into
   - A simple card or multi-row card visual with the `Product Name` column may be sufficient
   - Optionally, DAX measures can be used to create a text message advising of the product or item drilled into

```
Selected Product Name = SELECTEDVALUE('Product'[Product
Name],"Multiple Selected")
Product Name Message = "Product Name:" & " " & [Selected Product
Name]
```

6. Test the drillthrough report page by drilling to it from a visual on a separate report page.
   - In this example, right-click a matrix row containing the product name column and select **Drillthrough**.

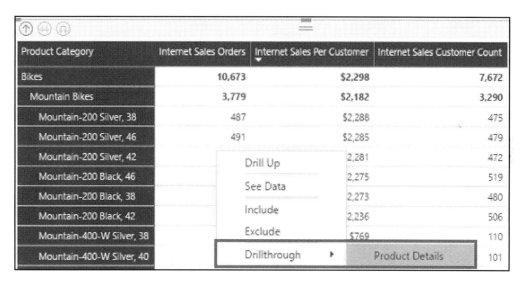

Drillthrough from a Matrix Visual to the Product Details Report Page

Drillthrough pages are especially valuable for high cardinality dimension columns since the individual values of these columns will likely not have their own dedicated reports or report pages. For example, the Product Category and Product Subcategory columns may already have their own reports and dashboards but an individual Product (third level of this hierarchy) may be a good candidate for one or multiple drillthrough report pages.

- Clicking the **Product Details** menu item (the name given to the report page from step 1) will access this page for the given product name represented on the selected row of the matrix visual.

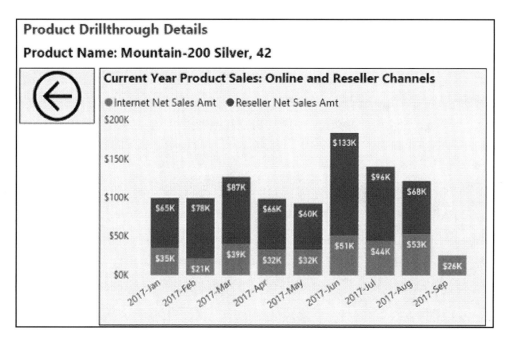

Sample of a Drillthrough Report Page Including the Default Drillthrough Back Button

- All visuals on the drillthrough report page should update to reflect the filter context of the given item (the product in this example).
    - Note that the drillthrough report page would contain several additional visuals relevant to analyzing a specific product beyond this limited example.

The back button is created automatically when a column is added to the **Drillthrough filters** field well per step 2. This button can be formatted or removed entirely but is often helpful, particularly with reports containing several pages. Alternatively, any Shape or Image that can be added via the Insert section of the Home ribbon in Power BI Desktop can also be used as a back button for a drillthrough page. A back button formatting toggle (**On/Off**) is available when selecting the given Shape or image.

Note that the same report, page, and visual level filters applicable to Power BI report pages can also be applied to drillthrough report pages. In the Product Details example of this recipe, a `Calendar Year Status` date dimension table column is used as a page filter to only show the current calendar year. See the *Applying Filters at Different Scopes* recipe later in this chapter for additional details on report filter scopes. Additionally, note that other visuals such as bar and column charts can also be used to access the drillthrough functionality via right-click.

Report themes

In this example, a report theme is applied to a report such that users with color vision deficiency can comprehend clearly.

1. Open the report in Power BI Desktop.
    - Report themes cannot be applied to reports in the Power BI Service .

2. Download the Color Blind Friendly Report Theme from the report theme gallery (`https://aka.ms/pbithemes`).
    - The Color Blind Friendly file is `ColorblindSafe-Longer.json`. Click on the download link and save the file.

3. From the Report View, click on the **Switch Theme** dropdown and select **Import Theme**:

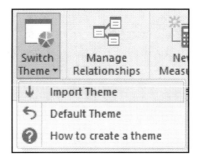

Report Color Theme Options

4. Navigate to the downloaded JSON file, select it, and click on **Open**. A message will appear: **Theme imported successfully**.
   - The standard Power BI Desktop visuals in the report pages will be updated to the colors of the theme.
   - The colors available for formatting visuals including table and matrix styles now reflect the theme colors.

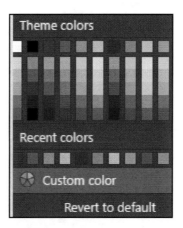

Report Theme Colors Applied to Formatting Pane of Power BI Report

5. Save and publish the report back to the Power BI Service for user access; the report theme colors will be retained.

Currently most custom visuals do not apply report themes. Additionally, report themes do not impact the colors of images and do not override any custom color applied to a specific data point in a visual.

How it works...

Report theme JSON files

- Each report theme JSON file has the following structure of elements to color code mapping:

```
"name": "ColorblindSafe-Longer",
"dataColors": ["#074650", "#009292", "#fe6db6", "#feb5da", "#480091", "#b66dff", "#b5dafe", "#6db6ff", "#914800", "#23fd23"],
"background":"#FFFFFF",
"foreground": "#074650",
"tableAccent": "#fe6db6"
```

Color Blind Report Theme JSON File Structure

- Only the `name` field is required in the JSON file. Any number of distinct codes can be entered in the datacolors field.

A popular tool for creating custom report themes (JSON files) such as a corporate colors theme, is available at `http://thememaster500.azurewebsites.net`.

There's more...

Conversational BI - mobile support for Q&A

- Q&A is also available for the Power BI mobile application that is referred to as **Conversational BI**
    - Open the dashboard and select the Q&A icon at the bottom of the screen.
    - Enter text such as `internet net sales by country as bar` to display a bar graph of this measure and dimension.
- A microphone on a mobile device can also be used to enter questions.

See also

- Words and Terminology that Q&A Recognized: `http://bit.ly/2pRIZdQ`
- Using Report Themes in Power BI Desktop: `https://aka.ms/pbithemes`

Integrating card visualizations

Card and Multi-row card visualizations are often positioned at the top and left sections of report pages given the importance of individual measures and small sets of measures. Although less graphically powerful and interactive than other visuals, cards are also the most common tiles pinned to Power BI dashboards and are also used frequently in phone layouts for mobile consumption. A common practice in report design is to start with a few high-level measures represented as card or KPI visuals and build additional chart and table visuals around these.

This recipe includes an example of a KPI visual as a more valuable alternative to a card visual and a multi-row card example. Additionally, a brief example of a gauge visualization is included in the *There's more...* section.

Getting ready

To most effectively integrate card visualizations, identify the following two items:

- Which measures does the user need to have maximum visibility to (such as all devices, reports and dashboards)?
- Which measures are available or can be created to serve as a target or goal to compare these measures to?

Numbers without well-defined targets and without any trending indicators such as standard card visualizations are simply less valuable than KPIs that provide this additional context. Goal and Target measures are one of the main benefits of integrating Plan and Budget fact tables into data models. If this integration isn't an option, a historical average of the indicator measure such as the trailing 3 or 6 months can be used as the KPI's target goal.

How to do it...

KPI visual

1. Identify the Indicator and Target measures
   - In this example the Internet Sales measure is the Indicator and the Internet Sales Plan measure is the Target
2. Identify the trend axis.
   - The Calendar Year-Month column (for example, 2017-Mar) is used for the trend. This is the grain of the Sales Plan.
3. Create KPI measures (if necessary).
   - The measure used as the Indicator will be filtered by the column used as the trend axis in the KPI visual.
   - It may be necessary to create measures for the Target Goals such as 20% above prior year.

4. Create the KPI visual.
   - Add the two measures and the dimension column to the canvas and select KPI from the **Visualizations** pane.

KPI Visual: Sales to Plan with Monthly Trend

- Four months are selected in the report page and reflected by the trend chart in the background of the KPI visual.
- Despite the increase from the previous month to $114K in sales, this was still a miss to the planned $120K.

If a card visual was used instead, the user would only see the 114K and have to search other areas of the report page for the variance to plan and trend information. The KPI can be easily viewed on a mobile device and pinned to a dashboard as well.

Multi-row card

1. Identify the measures:
   - In this example, the group manager wants visibility to margin % for each country and each product category.

2. Create the card measures (if necessary):

```
United Kingdom Margin % = CALCULATE([Internet Sales Margin
%],FILTER(ALL('Sales Territory'),'Sales Territory'[Sales Territory
Country] = "United Kingdom"))

Bikes Margin % = CALCULATE([Internet Sales Margin
%],FILTER(ALL('Product'),'Product'[Product Category] = "Bikes"))
```

The country and product category measures ignore any filter selection from the `Sales Territory` and `Product Category` dimension tables, respectively, to always display the measure in the multi-row card visual. This is common in dashboard reports to allow the user to see multiple dimensions at once and can avoid or limit the need to edit visual interactions.

3. Create the multi-row card visual:
   - Create one multi-row card visual for the countries and another for the Product Categories:

39.2 % France Margin %	62.6 % Accessories Margin %
40.6 % Germany Margin %	41.5 % Bikes Margin %
39.6 % United Kingdom Margin %	39.2 % Clothing Margin %

Two Multi-row Card Visualizations Grouped

4. Format the multi-row cards:
   - Use the category labels from the measure names rather than a title and apply a black font.
   - Use the general formatting to ensure both visuals have the same height and Y position.
   - See the *Formatting reports for publication* recipe for details on using a shape as a background and border.

Multi-row cards are best organized around a common dimension and measure, as in this example, and are often placed to the right of KPI or Gauge visuals as supplemental details.

There's more...

Gauge visualizations

- Power BI Desktop includes a gauge visualization that is a popular alternative to card and KPI visuals for dashboards.
- In this example a `Sales` measure is used as the value ($5.8M) and a `Sales Plan` measure as the target value ($6.1M).

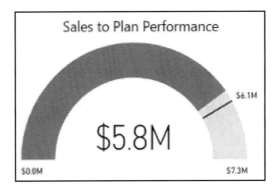

Gauge Visualization Comparing Two Measures (Value to Target Value)

- An additional measure that represents 20% above the plan amount is used as the maximum value ($7.3M).
- Gauge visualizations are considered less effective than KPIs given their curved shape and less efficient use of space.

Controlling interactive filtering between visuals

Power BI report pages are interactive by default with all visuals, excluding slicers, cross-filtered via the selections applied to one visual. While this dynamic filter context is often helpful in exploring and analyzing across dimensions, there's often also a need to exclude certain visuals from this behavior. For example, a high priority measure reflected in a card or KPI visual may be configured to ignore any filter selections from slicers and other visuals on the page. Additionally, rather than the default highlighting of cross-filtered visuals, it can be beneficial to exclusively display the related values in other visuals.

In this recipe, an example report page is provided, containing the three visual interaction behaviors: filter, highlight, and none.

How to do it...

Visual interaction control

In this example, the report is required to always display three current year measures while allowing for the filtering of other visuals with date dimension columns. Additionally, the sales for the subcategories of accessories and clothing should be easily accessible.

1. Create a report with three groups of visuals: cards, charts, and slicers.
   - The three cards must only show the current year and thus ignore or override the two slicers

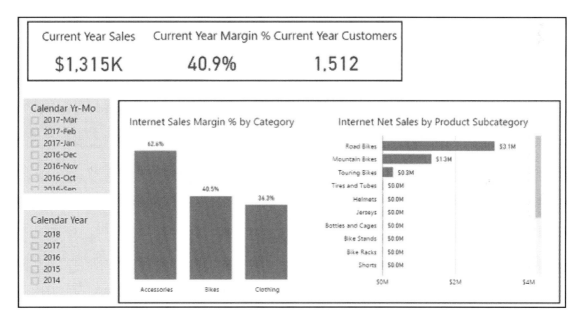

Edit Interactions Report Page

2. Select a visual on the canvas and click on **Edit interactions** from the **Format** tab.

3. Select the **Calendar Yr-Mo** slicer visual, and for each card visual click on the **None** circle icon

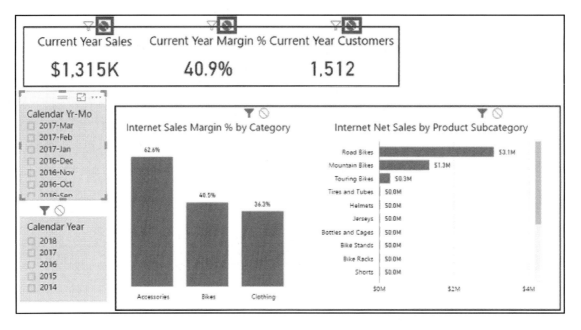

Removing Filter Interaction from Calendar Yr- Mo to the Card Visuals

4. With **None** selected for the card visuals, any selection from the **Calendar Yr-Mo** slicer will only effect the charts
    - It's not necessary to edit the interaction from from the calendar year slicer as the selection is overridden by the DAX CALCULATE() function used for each measure. See the How it works... for additional details.

5. Set the interactions to filter the product subcategory Chart.
    - Click on the **Internet Sales Margin % by Category** visual and switch the interaction from Highlight to Filter

 By default, the Product Subcategory chart is set to a 'Highlight' (pie chart) interaction behavior. Since the Accessories and Clothing subcategories represent a small portion of Net Sales, clicking on these categories from the Margin % chart doesn't expose these columns.

Internet Sales Margin % by Category

Internet Net Sales by Product Subcategory

62.6%

Tires and Tubes — $19K

Helmets — $18K

Interactions Switched from Highlight to Filter

- With Filter set as the interaction, clicking on **Accessories** displays the related subcategories on the Net Sales chart
- The default filter settings from the chart visuals to the current year measure cards at the top of the page is allowed
    - In this example, the three current year measures would update to reflect the accessories product category

This example illustrates the two most common use cases for editing interactions, but there are many scenarios in which a partially filtered view of data is necessary or beneficial. It's important to document and review any visual interaction changes with the users as nothing in Power BI advises of these settings. For example, a user could assume that the Current Year measures in the Card visuals reflect the selections of the Calendar Yr-Mo column.

How it works...

Current year Measures

- The current year measures apply filters from DAX variables based on the `TODAY()` and `YEAR()` functions:

```
Current Year Internet Net Sales =
VAR CurrentYear = YEAR(TODAY())
RETURN
CALCULATE([Internet Net Sales],'Date'[Calendar Year] = CurrentYear
)
```

- Because calendar year is filtered in the measure, it's not necessary to edit the interaction from the calendar year slicer.

Associating slicers with report pages

Slicer visuals are the primary means for users to apply filter selections to other visuals of a report page, and thus their implementation greatly affects usability and analytical flexibility. Although user interaction with other visuals also applies cross-filtering, slicers provide the fastest and most intuitive method to define specific filtering criteria such as three specific months and two product categories. Slicer visuals also have unique formatting options for defining the selection behavior including a **Select All** option.

In this recipe, we look at the primary use cases for slicers and the report design considerations, including selection properties and formatting options. The slicer filter configurations available for Date data types is also reviewed, and additional details on text search and alternative slicer visuals are included in the *There's more...* section.

How to do it...

Configure dimension slicers

1. Identify the slicer column(s).
    *   Typically this is a parent-level dimension such as year or region with few individual values.
    *   Choosing a column with few values allows these items to be exposed on the canvas without a dropdown.

 Using too many slicers or slicers with too many distinct values detracts from the usability of report pages. Without significant DAX customization to interpret filter selections, users can be uncertain what filters have been applied.

2. Align slicer visuals.
    *   It's recommended to position slicers to the left of all other visuals on the page.

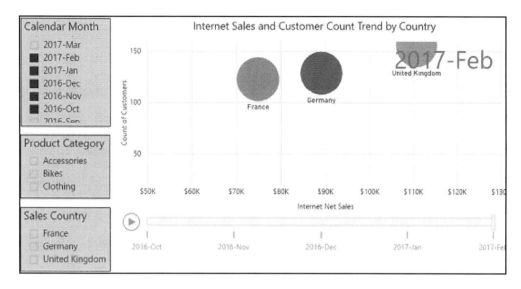

Left Aligned Slicer Visuals

3. Format the slicer visuals with borders and background colors.
   - Alternatively, a rectangle shape can group all slicer visuals.
   - Enlarged text is used for the titles instead of the default header and a black font color is applied to the items.

Horizontal slicers

- An alternative design is to set the orientation to horizontal under the General formatting options:

Slicer Visual with Horizontal Orientation

- Horizontal orientation slicers are often place along the top of report pages and can benefit mobile consumption.

4. Edit the interactions.
   - If necessary, use **Edit Interactions** from the **Format** tab and exempt certain visuals from the slicer selections
5. Configure the selection controls.
   - **Single Select** and **Select All** are turned on and off, respectively, under the **Selection Control** options.
      - With **Single Select**, holding down the *Ctrl* key is required to add items to the selection.

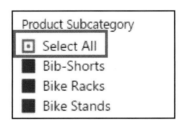

Select All Slicer Selection Control Turned On

- The **Select All** option can be helpful if the slicer contains more than 7-10 values.
   - With **Select All**, the user can easily construct a filter to exclude only a few items from a long list of items.

Customize a date slicer

Slicer visuals contain powerful filtering options when used with Date data types, including graphical date selection, before/after criteria, and Relative dates such as the last 4 weeks.

1. Add a date column to the canvas.
   - A hierarchy is created in the field well by default.
   - Click on the drop-down arrow for the date column in the field well and switch from **Date Hierarchy to Date.**

2. Switch to the slicer visualization.
    - By default, a timeline element is exposed below the start and end Date parameter inputs.

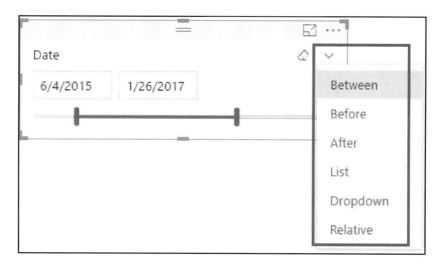

Slicer Visual Options for Date Data Types

- **Between** is the default filter setting, per the preceding screenshot (6/4/2015 through 1/26/2017--with both dates included).
    - The start and end points of the timeline can be selected and dragged to revise the filter condition
    - Alternatively, selecting the date input cells exposes a graphical calendar picker element for choosing a date
- The **Before** and **After** filter options gray out the start and end date input cells of the **Between** dialog, respectively

Relative date filters

1. Select the relative date filter option and use the three input boxes to configure a last 1 month (calendar) filter:

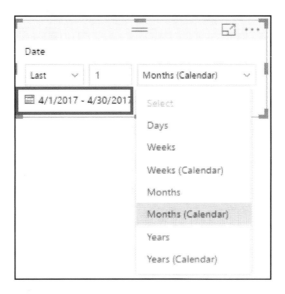

Standard Slicer based on a Date Column Configured for a Relative Date Filter

2. In the **Formatting** pane, specify whether the current day is included in the relative date filter:

Date Range Formatting Option with Relative Date Filters

Relative date filtering options of slicer visuals is also available as report, page, and visual level filters as well.

How it works...

Date slicer

- The calendar versions of the different date intervals reflect only whole or completed date periods
- The **Months** option (not calendar) includes the partially completed years, months, and weeks.
- The **Next** and **This** Relative Date options are also available in the first parameter of the relative date dialog
    - A `This` configuration can transparently filter a page to the current week, day, month, or calendar year

There's more...

Text search

- Slicers can be searched for specific text column values such as product or customer names

Slicer Text Value Search

- For long lists of text values, click on the ellipsis to expose the search bar and enter the text string

Numeric range slicers

- Slicers support similar custom filtering options for numeric data types as they do for `Date` datatypes:

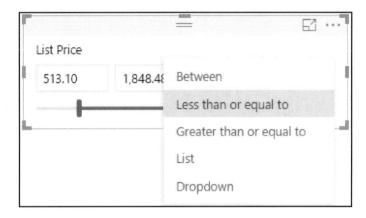

Numeric Data Type Slicer

- A slicer based on the **List Price** column offers the same range or timeline element and three custom filter settings

Applying filters at different scopes

Filters can be configured against Power BI reports at each level of the architecture: report, report page, and visual. As report filters are configured at design time and not exposed on the canvas like slicers, filters provide a powerful, efficient method of customizing elements of reports to specific needs. Report and page level filters that align with the user or team accessing the report, or with specific entities to be analyzed, deliver immediate focus and a level of organization. For example, a report page built for one product category can be duplicated for other product category pages, with each page containing a different page level filter. Visual level filters deliver maximum flexibility, as complex filtering conditions including measures can be defined in addition to any report and page level filters.

In this recipe examples are provided of implementing filters at the three different scopes. The Top N visual level filter condition is demonstrated and an example of the DAX queries generated by the filter types is shared in *How it works....*

How to do it...

Report and page level filters

In this example, report and page level filters are applied to the European Sales and Margin Monthly report. For this report, it's determined that the European team doesn't need to view other sales groups or countries.

Report and page level filters are most commonly implemented at different levels of a dimension hierarchy that is relatively static and with few unique values, such as the example in this recipe. Date range filters should generally be applied either in the data retrieval queries or the report canvas with visuals such as the date slicer. As these filters are applied to all visuals in the report or page, respectively, try to avoid filters against high-cardinality columns such as `Product ID` or `Sales Order`.

1. Create the report page structure.
    - Click on the New Page icon on the **Home** tab to create blank pages or duplicate report pages.
    - In this example, a standard country report layout can be created and duplicated for the three countries.

| Europe | Germany | France | United Kingdom | Cortana Monthly Metrics |

- The Cortana Monthly Metrics page is a supplementary page necessary for Windows Cortana natural language queries

2. Apply the report level filter.
- From the **Fields** pane, select the **Sales Territory Group** column such that it's highlighted.
- Drag the highlighted column to the **Report level filters** field well of the **Visualizations** pane.

Report level filter for European Sales and Margin Monthly Report

3. Select the **Europe** value from the **Basic filtering** type.
- All visuals in all pages of the report will respect this filter if a relationship to the dimension exists in the model and if DAX does not override the filter
4. Apply the **Page level filters**.
- Select the Germany report page and highlight the **Sales Territory Country** column from the **Fields** list
- Drag the highlighted column into the **Page level filters** field well
- Repeat this process for the France and United Kingdom report pages

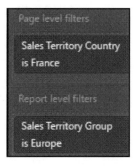

France Report Page with Report and Page level filters applied

DAX measures cannot be used to define Report and Page level filters. Additionally, Report and Page level filters can be overridden with DAX measures via the CALCULATE() and CALCULATETABLE() functions.

Visual level filter - top N

In this example, a visual level filter is applied based on the Internet Net Sales measure.

1. Select a blank space in the report canvas for the new visual and expose the **Fields** list.
2. Click on the measure and the dimension column name from the **Fields** list such that they're added to the same visual.
3. In the **Visual level filters**, click on the dropdown for the measure and select the expression **is greater than**.

Visual level filter based on measure

4. Click on **Apply filter** and the visual will be updated to the reflect the report, page, and visual level filters and slicers.

 Visual level filters can be based on both measures and columns from the data model that aren't present in the visual.

How it works...

DAX queries from report, page, and visual Filters

- The DAX queries created by Power BI reveal how the different layers of filters are implemented.
    - DAX variables are used to store the report and page level filters (as well as slicer selections):

```
VAR __DS0FilterTable = FILTER(KEEPFILTERS(VALUES('Sales
Territory'[Sales Territory Country])),
 'Sales Territory'[Sales Territory Country] = "United Kingdom")
```

- Visual level filters are also variables but use the report and page level variables as inputs.
- The DAX queries created by Power BI take advantage of the latest functions and features such as variables (VAR).

There's more...

Advanced report and page level filters

- The **Advanced filtering** filter type for report and page level filters can be used to create filter expressions.
- For example, an **is not blank** condition can be applied to text columns and greater than conditions can be applied to numeric columns.
- Both text and numeric columns support And and OR conditions to create more complex filter conditions.

 If complex filtering conditions are required, or if filters are needed against columns with many distinct values (for example, Product ID), it may be beneficial to account for this logic in the data retrieval or model, thus simplifying the DAX queries generated.

Formatting reports for publication

Power BI Desktop includes features to control and enhance the formatting and layout of reports at a detailed level. Prior to publishing reports to the Power BI Service, visuals can be aligned, sized, and evenly spaced to deliver an organized, symmetrical layout. Additionally, supplemental report elements such as shapes, textboxes, and images can be added to further organize and enrich report pages with textual and visual aids.

This recipe demonstrates how to control the positioning, alignment, and distribution of report visuals. An additional example is provided of using a Shape as a background color and border for a group of visuals. Further formatting techniques and examples, including embedding URLs in textboxes, are provided in the *There's more...* section.

How to do it...

Visual alignment and distribution

1. Identify the visuals to align.
   - In this example, three visuals on the right side of a page need to be aligned and distributed.

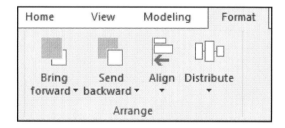

Align and distribute dropdowns in Report View

- Additionally, the top visuals on each side of the page need to be aligned to a common Y position (vertical).

2. Align left and right sides of page.
   - Select the top right visual, hold down the *Ctrl* key, and select the top visual from the left side of the page.
   - From the **Format** tab in the Report View, click on **Align top** from the **Align** drop-down icon.
   - The **Y Position** value of both visuals should now be equal in the **General** format options.

General Format Options Available for All Visuals

 The four input boxes under the **General** card in the **Format** options can be used to compare and directly control the position and size of all visuals. Additionally, report page height and width is available in the **Page Size** card of **Format** options.

3. Align and distribute visuals.
   - Press and hold the *Ctrl* key and select the three visuals on the right side of the page.
   - From the **Format** tab in the Report View, click on **Align left** from the **Align** drop-down icon.
     - All three visuals should now have the same X value in the **General** format options.
   - With the three visuals still selected, click on **Distribute vertically** from the **Distribute** drop-down icon.
     - The middle visual should adjust in height (**Y position**) to evenly space the three visuals.

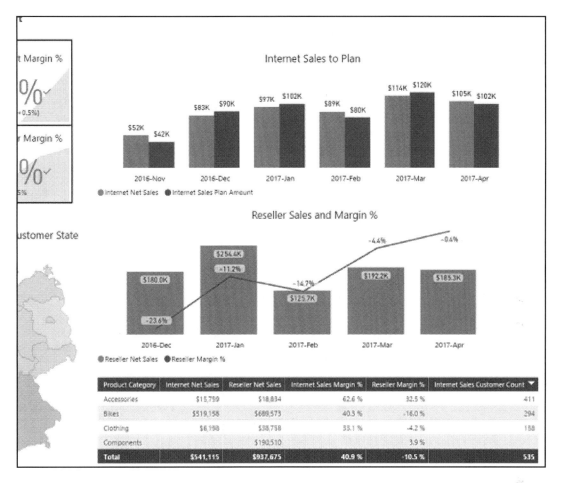

Aligned and Distributed Report

- With visuals aligned and distributed, it's easier for users to distinguish different sections and navigate pages.

Shapes as backgrounds and groups

1. Identify a set of visuals to be grouped.
   - Align and distribute the visuals:

Card Visuals with No Background or Border

2. Create a background shape.
   - From the **Home** tab of Report View, use the **Shapes** dropdown to select the rectangle shape.
   - From the **Format shape** formatting options, choose a fill color for the background.
   - Also from the **Format shape** formatting options, choose a line color and the weight for this line.
   - Increase the height and weight of the rectangle to fit over the visuals.
     - In this example, each card has a width of 209, so a width of 627 (209*3) is needed.

3. Place the background shape.
   - Move the background shape over the visuals such that it covers them.
   - With the shape selected, select the **Send to Back** option of the **Send backward** dropdown on the **Format** tab.

Rectangle Shape as Background and Border for Card Visuals

Shapes can better organize visuals and can improve report aesthetics relative to the borders and backgrounds of each visual. Shapes are commonly used for report title backgrounds and they can also customize the plot area of charts, such as splitting a scatter chart into four squares, each square having a distinct background color.

There's more...

Snap objects to grid and keyboard shortcuts

- From the **View** tab of the Report View, you can enable **Show Gridlines** and **Snap Objects to Grid.**
- With **Snap Objects to Grid** enabled, a visual aligns to X and Y coordinates as it's moved along the canvas.
- Visuals can also be moved by holding down the the *Ctrl* key and using the arrow keys in any.

 Whether moving visuals via snap to grid or the keyboard shortcuts, each movement represents 16 points on the X and Y coordinates. For example, a *Ctrl* + right-click could move a visual from X position 32 to X position 48.

Textbox with email link

- An email link (or other URL) can be embedded in a text box and exposed to report consumers in the Power BI Service

Support Email Link Provided via URL link in textbox

- Highlight the word and click on the URL icon to insert the link. In Power BI, the link will open a new email to the address

Format painter

- The **Format Painter** option on the **Home** tab of the Report View can be used to copy one visual's format to another:

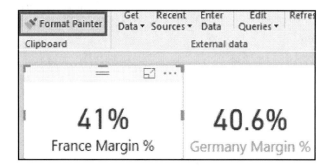

Format Painter Selected to Apply the Format from one Card Visual to Another

- In this example, select the **France Margin %** card, click on **Format Painter**, and then click on the **Germany Margin %** card.

See also

- Power BI Best Design Practices for Reports and Visuals: http://bit.ly/2poUeMv

Designing mobile report layouts

Power BI reports can be optimized for consumption on mobile devices via phone layout view in Power BI Desktop. This layout allows users accessing reports through the Power BI mobile applications to more easily view and interact with the most important content of these reports on iOS, Android, or Windows mobile devices. Given the importance of the mobile experience and the unique design considerations for reports with multiple pages, optimizing Power BI reports for mobile access is essential.

In this recipe, the Europe and United Kingdom report pages of the example report provided in the first recipe of this chapter are configured with the Phone Layout. Additional details for optimizing Power BI Dashboards are included in the *There's more...* section.

Getting ready

Plan for mobile consumption

The utilization of Power BI reports often varies significantly across devices. For example, a report page with multiple slicers and table or matrix visuals may be appropriate for a detailed, interactive experience on a laptop but may not lend itself well to mobile consumption. In many scenarios, the user prefers simple, easy access to only a few high-level visuals such as cards or KPIs on their mobile device, rather than a sub-optimal representation of all the visuals included on the page.

If mobile consumption is expected, the report's authors should collaborate with users on this layout and overall experience.

Given that phone layout is at the report page scope and visuals cannot be combined from multiple pages, a dedicated report page containing the most important measures or KPIs can be helpful. These report pages often contain only numbers via card, Gauge, or KPI visuals to provide a single "at a glance" mobile view of the most important data points.

How to do it...

Phone layout - Europe report page

1. Open **Phone Layout** in Power BI Desktop:
   - Select the Europe report page and click on **Phone Layout** from the **View** tab in the Report View

Phone Layout in Power BI Desktop Report View

- The phone layout presents a rectangular mobile device grid and a **Visualizations** pane containing the different elements of the given report page, including textboxes and shapes

Though it's possible to design mobile optimized layouts for each report page, for most reports it may only be necessary to design one or two mobile layouts that highlight the most important measures or trends of the report.

- The **Visualizations** pane of phone layout makes it easy to identify the elements to include or exclude.

2. Populate the phone layout view:
   - Click and drag the visualizations to the desired position in the device grid.
   - In this example, the KPIs, column and line chart are added.

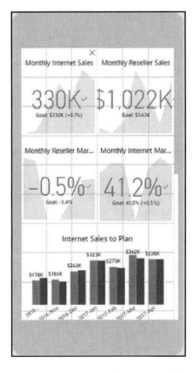

Populated Phone Layout View

- The visualizations snap to the grid at a default size and scale up or down on different sizes of mobile devices.

3. Organize, resize, and remove mobile tiles:
    - Click on the visuals added to the device grid and use any of the eight resizing icons to adjust the height and width.
        - Adjusting phone layout visuals is very similar to resizing tiles pinned to Power BI dashboards.
    - The scroll bar on the right of device grid can be used to add visuals below the main display.
    - Visuals can be removed from phone layout via the X icon in the top-right corner of each phone layout visual.

Phone layout - United Kingdom report page

For the United Kingdom mobile report page, the user or team would like to focus only on Internet Sales and retain filtering capability on the mobile device for product category and calendar month.

1. Add slicer visuals to the mobile layout for product category and calendar month:

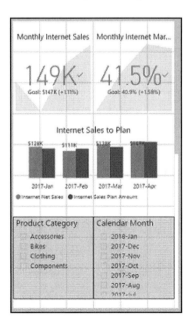

United Kingdom Sales and Margin Phone Layout

2. Set borders around the slicers and test the self-service user experience by applying multiple filter selections
    - Horizontal layout of slicers or a dedicated mobile report page could be additional design options

- See the *Enabling the mobile BI experience* recipe of `Chapter 13`, *Integrating Power BI with Other Applications*, for more details on mobile design and features

How it works...

- Once saved and published back to the Power BI Service, users accessing the report from mobile devices will see the defined phone layout.
- In the absence of a phone layout, mobile users will be advised that this has not been configured and can adjust the orientation of their devices (horizontally) to view the report page in landscape view.

 Switching to landscape orientation will open the report in the standard desktop view whether phone layout has been configured or not.

- The pages of a Power BI report can be accessed via swiping gestures from the side of the screen or the pages icon.

There's more...

Slicers and drill-down on mobile devices

Many of the same interactive features of Power BI reports such as drill mode and slicers are also available through Power BI mobile applications. However, given the form factor limitations, it's important to evaluate the usability of these elements and consider whether mobile-friendly visuals such as Cards or KPIs can provide the necessary visibility.

Mobile-optimized dashboards

As dashboards are created and modified in the Power BI Service, the Power BI service allows a similar mobile optimization authoring experience for dashboards. From a dashboard in Power BI, click on the **Web** dropdown in the top right.

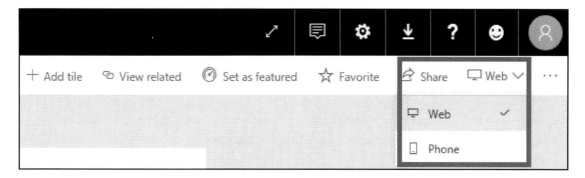

- The phone layout view and functionality is very similar to phone layout in Power BI Desktop

 A pinned live page to a dashboard becomes one dashboard tile and thus only one mobile visual. Therefore, pinning individual report visuals to tiles in dashboards is necessary to effectively configure mobile optimized dashboards.

See also

- Power BI apps for mobile devices: http://bit.ly/2q6SG8f

5
Creating Power BI Dashboards

In this chapter, we will cover the following recipes:

- Building a Power BI dashboard
- Constructing an enterprise dashboard
- Developing dynamic dashboard metrics
- Preparing datasets and reports for Q&A natural language queries
- Embedding analytical context into visualizations
- Exposing what matters - top N and percentage of total visualizations
- Leveraging Power BI reports in Power BI dashboards
- Deploying content from Excel and SSRS to Power BI
- Adding data alerts and email notifications to dashboards

Introduction

Power BI dashboards are collections of tiles created in the Power BI service, representing the visuals from one or many Power BI reports and optionally other sources, such as Excel and **SQL Server Reporting Services** (**SSRS**). Dashboards are best used to centralize essential measures and trends into a visually and mobile optimized layout, and to provide an entryway to other dashboards or reports with additional details. Additionally, dashboards can be enhanced with URL links, streaming data, images, web content, and interactivity.

> *"A dashboard is really a content aggregator. It lets you bring together lots of different data sources in one place so you can have a 360 degree view of your business on one dashboard."*

- Adam Wilson, group program manager for Power BI service

In this chapter, Power BI dashboards are constructed to provide simple at a glance monitoring of critical measures and high impact business activities. The unique features of dashboards, such as Q & A natural language queries, data alerts, and integration of other report types, such as Excel and SSRS, are also included.

Building a Power BI dashboard

With a robust data model and multiple reports created in Power BI Desktop, dashboards can be created in the Power BI service to consolidate the essential visuals from these reports onto one canvas. Additionally, the dashboard will provide an access point to the detailed reports supporting the tiles and will be optimized for mobile access through the Power BI mobile application.

This recipe walks through all the essential components of building a Power BI dashboard, from creating an app workspace to hold the dashboard to enhancing the layout and settings of the dashboard.

How to do it...

Dashboard design process

1. Define dashboard consumers and requirements.
   - The report design planning process described in Chapter 4, *Authoring Power BI Reports* is directly applicable to dashboards as well
   - Confirm that the existing data model (or models) supports the required business questions
2. Map dashboard tiles to reports and datasets.
   - In this example, a sales dashboard is created for the North American sales management team:

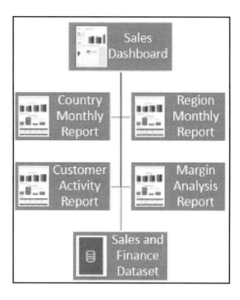

North America sales dashboard structure: 4 reports and 1 dataset

- Four reports are created from the same dataset (model) and one or more visuals from each report are pinned as tiles to the sales dashboard

Dashboard development process

1. Create an app workspace.
   - In the PBI service, click on **Create app workspace** from workspaces in the **Navigation** pane
   - Name the workspace and add team members with edit access who will be creating dashboard content
2. Import the dataset.
   - From the new app workspace, click on **Get Data** and then **Get** from the **File** menu to add the PBIX dataset
3. Create the dashboard.
   - From the app workspace in Power BI, click on dashboards and then click on **Create** in the top-right corner
   - Name the new dashboard and delete the dashboard that was created when the dataset was imported
     - Alternatively, a new dashboard can be created when a visual is pinned from a report

4. Create dashboard reports.
- From a blank PBIX file, connect to the published dataset hosted in the app workspace
- The Power BI service data source is available under online services

5. Copy the connected PBIX file for each report needed for the dashboard and develop the report visuals.

For better manageability and version control, the PBIX files can be stored and imported from OneDrive for business.

Design the report pages in context of the dashboard and app workspace. The report visuals should directly support the tiles of the dashboard, such that a user can instantly derive more useful details by clicking a dashboard tile.

6. Publish the reports.
- From the **Home** tab in Power BI Desktop, click on **Publish** from each of the reports
- The dashboard, reports, and dataset are now within the sales management app workspace in Power BI

7. Pin visuals to the dashboard.
- In the app workspace, open a report and select a visual to be pinned to the dashboard
- Click the pin icon and choose the existing dashboard; repeat this process for each report in the workspace

8. Refine dashboard layout.
- Move and resize the dashboard tiles such that most important visuals are in the top and left corners

North America sales dashboard

- The dashboard provides the at a glance visibility to the measures most important to the North America sales team
- The user can access any of the four detail reports (country, customer, margin, and region) by clicking a dashboard tile

Constructing an enterprise dashboard

Power BI dashboards are valuable assets for specific stakeholders and focused use cases, but their greatest strength is in consolidating important information from across an enterprise. These dashboards generally source from multiple datasets, such as SSAS tabular models, and often integrate on-premise with cloud-borne data. Enterprise dashboards typically utilize card and KPI visuals to focus on strategic objectives and maximize canvas space. Given the scale and breadth of data sources for a modern enterprise, a significant level of coordination is required to ensure that all datasets supporting the dashboard represent an appropriate level of data quality and governance.

In this recipe, an enterprise dashboard is constructed based off of four datasets (models) to include key measures across sales, inventory, general ledger, and customer service business processes.

How to do it...

Dashboard design process

1. Define dashboard requirements.
   - Map the required dashboard tiles to existing datasets (that is, data models) and source systems
   - For any new dataset to be created, evaluate readiness, scale, and data retrieval and modeling needed
   - The data warehouse bus matrix and model planning described in Chapter 3, *Building a Power BI Data Model*, can help guide this process to promote re-usability and version control

2. Map dashboard tiles to reports and datasets.

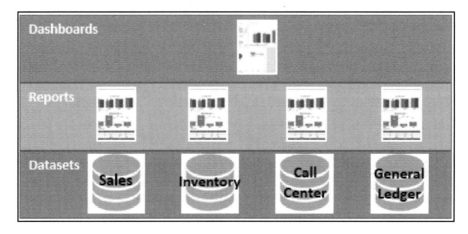

Enterprise dashboard supported by four datasets

   - The design process results in a logical architecture of the components needed in Power BI to support the dashboard

 As each report is tied to a single dataset, consolidating required schemas into fewer data models (datasets) can simplify manageability, and support richer analytics and visualizations.

An alternative dashboard architecture is for an executive dashboard to link to multiple dashboards (such as corporate divisions or product groups), which then link to individual reports. The option to link a dashboard tile to a separate dashboard is available in Tile details when set custom link is enabled.

3. Create an app workspace.
   - The same steps as in creating a workspace and adding team members from the previous recipe apply here
   - In the workspace, a blank dashboard can be created, and existing datasets and reports can be added

4. Create or augment datasets.
   - This could be a new Power BI Desktop file or additional queries and measures to an existing model
   - Publish or import the completed dataset to the new app workspace in Power BI

5. Create dashboard reports.
   - Connect PBIX report files to the data models, such as the published dataset or an SSAS tabular model
   - The visuals for the enterprise dashboard, such as Cards and KPIs, should follow a standard formatting scheme

The individual PBIX report files can be stored in OneDrive for business (if available) or at a secure network location. A single report page may be sufficient for certain tiles, while others (such as, sales) require robust report details.

6. Publish reports.
   - Publish each report to the workspace and then pin the required visuals to the existing dashboard

7. Refine dashboard layout.
   - Organize and resize the tiles to prioritize KPIs and make the best use of the canvas
   - Apply a mobile layout to the dashboard by switching from Web view to Phone view in the top right corner

The dual KPI chart types and color options (for both bottom and top charts) are used to help distinguish the different dashboard metrics. For example, sales metrics are displayed with green area charts, while the liabilities metrics are red, and the margin metrics are presented as line charts.

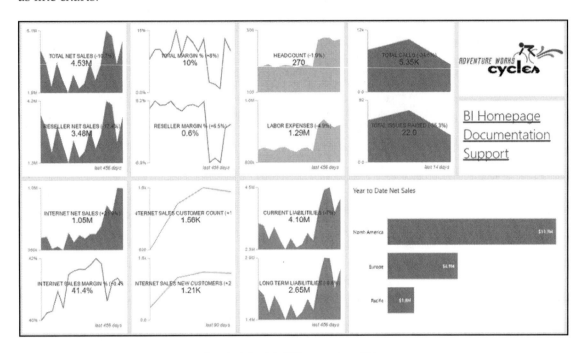

Enterprise dashboard: dual KPIs, corporate logo and links

8. Customize tile settings.
    - Click the ellipsis of the dashboard tiles and then the pencil icon to open the tile details form
    - Optionally, enter a title and subtitle for the tile, as well as a custom URL link, such as a SharePoint site

9. Add supporting tiles.
    - Optionally, click on **Add tile** to add text boxes, images, and other content to support the dashboard

How it works...

Dual KPI custom visual

- The dual KPI custom visual, developed by Microsoft, was used in this recipe to efficiently utilize dashboard canvas
- See `Chapter 9`, *Applying Advanced Analytics and Custom Visuals*, for additional details on this visual

Supporting tiles

- The corporate logo was pinned to the dashboard from an image that was inserted into a report
- The URL links were created within the **Add tile** feature in the Power BI Service for a textbox

Developing dynamic dashboard metrics

Dashboard tiles represent snapshots of report visuals. The values of the measures and columns used in the pinned report visual are refreshed, but modifications to the report, such as filters or formatting, are not reflected in the dashboard. Therefore, it's necessary to develop dynamic logic in the data model and measures that keep dashboard tiles current across time. Additionally, dynamic logic simplifies the user experience of interacting with reports and the dashboard report development process.

In this recipe, two columns are added to the date dimension table and used to drive dashboard report visuals. Additionally, a measure is created to provide a target value to support comparison with a KPI.

How to do it...

Dynamic date columns

1. Identify the grain(s).
    - Dashboards are usually focused on the current year, month, or week, and trends within the current year or recent history
    - Whether calendar or fiscal periods, columns associating dates to these values enhances and simplifies analysis
        - Time Intelligence measures, reviewed in Chapter 6, *Getting Serious with Date Intelligence,* enable the comparison of distinct time frames

2. Modify the date view.
    - Add columns to the SQL view supporting the date dimension table for the required grains with dynamic expressions

```
CASE
    WHEN YEAR(D.Date) = YEAR(CURRENT_TIMESTAMP) THEN 'Current
Calendar Year'
    WHEN YEAR(D.Date) = YEAR(CURRENT_TIMESTAMP)-1 THEN 'Prior
Calendar Year'
    WHEN YEAR(D.Date) = YEAR(CURRENT_TIMESTAMP)-2 THEN '2 Yrs Prior
Calendar Year'
    WHEN YEAR(D.Date) = YEAR(CURRENT_TIMESTAMP)-3 THEN '3 Yrs Prior
Calendar Year'
 ELSE 'Other Calendar Year'
 END AS [Calendar Year Status]

CASE
    WHEN YEAR(D.Date) = YEAR(CURRENT_TIMESTAMP) AND MONTH(D.Date) =
MONTH(CURRENT_TIMESTAMP)
        THEN 'Current Calendar Month'
    WHEN YEAR(D.Date) = YEAR(DATEADD(MONTH,-1,CAST(CURRENT_TIMESTAMP
AS date))) AND
        MONTH(D.Date) = MONTH(DATEADD(MONTH,-1,CAST(CURRENT_TIMESTAMP
AS date)))
        THEN 'Prior Calendar Month'
    WHEN YEAR(D.Date) = YEAR(DATEADD(MONTH,-2,CAST(CURRENT_TIMESTAMP
AS date))) AND
        MONTH(D.Date) = MONTH(DATEADD(MONTH,-2,CAST(CURRENT_TIMESTAMP
AS date)))
        THEN '2 Mo Prior Calendar Month'
    WHEN YEAR(D.Date) = YEAR(DATEADD(MONTH,-3,CAST(CURRENT_TIMESTAMP
```

```
AS date))) AND
     MONTH(D.Date) = MONTH(DATEADD(MONTH,-3,CAST(CURRENT_TIMESTAMP
AS date)))
     THEN '3 Mo Prior Calendar Month'
ELSE 'Other Calendar Month'
END AS [Calendar Month Status]
```

- Standard SQL syntax with `CASE` and `CURRENT_TIMESTAMP()` create two columns, each with five distinct values (Current Calendar Month, Prior Calendar Month, 2 Mo Prior Calendar Month, 3 Mo Prior Calendar Month, and Other Calendar Month)
- Since the date table query is executed on a schedule to support dataset refresh (or at run time if DirectQuery mode), these columns will be updated and available to the report author, thus avoiding stale or hard coded reports:
  - As an example, a report level filter could be set to only include the `Current Year` and `Prior Year` values of the `Calendar Year Status` column, and a page of the report could be set to only include the `Current Calendar Month` and `Prior Calendar Month` values of the `Calendar Month Status` column
  - The tables and charts of the report would update to respect the dates these values refer to as the dataset or report is refreshed

 Alternatively, if the date dimension table is updated daily via an ETL process, then the new dynamic columns could be included in this process and persisted in the table. Additionally, if both the source table and the SQL view cannot be modified, M queries with conditional expressions can be used to create the derived columns.

3. Implement in reports.
  - The new dynamic date columns can be used as filters in dashboard reports in the following methods:
    - As report level, page level, and visual level filters within the reports used to support dashboards
    - As slicer visuals in report pages to allow for further analysis of the dashboard tile

- Optionally, as filter arguments in time intelligence measures; see Chapter 6, *Getting Serious with Date Intelligence* for greater detail

```
Internet Net Sales (CY YTD) = CALCULATE([Internet Net Sales],
 FILTER(ALL('Date'),'Date'[Calendar Year Status] = "Current
Calendar Year" &&
'Date'[Date] <= MAX('Date'[Date])))
```

When used as a measure filter, the Calendar Year Status column can avoid the need to apply other filters (that is, slicers and page level filters) to produce the current or prior year value. This can be helpful for the fixed requirements of dashboard visuals but limits the use of these measures in self-service analysis with other date dimension columns. However, the standard and recommended date intelligence practice is to set the year column equal to the max value of this column in the current filter context, such as Date[Calendar Year] = MAX(Date[Calendar Year]). See Chapter 6, *Getting Serious with Date Intelligence* for examples of standard and more advanced custom date intelligence expressions.

For many dashboards, it's necessary to exclude the current month, given a large transaction or GL entry to be applied at the end of the month. A visual level filter, based on the dynamic month column, can support this scenario. Using the Calendar Month Status column from this recipe as example, four of the five computed values would be included, but the Current Calendar Month value would be filtered out of the visual.

KPI target measures

1. Identify the KPI.
    - These are dashboard measures which lack a relevant target to drive formatting (that is, red, yellow, green)
2. Define the target logic.
    - In the absence of a budget or plan, work with stakeholders to define upper and lower boundaries of the KPI
    - Without specific guidance or requirements, a trailing average measure of the KPI can be used

3. Develop the target measure.
   - In this example, the KPI trend axis is at the month grain and thus the target is needed at the month grain

```
Internet Sales Customer Count Average of Trailing 6 =
VAR LastNonBlankMonth =
LASTNONBLANK('Date'[CalYearMonthIndex],[Internet Sales Customer
Count])
VAR SixMonthsPrior = LastNonBlankMonth - 6
RETURN
CALCULATE(AVERAGEX(VALUES('Date'[CalYearMonthIndex]),[Internet
Sales Customer Count]),
FILTER(ALL('Date'),'Date'[CalYearMonthIndex] <= LastNonBlankMonth
-1 && 'Date'[CalYearMonthIndex] >=SixMonthsPrior))
```

- The target measure identifies the last month with customers and then only uses completed months for evaluation

How it works...

Target measure - trailing 6 months

- With CALCULATE(), the target measure can include prior months that are filtered out in the report via filters or slicers
- LASTNONBLANK() identifies the last month that has customer count in the current filter context
- Per earlier recipes, a sequentially increasing column can be used to drive Time Intelligence measures.

Preparing datasets and reports for Q & A natural language queries

Q & A can be a powerful method of enabling users to explore datasets, by directly submitting their own questions in both the Power BI service and through the Power BI mobile application. The tables and measures of each dataset, represented by a tile on the dashboard, are available to answer Q & A questions and per Chapter 4, *Authoring Power BI Reports*, *Enhancing exploration of reports* recipe, reports and featured questions can be configured to aid the Q & A experience.

This recipe provides data model design and metadata tips to prepare a dataset for Q & A. Additionally, synonyms are added to Power BI Desktop data model to improve the accuracy of natural language queries.

Getting ready

Determine use cases and feasibility

 Q & A may not be appropriate for certain dashboards and datasets. For example, the Q & A search bar "ask a question about your data" may be a distraction to users of the enterprise dashboard, who only want to view the KPIs. Additionally, if the dataset requires a gateway, such as an on-premises SSAS server or a DirectQuery Power BI Desktop model to an on-premises source, Q & A may be avoided given the additional (and potentially inefficient) queries and performance considerations.

1. Enable or disable Q & A.
   - In the Power BI service, access the app workspace containing the dashboard
   - Click the Gear icon and select **Settings**. From the **Dashboards** tab, click **Show the Q & A** search box.

 Currently, Q & A is not supported for Power BI Desktop Models in DirectQuery mode. Q & A is available for imported Power BI Desktop datasets and SSAS datasets. If supported in the future, this can be toggled on or off in the datasets' settings dialog. Additionally, all data models (Import or DirectQuery) with row level security roles applied cannot be used with Q & A.

How to do it...

Prepare a model for Q & A

Model metadata

1. Revise any columns with incorrect data types, such as dates or numbers that are stored as text data types.
2. Set the default summarization for dimension columns to do not summarize.
3. Associate geographical columns, such as states and zip codes, with a related data category.

Model design

1. Split columns containing multiple values into distinct columns.
2. Normalize tables such that entities within the tables are moved to their own distinct table.
   - For example, columns of a vendor in a products table can be moved to a vendor table
3. Q & A queries only work with active relationships of a model.
   - Consider dedicated role playing dimensions with active relationships
   - Alternatively, consider de-normalizing an inactive relationship dimension into a fact table

Apply synonyms

Analyze Q & a use cases

1. Define the top or most common natural language questions and test for accuracy in Power BI.
2. Identify the gaps between the names of data model entities and the names used in natural language queries.
   - Focus on entities with longer and less intuitive names, that aren't used casually by the users

Apply synonyms

1. Open the Power BI Desktop data model (or models) supporting the dashboard locally.
2. Select the relationships window and click the synonyms icon from the modeling tab.
3. The synonyms window will open on the right. Select a table in the diagram view to access its synonyms:

Synonym added to the reseller table

- Table names are at the top, measures are associated with their home tables. Names of the entities are synonyms by default.

4. Click in the input box of the table name, column name, or measure name and add synonyms separated by commas.

Avoid reusing the same synonym across multiple entities, as this can lead to incorrect query results. Ensure that the primary synonym for each entity of the model is unique.

Publish the dataset

1. Save and publish the dataset to the app workspace in Power BI:

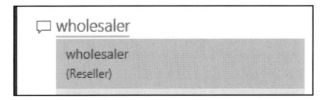

Wholesaler term entered in Q & A associated with the reseller table via the synonym

2. Test the query behavior with the synonyms and optionally create featured Q & A questions per `Chapter 4`, *Authoring Power BI Reports*.

Embedding analytical context into visualizations

Users of Power BI dashboards appreciate the linking of tiles to detailed reports to support further analysis. However, many users are not comfortable navigating through reports and would prefer that the dashboard itself provides all the essential information. Embedding Tooltips and conditional formatting logic into dashboard visuals are two powerful techniques to raise the insight to effort ratio mentioned in `Chapter 4`, *Authoring Power BI Reports*, while not compromising the performance or manageability of the solution.

In this recipe, a simple column chart of sales by month is enhanced with tooltip measures and conditional formatting logic. When pinned to a dashboard, the users instantly visualize a negative outcome and can hover over the bars for additional context.

How to do it...

Design the visual

1. Identify the essential components of a dashboard measure, such as group contributions to a total value.
2. Determine what rule or measure should drive any color changes, such as a negative variance to plan.

Create the visual

1. Open a Power BI Desktop report and create a clustered column chart visual with a measure and a dimension:
   - The measure will be added to the value field well and the dimension to the axis
2. Add a measure to the color saturation field well that will drive the color formatting of the value field.

3. From the formatting pane, open the data colors card and enter minimum and maximum values.

4. In the data colors formatting options, associate colors with these values, such as red with the minimum.

 The color saturation field could be the same measure as the value field or a different measure that provides even further context. In this example, internet net sales is used as the value and internet sales var to plan is used for color saturation. Color saturation can only be applied against a single value field—this option is not available when multiple values are used.

5. Add measures to the tooltips field well, that give context to either the value or the color saturation field:

- In this example, measures specific to the three sales regions are added to the tooltips field well:

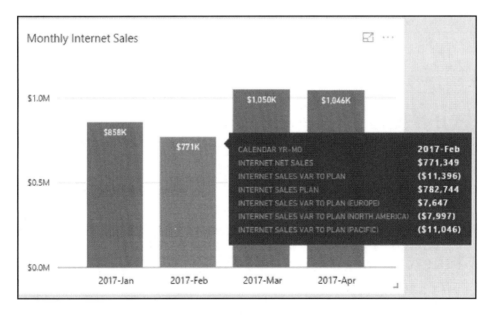

Dashboard tile with tooltips and conditional formatting

- Hovering over **2017-Feb** exposes the tooltip measures. The tooltips (by region) help explain the $11K miss to plan.

How it works...

Color saturation rule

The rule applied in this example is to color the bars red if sales misses the plan. Otherwise, use the default green theme.

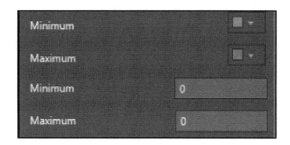

Data colors formatting

The internet sales var to plan measure used for color saturation is only negative for the 2017-Feb month.

Tooltip measures

Simple CALCULATE() functions can be used to create the tooltip measures if they don't exist in the dataset.

```
Internet Sales Var to Plan (Europe) =
CALCULATE([Internet Sales Var to Plan],'Sales Territory'[Sales Territory
Group] = "Europe")
```

If tooltip measures begin to clutter the fields list, they can be hidden or organized in dedicated measure group tables.

There's more...

See the recipes in Chapter 4, *Authoring Power BI Reports*, for further examples of conditional formatting, including line charts, tables, and matrix visuals.

Exposing what matters - top N and percentage of total visualizations

A common use case for dashboards is to highlight and monitor the drivers of significant events or business trends. For example, an enterprise dashboard may feature a reseller margin % KPI visualization, but a separate dashboard may identify the top and bottom 10 individual resellers and products by margin %.

In this recipe, dashboard visuals are created leveraging the top N filter type available to visual level filters and DAX measures to present focused, actionable information in Power BI dashboards.

How to do it...

Top 25 resellers with below -3% margin

1. Create a table visual with the dimension name (reseller) and two measures (reseller margin % and reseller net sales).
2. Add the dimension key column (reseller key) to the visual level filters pane.
3. In visual level filters, click the drop-down for reseller key and select top N as the filter type.
4. Enter 25 for **Show Items** and drag the reseller net sales measure to the **By Value** input box. Click **Apply Filter**.
5. In visual level filters, open the drop-down for the reseller margin % measure.
6. In the **Show items** when the value: input box, use the is less than option and enter (-.03). Click **Apply Filter**.

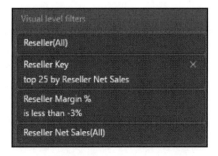

Top N and measure filters applied at visual level

7. Sort the table by margin % ascending and apply a format to the table visual that will align with the dashboard.

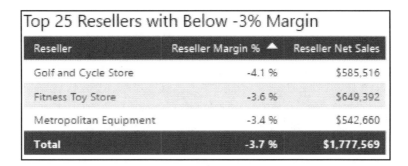

Top 25 Resellers with Below -3% Margin		
Reseller	**Reseller Margin %** ▲	**Reseller Net Sales**
Golf and Cycle Store	-4.1 %	$585,516
Fitness Toy Store	-3.6 %	$649,392
Metropolitan Equipment	-3.4 %	$542,660
Total	**-3.7 %**	**$1,777,569**

Formatted table visual reflecting low margin, high impact resellers

- In this example, only three of the larger (top 25) resellers are included in the visual

Only a single top N filter condition can be applied to a visual. As an alternative or supplement to top N, ranking measures can be created and used as visual level filters.

Last year's top 50 products with below -10% growth

1. Create a table visual with the product name column and a year-to-date growth measure.
2. Add a prior year, year-to-date ranking measure to the visual level filters field well:
    - Enter 101 in the is less than condition and click on **Apply Filter**

3. In the visual level filters pane, click the dropdown for the year-to-date growth measure:

   - Enter −1 for an is greater than condition and −.1 for an is less than condition. Click on **Apply filter**.

Product Total Sales Rank (PY YTD)	×
is less than 51	
Total Net Sales (YOY YTD %)	
is greater than -100% and is less than -10%	

Visual level filters applied to ranking measure and YOY YTD % growth measure

- The greater than -100% condition accounts for products which aren't being sold this year.

4. Sort by growth measure ascending and optionally add additional supporting measures and apply a format.

The finished table visual displays only the top (50) products from last year which are still being sold in the current year but with declining sales revenue of 10% or more.

Last Year's Top 50 Products with Below -10% Growth

Product Name	Total Net Sales (YOY YTD %)	Total Net Sales (CY YTD)	Total Net Sales (PY YTD)
Road-250 Red, 58	-15.9 %	$298,089	$354,286
ML Road Frame-W - Yellow, 38	-12.5 %	$59,602	$68,135
ML Road Frame-W - Yellow, 48	-12.4 %	$59,959	$68,460
Total	**-14.9 %**	**$417,650**	**$490,880**

Formatted table visual reflecting high value products from last year with declining sales

Look to leverage drill through report pages for deep analysis of individual dimension values such as products or vendors. In this example, after the user has accessed the underlying report from the dashboard, the user could right-click one of the three rows displaying the Product Name column and drill through to a report page that provides great detail about the specific product. See the *Enhancing the exploration of reports* recipe in Chapter 4, *Authoring Power BI Reports* for additional details.

5. Publish the report to the app workspace in the Power BI service and pin the exception visual to a dashboard tile.

How it works...

Prior year rank measure

- The ranking measure removes filters on the product name and the alternate key via ALL(), prior to the RANKX() evaluation.

```
Product Total Sales Rank (PY YTD) =
IF(HASONEVALUE('Product'[Product Alternate Key]),
RANKX(ALL('Product'[Product Name],'Product'[Product Alternate Key]),
[Total Net Sales (PY YTD)],,DESC,Skip),BLANK())
```

- The HASONEVALUE() function is used to check if a single product is in the filter context. If not, a blank is returned.

Visualizing performance relative to targets with KPIs and gauges

KPI and gauge visuals are frequently used to present the most critical performance measures in dashboards. Given their compact size and supporting context, such as trend graphs and target values, users can quickly obtain useful insights from these visuals alone, on any device. However, to derive the most value out of these visuals, it's often necessary to apply Visual level filters, create supporting target measures, and group related visuals.

In this recipe, a KPI and gauge visual are developed to present growth relative to planned growth. Groups of KPI visuals are then created to provide visibility to current period, prior period, and year-to-date.

How to do it...

1. Identify the measure:
   - This measure will serve as the Indicator input for the KPI visual and the value input for the gauge visual

2. Define the grain:
   - For the KPI visual, the date dimension column used in the trend axis input will determine
   - For example, a period trend axis will result in the value of the indicator for the latest period

Per `Chapter 3`, *Building a Power BI Data Model*, it's essential that Sort By columns are applied to date dimension columns, such as month and year-month. Without this configuration, the default sort order will cause the KPI visual to select the value for the last alphabetical month rather than the last chronological month via the trend axis input.

3. Identify the target:
   - This measure will serve as the target goal for the KPI visual at the grain of the trend axis input
   - For the gauge visual, this measure will be the target value input, and optionally, the maximum value as well

Create the visuals

1. Create a new Power BI report, connect to the dataset, and create two blank visuals: a KPI and a gauge.
2. Add the measures identified in steps 1 through 3 to their designated field wells.

3. Provide a custom title and apply any other helpful formatting, such as enlarging the target on the gauge visual.

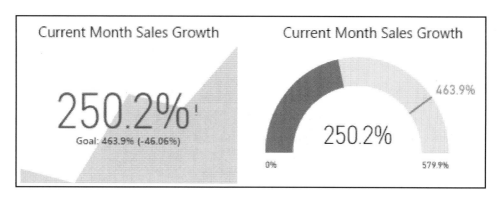

Standard KPI and gauge visuals: current month growth versus planned growth

 In this example, the trend axis on the KPI is monthly, and since the month isn't complete, the current growth of 250 percent is well below the 463 percent growth planned for the given month. As the month progresses (and data refreshes), the 250 percent will increase.

Grouping KPIs

Create a prior month and a year-to-date KPI visual to supplement the current month KPI visual:

Year-to-date and and prior month KPI visuals created to support the dashboard

The same monthly trend axis column (for example, 2017-May) is used for the two new KPI visuals. The year-to-date KPI simply substitutes year-to-date measures for the indicator and target goals. The prior month sales growth KPI uses the same inputs but the `Calendar Month Status` column is used as a visual level filter for both this visual and the year-to-date KPI.

Publish KPIs to dashboard

1. When complete, publish the report with the KPI visuals to the App Workspace containing the dashboard.
2. Pin the visual(s) to the dashboard and re-organize the layout.

Per the *Data alerts* recipe in this chapter alerts can be configured for standard card, KPI, and gauge visuals published to dashboards. See this recipe for an example of setting a notification, and optionally an email message, based on these visuals.

How it works...

Current month filter

- For the gauge visual, the `Calendar Month Status` dynamic date dimension column, described earlier in this chapter, is used a Visual level filter. This filter is set to `Current Calendar Month`.
- For both the year-to-date and the prior month sales growth KPI visuals, the `Calendar Month Status` column is used as a visual level filter. This filter is set to `Current Calendar Month`.
  - The prior month sales growth KPI therefore defaults to the next latest month-the prior month
  - The YTD KPI provides an apples-to-apples comparison by only comparing completed months against plan

Time intelligence measures

- Year over year, percentage measures are used for both the indicator and target input fields of the visuals
- These measures, in turn, reference current year, prior year, current year to date, and prior year to date measures
    - For example, the year-to-date target measure compares the sales plan (YTD) versus sales (prior YTD)
- See `Chapter 6`, *Getting Serious with Date Intelligence*, for additional detail on developing time intelligence measures

Leveraging Power BI reports in Power BI dashboards

By default, the tiles of a dashboard are independent of each other and cannot be filtered or interacted with. Additionally, modifications to reports after visuals have been pinned to dashboards, such as filter and layout changes, are not automatically reflected in the dashboards. In many scenarios, the users consuming a dashboard want to retain the interactive filtering experience of Power BI reports from within their dashboard and it can be helpful to automatically synchronize reports with dashboards.

In this recipe, a fully interactive live page of visuals is pinned to a dashboard, along with additional supporting visuals.

How to do it...

Define live page requirements

1. Determine the top business questions and thus measures and visuals to include in the page:
    - As report pages (and reports) are limited to a single dataset, confirm feasibility with existing models

2. For a single report page, identify the essential dimensions that will be used as slicer visuals:
   - Additionally, identify report and page level filters to align the page with other dashboard visuals

 In this example, the USA sales management team wants to easily view and filter high level sales measures and KPIs by sales region and time period, without having to navigate from the dashboard to detail level reports.

Create and publish to the dashboard

1. Create a Power BI report and connect to the published dataset in the app workspace of the dashboard.
2. Construct the report page according to the requirements, and to maximize the user experience with the dashboard.
3. Publish the report with the live page to the App Workspace in Power BI.
4. In the workspace in Power BI, open the published report in the given workspace and select the page to pin.

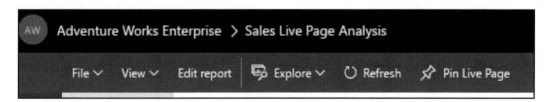

The Sales Live Page Analysis Report in the Adventure Works Enterprise Workspace

5. Click the **Pin Live Page** option in the preceding image and choose either a new or existing dashboard.
6. Pin any additional visuals from other pages of this report or other reports to the dashboard.

Refine dashboard layout

1. Position the live page at the top left of the dashboard, with separate visual tiles to the right:

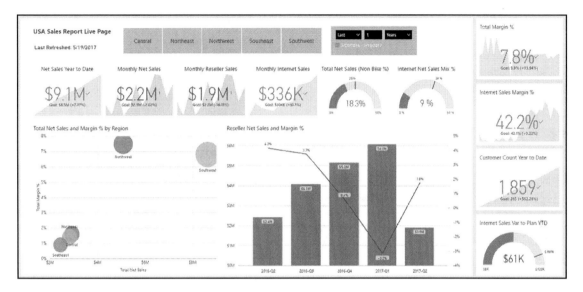

Dashboard with pinned live page and additional visuals

*   If a title and refresh message is included in the page, per this example, then those values can be excluded in tile details.

2. Switch from web view to phone view at the top right of the dashboard:
    *   Given the size of the live page, it may be necessary to hide this tile from Phone view or move it to the bottom

*   The user of the dashboard can interact with the region and date slicers and other visuals on the live page

 The ellipsis in the top right of the live page tile includes a go to report link to access all pages of the live page report. Modifications to the underlying report will be reflected in the pinned live page. The other visuals link to their report pages.

How it works...

Live page slicers

- The sales region slicer at the top has the orientation option in the formatting pane set to horizontal
- The date slicer is based on the calendar date from the date dimension and uses the relative slicer visual option

Deploying content from Excel and SSRS to Power BI

Dashboards in Power BI can consolidate much more than Power BI report visuals. Microsoft Excel objects, such as pivot tables, charts, and workbook ranges, and SSRS report items can also be pinned as dashboard tiles. This integration with Power BI allows teams to utilize existing reports and skills, and to leverage the unique capabilities of these tools as part of overall BI solutions.

In this recipe, a pivot table and pivot chart from an Excel workbook are integrated into an existing Power BI dashboard for the Australian sales team. Additionally, an SSRS report item is also pinned to this dashboard. For more advanced integration examples, see Chapter 13, *Integrating Power BI with Other Applications*.

Getting ready

1. Install Power BI Publisher for Excel:
    - See Chapter 1, *Configuring Power BI Development Tools*, for details on this process
    - If the Power BI tab is not visible in Excel, check that the COM Add-in in Excel options is visible and enabled
2. Configure Report Server for Power BI:
    - Open reporting services configuration manager
    - Click on the **Power BI Integration** tab and select **Register with Power BI**

How to do it...

Publish and pin excel objects

1. Open a new Excel workbook and select **Connect to Data** from the Power BI tab (Power BI Publisher for Excel).
2. Choose the Power BI workspace and dataset to be used as the source for the Excel report.
3. Click **Connect** and a blank pivot table will be created with the field list exposed on the right.
4. Create and format a pivot table. Apply a slicer based on a dynamic date column, such as current year.
5. Create additional slicers, such as `Sales Territory Country = Australia`:
   - To create a slicer, right-click a column in the field list and select **Add as Slicer**

Using slicers rather than the filters field well for pivot tables allows for a better presentation on the dashboard tile.

6. Select any cell outside of the pivot table, and from the Insert tab, click **PivotChart**:
   - Select **Use an External Data Source** from the **Create PivotChart** dialog. Click the Power BI connection.

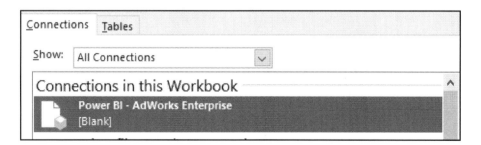

Existing Connections Window in Excel: Connection to the Power BI dataset

7. Select the Power BI connection from the existing connections window and click on **Open**.
8. Build and format the pivot chart. With the pivot chart selected, click on **Filter Connections** from the **Analyze** tab:
   - Ensure that the same slicers filtering the pivot table are also filtering the pivot chart

 Click on **Options** under the **Analyze** tab for each new report object and enable evaluate calculated members from OLAP server in filters on the Totals and Filters tab. Additionally, from the Display tab of Options, enable show calculated members from OLAP server for both objects. It is necessary to apply the same slicer to both the chart and the table.

9. Save the Excel report file to either a OneDrive for business folder or at a secure network location.
10. Select the chart and and click **Pin** from the Power BI tab. Choose the workspace and the dashboard, and then click **OK**.

Pinning a chart from an Excel workbook to a Power BI dashboard in an App Workspace of the Power BI Service

11. Now select the full range of cells of the pivot table and pin this to the dashboard as well.

12. In the Power BI service, navigate to the workspace and dashboard to adjust the size and layout of the tiles.

13. Optionally, adjust the tile details for the pinned Excel tiles, such as title and subtitle.

> Excel online does not currently support the refresh of external data connections. Therefore, though it's possible to publish the workbook from Excel to Power BI and then pin items from the workbook report in the Power BI service, once published, the workbook would not be refreshed. By pinning items directly from the Excel workbook to the dashboard, the connection to the dataset hosted in the Power BI service must be periodically refreshed and the **Pin Manager** dialog in the Power BI Publisher for Excel can be used to update pinned tiles.
>
> To avoid this manual and local refresh process, Excel report visuals can be built on top of an Excel data model, and this Excel workbook can be published to the Power BI Service. Published workbooks, containing data models, can be configured for scheduled refresh in the Power BI Service, and their dependent reports will be updated to reflect these refreshes.

Pin SSRS report items

1. Create or identify the SSRS report to support the dashboard.

2. Publish this report to the SSRS report server or open this report on the report server.

3. From the report server browser window, click the Power BI icon and sign in with the appropriate Power BI account.

4. Click on the SSRS report item to pin:

Pin to Power BI from SSRS 2016

5. From the Pin dialog, choose the workspace and dashboard to pin the item to.
   - The update frequency creates an SSRS subscription to keep the tile updated in Power BI

In this example, the reseller freight expense tile (lower left) is from an SSRS report. The Australia headcount chart and Australia sales to plan pivot table tiles are both from an Excel workbook.

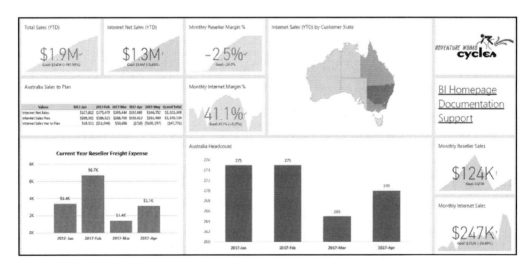

Excel objects and SSRS report items pinned to a Power BI dashboard

You can pin charts, gauge panels, maps, and images from SSRS reports to Power BI dashboards provided these items are within the report body (not page header or footer). You cannot currently pin tables, matrix, or list report items from SSRS reports.

Adding data alerts and email notifications to dashboards

Alerts can be configured on the tiles of dashboards to provide notification that a specific condition has been met. Alert rules and options can be managed in the Power BI service, and notifications can be limited to the notification center in Power BI or shared via email. Data-driven alerts enhance the value of Power BI dashboards, as they immediately bring attention to significant events or outcomes as the dataset supporting the dashboard tile is refreshed.

In this recipe, an alert is configured on a KPI visual represented in a dashboard tile. Additionally, an example is provided of automating email delivery of notifications via Microsoft Flow based on a Power BI data alert.

How to do it...

Configure data alert

1. Open the App Workspace in Power BI and select the dashboard containing the tile to be used for the alert.
2. Click on the ellipsis in the top right of the tile and select the bell icon to open the **Manage Alerts** window.

 Alerts can only be configured on dashboard tiles of standard gauge, KPI, and card visuals, and they only work with numeric data types. Custom visuals, streaming data tiles, and date datatypes are not currently supported.

Only the user who configures the alert can see the alerts in the Power BI Service.

3. Click on the **Add alert rule** button and enter a title for the alert that describes the measure and the condition.

4. Set the **Condition** and **Threshold** parameters for the alert:

Manage alerts

5. Repeat this process for other tiles in the dashboard or other dashboards.

 Multiple alerts can be configured for the same dashboard tile with each alert having a separate condition and/or threshold, such as a maximum and a minimum accepted value. Click the Gear icon in Power BI and select **Settings** to access all the alerts configured across the workspaces.

Data alerts can also be set and viewed in the Power BI mobile apps.

Automate email notification

1. Open Microsoft Flow in Office 365.
2. Enter `Power BI` in the search bar and select **Trigger a flow with a Power BI data-driven alert:**
   - Click on **Continue** to use this template. Ensure your Power BI account is associated with the Power BI trigger.

3. In the **Flow name** input box at the top, provide a a descriptive title (for example, email sales team based on margin % alert).

4. From the **Alert ID** dropdown, choose the specific Power BI data alert to trigger the Flow and click on **New Step**.

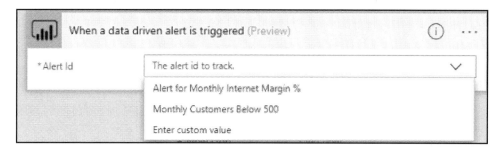

Associating the Power BI alert with the flow

5. Click on **Add an Action** and then select **Office 365 Outlook**. Click n the **Send an email** action available for this service:
   - Customize the send an email action to specify users or groups and what alert content and text to include:

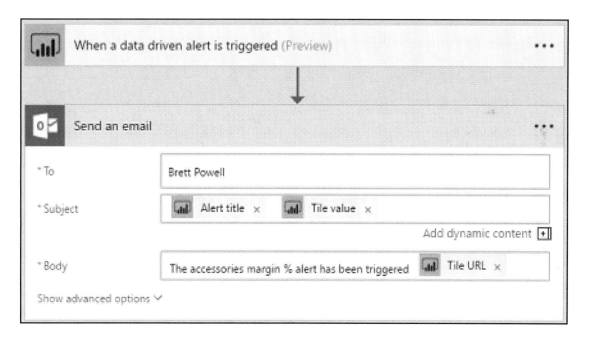

Outlook send an email action step in MS Flow

6. Click on **Create flow** from the top menu. The flow will be saved and will begin working immediately. Click on **Done**.
   - From My flows, this new alert flow can be saved as to create additional flows which leverage the same triggers, logic, and actions

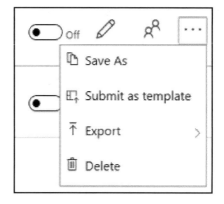

Save as option in my flows

- Save as will create a copy of the flow and add it the my flows page

Given the value of alerts to stakeholders and the low effort required in creating and managing alerts and notifications in Power BI and Flow, dedicated alert dashboards can be developed to reduce the amount of analysis and monitoring required.

How it works...

Power BI evaluates the alert rule when the dataset supporting the dashboard is refreshed.

If the alert is triggered, an icon and message will appear in the notification center in the Power BI service containing a link to the dashboard tile configured for the alert.

Alert notification from notification center in Power BI

Notifications are also visible in Power BI mobile. For example, a notification message is visible on the Apple watch.

6
Getting Serious with Date Intelligence

In this chapter, we will cover the following recipes:

- Building a complete date dimension table
- Prepping the date dimension via the Query Editor
- Authoring date intelligence metrics across granularities
- Developing advanced date intelligence metrics
- Simplifying date intelligence with DAX queries and calculated tables
- Adding a metric placeholder dimension

Introduction

Date intelligence refers to a broad set of data modeling patterns and functions that enable analysis across time periods. Fundamental measures, such as Reseller Net Sales as created in `Chapter 3`, *Building a Power BI Data Model*, are supplemented with date intelligence measures to calculate Year-to-Date, Prior Period, and many other custom time period calculations. These measures are then used in combination to support growth and variance measures and are often utilized as **Key Performance Indicators (KPIs)** in Power BI dashboards given their ability to convey additional context and insight. When implemented properly, date intelligence dramatically expands the analytical power of a data model and simplifies report and dashboard development.

This chapter contains three recipes for preparing a data model to support robust date intelligence and two recipes for authoring custom date intelligence measures.

Building a complete date dimension table

As a date dimension and the date intelligence it supports is needed by almost all data models building a robust date table in the source system provides significant long term value across BI projects and tools. A complete date table accounts for all the required grains or hierarchy levels of both the standard (Gregorian) calendar and any fiscal calendar specific to the organization. Additionally, surrogate key columns aligned to each grain are included to drive the sort order of report attributes and to enable date intelligence expressions.

This recipe includes a design phase to identify required date dimension columns and a process for adding a date intelligence surrogate key column to a dimension. Reference date dimension templates and examples of related T-SQL date functions are included in the *Getting ready* and *There's more...* sections, respectively.

Getting ready

- If you don't have a date table in your source database, there are tools and templates to help you get started:
  - The Kimball Group provides a downloadable Excel file with date formulas: http://bit.ly/2rOchxt
  - A T-SQL approach to building a date table is available on PowerPivotPro: http://bit.ly/2s6tuPT
- The date table should contain a single row for every calendar date (no gaps)
- Given the small size (20 years, approximately 7,300 rows), include all necessary history and three or more future years

How to do it...

Date dimension design

1. Identify and document the required columns of the date dimension and identify any gaps with the existing table:
   - The following two sections advise of the types of columns to include.

Like other dimension tables, teams can often incrementally improve their date dimension table over time with additional logic. For example, if the great majority of analysis revolves around a fiscal calendar and at a certain granularity then these columns can be targeted first. Mature date tables inclusive of standard and financial calendars, sequential surrogate columns, and logical or dynamic columns such as `Fiscal Period Status` are often quite wide with over 40 columns.

Required date dimension columns

- The `Prior Year Date` and `Prior Period Date` columns for both standard and financial calendars
- Natural hierarchy attributes for all levels, such as `2013`, `2013-Q3`, `2013-Sep`, `2013-Wk39`, and `9/25/2013`

The natural hierarchy (one parent for each child value) allows users to easily navigate Power BI report visuals via drill down and next level commands. Without natural hierarchies, the context of the parent value is lost when drilling into the given parent. For example, drilling into the year 2017 would display each month name but the year associated with this month would only be visible in the tooltips by hovering over the chart. With natural hierarchies, this context is not lost as the Calendar Yr-Mo column contains values such as `2017-Aug`.

Power BI provides a method of working around unnatural hierarchies in report visuals via the Expand All down one level drilling feature. However, this can lead to dense axis labels when multiple levels of a hierarchy are used and given time intelligence requirements and the needs of other visualizations it's recommended to support natural hierarchies.

- An integer column that corresponds to the chronological order of each string column, such as Weekday:
    - For example, a `Weekday Number` column, with values of 1 through 7, will set the **Sort By** property of **Weekday**
- Multiple "X in Y" columns, such as `Day in Year`, `Day in Month`, `Week in Month`, and `Week in Year`, stored as integers

- Indicator columns, such as `Weekday Indicator`, `Holiday Indicator`, and `Working Day Indicator`:
    - The values for these columns should be report-friendly, such as `Holiday` and `Non-Holiday`
- Starting and ending date columns for the different grains supported, such as `Week Ending Date` and `Period Ending Date`

Date dimension planning and design

1. Look to integrate other calendars, such as a periods or fiscal calendar, into the same date table in the source database:
    - Distinct views can be created to support role playing dimensions. See the *There's more...* section
2. Identify common date manipulations taking place in the existing reports or by business users in Excel or Power BI, and consider adding a date dimension column to eliminate or simplify this work.
3. Ensure that date columns (for example, `Prior Year Date`) and number columns (for example, `Calendar Year`) are stored as date and integer data types, respectively, as this allows arithmetic and DAX functions, such as `MAX()` and `MIN()`, to operate without any type conversion.

 If the date dimension table is updated daily as part of a data warehouse **Extract-Transform-Load** (ETL) process, columns identifying the current and prior periods such as the `Calendar Year Status` and `Calendar Month Status` columns from the *Developing Dynamic Dashboard Metrics* recipe in *Chapter 5*, *Creating Power BI Dashboards* can further simplify date intelligence. Columns such as `IsCurrentFiscalPeriod` and `IsPrior60Days` are also common.

Add date intelligence columns via SQL

1. Add two columns to the date table stored in the relational database:
    - A natural hierarchy string (`2009-Jan`) and an integer column, such as `Calendar Year Month Number`
2. Execute an `UPDATE` statement that populates the string column via the concatenation of the `Year` and `Month` columns.

3. Create a table with three columns, `Year`, `Month Number`, and an `Identity` column, with an increment value of 1:

```
Create Table dbo.TempTblYearMo
( [Calendar Year] int not null
, [Calendar Month Number] tinyint not null
, [Calendar Yr Mo Index] smallint identity(1,1) not null)
```

4. Execute an Insert Into SQL statement to load this table:
   - Select, group, and order the `Calendar Year` and `Calendar Month Number` columns from the existing date table
   - The `Order By` clause of the `Select` statement should order by Year and then by Month Number
   - The temporary table's index column (`Calendar Yr Mo Index`) is now populated in sequential order by Month across years per the following image:

Calendar Year	Calendar Month Number	Calendar Yr Mo Index
2016	11	95
2016	12	96
2017	1	97
2017	2	98

TempTblYearMo Table Loaded from Insert Into Statement

5. Execute an `UPDATE` statement that populates the `Calendar Year Month Number` column with the Identity value:

```
UPDATE DBO.DimFinDateTestTbl
SET [Calendar Year Month Number] = T.[Calendar Yr Mo Index]
FROM
DBO.DimFinDateTestTbl as D INNER JOIN dbo.TempTblYearMo as T
ON D.[Calendar Year] = T.[Calendar Year] AND D.[Calendar Month
Number] = T.[Calendar Month Number]
```

The following query displays the sequentially increasing Calendar Year Month Number column on the Date table:

Date	Calendar Yr-Mo	Calendar Year Month Number
2017-12-30	2017-Dec	108
2017-12-31	2017-Dec	108
2018-01-01	2018-Jan	109
2018-01-02	2018-Jan	109

Date table with Calendar Year Month Number column Updated

6. Repeat this process for other natural hierarchy columns, such as `Year-Qtr` and `Year-Wk`, and drop the temporary tables.

7. When loaded to the model, the surrogate columns should be hidden from Report View and used as the `Sort By` column.

8. Implement hierarchies in the **Fields** list as per the *Creating browsable model hierarchies and groups* recipe, shared in `Chapter 3`, *Building a Power BI Data Model*.

Window functions can be helpful in creating certain X in Y date dimension columns. For example, the following `DENSE_RANK()` function returns the calendar week number of the given calendar month.

DENSE_RANK() `OVER(PARTITION BY D.[CALENDAR YEAR MONTH NUMBER] ORDER BY D.[Calendar Week Number in Year])`

For DirectQuery data models in which the SQL queries defining the tables of the model are executed at runtime, it's best to move as much data transformation logic back to the source system. Complex SQL queries, DAX calculated columns, and M query expression logic can all lead to inefficient query plans, and negatively impact the performance of DirectQuery solutions.

How it works...

Date intelligence columns

- Date intelligence measures reference the surrogate key columns to easily define specific time period filter conditions

```
Internet Net Sales (Trailing 3 Periods) = CALCULATE([Internet Net
Sales],FILTER(ALL('Date'),
 'Date'[Calendar Year Month Number] >= MAX('Date'[Calendar Year
Month Number])-2 && 'Date'[Calendar Year Month Number] <=
MAX('Date'[Calendar Year Month Number])))
```

Calendar Yr-Mo ▼	Calendar Year Month Number	Internet Net Sales	Internet Net Sales (Trailing 3 Periods)
2017-May	101	$1,169,589	$3,265,519
2017-Apr	100	$1,046,023	$2,867,279
2017-Mar	99	$1,049,907	$2,678,946

Trailing 3 Period Measure includes Calendar Year Month Numbers 99 through 101 for 2017-May

- If the `Calendar Year Month Number` column wasn't sequential, it wouldn't be possible to refer to months across years, such as the trailing 3-month average of 2017-Jan
- Note that in this example, May of 2017 is the current month and was included, but often only the completed (or previous) months are included in these calculations

Loading the date dimension

- The SQL view used by the data model should dynamically filter the required dates, such as the trailing three years

```
FROM DBO.DimFinDate as D
WHERE
D.[Date] BETWEEN DATEADD(YEAR,-3,CAST(CURRENT_TIMESTAMP AS date))
AND CAST(CURRENT_TIMESTAMP as date)
```

- In this example, only the current system date and three prior calendar years are loaded to the data model

There's more...

Role playing date dimensions

- An alternative to "secondary relationships" (inactive relationships) via the USERELATIONSHIP() function described in Chapter 3, *Building a Power BI Data Model,* is to have multiple date dimension tables in the data model, each with a single, active relationship based on a different date column of the fact table.
- For example, a model would have Order Date, Ship Date, and Delivery Date dimension tables. This approach reduces the volume of custom measures that must be developed and maintained in the model.
- If chosen, create separate views against the source date dimension table, corresponding to each role playing table. Apply column aliases in each view associating the attribute to the date (for example, Ship Date Year or Ship Date Month).

Surrogate key date conversion

- Per Chapter 3, *Building a Power BI Data Model,* the relationship between fact tables and the date table should use a Date data type column
- If the source fact table only contains a surrogate key, commonly in the YYYYMMDD format, the source views utilized by the data model can include the conversion logic:

```
CONVERT(date,(CAST(F.OrderDateKey AS nvarchar(8)))) as [Order Date-
Convert]
```

- The DATEFROMPARTS() function in SQL Server can be used for many other date conversion or logical needs

Prepping the date dimension via the Query Editor

In some BI environments, it's not feasible to alter the source date table per the previous recipe or even modify the SQL view used to load the date dimension table; at least, not in the short term. In these situations, Power BI Desktop's Query Editor and M expressions can serve as an effective alternative to deliver the same columns necessary to drive robust date intelligence analysis.

In this recipe, an example date dimension M query is shared, which builds common date attributes as well as dynamic logical columns. Additionally, a process for adding sequential date intelligence columns via M expressions is also included.

How to do it...

Date dimension M Query

1. Create an M query that accesses an existing SQL date table view, retrieves the last three years of dates, and computes 11 additional columns via M functions:
    * A filter is applied via `Table.SelectRows()` to only retrieve the last three years of dates, and conditional logic is used to populate dynamic `Year Status` and `Month Status` columns (for example, `Current Year`):

```
let Source = AdWorksProd, Dates = Source{[Schema = "BI", Item =
"vDim_FinDate"]}[Data],
 CurrentDate = DateTime.Date(DateTime.LocalNow()),
 CurrentYear = Date.Year(DateTime.Date(DateTime.LocalNow())),
 CurrentMonth = Date.Month(DateTime.Date(DateTime.LocalNow())),
 FilteredDates = Table.SelectRows(Dates, each [Date] >=
Date.AddYears(CurrentDate,-3) and [Date] <= CurrentDate),
 DateCol = Table.SelectColumns(FilteredDates,"Date"),
 YearCol = Table.AddColumn(DateCol, "Year", each Date.Year([Date]),
Int64.Type),
 MonthNameCol = Table.AddColumn(YearCol, "Month Name", each
Date.MonthName([Date]), type text),
 YearMonthCol = Table.AddColumn(MonthNameCol, "Year-Mo", each
Text.From([Year]) & "-" & [Month Name], type text),
 MonthNumberCol = Table.AddColumn(YearMonthCol, "Month Number",
each Date.Month([Date]), Int64.Type),
```

```
    WeekdayNameCol = Table.AddColumn(MonthNumberCol, "Weekday", each
Date.DayOfWeekName([Date]), type text),
    DayNumberOfWeekCol = Table.AddColumn(WeekdayNameCol, "Weekday
Number", each Date.DayOfWeek([Date]), Int64.Type),
    YearStatusCol = Table.AddColumn(DayNumberOfWeekCol, "Year Status",
each
    if Date.IsInCurrentYear([Date]) = true then "Current Year"
    else if [Year] = CurrentYear - 1 then "Prior Year" else "Other
Year", type text),
    MonthStatusCol = Table.AddColumn(YearStatusCol, "Month Status",
each
    if [Year Status] = "Current Year" and [Month Number] =
CurrentMonth then "Current Month"
    else if [Year] =
Date.Year(Date.AddMonths(DateTime.Date(DateTime.LocalNow()),-1))
and
    [Month Number] =
Date.Month(Date.AddMonths(DateTime.Date(DateTime.LocalNow()),-1))
then "Prior Month"
    else "Other Month", type text),
    DayInMonthCol = Table.AddColumn(MonthStatusCol, "Day in Month",
each Date.Day([Date]), Int64.Type),
    WeekOfYearCol = Table.AddColumn(DayInMonthCol, "Week of Year",
each Date.WeekOfYear([Date]), Int64.Type),
    WeekOfMonthCol = Table.AddColumn(WeekOfYearCol, "Week of Month",
each Date.WeekOfMonth([Date]), Int64.Type) in WeekOfMonthCol
```

Despite a minimal date table available in the source system (for example, SQL Server), the M query generates a useful date dimension table for a model with many of the most common and important columns:

8 of the 11 Date Dimension Columns Produced via the M Query. Day In Month, Week of Year, and Week of Month Not Displayed

- Per Chapter 2, *Accessing and Retrieving Data,* the CurrentDate, CurrentMonth, and CurrentYear expressions can be stored as separate queries

Add the date intelligence column via join

1. Develop an M query which creates a surrogate sequential column to be used in Date Intelligence measures:

   - Two columns (`Calendar Year` and `Calendar Month Number`) are accessed from an existing SQL view and the `Table.AddIndexColumn()` function is applied to this sorted table to create the sequential column

   ```
   let Source = AdWorksProd, DateDim = Source{[Schema = "BI",Item =
   "vDim_FinDate"]}[Data],
   YearMonthCols = Table.Distinct(Table.SelectColumns(DateDim,
   {"Calendar Year","Calendar Month Number"})),
   YearMonthColSort = Table.Sort(YearMonthCols,{{"Calendar Year",
   Order.Ascending}, {"Calendar Month Number", Order.Ascending}}),
   YearMonthColIndex = Table.AddIndexColumn(YearMonthColSort,
   "YearMonthIndex",1,1),
   JoinedDateTable =
    Table.NestedJoin(#"M Date Query", {"Year", "Month
   Number"},YearMonthColIndex, {"Calendar Year","Calendar Month
   Number"}, "Year-Mo Index", JoinKind.Inner),
   IndexColumnAdded =
   Table.ExpandTableColumn(JoinedDateTable,"Year-Mo
   Index",{"YearMonthIndex"},{"Year Month Number"})
   in IndexColumnAdded
   ```

   - The date dimension query from the previous example (# "M Date Query") is joined to the three column tables:
     - See Chapter 2, *Accessing and Retrieving Data*, for examples and details on the `Table.NestedJoin()` and `Table.Join()` functions
   - Only this query with the new date intelligence column (`Year Month Number`) needs to be loaded to the data model
   - Disable the load for the other query in the join, but it must continue to refresh to support the retrieval
   - The `Year-Mo` column (that is, `2016-Dec`) can now be sorted by the `Year Month Number` column in the data model and DAX measures can reference the `Year Month Number` column (that is, 96) to apply date intelligence filter conditions such as the trailing 6 months. See the *Configuring default summarization and sorting* recipe in Chapter 3, *Building a Power BI Data Model* for additional details on default sorting.

How it works...

Date dimension M query

- The `AdWorksProd` source variable is a `Sql.Database()` function containing the server and database names
- The `DateTime.LocalNow()` function is used in dynamic M date logic, similar to the `CURRENT_TIMESTAMP` function used in SQL statements

DirectQuery support

The `Table.AddIndexColumn()` function used in this recipe is not currently supported in DirectQuery mode for SQL Server

The full M query from the date dimension M query section of this recipe cannot be used in DirectQuery data models

Since the data access queries defining the dimension and fact tables in DirectQuery models are executed at run time, these queries should be as simple as possible. For example, these queries should avoid joins, derived tables, subqueries, data type conversions, case statements, and so on. Simple, performant or optimized queries are especially important for the queries used to access the largest tables of the model. To ensure sufficient performance in Power BI with DirectQuery models, large source tables of DirectQuery models should be optimized for read performance with features such as the Columnstore Index of SQL Server and table partitions.

Authoring date intelligence metrics across granularities

With a complete date dimension table in place, date intelligence measures can be developed to support common requirements, such as `Year-to-Date`, `Year-over-Year`, and rolling history, as well as more complex, context-specific behaviors. The date intelligence patterns described in this recipe are applicable to both standard and non-standard financial calendars as they leverage fundamental DAX functions and the sequential date intelligence columns created earlier in this chapter.

This recipe includes examples of core `Year-to-Date` and `Prior Year` measures, as well as a more advanced dynamic prior period measure that adjusts to all grains of the date dimension.

Getting ready

1. Plan for a standard measure naming convention to identify the date intelligence logic, such as `Sales (PYTD)`:
   - Symbol characters, such as currency ($) or percentage (%), can also help users browse the measures
2. Document the types of date intelligence measures to be implemented and for which measures of the model.
3. Create a date intelligence measure matrix for documentation and to support communication with stakeholders:

Date Intelligence Measures	YTD	MTD	WTD	PY	PM	PYTD	PMTD	YOY	YOY %	YOY YTD	YOY YTD %	Rolling 12
Internet Sales	✓	✓	✓	✓	✓	✓	✓	✓	✓	✓	✓	✓
Internet Orders	✓	✓	✓	✓	✓	✓	✓	✓	✓	✓	✓	✓
Reseller Sales	✓	✓	✓	✓	✓	✓	✓	✓	✓	✓	✓	✓

Date Intelligence Measure Matrix

Conduct reviews and/or QA testing with business users to validate the logic, and walk through use cases in report design. Given the volume of new measures to be developed, it's best to receive business approval for one or two measures prior to applying the date intelligence logic to other measures.

How to do it...

Current time period measures

1. Open the Power BI Desktop model locally and create `Year-to-Date`, `Period-to-Date`, and `Week-to-Date` measures:

```
Internet Sales (YTD) = CALCULATE([Internet Sales],
FILTER(ALL('Date'),
'Date'[Calendar Year] = MAX('Date'[Calendar Year]) && 'Date'[Date]
<= MAX('Date'[Date])))

Internet Sales (MTD) = CALCULATE([Internet Sales],
FILTER(ALL('Date'),'Date'[Calendar Year Month Number] =
MAX('Date'[Calendar Year Month Number]) && 'Date'[Date] <=
MAX('Date'[Date])))

Internet Sales (WTD) = CALCULATE([Internet Sales],
FILTER(ALL('Date'),'Date'[Calendar Year Week Number] =
MAX('Date'[Calendar Year Week Number]) && 'Date'[Date] <=
MAX('Date'[Date])))
```

Each measure expression sets an "equal to" condition on the column representing the intended granularity and this column respects the filter context of the report query via `MAX()`. If the source query to the date table is filtered to only retrieve dates equal to or less than the current date, these measures will default to the current year, month (or period), and week when added to reports.

Note that the `Calendar Year Month Number` and `Calendar Year Week Number` columns should be sequentially increasing integers per the *Building a complete date dimension table* recipe earlier in this chapter. For example, the `Calendar Year Month Number` column may have the values 96 and 97 for the months of December in 2016 and January in 2017, respectively.

DAX includes a full set of Time Intelligence functions, such as `DATESYTD()` and `SAMEPERIODLASTYEAR()`, which, given a standard (Gregorian) calendar, can compute the same values as the expressions in this recipe. Although these functions generally improve readability relative to the examples in this recipe, the use (and knowledge) of core DAX functions, such as `FILTER()` and `ALL()`, is necessary when working with non-standard calendars, such as fiscal calendars and more complex scenarios.

Prior time period measures

1. Create Prior Year (PY), Prior Year to Date (PYTD), and Prior Month to Date (PMTD) measures:

   Internet Sales (PY) = CALCULATE([Internet Sales],FILTER(ALL('Date'), 'Date'[Date] >= MIN('Date'[Prior Calendar Year Date]) && 'Date'[Date] <= MAX('Date'[Prior Calendar Year Date])))

   Internet Sales (PYTD) = CALCULATE([Internet Sales], FILTER(ALL('Date'),'Date'[Calendar Year] = MAX('Date'[Calendar Year])-1 && 'Date'[Date] <= MAX('Date'[Prior Calendar Year Date])))

   Internet Sales (PMTD) = CALCULATE([Internet Sales],FILTER(ALL('Date'),'Date'[Calendar Year Month Number] = MAX('Date'[Calendar Year Month Number])-1 && 'Date'[Date] <= MAX('Date'[Prior Calendar Month Date])))

- Applying both the MIN() and MAX() filter conditions against the prior date columns selects the corresponding date ranges.
- Subtracting a value (1 in this example) from MAX() of the column shifts the selected time period backwards.
- Growth or variance measures which calculate the difference between the current time period value of a measure to a prior time period such as **Year-over-Year (YOY)** Growth can be created with new measures which subtract the previous time period measure from the current period measure. Additional growth or variance measures expressed in percentages can use the **DIVIDE()** function for computing this difference as a percentage of the previous time period value.

   Internet Net Sales (YOY YTD) = [Internet Net Sales (CY YTD)] - [Internet Net Sales (PY YTD)]

   Internet Net Sales (YOY YTD %) = DIVIDE([Internet Net Sales (YOY YTD)],[Internet Net Sales (PY YTD)])

Prior period date columns allow the prior time period measures to apply simple filter expressions relative to the active date filter context down to the individual date granularity. In the absence of these columns and for period or month level date tables, measure filter conditions can be written as follows:

```
Prior Year (PY) = 'Date'[Calendar Year Month Number] =
MAX('Date'[Calendar Year Month Number]) - 12)
Prior Month (PM) = 'Date'[Calendar Year Month Number] =
MAX('Date'[Calendar Year Month Number]) - 1)
```

Dynamic prior period measure

1. Build logic into date intelligence measures to account for alternative subtotal filter contexts, such as when a prior period measure is calculated in a yearly, quarterly, or weekly subtotal context:

    ```
    Internet Sales (Prior Period) = VAR Periods =
    DISTINCTCOUNT('Date'[Calendar Year Month Number])
    RETURN SWITCH(TRUE(),
    HASONEVALUE('Date'[Date]),CALCULATE([Internet
    Sales],FILTER(ALL('Date'),'Date'[Date] = MAX('Date'[Date])-1)),
    HASONEVALUE('Date'[Calendar Year Week Number]),CALCULATE([Internet
    Sales],FILTER(ALL('Date'),'Date'[Calendar Year Week Number] =
    MAX('Date'[Calendar Year Week Number])-1)),
     CALCULATE([Internet Sales],FILTER(ALL('Date'),
     'Date'[Calendar Year Month Number] >= MIN('Date'[Calendar Year
    Month Number]) - Periods &&
     'Date'[Calendar Year Month Number] <= MAX('Date'[Calendar Year
    Month Number]) - Periods )))
    ```

The DAX variable (Periods) computes the number of periods in the current filter context, such as 12 if a year is the subtotal, 3 if it is a quarter, or 1 for an individual period. Test conditions with HASONEVALUE() check if a single date or week is selected and return the corresponding previous day or week, respectively. The remaining date grains (Year, Quarter, Period) are accounted for by the Periods variable; this value is subtracted from both the MIN() and the MAX() of the period number of the given context. This example underscores the importance of sequential date intelligence columns, for accessing specific time frames across grains to apply custom filter conditions.

How it works...

Current and prior time period measures

- The `FILTER()` function iterates each row (a date) to determine which rows are passed to the `CALCULATE()` function
- The `ALL()` function removes all existing date table filters, thereby allowing filter conditions in the measure to access all rows of the date table

Developing advanced date intelligence metrics

Date intelligence measures are often at the center of the most visible Power BI reports and dashboards as well as more complex business analyses. Therefore, given the unique requirements of each organization and BI project, it's important to understand how to go beyond the standard patterns described in the previous recipe to efficiently embed custom logic. Additionally, the ability to answer the business question "When did X occur (or not occur)?" is a powerful supplement to data models that can be supported via DAX measure logic.

In this recipe, an example is provided of a measure that identifies the dates in which sales were not recorded for a specific region and product category. In the second example, a custom Prior Year-to-Date measure is described with default (no filter) behavior and the exclusion of incomplete periods from the current year.

How to do it...

Count of days without sales

In this example, a new measure must count the days in which the Northwest Sales region didn't have any online sales for the Bikes product category.

1. Create a measure that counts the rows (days) that don't have corresponding fact table rows given the conditions

```
Days Without Northwest Bike Sales =
COUNTROWS(FILTER('Date', ISEMPTY(CALCULATETABLE('Internet Sales',
FILTER(CROSSJOIN(ALL('Sales Territory'),ALL('Product')),'Sales
Territory'[Sales Territory Region] = "Northwest" &&
'Product'[Product Category] = "Bikes")))))
```

Any existing filters on the Product and Sales Territory tables are removed via CROSSJOIN() of the ALL() functions. The Internet Sales fact table is then filtered for the Northwest region and the Bikes category, and ISEMPTY() is applied for each date in the filter context. Only the dates with no rows are returned by FILTER() to be counted.

The use of CROSSJOIN() is necessary to remove filters on columns from separate tables of the model. A single ALL() function can be used to remove one or more columns from the filter context of a single table such as ALL('Product'[Product Color],'Product'[Product Class]).

2. Create Power BI report visuals to analyze the measure:

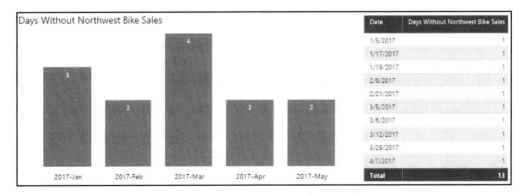

With a Page level filter for the current year, the measure identifies the 13 days in 2017 in which the Northwest region didn't generate any Bike sales

- The date attribute column can be drilled into from higher level trend visuals or detail reports at the date level can be designed with visual level filters applied to the new measure, such as `[Measure] is greater than or equal to 1`

Dynamic Prior Year-to-Date

In this Prior Year-to-Date example, which is at the monthly grain, the business requirements are as follows:

- Filter the prior year by only the completed periods of the current year (only compare completed against completed)
- Calculate the Prior Year-to-Date value (completed periods only) automatically without any date columns in the report
- Return a blank if the current period, which is incomplete, is selected in report visuals

1. Create a measure with multiple pairs of conditions and results to account for the filter contexts and requirements:

```
Sales (PYTD-Custom) =
SWITCH(TRUE(),NOT(ISCROSSFILTERED('Date')),
 CALCULATE([Internet Sales],FILTER(ALL('Date'),'Date'[Calendar
Year] = MAX('Date'[Calendar Year])-1 && 'Date'[Calendar Month
Number] <= [Last Complete Month])),
 HASONEVALUE('Date'[Calendar Year Month Number]) &&
MAX('Date'[Calendar Year Month Number]) > [Last Complete
Period],BLANK(),
 HASONEVALUE('Date'[Calendar Year Month Number]) &&
MAX('Date'[Calendar Year Month Number]) <= [Last Complete Period],
 CALCULATE([Internet Sales],FILTER(ALL('Date'),'Date'[Calendar
Year] = MAX('Date'[Calendar Year])-1 && 'Date'[Calendar Year Month
Number] <= MAX('Date'[Calendar Year Month Number])-12)),
 MAX('Date'[Calendar Year]) = [Current Year],
 CALCULATE([Internet Sales],FILTER(ALL('Date'),'Date'[Calendar
Year] = [Current Year]-1 && 'Date'[Calendar Month Number] <= [Last
Complete Month])),
 CALCULATE([Internet Sales],FILTER(ALL('Date'),'Date'[Calendar
Year] = MAX('Date'[Calendar Year])-1 && 'Date'[Calendar Year Month
Number] <= MAX('Date'[Calendar Year Month Number])-12)))
```

DAX Formatter in DAX Studio can be used to improve the readability of long, complex measures, such as this example. Clicking on **Format Query** from the Home tab of DAX Studio isolates functions to individual lines and applies indentations to inner functions. An example of using this tool, also available at `http://www.daxformatter.com/`, is described in the *There's more...* section of the *Isolating and documenting DAX expressions* recipe in `Chapter 11`, *Enhancing and Optimizing Existing Power BI Solutions*.

The first condition `NOT(ISCROSSFILTERED())` handles whether any date filter has been applied from any date column. The second condition tests for individual periods that are not yet complete and returns a `BLANK()`. The third condition accounts for individual periods prior to or equal to the last complete period. The fourth condition is specific to the subtotal of the current year (`= [Current Year]`); this rule excludes the incomplete period. All other filter contexts are accounted for in the final expression--a standard Prior Year-to-Date calculation at the period grain. See *How it works* for details on the measures referenced, such as `[Last Complete Month]` and `[Last Complete Period]`.

	Calendar Yr-Mo	Sales (PYTD-Custom)	Internet Sales		Calendar Year	Sales (PYTD-Custom)	Internet Sales
$2,135,055	2017-Jun		$114,259		2017	$2,135,055	$5,123,821
Sales (PYTD-Custom)	2017-May	$2,135,055	$1,284,593		2016	$7,075,526	$5,842,485
	2017-Apr	$1,776,177	$1,046,023		2015	$43,421	$7,075,526
	Total	**$2,135,055**	**$18,085,253**		**Total**	**$2,135,055**	**$18,085,253**

Custom PYTD measure computes the correct value without any filter (Card visual) and across date hierarchy levels

- Note that a blank is returned for the current period (2017-Jun) per requirements

Remember that the data models created in Power BI can be consumed in self-service scenarios, such as with Excel pivot tables, and business users will want or expect the new measures to 'just work' across filter conditions. However, in a rapid, agile delivery of Power BI, only the most important or core filter contexts can be implemented in the first iterations.

How it works...

Dynamic prior period intelligence

- By passing TRUE() as the expression parameter to SWITCH(), the first <value> condition (such as no filters applied) that evaluates to true will result in the corresponding result expression.
- The three measures referenced in the PYTD-Custom measure are simple LOOKUPVALUE() scalar functions that can be hidden from Report View. Unlike DAX variables, measures can be re-used by many other measures in the model.

```
Last Complete Period = LOOKUPVALUE('Date'[Calendar Year Month
Number],
'Date'[Calendar Month Status],"Prior Calendar Month")
Last Complete Month = LOOKUPVALUE('Date'[Calendar Month Number],
'Date'[Calendar Month Status],"Prior Calendar Month")
Current Year = LOOKUPVALUE('Date'[Calendar Year],'Date'[Calendar
Year Status], "Current Calendar Year")
```

Simplifying date intelligence with DAX queries and calculated tables

In addition to the M query transformations described earlier in this chapter, DAX table functions can also be used in Power BI import mode models to enhance and simplify date intelligence. DAX queries can access existing tables in the data model, and the tables evaluated during refresh can be used in relationships and measure calculations like all other tables. Similar to calculated columns, calculated tables should be rarely used given the transformation capabilities of M, SQL, and ETL tools, but can be valuable supplements to models for small tables, such as role playing date dimensions and bridge tables.

This recipe provides an example of using DAX Calculated Tables to support role playing date dimensions. Additionally, a single row table is created via DAX to simplify common date intelligence measures.

How to do it...

Role playing date dimensions via calculated tables

1. Open a Power BI Desktop import mode model locally.
2. From Report View, click on **New Table** from the **Modeling** tab.
3. In the formula bar, assign a name to the date dimension table, such as `Shipment Dates`:
    - Use the `SELECTCOLUMNS()` function to retrieve date columns from the existing date dimension table:

```
Shipment Dates = SELECTCOLUMNS('Date',
"Shipment Date", 'Date'[Date], "Shipment Year", 'Date'[Calendar Year],
"Shipment Month", 'Date'[Calendar Month], "Last Refreshed", NOW())
```

4. Per the example, apply column aliases (`Shipment ...`) to avoid confusion with other date tables in the model.
5. Optionally, use additional DAX functions, such as `NOW()`, to enrich the new table with additional or modified columns.
6. From the Data View, apply any necessary metadata changes, such as **Sort by Column** and **Default Summarization**:

Shipment Date	Shipment Year	Shipment Month	Last Refreshed
2/1/2016	2016	Feb	5/30/2017 3:21:00 PM
2/2/2016	2016	Feb	5/30/2017 3:21:00 PM
2/3/2016	2016	Feb	5/30/2017 3:21:00 PM

Data View of Calculated Table

7. From the **Modeling** tab, click on **Manage Relationships** and select **New**.
8. Create a relationship between the new date table and the fact table based on the date column (date data type).

The model now has two date dimension tables with active relationships to the fact table; order date and shipment date in this example. Generally, when role playing date dimensions are used, aliases are applied to all tables and columns, thus requiring the date table and its columns to be renamed as Order Dates. However, if the new role playing date tables will be rarely used, then aliases may only be necessary for these tables.

Date table logic query

One option to further simplify date intelligence measures is to embed a calculated table in a model that generates values frequently used as filter conditions.

1. Identify the target columns (filter conditions) of the table and test DAX expression logic to compute these scalar values.

Using DAX Studio connected to the Power BI Desktop model may be helpful for more complex table queries and measures. Similar to the Date table in this example, the ROW() function with a calculated table is also useful for storing model metadata, such as table row counts and the number of blank or null values in columns.

2. From the **Modeling** tab in Power BI Desktop, click on **New Table** and enter the DAX query:

```
Date Parameters =
VAR Today = TODAY()
VAR CurrentFiscalYear = LOOKUPVALUE('Date'[Fiscal Year],
'Date'[Date],Today)
VAR FiscalYearPeriodSort = LOOKUPVALUE('Date'[Fiscal Yr-Period
Sort], 'Date'[Date],Today)
VAR FiscalYearQtrSort = LOOKUPVALUE('Date'[Fiscal Yr-Qtr Sort],
'Date'[Date],Today)
RETURN
ROW
("Last Refreshed", NOW(),"Today", Today,"30 Days Prior", Today -
30,"90 Days Prior",Today - 90,
"Current Fiscal Year", CurrentFiscalYear, "Prior Fiscal Year",
CurrentFiscalYear-1,
"Current Fiscal Year-Period",
LOOKUPVALUE('Date'[Fiscal Yr-Period],'Date'[Fiscal Yr-Period
Sort],FiscalYearPeriodSort),
"Prior Fiscal Year-Period",
LOOKUPVALUE('Date'[Fiscal Yr-Period],'Date'[Fiscal Yr-Period
Sort],FiscalYearPeriodSort-1),
```

```
"Current Fiscal Yr-Qtr",
LOOKUPVALUE('Date'[Fiscal Yr-Qtr],'Date'[Fiscal Yr-Qtr
Sort],FiscalYearQtrSort),
"Prior Fiscal Yr-Qtr",
LOOKUPVALUE('Date'[Fiscal Yr-Qtr],'Date'[Fiscal Yr-Qtr
Sort],FiscalYearQtrSort-1))
```

3. Hide the parameters table from the Report view.

Last Refreshed	Today	30 Days Prior	90 Days Prior	Current Fiscal Year	Prior Fiscal Year	Current Fiscal Year-Period
5/30/2017 5:14:46 P	5/30/2017	4/30/2017	3/1/2017	2017	2016	2017-P5

Sample of the Single Row Table ('Date Parameters') Created via the DAX Calculated Table Query

4. Create date intelligence measures which leverage the values stored in the calculated table:

```
Current Period Internet Sales = CALCULATE([Internet Sales],
'Date'[Fiscal Yr-Period] = VALUES('Date Parameters'[Current Fiscal
Year-Period]))
Last 90 Days Sales = CALCULATE([Internet Sales],'Date'[Date] >=
VALUES('Date Parameters'[90 Days Prior]))
```

How it works...

Date table logic query

- The Sort' columns referenced by the LOOKUPVALUE() functions are sequential surrogate key columns
- Variables are computed based on the TODAY() function and used to simplify the column expressions
- VALUES() retrieves the single value from the table for comparison to the corresponding date dimension column in the filter condition of CALCULATE()

Adding a metric placeholder dimension

As date intelligence and other measures are added to a data model, it becomes necessary to organize measures into dedicated measure group tables in the Fields list. These tables, displayed with calculator symbols at the top of the **Fields** list, make it easier for users and report developers to find measures for building and modifying Power BI reports. The *Setting the visibility of columns and tables* section of Chapter 3, *Building a Power BI Data Model* briefly introduced the concept of measure group tables in the *How it works...* section, but didn't specify the process to implement these objects.

This recipe provides step-by-step guidance for a method of implementing measure group tables that works with both DirectQuery and Import data models.

How to do it...

Metric placeholder dimension query

1. Open the Power BI Desktop model file locally (Import or DirectQuery modes).
2. From Report View, click on the **Edit Queries** icon on the **Home** tab to open the Query Editor.
3. Select an existing query in the Queries pane on the left, right-click the query, and select **Duplicate**.
4. With the duplicated query selected, enter a name, such as Date Intelligence, in the Query Settings pane on the right.
5. Click on the Advanced Editor icon on the **Home** tab and revise the M expression as follows:

```
let
  Source = AdWorksProd,
  DateIntelligence = Value.NativeQuery(Source, "Select 1 as Dummy")
in
  DateIntelligence
```

- The Value.NativeQuery() function passes a T-SQL statement against the database specified by the AdWorksProd query

The `AdWorksProd` query used as the source of the `Value.NativeQuery()` function contains the server and database names in a `Sql.Database()` function. See `Chapter 2`, *Accessing and Retrieving Data* for detailed examples of isolating source system information from individual queries.

- If **Require user approval for new native database queries** is set in the **Global Security** options, a warning will appear, advising that permission is required to run the new query

6. Click on the **Edit Permission** button and then click on **Run** to authorize the new native database query.
7. Right-click the query and disable **Include in Report Refresh**.
8. **Enable load** is needed but as a measure placeholder there's no reason to run the query during refresh.
9. Click on **Close and Apply** from the **Home** tab of the Query Editor.

Measure group table

1. From the Report View, right-click the column from the new table created earlier (Dummy) and select **Hide**.
2. With the only column of the table hidden, the table will not be visible in the Fields list.
3. Select a date intelligence measure in the **Fields** list.
4. With the measure selected, click on the **Modeling** tab and change the **Home Table** of the measure to date intelligence:

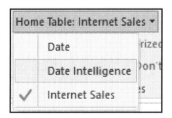

Measure Home Table Setting

5. Click on the Show/Hide pane arrow above the search box to refresh the **Fields** list:

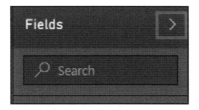

Show/Hide arrow refreshes Fields List

- With only measures of a table visible, the table will be moved to the top of the Fields list with a calculation icon:

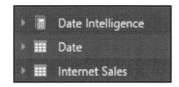

Date Intelligence measure group table moved to the top of the Fields list and updated with a calculator icon

6. Optionally, add more measure tables and re-assign the Home Table of measures to better organize the Fields list.

- Per `Chapter 3`, Bu*ilding a Power BI Data Model*, the **Display Folders** feature of **SQL Server Analysis Services** (**SSAS**) isn't currently available for Power BI

7
Parameterizing Power BI Solutions

In this chapter, we will cover the following recipes:

- Creating dynamic and portable Power BI reports
- Filtering queries with parameters
- Preserving report metadata with Power BI templates
- Converting static queries into dynamic functions
- Parameterizing your data sources
- Generating a list of parameter values via queries
- Capturing user selections with parameter tables
- Building a forecasting process with What if analysis capabilities

Introduction

With the foundation of a Power BI deployment in place, components of the data retrieval and report design processes, as well as the user experience, can be parameterized to deliver greater flexibility for both IT and users. For example, query parameters can isolate and restrict data sources to support changing source systems, templates can enable parameterized report development against pre-defined metadata, and M and DAX functions can deliver custom integration and analytical capabilities.

The recipes in this chapter cover both standard parameterization features and techniques in Power BI as well as more advanced custom implementations. Examples of parameterizing data sources, queries, user-defined functions, and reports further express the power of the M language and its integration with other Power BI Desktop features. Additional examples, such as URL-based parameter filters, a dedicated forecasting or What if? tool, and user selection parameter tables, utilize both the transformation and analytical features of Power BI, to empower users with greater control over the analysis and visualization of Power BI data models.

Creating dynamic and portable Power BI reports

In addition to the report filter options in Power BI Desktop, covered in Chapter 4, *Authoring Power BI Reports*, filters can also be applied to published Power BI reports via the URL string. Rather than multiple, dedicated reports and report pages with distinct filter conditions, URL links with unique query strings can leverage a single published report in the Power BI Service. Additionally, URL links can be embedded within a dataset such that a published report can expose links to other reports with a pre-defined filter condition.

In this recipe, two URL strings are created to demonstrate single and multiple filter parameter syntax. The second example creates a URL string for each row of the Product dimension table via an M query and exposes this dynamic link in a report visual.

Getting ready

1. Identify the tables and columns that will be used for the URL filtering and, if necessary, create hidden tables and/or columns with no spaces.

 Table and field names in URL query parameters cannot have any spaces. Therefore, since it's a best practice to include spaces in column names for usability, creating new columns and/or tables is often necessary to enable URL filtering.

- In this example, the Product Category and Calendar Year Status columns from the Product and Date dimension tables are to be used for the URL filters

How to do it...

Single and multiple URL parameters

1. Add columns to the `Product` and `Date` dimension queries that don't contain spaces:

```
let Source = AdWorksProd,
FinDate = Source{[Schema = "BI", Item = "vDim_FinDate"]}[Data],
CalYearStatusColumn = Table.AddColumn(FinDate,
"CalendarYearStatus", each [Calendar Year Status], type text)
in CalYearStatusColumn
```

- An additional M expression with the `Table.AddColumn()` function creates a column in each dimension table query that doesn't contain spaces (for example, `CalendarYearStatus`)

 This additional column can also be created in the SQL view accessed by the M query. If rights to the source SQL view are available, this is where the new column should be added.

2. From the Data View in Power BI Desktop, right-click the new columns and select **Hide in Report View**.

 URL filters can be applied to any column in the data model that is of a text data type. The column doesn't have to be visible in the Fields list or used in one of the **Filtering** field wells in Report view to be used in a URL filter.

3. Create a report connected to a published Power BI dataset that is impacted by filters applied on the new columns.

The **Product Subcategory** visual (left) will update to reflect the URL filter selections for the new product category column (with no spaces). Likewise, the **Calendar Yr-Qtr** visual (right), will be impacted by the URL filter selection of the new calendar year status column created in step 1 (for example, `Current Year`):

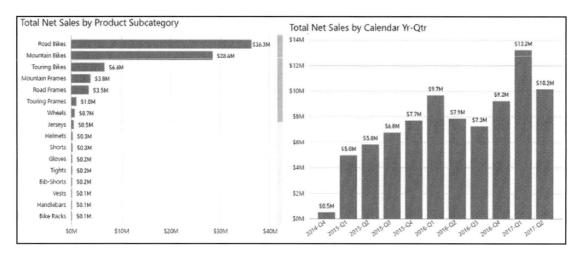

Total Net Sales by Product Subcategories and Quarters Without Any URL Filter Applied

 Published datasets are available as sources for new Power BI reports from the Power BI service connection within the Online Services category of the Get Data interface. The new report will not contain filter conditions; filters will be applied via URL.

4. Publish the report to the Power BI Service.
5. Open the report in the Power BI Service and copy the full URL to a text editing application.
6. Append filter condition syntax at the end of the URL, as follows:

```
...ReportSection2?filter=Product/ProductCategory eq 'Bikes'
```

 The syntax is `<Report URL>?filter=Table/Field eq 'value'`. The table and field names (without spaces) are case sensitive and the `'value'` must be enclosed in single quotes.

7. Open a new browser tab or page and paste the updated URL to observe the report filtered by the single URL condition.

8. To apply multiple URL filter parameters, separate the column filters with an `and` operator, as in the following example:

```
...ReportSection2?filter=Product/ProductCategory eq 'Bikes' and
Date/CalendarYearStatus eq 'Current Calendar Year'
```

The report will respect the URL filters to only show the `Bikes` product subcategories and the `Current Calendar Year` quarters:

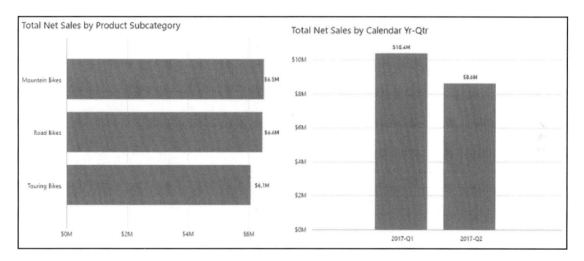

Filtered Power BI report via URL Parameters: Product Category = 'Bikes' and Calendar Year Status = 'Current Calendar Year'

 Multiple URL strings can be created and then distributed to business users or teams such that filters relevant to the given user or team are applied via the URL and not in the report itself.

Dynamic embedded URLs

1. Create a column in the product table M query that contains the URL to a report and a filter for the given product name:

```
Table.AddColumn(ProdNameColumn, "Product URL", each
"https://app.powerbi.com/groups/...../ReportSection" &
"?filter=Product/ProductName eq " & "'" & [Product Name] & "'",
type text)
```

First, a new hidden column with no spaces (`ProductName`) is created to be used by the URL filter, like the first example in this recipe. Multiple ampersand symbols are then used within a `Table.AddColumn()` function to concatenate the string values to meet the required URL filter syntax.

The end of the `Product URL` column for the `'BB Ball Bearing'` product appears as follows:

```
/ReportSection?filter=Product/ProductName eq 'BB Ball Bearing'
```

Query Preview of the new 'Product URL' column created in the M Query

2. Hide the single space column and click on **Close and Apply** to load the `Product URL` column to the data model.
3. Select the new column in the Data View and set the data category to `Web URL`.
4. In the Report view, create a table visual with the product name, measures, and the `Product URL` column.
5. With the table visual selected, go to the Format pane and enable the URL icon setting under **Values**:

Product Name	Total Net Sales	Product URL
Mountain-200 Black, 38	$3,038,211	⬬
Mountain-200 Black, 42	$2,810,396	⬬
Mountain-200 Silver, 38	$2,526,896	⬬

Product URL Column Exposed in Table Visual

With the product-specific URL filter column added to the report, the user can select the icon to navigate to a detailed product report that would be filtered for the given product.

There's more...

Dashboards with custom URLs

- A report visual from a custom URL with a query string can be pinned to a dashboard and the dashboard tile will reflect the filter condition in refreshes. However, by default, selecting the pinned dashboard tile will navigate to the unfiltered source report.
- The custom URL can be associated with a dashboard tile to control the dashboard navigation:

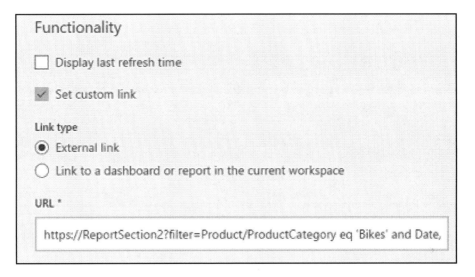

Custom URL Link for a Power BI Dashboard Tile

In the future, the Power BI team may remove the requirement for table and column names without spaces. In the interim, given the additional resources required of the new column(s), try to limit the columns to those with few distinct values. Additionally, a single hidden column with no spaces can be created based on the concatenation of multiple columns to simplify the URL strings.

See also

- Power BI Documentation on Report URL Query String Filters at http://bit.ly/2s5hXSW

Filtering queries with parameters

Parameters are a primary component in building flexible, manageable query retrieval processes, as well as enabling simple filter selections. Hard coded values in queries can be replaced with parameters and a single parameter can be leveraged by multiple queries, thus reducing development time and maintenance. Additionally, parameters can be assigned data types to match data sources and can be easily adjusted via lists of predefined values, both in the Query Editor and in the Report View.

In this recipe, a parameter is used to filter a fact table query for a specified number of days relative to the current date. An additional, more advanced example is shared to apply parameters to a fact table query on both a dimension column as well as a date range.

Getting ready

1. Identify candidates for query parameters, such as hard coded date filters and dimension attributes with few distinct values (for example, department groups).
2. Identify scenarios in which certain business users or teams require edit rights to a dataset (that is, source queries, model relationships, and measures), but only need a small, highly filtered model for self-service development.

Per `Chapter 4`, *Authoring Power BI Reports*, Power BI reports can be developed against published datasets hosted in the Power BI service. In the event that new metrics are required for a report, these DAX measures can be added to the source dataset and used in these reports once the dataset is re-published to the Power BI service. Alternatively, and particularly for rare or very narrow use cases, DAX measures can be created specific to a given Power BI report and not added to the source dataset.

Providing a separate, business team-controlled dataset for report development can increase version control risks and manageability costs. Minimizing the number of datasets, avoiding overlapping datasets, and maintaining central control of M and DAX logic is recommended to promote consistent, efficient Power BI projects.

How to do it...

Trailing days query parameter filter

1. Open a Power BI Desktop file locally and access the Query Editor by clicking on **Edit Queries** from the **Home** tab.
2. Create a blank query to retrieve the current date via the following M expression:

The Current Date is returned as a Date type

- Name the new query `CurrentDate` and disable its load to the data model

3. From the **Home** tab of the Query Editor, click on the **Manage Parameters** dropdown and select **New Parameter**:

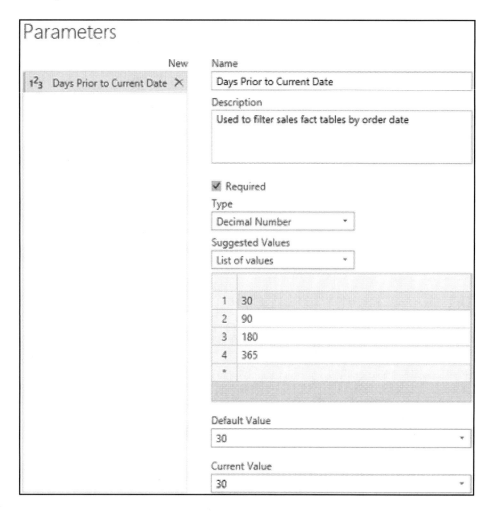

New Parameter Created for Filtering Fact Table Queries

4. Give the query a name, a data type, and, for this example, enter a list of suggested values:
    - Values outside this suggested list can also be applied to the parameter when necessary

5. Based on the **List of values**, enter a **Default Value** and **Current Value**.

6. Create a new blank query that computes a date value based off the `CurrentDate` query and the new parameter:

```
let MyDate = Date.AddDays(CurrentDate,- #"Days Prior to Current
Date")
in MyDate
```

- In this example, a date 30 days prior to the current date is returned based on the default parameter value:
  - Name this query `StartDate`

7. Add a filtering step (expression) to the fact table query that references the `CurrentDate` and `StartDate` queries:

```
let Source = AdWorksProd,
ISales = Source{[Schema = "BI", Item =
"vFact_InternetSales"]}[Data],
RowFilter = Table.SelectRows(ISales, each [Order Date] >= StartDate
and [Order Date] <= CurrentDate)
in RowFilter
```

- `Table.SelectRows()` filters the sales table order date for greater than or equal to the `StartDate` (a date value)

8. Click on **Close & Apply** from the **Home** tab of the Query Editor.
9. Optionally, build a report or query against the refreshed fact table to validate the filter.
10. From the **Home** tab of the report view, click on the **Edit Queries** dropdown and select **Edit Parameters**:

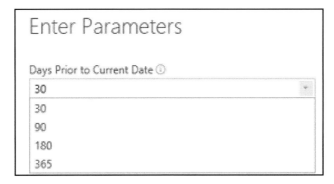

Edit Parameters from Report View

11. Either select a suggested value from the dropdown menu or enter a number in the input box and click on **OK**.

12. Click on **Apply Changes** from the warning dialog. The StartDate and the fact table queries impacted by the parameter change will both be refreshed.

Multi-parameter query filters

In this example, the goal is to filter the fact table by both a time frame (start and end dates) as well as a dimension:

1. From a Power BI Desktop file, open the Query Editor and click on **New Parameter** from the **Manage Parameters** dropdown.

2. Create a parameter for the Sales Territory Group with a text data type:

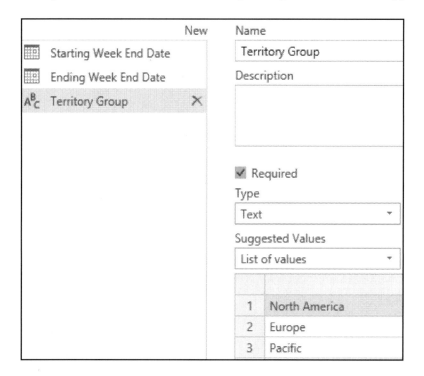

3. Name the parameter **Territory Group** and enter the names (North America, Europe, or Pacific) as **Suggested Values**.

4. Create a new query (from a blank query) that selects the unique key values associated with this dimension:

```
let ParamFilter = Table.SelectRows(#"Sales Territory", each [Sales
Territory Group] = #"Territory Group"),
KeyColumn =
Table.Distinct(Table.SelectColumns(ParamFilter,{"SalesTerritoryKey"
}))
in KeyColumn
```

- The existing Sales Territory dimension table is filtered by the Territory Group parameter value.
- Only the key column used in the relationship with the fact table is selected and Table.Distinct() removes any duplicate values. Name this query ParamTerritoryKey.

5. Within the sales fact table query, create an inner join expression step against the new ParamTerritoryKey query:

```
SalesTerritoryJoin =
Table.Join(ISales,"SalesTerritoryKey",ParamTerritoryKey,"SalesTerri
toryKey",JoinKind.Inner),
```

6. Create two new parameters with a Date data type: Starting Week End Date and Ending Week End Date:
    - For now, Any value can be used for the Suggested Values property

7. Finally, add a filtering expression to the sales fact table query that reflects both date parameter values:

```
RowFilter = Table.SelectRows(SalesTerritoryJoin,
each [Order Date] >= #"Starting Week End Date" and [Order Date] <=
#"Ending Week End Date")
```

Note that the `RowFilter` variable references the `SalesTerritoryJoin` variable from step 5. At this point, the internet sales fact table query must respect both the sales territory parameter (via inner join) and the two date parameters. Both operations, the join and the filter, are merged into a single SQL statement and executed by the source database per the *How it works...* section.

- The parameter values, optionally submitted from a template, are passed into the M query retrieval process:

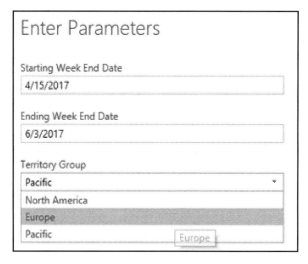

Timeframe and Territory Group Parameters from Report View

8. Per the prior example, modify the values and click on **Apply Changes** to refresh the queries and validate the parameters.

How it works...

Query folding of parameter value filters

- Both the join and the filter conditions applied via parameter values in these examples are converted into SQL statements for processing by the source database.

- Click on **View Native Query** on the final step or expression of the sales fact table query to view the SQL statement:

```
    from [BI].[vFact_InternetSales] as [_]
    where [_].[Order Date] >= convert(datetime2, '2017-05-06 00:00:00') and [_].[Order Date] <= convert(datetime2, '2017-06-03 0
) as [$Outer]
inner join
(
    select distinct [_].[SalesTerritoryKey]
    from [BI].[vDim_SalesTerritory] as [_]
    where [_].[Sales Territory Group] = 'Europe' and [_].[Sales Territory Group] is not null
) as [$Inner] on ([$Outer].[SalesTerritoryKey] = [$Inner].[SalesTerritoryKey])
```

SQL Query generated by by the Multi-Parameter Query Filters example

There's more...

Power BI Service support

- Currently, parameters cannot be created or edited in the Power BI service
- The parameter values configured when published will be used for each refresh

Preserving report metadata with Power BI templates

Power BI templates can be created from Power BI Desktop files as a means of providing users and other report authors with access to pre-defined metadata such as M queries, DAX measures, model relationships, and report visualizations. As the template files do not contain actual data, they're very lightweight and, for import mode models, data is only retrieved when the template is opened. Additionally, if query parameters have been configured, a user interface is provided for entering parameter values and these parameters can be integrated with the source queries and other components of the dataset.

In this recipe, a parameter and supporting query is added to a Power BI Desktop file to support the distribution of a Power BI template.

Getting ready

Per the previous recipe's *Getting ready* section, distributing templates can introduce version control and manageability issues. Therefore, prior to designing parameters and creating templates, confirm that the report authoring capabilities of Power BI Desktop against a published dataset in Power BI is insufficient. If insufficient, identify the modifications that users need to implement, such as additional data sources or query transformations, and consider if these changes can be implemented in the existing dataset.

1. Identify the scope and goals of the templates, such as the years of data and specific dimensions needed:
    * Parameters will be designed based on these requirements to retrieve the minimum amount of data needed

How to do it...

In this example, the goal is to provide Power BI templates that retrieve a maximum of two years of sales data relative to the current date, and that only retrieve data for a single customer country.

Template parameters

1. Open the Power BI Desktop file and click on **New Parameter** from the **Manage Parameters** dropdown in the Query Editor.
2. Create a date type parameter with the name Start Date and a text parameter named Customer Country.
3. Both parameters should be **Required**, and the **Suggested Values** property can be left at **Any value**:
    * Enter a valid current value for each parameter
4. Create a query for the customer key values that references the Customer Country parameter:
    * Name this query CustomerCountryKeys and disable the load:

```
let CountryParamFilter = Table.SelectRows(Customer, each [Country]
= #"Customer Country"),
CustomerKeys = Table.SelectColumns(CountryParamFilter,
{"CustomerKey"})
in CustomerKeys
```

Since the `CustomerKey` column is the surrogate key used in the customer to sales relationship, it's not necessary to apply any transformations to remove duplicates, as each value is already unique.

5. Create a query that returns a list of the unique customer countries:

```
let CountriesList = Customer[Country],
DistinctCountriesList =
List.RemoveNulls(List.Distinct(CountriesList))
in DistinctCountriesList
```

- Disable the load for this query

6. Click on **Manage Parameters** and associate this query with the **Suggested Values** for the **Customer Country** parameter.

7. Create a query to return the date from two years prior to the current date. Name this query `TwoYearsPriorToToday`:

```
Date.AddYears(CurrentDateQry,-2)
```

- The `CurrentDateQry` referenced is defined as follows:

```
DateTime.Date(DateTime.LocalNow())
```

- Disable the load for this query

8. Create a list query that returns the week ending dates later than or equal to the query `TwoYearsPriorToToday`:

```
let DateFilter = Table.SelectRows(Date, each [Calendar Week Ending
Date] >= TwoYearsPriorToToday),
DistinctList = List.Distinct(DateFilter[Calendar Week Ending Date])
in DistinctList
```

9. Associate this query with the **Suggested Values** of the **Start Date** parameter and disable its load.

10. Modify the internet sales fact table query to respect the parameter selections:

```
let Source = AdWorksProd,
ISales = Source{[Schema = "BI", Item =
"vFact_InternetSales"]}[Data],
 CustomerKeyJoin = Table.Join(ISales,
"CustomerKey",CustomerCountryKeys,"CustomerKey",JoinKind.Inner),
 OrderDateFilter = Table.SelectRows
(CustomerKeyJoin, each [Order Date] >= #"Start Date" and [Order
Date] <= CurrentDateQry)
in OrderDateFilter
```

- An inner join of the view used to load the `Internet Sales` fact table with the `CustomerCountryKeys` query in effect filters the internet sales rows by the country parameter. For example, a parameter selection of United States will filter the `CustomerCountryKeys` query to only include these customer rows and the inner join to this filtered query will remove internet sales rows associated with other customer countries.
- The `Start Date` parameter is passed to the `Table.SelectRows()` function to apply the additional parameter filter.

11. Right-click the final variable step (`OrderDateFilter`) of the internet sales query and select **View Native Query**:

```
    [_].[Product Standard Cost]
    from [BI].[vFact_InternetSales] as [_]
    where [_].[Order Date] >= convert(datetime2, '2017-04-29 00:00:00') and [_].[Order Date] <= convert(datetime
) as [$Outer]
inner join
(
    select [_].[Customer Key] as [CustomerKey]
    from [BI].[vDim Customer] as [_]
    where [_].[Customer Country] = 'United States' and [_].[Customer Country] is not null
) as [$Inner] on ([$Outer].[CustomerKey] = [$Inner].[CustomerKey])
```

Native Query of Parameterized Internet Sales Query

The inner join and the `Where` clause of the SQL statement both implement the parameter steps added to the M query. The `United States` value reflects the current value of the `Customer Country` parameter.

12. Click on **Close and Apply** and return to the Report View.
13. Use the **Edit Parameters** option of the **Edit Queries** dropdown to validate the lists of parameter values and the filters.
14. Save the Power BI Desktop file (`.pbix`).

Export template

1. From the **File** menu of Report View, select **Export to Power BI template**.
2. Optionally, give the template a description describing the parameter logic.
3. Choose a folder path for the template (`.pbit`).
4. Open the template file to observe performance, file size, and confirm that all required tables of the model are retrieved:

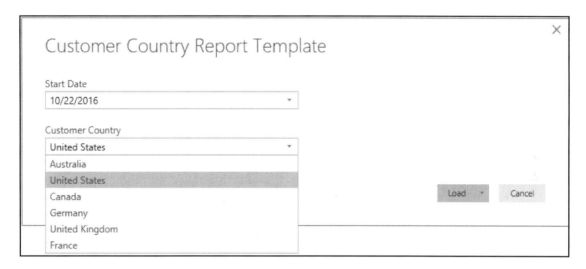

Parameter Dialog when opening the Power BI template (.PBIT)

5. Click on **Load** and save the file as a new Power BI Desktop (`.pbix`) file.

Converting static queries into dynamic functions

In addition to the standard library of functions available to M queries, user defined functions can be created to encapsulate the logic of queries for dynamic application against parameter inputs. Similar to SQL stored procedures, M functions can be created with or without input parameters and these parameters can be required or optional. Additionally, as functions are values in the M language, just like table and list values, they can be invoked on demand and in multiple areas within a given Power BI data model.

In this recipe, a function is created to support the integration of a list of employee IDs maintained outside the data warehouse environment. The function accepts the employee ID values as parameter inputs and retrieves related column values.

How to do it...

In this example, a business team maintains a list of employee IDs in an Excel workbook and wants the ability to access several columns from the employee dimension table in the data model related to these IDs.

1. Create an M query that retrieves the employee IDs from the Excel workbook:

```
let Source =
Excel.Workbook(File.Contents("J:\Finance\TeamFiles\EmployeeIDs.xlsx
"), null, true),
ExcelTable = Source{[Item="EmployeeTbl",Kind="Table"]}[Data],
TypeConversion = Table.TransformColumnTypes(ExcelTable,{{"Employee
Alternate Key", type text}}),
RemoveNullsAndDuplicates =
Table.Distinct(Table.SelectRows(TypeConversion, each [Employee
Alternate Key] <> null))
in RemoveNullsAndDuplicates
```

- The employee IDs are stored in an Excel table object (Kind="Table") for easier access from external applications
- Three M transformation functions are applied to protect the integration process: a data type conversion to text, the removal of any null values, and the removal of any duplicates

2. Name this query EmployeeKeysAdHoc and disable its load to the model.

Data cleansing operations are always recommended when importing from files and unstructured data sources. Additionally, per the *Parameterizing your data sources* recipe in this chapter, parameters can be created and substituted for the folder path and the name of the Excel workbook file.

3. Create a function that retrieves the required Employee column values for a given Employee ID input parameter:

```
(EmployeeCode as text) =>
let EmployeeDimFilter = Table.SelectRows(Employee,
each [Employee Alternate Key] = EmployeeCode and [Employee Row End
Date] = null),
EmployeeColumnSelection = Table.SelectColumns
(EmployeeDimFilter, {"Employee Name", "Employee Department",
"Employee Email Address"})
in EmployeeColumnSelection
```

- The `EmployeeCode` parameter is first defined as a required text type input parameter. The parameter is then used in the `EmployeeDimFilter` expression as part of a `Table.SelectRows()` filtering function.

Given that the Employee table has a Type 2 slowly changing dimension logic applied with multiple rows possible per employee, it's necessary to filter for the current employee row per the `EmployeeDimFilter` variable expression (`[Employee Row End Date = null]`). Setting this filter condition ensures that only the current or 'active' row (no end date) for the employee is returned.

Slowly changing dimension logic that inserts and/or updates rows for core dimensions such as products and employees as these entities change is an essential feature of data warehouses. Power BI dataset designers must be aware of this logic as represented in dimension columns such as surrogate keys and alternate or business keys and develop M and DAX expressions accordingly.

- With the filters applied, a simple `Table.SelectColumns()` is used to retrieve the three required columns

4. Name this function `EmployeeDetailFunction`. A formula icon in the Query Editor will identify the value as a function.
5. Create a new blank query that references the query `EmployeeKeysAdHoc` created in the first step of this recipe:
    - Name this new query `EmployeeIDLookup`

6. Add an expression that invokes the `EmployeeDetailFunction` in a `Table.AddColumn()` function:

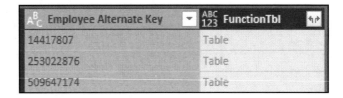

The Employee Alternate Key column from the Excel workbook is used as the parameter input to the EmployeeDetailFunction

- A Table value will be returned for each row per the preceding screenshot. Each table contains columns for the given employee ID from the Excel workbook.

7. Use the `Table.ExpandTableColumn()` function to expose the three columns from the `EmployeeDetailFunction`:

```
let PassKeysToFunction = Table.AddColumn(EmployeeKeysAdHoc,
"FunctionTbl", each EmployeeDetailFunction([Employee Alternate
Key])),
ExpandColumns = Table.ExpandTableColumn(PassKeysToFunction,
"FunctionTbl",
{"Employee Name", "Employee Department", "Employee Email Address"},
{"Employee Name", "Employee Department", "Employee Email Address"})
in ExpandColumns
```

- Per the M expression code, the `EmployeeDetailFunction` accepts the values from the `Employee Alternate Key` column as its parameter inputs

8. Click on **Close and Apply**, and build a simple table visual in Power BI to display the integrated results:

Employee Alternate Key	Employee Name	Employee Department	Employee Email Address
10708100	Frank Miller	Production	frank1@adventure-works.com
367453993	Frank Pellow	Purchasing	frank2@adventure-works.com
947029962	Frank Martinez	Production	frank3@adventure-works.com
295971920	Fred Northup	Production	fred0@adventure-works.com

The EmployeeID Lookup Query Loaded to the Model and Visualized via the standard table visual

- Changes to the list of employee keys in the Excel workbook will be reflected in the Power BI report with each refresh

 Additional columns and logic can be added to the function and, as the function is only metadata, it can be used in other data transformation scenarios, in this model or in other models with access to the Employee table.

There's more...

Local resource usage

The function in this recipe (Excel-based list) as well as functions applied against relational database sources that support query folding still requires local resources of the M engine:

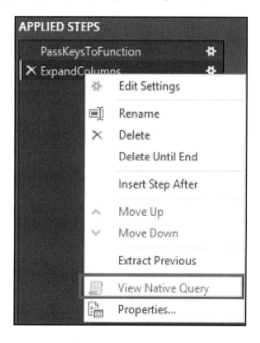

No Query Folding for Invoked M Function

Given local resource usage and the iterative nature of functions, try to limit or avoid the use of functions against many rows, as well as functions with complex, multi-step logic. In this recipe, for example, the list of employees was very small and the function only selected a few columns from a small dimension table. Since join functions (`Table.Join()`, `Table.NestedJoin()`) and filter expressions are folded back to relational database sources, design query processes that achieve the same results as functions, but without row-by-row iterations and local or gateway resource usage.

Parameterizing your data sources

Parameters can be used to store data source information, such as server and database names, file paths, filenames, and even input parameters to SQL stored procedures. With multiple queries leveraging the same M query parameter values, implementing changes, such as migrations from development or QA environments to production environments, becomes very straightforward.

Two examples of parameterized data sources are described in this recipe, including the server and database of an SQL Server database and the directory path and file name for an Excel workbook. Additionally, M query parameters are assigned to the input parameters of a SQL stored procedure.

Getting ready

1. Identify the components of data sources that are subject to change and, if available, the list of possible values for these parameters, such as servers, databases, Windows directories, and filenames.

2. Create a group folder in Power BI Desktop to store parameter values and related queries:

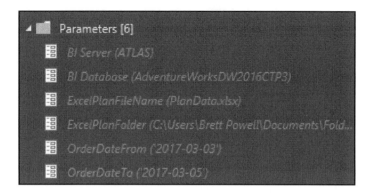

Query Group of Parameter Values in Query Editor

- Queries will reference these query names and the values of each parameter can be changed by selecting each icon

How to do it...

SQL Server database

1. Create two parameters of text data types, BI Server and BI Database, from the Query Editor in Power BI Desktop:
    - Click on **New Parameter** from the **Manage Parameters** dropdown on the **Home** tab

2. If known, enter the list of alternative values for these parameters:

SQL Database Name Parameter with two Suggested Values

3. Create a new query that accepts the server and database parameters as inputs to
   the `Sql.Database()` function for connecting to SQL Server:

```
let Source = Sql.Database(#"BI Server", #"BI Database") in Source
```

4. Name this query `AdWorksParam` and reference this source query in other queries
   in the model, such as `Employee`:

```
let Source = AdWorksParam,
Employee = Source{[Schema = "dbo", Item = "DimEmployee"]}[Data] in
Employee
```

5. Alter the value of one of the parameters (`Server` or `Database`) to confirm that the query results change:

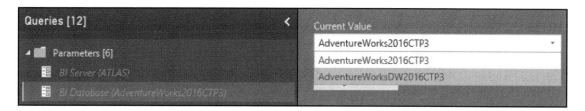

Switching Current Value of Database Name Parameter in Query Editor

- Per prior recipes in this chapter, a parameter value (of Text type) can also be entered into the input box

Excel filename and path

1. Create two parameters of text data types, `ExcelPlanFolder` and `ExcelPlanFileName`:
   - The current value of the Excel file parameter should include the extension (`.xlsx`), and the current value of the folder should include the complete path to the Excel file (all subfolders)

2. Create a new query, which merges these two parameters into a single text value. Name this query `ExcelPlanQry`:

```
let ExcelBudget = ExcelPlanFolder & "\" & ExcelPlanFileName
in ExcelBudget
```

3. Reference the `ExcelPlanQry` in the query (or queries) used to access the Excel workbook:

```
let Source = Excel.Workbook(File.Contents(ExcelPlanQry), null,
true),
ExcelBudgetTbl = Source{[Item="BudgetTbl",Kind="Table"]}[Data]
in ExcelBudgetTbl
```

- Any changes to the name of the Excel file or its folder location can now be applied to the parameters:

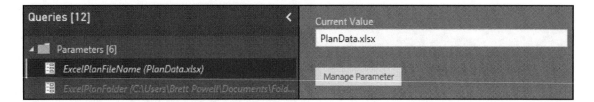

Excel Workbook File Parameter Value

Stored procedure input parameters

In this example, a simple stored procedure with two input parameters is used by the sales fact table query:

```
CREATE PROC [BI].[spFactInternetSales]
 @orderdatefrom AS DATE,
 @orderdateto AS DATE
AS
SELECT * FROM BI.vFact_InternetSales AS F
WHERE F.[Order Date] BETWEEN @orderdatefrom AND @orderdateto
```

1. Create two parameters of text data types, OrderDateFrom and OrderDateTo.
2. Enter a current value in the non-ambiguous form YYYY-MM-DD or YYYYMMDD for the DATE type in SQL Server.
3. Modify the M query used to execute the stored procedure to pass these parameters from Power BI:

```
let Source = AdWorksProd,
SalesFactProc = Value.NativeQuery(Source,
"EXECUTE BI.spFactInternetSales @orderdatefrom = "& OrderDateFrom &
"," &" @orderdateto = "& OrderDateTo)
in SalesFactProc
```

- Ampersands and double quotes are used to construct a single query string, inclusive of the parameter values

4. Change the Current Value of one or both of the input parameters and grant approval to the new native database query:

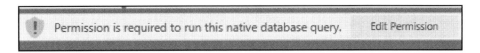

Click on Edit Permission and then 'Run' to approve of the revised stored procedure parameters

Per the *Filtering queries with parameters* recipe, shared earlier in this chapter, filter (the WHERE clause) parameters defined in M queries are converted into SQL statements via Query Folding. Additionally, per Chapter 2, *Accessing and Retrieving Data*), any transformations applied after the Value.NativeQuery() function will not be folded back to the source system.

Generating a list of parameter values via queries

The parameter values available for selection, such as dates and product subcategories, can also be parameterized via M queries. This data-driven approach to parameters exposes the current or relevant values from data sources and avoids error-prone manual entry, and stale or outdated values.

This recipe includes two examples of query-driven parameter values. One example retrieves the week end dates from the prior two years and another selects the product subcategories of a product category.

How to do it...

Dynamic date parameter query

1. In the Query Editor, create a new blank query and name it WeekEndDatesParamList.

2. Reference the existing date dimension query and use standard M functions to select the week ending date column and the dynamic `Calendar Month Status` column described in `Chapter 5`, *Creating Power BI Dashboards* and `Chapter 6`, *Getting Serious with Date Intelligence*:

```
let DateColSelect = Table.SelectColumns(Date,{"Calendar Month
Status","Calendar Week Ending Date"}),
DateFilter = Table.SelectRows(DateColSelect,
each [Calendar Month Status] = "Current Calendar Month" or
[Calendar Month Status] = "Prior Calendar Month"),
ListOfDates = List.Distinct(DateFilter[Calendar Week Ending Date])
in ListOfDates
```

- The `List.Distinct()` function is necessary, as only List values (not tables) can be used by M parameters

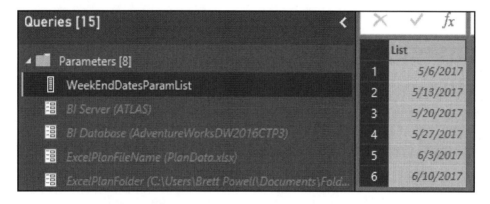

The 'WeekEndDatesParamList' query returning a list of week end date values for use by date parameters

3. Right-click on the `WeekEndDatesParamList` query and disable the load, but include the query in report refresh.

4. Either create a new date type parameter or click on **Manage Parameter** of an existing date type parameter:
    - See the *Filtering Queries with Parameters* recipe for details on associating parameters with queries

5. From the **Suggested Values** dropdown, select **Query** and then choose the new List query created earlier:

WeekEndDatesParamList used as the Query source to a Date Parameter

6. From Report View, click on **Edit Parameters** from the **Edit Queries** dropdown on the **Home** tab.

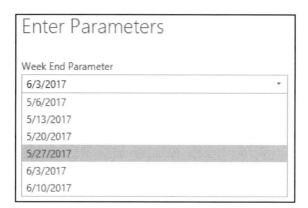

Week End Parameter Values Exposed in the Report View

 Business users often prefer to remain in the Report View rather than access the Data or Relationships Views and particularly the more complex Query Editor interface. The **Edit Parameters** option from the Report View and other modeling options available in Report view, such as hierarchies and groups, are helpful in self-service deployments of Power BI.

- As the report (and the list query) is refreshed, the parameter selections are updated

Product subcategories parameter query

1. Create a new blank query titled `BikeSubcategoriesParamList`.
2. Reference the existing Products dimension query and apply filters to return a List of distinct bike subcategories:

```
let Source = Product,
SelectCols = Table.SelectColumns(Source,{"Product
Category","Product Subcategory"}),
SelectRows = Table.SelectRows(SelectCols, each [Product Category] =
"Bikes" and [Product Subcategory] <> null),
DistinctSubcats = List.RemoveNulls(List.Distinct(SelectRows[Product
Subcategory]))
in DistinctSubcats
```

- Similar to the week ending date example, standard M table functions are used to prepare a filtered table of the required columns, and `List.Distinct()` returns a list value for the parameter to access
    - `List.RemoveNulls()` further protects the query from exposing any null values to the user interface

The Three Subcategories of the Bikes Category Returned by the List Query

3. Associate the list query with the **Suggested Values** of a **Product Subcategory** parameter.

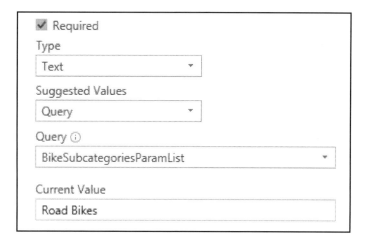

Bike Subcategories Parameter List Query

4. If necessary, associate the **Product Subcategory** parameter with queries used to load the data model, per the *Filtering queries with parameters* recipe earlier in this chapter.

5. Disable the load of the list query and validate that query results are impacted by parameter value changes.

There's more...

DirectQuery support

List queries can also be used to support the parameter values of DirectQuery data models:

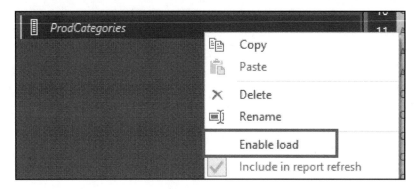

List Query Used for Suggested Parameter Values in DirectQuery Model with Enable load disabled

The list query, like all list queries in DirectQuery data models, must not be loaded to the data model

Capturing user selections with parameter tables

An alternative method of providing parameter functionality to users of Power BI reports is via dedicated parameter tables. In this approach, the parameter values of a table are either computed during the dataset refresh process, or are loaded as a one-time manual operation, such as in the Virtual Table Relationship recipe in Chapter 3, *Building a Power BI Data Model*. DAX measures reference this parameter table and other tables and expressions of the model to enrich the self-service analysis experience and support Power BI report development.

The example in this recipe involves providing simple visibility to four alternative scenarios to the baseline annual sales plan--10 and 20 percent above and below the baseline plan. An inline set of scenario values are embedded in the data model and DAX measures are used to capture filter context, such as business user selections, and compute the corresponding scenario logic.

How to do it...

Sales plan growth scenarios

1. Open a Power BI Desktop model locally, and from the **Modeling** tab of the Report View, click on **New Table**.
2. Use the `DATATABLE()` DAX function to create a calculated table with the scenario name, scenario value, and a sort key:

```
Plan Scenarios = DATATABLE
("Plan Scenario",STRING, "Var to Plan",DOUBLE, "Scenario
Sort",INTEGER,
 {{"Plan",1,3},{"10% Above Plan",1.1,2},{"20% Above Plan",1.2,1},
{"10% Below Plan",.9,4},
{"20% Below Plan",.8,5}})
```

Ideally, the new scenario table can be persisted within a data warehouse and the Power BI solution can be resilient to changes in scenario names and values. Per other recipes, using DAX to create tables or columns should generally be thought of as a secondary and temporary option, such as in proof-of-concept scenarios or in narrow, static use cases, such as a Power BI model owned and maintained by a business team.

- The column names and types are declared and each row is enclosed in curly braces, like List values in M queries

3. Select the new table (`Plan Scenarios`) in Data View and set the `Plan Scenario` column to sort by the `Scenario Sort` column:

Plan Scenario	Var to Plan	Scenario Sort
Plan	1	3
10% Above Plan	1.1	2
20% Above Plan	1.2	1
10% Below Plan	0.9	4
20% Below Plan	0.8	5

Plan Scenarios Table in Data View

4. Right-click on the `Scenario Sort` and `Var to Plan` columns and select **Hide in Report View**.

5. Return to Report View and create a measure that retrieves the filter context of the `Plan Scenario` column:

```
Sales Plan Scenario Filter Branch =
SWITCH(TRUE(),
NOT(ISFILTERED('Plan Scenarios'[Plan Scenario])),"No Selection",
NOT(HASONEFILTER('Plan Scenarios'[Plan Scenario])),"Multiple
Selections","Single Selection")
```

- The intermediate measure simplifies the parameter selection measure by computing one of the three possible filter contexts: **No Selection**, **Single Selection**, or **Multiple Selections**. Hide this measure from the **Fields** list.

6. Now create a measure that dynamically calculates a budget/plan amount based on the filter context (slicers, visuals):

```
Internet Sales Plan Scenario =
VAR FilterContext = [Sales Plan Scenario Filter Branch] RETURN
SWITCH(TRUE(),
FilterContext = "Single Selection",MIN('Plan Scenarios'[Var to
Plan]) * [Internet Sales Plan Amount],
FilterContext = "No Selection",[Internet Sales Plan Amount],
FilterContext = "Multiple Selections", BLANK())
```

The scenario measure passes the intermediate measure into a variable and leverages the existing `Internet Sales Plan Amount` measure. If a single scenario selection has been made, such as on a slicer visual, then only a single value will be active in the Plan Scenarios table and this will be retrieved via the `MIN()` function. Generally, defaulting to a standard or base value if no selections have been made and returning a blank if multiple selections are made, is appropriate to minimize complexity and user confusion. Per the *There's more...* section, however, additional measures and logic can be added to support the comparison of multiple scenarios when multiple scenarios are selected.

7. Apply a currency format and create report visualizations that use the new measure and `Plan Scenarios` table:

Plan Scenario	Accessories	Bikes	Clothing	Total
20% Above Plan	$346,396	$7,096,765	$162,065	$7,605,226
10% Above Plan	$317,529	$6,505,368	$148,559	$6,971,457
Plan	$288,663	$5,913,971	$135,054	$6,337,688
10% Below Plan	$259,797	$5,322,574	$121,549	$5,703,919
20% Below Plan	$230,930	$4,731,177	$108,043	$5,070,150
Total	$288,663	$5,913,971	$135,054	$6,337,688

Plan Scenario slicer:
- 20% Above Plan
- 10% Above Plan
- Plan
- 10% Below Plan
- 20% Below Plan

A Slicer visual of the Plan Scenario column and Matrix visual of the Internet Sales Plan Scenario Measure

A standard slicer is the most straightforward method of exposing the parameter values in reports and the descending order of scenario values (based on the Sort By column) makes the slicer intuitive for users. Per the matrix visual, the `Plan Scenario` column can also be used within report visuals. Additionally, any dimension table with a relationship to the plan/budget fact table, such as the `Product` table in this example, can be used in report visualizations with the new scenario measure as well.

- Visual level filters can be applied to only display one or a few of the five scenario values:

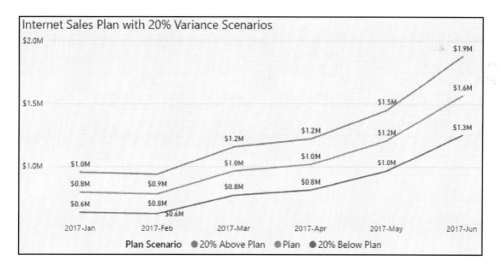

Line Chart Visual with the two 10% Variance Scenario's Excluded via Visual level filters

Disconnected parameter tables is one of the more powerful and easy to implement patterns in Power BI with many published examples available such as enabling the user to filter reports for their own TOP criteria (ie Top 5, 10, 15, 20) through slicers. A more dynamic and analytical approach involves computing parameter values via M queries with each refresh, such as the standard deviation, median, and average of prices, and then using these query results in DAX measures.

There's more...

Scenario specific measures

It may be necessary to create scenario-specific measures such that multiple scenarios can be visualized concurrently

```
Internet Sales Plan 20% Above Plan =
VAR FilterContext = [Sales Plan Scenario Filter Branch]
VAR ScenarioValue = [Internet Sales Plan Amount]*CALCULATE(MIN('Plan
Scenarios'[Var to Plan]),FILTER(ALL('Plan Scenarios'),'Plan Scenarios'[Plan
Scenario] = "20% Above Plan"))
VAR PlanScenario = "20% Above Plan"
RETURN SWITCH(TRUE(), FilterContext = "No Selection",ScenarioValue,
CONTAINS(VALUES('Plan Scenarios'[Plan Scenario]),'Plan Scenarios'[Plan
Scenario], PlanScenario), ScenarioValue,BLANK())
```

This measure defaults to its scenario (**20% Above Plan**) if no scenario filter has been applied and, more importantly, will also return its 20% above plan value when the **20% Above Plan** scenario is one of multiple scenario filter selections. A blank will be returned if a scenario filter has been applied and **20% Above Plan** is not included in the filter context.

Building a forecasting process with What if analysis capabilities

Power BI can be used to directly support the creation of forecasts, budgets, and other planned values of future business measures and events. The relationships and logic of these datasets, which are commonly implemented in Excel formulas and maintained by business teams, can be efficiently replicated within a dedicated Power BI Desktop file. Isolating the What if input variables from the forecast creation, storage, and visualization in Power BI enables users to more easily create, analyze, and collaborate on business forecasts.

In this recipe, a Power Desktop model is used to ingest forecast variable inputs from Excel and process these variables with a dynamic transformation process to generate a forecast table available for visualization. This design enables business teams to rapidly iterate on forecasts, and ultimately supports an official or approved forecast or Plan that could be integrated in other data models.

Getting ready

1. Identify the measures and grain of the target dataset produced by the forecast process, such as `Sales` and `Sales Orders per Calendar Month`, `Sales Region`, and `Product Subcategory`.
2. Determine the logic of the current forecast or budget process, including data sources, variable inputs, and calculations.

 Typically, a forecast process will have a direct relationship to actual or historical data sources, such as a series of monthly reports or a SQL query with results exported to Excel. It's important to thoroughly study and document this process, including Excel formulas and any manual processes, to provide a seamless transition to a new forecasting tool.

How to do it...

Forecast variables from Excel

1. Create an Excel workbook that contains tables of the input variables and scenario metadata such as Forecast Name:

Forecast Name	Base Forecast
Forecast Year	2018

Total Sales Growth: Base Forecast												
YOY Growth %	Jan	Feb	Mar	Apr	May	Jun	Jul	Aug	Sep	Oct	Nov	Dec
Internet Sales	4.0%	8.0%	5.0%	7.0%	6.0%	8.0%	9.0%	6.5%	9.0%	10.0%	11.0%	12.0%

Sales Group Allocation												
Group	Jan	Feb	Mar	Apr	May	Jun	Jul	Aug	Sep	Oct	Nov	Dec
North America	40.0%	40.0%	40.0%	40.0%	40.0%	40.0%	40.0%	40.0%	40.0%	40.0%	40.0%	40.0%
Europe	50.0%	50.0%	50.0%	50.0%	50.0%	50.0%	50.0%	50.0%	50.0%	50.0%	50.0%	50.0%
Pacific	10.0%	10.0%	10.0%	10.0%	10.0%	10.0%	10.0%	10.0%	10.0%	10.0%	10.0%	10.0%
Total	100%	100%	100%	100%	100%	100%	100%	100%	100%	100%	100%	100%

Sample Forecast Variable Input Tables from an Excel Workbook

In this example, the forecasting tool computes the internet sales for the next year at the grain of sales region by month. An overall growth rate variable over the previous year period serves as the starting point and this amount is then allocated to the Sales Groups (Europe, North America, and Pacific) and then to to the countries within these Sales Groups, and finally to individual sales regions within countries based on allocation variables. The Excel tables provide a simple, familiar interface for adjusting the growth rates and allocation percentages among these dimensions.

As an example, suppose that October of the prior year had an overall company sales total of $100. Given the 10% growth variable per the image, $110 would be the planned value for October in the given scenario. North America would be allocated 40% of the $110 ($44) and this $44 would be further distributed between the United States and Canada based on the country allocation variables. Finally, this country level forecast amount is further distributed to sales territories regions of the country based on regional variable inputs. To close this example, the United States is modeled to receive 50% of North American sales ($22) for October and the Southwest region is modeled to receive 60% of the United States sales for October ($13.2).

2. For each table, create named ranges by highlighting the table and clicking on **Define Name** from the **Formulas** tab:

- The **Name Manager** available on the **Formula** tab exposes all the defined names and the cell references:

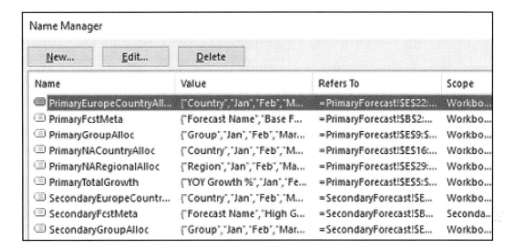

Named Ranges Applied to Forecast Variable Tables

Data validation and integrity can be built into the Excel input workbook such as using **Protect Sheet** from the **Review** tab to only allow the user to select unlocked cells (the variables). Addtionally, the variables can be limited to a range or list of possible values (that is, 0 to 100%) via the **Data Validation** options under the **Data** tab. Moreover, a simple conditional formatting rule can highlight the total row for each table if the sum of the components (for example, regions) doesn't equal 100 percent.

In the following example, the conditional formatting identifies needed revisions to the sales region allocation variables for April and June:

Region	Sales Regional Allocation: North America							
	Jan	Feb	Mar	Apr	May	Jun	Jul	Aug
Central	10.0%	10.0%	10.0%	10.0%	10.0%	10.0%	10.0%	10.0%
Northeast	10.0%	10.0%	10.0%	10.0%	10.0%	10.0%	10.0%	10.0%
Northwest	10.0%	10.0%	10.0%	10.0%	10.0%	10.0%	10.0%	10.0%
Southeast	10.0%	10.0%	10.0%	9.0%	10.0%	10.0%	10.0%	10.0%
Southwest	60.0%	60.0%	60.0%	60.0%	60.0%	61.0%	60.0%	60.0%
Total	100%	100%	100%	99%	100%	101%	100%	100%

Excel conditional formatting identifies two incorrect variable inputs

Optionally, per the example in this recipe, a second group of variable input tables can be included in the workbook to allow the users to create a second or alternative forecast scenario. This enables the team to visualize and more easily compare multiple forecast scenarios based on the different input variables provided such as comparing a Base Plan to a High Growth Plan.

Power BI Desktop forecast model

Source connection and unpivoted forecast tables

1. Create a new Power BI Desktop model file and establish a data source query to the data warehouse or source system.
2. Create essential dimension and fact table M queries, such as `Date`, `Sales Territory`, and `Internet Sales`.
3. Create a connection to the Excel forecast file and build queries that unpivot the columns of each forecast table.

See the *Parameterizing your data sources* recipe in this chapter for examples of storing data source information such as folder paths and filenames as parameter values. This approach is recommended for all data sources and is especially valuable with file data sources maintained by business teams on network directories. The owner of the Power BI forecasting file (PBIX) can easily revise the data source parameter to update all dependent M queries.

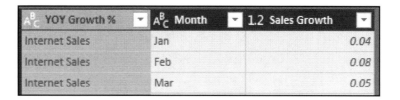

An M query that unpivots the columns of an Excel forecast table and applies data types

An example forecast table connection query (Primary-TotalGrowth) with columns unpivoted:

```
let Source = ExcelForecastItems,
 PrimaryGrowth =
Source{[Name="PrimaryTotalGrowth",Kind="DefinedName"]}[Data],
 PromoteHeaders = Table.PromoteHeaders(PrimaryGrowth),
 UnpivotColumns = Table.UnpivotOtherColumns(PromoteHeaders, {"YOY Growth
%"}, "Month", "Sales Growth"),
 ColumnTypes = Table.TransformColumnTypes(UnpivotColumns,{{"YOY Growth %",
type text},{"Month", type text},{"Sales Growth", type number}}) in
ColumnTypes
```

The `ExcelForecastItems` is a dedicated source query that exposes the tables of the source, similar to the `AdWorksProd` SQL Server query in other recipes. Observe that the `Name` and `DefinedName` fields are used to identify the record of this table, similar to the `Schema` and `Item` fields used with the SQL Server database source query. `UnpivotOtherColumns()` converts each month column into a row and applies column names for Month and Sales Growth.

Apply the forecast to historical values

1. Develop a dynamic `Sales by Month` query to be used by the forecast variables. The query must use the current year history if it's available or, if the month isn't completed in the current year, use the prior year value.
2. To simplify this query, create a `PriorYearMonthlySales` query and a `CurrentYearMonthlySalesQuery`:

Current and Prior Year Queries used by the PrimarySalesForecastBase query

The following expression of the `PriorYearMonthlySales` query only retrieves the prior year months that haven't been completed in the current year:

```
let CurrentYear = Date.Year(DateTime.Date(DateTime.LocalNow())),
CurrentMonth = Date.Month((DateTime.LocalNow())),
PYJoin = Table.Join(#"Internet Sales","Order Date",Date,
"Date",JoinKind.Inner),
PYFilter = Table.SelectRows(PYJoin, each [Calendar Year] = CurrentYear-1
and
[Calendar Month Number] >= CurrentMonth),
PYGroup = Table.Group(PYFilter,{"Calendar Year", "Calendar Month"},
{"Sales", each List.Sum([Sales Amount]), Currency.Type}) in PYGroup
```

- The `Table.SelectRows()` filter function is used in the `PriorYear` and `CurrentYear` queries to ensure that the total (merge) of the two queries always equals the full 12 months. For example, in June of 2017, only January through May would be retrieved by the `Current Year` query, with the remaining months retrieved by the Prior Year query.
- The `PrimarySalesForecastBase` query combines the current and prior year queries via `Table.Combine()` resulting in 12 rows.

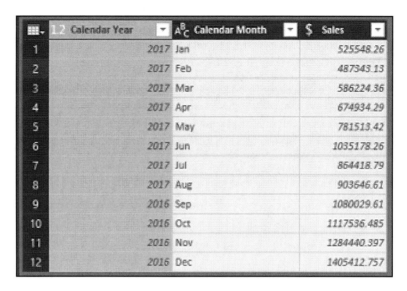

History Variable of the PrimarySalesForecastBase query

The combined table includes current year sales for months that have completed in the current year and prior year sales for any future or incomplete months of the current year.

- This table is then joined to the `Primary-TotalGrowth` query to allow for the multiplication of the growth rate by the historical sales value for the given month:

```
let History =
Table.Combine({CurrentYearMonthlySales,PriorYearMonthlySales}),
JoinForecast = Table.NestedJoin(History, "Calendar Month", #"Primary-
TotalGrowth","Month", "Fcst Column", JoinKind.Inner),
 ForecastColumns = Table.ExpandTableColumn(JoinForecast, "Fcst Column",
{"Sales Growth"}, {"Sales Growth"}),
 MonthlyForecast = Table.AddColumn(ForecastColumns, "Forecast Sales", each
([Sales Growth]+1) * [Sales], Currency.Type) in MonthlyForecast
```

The final step (`MonthlyForecast`) results in a `Forecast Sales` column populated at the monthly gain. This value can then be allocated to sales groups, countries, and regions based on scenario variables to produce the forecast table.

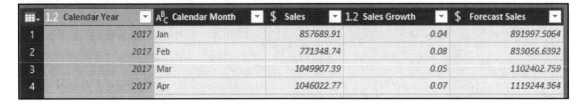

1.2 Calendar Year	A♭C Calendar Month	$ Sales	1.2 Sales Growth	$ Forecast Sales
2017	Jan	857689.91	0.04	891997.5064
2017	Feb	771348.74	0.08	833056.6392
2017	Mar	1049907.39	0.05	1102402.759
2017	Apr	1046022.77	0.07	1119244.364

The PrimarySalesForecastBase Query Integrates the dynamic Current and Prior Year grouped queries with the Forecast Query

- The `PrimarySalesForecastBase` query contains 12 rows and the `Forecast Sales` column, which can be allocated to the `Sales Groups`, `Countries`, and `Regions`.

Allocate the forecast according to the dimension variable inputs

The final forecast query that's loaded to the data model for analysis and visualization will contain 120 rows in this example. This represents 12 months for the 6 regions in North America, 3 regions in Europe, and 1 Pacific region. If an additional variable were to be added to the forecast logic, such as product category allocation, the row count of the forecast query would be multiplied by the count of distinct values of this dimension.

1. Create integration queries for each member of the highest level of the hierarchy (Europe, Pacific, and North America).
2. Apply the forecast allocation variables at each level in the M queries to construct a common report data structure (which can later be appended together), such as the following `PrimaryEuropeRegions` query:

```
let GroupColumn = Table.AddColumn(#"Primary-EuropeCountries",
"Group", each "Europe", type text),
RegionColumn = Table.AddColumn(GroupColumn, "Region", each
[Country], type text),
RegionJoin = Table.NestedJoin(RegionColumn,{"Group",
"Month"},#"Primary-SalesGroups",{"Group", "Month"},"Sales Group
Column", JoinKind.Inner),
GroupAllocation = Table.ExpandTableColumn(RegionJoin,"Sales Group
Column", {"Sales Allocation"}, {"Sales Group Allocation"}),
ForecastJoin = Table.NestedJoin(GroupAllocation, "Month",
```

```
PrimarySalesForecastBase,"Calendar Month", "Forecast Column",
JoinKind.Inner),
ForecastColumn = Table.ExpandTableColumn(ForecastJoin, "Forecast
Column", {"Forecast Sales"}, {"Total Forecast Sales"}),
EuropeRegionForecast = Table.AddColumn(ForecastColumn, "Forecast
Sales", each
[Sales Allocation]*[Sales Group Allocation]*[Total Forecast Sales],
Currency.Type),
 EuropeColumns = Table.SelectColumns(EuropeRegionForecast,
{"Group", "Country", "Region", "Month", "Forecast Sales"}) in
EuropeColumns
```

The `EuropeRegions` query starts with the allocation at the country level (France, UK, Germany) and adds the group level allocation. With these two allocation percentage columns available, the forecast is also added via join and a `Forecast Sales` column is computed for each country by month (*Total Forecast Sales * Group Allocation * Country Allocation*).

A⁸C Group	A⁸C Country	A⁸C Region	A⁸C Month	$ Forecast Sales
Europe	France	France	Jan	178399.5013
Europe	Germany	Germany	Jan	222999.3766
Europe	United Kingdom	United Kingdom	Jan	44599.87532

The European Forecast Query with Sales Allocated to Country by Month (36 Rows)

3. Create a Forecast query (`Sales Forecast`) that merges the individual hierarchy queries (Europe, North America, Pacific) and applies the forecast metadata (name, year) for the load to the data model:

```
let ForecastYear = #"Forecast Metadata-Primary"[Forecast Year]{0},
ForecastName = #"Forecast Metadata-Primary"[Forecast Name]{0},
PrimaryForecastTable =
Table.Combine({PrimaryEuropeRegions,PrimaryPacificRegions,PrimaryNo
rthAmericaRegions}),
ForecastYearColumn = Table.AddColumn(PrimaryForecastTable,
"ForecastYear", each ForecastYear, Int64.Type),
ForecastNameColumn = Table.AddColumn(ForecastYearColumn, "Forecast
Name", each ForecastName, type text),
MonthColumn = Table.AddColumn(ForecastNameColumn, "Calendar Year-
Mo", each Number.ToText([ForecastYear]) & "-" & [Month], type text)
in MonthColumn
```

The name assigned to the given Forecast in Excel is added as a column as well as the forecast year. `Table.Combine()` builds the 120 row query based on the three Sales Group queries, and a `Calendar Year-Mo` column is created to allow the forecast to be related, via a bridge table, to the `Date` dimension table in the model.

Group	Country	Region	Month	Forecast Sales	ForecastYear	Forecast Name	Calendar Year-Mo
Europe	France	France	Jan	178399.5013	2018	Base Forecast	2018-Jan
Europe	Germany	Germany	Jan	222999.3766	2018	Base Forecast	2018-Jan
Europe	United Kingdom	United Kingdom	Jan	44599.87532	2018	Base Forecast	2018-Jan

The Sales Forecast Query Loaded to the Data Model for Analysis and Visualization

- Only this query should be loaded to the data model; all other queries should only be included in report refresh

If a secondary or additional forecast scenario is to be supported by the tool, duplicate the queries created to support the primary forecast and revise the input variables to reference the secondary/alternative inputs. This implies a second group of Excel tables and named ranges in the forecast input workbook.

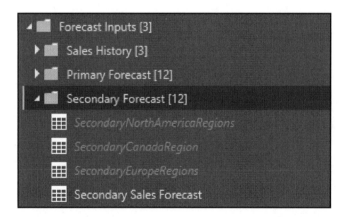

Secondary Sales Forecast Queries

In the absence of a secondary forecast scenario, each refresh will always reflect the latest variables and thus overwrite any prior assumptions. Given the additional M queries and Excel objects, confirm that the secondary forecast or scenario is indeed necessary.

Create relationships, measures, and forecast visuals

1. Create relationships in the model to enable filtering the forecast table(s) by dimension tables:

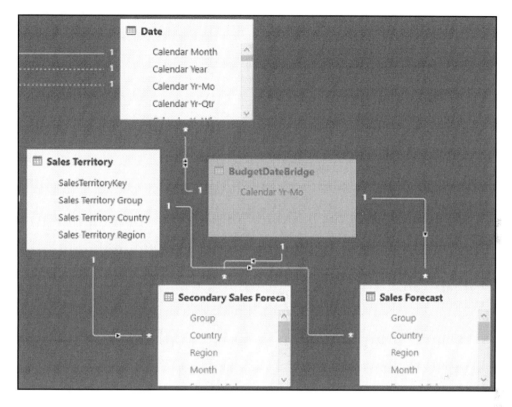

Sales Forecast and a Secondary Sales Forecast table related to the Sales Territory table and the Date table via the hidden BudgetDateBridge table

See the *Building analytics into data models with DAX* recipe in Chapter 3, *Building a Power BI Data Model,* for details on Budget versus Actual data models. The *Actual versus budget model and measures* section of this recipe includes design guidance on bridge tables and relationship types (single or bidirectional cross filtering).

2. Create DAX measures for analyzing the two forecast scenarios supported.

   In addition to sums of sales for both scenarios, FIRSTNONBLANK() is used to retrieve the name given to each scenario (that is, High Growth or Base Plan):

```
Forecast Sales Amount = sum('Sales Forecast'[Forecast Sales])
Secondary Sales Forecast Amount = sum('Secondary Sales
Forecast'[Forecast Sales])
Forecast = FIRSTNONBLANK('Sales Forecast'[Forecast Name],0)
Secondary Forecast Name = FIRSTNONBLANK('Secondary Sales
Forecast'[Forecast Name], 0)
```

3. Create Power BI Report visuals that analyze the forecast or the two forecast scenarios generated:

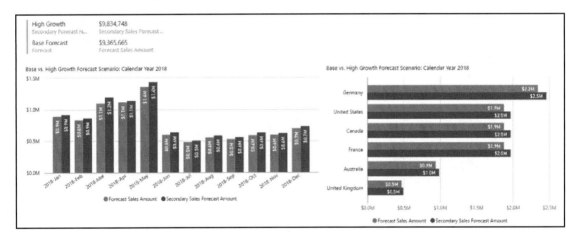

The Base Forecast compared to the 'High Growth' forecast as computed based on the forecast variables from the Excel workbook

Test and deploy forecasting tool

1. Test the forecasting tool by modifying input values in the Excel workbook, such as the allocation percentage for a country or growth for a month, saving the updated file, and then refreshing the Power BI Desktop model to observe the changes reflected in report visuals.

2. As an additional test, choose one of the most granular forecast amounts (forecast for a given region and month) and use the associated input variables (that is, growth rate, allocation percentages) to calculate the same amount manually and confirm that that Power BI process generates the same value.

3. Once tested, the Power BI model could then be deployed to an App Workspace in the Power BI Service and a gateway could be used to support the local workbook data source in scheduled dataset refreshes.

4. Additional Power BI and Excel reports could be created based on a connection to the published model.

Pivot table reports within the Excel variable input workbook via the Power BI Publisher for Excel may be helpful to the user(s) and teams creating forecast scenarios. This allows the user or modeler to iterate quickly on new scenarios by observing the impacts of variable inputs.

How it works...

- The date dimension table query in this recipe is filtered to include dates in the future year (the forecast year)
- The date bridge table (BudgetDateBridge) was also revised to include future months:
    - Typically, per previous recipes, the date dimension is filtered to exclude future dates
- For the North America forecast, conditional logic was applied to handle Canada differently than United States regions:

```
RegionalForecast = Table.AddColumn(TotalForecastColumn, "Forecast
Sales", each
 if [Country] = "United States" then [Sales Allocation] * [Group
Sales Allocation] * [Country Sales Allocation] * [Total Forecast
Sales]
 else if [Country] = "Canada" then [Group Sales Allocation] *
[Country Sales Allocation] * [Total Forecast Sales] else null,
Currency.Type)
```

- Just like the European countries, Canada isn't split into regions, and thus only the Group and Country allocation variables are used to compute its forecast. Only the United States has all three allocation variables applied.

8

Implementing Dynamic User-Based Visibility in Power BI

In this chapter, we will cover the following recipes:

- Capturing the current user context of your Power BI content
- Defining RLS roles and filtering expressions
- Designing dynamic security models in Power BI
- Building dynamic security in DirectQuery data models
- Displaying the current filter context in Power BI reports
- Avoiding manual user clicks with user-based filtering logic

Introduction

Data security in which certain users or groups of users are prevented from viewing a portion of a dataset is often a top requirement in Power BI deployments. Security implementations can range in complexity from mapping user or security group accounts to simple security roles based on a single dimension value, to dynamic, user-based security with dedicated user permissions tables and dynamic DAX functions embedded in the dataset. Given the variety of use cases and the importance of this feature to securely share a dataset across stakeholders, it's important to understand the process and techniques available for developing, testing, and operationalizing data security roles.

In addition to **row level security** (**RLS**) roles, dynamic user-based filter context techniques can also be used to simplify and personalize the user experience. For example, the filter conditions built into reports, as well as the interactive filter selections from end users, can be dynamically updated and displayed in intuitive visuals to aid comprehension. In more advanced scenarios, DAX measures themselves can be filtered based on information about the user interacting with the content to deliver a personalized experience. This chapter contains detailed examples of building and deploying dynamic, user-based security for both import and DirectQuery datasets, as well as developing dynamic filter context functionality to enhance the user experience.

Capturing the current user context of Power BI content

The foundation of dynamic user security and visibility in Power BI is the ability to extract the **user principal name** (**UPN**) or login credential of the business user connected to content in the Power BI service. The USERPRINCIPALNAME() DAX function retrieves this text value and thus enables filter expressions to be applied to the tables of a model in security roles. In addition to RLS roles which override and impact all DAX measures of a dataset, the UPN or "current user" text value can be used by other DAX measures, such as retrieving the UPN prefix and suffix and even filtering other measures per the final recipe in this chapter, *Avoiding manual user clicks with user-based filtering logic*.

In this recipe, DAX measures are added to a data model to dynamically retrieve the UPN, as well as its prefix and suffix. Additional detail on authentication in Power BI and the USERNAME() function, an alternative dynamic DAX function which also retrieves the UPN in the Power BI service, is available in the *How it works...* and *There's more...* sections, respectively.

Getting ready

1. Create a new measure group table via a blank query to organize dynamic user context measures.

2. Use the `Value.NativeQuery()` function to select one blank column, give the table a name such as `Dynamic User Measures`, and disable the include in report refresh property.

```
let DynamicMeasureTbl = Value.NativeQuery(AdWorksProd, "Select 0 as
dummy") in DynamicMeasureTbl
```

3. In the report view, hide the blank column (dummy) and set the home table of a measure to this new table.

Dedicated measure group table for new dynamic measures

- The new measure group table can be hidden from report view when development and testing is complete

How to do it...

1. Create three new DAX measures to extract the connected user's user principal name:

```
User Principal Name = USERPRINCIPALNAME()
```

```
UPN Prefix =
VAR UPNAT = SEARCH("@",[User Principal Name]) RETURN LEFT([User Principal
Name],UPNAT-1)
```

```
UPN Suffix =
VAR UPNLENGTH = LEN([User Principal Name]) VAR UPNAT = SEARCH("@",[User
Principal Name])
RETURN MID([User Principal Name],UPNAT+1,UPNLENGTH-UPNAT)
```

 It's not technically necessary to create these measures in a data model to implement dynamic security or visibility, but per other recipes, this approach simplifies development, as measure expressions can be reused and hidden from users.

2. Publish the updated dataset to an app workspace in the Power BI service.

3. In the Power BI service, create a new report based on the updated dataset and apply the new measures to simple visuals that can represent text, such as a card or table.

User Principal Name	UPN Prefix	UPN Suffix
BrettP@FrontlineAnalytics.onmicrosoft.com	BrettP	FrontlineAnalytics.onmicrosoft.com

UPN measures in Power BI service

The USERPRINCIPALNAME() DAX function returns the email address used to login to Power BI. For organizations that use work email addresses for Power BI login, this effective user name maps to a UPN in the local active directory. In this scenario, a separate, non-work email address (@...onmicrosoft.com) was used for the Power BI account.

4. Add a separate user to the App Workspace containing the dataset.

5. Request this user to login to the workspace to view the new report or login to Power BI with this user's credentials:

User Principal Name	UPN Prefix	UPN Suffix
JenLawrence@FrontlineAnalytics.onmicrosoft.com	JenLawrence	FrontlineAnalytics.onmicrosoft.com

The function returns the UPN of the different logged in user

If security roles have not been configured on the dataset, the member of the workspace (JenLawrence) will see her UPN via either read or edit rights in the workspace. If security roles have been configured for the dataset, the member will either require edit rights in the workspace or can be added to one of the security roles defined for the dataset and granted read access to the workspace. Security roles are applied to read-only members of app workspaces. Alternatively, the app workspace admin or workspace members with edit rights can test the security of users who are mapped to a security role but are not members of the workspace.

How it works...

Power BI authentication

- Power BI uses **Azure Active Directory** (**AAD**) to authenticate users who login to the Power BI service, and the Power BI login credentials (such as `BrettP@FrontlineAnalytics.onmicrosoft.com`) are used as the effective user name whenever a user attempts to access resources that require authentication
- In Power BI service to on-premises scenarios, such as with SSAS cubes on-premises, the effective username (login credentials) from the Power BI service is mapped to a UPN in the local active directory and resolved to the associated Windows domain account

There's more...

USERNAME() versus USERPRINCIPALNAME()

- The `USERNAME()` DAX function returns the user's domain login in the format domain\user) locally, but returns the user principal name (the user's login credential) in the Power BI service. Therefore, security role filter expressions, user permissions tables, and any other dynamic user functionality added to Power BI datasets should align with the UPN email address format provided by `USERPRINCIPALNAME()`.
- In locally shared data models, DAX text functions can be used to extract the domain and username from `USERNAME()`, like with `USERPRINCIPALNAME()` in this recipe's example:

User Name	User Name Domain	User Name Login
ATLAS\Brett Powell	ATLAS	Brett Powell

The USERNAME() function used locally and outside of the Power BI service

```
User Name = USERNAME()
User Name Domain =
VAR Slash = SEARCH("\",[User Name]) RETURN LEFT([User Name],Slash-1)
```

```
User Name Login =
VAR Slash = SEARCH("\",[User Name]) VAR Length = LEN([User Name]) RETURN
RIGHT([User Name],Length-Slash)
```

 The USERNAME() is commonly used in dynamic security implementations with SSAS tabular models. The USERPRINCIPALNAME() was introduced to simplify user identity, as it returns the UPN (email address format) locally and in the Power BI service. A rare exception to this is when a PC is not joined to a domain. In this unlikely scenario, the USERPRINCIPALNAME() returns the domain and username in (domain\user) format, just like USERNAME().

See also

- Power BI security documentation and whitepaper at http://bit.ly/22NHzRS

Defining RLS roles and filtering expressions

The data security of Power BI models is comprised of security roles defined within the model, with each role containing a unique set of one or more filter expressions. Roles and their associated filter expressions are created in Power BI Desktop, and users or groups are mapped to security roles in the Power BI service. A single DAX filter expression can be applied to each table of a model within a given security role, and users can optionally be mapped to multiple security roles. The filter expressions applied to tables within a security role also filter other tables in the model via relationships defined in the model, like the filters applied to Power BI reports, and are applied to all queries submitted by the security role member.

This recipe contains an end-to-end example of configuring, deploying, and validating RLS roles, applicable to both Import and DirectQuery data models. Additional guidance on a consolidated security role table to improve the manageability of changing security requirements is included in the *There's more...*section. Examples of dynamic security, in which a single security role applies filter expressions based on the logged in user, are included in the following two recipes of this chapter.

Getting ready

1. Define and document the security role requirements to be implemented, and the members or groups of these roles.
2. Use the bus matrix diagrams described in `Chapter 3`, *Building a Power BI Data Model* to help communicate what data is currently stored in the model.
3. Validate that role security is indeed required (not report or model filters), given the risk or sensitivity of the data.

Do not confuse security role filters with the various other forms of filters in Power BI, such as report, page, and visual level filters, as well as filter logic in DAX measures. RLS role filters are applied to all queries of security role members, effectively producing a virtual subset of the data model for the given role at query time. Given the performance implications of compounding security role filters with report query filters, all user experience and analytical filters should be implemented outside of the security role filters. Security filters should be exclusively used for securing sensitive data.

How to do it...

In this example, the following two security roles must be created, deployed to the Power BI service, and tested:

- United States online bike sales
- Europe reseller sales-mountain and touring

The data model contains both internet sales and reseller sales, but each role should be restricted to their specific business process (fact table). Additionally, the United States online bike sales role should be able to view North America customer details (Canada and United States), but only sales for United States customers purchasing bike category products.

1. Open the data model and create a simple table visual containing row count measures of the different tables:

Internet Sales Row Count	Product Row Count	Customer Row Count	Sales Territory Row Count	Promotion Row Count	Reseller Sales Row Count	Reseller Row Count
26,608	606	18,484	11	16	47,572	701

Row count measures in a table visual of the Power BI data model

Each measure uses the COUNTROWS() DAX function, and generic tables that don't require security, such as date and currency, can be excluded. See the *Handling one-to-many and many-to-many* recipe in Chapter 3, *Building a Power BI Data Model*, for an additional use case for including row count measures in a data model. Like other testing and intermediary DAX measures, a dedicated measure group table may be needed, and this table or the individual measures can be hidden from the fields list.

United States online Bike Sales Role

1. From the **Modeling** tab of report view, click **Manage Roles** to open the security roles interface.
2. Click **Create** and give the new role the name United States Online Bike Sales.
3. Apply the following four DAX expressions to the Sales Territory, Customer, Product, and Reseller tables, respectively:

```
[Sales Territory Country] = "United States"
[Customer Sales Territory Group] = "North America"
[Product Category] = "Bikes"
FALSE()
```

The Sales Territory filter ensures that members will only see sales data associated with United States customers. The Customer table filter allows the security members the option to view Canada customer dimension table details only. The FALSE() function is used to filter every row of the Reseller table, which also filters the related Reseller Sales table.

The manage roles dialog displays filter icons to indicate which tables contain security filter conditions.

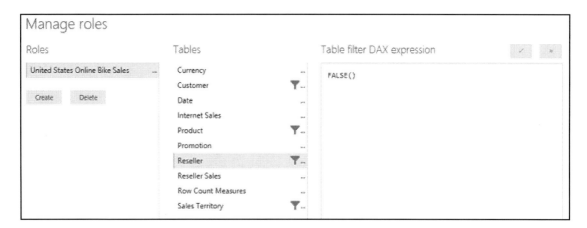

Role security definitions for United States Online Bike Sales

4. The ellipses next to the table names provide access to the columns for filtering, and the check mark can be used to validate the filtering expression. Click **Save**.

5. From the **Modeling** tab of report view, click **View as Roles** and select the new United States Online Bike Sales role:

Viewing the table visual of row count measures in Power BI Desktop as a member of the United States Online Bike Sales role

The two reseller table measures return a blank value, given the FALSE()
security filter. The Internet Sales table is filtered by both the Product filter
(Bikes) and the Sales Territory filter (United States). 9,390 customer
rows split between United States and Canada sales territory countries are
available given the customer table filter. The Promotion table is not
impacted by any of the security filters given its single direction, one-to-
many relationship to the Internet Sales fact table.

Even for experienced Power BI developers and for relatively simple
requirements, it can be helpful to apply a single security filter at a time
and to observe the impact on row counts. A standard testing report page
with row counts, and possibly fact table measures, can help expedite the
process.

Europe reseller sales - mountain and touring

1. Create a new role with the name Europe Reseller Sales-Mountain and
   Touring.
2. Apply the following DAX security filter expressions to the Customer, Sales
   Territory, and Reseller tables, respectively:

```
FALSE()
[Reseller Product Line] IN {"Mountain","Touring"}
[Sales Territory Group] = "Europe"
```

The Customer table is only related to the Internet Sales table, and
since every internet sales transaction has a Customer row, all rows from
the Internet Sales table are filtered. The IN DAX operator is a more
intuitive and sustainable expression than the | | symbol used as a logical
OR operator in older versions of the language.

3. Click on **Save** and then choose the new role from **View as Roles** on the **Modeling** tab:

Internet Sales Row Count	Product Row Count	Customer Row Count	Sales Territory Row Count	Promotion Row Count	Reseller Sales Row Count	Reseller Row Count
	606		3	16	3,843	401

Viewing the table visual of row count measures in Power BI Desktop as a member of the Europe Reseller Sales - Mountain and Touring role

The `Internet Sales` and `Customer` tables are blank due to the `FALSE()` expression for the customer dimension table. Customer has a one-to-many single direction relationship with Internet Sales. Therefore, filters on the `Customer` table impact Internet Sales but not other tables.

The `Sales Territory` table has three rows remaining (France, Germany, and United Kingdom) due to the Europe filter. The `Reseller Sales` fact table is impacted by the both the Sales Territory filter and the `Reseller Product Line` filter (`Mountain` or `Touring`). Just like the United States Online Bike Sales role, the Promotion table is not impacted given its single direction, one-to-many relationship with Reseller Sales. The filters from the `Reseller` and `Sales Territory` tables flow to the `Reseller Sales` table but stop there and don't impact other tables.

Deploy security roles to Power BI

1. Identify or create an App Workspace in Power BI with Edit or Admin rights.
2. Save the model, click **Publish**, and choose the App Workspace in Power BI to host the data model.

3. Log in to the Power BI service and navigate to the workspace of the published dataset:

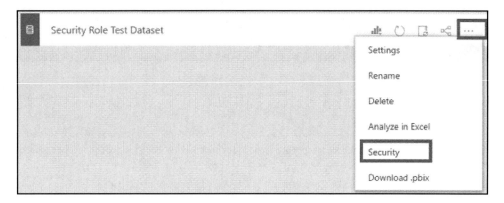

Opening security for published Power BI dataset in an App Workspace

4. Click the ellipsis next to the dataset and select Security to bring up the RLS dialog:

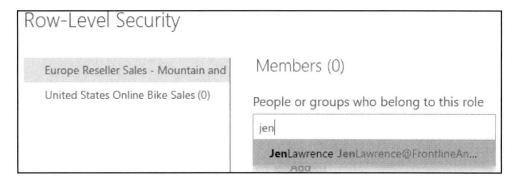

5. Select each role and add members or security groups via the **Members** input box.

Per the dynamic security recipes in this chapter, you can also test security roles in the Power BI Service. This includes viewing a dataset and its dependent reports from the perspective of an individual user. It's also possible to view a model from the perspective of multiple security roles simultaneously; the combined visibility provided to each role is available to any user or group mapped to these roles.

How it works...

Filter transfer via relationships

- Filters applied in security roles traverse relationships just like filters in Power BI reports and filters applied in DAX measures. For example, a security filter on a product dimension table will flow from the product table (one side of a relationship) to the many side (Sales) but will stop there and not also flow to other tables related to Sales unless bidirectional relationships have been enabled between Sales and these other dimension tables.

In gathering security requirements, and again in a testing or QA phase, communicate which tables are not impacted by the security filters. Users may falsely believe that a `Product` table security filter will also filter a Store dimension table since only certain products are sold in certain stores. However, if the Store table is queried directly and there is not a bidirectional relationship between Store and Sales, all the stores would be accessible. Only when a sales measure is used in a visual would stores with blank values (given the product filter) be discarded by default and even then a user could access these stores via the **Show items with no data** setting. To secure these tables and avoid bidirectional cross filtering for these relationships additional table-specific security filters may be needed.

There's more...

Managing security

Per the introduction, security role definitions are specific to a given Power BI model (dataset). If multiple models are deployed, consistent security roles (and measure definitions) need to be applied to these models as well. The management overhead and risk of maintaining common security roles and business definitions across multiple Power BI models can motivate IT/BI teams to consolidate data models when feasible and to consider a **SQL Server Analysis Services (SSAS)** or AAS model as a more efficient and secure long term solution.

Dynamic columns and central permissions table

- Any dynamically computed columns, such as the `Calendar Year Status` and `Calendar Month Status` columns described in `Chapter 6`, *Getting Serious with Date Intelligence*, can make security roles more robust and resilient to changes.
- As more roles and role filter requirements are required of a data model, a central security role table can be built into a data warehouse with the names of distinct roles associated with the values of the columns to be secured. Queries against this table can be used by Import or DirectQuery data models to implement these roles via relationships. See the *Building dynamic security into DirectQuery data models* recipe later in this chapter for additional details.

Designing dynamic security models in Power BI

Dynamic security models in Power BI filter tables based on the relationship of the logged in user to a column or columns stored in the data model. The `USERPRINCIPALNAME()` DAX function returns the user's UPN per the first recipe of this chapter, and a filter expression of a security role accepts this value as a parameter. Like all filters in Power BI data models, the filters applied in security roles also filter other tables via one-to-many and bidirectional relationships. Security roles can also blend dynamic, user-based filters with standard security filters to further restrict the visibility of members mapped to these roles.

This recipe implements dynamic security on an Employee dimension table such that users (employees) logged into Power BI can only view their own data and the data of those who report to them directly or indirectly via other managers.

Getting ready

The DAX functions used in this recipe are specific to a parent-child hierarchy that exists in the Employee source table. The `Employees` table contains an email address column, which corresponds to the `User Principal Name` credential used to log into the Power BI Service. Additionally, this recipe is exclusive to import mode datasets as parent-child DAX functions are not currently supported in DirectQuery mode models for either calculated columns or security filter expressions.

Establish the technical feasibility of dynamic security early in a Power BI deployment, such as the existence and quality of employee-manager hierarchy sources and the role security implications/options of Import versus DirectQuery models. Per the Building dynamic security in DirectQuery models recipe in this chapter, simple tables and relationships can be used as an alternative to relatively complex DAX expressions such as `PATHCONTAINS ()`. Additionally, for DirectQuery models, consider the option to leverage the existing security model of the source database rather than defining new RLS roles.

How to do it...

1. Open the import mode Power BI Desktop file and confirm that the two key columns (`EmployeeKey` and `ParentEmployeeKey`) exist in the Employee dimension table. If they don't, they can be added and hidden from Report view.

2. In the data view, select the `Employee` table and add two calculated columns to expose the hierarchy path and length:

```
ManagementPath =
PATH(Employee[EmployeeKey],Employee[ParentEmployeeKey])
ManagementPathLength = PATHLENGTH([ManagementPath])
```

The `Employees` table has 299 rows, but a logged in user should only see her data and the data of those that report to her directly or indirectly. For example, a vice president should still have visibility to a manager even if the manager reports to a senior manager who reports to the vice president. The senior manager, however, should not be able to view the vice president's data or the data of a different senior manager. Visibility is limited to the current user's level and the current user's management hierarchy.

3. In Power BI Desktop, create a simple table visual containing the new columns and related `Employee` columns:

Filtered table visual of Employee table columns

- In this example, Brett reports to Robert, Jennifer reports to Brett, and John reports to Jennifer. Therefore, Brett should only be able to view the data related to three employees (himself, Jennifer, and John).

- The `EmployeeKey` value is the last item in the `ManagementPath` column via the `PATH()` function

4. Create the following DAX Measures:

User Principal Name = USERPRINCIPALNAME()

Current User EmployeeKey = LOOKUPVALUE(Employee[EmployeeKey], Employee[Employee Email Address],[User Principal Name])

Current User Name =
LOOKUPVALUE(Employee[Employee Name],Employee[Employee Email Address],[User Principal Name])

Current User Manager = LOOKUPVALUE(Employee[Manager Name], Employee[EmployeeKey],[Current User EmployeeKey])

```
Current User Org Level =
CALCULATE(MAX(Employee[ManagementPathLength]),
FILTER(ALL(Employee),Employee[EmployeeKey] = [Current User
EmployeeKey]))

Employee Row Count = COUNTROWS('Employee')
```

 Not all of these measures are required to implement the desired RLS filter but they can be useful in testing/validation and potentially for other projects. Simple row count measures for all tables of a data model make it easy to validate the impact of security filters, similar to the bidirectional relationship example in Chapter 3, *Building a Power BI Data Model*.

5. Select **Manage Roles** from the **Modeling** tab of either the report view, the data view, or the relationships view.

6. Create a new security role, give it a name, and select the Employee table.

7. Add the following DAX expression in the table filter DAX expression window:

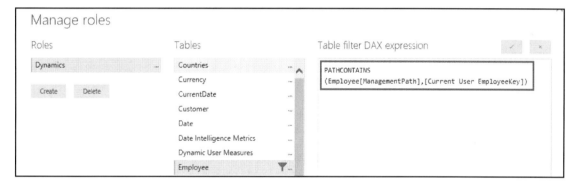

Dynamic filter expression applied to Employee table for security role dynamics

 The [Current User EmployeeKey] measure, which uses the user principal name measure to retrieve the Employee Key value, is passed as the item parameter to the PATHCONTAINS() function. The calculated column created in the first step, ManagementPath, provides the string of values for each Employee row to be evaluated against.

8. Create a simple report page of visuals that exposes the dynamic security measures.

9. Deploy the updated data model to an App Workspace in the Power BI service.

10. Per the previous recipe, click the ellipsis next to the **Dataset** and select **Security** to add individual user accounts or security groups to security roles.

Recall from the first recipe of this chapter that security can be tested for security role member accounts, despite the associated users not being members of the app workspace hosting the secured dataset. Workspace administrators and members of app workspaces that allow members to edit content can add and remove members from security roles and test security roles, including individual Power BI accounts per the following example.

11. Click on the ellipsis next to the **Dynamics** security role and select **Test** as role:

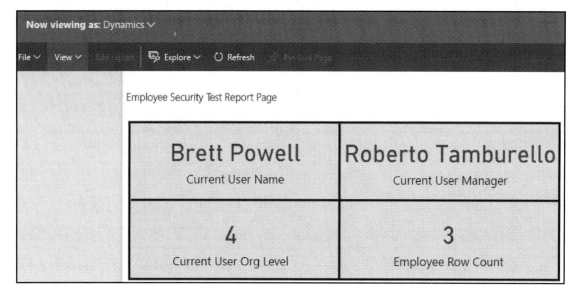

Given the security role (Dynamics) filter, all four measures are updated reflecting Brett Powell's position in the hierarchy

12. Add a different user to the security role and select the **Now viewing as** dropdown to test their visibility:

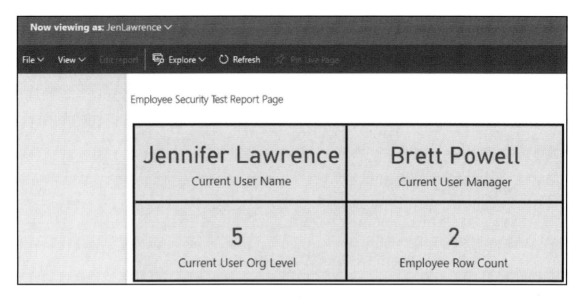

File ∨   View ∨   Edit report   🖥 Explore ∨   ↻ Refresh   Pin Live Page

Employee Security Test Report Page

Jennifer Lawrence	Brett Powell
Current User Name	Current User Manager
5	2
Current User Org Level	Employee Row Count

Viewing the same report as JenLawrence, all measures are updated to reflect her position in the hierarchy

The `Employee` table has 299 rows, but when Jennifer Lawrence logs into Power BI, she only sees her data and the one employee below her in her hierarchy (John Jacobs); hence, the `Employee Row Count` of 2. Likewise, Brett can see his data, Jennifer's data, and John Jacob's data, but is prevented from accessing any other employee data. Tables related to the Employee table with relationships that support cross filtering, such as one-to-many (employee to sales) or bidirectional cross filtering relationships, will also be filtered by the security filter and all DAX measures in report and dashboard visuals will reflect this filter context. For example, Jennifer would only see sales associated with her and John Jacobs.

13. Test the performance impact of the security role by comparing a baseline response time for reports that use (or are impacted by) the `Employees` table against the security role. For example, the administrator in the workspace or a member with edit rights can view the reports without the security role filter in effect to establish a baseline.

There's more...

Performance impact

- RLS expressions can significantly degrade query performance, as these filters will be applied in addition to other filters and expressions from Power BI reports when members of security roles access this content
- As a general rule, try to use relationships between tables with low cardinality to implement dynamic security per the following recipe in this chapter
- Utility or information functions, such as LOOKUPVALUE(), CONTAINS(), and PATHCONTAINS(), can meet complex security rules in import mode models but can be very expensive from a performance standpoint when applied against larger dimension tables, such as 1M+ row customer and product tables

Building dynamic security in DirectQuery data models

Dynamic row level security roles can be implemented in DirectQuery models via relationships and with specifically bidirectional cross-filtering between user security tables and the dimension tables to be secured. DAX information functions, commonly used in the role security expressions of import mode models, such as CONTAINS() and LOOKUPVALUE(), are not supported in DirectQuery mode models, thus requiring a relationship-based security design. However, though limited to this single approach, dynamic security can be developed for DirectQuery models quickly and maintained easily, given the avoidance of complex DAX security expressions.

This recipe walks through the essential steps and settings necessary to support dynamic security in a DirectQuery model. Additional details describing the filter context applied by the security role created in this example are included in the *How it works...* and *There's more...* sections.

Getting ready

1. Create a users table in the source database of the DirectQuery model:
   - Each row of this table must contain a unique UPN
2. Create one (or more) security tables that map UPNs to a single dimension table column to be secured.
3. For this table, a single UPN can be associated with one or more dimension table values.

User Name	User Email Address	User Employee Key
Jennifer Lawrence	JenLawrence@FrontlineAnalytics.onmicrosoft.com	888888888
Brett Powell	BrettP@FrontlineAnalytics.onmicrosoft.com	999999999

Users table created in SQL Server database for dynamic security

In this example of the users Table, the `User Employee Key` column is used as the primary key and the `User Email Address` column stores the UPN value used by the user in Power BI. If a single user to be secured will be using multiple UPNs, the primary key can be extended to include both the `User Employee Key` and the `User Email Address` columns, and the SQL statement used by the DirectQuery model can select only the distinct `User Email Address` values.

User Email Address	Sales Territory Country
BrettP@FrontlineAnalytics.onmicrosoft.com	United States
BrettP@FrontlineAnalytics.onmicrosoft.com	Canada
JenLawrence@FrontlineAnalytics.onmicrosoft.com	Australia
JenLawrence@FrontlineAnalytics.onmicrosoft.com	United Kingdom

User security table created in SQL Server for dynamic security

4. Create SQL views for both the new tables in the same schema as the views used by other data model tables.

- In this example, the `Sales Territory Country` column will be secured in the data model for the given user. If an additional column needs to be secured, a separate two-column table should be created with this column and the UPN.

As of writing this, enable cross filtering in both directions for DirectQuery is a preview feature that must be enabled in the global options of Power BI Desktop. This feature and a technique for implementing row level security in DirectQuery models (SSAS or Power BI) is further described in the official whitepaper, *Bidirectional Cross-Filtering in SQL Server Analysis Services 2016 and Power BI Desktop.*

 Plan ahead for the data sources, owners, and maintenance of user and security tables used by Power BI models. In some scenarios, only a static user table or manual update process is initially available, while in other situations, a complex SQL query is needed to meet the required structure and quality. A robust and recurring ETL process to update these tables with changes in users and user responsibilities is necessary to deliver dynamic security and visibility over the long term.

How to do it...

1. Open a local DirectQuery Power BI data model and select **Edit Queries** from report view to open the Query Editor.
2. Create queries against the users and security views developed in *Getting ready*.

```
let Source = AdWorksProd,
UserSalesCountry = Source{[Schema = "BI", Item =
"vDim_UserSalesCountrySecurity"]}[Data]
in UserSalesCountry
```

3. Duplicate an existing query via the right-click context menu and revise the Item value to the name of the SQL view.
4. Create one additional query, which retrieves the unique values of the column to be secured (Countries):

```
let Source = AdWorksProd,
Territory = Source{[Schema = "BI", Item =
"vDim_SalesTerritory"]}[Data],
Countries = Table.SelectColumns(Territory,{"Sales Territory
Country"}),
DistinctCountries = Table.Distinct(Countries)
in DistinctCountries
```

- Two additional table functions in *M* are used to produce a single column of the unique sales territory countries

---

Per the view native query dialog in **Query Settings**, the following SQL statement is generated based on the preceding M query: `"select distinct [Sales Territory Country] from [BI].[vDim_SalesTerritory] as [$Table]"`

5. Provide intuitive names for the new queries and ensure **Enable load** and **Include in report refresh** is selected:
   - The names `Users`, `Countries`, and `User Sales Country Security` are given in this example

6. Click **Close and Apply** and hide the three new tables, either via right-click in report view or the relationships view.

7. Open the relationships view and position the `Users`, `User Security`, `Countries`, and `Sales Territory` tables near each other.

8. Create a one-to-many single direction relationship from the `Users` table to the `User Security` table.

9. Create a many-to-one bidirectional relationship from the `User Sales Country Security` table to the `Countries` table.

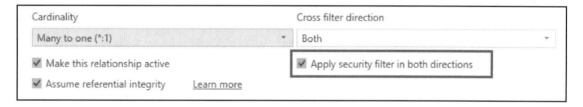

Bidirectional relationship from user sales country security to

Ensure that **Apply security filter in both directions** is selected for this bidirectional (both) cross filter relationship. Bidirectional cross filtering for DirectQuery models is currently a preview feature that must be enabled in the global options of Power BI Desktop. Per other recipes, the **Assume referential integrity** setting causes the DirectQuery data model to send inner join SQL queries to the source database and this, of course, significantly improves performance with larger models.

10. Create a one-to-many single direction relationship between the Countries and Sales Territory tables:

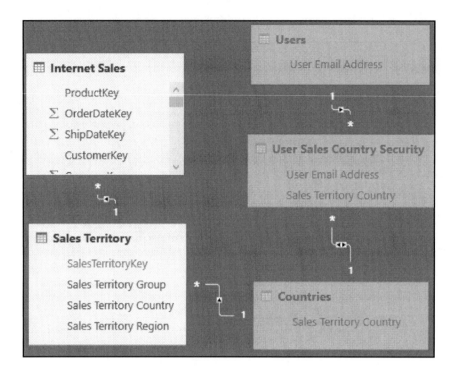

Dynamic user security relationships

- See the *How it works...* section for an explanation of how the relationships drive the filter context of the security role
- In short, the Users table is filtered by the current user measure (step 11) and this filter flows to the Security table, the Countries table, and finally the Sales Territory and Internet Sales table

11. Add a DAX measure named UPN that simply calls the `USERPRINCIPALNAME()` function.
12. In the **Modeling** tab of either report or relationships view, select **Manage Roles**.
13. In the **Manage Roles** interface, click **Create** and give the new role a name, such as `Dynamic User`.

14. Apply a filter on the `Users` table that matches the UPN measure with the `User Email Address` column:

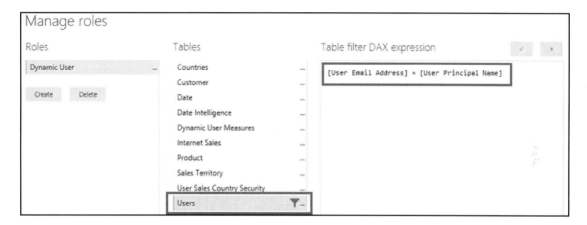

Dynamic user security role created with filter expression applied to UPN (email address) column of Users table

15. Save the dataset and publish the DirectQuery model to an app workspace in the Power BI service.
16. Test the security role(s) in the Power BI service and optionally map user accounts or security groups to the new role.

Per the following image, the user (JenLawrence) only sees Internet Net Sales for Australia and the United Kingdom via RLS:

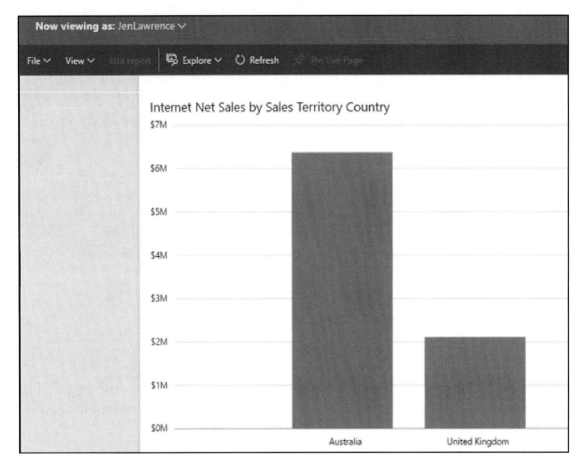

The member of the Security Role (JenLawrence) only sees sales for Australia and the United Kingdom per the security table

17. With functional requirements tested, also test for the performance impact of the security role relative to baseline performance. Reports must respect both their own filter contexts, such as slicers and DAX measures, as well as RLS role filters. Therefore, particularly for larger datasets, complex RLS conditions can cause performance degradation.

How it works...

Dynamic security via relationship filter propagation

When a user mapped to the dynamic security role connects to the DirectQuery dataset, their UPN is computed via the `USERPRINCIPALNAME()` function. This value filters the Users table to a single row which then filters the `User Sales Country Security` table via the one-to-many relationship. The filter is then transferred to the `Countries` table via the bidirectional many-to-one relationship between the `User Sales Country Security` and `Countries` tables. The filtered countries, such as Australia and the United Kingdom per the example with JenLawrence, then filter the `Sales Territory` dimension table. As a fourth and final step, the `Internet Sales` fact table is filtered by `Sales Territory` and thus all `Internet Sales` measures reflect the given `Sales Territory Countries`.

Note that the `Countries` table, which contains only the distinct country values, is necessary since the `Sales Territory` table contains many regions for the same country and all relationships must have a side that identifies each row of a table.

There's more...

Bidirectional security relationships

The approach from this recipe can be implemented in the same way for an import mode model and can also be used with a consolidated security role table. For example, instead of a users table containing UPNs (email addresses), a permissions table could be loaded to the model containing the names of each RLS role and the columns to secure. For each role, a simple security filter could be applied referencing the name of the role. Like this recipe, bridge tables containing the unique values of the secured columns could be created and security filters would flow across relationships from the permissions table to the dimension and fact tables via the bridge table(s).

Security Role	Sales Country	Product Category
European Bike	France	Bikes
European Bike	United Kingdom	Bikes
European Bike	Germany	Bikes
USA Non Bikes	United States	Accessories
USA Non Bikes	United States	Clothing
USA Non Bikes	United States	Components

RLS permissions table

Given the performance advantage of relationship filtering (including bidirectional relationship filtering), as well as the avoidance of relatively complex DAX, there could be value for organizations to follow this approach to dynamic security for both Import and DirectQuery models.

Displaying the current filter context in Power BI reports

DAX measures can be created to dynamically display the current filter context to report users. These measures can detect, retrieve values, and apply conditional logic to the filters applied to both slicer visuals and report and page level filters. With the filter context as a visual aid, users consuming or interacting with Power BI reports can focus on the data visualizations to obtain insights more quickly and with greater confidence.

In this recipe, DAX measures are created to detect and display the filter selections applied to a specific column, either on the report canvas itself or as a report or page level filter. An additional example displays the values of a column that are 'remaining' given the filters applied to the column directly and indirectly via other filters.

How to do it...

Dimension values selected

1. Create a DAX measure that returns a formatted text string of the filters applied on the `Sales Territory Region` column.

```
Regions Selected =
VAR SelectedRegions = FILTERS('Sales Territory'[Sales Territory
Region])
VAR RegionString = "Regions Selected: " &
CONCATENATEX(SelectedRegions,[Sales Territory Region],", ",[Sales
Territory Region])
VAR StringLength = LEN(RegionString)
VAR NumOfRegions = COUNTROWS(SelectedRegions)
RETURN
SWITCH(TRUE(),
   NOT(ISFILTERED('Sales Territory'[Sales Territory Region])),"No
Regions Selected",
   StringLength < 45, RegionString,
```

```
NumOfRegions & " Regions Selected" )
```

Four DAX variables and a `SWITCH()` function are used to support three separate conditions. When no filters are applied, the message `No Regions Selected` is returned. When many regions are selected, resulting in a long text string (over 45 characters in this example), a short message is returned advising of the number of regions selected. Otherwise, an ordered and comma separated list of the selected region values is returned.

2. Create a card or multi-row card visual and add the new DAX measure. Add a slicer visual for the same column:

Regions Selected: Australia, Canada, Germany	
Categories Selected: Bikes, Components	

Sales Territory Region	Product Category
■ Australia	☐ Accessories
■ Canada	■ Bikes
☐ Central	☐ Clothing
☐ France	■ Components
■ Germany	
☐ Northeast	
☐ Northwest	
☐ Southeast	
☐ Southwest	
☐ United Kingdom	

Two multi-row card visuals displaying the filter context from two slicer visuals

In this example, a separate measure was created for the `Product Category` column on the `Product` table, and both columns are being filtered by slicer visuals. The two measures displayed in the Multi-row card visuals will also reflect filters applied via report and page level filters. For example, if there were no selections on the `Product Category` slicer, or if this slicer was removed completely, the categories selected measure would still detect and display product category filters from page and report level filters. See `Chapter 4`, *Authoring Power BI Reports*, for details on filter scopes and slicers in Power BI reports.

3. Confirm that all three conditions (no filters, too long of a text string, and text string) return the expected results by altering the filters applied to the slicer(s).

4. Revise the `StringLength` rule of 45 characters and the supporting text to suit the use case. For example, the name of the measure itself can be used in report visuals instead of the extra text string `Regions Selected:`.

5. Apply formatting to the text visuals, such as this example with a shape used for background color and a border.

Dimension values remaining

1. Create a DAX measure that identifies the sales territory regions remaining given all other filters applied.

```
Regions Remaining =
VAR RemainingRegions = VALUES('Sales Territory'[Sales Territory
Region])
VAR RegionString = "Regions Remaining: " &
CONCATENATEX(RemainingRegions,[Sales Territory Region],", ",[Sales
Territory Region])
VAR StringLength = LEN(RegionString)
VAR NumOfRegions = COUNTROWS(RemainingRegions)
RETURN
SWITCH(TRUE(),
    NOT(ISCROSSFILTERED('Sales Territory')),"No Sales Territory
Filters",
    StringLength < 55, RegionString,
    NumOfRegions & " Regions Remaining")
```

The VALUES() function replaces the FILTERS() function used in the earlier example to return the unique values still active despite filters on other columns. The ISCROSSFILTERED() function replaces the ISFILTERED() function used in the example earlier to test if any column from the Sales Territory dimension table is being used as a filter. Per several other recipes, a hierarchy exists within the Sales Territory table with one Sales Territory Group having one or more Sales Territory Countries, and one Sales Territory Country having one or more Sales Territory Regions.

2. Test the new measure by applying filters on columns that would reduce the available or remaining values:

Three sales territory regions displayed based on the Europe selection and 15 product subcategories identified given the bikes and accessories selections

- The `Sales Territory Region` and `Product Subcategory` columns are impacted by filters applied to the the `Sales Territory Group` and `Product Category` columns, respectively
- Given the number of characters in the text string of 15 product subcategories, only the number remaining is displayed

Note that these remaining expressions will return the same string values as the first example, when filters are applied directly on the given column. For example, if the Northwest and Northeast regions were selected on a sales territory region slicer, these would be the only two regions remaining.

The techniques applied in these two examples can be blended or enriched further, such as by associating a measure with each dimension value returned by the delimited string. The following example integrates an internet sales amount measure:

```
RemainingRegions,
[Sales Territory Region] & " " & FORMAT([Internet Net
Sales],"$#,###"),", ",[Sales Territory Region])
```

Without the use of `FORMAT()`, the raw unformatted value of the measure is included in the text.

How it works...

FILTERS() and CONCATENATEX()

- The FILTERS() function returns a table of the values that are directly applied as filters to a column
- The third parameter to CONCATENATEX() is optional but it drives the sort order of the text values returned, and thus is recommended to aid the user when accessing the report. Per the preceding image, the values are sorted alphabetically.

Avoiding manual user clicks with user-based filtering logic

A very common scenario in BI projects is the need to customize a core set of reports and dashboards to better align with the responsibilities and analytical needs of specific roles or users within a larger team or organizational function. A given business user should, ideally, have immediate and default visibility to relevant data without the need to interact with or modify content, such as applying filter selections. Power BI's extensive self-service capabilities are sometimes a solution or part of a solution to this need, and additional role-specific, IT supported reports and dashboards are another realistic option.

A third option and the subject of this recipe is to embed user-based dynamic filtering logic into DAX measures. With this approach, a single or small group of reports and dashboards can be leveraged across multiple levels of an organization, thus avoiding the need for new report development.

Getting ready

1. Create a table, preferably in a source data warehouse system, that stores the UPN, the user's role, and a dimension key value.

User Email Address	Sales TerritoryKey	User Role
BrettP@FrontlineAnalytics.onmicrosoft.com	2	Country
JenLawrence@FrontlineAnalytics.onmicrosoft.com	4	Region

A table (BI.AdWorksSalesUserRoles) created in SQL Server to support dynamic filter context

- Each row should be unique based on the UPN (email address) column only
- The User Role column should contain the values of a hierarchy; such as Group, Country, and Region in this example
- The dimension column should map the user to a specific member of the hierarchy, such as a store within a region

 Per the guidance regarding User and Security tables in the *Building dynamic security into DirectQuery data models* recipe earlier in this chapter, it's essential to define the ownership and management of this table. For example, a new SQL stored procedure or SSIS package could be developed and scheduled to update this new table nightly, along with other BI assets. Like all table sources to data models, a SQL view should be created and the view should be used by the data model.

How to do it...

1. Load or connect to the user role table described in the *Getting ready* section, from a Power BI data model:
   - The user table should be hidden from the Fields List and should not have relationships to any other table
2. Create DAX measures to return the user's role and sales territory values for group, country, and region:

```
User Principal Name = USERPRINCIPALNAME()

User Sales Territory Key = LOOKUPVALUE('Sales User
Roles'[SalesTerritoryKey],
'Sales User Roles'[User Email Address],[User Principal Name])
```

```
User Sales Role =
VAR RoleLookup = LOOKUPVALUE('Sales User Roles'[User Role],
'Sales User Roles'[User Email Address],[User Principal Name])
RETURN IF(ISBLANK(RoleLookup),"Role Not Found",RoleLookup)
```

```
User Sales Group =
IF([User Sales Role] = "Role Not Found", "Role Not Found",
LOOKUPVALUE('Sales Territory'[Sales Territory Group],'Sales
Territory'[SalesTerritoryKey],[User Sales Territory Key]))
```

```
User Sales Country =
IF([User Sales Role] = "Role Not Found", "Role Not Found",
LOOKUPVALUE('Sales Territory'[Sales Territory Country],'Sales
Territory'[SalesTerritoryKey],[User Sales Territory Key]))
```

```
User Sales Region =
IF([User Sales Role] = "Role Not Found", "Role Not Found",
LOOKUPVALUE('Sales Territory'[Sales Territory Region],'Sales
Territory'[SalesTerritoryKey],[User Sales Territory Key]))
```

The purpose of these measures is to provide a specific default filter context to apply to a measure (sales). A country role member, for example, should see data filtered by her country by default when opening the report. However, conditional logic can also allow for user filter selections to be applied, allowing for additional visibility as well, as an option.

3. Create two DAX measures to detect the filter context of the Sales Territory table and to filter the sales measure.

```
Sales Territory Detection =
IF(ISCROSSFILTERED('Sales Territory'),"Filters Applied","No
Filters")
```

```
Internet Sales Amount =
SWITCH(TRUE(), [Sales Territory Detection] = "Filters Applied" ||
[User Sales Role] = "Role Not Found",[Internet Net Sales],
[User Sales Role] = "Group",CALCULATE([Internet Net Sales],
Filter(ALL('Sales Territory'),'Sales Territory'[Sales Territory
Group] = [User Sales Group])),
[User Sales Role] = "Country",CALCULATE([Internet Net Sales],
Filter(ALL('Sales Territory'),'Sales Territory'[Sales Territory
Country] = [User Sales Country])),
[User Sales Role] = "Region",CALCULATE([Internet Net Sales],
Filter(ALL('Sales Territory'),'Sales Territory'[Sales Territory
Region] = [User Sales Region])) )
```

The `Sales Territory Detection` measure is fundamental to this approach. If no columns on the `Sales Territory` table have been filtered on, such as via slicers, then the sales measure should default to a specific filter context based on the user. If filter selections have been made on Sales Territory columns, then these selections should be used by the measure.

The Internet Sales Amount measure also passes the standard `[Internet Net Sales]` measure if the current user is not found in the `Users` table. If a role is identified for the user and no filters have been applied on the `Sales Territory` table, a filter at the user's role level (`Group`, `Country`, `Region`) and the specific dimension member is applied.

4. Hide the new measures except for internet sales amount.
5. Optionally, create additional status DAX measures to inform the user of the filter logic applied.
6. Create a standard report with the new measure and the sales territory table to test or demonstrate the logic.

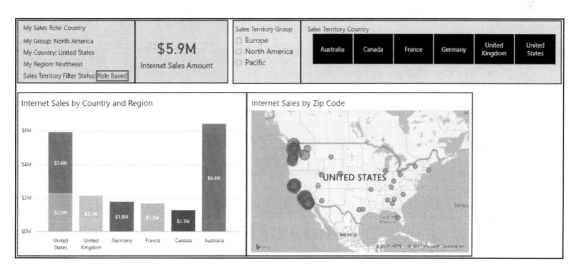

Default filter context for user Brett: a country role member for the United States

When the user Brett accesses the report, the card visual updates to $5.9M (United States) and the map visual zooms in on the United States, since both visuals use the internet sales amount measure and no filter from the `Sales Territory` table is applied. The country and region chart uses columns from the `Sales Territory` table and thus this visual breaks out internet sales across the hierarchy. The five text strings in the top left multi-row card visual are simple measures used to aid the user. See *How it works...* for the specific expressions used.

7. Test all three user roles and confirm that filter selections applied to the `Sales Territory` columns, such as the two slicers at the top of the report page, are reflected accurately.

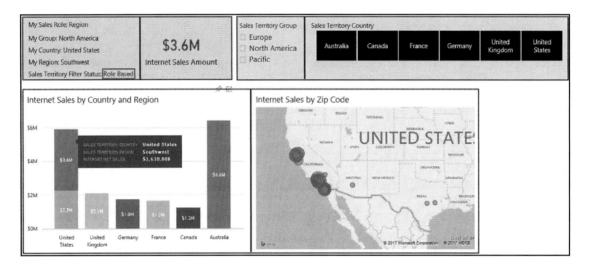

Default filter context for user Jennifer: a Region role member for the Southwest Region of the United States

When Jennifer, a region role member from the user table described in the *Getting ready* section, accesses the report, filters are applied for her Southwest region to compute $3.6M. Jennifer can still navigate away from this default by either clicking one of the bars on the lower left chart or using one of the two Sales Territory slicers at the top. The card and map would update to reflect these selections and the `Sales Territory Filter Status` message in the top left table would change to `User Defined` per the *How it works...* section.

How it works...

The five DAX measures exposed in the top left card visual of the sample reports are defined as follows:

```
User Role Status = "My Sales Role: " & [User Sales Role]
Sales Group Status = "My Group: " & [User Sales Group]
Sales Country Status = "My Country: " & [User Sales Country]
Sales Region Status = "My Region: " & [User Sales Region]
Filter Status =
VAR Prefix = "Sales Territory Filter Status: "
RETURN
IF([Sales Territory Detection] = "No Filters",Prefix & "Role Based",Prefix
& "User Defined")
```

There's more...

12 of the 13 measures created in this recipe only need to be developed once. The conditional logic applied to the internet sales amount measure can be applied to other measures to support much richer, personalized reports and dashboards with multiple dynamic measures. Given lazy evaluation behavior of DAX, small tables being queried to look up the user's values, and the use of DAX variables, performance should not be significantly impacted by this logic in most scenarios, but this should be tested.

Personal filters feature coming to Power BI apps

The Power BI team has announced that a personal filters feature is on the product roadmap related to the deployment of apps. As this feature becomes available, it may eliminate the need for user-specific DAX measures, such as the examples in this recipe.

9
Applying Advanced Analytics and Custom Visuals

In this chapter, we will cover the following recipes:

- Incorporating advanced analytics into Power BI reports
- Enriching Power BI content with custom visuals and quick insights
- Creating geospatial mapping visualizations with ArcGIS maps for Power BI
- Configuring custom KPI and slicer visuals
- Building animation and story telling capabilities
- Embedding statistical analyses into your model
- Creating and managing Power BI groupings and bins
- Detecting and analyzing clusters
- Forecasting and visualizing future results
- Using R functions and scripts to create visuals within Power BI

Introduction

Power BI Desktop's standard report authoring tools provide a robust foundation for the development of rich BI and analytical content. Custom visualization types developed by Microsoft and third parties further supplement these capabilities with their own unique features and can be integrated with standard visuals in Power BI reports and dashboards. Additionally, geospatial analysis features such as the ArcGIS Map visual for Power BI, custom dimension groupings, and animation and annotation options, further aid in the extraction of meaning from data and also support sharing these insights with others.

Power BI desktop also includes advanced analytics features reflecting modern data science tools and algorithms including clustering, forecasting, and support for custom R scripts and visuals. For example, an analytics pane is available to enrich visuals with additional metrics such as a trend line and the Quick Insights feature empowers report authors to rapidly analyze specific questions and generate new visualizations.

This chapter contains a broad mix of recipes highlighting many of the latest and most popular custom visualization and advanced analytics features of Power BI. This includes top custom visuals, such as the Dual KPI, Chiclet Slicers, Bullet charts, the ArcGIS map visual for Power BI, and data storytelling via animation and annotation. Additionally, examples are provided of leveraging Power BI datasets and the DAX and R languages to embed custom statistical analyses and visualizations, respectively.

Incorporating advanced analytics into Power BI reports

The standard line, scatter, column, and bar chart visualization types available in Power BI Desktop, which generally represent the majority of Power BI report content, given their advantages in visual comprehension, can be further enhanced via a dedicated analytics pane. Similar to visual level filters, the Power BI analytics pane creates measures scoped to the specific visual such as a trend lines, constant lines, percentile lines, min, max, and average. This additional logic provides greater context to the visual and avoids the need to author complex or visual-specific DAX measures.

> *"This pane is our home for all of our analytics features and you'll be able to use this to augment your charts with any kind of additional analytics that you need."*
> *- Amanda Cofsky, Power BI Program Manager*

This recipe includes two examples of leveraging the analytics pane in Power BI Desktop to raise the analytical value of chart visuals: one for a clustered column chart and another for a line chart. The predictive forecasting feature built into the analytics pane is described in the *Forecasting and visualizing future results* recipe later in this chapter.

How to do it...

Clustered column chart

1. In Power BI Desktop, select the clustered column chart visualization type from the visualizations pane.
2. Select a measure, such as **Average Unit Price**, from the **Fields** list and drop the measure into the **Value** field well.
3. Select a date column from the **Date** or **Calendar** dimension table and drop this column into the **Axis** field well.
4. In the **Axis** field well, select the dropdown under the **Date** column and switch from the hierarchy to the **Date** column:

The Automatic Date Hierarchy when a Date Column is added to a Visual

5. Click the Analytics Pane icon to the right of the Format pane (chart symbol).
6. Open the **Trend Line** card, click **Add**, and apply a black color with a dotted style and 0% transparency.
7. Add **Min**, **Max**, and **Median** lines to the visual from their respective cards in the Analytics pane.
8. Set the data label property for these three lines to **On** and use the **Name and Value** text option.

9. Finally, apply a black color with a solid Style and 0% transparency for these three lines:

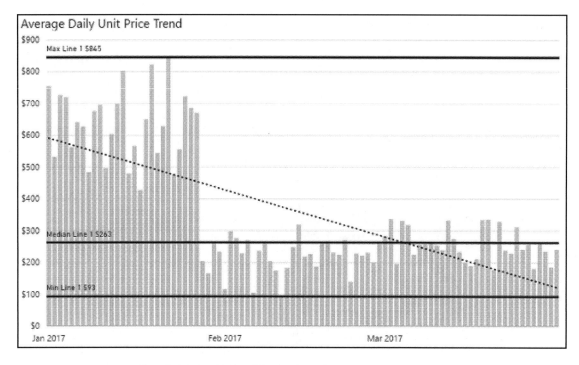

Clustered column chart with 4 dynamic lines from the analytics pane: Trend, Min, Max and Median

10. Format the colors of the columns to contrast with the analytics lines, format the x and y axes, and enter a title.

In this example, since a Date column was used as the axis, the trend line calls out the decline in daily prices in the first quarter of 2017, when lower priced accessory products were first sold. Given the volume of individual dates, the **Min**, **Max**, and **Median** lines give the user quick takeaways, such as the median daily unit price for an entire quarter and the option to further analyze sales activity on February 11th, when daily unit prices reached a low (Min) of $93 per unit.

Line chart

1. Create a line chart visual in Power BI Desktop.
2. Drag a margin percentage measure to the **Values** field well and a weekly column from the date table to the axis.
3. In the **Analytics Pane**, add a constant line and enter a percentage represented as a number in the **Value** input box.
4. Add a **Percentile Line** in the **Analytics Pane** and enter the percentage value of 75 in the **Percentile** input box.
5. Add **Min** and **Max** lines and turn set the **Data label** property to **On** for all four lines.
6. Set the text property of each data label to **Name and Value**, and the position property to **In Front**.
7. Apply a solid style to all lines except for the **Percentile Line**—use a dashed style for this line.
8. Use colors and the stroke width of the margin percentage line to contrast the analytics lines.

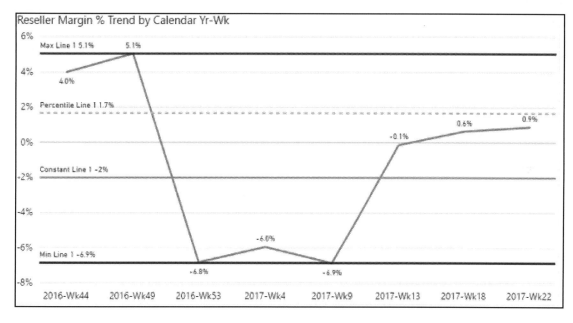

A line chart with 4 lines from the analytics pane: Percentile, Min, Max, and Constant

In this example, negative (-2 percent) is considered a key profitability threshold and thus a constant line helps to call out values below this level. Additionally, the percentile line set at 75 percent helps to identify the top quartile of values (above 1.7 percent). The four lines from the Analytics pane (and their formatting) provide more analytical value to users without requiring additional DAX measures for the model or cluttering the visual.

How it works...

Analytics pane measures

- The selections applied in the **Analytics** pane result in new expressions added to the DAX query of the visual:

```
EVALUATE
  GROUPBY(
    __DSOCore,
    "MinInternet_Net_Sales", MINX(CURRENTGROUP(), [Internet_Net_Sales]),
    "MaxInternet_Net_Sales", MAXX(CURRENTGROUP(), [Internet_Net_Sales]),
    "AverageInternet_Net_Sales", AVERAGEX(CURRENTGROUP(), [Internet_Net_Sales]),
    "MinMinDate", MINX(CURRENTGROUP(), [MinDate])
  )
```

A SQL Server profile trace of a Power BI Desktop file using the Analytics pane for Min, Max, and Average

- The analytics calculations are translated into the equivalent DAX expressions (ie MINX(), AVERAGEX()) and passed into the GROUPBY() table function.

Running a SQL Server Profiler trace against a Power BI Desktop file and viewing the full DAX query associated with a given visual (including all filters applied) is a great way to understand advanced DAX functions and filter context. In Windows Task Manager, you can identify the **Process ID** (**PID**) associated with Power BI Desktop's msmdsrv.exe process. You then run netstat - anop tcp from a command prompt, find the local port (in the local address column) associated with this process and pass this value to SQL Server Profiler. See the blog post referenced in the *See also* section for full details.

There's more...

Analytics pane limitations

- The analytics pane features are not available for custom, third-party supported visuals or combination visuals
- The predictive forecast is only available to the line chart and requires a date/time data type as the x axis
- The trend line is available to the clustered column and line chart if a date/time data type is used as the x axis
- Combination chart visuals are currently not supported and only a constant line is available for stacked chart visuals
- There's no option to apply a name or title to the analytics lines

See also

- Power BI analytics pane documentation: `http://bit.ly/2s2fA0P`
- How to trace a Power BI Desktop file: `http://bit.ly/2tYRLZg`

Enriching Power BI content with custom visuals and quick insights

Custom visuals for Power BI can be reviewed and downloaded from the Office Store gallery to provide additional features and options beyond those supported by the standard visuals of Power BI Desktop. Over 90 custom visuals are currently available in the Office Store and many of these have been developed by Microsoft to address common needs, such as the bullet, histogram, and gantt charts. Other custom visuals available in the Office Store have been developed by third parties but validated for security by Microsoft, and they deliver unique and powerful capabilities, such as the Flow map network visualization and the interactive visuals developed by ZoomCharts. In addition to custom visuals, Quick Insights can be used in the Power BI service and in Power BI Desktop to apply advanced analytics algorithms against datasets to extract insights such as trends or relationships, and rapidly generate new visualizations for use in reports and dashboards.

This recipe includes an example of accessing and utilizing the Bullet chart custom visual in Power BI Desktop and an example of the quick insights feature in the Power BI service. Additional details on Quick Insights within Power BI Desktop are included in the *There's more...* section.

Getting ready

1. Download the sample Power BI report associated with the Bullet custom chart visual from the Office Store (`http://bit.ly/2pS7LcH`).
2. In the Office Store, selecting the bullet chart and clicking on **Add** exposes a download the sample report hyperlink.
3. Open the Power BI Desktop sample report and review the field wells, formatting options, and any notes available.

Technically, it's only necessary to import the custom visual (.pbiviz file) to Power BI Desktop, but reviewing the associated sample report, which often includes multiple examples and a hints page, helps to expedite the report design process and derive the most value from the custom visual.

How to do it...

Bullet chart custom visual

1. Open Power BI Desktop and click the from store icon on the **Home** tab of the ribbon.

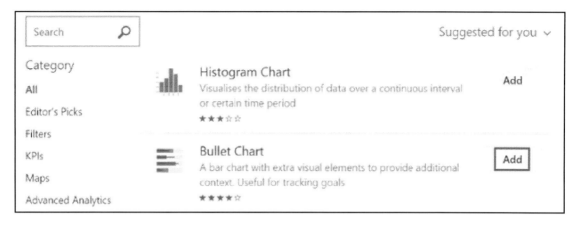

Adding a custom visual from Power BI Desktop

2. Search or navigate to the **Bullet Chart** and click **Add**. The bullet chart icon will appear in the visualizations pane.

 If the from store icon isn't available in Power BI Desktop, you can access the Office Store gallery via an internet browser per the *Getting ready* section. The custom visual (`.pbiviz` file) can be downloaded from the Store to a local directory and then, in Power BI Desktop, you can click the ellipsis in the visualizations pane to import the visual from this file.

3. Select the bullet chart icon in the visualizations pane to add it to the report canvas.

4. Add the measures Internet Net Sales (CY YTD) and Internet Net Sales Plan (CY YTD) to the `Value` and `Target Value` field wells, respectively.

5. Apply additional measures to the `Needs Improvement`, `Satisfactory`, `Good`, and `Very Good` field wells that represent threshold values relative to the Target value.

6. Add the `Sales Territory Country` column to the `Category` field well to expose an individual bullet for each country.

7. Optionally, apply measures to the `Minimum` and `Maximum` field wells to focus the visualization on the most meaningful ranges of values.

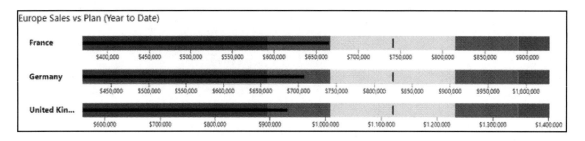

Bullet chart custom visual with data driven ranges and threshold values

- Other additional formatting options for this visual include customizing the colors and the orientation

In this example, six DAX measures, reflecting different values relative to the target measure (internet net sales plan (CY YTD)), were used to drive the color thresholds and the min and max values of the bullets. A 10 percent below plan (YTD) measure was used for the `Satisfactory` field well, and this represents the minimum value for the default yellow color, while a 10 percent above plan (YTD) measure was used for the `Good` field well (Green). 20 percent below and above plan measures were used for the needs improvement (dark red) and very good (dark green) field wells, respectively. A 50 percent below plan (YTD) measure was used for the `Minimum` field well value and a 25 percent above plan (YTD) measure was used for the `Maximum` field, to focus the range of the bullets.

The bullet chart also supports manually entered target values and percentage of target values in the formatting pane. However, the data driven approach with DAX measures is recommended, as this allows for the reuse of the calculations across other visuals and makes it easy to adjust multiple reports when the target and threshold value logic changes.

Scoped quick insights

1. Open a dashboard in the Power BI service.
2. Click the focus mode icon in the top right corner of a dashboard tile.
3. Select `Get Insights` in the top right corner of the Power BI service:

Power BI service with a dashboard tile opened in focus mode

4. The insights engine will produce a summary and insights visuals related to the data in the dashboard tile:

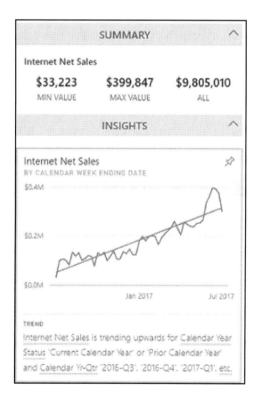

Quick insights generated based on a single dashboard tile

- Additionally, quick insights can be executed against a visual that was previously generated by quick insights

  Quick insights visuals can be pinned to new and existing dashboards like other Power BI report and dashboard tiles. Additionally, quick insights can be executed against a visual that was previously generated by quick insights. This example focuses on (scopes) the search process of the quick insights engine against the data in a single dashboard tile. However, Quick Insights can also be executed in Power BI Desktop and against an entire published dataset in the Power BI service. See the *'There's more...'* section for more details on these two use cases.

  The results from quick insights can be improved by hiding or unhiding columns. Quick insights does not search hidden columns, so hiding (or removing) unnecessary columns can focus the insights algorithms on only important columns. Likewise, any duplicate columns can be removed or hidden such that the time available for quick insights to run is used efficiently.

How it works...

- Quick Insights applies sophisticated algorithms against datasets, including category outliers, correlation, change points in a time series, low variance, majority, seasonality in time series, and overall trends in time series
- The insights engine is limited to a set duration of time to render its results

There's more...

Quick insights in Power BI Desktop

- The quick insights feature and analytics engine is now available in Power BI Desktop:

Quick insights in Power BI Desktop: right-click context menu of a data point in a line chart

- An **Analyze** option appears when right-clicking a specific data point, enabling additional visualizations to be generated specific to the selected item, such as a date on a line chart or a dimension value on a bar chart
- The generated visuals can then be added to the Power BI Desktop file and edited just like all other visuals

A *what's different?* option is available in the analyze right-click context menu, when two items are selected from the same visual. For example, select two product categories represented by their own bars in a sales by product category bar chart and use the what's different? Quick insights feature to generate visualizations that further compare and explain the difference in sales.

Quick insights on published datasets

- Quick insights can also be executed against an entire dataset in the Power BI service:

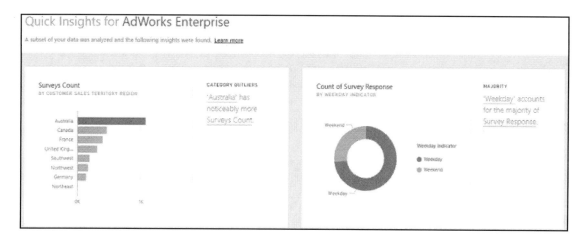

Quick Insights generated in the Power BI service for the AdWorks Enterprise Dataset

To run quick insights against a dataset, click the ellipsis under the **Actions** category for the given dataset and select **Get quick insights**. The insights generated can be accessed from the same context menu via a **View Insights** option. Each insight contains a Power BI visual, the title of the insight (algorithm) applied, such as outliers and correlation, and a short description. Visuals from **View Insights** can also be pinned to new and existing dashboards.

Creating geospatial mapping visualizations with ArcGIS maps for Power BI

ArcGIS mapping and spatial analytics software from ESRI, the market leader in **geographic information systems (GIS)**, is built into Power BI Desktop to generate greater insights from the spatial component of data. Familiar report visualization field wells and the cross filtering capabilities of Power BI can be combined with ArcGIS geospatial features and datasets, such as classification types, pins, and reference layers, to build custom, intelligent geographical visualizations into Power BI solutions.

In this recipe, a custom geographical column is created to include multiple geographical attributes (ie Street Address, City, State) to support accurate geocoding by the ArcGIS service. The ArcGIS visualization in Power BI Desktop is then used to plot customer addresses into a Cluster theme map visualization with supporting Pins and Infographics. See the *There's more...* section for greater detail on using the ArcGIS Map visualization, including options for applying custom conditional formatting logic.

Getting ready

1. In the Power BI service, click on Settings (gear icon) in the top right and enable ArcGIS maps on the **General** tab:

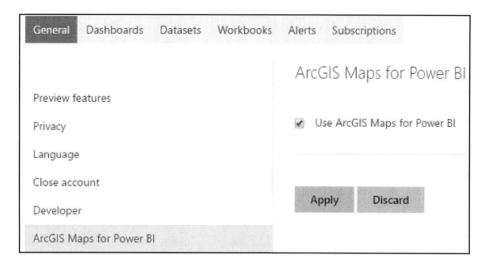

General settings dialog in Power BI service

- In Power BI Desktop, the ArcGIS map visualization should be available (globe icon) in the visualizations pane if you have the June 2017 version or later of Power BI Desktop installed. For earlier versions of Power BI Desktop, open preview features in options to enable the ArcGIS visual.

How to do it...

Single field address

1. Identify the following source columns for a new column `Full Address` to be used by the ArcGIS visual: street address (line 1), city, state or province, and postal or zip code. (Providing only a street address will result in inaccurate results.)
2. Include these columns in the SQL view used by the dimension table in the data model.
3. Create the `Full Address` column in the data model, either within the SQL view or by adding an M expression per the following example:

```
let
  Source = AdWorksProd,
  Customer = Source{[Schema = "BI", Item = "vDim_Customer"]}[Data],
  FullAddress= Table.AddColumn
```

```
(Customer, "Customer Full Address",
each Text.Combine({[Address Line 1], [Customer City], [Customer
State Province Code]}, ", ") & " " & [Customer Postal Code], type
text)
in FullAddress
```

The `Text.Combine()` is used for three columns separated by comma and space. This value is then concatenated with an additional space and the `Customer Postal Code` column via ampersand operators.

 Per other recipes, it's always recommended to move data transformation processes, particularly resource-intensive operations, back to the source system. In this example, the operation was applied to a small table (18,484 rows), but per the **Query Settings** window, the final step was not folded back to the SQL Server source system-local resources were used against the results of the `vDim_Customer`.

AB𝒸 Address Line 1	AB𝒸 Customer City	AB𝒸 Customer State Province Code	AB𝒸 Customer Postal Code	AB𝒸 Customer Full Address
7902 Hudson Ave.	Lebanon	OR	97355	7902 Hudson Ave., Lebanon, OR 97355
9011 Tank Drive	Redmond	WA	98052	9011 Tank Drive, Redmond, WA 98052
244 Willow Pass Road	Burbank	CA	91502	244 Willow Pass Road, Burbank, CA 91502

Customer Full Address column created in M query for Customer Dimension table

4. Load the updated customer query to the model and select the new column (`Customer Full Address`) in the `Fields` list.

5. Set the `Data Category` for the new column to `Address` via the **Modeling** tab of report view or data view.

 Per the *Assigning data formatting and category properties* recipe in `Chapter 3,` *Building a Power BI Data Model,* data categories assigned to columns are used by Power BI Desktop and Q & A in the Power BI service, in determining default visualizations and to better plot this data in map visuals. ArcGIS also benefits from geographical data categories.

Customer clustering Map

1. Apply page level filters to reduce the volume of data points to below the 1,500 limit when a location field is used (rather than latitude and longitude). In this example, the current year and Southwest region values from the `Date` and `Sales Territory` tables, respectively, are used as page level filters.

2. In report view, add an ArcGIS visual to the canvas and drop the `Full Address` column into the `Location` field well.

3. If the location data points are in one country, click the ellipsis in the top right of the visual and select **Edit**.

4. From the **Edit** menu, click **Location Type** and then set the **Locations are in** options to the given country.

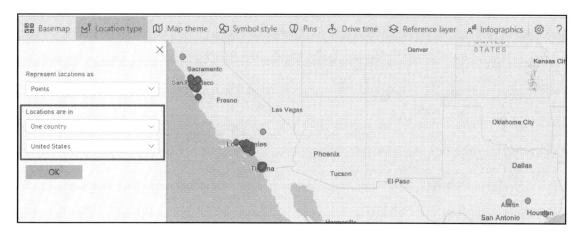

Location Type options in ArcGIS maps visual: setting the locations to United States

Setting the **Locations are in** geographic hint option significantly improves the accuracy of the plotted points returned by the ESRI service. Note that locations can also be represented as boundaries, such as states or postal codes. Almost all the advanced report development features provided by ArcGIS are exposed via this Edit window.

If latitude and longitude columns are already available for the dimension to be mapped, then these columns should be used in the ArcGIS visual instead of the Location field well. Providing latitude and longitude source data significantly improves performance as this eliminates the need for ESRI to compute these values. Additionally, a limit of 1,500 plotted data points is applied when the Location field well is used. Many more data points can be plotted via latitude and longitude inputs.

5. Enter a title, such as Current Year Customer Distribution: Los Angeles, CA, in the formatting pane of the visual.
6. Select the **Map theme** menu and change the theme to **Clustering**.
7. Use the **Symbol style** menu to configure the radius, and background and text colors of the clusters.
8. Click on the **Pins** menu and search for one or more points of interest, such as a headquarters city, and format the pin.
9. Click on the **Drive time** menu and individually select the pins by holding down the *Ctrl* key.
10. With the pinned locations selected, revise the search area to radius and choose a distance of five miles.
11. Optionally, apply formatting to the radius, such as a bright, bold fill color, and reduce the transparency.

The default formatting settings are based on ESRI's deep experience and should be sufficient for most scenarios. If the map's formatting has an analytical component, such as the classification type and color ramp, applied to measures used in the Color field well per the *There's more...* section, this logic should receive greater attention.

12. Finally, open the **Infographics** menu and add total population and household income. Click **Back to Report**.

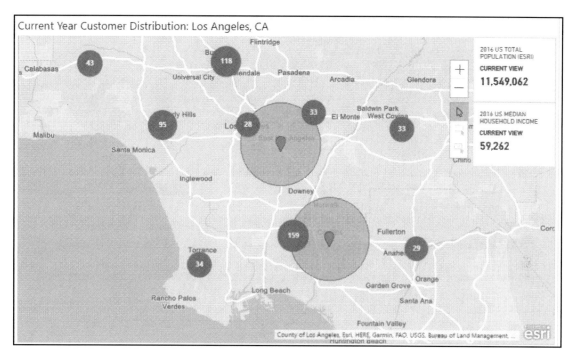

Formatted cluster theme map with pins, a drive time radius, and two infographics

- The relationship between relatively few clusters of customers and the pins makes the map easy to view and analyze

13. When complete, publish the Power BI Desktop report to an App Workspace in the Power BI Service.

 The visual is fully interactive; the clusters and the infographic numbers all update dynamically as the zoom of the visual is changed and as different geographic areas are navigated to, such as San Francisco, CA. A common alternative to the clustering theme is the heat map and the dark gray canvas basemap is an alternative basemap that can help visualize bright colors.

There's more...

ArcGIS map field wells

- Only the location was used in this example, but size, color, time, and tooltips can also be used by ArcGIS Map visuals
- Numerical measures can be for size, but both numerical measures and text values can be used for color
- Tooltips cannot be used with clustering themes but are very helpful with individual data points
- See the recipe *Building animation and story telling capabilities* in this chapter for details on the Time field well

Conditional formatting logic

- A powerful analytical capability of ArcGIS for Power BI is its ability to set the classification algorithm:

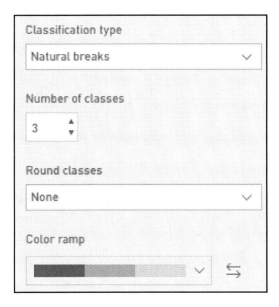

Classification

Use a measure such as sales in the `Color` field well of the ArcGIS visual and open the **Symbol Style** menu to customize how the data points are colored. For example, a **Manual Breaks** classification could be set to define specific threshold values that separate the different classes, such as locations above $2,000 as dark green. There are multiple classification types supported, including standard deviation, and up to 10 distinct classes (similar to bins) can be set in addition to a rich variety of color ramps to associate with these classifications.

See also

- ArcGIS for Power BI documentation: `https://doc.arcgis.com/en/maps-for-powerbi/`

Configuring custom KPI and slicer visuals

Per previous chapters, the KPI visualization type is commonly used to provide at-a-glance insights in Power BI dashboards and from the Power BI mobile application via mobile-optimized reports and dashboards. Additionally, the slicer visualization type delivers a robust self-service filtering capability to consumers of Power BI content across all data types. Given the importance of these two use cases Microsoft has developed the dual KPI and chiclet slicer custom visualizations to provide even more analytical features and design options such as the percentage change of a KPI value relative to a specific date and the use of images as slicer items.

In this recipe, the steps required to create the headcount and labor expenses dual KPI from enterprise dashboard example in `Chapter 5`, *Creating Power BI Dashboards*, are fully described. Additionally, a chiclet slicer custom visual is configured to expose images of flags associated with specific countries as filtering items via URL links. Further details on the cross highlighting and color formatting features of the Chiclet Slicer are included in the *There's more...* section.

Getting ready

1. Import the dual KPI and chiclet slicer custom visuals (`.pbiviz` files) to Power BI Desktop.
2. Identify the online source and specific URLs to use for the Chiclet Slicer images.
3. Update the table in the source database of the data model with a string column containing the image URL:

SalesTerritoryKey	SalesTerritoryGroup	SalesTerritoryCountry	SalesTerritoryRegion	SalesTerritoryCountryURL
4	North America	United States	Southwest	http://www.crwflags.com/fotw/images/u/us.gif
7	Europe	France	France	http://www.crwflags.com/fotw/images/f/fr.gif
8	Europe	Germany	Germany	http://www.crwflags.com/fotw/images/d/de.gif
9	Pacific	Australia	Australia	http://www.crwflags.com/fotw/images/a/au.gif
10	Europe	United Kingdom	United Kingdom	http://www.crwflags.com/fotw/images/g/gb.gif

Image URL column (SalesTerritoryCountryURL) added to the SQL Server Sales Territory table

4. Revise the SQL view used by the Power BI data model to retrieve the new image URL column.
5. Create a date column to support the percentage change since start date component of the dual KPI visual.

For this recipe, a column is added to the `Date` table's SQL view, reflecting the date one year prior to the current date:

```
DATEADD(YEAR,-1,CAST(CURRENT_TIMESTAMP as date)) as 'One Year Prior
Date'
```

In the absence of a date column for the percentage change start date field wells of the dual KPI Slicer, the first date available in the filter context will be used by the `% change since` data label and tooltip. Additionally, date values can be manually entered in the two start date input boxes available in the dual KPI Properties formatting card. These two options may be sufficient for certain scenarios, but since the dual KPI is likely to be used on highly visible dashboards, it's generally recommended to avoid hard coded values and provide a dynamic column to expose the most relevant trend.

How to do it...

Dual KPI - headcount and labor expense

1. In Power BI Desktop, select the dual KPI custom visual to add it to the report canvas.
2. Apply a column of the date datatype to the `Axis` field well. A text column in the format 2017-Jan can also be used.
3. Drop the headcount and labor expenses measures into the top and bottom values field wells, respectively.
4. Apply a date column to the top and bottom percentage change start date field wells. A measure cannot be used.

> In this example, the `One Year Prior Date` column created in the *Getting ready* section is used for both the top and bottom percentage change start date field wells. As this column only contains one value, it can be hidden from the `Fields` list after being added to the dual KPI. Although it's possible to create distinct percentage change calculations for the top and bottom KPIs, such as Year-over Year for the top KPI and year-to-date for the bottom KPI, this customization requires a second additional date column and could easily confuse users as the KPIs would share the same axis but the data labels would reflect different calculations.

5. Open the formatting pane of the visual and expose the dual KPI properties card settings.
6. Disable the title formatting property.
7. In the dual KPI properties card, delete the default text `Title` in the `Title` text property and set the **Abbreviate values** properties to **On**:

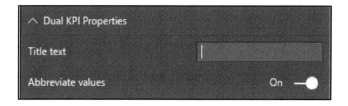

Dual KPI properties

8. In the dual KPI colors card, set the data color to the tan theme color, the text color to black, and chart opacity to 70.

9. Optionally, revise the dual KPI axis settings and the dual KPI chart type properties. For example, one or both KPIs could be displayed as a Line chart instead of an area chart and a custom axis could be used to focus the visual to a specific range of KPI values.

Related KPI measures of headcount and labor expense on the dual KPI visual with the hover tooltip highlighted:

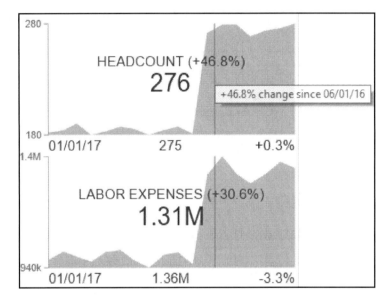

Dual KPI slicer configured with One Prior Year Date column as % start date

- Although the labor expense of 1.31M is 30.6 percent higher since the prior year (6/1/2016), it's 3.3 percent lower than January of 2017

In this example, the Power BI report is filtered to the current and prior calendar year dates, so all periods from January 2016 through the current month of June of 2017 are included in the Dual KPI charts. However, the (+46.8%) and (+30.6%) data labels are based on the percentage change start date parameters which use the `One Prior Year Date` column created in the *Getting ready* section. Since the KPI values of 276 and 1.31 M reflect the latest date in the filter context, the `% change since` values represent year-over-year calculations (June of 2017 versus June of 2016 in this example). By hovering over January of 2017 in one of the charts, the bottom tooltips display the values for this time period and compares it to the current KPI value.

Per `Chapter 5`, *Creating Power BI Dashboards*, data alerts on Power BI Dashboard tiles can only be configured on standard KPI, gauge, and card visuals. Until data alerts are supported for custom visuals, such as the Dual KPI, a work-around option is a dedicated alerts dashboard comprised of standard KPI visuals. Business users can continue to view the Dual KPIs in their dashboard but alerts could be triggered from the separate dashboard.

Chiclet Slicer - Sales Territory Country

1. In Power BI Desktop, select the `Sales Territory URL` column in the `Fields` list and set the **Data Category** to `Image URL`.
2. Select the Chiclet Slicer custom visual to add it to the report canvas.
3. Drag the `Sales Territory Country` text column to both the `Category` field well and the `Values` field well.

The images will not appear in the Chiclet Slicer unless the `Values` field well is populated. Likewise, per the *'There's more...'* section, cross highlighting will not be enabled unless the `Values` field well is populated. Other columns beyond the `Category` column can also be used in the `Values` field well, and in some cases, the columns contain business meaning such as a score value of 10 being associated with a smiling image.

4. Drag the `Sales Territory URL` column to the `Image` field well and open the formatting options of the Chiclet Slicer.

5. Set the orientation to horizontal and enter the values of `6` and `1` for the `Columns` and `Rows` properties, respectively.

6. Increase the size of the header text and apply a black font color. The title can be left off per its default setting.

7. Open the Chiclets card and set the outline color to match the background color of the report page.

8. Open the images formatting card, set the `Image Split` to `80`, and turn on the `Stretch image` property.

9. Optionally, adjust the other colors in the Chiclets card, such as the disabled color, and revise the Chiclet text size.

The chiclet slicer with images such as flags and corporate logos provides an eye-catching and intuitive user experience.

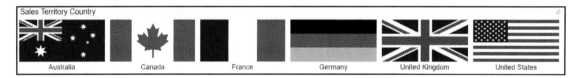

Chiclet Slicer custom visual with image URLs

- The 80 percent image split leaves just enough space for the country name. Additionally, the white outline color of the chiclets makes these cells invisible to the interface, such that only the flag and country name is exposed.

There's more...

Chiclet slicer custom visual

1. Customized row, column, and color formatting options are also useful features of the Chiclet Slicer.

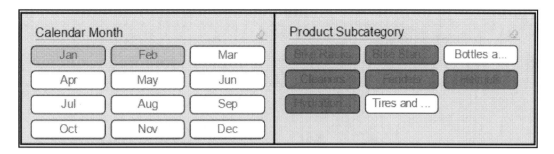

Two Chiclet Slicers with horizonal orientation and 3 columns

2. A rectangle shape provides the gray background color and a line shape is used to divide the Chiclet slicers.

For basic filtering features via chiclet slicers, only the `Category` field well is required. However, to enable cross highlighting, a column is also required in the `Values` field well. In the preceding example, the light blue shading of the January and February slicer items indicate that these values have been selected. No selections have been made via the product subcategory chiclet slicer, but given a customer selection made on a separate visual, subcategories without related data are automatically grayed out through cross highlighting. In this example, only the bottles and cages and tires and tubes product subcategories are associated with both the calendar selections and the customer selection. The default gray disabled color property can be modified along with the selected and unselected chiclet colors.

Note that cross highlighting relies on the filter context to impact the column used by the Chiclet slicer. In this example, a bidirectional relationship between internet sales and the `Product` table enables a filter selection made on the `Customer` table to impact the `Product` table. The Calendar table has a single direction relationship with internet sales and therefore it's not impacted by the other dimension filters and not cross-highlighted in the Chiclet Slicer.

Though powerful from an analytical and visualization standpoint, updating the individual Chiclet items through cross highlighting requires additional queries, just like chart and table visuals on the same report page. Therefore, this feature should be used prudently, particularly with larger and more complex data models or those with many distinct chiclet items.

Building animation and story telling capabilities

Business teams and analysts are commonly responsible for sharing or "walking through" business results, trends, and the findings from their analyses with other stakeholders such as senior management. To most effectively support the message delivery process in these scenarios, Power BI provides built-in animation capabilities for the standard scatter chart and ArcGIS map visualization types. Additionally, custom visuals such as the pulse chart further aid the storytelling process by embedding user-defined annotations into the visual and providing full playback control over the animation.

> *"We're bringing storytelling into Power BI. We're making Power BI into the PowerPoint for data"*
> *- Amir Netz, Microsoft Technical Fellow*

This recipe includes examples of preparing the standard Scatter chart visualization for animation, leveraging the date animation feature of the ArcGIS map visual, and utilizing the Pulse Chart custom visual with annotations. Details on the new Bookmarks Pane in Power BI Desktop, as well as additional story telling custom visuals, are included in the *'There's more...'* section.

Getting ready

1. Find and add the pulse chart custom visual (`.pbiviz`) to Power BI Desktop from the Office Store.
   - Click **From Store** on the **Home** tab of report view:

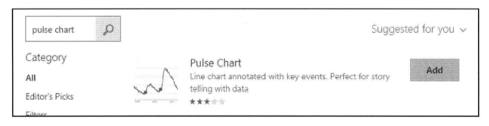

Pulse chart custom visual via the Office Store integrated with Power BI Desktop

2. Identify specific events and details to be included in the pulse chart annotations, such as marketing campaigns.

How to do it...

Scatter chart with play axis

1. In Power BI Desktop, apply a report or page level filter for the `Sales Territory Group` column to the value `Europe`.

2. Select the scatter chart visualization type and re-position the blank visual on the canvas.

3. Drag the internet sales customer count and internet net sales measures into the *X* and *Y* field wells, respectively.

4. Drag the `Sales Territory Country` column to the `Details` field well and open the Formatting pane.

5. Open the Bubbles card and set the **Size** to 100 percent.

 An alternative method of displaying bubbles is by using a measure for the Size field well. Applying this third measure converts the scatter chart to a bubble chart with the size of the bubbles being used to visually emphasize a certain measure. Similar to pie and donut charts, it's difficult to visually determine differences in bubble sizes. Additionally, even a small number of dimension items, such as product categories, can lead to a cluttered visualization when presented as a bubble chart.

6. In the formatting pane, set the fill point and color by category properties to on.

7. Set the **Category labels** setting to **On**, increase the text size to 11 points, and specify a black font color.

8. Give the visual a title and format the *X* and *Y* axes with a larger text size and a black font color.

9. Optionally, identify supplemental measures, such as margin percent, and drop these measures into the `Tooltips` field well.

10. Finally, drag the `Year-Mo` column from the `Date dimension` table to the `Play Axis` field well.

11. Note that any manually applied colors in the Data colors formatting card will be overridden when the Play Axis is used.

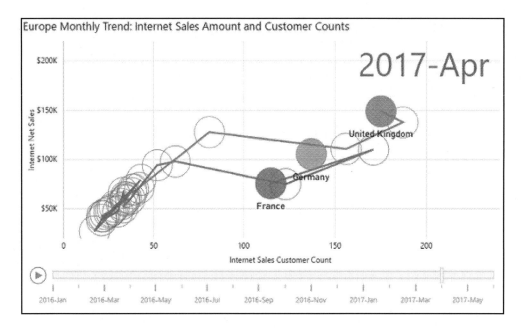

12. Test the animation behavior and tracing capability by clicking play, pausing on a play axis value, and selecting one or more of the categories in the scatter chart.

In the preceding example, the animation (filter) is paused at 2017-April, and both United Kingdom and France have been selected. Multiple items can be selected or unselected by holding down the *Ctrl* key and clicking a bubble from a separate series. When selected, the Scatter chart highlights the path of the given item (or items) up to the currently selected or filtered point on the play axis. Playing and pausing the Play axis and selecting the dimension(s) in the Scatter chart makes it easy for presenters to address a significant outlier or a point in time at which a relevant trend began.

Microsoft has also created the enhanced scatter custom visual which supports a background image URL, such as a business location or diagram and images for the individual plotted categories similar to the Chiclet Slicer example in the previous recipe. However, this visual does not include a Play Axis or any visual animation like the standard scatter chart used in this recipe.

ArcGIS map timeline

1. Open a Power BI Desktop report with an ArcGIS map visual, such as the example from earlier in this chapter.
2. Select this visual and add a date column to the `Time` field well.

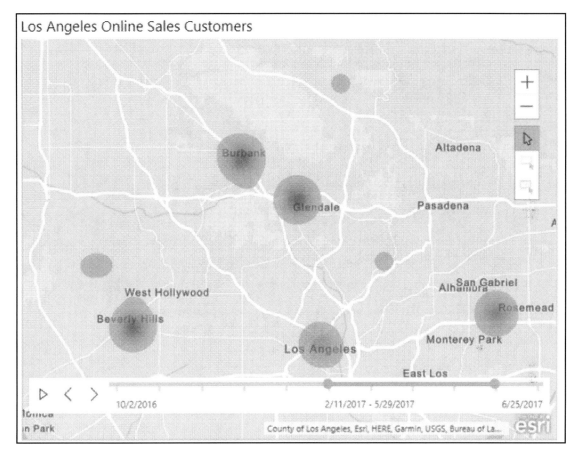

ArcGIS Map for Power BI visual using the heat map theme and the timeline

The column used for the `Time` field well must be of the date or the date/time data type, such as an individual calendar date or a week ending date. Text and numeric data type columns, such as calendar year, are not currently supported.

The timeline at the bottom of the visual can be used to play through each individual date value or, per the preceding example, a custom time interval can be set by modifying the start and end points of the timeline. For instance, a date interval representing four weeks could be set at the beginning of the timeline, and clicking the play icon would sequentially display each interval. The forward and backward icons can be used to quickly navigate to different time periods or intervals.

Pulse chart custom visual

The Pulse Chart custom visual, developed by Microsoft, also supports animated playback, but adds rich support for storytelling via customized popup text boxes and controls for automatically pausing an animation at particular data points.

1. Create a table in the source database with the following columns: `Event Date`, `Event Title`, and `Event Description`:

Event Date	Event Title	Event Description
2016-12-24	New Product Category	Accessories category made available online
2017-02-11	New Product Release	New Road and Touring models released
2017-05-20	Marketing Campaign	Launched summer marketing campaign

Event table with annotations to support data storytelling

2. Insert event detail rows into this table and create a view for access by the Power BI data model.
3. Expose this new view as an M query in Power BI Desktop (`EventAnnotations`).

4. Use an outer join M function from the date query to the `EventAnnotations` query and add the two event columns.

> In this example, the visualization to create is at the weekly grain, so the join from the Date query to the `EventAnnotations` query uses the calendar week ending date column. If event annotation requirements are known and stable, the integration of the annotation columns can be implemented in the SQL views or an ETL process. See `Chapter 2`, *Accessing and Retrieving Data*, and other recipes for examples on merging queries via M functions.

5. Add the Pulse Chart visual to the report canvas and drop a measure into the `Value` field well.

6. Now drop the `Calendar Week Ending Date` column (a `Date` datatype) into the `Time Stamp` field well.

7. Add the `Event Title` and Event Description columns, now merged into the date dimension table, to the `Event Title` and `Event Description` field wells.

8. Open the formatting pane and set the series color to black and the fill of the dots to red.

9. Set the position of the X axis to bottom, unless you have negative values in the data set.

10. In the popup card, adjust the width, height, fill, and text size to align with the annotations being displayed.

11. Finally, apply black color to the playback controls, a border, a background color, and enter an intuitive title.

12. Optionally, revise the speed, pause, and delay playback settings to suit the specific use case.

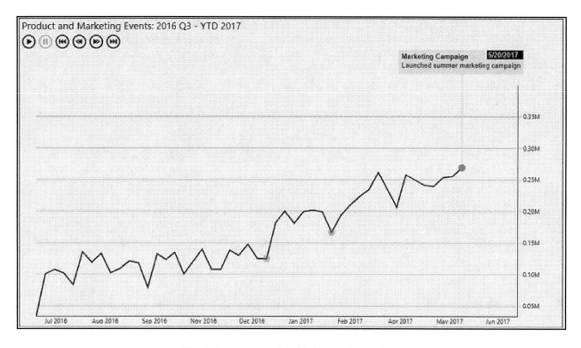

Pulse Chart paused on an event with data-driven annotation displayed

The Pulse Chart only supports a single data series and far fewer axis controls than the standard Line chart visual, but offers fine grained control over Playback, including an auto play option that initiates the animation when the report is opened. In this example, the running animation is automatically paused for the default 10 seconds when the third event (Marketing campaign on 5/20/17) is reached and the annotation (Event Title, Event Description) is displayed during the pause. The playback controls in the top left of the visual can be used to quickly navigate to individual events (three in this example) or the beginning and end of the time series.

There's more...

Bookmarks

- Bookmarks enable the saving of specific report states including filter context and the visibility of specific items on the report canvas
- The **Bookmarks** pane can be accessed from the **View** tab in the report view of Power BI Desktop:

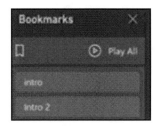

Bookmarks pane in Power BI Desktop

- A new bookmark can be created via the left icon and animation through bookmarks is available via **Play All**

 A **Canvas Items** pane, also available in the **View** tab, can be used with bookmarks to set the visibility of visuals to align with the sequence of the presentation. Playing through bookmarks in Power BI reports resembles Microsoft PowerPoint presentations (in presentation mode) which leverage animation. Additionally, bookmarks can be linked with other objects in the report such as images making it possible to create an intuitive navigation experience across report pages.

Play axis custom visual

- The Play Axis custom visual filters multiple visuals on the report page like a slicer but also supports animation.

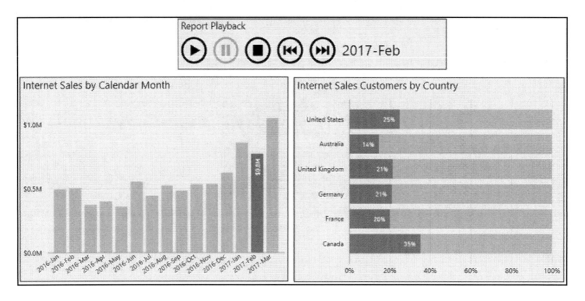

Play Axis custom visual filtering two charts and paused on 2017-Feb

- The play axis is best used in combination with column and bar charts that allow the highlight visual interaction

Storytelling custom visuals

- Two additional custom visuals focused on integrating explanatory text or annotations with data from the data model include Narratives for Business Intelligence and enlighten data story
- Enlighten data story provides a text input box and allows for measures and columns to be built into a single text value
- Narratives for business intelligence applies advanced analytics to a user-defined set of dimensions and measures to discover insights and presents these findings in a well formatted annotation form:

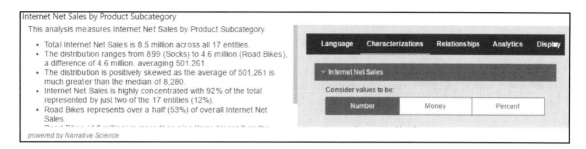

Internet Net Sales by Product Subcategory

This analysis measures Internet Net Sales by Product Subcategory.

- Total Internet Net Sales is 8.5 million across all 17 entities.
- The distribution ranges from 899 (Socks) to 4.6 million (Road Bikes), a difference of 4.6 million, averaging 501,261.
- The distribution is positively skewed as the average of 501,261 is much greater than the median of 8,280.
- Internet Net Sales is highly concentrated with 92% of the total represented by just two of the 17 entities (12%).
- Road Bikes represents over a half (53%) of overall Internet Net Sales.

powered by Narrative Science

Narrative for business intelligence custom visual with options dialog open

- The resulting text updates dynamically as the data changes and a verbosity property controls the level of detail

Embedding statistical analyses into your model

Statistical analysis, beyond basic measures, is typically implemented outside of business intelligence data models via data analytics professionals and dedicated statistics and data science applications. When possible, however, it's much more efficient to leverage existing data models, Power BI skills, and the features used for other Power BI reports and dashboards, such as the analytics pane described earlier in this chapter.

In this recipe, the data points supporting a linear regression model are created from an existing Power BI data model. This model is then analyzed and described via DAX measures with values such as slope, Y intercept, and the Z-score for residuals. Finally, a rich report page is constructed to visualize the strength and accuracy of the regression model and to detect outliers. See the *How it works...* section for additional details on the equations used in this recipe.

Getting ready

1. Identify the X or predictive, independent variable(s) and the Y or dependent variable to be predicted.
2. Determine if the required data of the model is available in the Power BI data model.

In this example, monthly marketing spend from a `General Ledger` fact table is used to predict monthly internet sales from an internet sales transaction fact table. Simple (single variable) regression models are often insufficient to estimate Y values accurately, but many of the concepts and techniques used in this recipe are applicable to more complex, multiple linear regression models.

How to do it...

Regression table and measures

1. From the **Modeling** tab in Power BI Desktop, click **New Table**.
2. Create a table named `MktSalesRegression` which retrieves the `X` and `Y` variables at the monthly grain.

```
MktSalesRegression =
FILTER(
SUMMARIZECOLUMNS(
'Date'[Calendar Yr-Mo],
'Date'[Calendar Year Month Number],
CALCULATETABLE('Date','Date'[Calendar Month Status] <> "Current
Calendar Month"),
"Marketing Amount", [Marketing Fin Amount],
"Internet Sales", [Internet Net Sales]
),
NOT(ISBLANK([Internet Sales]) || ISBLANK([Marketing Amount])))
```

 `SUMMARIZECOLUMNS()` groups the table at the monthly grain and `FILTER()` removes any rows (months) which don't have both internet sales and marketing values. `CALCULATETABLE()` passes a filtered date table to `SUMMARIZECOLUMNS()` to exclude the current calendar month. The dynamic `Calendar Month Status` column in the `Date` table is described in Chapter 6, *Getting Serious with Date Intelligence* and `Marketing Fin Amount` is a simple measure defined in the model as follows:
`CALCULATE([Finance Amount],Account[Parent Account] = "Marketing")`

Calendar Yr-Mo	Marketing Amount	Internet Sales	Calendar Year Month Number
2014-Dec	838.0053	43421.0364	72
2015-Jan	8738.7364	469823.9148	73

The MktSalesRegression table created to support linear regression

A new SQL view could be developed in the source system to meet the regression table requirements and, as another alternative, M queries within the dataset could leverage the existing general ledger, internet sales, and date queries. Small DAX tables such as this example (31 rows) are a good option for supporting custom or advanced analysis and functionality.

3. Create measures for the correlation coefficient, slope, Y intercept, and coefficient of determination (R squared).

```
MktSalesCorrelNum = SUMX(MktSalesRegression,MktSalesCorrelNum =
SUMX(MktSalesRegression, ((MktSalesRegression[Marketing Amount]-
AVERAGE(MktSalesRegression[Marketing
Amount]))*(MktSalesRegression[Internet Sales]-
AVERAGE(MktSalesRegression[Internet Sales])))))
```

```
MktSalesCorrelDenomX =
SUMX(MktSalesRegression,(MktSalesRegression[Marketing Amount] -
AVERAGE(MktSalesRegression[Marketing Amount]))^2)
```

```
MktSalesCorrelDenomY =
SUMX(MktSalesRegression,(MktSalesRegression[Internet Sales] -
AVERAGE(MktSalesRegression[Internet Sales]))^2)
```

```
Mkt-Sales Correl =
DIVIDE([MktSalesCorrelNum],SQRT([MktSalesCorrelDenomX]*[MktSalesCor
relDenomY]))
```

```
Mkt-Sales R Squared = [Mkt-Sales Correl]^2
```

```
MktSalesSlope = DIVIDE([MktSalesCorrelNum],[MktSalesCorrelDenomX])
```

```
MktSales Intercept = AVERAGE(MktSalesRegression[Internet Sales])-
([MktSalesSlope]*AVERAGE(MktSalesRegression[Marketing Amount]))
```

The correlation coefficient is split into three separate intermediate measures (Num, DenomX, and DenomY) and these measures are referenced in the Mkt-Sales Correl measure. With the correlation and its components defined in the model, the slope (MktSalesSlope) measure can leverage the same numerator measure and the DenomX measure as well. See the *How it works...* section for details on the mathematical functions these measures reflect.

Residuals table and measures

1. From the modeling tab, click **New Table** and create a Residuals table:

```
Residuals =
VAR Intercept = [MktSales Intercept]
VAR Slope = [MktSalesSlope]
Return
ADDCOLUMNS(MktSalesRegression,"Y
Intercept",Intercept,"Slope",Slope,
    "Predicted Internet Sales", ([Marketing Amount]*Slope) +
Intercept,
    "Residual",[Internet Sales] - ((([Marketing Amount]*Slope) +
Intercept))
```

- The regression table and measures created earlier are referenced to support analysis of the model

Calendar Yr-Mo	Marketing Amount	Internet Sales	Slope	Calendar Year Month Number	Y Intercept	Predicted Internet Sales	Residual
2014-Dec	$838	$43,421	47.47	72	34,447	$74,232	($30,811)
2015-Jan	$8,739	$469,824	47.47	73	34,447	$449,317	$20,506
2015-Feb	$9,094	$466,335	47.47	74	34,447	$466,161	$174

The Residuals table created via

DAX variables are used to store the computed values of the Slope and intercept measures, such that the same values (47 and 34,447, respectively) are applied to each of the 31 rows. The Predicted Internet Sales column implements the equation of a line ($Y = MX + B$) by referencing the marketing amount (X), the slope (M), and the Y intercept (B). Finally, the Residual column is computed to subtract the predicted sales value from the observed (actual) value in the internet sales column.

2. Create measures to evaluate the residuals and support the visualization.

```
Residuals Amount = SUM(Residuals[Residual])
Residuals Average =
CALCULATE(AVERAGE(Residuals[Residual]),ALL(Residuals))
Residuals Sample Std Dev =
CALCULATE(STDEV.S(Residuals[Residual]),ALL(Residuals))
Residuals Z Score = DIVIDE([Residuals Amount] - [Residuals
Average],[Residuals Sample Std Dev])
Regression Line Message = "Regression Line: Y= " &
FORMAT([MktSalesSlope],"#,###") & "X" & "+" & FORMAT([MktSales
Intercept],"#,###")
Last Month Predicted Internet Sales = CALCULATE([Predicted Internet
Sales Amount],FILTER(ALL(Residuals),Residuals[Calendar Year Month
Number] = MAX(Residuals[Calendar Year Month Number])))
Last Month Internet Sales = CALCULATE([Internet Net
Sales],'Date'[Calendar Month Status] = "Prior Calendar Month")
Actual Internet Net Sales = sum(Residuals[Internet Sales])
```

 A Z-score is computed for each residual data point (a month) to determine if the variation (or 'miss') between predicted and observed values is large relative to other data points. To support the visualization, a measure returns a text string containing the equation of the regression model's line. Additionally, two measures are created to display actual and predicted internet sales for the prior or 'last month'. Given that the regression table is filtered to exclude the current month, the maximum value from the `Calendar Year Month Number` column can be used as a filter condition.

Regression report

1. From the report view of Power BI Desktop, create card visuals to display the actual and predicted internet sales measures for the last month, as well as the correlation coefficient and R squared measures.
2. Create a scatter chart that plots actual marketing spend as the *X* axis and actual internet sales as the *Y* axis.
3. Add the `Calendar Yr-Mo` column to the `Details` field well and add the trend line from the analytics pane.

The two measures and one column used for this scatter chart are pulled from the existing data model to help visualize the relationship. All other visualizations in the report use the new measures and columns created in this recipe.

4. Create an additional scatter chart that plots predicted internet sales as the *X* axis and the residual *Z*-score as the *Y* axis.

5. Add the residual amount and actual internet net sales measures to the `Tooltips` field well.

6. In the analytics pane for this visual, enable the trend line.

7. Finally, add a card visual to hold the regress line message measure and format the report page with a title, a `Last Refreshed` message, and use rectangle and line shapes to provide background colors and borders.

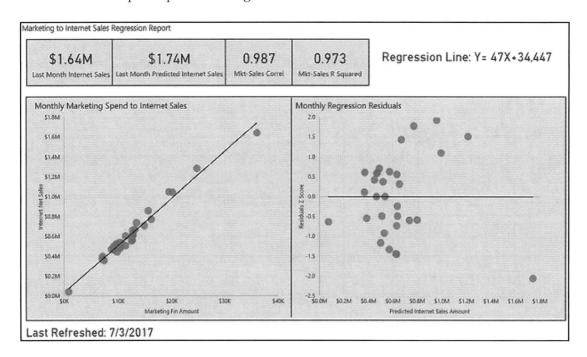

Regression report page

8. Optionally, hide the two calculated tables and the regression measures created from the Fields List.

With this report design, the user can instantly perceive the strength of the relationship via the marketing Spend to Internet Sales Scatter chart and the high values for the correlation and R Squared cards. The Residuals Scatter chart helps to identify the months with relatively large variations. In this example, the predicted value of $1.74 M for June of 2017 resulted in a (-100K) residual value (observed minus predicted), and this data point is plotted at the bottom right of the Residuals Scatter chart, given its low residuals Z-score.

Building measure values into text strings, such as the regression line and the Last Refreshed message, is useful in many scenarios to raise usability. The Last Refreshed message is described in the first recipe of Chapter 4, *Authoring Power BI Reports*. The *Displaying the current filter context in Power BI reports* recipe in Chapter 8, *Implementing Dynamic User-Based Visibility in Power BI* contains more advanced examples.

How it works...

Statistical formulas

- The created DAX measures correspond to the CORREL(), INTERCEPT(), AND SLOPE() functions in Microsoft Excel:

$$Correl(X,Y) = \frac{\sum (x-\bar{x})(y-\bar{y})}{\sqrt{\sum (x-\bar{x})^2 \sum (y-\bar{y})^2}}$$

Correlation Coefficient for a Sample (Pearson's Correlation Coefficient)

$$b = \frac{\sum (x-\bar{x})(y-\bar{y})}{\sum (x-\bar{x})^2}$$

Slope of the Regression Line

$$a = \bar{y} - b\bar{x}$$

Intercept of the Regression Line

- The same results from the DAX measures can also be retrieved via Excel formulas

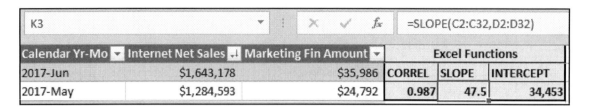

Calendar Yr-Mo ▾	Internet Net Sales ↓	Marketing Fin Amount ▾	Excel Functions		
			CORREL	SLOPE	INTERCEPT
2017-Jun	$1,643,178	$35,986			
2017-May	$1,284,593	$24,792	0.987	47.5	34,453

K3 f_x =SLOPE(C2:C32,D2:D32)

Applying CORREL(), SLOPE(), and INTERCEPT() lines in Excel 2016

- Simply add the regression table columns to a table visual in Power BI Desktop and click **Export data**
- Per the residuals Z-score measure, a Z-score is computed by subtracting the sample average from the value for a given data point and dividing this number by the sample standard deviation

DAX calculated tables

- The two calculated tables in this recipe do not have any relationships to other tables in the model
- Refreshing the source tables (queries) of the two DAX tables also refreshes the calculated tables

See also

- Slope and intercept equation descriptions: http://bit.ly/2tdzrgA

Creating and managing Power BI groupings and bins

Power BI grouping was introduced in the *Creating browsable hierarchies and groups* recipe in Chapter 3, *Building a Power BI Data Model* as a means to consolidate the values or members of columns in your data model into dedicated group columns. These group columns can then be utilized like other columns in the model to simplify report visualizations and self-service analysis, given their reduced granularity. Additionally, groups can be managed and edited in Power BI Desktop, providing a flexible option for dataset owners to respond quickly to changing requirements or preferences.

In this recipe, a customer attrition analysis is supported by a quarterly group based on a First Purchase Date column of a Customer dimension table. In the second example, a Number of Days Since Last Purchase column is created via M queries and then grouped to support further customer behavior analysis. These two examples represent the grouping of Date and Number datatype columns; example in Chapter 3, *Building a Power BI Data Model* was based on a text data type column.

How to do it...

First purchase date grouping

In this example, the Customer dimension table has a First Purchase Date column with over 1,000 distinct date values. The business wants the ability to segment customers based on this date in report visualizations.

1. In report view of Power BI Desktop, select the First Purchase Date column in the **Fields** list.
2. With the column selected, click **New Group** from the **Modeling** tab in the toolbar.

   - Alternatively, you can right-click the column and select **New Group**

- The groups dialog appears as follows, given the `Date` datatype:

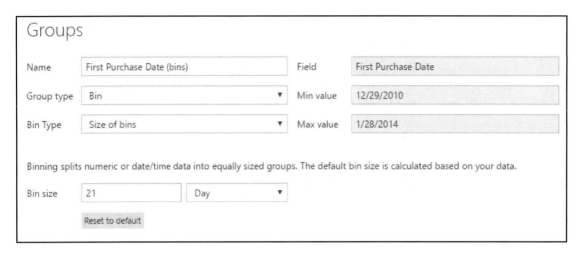

Default groups dialog for first purchase date column: 21 day Bin size

By default, the groups feature calculates a bin size that evenly splits the rows of the table. In this example, 55 bins would be created containing close to 21 days. Each bin would be identified by a specific date representing the first date of the given bin. Since 55 distinct bins is too many to support intuitive visualizations, and given that 21 days is not a normal business grouping, the recommendation is to adjust the bin size values.

3. Enter the value 3 in the **Bin size** input box and revise the drop-down from **Day** to **Month**.
4. Enter the name `Customer First Purchase Calendar Quarter` in the **Name** input box. Click **OK**.
   - A column will be added to the `Customer` table with the date format of `July 2013` by default, given the monthly bin size

5. Create a matrix visual that analyzes the sales of these quarterly customer bins across the past three years.

Customer First Purchase Calendar Quarter	2015	2016	2017	Total
April 2013			$914,359	$914,359
January 2013			$994,870	$994,870
October 2012		$1,620,094	$298,288	$1,918,382
July 2012		$1,461,896	$374,907	$1,836,803
April 2012		$1,320,543	$357,780	$1,678,322
January 2012		$1,378,995	$482,960	$1,861,955
October 2011	$2,038,185	$3,485	$466,062	$2,507,732
July 2011	$1,814,388	$16,952	$580,050	$2,411,390
April 2011	$1,801,595	$22,953	$387,781	$2,212,329
January 2011	$1,421,357	$17,567	$248,434	$1,687,358
October 2010			$18,330	$18,330

First Purchase Date Quarterly Grouping used in Matrix Visual

 By grouping the customers into quarterly bins, the new grouping column (`Customer First Purchase Calendar Quarter`) has only 14 unique values and can be used in report visualizations. In this analysis, it's clear that sales in 2017 are being driven by customers that first purchased in the first and second quarters of 2013 (January 2013, April 2013). Interestingly, customers that first purchased in 2011 were large buyers in 2015, but then generally disappeared in 2016, and are now coming back in 2017.

Days since last purchase grouping

In this example, the goal is to group (bin) customers based on the number of days since they last purchased.

1. Create a new M query in Power BI Desktop that groups the customer keys by their last order date and computes the date difference between this order date and the current date:

```
let
    Source = AdWorksProd,
    ISales = Source{[Schema = "BI", Item =
"vFact_InternetSales"]}[Data],
    CurrentDate = DateTime.Date(DateTime.LocalNow()),
    CustomerGrouping = Table.Group(ISales, {"CustomerKey"}, {{"Last
Order Date", each
```

```
List.Max([Order Date]), type date}}),
    DaysSinceLastPurchase = Table.AddColumn(CustomerGrouping, "Days
Since Last Purchase", each    Duration.Days(CurrentDate - [Last
Order Date]), Int64.Type)
in
    DaysSinceLastPurchase
```

The view used to load the Internet Sales fact table is grouped by the customer key and **List.Max()** is used to compute the last order date for the given customer key. This simple grouping is folded back to the source SQL Server database and a Days Since Last Purchase column is added, based on the difference between the CurrentDate variable and the Last Order Date column from the grouping. Note that subtracting two date columns results in a duration value, hence Duration.Days() is used to convert the duration to the number of days.

1²₃ CustomerKey	▼	⊞ Last Order Date	▼	1²₃ Days Since Last Purchase	▼
15652		3/31/2017		88	
14324		9/4/2016		296	
18569		2/6/2017		141	

New M query DaysSinceLastPurchase created to support a customer grouping

2. Give the query a name and disable the load of the query to the data model, but include the query in report refresh.

3. Join the customer dimension table query to the new query and load the two new columns to the data model.

```
let
    Source = AdWorksProd,
    Customer = Source{[Schema = "BI", Item =
"vDim_Customer"]}[Data],
    LastPurchaseJoin =
        Table.NestedJoin(Customer, {"Customer
Key"},DaysSinceLastPurchase,{"CustomerKey"},"DaysSincePurchase",Joi
nKind.LeftOuter),
    LastPurchaseColumns =
Table.ExpandTableColumn(LastPurchaseJoin,"DaysSincePurchase",{"Last
Order Date","Days Since Last Purchase"},{"Last Order Date","Days
Since Last Purchase"})
in
    LastPurchaseColumns
```

- A left outer join is used to retain all the Customer table rows and Table.ExpandTableColumn() is used to expose the two new columns to the customer table

4. Finally, create a numerical grouping based on the Days Since Last Purchase Column to help analyze this data:

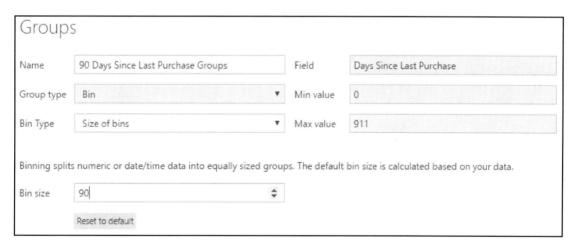

Grouping created based on days since last purchase column

- The configured bin size of 90 results in 12 distinct bins—a small enough number to be used to analyze customer sales

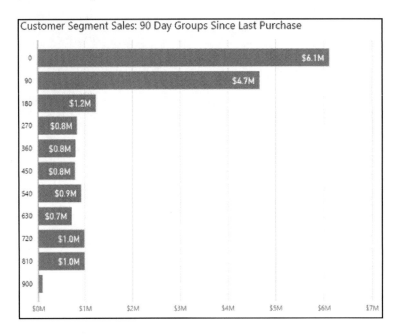

Clustered Bar Chart of Internet Sales by the 90 Days Since Last Purchase Grouping

The new grouping column (90 Days Since Last Purchase Groups) helps determine that $10.8 M of total historical internet sales is comprised of customers that have purchased within the past 180 days ($6.1 M for the 0 to 90 group and $4.7 M for the 90 to 180 group). Note that the Last Order Date column added in this example could also be used to create a grouping or even used as a child column in a hierarchy with the 90 Days Since Last Purchase Groups column as the parent.

As groupings are effectively calculated columns within the data model and not visible to source systems, their logic should eventually be migrated to new columns in a source data warehouse. Groups can be very helpful for proof-of-concept scenarios and short term solutions, but per other recipes, data transformation processes should be limited in Power BI Desktop to keep the dataset as manageable and scalable as possible. If a data warehouse option is not available, M query transformations can be used rather than DAX calculated columns.

Detecting and analyzing clusters

Clustering is a data mining and machine learning technique used to group (cluster) the items of one dimension based on the values of one or more measures. Given the number of distinct dimension items, such as products or customers, and the number of measures describing those items, clustering is a powerful method of exploring data to discover relationships not easily detected with standard reporting and analysis techniques. Power BI Desktop provides built-in support for the creation of clusters and allows these clusters to be managed, revised, and used in Power BI reports like other columns in the data model.

In this recipe, a customer cluster is created based on sales amount, the count of orders, and the count of days since last purchase. DAX measures are created to support this analysis and a Scatter Chart visual is created to further analyze the clusters.

Getting ready

1. Identify measures that add the most value to the algorithm by representing the dimension in different ways.
2. Create the DAX measures, and if necessary, enhance the data retrieval process to provide these measures to the model.

 Feature engineering is a common practice in data science in which new columns are added to a dataset to produce more accurate models. The new columns often contain built-in logic and features (columns) are added, removed, and modified iteratively based on the models produced.

How to do it...

Create clusters

1. Add the customer dimension key column to a table visual in Power BI Desktop. This should be the natural or business key if slowly changing dimension ETL processes are in effect and multiple rows refer to a given customer.
2. Add (or create) the following measures: Internet Net Sales, Internet Sales Orders, and Days Since Last Purchase:

   Internet Net Sales = [Internet Gross Sales] - [Internet Sales Discounts]

```
Internet Sales Orders = DISTINCTCOUNT('Internet Sales'[Sales order
number])
Last Purchase Date = LASTNONBLANK('Date'[Date],[Internet Net
Sales])
Days Since Last Purchase = DATEDIFF([Last Purchase
Date],TODAY(),DAY)
```

 `Last Purchase Date` is an intermediary measure created to support the `Days Since Last Purchase` measure. `Days Since Last Purchase` uses this measure and a `TODAY()` function as parameter inputs to `DATEDIFF()`.

3. Add the three measures to the table visual. Only the four columns should be in the table.

4. Apply any filtering logic to reduce the list of customers, such as a page level filter. In this example, the customer cluster is specific to the `Europe Sales Group`, so the `Sales Territory Group` column is added to a page level filter.

5. Click the ellipsis in the top right of the visual and select **Automatically find clusters**.

6. In the clusters dialog, provide a name for the clusters that will serve as the column name in the model.

7. In the description input box, enter the measure names (from the table) that were used to create the clusters.

8. Click **OK** to let the clustering algorithm create as many clusters as it determines necessary.

Customer Alternate Key	Internet Net Sales	Internet Sales Orders	Days Since Last Purchase	Europe Customers (RFM)
AW00012132	$10,896	4	71	Cluster2
AW00012301	$10,876	4	55	Cluster2
AW00012308	$10,841	4	44	Cluster2
AW00012323	$10,837	4	41	Cluster2

Cluster created: Europe customers (RFM)

 Four clusters were created in this example. Additionally, a column was added to the customer table of the data model with the name provided in the clusters dialog. The cluster column is identified in the Fields list with two overlapping square shapes, and an **Edit clusters** option is available by either right-clicking the column or selecting the ellipsis next to the column.

Analyze the clusters

1. Create three additional measures to help describe the clusters created and use a simple table to visualize them.

   Average Customer Sales = AVERAGEX(VALUES(Customer[Customer Alternate Key]),[Internet Net Sales])
   Average Customer Orders = AVERAGEX(VALUES(Customer[Customer Alternate Key]),[Internet Sales Orders])
   Average Days Since Last Purchase =
   AVERAGEX(VALUES(Customer[Customer Alternate Key]),[Days Since Last Purchase])

- AVERAGEX() is used to iterate over the unique customer keys provided by VALUES() to compute the customer-specific value (sales, orders, and days since purchase) and then return the average of the customers from each cluster:

Europe Customers (RFM)	Internet Net Sales	Internet Sales Customer Count	Average Customer Sales	Average Customer Orders	Average Days Since Last Purchase
Cluster2	$2,483,246	534	$4,650	2	88
Cluster4	$904,352	297	$3,045	1	727
Cluster3	$1,085,424	597	$1,818	1	364
Cluster1	$732,915	1,517	$483	1	97
Total	**$5,205,937**	**2,945**	**$1,768**	**1**	**213**

Average Customer Measures used with the Europe Customers (RFM) Cluster

Per the table, Cluster2 contains high value customers ($4,650 average) that have purchased recently (88 day average). Cluster1 contains low value customers that have purchased recently. Cluster4 contains high value customers that have not purchased recently and Cluster 3 contains average customer value and average time since the last purchase.

2. Create a scatter chart to better illustrate the four clusters:

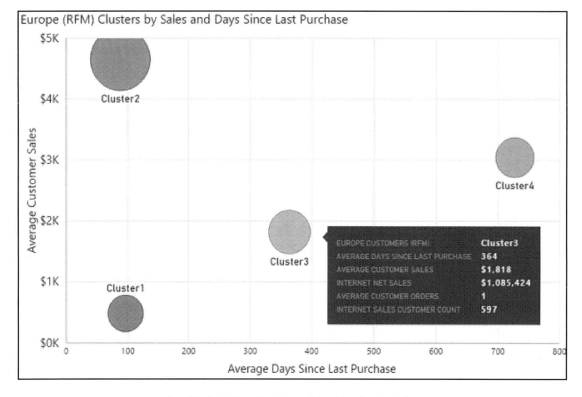

Clusters Visualized in Scatter Chart by Internet Sales and Days Since Last Purchase

- The average days and average sales measures are used as the X and Y axis variables, respectively
- The other average measure, total sales, and customer count measures are added to the tooltips

A potential use case or action based on these clusters is to focus marketing efforts on converting the Cluster1 customers, who've purchased recently, to higher value Cluster2 customers. Additionally, efforts could be made to reach the Cluster3 customers and maintain this relationship, given the 1 year (364) average duration since their last purchase. Finally, the 297 customers in Cluster4 may have already committed to a new bike supplier or, more optimistically, may have purchased a bike 2-3 years ago and may not be aware of what bike related accessories and clothing are available.

How it works...

RFM - recency, frequency, monetary

- The three measures used to support the clustering in this example follow the RFM technique, identifying the recency, frequency, and value of the customer's purchase history
- Adding measures (feature engineering) that covers each component of RFM is useful for various marketing and customer attrition analyses

Clustering algorithm and limits

- The Power BI clustering feature uses a K-Means algorithm to determine the optimal number of clusters to create
- Currently a cluster is limited to 15 measures and 1 dimension; an error message is returned if these limits are exceeded

There's more...

R clustering custom visuals

In addition to the standard Power BI clustering from this recipe, a Clustering and a Clustering with Outliers custom visual are also available to support similar analysis. Both these custom visuals are built with the R statistical programming language.

Scatter chart-based clustering

- Like the table visual from the example, clusters can also be automatically created from a Scatter chart visual
- These clusters are limited to two input measures (X and Y) but the clusters are automatically added to the Details field:

Clusters automatically added to the Legend of a Scatter chart based on the Dimension (Product Name) and X and Y variables

- This can be a quick method of discovering simple relationships (2 measures) and visualizing the dimension

Forecasting and visualizing future results

Standard Power BI report and dashboard visualizations are great tools to support descriptive and diagnostic analytics of historical or real-time data but ultimately, organizations need predictive and prescriptive analytics to help guide decisions involving future outcomes. Power BI Desktop provides a time series forecasting tool with built-in predictive modeling capabilities that enables report authors to quickly create custom forecasts, evaluate the accuracy of these forecasts, and build intuitive visualizations that blend actual or historical data with the forecast.

This recipe contains two complete forecasting examples. The first example builds a monthly forecast for the next three months utilizing an automatic date hierarchy. The second example builds a weekly forecast of the next eight weeks and evaluates the forecast's accuracy when applied to recent data.

Getting ready

1. Ensure that the Auto Date/Time setting in the Current File Data Load options is enabled in Power BI Desktop.
2. Create column(s) in the date dimension, such as `IsCurrentWeek`, that identifies the status of the level or grain required of the forecast. See the *Developing Dynamic Dashboard Metrics recipe* in `Chapter 5`, *Creating Power BI Dashboards,* for examples of creating these date dimension table columns within SQL views. Additionally, see the first recipe of `Chapter 6`, *Getting Serious with Date Intelligence,* for Date table design considerations.

A 'Calendar Week Status' column from the Date table is used to filter the weekly sales forecast in the second example of this recipe.

Page level filter of a report set to exclude the Current Calendar Week value

 The Forecast tool in Power BI includes an Ignore last feature which allows for the exclusion of incomplete periods (months, weeks, and days) from the forecast and this feature is utilized in the first example of this recipe. However, for common additive measures, such as Sales Amount, not filtering out the current period often significantly detracts from the usability of the visual given the steep decline represented by the current (incomplete) period. Dynamically updated date columns resolve this issue and persisted static date range filters generally.

How to do it...

Monthly forecast via date hierarchy

1. In Power BI Desktop, select the Line chart visualization type and position it on the report canvas.
2. With the empty Line chart selected, click on a measure from the **Field** List, such as Internet Net Sales.

3. Now add the date column (Date or Date/Time data type) from your Date table to the axis field well of this visual.
   - By default, a calendar hierarchy should be added to the axis with columns for Year, Quarter, Month, and Day

4. In the top left of the visual, click on the **Expand All Down One Level** button twice to navigate to the monthly grain:

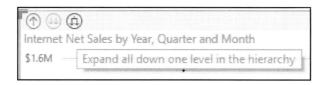

Internet Net Sales by Year, Quarter and Month

$1.6M — Expand all down one level in the hierarchy

Expand All Down Used to Display the Line Chart Visual by Month

5. With the chart still selected, open the **Analytics** pane to the right of the Format pane.

6. Expose the forecast options are at the bottom of the analytics pane and click on **Add**.
   - By default, a forecast of the measure for 10 points (months) in the future is created with a 95 percent Confidence interval

   - In this example, no filters have been applied to the report, report page, or visual, therefore the forecast is using the current month its algorithm

By default, a forecast of the measure for 10 points (months) in the future is created with a 95 percent Confidence interval. The forecast automatically determined the step (monthly grain) and also determined a seasonality factor to apply to the forecast. In this example, no filters have been been applied to the Report and thus the current month, which is incomplete, is being used by the forecast and should be excluded per step 7.

7. Enter the value 1 in the Ignore last input box and reduce the Forecast length to 3 Points (or Months).

8. Enter the value 12 in the Seasonality input box and click on **Apply**.

The forecast will now shorten and include a forecasted value for the current (incomplete) month. For example, if June is the current month, the revised forecast will include values for June, July, and August, based on the historical data from May and earlier data points. Applying the seasonality variable for its known grain (12 per year) overrides the default seasonality factor. When the seasonality (points per cycle) is known, it's recommended to apply this value manually to improve accuracy.

9. Finally, use the Color, Style, Transparency, and Confidence band style formatting options to highlight the forecast.

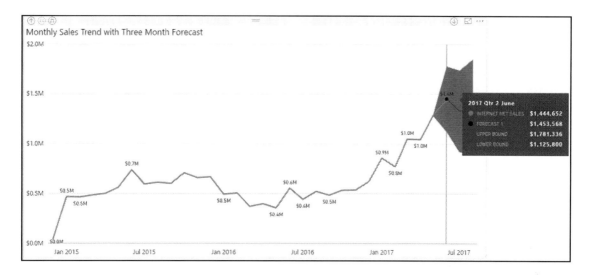

Monthly Forecast with Three Forecast Points Excluding the Current Month

Hovering over the June 2017 data points exposes both the Forecast and the upper and lower boundary values, given the 95 percent confidence interval. In this example, there are still 4 days remaining in June 2017, so it appears that actual sales will be higher than the forecasted value, but below the Upper Bound. In terms of formatting, a dark color with low transparency and the Fill Confidence band style is used to easily distinguish the forecast from the lighter color of the Internet Sales measure.

Weekly sales forecast analysis

The goal in this example is to produce a three week forecast based on weekly sales data and to evaluate whether the forecast would have predicted the recent increase in sales.

1. Follow the same steps from the first example to build a line chart with a forecast but now use a date column that represents the week ending date.
2. Apply a filter that excludes the current (incomplete) week, such as the example described in the *Getting ready* section.
3. In the **Forecast** options of the Analytics pane, enter a value of 8 for Forecast length and the value 5 for Ignore last.
4. Enter the value '52' for Seasonality and click on **Apply**.

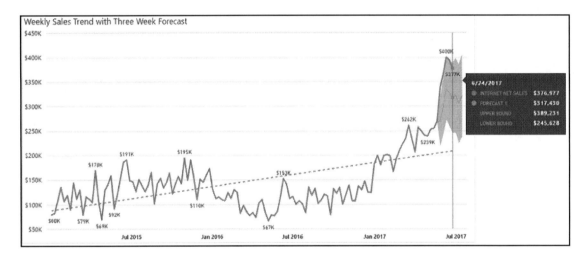

Weekly Sales Trend and Three Week Forecast which excludes the prior 5 Completed Weeks

In this example the last completed week ending date is 6/24/17. Therefore, given '5' points to ignore from Step 3, this point and four previous weeks are excluded from the forecasting algorithm such that the forecast can only use the weeks ending on 5/20/17 and earlier to generate its projections. Three additional forecast points (8 (Forecast Length) — 5 (Ignore Last)) are computed for the weeks ending on 7/1, 7/8, and 7/15. At the default 95 percent confidence interval, the Tooltips (and exported detail data) reveal that actual sales for the recent week are at the very top and, for certain weeks, in excess of the upper boundary. Only raising the confidence interval to 99 percent would maintain the recent weeks within the boundaries of the forecast.

This second example highlights the limitations of forecasts based exclusively on historical data. If and when business circumstances significantly change, such as in May of 2017 in this example, the historical data loses its predictive value. Nonetheless, building predictive forecasts into Power BI reports and dashboards raises the analytical value of these assets by drawing attention to trends and projected outcomes.

How it works...

Exponential smoothing

The Power BI Forecast tool uses the exponential smoothing time series predictive algorithm. This method is widely used in multiple domains and helps to suppress outlier values while efficiently capturing trends.

Dynamic week status column

The `Calendar Week Status` column used as a filter in the second example was created via T-SQL

```
CASE
      WHEN YEAR(D.Date) = YEAR(CURRENT_TIMESTAMP) AND DATEPART(WEEK,D.Date)
=      DATEPART(WEEK,CURRENT_TIMESTAMP) THEN 'Current Calendar Week' WHEN
YEAR(D.Date) = YEAR(DATEADD(WEEK,-1,CAST(CURRENT_TIMESTAMP AS date))) AND
DATEPART(WEEK,D.Date) =
DATEPART(WEEK,DATEADD(WEEK,-1,CAST(CURRENT_TIMESTAMP AS date))) THEN 'Prior
Calendar Week'
ELSE 'Other Calendar Week'
End As [Calendar Week Status]
```

Two additional values (`2 Wk Prior Calendar Week` and `3 Wk Prior Calendar Week`) are not included in this excerpt from the T-SQL view used to load the date dimension table in the Power BI data model. Unlike the dynamic year and month columns described in `Chapter 6`, *Getting Serious with Date Intelligence*, which used the `YEAR()` and `MONTH()` T-SQL functions, respectively, this column uses the `DATEPART()` T-SQL function to extract the calendar week value, since a calendar week function isn't currently supported by SQL Server.

There's more...

Forecast requirements

- The forecast tool is currently only available to the Line chart visual and only one measure (line) on this visual
- The x-axis value needs to have a date/time data type or be a uniformly increasing whole number
- A minimum of six (6) date points are required

Using R functions and scripts to create visuals within Power BI

The R programming language, including its powerful and extensible features in data processing, advanced analytics, and visualization, is deeply integrated with Power BI. An R script can be used as a data source for a Power BI dataset, as a data transformation and shaping process within an M query, and as its own visualization type within Power BI reports and dashboards. Like standard Power BI visuals, R script visuals directly leverage the relationships defined in the data model and can be dynamically filtered via other visuals, such as slicers.

In this recipe, two histogram visualizations are created in Power BI Desktop with R scripts, one with R's standard distribution base graphics and another with the popular ggplot2 visualization package. The R Script Showcase, referenced in the *See also* section, contains many additional examples of R script visuals for Power BI, such as Correlation Plots, Clustering, and Forecasting.

Getting ready

1. Download and install the R engine on the local machine (`https://cran.r-project.org/bin/windows/base/`).

2. Install the `ggplot2` package for R via the following command:
   `install.packages("ggplot2")`.

3. Optionally, install an IDE for editing R scripts, such as R Studio (`https://www.rstudio.com/`) or R Tools for Visual Studio.

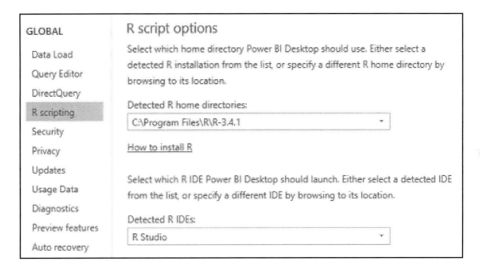

R Scripting Options in Power BI Desktop

 Confirm that the local R installation directory path is reflected in the R Scripting options in Power BI Desktop. The Detected R IDEs dropdown can be used to choose between multiple installed IDEs. If an R script visual has not been used in Power BI Desktop, an **Enable script visuals** prompt will appear. Click on **Enable**.

How to do it...

The requirement for both visualizations in this recipe is to display a distribution of the product list prices that have been sold online in the current calendar year. The first example uses the standard `hist()` function with R's base graphics and the second example uses the `ggplot()` function provided by the `ggplot2` package for R.

Base graphics histogram

1. In Power BI Desktop, unhide the Product Key column of the Product table--the column used in relationships to fact tables.
2. Add the Calendar Year Status column from the Date dimension table to a Page or Report level filter and set the filter condition to the current calendar year.

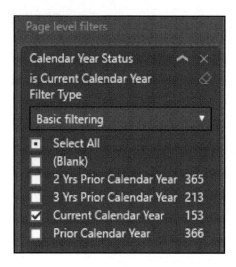

Page Level Filter

- See `Chapter 6`, *Getting Serious with Date Intelligence* for details on dynamic date columns.

3. Click on the R script visual from the Visualizations pane to add it to the canvas.
4. Add the Product Key and List Price columns from the Product table to the Values field well of the R script visual.
5. Now add the Internet Net Sales measure to the Values field well. This ensures that the products have been sold.
    - The R script editor will automatically create a data frame of the three fields and remove duplicates

If a supported external R IDE is installed and selected in the Detected R IDEs R scripting options per the the *Getting ready* section, you can now click on **Edit script in External R IDE** (up arrow icon). This will launch the IDE application (such as R Studio) and export the data frame from Power BI Desktop. Common features of R scripting IDEs, such as Intellisense and Variable History, are helpful (if not essential) for developing complex R script visuals. Currently, the external R script must be pasted back into Power BI Desktop's R script editor.

6. Enter (or paste) the following R script into the R script editor and click the 'Run script' icon:

```
par(bg = "#E6E6E6")
hist(dataset$'List Price', breaks = seq(from=0, to = 2500, by = 500), col =
"#2C95FF",
main = "Current Year Online Sales List Price Distribution", cex.main =
1.75, cex.axis = 1.2, cex.lab = 1.4, ylab = "Count of Products", xlab =
"Product List Price Bins", las = 1, labels = TRUE, border = "black",
ylim=c(0,50))
```

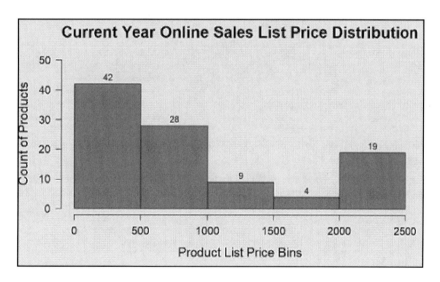

R script visual rendered in Power BI via Base Graphics

The light gray background color is set via the par() function, and arguments to the hist() function define the X and Y axes, the text strings for the titles, data labels, font sizes, and the light blue color of the bars. The seq() function is used to configure the X axis intervals (bins) with a width or bin size of $500 and a max price of $2,500.

ggplot2 histogram

1. With the ggPlot2 package for R installed per the *Getting ready* section, create a new R script visual in Power BI Desktop.
2. Add the same columns and measures to the visual as the previous example (List Price and Product Key from the Product table, Internet Net Sales Measure from Internet Sales).

3. If the new R script visual is on a separate page as the previous example (Base Graphics Histogram) and if a report level filter for current year has not been set, apply a page level filter for current calendar year just like in step 2 of the previous example.
4. Enter or paste the following script into the R script editor window and click on the Run script icon:

```
prices <- as.numeric(as.character(dataset$'List Price'))
breakpoints <- seq(from=0, to = 2500, by = 500)
library("ggplot2")
ggplot(dataset, aes(x = prices)) + geom_histogram(breaks =
breakpoints, fill = "#2C95FF", color = "black") + xlab("Product
List Price Bins") + ylab("Count of Products") + ggtitle("Current
Year Online Sales List Price Distribution") + stat_bin(breaks =
breakpoints, geom="text", aes(label=..count..), vjust = -1) +
coord_cartesian(ylim=c(0,50)) + theme(text = element_text(size =
16)) + theme(plot.title = element_text(hjust = .5))
```

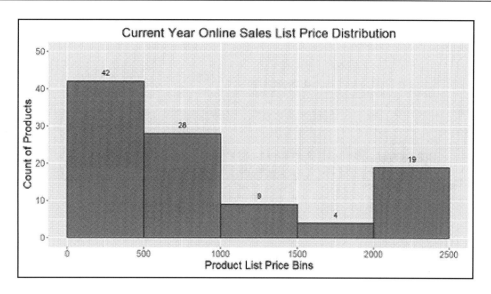

R script visual rendered in Power BI via ggplot2 package

The ggplot2's `geom_histogram()` requires a continuous variable and thus the `List Price` column is converted to a numeric data type in the `prices` variable. The same vector expression (`seq()`) used for the x axis (bins by 500 to 2,500) in the prior example is used as the parameter to the breaks argument of `geom_histogram()` and `stat_bin()`. Likewise, the same expression for the Y axis in the prior example is re-used, but passed as a parameter to the `coord_cartesian()` function.

The `qplot()` function, short for quick plot, is also available in the `ggplot2` package and can provide faster development of relatively complex visualizations with less code-often just one line.

How it works...

Automatic duplicate removal

The R script editor in Power BI Desktop automatically creates a data frame and removes duplicate rows based on the columns loaded to the Values field well.

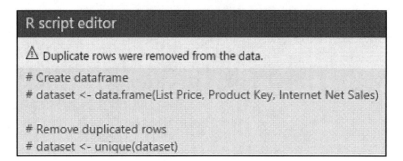

R script editor

⚠ Duplicate rows were removed from the data.

\# Create dataframe
\# dataset <- data.frame(List Price, Product Key, Internet Net Sales)

\# Remove duplicated rows
\# dataset <- unique(dataset)

Power BI Desktop R script editor: Data Frame and Duplicate Removal

In this example, in which the intent is to count individual products (including those with the same list price), it's necessary to add a separate column in the data frame (the product key column) that makes each row of the data frame unique. In other scenarios, the `Table.AddIndexColumn()` M function could be used to create uniqueness.

Filter context

- Including the Internet Net Sales measure in the R script visuals data frame allows the visual to be filtered by the Date dimension column (`Calendar Year Status = Current Calendar Year`) and other dimension tables on the report page.
- By default, the products without any sales, given this filter context, will not be included in the data frame per the requirements of this recipe. The **show items with no data** option for the Product Key column in the Values field well can be used if the products without sales are to be included in this visualization.

There's more...

- The R script data source connector is available in the Other category of the Get Data dialog
- A Run R Script command icon is available in the Transform window of the Query Editor
- Many custom visuals built with R are already available in the Office Store, and as of July 2017, R custom visuals can include interactive features, such as selection and zoom

See also

- R Script Visual Showcase for Power BI: `https://community.powerbi.com/t5/R-Script-Showcase/bd-p/RVisuals`

10
Developing Solutions for System Monitoring and Administration

In this chapter, we will cover the following recipes:

- Creating a centralized IT monitoring solution with Power BI
- Constructing a monitoring, visualization, and analysis layer
- Importing and visualizing dynamic management view (DMV) data of SSAS and Power BI data models
- Increasing the SQL Server DBA's productivity with Power BI
- Providing documentation of Power BI and SSAS data models to BI and business teams
- Analyzing performance monitor counters of the Microsoft on-premises data gateway and SSAS tabular databases
- Analyzing Extended Events trace data with Power BI
- Visualizing log file data from SQL Server agent jobs and Office 365 audit searches

Introduction

In addition to solutions targeting business processes and entities such as sales and customers, Power BI can also serve as a platform for system monitoring and administration. Diverse data sources, including performance monitor counters, log files, and events can be integrated into Power BI datasets to deliver robust visibility to system health, performance, and activity. Although there are several dedicated monitoring tools available, such as Operations Manager in Microsoft System Center, building a custom solution with Power BI provides full flexibility and control over all layers of the solution while leveraging relevant Power BI features such as data-driven alerts, email notifications and subscriptions, and Power BI mobile. Additionally, as more organizations adopt and deploy Power BI, existing licenses and experience can significantly reduce the costs of developing and maintaining these solutions.

This chapter's recipes highlight the most common and impactful administration data sources, including Windows Performance Monitor, SQL Server Query Store, the Microsoft On-Premises Data Gateway, the MSDB system database, and Extended Events. Power BI solutions built on top of these sources proactively assess usage trends and resource bottlenecks and deliver the detailed analysis necessary to identify root causes. Additionally, the metadata of existing Power BI and SSAS data models exposed via **dynamic management views** (**DMVs**) such as measure and relationship definitions and resource consumption can be integrated to provide a simplified reference or documentation asset for both BI and business teams. Erin Stellato, principal consultant from SQL skills and Microsoft Data Platform MVP, has contributed to several of these recipes, including references to the setup and utilization of relational database monitoring and administrative data sources.

Creating a centralized IT monitoring solution with Power BI

Power BI's rich data connectivity and transformation capabilities are very well suited for the integration needs of system and database administrators. A collection of log files containing performance monitor counter statistics can be retrieved from a file directory (or multiple directories), consolidated, and further enhanced to support reporting. Additional sources, such as snapshots of performance and configuration data stored in a dedicated administrator database, can also be included in a scheduled data refresh process, and the inclusion of existing BI dimension tables such as date and time further simplifies the overall monitoring solution.

In this recipe, a set of Windows Performance Monitor counter files containing statistics on CPU, Memory, and more are integrated with administrative data stored in a SQL Server database including query wait statistics and instance configuration values. This recipe documents the data retrieval and integration of the monitoring data, and the following recipe, *Constructing a monitoring visualization and analysis layer,* utilizes this dataset in building Power BI report and dashboard content. Details and references on implementing the three data sources featured in this recipe are included in the *How it works..., There's more..., and See also* sections.

Getting ready

1. Identify the administrative stakeholders familiar with the current state of monitoring and the top priorities of the solution such as "How is performance today?" and/or "Has a configuration changed?"
2. Sharpen the meaning of these questions to identify the required data sources including performance counters and system views.
3. Create a dedicated database named Admin in SQL Server that will exclusively store system and administrative data.
4. Create two tables in the admin database, `WaitStats` and `ConfigData`, with columns that correspond to the `sys.dm_os_wait_stats` and `sys.configurations` system views, respectively.

5. Use Windows Performance Monitor to design and schedule a new data collector set containing the following performance monitor counters.

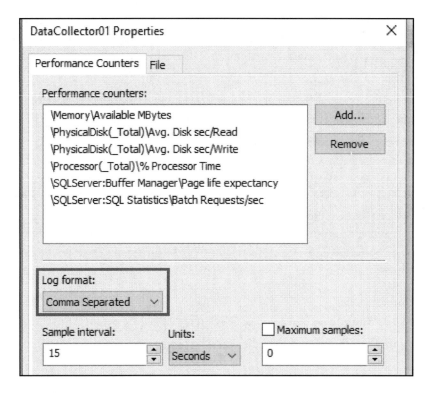

Custom Data Collector set with CSV Log Format

Performance Monitor defaults to `.blg` log files but Power BI can only consolidate files in text, CSV, and Excel format.

Windows Performance Monitor is well documented and understood by most administrators; best practices and automation via PowerShell are outside the scope of this recipe. Details of the scheduled processes and design considerations supporting the `WaitStats` and `ConfigData` tables are included in the *How it works...* section. Essentially, these tables contain snapshots of performance or configuration data, just as performance counters represent point-in-time values at the intervals chosen. Maintaining these data collection processes enables tools such as Power BI to generate insights and drive appropriate responses.

An iterative development approach in which more readily available data such as performance counters is targeted first may benefit the monitoring solution. In some scenarios, performance counters alone may be of significant value and additional monitoring data sources such as `WaitStats` and `Configuration` values can be added later once the necessary supporting processes/jobs are in place.

How to do it...

1. Open a new Power BI Desktop file (`.pbix`) and create parameters for the source servers and databases.
2. Create queries against the admin and BI/DW databases with the `Sql.Database()` function and these parameters.

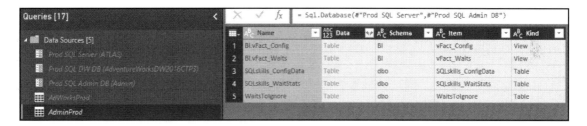

Server and database parameters and Queries with Load Disabled

As per some of the previous recipes, Power BI does not isolate data sources from individual queries by default, and thus dedicated database queries are used to expose table and view objects. Individual queries reference these database queries such that many queries can be adjusted by modifying the server and database parameter values referenced by the database query.

3. Add a `Date` and a `Time` query from the existing dimension views available in the BI/DW database.
4. Create a parameter named `CounterHistoryDays` and assign a current value such as 7 or 30 to limit the history retrieved.

5. Retrieve the performance counter log files by creating a new query and using the folder data source.

C:\PerfLogs\AdminMonitoringCounters

Content	Name	Extension	Date accessed	Date modified	Date created	Attributes	Folder Path
Binary	DataCollector01.csv	.csv	7/11/2017 11:21:24 AM	7/11/2017 11:21:24 AM	7/11/2017 11:21:24 AM	Record	C:\PerfLogs\AdminMonitoringCounters\ATLAS_201707...
Binary	DataCollector02.csv	.csv	7/11/2017 10:39:31 PM	7/11/2017 10:39:31 PM	7/11/2017 10:24:13 PM	Record	C:\PerfLogs\AdminMonitoringCounters\ATLAS_201707...

Performance Counter collector set files exposed in both root and subdirectories

The scheduled data collector set will automatically generate a subdirectory for each new file output. The Power BI M query references the root directory (or parent) and all supported file formats in subdirectories of this query are available for retrieval. Depending on the volume of counters, their time interval (that is, 15 seconds), and the schedule and duration of the collector set, a significant volume of files can accumulate.

6. Add a filter expression to the performance counter query that requires CSV files and "date modified" dates later than or equal to the `EarliestDate` variable.

```
CurrentDate = DateTime.Date(DateTime.LocalNow()),
EarliestDate = Date.AddDays(CurrentDate,-CounterHistoryDays),
SourceFolder =
Folder.Files("C:\PerfLogs\AdminMonitoringCounters"),
ReportFiles = Table.SelectRows(SourceFolder, each [Extension] =
".csv" and
DateTime.Date([Date modified]) >= EarliestDate)
```

- The `EarliestDate` variable is evaluated based on the `CounterHistoryDays` parameter and the current system date

7. Click on the double arrows pointed down on the `Content` column to combine the files remaining into one query:

- Power BI will automatically create a sample query, file, parameter and a new function to combine the files. The official documentation on combining binaries in Power BI Desktop is referenced in the *See also* section.

8. Open the sample query created and add a `Date` and a `Time` column based on the data collector Set Date column.

```
ParsedDate = Table.AddColumn(Columns, "Date", each
Date.From(DateTimeZone.From([#"(PDH-CSV 4.0) (Eastern Daylight
Time)(240)"])), type date),
ParsedTime = Table.AddColumn(ParsedDate, "Time", each
Time.From(DateTimeZone.From([#"(PDH-CSV 4.0) (Eastern Daylight
Time)(240)"])), type time)
```

9. Add a `Table.RenameColumns()` expression to the sample query that applies report friendly names.

- These revisions to the sample query will be reflected in the performance counters query that will be loaded
- If automatic type detection for unstructured data sources is turned off as recommended, it will be necessary to add a data type conversion step to avoid the counter columns from being loaded as a text data type

```
TypeChanges =
Table.TransformColumnTypes(ExpandedTable,{{"Date", type date},
{"Time", type time}, {"Page life expectancy", Int64.Type}, {"Avg.
Disk sec/Write", type number},
{"Avg. Disk sec/Read", type number}, {"Batch Requests/sec", type
number}, {"% Processor", Int64.Type}, {"Available MBytes",
Int64.Type}})
```

If the source `DateTime` column is already rounded to whole seconds, such as SQL Server `datetime2(0)`, then a Time column created via the `DateTime.Time()` M function can be used for the relationship to the `Time` dimension table. Casting SQL Server datetime data type columns to `datetime2(0)` in the SQL view used to import to Power BI is recommended, to avoid additional rounding logic implemented in the Power BI query. In the case of Performance Monitor Counter log files, the `DateTime` column is not rounded to the second, and therefore, rounding logic is applied within the M query to create a six-character text column.

10. Create a six-character column rounded to the individual second based on the `Time` column:
    - Note that the `Time` column is of the `Time` data type

```
HourText = Table.AddColumn(TimeCol, "TextHour", each
  if Time.Hour([Time]) < 10 then "0" & Text.From(Time.Hour([Time]))
else
  Text.From(Time.Hour([Time])), type text),
MinText = Table.AddColumn(HourText, "TextMin", each
  if Time.Minute([Time]) < 10 then "0" &
Text.From(Time.Minute([Time])) else
  Text.From(Time.Minute([Time])), type text),
SecText = Table.AddColumn(MinText, "TextSec", each
  if Number.RoundDown(Time.Second([Time]),0) < 10 or
Number.RoundUp(Time.Second([Time]),0) < 10 then "0" &
Text.From(Number.RoundDown(Time.Second([Time]),0))
else Text.From(Number.RoundDown(Time.Second([Time]),0)), type
text),
SecondCol = Table.AddColumn(SecText,"SecondOfDay", each [TextHour]
& [TextMin] & [TextSec], type text)
```

The concatenated `SecondOfDay` column will be used for the relationship with the `Time` dimension.

In this example, the `DimTime` dimension table in the data warehouse has 86,400 rows--1 row for each second. The detail of this granularity can be helpful in troubleshooting and deeper analysis, but a time dimension at the minute grain with only 1,440 may be sufficient. Whether in seconds or minutes, a Time dimension table is especially recommended for filtering multiple fact tables (for example, `Wait Stats` and `Counter Data`) in the same report and for providing useful groupings such as the 7 AM to 9 AM timeframe.

11. SQL views should be created in the admin database for both `Wait Stats` and the `Config Data` tables:
    - Each view should apply report-friendly column aliases and `WHERE` clauses to only import the timeframes required

12. In the `BI.vFact_Waits` SQL view, cast the capture date column to `datetime2(0)` to round this column to seconds.

13. In the `Wait Stats` M query, add a column named `Time` of the time data type via the `DateTime.Time()` function based on the capture date column (`datetime2(0)`).

Similar to other SQL views described in previous recipes the SQL view predicate, or WHERE clause, reduces the workload of the Power BI retrieval process and avoids unnecessary M query transformations such as column aliases and any data type conversions.

14. Duplicate either the Date or Time table and revise the source, schema, and item variables to expose the Wait Stats and Configuration Values views in their own M queries:

```
Source = AdminProd,
Config = Source{[Schema = "BI", Item = "vFact_Waits"]}[Data]
```

15. Ensure that only the five tables (Date, Time, Wait Stats, Configuration Values, and Performance Counters) are enabled for load (all other queries and parameters should have a gray font, indicating that they exist only in the Query Editor).
16. Click on **Close & Apply** to exit the Query Editor.
17. Create five single-direction relationships between the monitoring tables and the Date and Time tables.

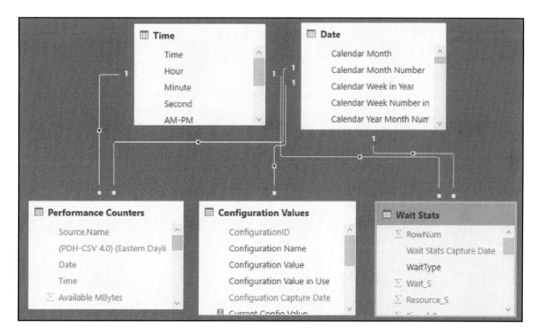

Relationships View - Single-direction relationships from Date and Time dimension tables to Monitoring fact tables

- The three date table relationships should be based on date data types to enable time intelligence DAX functions
- The `SecondOfDay` six-character text column is used for the `Performance-Monitor-to-Time` table relationship
- The `Time` column of the time data type is used for the `Wait-Stats-to-Time` table relationship

 In this example, the `Configuration Values` job runs only on a daily basis and is cast as a date data type in its SQL view. In most scenarios, this should be sufficient as configuration values change infrequently--a time column and relationship would not be useful. As the monitoring solution expands, say with Query Store statistics and system logic files, additional dimension tables describing and grouping the monitoring data may be helpful.

18. Hide all columns that won't be exposed in reports, including the numerical columns, as measures will be created.
19. Create hierarchies in the `Date` and `Time` dimension tables to support drill-up and drill-down navigation.
20. Set the **Default Summarization** column property to **None** and set the **Sort By Column** property where appropriate, such as **Month** and **Weekday** text columns.
21. Optionally, create dedicated measure tables to store all monitoring measures or measures specific to a fact table.

How it works...

Wait Stats and instance configuration data source setup

- The setup of the wait statistics data store and the capture of wait statistics are described by Erin Stellato in the following blog post: https://sqlperformance.com/2015/10/sql-performance/proactive-sql-server-health-checks-5
- The setup of the instance configuration data store and the capture of these values are also described by Erin Stellato in this blog post: https://sqlperformance.com/2015/02/system-configuration/proactive-sql-server-health-checks-3

The `value` and `value_in_use` columns in the `sys.configurations` view and table to be created in the admin database are stored in a `sql_variant` data type. The view used to import this data to Power BI casts these columns as an Integer data type and casts the datetime `CaptureDate` column as a date data type.

There's more...

Query Store integration

- The dataset created in this recipe is extended to include Query Store performance statistics in the *Increasing SQL Server DBA Productivity with Power BI* recipe later in this chapter
- Additional inputs such as SQL Server Agent and backup log files can also be integrated to aid administrators in assessing the causes and impacts of changes in available resources, workloads, and system configurations.

DirectQuery real-time monitoring datasets

 DirectQuery datasets require a single database on a single supported data source, such as SQL Server, Oracle, and Teradata. Therefore, to support a DirectQuery dataset in which SQL queries would be passed from Power BI to the data source as users accessed and interacted with the reports in Power BI, a process or job needs to be scheduled to load a single database with the three data inputs (performance counter files, configuration values, and wait statistics).

See also

- Combine binaries in Power BI Desktop: `http://bit.ly/2oL2nM4`

Constructing a monitoring visualization and analysis layer

Monitoring and administration tools such as Performance Monitor, SQL Server Activity Monitor, Query Store, and Extended Events include their own graphical interfaces for viewing and analyzing their own specific datasets. However, these features are limited relative to the data exploration and visualization capabilities provided by dedicated BI tools such as Power BI. Additionally, as per the first recipe of this chapter, system and database administrators require an integrated view over distinct data sources with a common and flexible visual surface. The ability to define logic on top of monitoring source data, along with the "anywhere" availability of Power BI content and its data alert and advanced analytics features, further enhances the value of integrated monitoring datasets.

In this recipe, the monitoring dataset created in the first recipe of this chapter is leveraged to develop reporting content that addresses top stakeholder priorities, such as "How is the performance today?" and "Has any configuration value changed?" A report visualization specific to SQL Server Query Store is included in the *There's More...* section and additional monitoring visualizations are included in later recipes in this chapter.

Getting ready

1. Obtain guidance from stakeholders and **subject matter experts (SMEs)** on performance baselines and threshold values.
2. For example, should the metric available memory be compared to the last 7, 30, or more days? Are there good (green), satisfactory (yellow), and problem (red) values associated with `Wait Statistics` measures or CPU time?

How to do it...

1. Create simple DAX measures (`Average`, `Min`, and `Max`) and then `Date` Intelligence measures to support a comparison of performance monitoring counters against prior time periods or baselines:

   Available Memory MB (Today) = CALCULATE([Available Memory (MB)],
   FILTER(ALL('Date'),'Date'[Date] = [Current Date]))
   Batch Requests per Sec (Yesterday) = CALCULATE([Batch Requests Per Sec],
   FILTER(ALL('Date'),'Date'[Date] = [Yesterday]))
   Min Available Memory MB (Today) = CALCULATE([Min Available Memory (MB)],
   FILTER(ALL('Date'),'Date'[Date] = [Current Date]),ALL('Time'))

2. Create a report page based on the performance monitor counters that addresses top visibility needs such as "How is performance today?" and "How close are we to resource thresholds?"

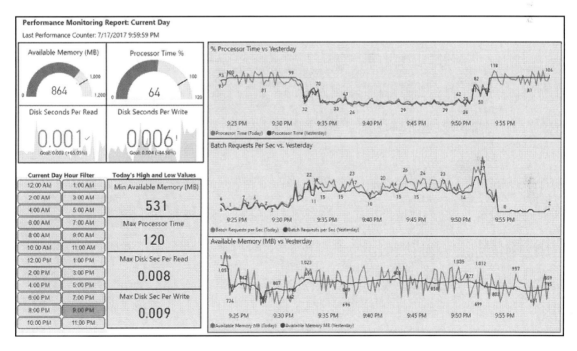

Performance Monitoring Report Page Leveraging Windows Performance Monitor Counters

Two gauge visuals and two KPI visuals are used to display the highest priority counters relative to predefined thresholds or baselines. For example, Disk Seconds per Read is highlighted in green given the lower value than the goal of .003, and disk seconds per write is highlighted in red due to the higher value than the goal of .004. All four visuals respect the hour filter control (a custom Chiclet Slicer) from the lower left, and a `Minute of Day` Time data type column from the Time dimension table is used for the KPI Trend. A **Today's High and Low Values** group of Card visuals ignores the Time filter selection (for example, 9:00 PM from the slicer) but applies the current date filter. CPU (% processor), batch requests per second, and available memory are plotted against the prior day values in the line charts in this example. Seven-day and 30-day average measures are commonly used for the performance baseline.

3. Create DAX measures to identify database instance configuration changes:

```
Config Value = If(AND(HASONEVALUE('Configuration
Values'[ConfigurationID]),HASONEVALUE('Date'[Date])),
MAX('Configuration Values'[Configuration Value]),BLANK())
Config Value (Today) = CALCULATE([Config
Value],FILTER(ALL('Date'),'Date'[Date] = [Current Date]))
Config Value (Yesterday) = CALCULATE([Config
Value],FILTER(ALL('Date'),'Date'[Date] = [Yesterday]))
Config Change (Today) = IF([Config Value (Today)] <> [Config Value
(Yesterday)],
"Config Change", "No Change")
Config Changes = IF([Config Value] = [Prior Day Config],0,1)
```

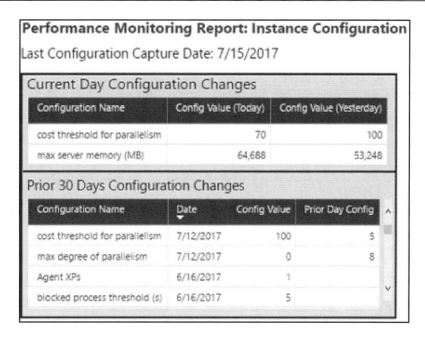

Performance Monitoring Report: Instance Configuration

Last Configuration Capture Date: 7/15/2017

Current Day Configuration Changes

Configuration Name	Config Value (Today)	Config Value (Yesterday)
cost threshold for parallelism	70	100
max server memory (MB)	64,688	53,248

Prior 30 Days Configuration Changes

Configuration Name	Date	Config Value	Prior Day Config
cost threshold for parallelism	7/12/2017	100	5
max degree of parallelism	7/12/2017	0	8
Agent XPs	6/16/2017	1	
blocked process threshold (s)	6/16/2017	5	

Instance Configuration Report Page: Current Day and Trailing 30-Day History of Changes

The Current Day Configuration Changes table visual uses a visual-level filter on the Config Change (Today) measure created earlier such that only changed configurations (for the current day) are displayed. The Prior 30 Days Configuration Change table visual uses two Visual level filters. One filter is applied to the date column from the Date dimension table and uses the relative date filtering feature to retrieve the past 30 days but exclude the current day. The other filter condition is applied against the Config Changes measure created earlier; this filter is set to **is 1**.

4. Create similar DAX measures for the Wait Statistics table, such as current day average wait seconds.

5. On a new page, compare the average of the current day's wait statistics capture data against a prior date.

"Wait statistics are probably the single best way to start troubleshooting a SQL Server performance issue. SQL Server knows why execution is being stalled (i.e. why threads are having to wait) so using this information to identify bottlenecks and avenues for further investigation can dramatically reduce the time it takes to diagnose the cause of workload degradation."

- Paul Randal, CEO of SQLskills, Microsoft Data Platform MVP

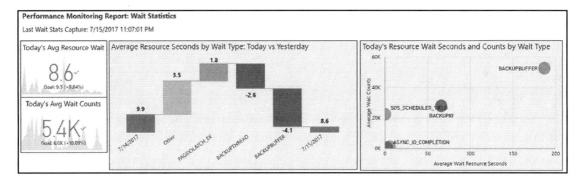

Wait Statistics Report Sample: KPIs, Waterfall, and Scatter Chart visuals

In this limited sample of a wait statistics report, relative date filtering is applied at the page level, to only include the past 30 days, and thus the 30 day trend is displayed in the background of the two KPI visuals. Relative date filters are also applied at the visual level to the waterfall and scatter charts to include only the last two days and only the current day, respectively. The breakdown field well of the waterfall chart is used to automatically identify the largest drivers of the change in wait seconds (wait types) from the prior day to the current day.

A high-level wait statistics report can be used as a quick starting point of analysis to identify bottlenecks in a system. Additionally, with mature and predictable baseline data in place, the report can be used to troubleshoot performance degradation issues. For example, a sudden spike in PAGEIOLATCH_EX waits may indicate a missing index issue or related database schema or code change.

How it works...

Relative date filtering

- The July 2017 release of Power BI Desktop made relative date filtering available to all report scopes: visual, page, and report.

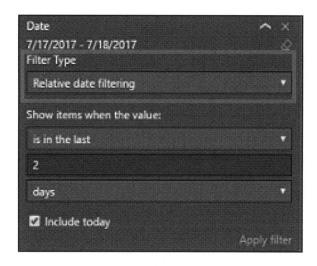

Relative Date Filtering

- Relative date filtering was previously only available in the slicer visual for date data types. In many scenarios, this functionality can eliminate the need to write additional custom DAX measures for specific visuals or report pages.

There's more...

Top 10 slowest queries via Query Store

- Individual SQL query statements can also be retrieved from Query Store and Extended Events

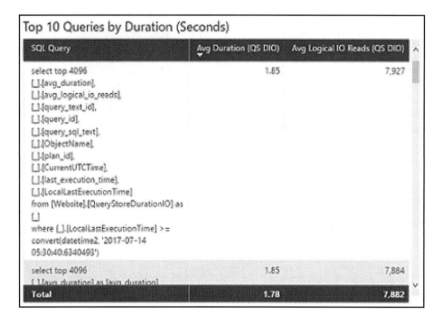

A Table Visual filtered for the top 10 SQL Query values based on the Duration measure

- The top N visual level filter is applied to a table visual based on the `Avg Duration` measure

This recipe focused primarily on dashboard content that addresses top, high-level monitoring questions. However, a layer of detailed reports, including visuals such as this top X queries by duration (or I/O, CPU, and so on), would likely be valuable complements in the summary-level reports and dashboards. Note that table visuals support cross-highlighting such that clicking on an individual SQL query would cross-highlight other visuals on the report page. See the *Query Store and Extended Events* recipes later in this chapter for additional details and examples of exposing the SQL statement on the report canvas.

See also

- SQL Server Wait Types Library: `https://www.sqlskills.com/help/waits/`

Importing and visualizing dynamic management view (DMV) data of SSAS and Power BI data models

SSAS and Power BI instances include many **dynamic management views** (**DMVs**), which can be used to retrieve both schema metadata and resource usage associated with the various database objects. As query performance for imported data models is directly impacted by the amount of memory consumed, visibility to memory and related information, such as compression and cardinality, is essential in performance tuning efforts. Power BI integration and visualization tools can enhance the value of the system information provided by DMVs to provide owners of Power BI and SSAS datasets with an intuitive, sustainable reporting layer in support of these assets.

In this recipe, M queries are created to retrieve and transform DMV information from a Power BI dataset. Essential relationships, measures, and report visuals are then built to support memory usage analysis.

How to do it...

1. Open the Power BI Desktop file containing the dataset to be analyzed. This file must remain open during data retrieval.
2. Open DAX Studio and connect to the open Power BI Desktop file (`.pbix`).
3. Retrieve the server and database name associated with the running Power BI Desktop file.

The server name will be in the bottom right of the DAX Studio Status Bar, such as `localhost:56514`. The following SQL statement will retrieve the system name of the database to be queried:

```
Select [CATALOG_NAME] From $System.DBSCHEMA_CATALOGS
```

In this example, `56514` represents the local port being used by the Power BI Desktop file and the following 36 character string is the catalog name: `7f1e8568-4281-4c17-a990-dbe7b6199163`.

4. Open a new Power BI Desktop file and click on **Edit Queries** to open the Query Editor window.

5. Create two parameters, `Server` and `Database`, and apply the values retrieved from DAX Studio as the current values.

Query Parameters with values for the local Power BI Model

6. Create two new M queries, segments and columns, which use the `Server` and `Database` parameters to access SQL Server analysis services **dynamic management views (DMVs)**.

Following is the segments query:

```
let Source = AnalysisServices.Database
(Server, Database,[Query="Select * From
$SYSTEM.DISCOVER_STORAGE_TABLE_COLUMN_SEGMENTS"]),
    Segments = Table.AddColumn(Source, "Structure Type", each
        if Text.Range([TABLE_ID],1,1) <> "$" then "Data"
        else if Text.Start([TABLE_ID],2) = "H$" then "Column
Hierarchy"
        else if Text.Start([TABLE_ID],2) = "U$" then "User
Hierarchy"
        else if Text.Start([TABLE_ID],2) = "R$" then "Relationship"
        else "unknown", type text),
    RenameTable = Table.RenameColumns(Segments,{{"DIMENSION_NAME",
"Table"}}),
    KeyColumn = Table.AddColumn(RenameTable, "ColumnKey", each
[Table] & "-" & [COLUMN_ID], type text)
in KeyColumn
```

The `Server` and `Database` parameters, along with a SQL statement against the `Discover_Storage_Table_Column_Segments` DMV, are used to extract access memory usage data from the running Power BI Desktop file (which contains an analysis services instance). The conditional column (`Structure Type`) is added to identify the memory structure represented by each row, and a concatenated column (`ColumnKey`) is created to support a relationship to the `Columns` table.

Following is the columns query:

```
let Source = AnalysisServices.Database
(Server, Database,[Query="Select * From
$SYSTEM.DISCOVER_STORAGE_TABLE_COLUMNS"]),
    BasicData = Table.SelectRows(Source, each ([COLUMN_TYPE] =
"BASIC_DATA")),
    RenameTable = Table.RenameColumns(BasicData,{{"DIMENSION_NAME",
"Table"},{"ATTRIBUTE_NAME","Column"}}),
    KeyColumn = Table.AddColumn(RenameTable, "ColumnKey", each
[Table] & "-" & [COLUMN_ID], type text),
    DateRetrieved = Table.AddColumn(KeyColumn, "Date Retrieved",
each DateTime.Date(DateTime.LocalNow()), type date)
in DateRetrieved
```

The `Discover Storage Table Columns` DMV is filtered based on the `Column_Type` column and a concatenated column (`ColumnKey`) is created for the relationship to the `Segments` table. Additionally, a dynamic `Date Retrieved` column is added to support the reporting layer.

7. Load the two queries and create a bidirectional many-to-one relationship between segments and columns based on the `ColumnKey` column that was created for both queries.

8. Create DAX measures that calculate the memory usage of the objects in the model in terms of **megabytes (MB)**:

```
Segment Size (MB) = DIVIDE(SUM(Segments[USED_SIZE]),1048576)
Dictionary Size (MB) =
DIVIDE(SUM('Columns'[DICTIONARY_SIZE]),1048576)
Data Size (MB) = CALCULATE([Segment Size (MB)],Segments[Structure
Type] = "Data")

Column Hierarchies Size (MB) =
CALCULATE([Segment Size (MB)],Segments[Structure Type] = "Column
Hierarchy")
User Hierarchy Size (MB) = CALCULATE([Segment Size
(MB)],Segments[Structure Type] = "User Hierarchy")
```

```
User Hierarchy Size (MB) = CALCULATE([Segment Size
(MB)],Segments[Structure Type] = "User Hierarchy")
Relationship Size (MB) = CALCULATE([Segment Size
(MB)],Segments[Structure Type] = "Relationship")
Total Column Size (MB) = [Data Size (MB)] + [Dictionary Size (MB)]

Total Size (MB) = [Column Hierarchies Size (MB)] + [Relationship
Size (MB)] + [User Hierarchy Size (MB)] + [Dictionary Size (MB)] +
[Data Size (MB)]

Last Refresh Message = VAR RefreshDate = MAX('Columns'[Date
Retrieved]) RETURN
"Last Refreshed: " & RefreshDate
```

The memory columns for both source DMVs are in terms of bytes.
Megabytes (MB) are more intuitive and presentable given that they have
fewer digits; thus, DIVIDE() by 1,048,576 is applied. The Structure
Type column created in the segments query is used to support different
components of overall memory usage and two total measures are created
for summary-level reports.

9. Create a Power BI report page based on the retrieved and modeled DMV data.

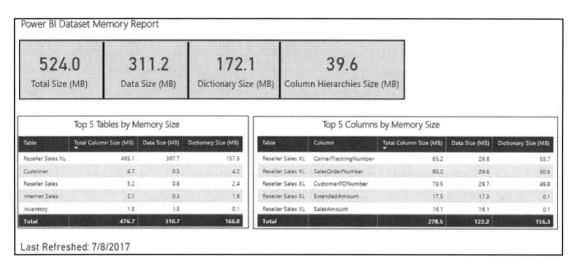

Summary Memory report of the Power BI dataset

Card visuals are used to display overall memory usage, and two table visuals with top *N* visual level filters provide additional details. In this example, the `Reseller Sales XL` table is by far the largest table in the model, and specifically the `CarrierTrackingNumber`, `SalesOrderNumber`, and `CustomerPONumber` columns of this table are consuming the most memory. Clicking on a table name in the Top 5 Tables visual will cross-filter the Top 5 Columns visual.

More DMVs and logic can be added to build a more robust template report for use across Power BI projects. Note that the port number and catalog name (database) parameters will also need to be updated when a PBIX file being analyzed has been closed and reopened. See `Chapter 7`, *Parameterizing Power BI Solutions* for more examples of working with query parameters.

How it works...

Memory structures

- In addition to the compressed data memory structure for each column, dictionary and column hierarchy structures (H$) are also created internally for imported data models to support queries. The dictionary structure, retrieved via the columns DMV, stores the unique values of a column, and so it is larger for high-cardinality columns.
- Two additional memory structures include user-defined hierarchies (U$) and table relationships (R$).

In this recipe, the memory allocated to column hierarchy structures (H$) is excluded from the Total Column Size measure but included in Total Size measure. This is intended to focus analysis on the larger components of memory that can be directly impacted by revisions to the data model. Likewise, the memory used for relationships and user-defined hierarchies is small relative to the data and dictionary size of the model's columns. Basic performance tuning of imported data models largely focuses on minimizing high cardinality columns and relationships to reduce the memory scanned. More advanced tuning, generally reserved for SSAS models, involves the partitioning of tables, segment sizes, and the optimal sorting order used by the engine during compression; only the sort order is available to Power BI datasets.

See also

- Kasper de Jonge has published a blog on building an SSAS memory report with Power BI: `http://bit.ly/2tDumgk`
- A Power Pivot for Excel-based memory analysis report is provided by SQL BI: `http://bit.ly/2sTTuSO`

Increasing SQL Server DBA productivity with Power BI

SQL Server Query Store is a monitoring feature available to all editions of SQL Server 2016 and later; it significantly simplifies and expedites query tuning and troubleshooting. The Query Store database provides aggregated metrics regarding query executions, query plans, and wait statistics to enable visibility to performance trends and usage patterns.

"Query Store is a fantastic flight data recorder for your execution plans. It will help you troubleshoot parameter sniffing issues, connection settings issues, plan regressions, bad stats, and much more."

- Brent Ozar, Author and Microsoft Certified Master in SQL Server

Query Store includes a graphical interface of charts and user controls and its schema lends itself to custom T-SQL queries such as "10 longest running queries in the past hour". While these are great features and sufficient for certain scenarios, administrators often have to make trade-offs between the flexibility of T-SQL and the graphical controls provided by Query Store. In this recipe, simple T-SQL statements are passed from Power BI to SQL Server Query Store, to identify and analyze recent performance issues as well as the performance of a specific stored procedure.

Getting ready

1. Enable Query Store in the latest version of **SQL Server Management Studio** (**SSMS**), either via the Database Properties dialog in the Object Explorer interface (right-click on on the database) or via the following T-SQL statement:

```
ALTER DATABASE WideWorldImporters SET QUERY_STORE = ON;
```

2. Configure Query Store settings such as Statistics Collection Intervals, Retention, and Max Size (MB) according to your requirements.

 In this example, the performance of individual queries will be aggregated or summarized into 5-minute time frames. Smaller collection time intervals provide greater details but also require more storage and collection resources. For maximum detail with no grouping of queries, an Extended Events session can be scheduled. See the *Consolidating SQL Server Extended Events Trace Event Data into Power BI* recipe later in this chapter for more details.

How to do it...

1. Build and test the T-SQL statements to retrieve the required Query Store statistics:

```
SELECT
[rs].[avg_duration], [rs].avg_logical_io_reads,
[qst].[query_text_id], [qsq].[query_id],
[qst].[query_sql_text], CASE WHEN [qsq].[object_id] = 0 THEN N'Ad-
hoc' ELSE OBJECT_NAME([qsq].[object_id])  END AS [ObjectName],
[qsp].[plan_id],  GETUTCDATE() AS CurrentUTCTime,
[rs].[last_execution_time], CAST((DATEADD(MINUTE, -
(DATEDIFF(MINUTE, GETDATE(), GETUTCDATE())), CAST((DATEADD(MINUTE,
-(DATEDIFF(MINUTE, GETDATE(), GETUTCDATE())),
[rs].[last_execution_time])) AS datetime2(0)) AS
[LocalLastExecutionTime]
FROM
[sys].[query_store_query] [qsq] JOIN [sys].[query_store_query_text]
[qst] ON [qsq].[query_text_id] = [qst].[query_text_id]JOIN
[sys].[query_store_plan] [qsp]  ON [qsq].[query_id] =
[qsp].[query_id]JOIN [sys].[query_store_runtime_stats] [rs]  ON
[qsp].[plan_id] = [rs].[plan_id] WHERE [rs].[last_execution_time] >
DATEADD(hour, -8, GETUTCDATE())
```

This query retrieves the average duration and logical IO reads of the Query Store intervals collected over the previous 8 hours, as well as the SQL statement itself and the Query ID. A parameter can be set for the hours value in Power BI, and thus the SQL view created for retrieving this data does not require a WHERE clause. Power BI will dynamically build a T-SQL statement with a WHERE clause filter containing the parameter via Query Folding. Note that the LocalLastExecutionTime column is cast to a datetime2(0) data type to provide a date value rounded off to the nearest second.

2. Create an additional T-SQL statement containing similar performance-related columns, filtered to a specific stored procedure that also retrieves the collection interval times:

```
SELECT.....FROM
[sys].[query_store_query] [qsq] JOIN [sys].[query_store_query_text]
[qst] ON [qsq].[query_text_id] = [qst].[query_text_id]JOIN
[sys].[query_store_plan] [qsp]  ON [qsq].[query_id] =
[qsp].[query_id]JOIN [sys].[query_store_runtime_stats] [rs] ON
[qsp].[plan_id] = [rs].[plan_id]JOIN
[sys].[query_store_runtime_stats_interval] [rsi] ON
[rs].[runtime_stats_interval_id] =
[rsi].[runtime_stats_interval_id]
WHERE [qsq].[object_id] =
OBJECT_ID(N'Sales.usp_GetFullProductInfo')
```

The Query Store user interface does not support analyzing any activity specific to a stored procedure. Additionally, administrators often require visibility to both the specific timeframes and the overall performance to pinpoint when a performance issue occurred and its significance relative to a baseline.

3. Create a view and a parameterized stored procedure in SQL Server for the two Query Store queries:

- To reiterate, the view will not include the WHERE clause filter as this condition will be driven by a Power BI parameter

4. Design the SQL Server stored procedure to include a WHERE clause with a parameter that will be passed from Power BI, such as the following:

```
CREATE PROCEDURE [Website].[QueryStoreProc]
@QSProcedure nvarchar(55)
AS ......
WHERE [qsq].[object_id] = OBJECT_ID(@QSProcedure)
```

5. Open a Power BI Desktop file locally and add server and database parameters for the Query Store database.
6. Create a new query with the Sql.Database() function that references these two parameters.
7. Create a parameter (HoursInPast) of a decimal number data type and a QueryStoreProcedure text parameter.

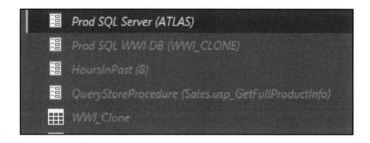

Server, Database, Database Query (WWI_Clone), and Two Parameters

The HoursInPast parameter will be embedded in the Query Store duration the I/O query, and likewise the QueryStoreProcedure parameter will be referenced in the Query Store Procedure query. This design allows for simple modification of the data retrieval process to control the timeframe of data retrieved and the specific stored procedure. As per Chapter 7, *Parameterizing Your Power BI Solutions*, Power BI Template files can also be used with parameters to quickly create new reports based on a common metadata design (M queries, DAX measures, relationships, and so on) but with different data imported.

8. Create a new M query that retrieves the I/O and duration statistics for all queries:

```
Source = WWI_Clone, SQLView = Source{[Schema = "Website", Item =
"QueryStoreDurationIO"]}[Data],
ParamFilter = Table.SelectRows(SQLView, each
[LocalLastExecutionTime] >= (DateTime.LocalNow() -
#duration(0,HoursInPast,0,0))),
ExecutionDate = Table.AddColumn(ParamFilter, "Last Execution Date",
each DateTime.Date([LocalLastExecutionTime]), type date),
ExecutionTime = Table.AddColumn(ExecutionDate,
"Time", each DateTime.Time([LocalLastExecutionTime]), type time)
```

- The `LocalLastExecutionTime` column is filtered by the `DateTime` value that is based on the current local `DateTime` and the value in the `HoursInPast` parameter. You may click on **View Native Query** to confirm that the query was folded to the server.
- A `Date` and `Time` column are added via the `DateTime.Date()` and `DateTime.Time()` M functions. These added columns will be used in relationships to the Date and Time dimension tables, respectively.

9. Name this query `Query Store DurationIO`.

10. Create a new M query that retrieves the Query Store statistics associated with a specific stored procedure:

```
let Source = WWI_Clone,
Procedure = Value.NativeQuery(Source,
"EXECUTE Website.QueryStoreProc @QSProcedure = " & "'" &
QueryStoreProcedure & "'"),
InsertedDate = Table.AddColumn(Procedure, "Date", each
DateTime.Date([end_time]), type date),
InsertedTime = Table.AddColumn(InsertedDate, "Time", each
DateTime.Time([end_time]), type time)
```

The SQL Server stored procedure `Website.QueryStoreProc` is executed via the `Value.NativeQuery()` function and the Power BI parameter `QueryStoreProcedure` is passed into the concatenated text string. `Date` and `Time` columns are also added to support relationships to the `Date` and `Time` dimension tables. Like the `DurationIO` Query Store query, the `end_time` in the stored procedure is of the `datetime2(0)` data type, such that `Time` columns created via `DateTime.Time()` will be rounded off to seconds.

11. Name this query `'Query Store Procedure'` and click on Close & Apply to exit the Query Editor.

12. Create many-to-one, single-direction relationships from the Query Store `DurationIO` table and the Query Store Procedure table to the `Date` and `Time` tables.

13. Add core DAX measures to the Query Store statistics (fact) columns such as `Min`, `Max`, and `Average Duration`:

    Average CPU Time (QS Proc) = AVERAGE('Query Store
    Procedure'[avg_cpu_time])
    Average Duration (QS Proc) = AVERAGE('Query Store
    Procedure'[avg_duration])
    Average Logical IO Reads (QS Proc) = AVERAGE('Query Store
    Procedure'[avg_logical_io_reads])

14. Create dedicated report pages for the two Query Store tables leveraging the measures and relationships.

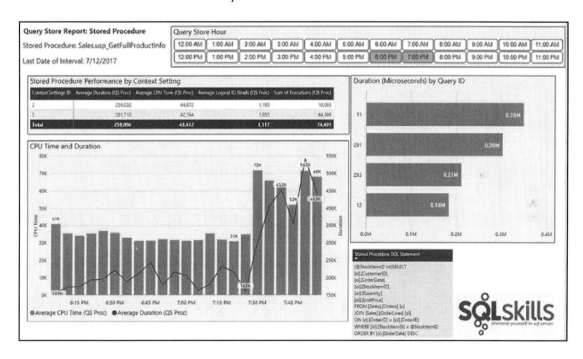

Query Store Sample report page - Stored Procedure

The Query Store Stored Procedure report page breaks out measures of performance by context settings ID and individual query IDs. A combination chart displays the trend of CPU and duration performance across the intervals and the SQL statement associated with the procedure is displayed via a table visual. Additionally, a custom Chiclet slicer is used to give the user simple filtering control for the hourly time frames.

How it works...

Query Store

- SQL Server Query Store collects compile and runtime information related to the queries and query plans of a database like a flight data recorder. This persisted data is made available for analysis via three separate data stores:
    - A plan store containing query execution plan information
    - A runtime stats store of execution statistics
    - A wait stats store of query wait statistics
- The wait stats store is currently exclusive to Azure SQL
- These three data stores can be queried in SQL Server 2016 or later via the following system views: `sys.query_store_plan`, `sys.query_store_runtime_stats`, and `sys.query_store_wait_stats`

See also

- MS Docs: Monitoring Performance by using the Query Store (`http://bit.ly/2s9Cx5r`)

Providing documentation of Power BI and SSAS data models to BI and business teams

As data models grow and change to support new business processes and logic, access to current documentation becomes imperative. Visibility to basic metadata such as the relationships of the model, columns of the tables, and the filtering logic built into measures can significantly aid business teams in utilizing Power BI datasets. Additionally, business intelligence and IT professionals who may be new to a specific model or unfamiliar with a component of the model can benefit greatly from direct access to technical metadata such as data source parameters, SQL and M queries, and the configured security roles.

In this recipe, several **dynamic management views** (**DMVs**) related to the schema of a Power BI dataset are accessed and integrated into a Power BI report. A template is then created with parameters, enabling standard documentation reports across multiple Power BI datasets.

Getting ready

1. Identify the top use cases and consumers of the documentation and align this with the data contained in the DMVs.
2. If the use cases and consumers are significantly varied, such as business users and BI or IT professionals, separate dedicated reports may be necessary to retrieve the relevant metadata and avoid a cluttered or excessively large report.

How to do it...

1. Open the Power BI Desktop file containing the dataset to be documented. This file must remain open during data retrieval.
2. Open DAX Studio and connect to the open Power BI Desktop file.
3. Retrieve the server and database name associated with the running Power BI Desktop (PBIX) dataset.

The server name will be in the bottom right of the DAX Studio status bar such as `localhost:57825`. The following SQL statement will retrieve the system name of the database to be queried:

```
Select [CATALOG_NAME] From $System.DBSCHEMA_CATALOGS
```

In this example, `57825` represents the local port being used by the Power BI Desktop file and the following 36-character string is the catalog name: `59eb0067-25f9-4f07-a4e2-54d2188ebc43`.

4. Open a new Power BI Desktop file and click on **Edit Queries** to open the Query Editor window.
5. Create two parameters, `Server` and `Database`, and apply the values retrieved from DAX Studio as the current values.
6. Create a new blank M query that retrieves the `TMSCHEMA_TABLES` DMV via the server and database parameters.

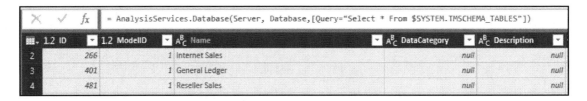

Table metadata of the running Power BI Desktop file

7. Name the query `TablesDMV` and disable the load of the query, as it will be referenced by other queries.

As of July 2017, official documentation is not available for the new TMSCHEMA DMVs associated with SSAS Tabular databases (and thus Power BI datasets). Analysis Services Schema Rowset documentation can be found at `https://docs.microsoft.com/en-us/sql/analysis-services/schema-rowsets/analysis-services-schema-rowsets`.

8. Duplicate the `TablesDMV` query to retrieve the following five schema DMVs as well: `COLUMNS`, `MEASURES`, `ROLES`, `TABLE_PERMISSIONS`, and `RELATIONSHIPS`:

- Each DMV follows the same naming convention (`SYSTEM.TMSCHEMA_`)

9. In the query editor, grant permission to run each native query by clicking on **Edit Permission** and then on **Run**.

10. Name the queries according to their source and organize the queries and parameters into their own folders:

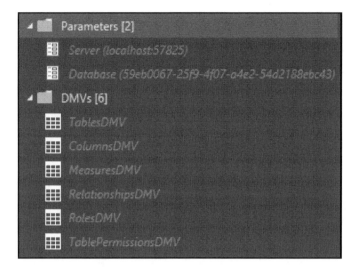

Parameters and DMV Queries Used to Support Model Documentation

11. Create a third query group named `Documentation` and a new blank query named `Columns`:

```
let Tables = TablesDMV, Columns = ColumnsDMV,
    Join =
Table.NestedJoin(Columns,{"TableID"},Tables,{"ID"},"TableColumns",J
oinKind.LeftOuter),
    TableExpand =
Table.ExpandTableColumn(Join,"TableColumns",{"Name"},{"Table"}),
    DataType = Table.AddColumn(TableExpand, "Data Type", each
        if [ExplicitDataType] = 2 then "Text" else
        if [ExplicitDataType] = 6 then "Whole Number" else
        if [ExplicitDataType] = 8 then "Decimal Number" else
        if [ExplicitDataType] = 9 then "Date" else
        if [ExplicitDataType] = 10 then "Fixed Decimal Number" else
"Other", type text),
    ColumnType = Table.AddColumn(DataType, "Column Type", each
        if [Type] = 1 then "Standard" else
        if [Type] = 2 then "Calculated" else "Other", type text),
    Filter = Table.SelectRows(ColumnType, each
        not Text.StartsWith([ExplicitName], "RowNumber")
```

```
            and not Text.StartsWith([Table],"LocalDate")
            and not Text.StartsWith([Table], "DateTableTemplate")),
    Rename = Table.RenameColumns(Filter,{{"ExplicitName","Column"},
{"DataCategory", "Data Category"},
        {"IsHidden", "Is Hidden"}, {"FormatString", "Column
Format"}})
in Rename
```

The columns query joins the `Columns` and `Tables` DMV queries and creates two new columns to identify data types and any calculated columns. Additionally, filters are applied to remove metadata associated with the internal date tables that Power BI creates for date columns, and a few columns are renamed to support the documentation reports.

Columns and measures can be renamed within report visuals as of the July 2017 release of Power BI Desktop. Double-clicking on the field name in the `Values` field well creates a textbox for us to enter the alias. Since the alias is specific to the given visual, applying user-friendly, succinct names in datasets is still important.

12. Create a new blank query named `Relationships` and identify the tables and columns for each relationship:

```
let Relationships = RelationshipsDMV, Tables = TablesDMV, Columns =
ColumnsDMV,
    FromTableJoin =
Table.NestedJoin(Relationships,{"FromTableID"},Tables,
{"ID"},"FromTableCols",JoinKind.Inner),
    FromTable =
Table.ExpandTableColumn(FromTableJoin,"FromTableCols",{"Name"},{"Fr
om Table"}),
    ToTableJoin =
Table.NestedJoin(FromTable,{"ToTableID"},Tables,{"ID"},"ToTableCols
",JoinKind.Inner),
    ToTable =
Table.ExpandTableColumn(ToTableJoin,"ToTableCols",{"Name"},{"To
Table"}),
    FilterDateTbls = Table.SelectRows(ToTable, each not
Text.StartsWith([To Table],"LocalDateTable")),
    FromColumnJoin =
Table.NestedJoin(FilterDateTbls,{"FromColumnID"},Columns,{"ID"},"Fr
omColumnCols",JoinKind.Inner),
    FromColumn =
Table.ExpandTableColumn(FromColumnJoin,"FromColumnCols",{"ExplicitN
ame"},{"From Column"}),
    ToColumnJoin =
```

```
Table.NestedJoin(FromColumn,{"ToColumnID"},Columns,{"ID"},"ToColumn
Cols",JoinKind.Inner),
    ToColumn =
Table.ExpandTableColumn(ToColumnJoin,"ToColumnCols",{"ExplicitName"
},{"To Column"}),
    CrossFiltering = Table.AddColumn(ToColumn, "Cross Filtering",
each if [CrossFilteringBehavior] = 1 then "Single Direction" else
"Bidirectional", type text),
    Rename =
Table.RenameColumns(CrossFiltering,{{"ID","Relationship ID"}})
in Rename
```

The `Relationships` DMV contains the `Table` and `Column  ID` keys for each side of every relationship defined in the model. Therefore, four separate join expressions are used to retrieve the `from` table and column as well as the `to` table and column. Additionally, a column is added to identify any bidirectional cross-filtering relationships and filters are applied to remove internal date tables.

13. Create a simple query based on `MeasuresDMV` that adds the table name via a join to the `TablesDMV`. Name this query `Metrics` as `Measures` is a reserved word.

14. Add a query that joins the `RolesDMV` with the `TablePermissionsDMV` and the `TablesDMV` such that the name of the security role, the filter condition, and the table of the filter condition are included in the query.

15. Name this last query `Security  Roles` and click on **Close & Apply** to return to the Report view.

16. Create four report pages: `Columns`, `Relationships`, `Measures`, and `Security`.

17. Use table visuals to expose the most important columns from each integrated M query in each page.

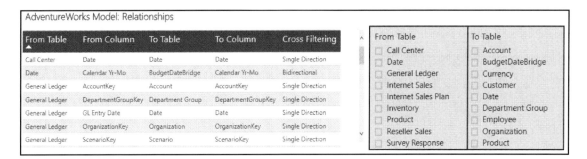

Relationships Metadata Report Page

The `Alternating rows` Matrix style is useful for simple table lists such as metadata documentation. For larger, more complex models, slicer visuals give users the ability to quickly answer their own questions about the model such as "Which tables are related to Internet Sales?" or "Which measures are hidden from the Fields list?"

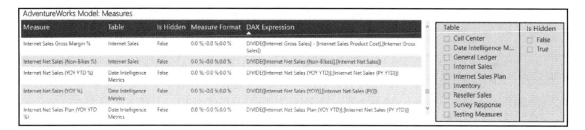

Measures Metadata Report Page

`Table` and `Matrix` visuals support word wrap for both headers and individual values. For table visuals exposing the **DAX Expression** column and other long columns such as SQL Statements, enable word wrap in the Values card of the formatting pane.

18. With the report pages completed, save the Power BI Desktop file and publish the report to the Power BI service.

19. Click on **File** and then on **Export** to save a Power BI Template file (`.pbit`).

20. Test the template by retrieving the port and catalog name for a separate dataset and opening the template.

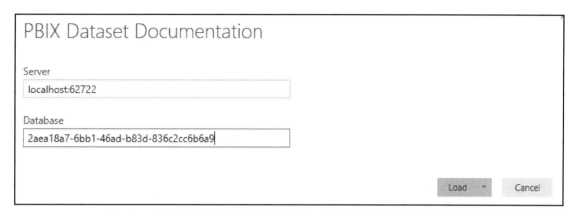

Opening the Template (.pbit) File to generate documentation on a separate Power BI dataset

- With the target dataset open, the queries will prompt for authorization but will then load the report pages.

How it works...

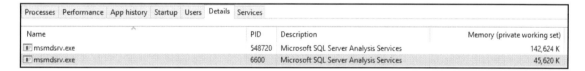

Windows Task Manager: SQL Server Analysis Services processes associated with open PBIX datasets

When used as a dataset rather than a report with a live connection, an open Power BI Desktop file includes an instance of **SQL Server Analysis Services (SSAS)**. Therefore, all data model objects (including DMVs) contained within a Power BI Desktop file can be accessed as an SSAS Data Source. For example, SQL Server Profiler, SQL Server Management Studio, and Microsoft Excel can all reference the same port and catalog name to establish a connection to the data source. Additionally, the same approach in this recipe is applicable to Power BI Desktop models in DirectQuery mode.

There's more...

Power BI documentation reports via Excel

- As a published Power BI dataset, documentation can be displayed in standard Excel table and PivotTable formats.

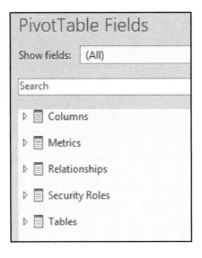

Power BI documentation dataset accessed from Excel

- See the *Accessing and Analyzing Power BI Datasets from Excel* recipe in `Chapter 13,` *Integrating Power BI with Other Applications* for details on the analyze in Excel feature.

SQL Server Analysis Services (SSAS) Metadata

For SSAS Tabular documentation, additional DMVs such as `TMSCHEMA_KPIS` and `TMSCHEMA_PERSPECTIVES` may be utilized along with more details on the display folders of columns and measures, the descriptions entered by model authors for various objects, and partitions. It's possible that metadata currently specific to SSAS such as perspectives and KPIs will also be utilized by Power BI datasets in the future.

Analyzing performance monitor counters of the Microsoft on-premises data gateway and SSAS tabular databases

The Microsoft on-premises data gateway enables specific cloud services including Power BI, Azure Analysis Services, PowerApps and Microsoft Flow to securely connect to on-premises data sources. In the context of Power BI, these connections support both the scheduled refresh of imported datasets stored in Power BI, as well as DirectQuery and Live Connection datasets in which only report queries and their results are exchanged between Power BI and the on-premises source. As the availability and performance of the gateway is critical for any Power BI and other supported cloud service deployment requiring on-premises data, regular monitoring of both the gateway service and its host server(s) is recommended. Additionally, given that Power BI datasets are often migrated to **SQL Server Analysis Services** (**SSAS**) to take advantage of enterprise BI features such as source control and a programmatic interface, visibility to SSAS server resources is important to isolate performance bottlenecks.

In this recipe, performance monitor counters specific to the on-premises data gateway and SQL Server Analysis Services are integrated into a single Power BI dataset. This source data is dynamically retrieved and enhanced via M queries and sample report visualizations are created to support monitoring and analysis.

Getting ready

1. For the initial deployment or planning phases, review the available documentation, tips, and best practices on both SSAS Tabular and the on-premise data gateway, including the recommended hardware and network configuration.

   SSAS Tabular servers should have 2.5X the RAM of their compressed in-memory databases, and outbound ports 9350-9353 should be opened to run the On-Premises Data Gateway in the default TCP mode (443 if HTTPS mode). Despite sufficient hardware, the design and complexity of data models, M queries, and DAX measures can significantly impact resource usage and performance. See Chapter 11, *Enhancing and Optimizing Existing Power BI Solutions*, for more details.

2. Identify a secure network location directory to store the performance counter file. This path could use a common network drive and the parent folder of other monitoring log files.

How to do it...

SSAS tabular memory reporting

1. Create a new data collector set in Windows Performance Monitor to capture SSAS tabular memory counters:

SSAS Memory Counters in a Performance Monitor Data Colletor Set

2. Set the **Log format** of the collector set to **Comma Separated**.
3. Open a new Power BI Desktop file to be used for both the SSAS Tabular and on-premise data gateway counters.
4. Create data source parameters for the server, database, and number of days of history to retrieve.

5. Define a query that exposes the database objects (`AdWorksProd`) and `Date` and `Time` queries that retrieve these views.

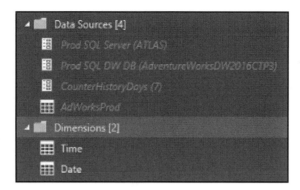

Parameters and Queries Used to Retrieve Date and Time Dimension Tables from SQL Server

6. Disable the refresh of the `Time` table as this always has 86,400 rows (per second).
7. Create a new query that selects the parent folder location of the SSAS tabular performance counters.
8. Follow the same steps of importing performance monitor counter files described in the *Creating a centralized IT monitoring solutions with Power BI* recipe earlier in this chapter.

 The result of the import process should be a dynamic filter based on the `CounterHistoryDays` parameter, revised data types, report-friendly column names, and Date and Time columns to support the relationships to `Date` and `Time` dimension tables.

9. Name the query `SSAS Memory` and click on **Close & Apply**.
10. Create single direction relationships between SSAS Memory and the `Date` and `Time` dimension tables.
11. Create DAX measures to support reporting and analysis such as the following:

```
Avg Memory Limit Hard (GB) = DIVIDE(AVERAGE('SSAS Memory'[Memory
Limit Hard KB]),[KB to GB Conversion])
Avg Memory Usage GB (Today) = CALCULATE([Avg Memory Usage (GB)],
FILTER(ALL('Date'),'Date'[Date] = [Current Date]))
Max Memory Usage GB (Today) = CALCULATE([Max Memory Usage
(GB)],FILTER(ALL('Date'),'Date'[Date] = [Current Date]))
Max Memory GB (Today, All Time) = CALCULATE([Max Memory Usage GB
(Today)],ALL('Time'))
```

The DAX measures convert the memory counter values from KB to GB and make it easy to compare the current day versus the prior day in different filter contexts. For example, the `Avg Memory Usage GB (Today)` measure is filtered to the current date but will respect user or report filter selections on the `Time` dimension table. The `Max Memory GB (Today, All Time)` measure, however, will ignore both `Date` and `Time` filter selections to always show the highest memory usage value for the current day.

12. Create an SSAS tabular memory report leveraging the consolidated counter files, model relationships, and measures.

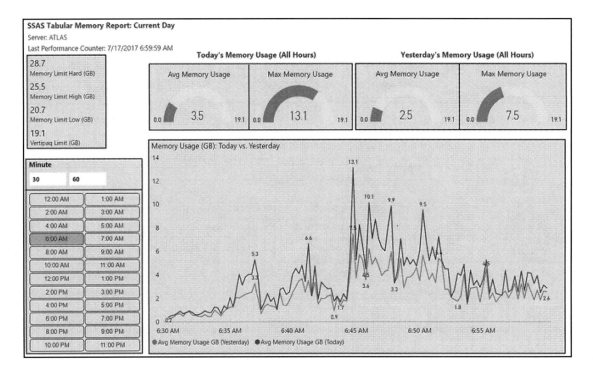

In this example, two slicers are used for the `Hour of Day` and `Minute` columns of the `Time` dimension table to provide the user with the option to focus the line chart on intervals within an hour (for example, 6:30 to 7:00 AM). A multi-row card is used to display the different memory thresholds as indicated by the corresponding performance monitor counters. Four gauge visuals are used to display measures that ignore the filters from the `Time` dimension in order to show the average and max values for the current and previous date.

Name	Value	Current Value	Default Value	Restart	Type	Units	Category
Memory \ HardMemoryLimit	0	0	0		dou...		Basic
Memory \ HeapTypeForObjects	0	0	0	yes	int		Advanc...
Memory \ LowMemoryLimit	65	65	65		dou...		Basic
Memory \ MemoryHeapType	-1	-1	-1	yes	int		Advanc...
Memory \ TotalMemoryLimit	80	80	80		dou...		Basic
Memory \ VertiPaqMemoryLimit	60	60	60		dou...		Basic
Memory \ VertiPaqPagingPolicy	1	1	1	yes	int		Advanc...

SQL Server Analysis Services Server Properties - memory properties

Significant spikes in memory usage may indicate sub-optimal DAX measures or inefficient report queries which require large, temporary memory structures. BI teams would want to ensure that memory usage does exceed the memory limits identified by the counters, to avoid performance degradation. Increases in the SSAS memory limit property settings or simply more overall RAM for the SSAS server are two options to avoid memory shortages.

On-premises data gateway counters

1. Create and schedule a new performance monitor data collector set containing the on-premises data gateway counters.

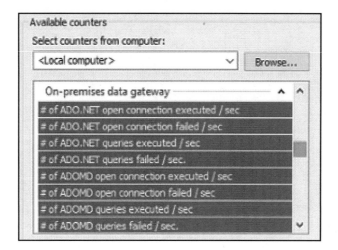

On-premises data gateway performance counters

2. In the same Power BI Desktop file containing the SSAS counters, create an additional query to the parent folder of the gateway counter files.
3. Apply the same M query transformations to filter the files imported (via parameter), adjust data types, rename columns, and add `Date` and `Time` columns to support relationships to the `Date` and `Time` dimension tables.
4. Build basic (`Average` or `Max`) aggregation measures against the different gateway counter columns.
5. Build additional DAX measures that apply or remove filter contexts from the `Date` and `Time` tables following the same expression patterns as the SSAS Tabular Memory DAX measures.
6. Design a dedicated gateway report page that addresses the top monitoring priorities such as query volumes and failures.

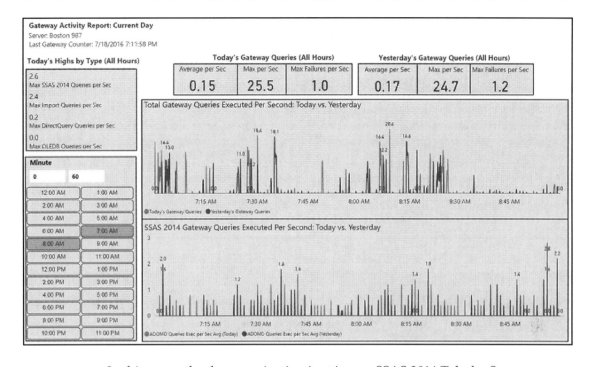

In this example, the organization is using an SSAS 2014 Tabular Server as a primary data source for Power BI report and dashboard content. Therefore, measures based on the ADOMD gateway counters are used to expose the volume of this workload (bottom chart). The `# of all queries executed / sec` performance counter is used by the top chart as well as the average and max card visuals above the line chart. Though less common, the organization also uses this gateway to support certain import refreshes of Power BI datasets (Mashup counters) and DirectQuery datasets (ADO.NET counters).

As per the *Adding data alerts and email notifications to dashboards* recipe of `Chapter 5`, *Creating Power BI Dashboards*, card, gauge, and standard KPI visuals pinned as tiles to dashboards can drive data alerts and e-mail notifications. In the context of this recipe, memory usage in excess of the Vertipaq and other memory limits could warrant a data alert. Likewise, a high number of query failures or an unexpected query type activity reported by the gateway counters could also drive a data alert. For example, if a particular gateway is intended to be dedicated to Import (Mashup) workloads, the counters shouldn't report query activity for ADO.NET (DirectQuery) or OLEDB connections.

How it works...

SSAS tabular memory limits

SSAS Tabular requires memory during processing operations to load new data in addition to the memory used for existing data. Additionally, temporary memory structures are sometimes created to resolve certain queries. These three components comprise the 2.5X RAM recommendation (2X for current and new data and .5X for temporary structures).

As the memory required by the SSAS instance exceeds certain memory limits or thresholds, given the amount of RAM available to the server and the memory properties defined in analysis server properties, SSAS takes various actions ranging from clearing out low-priority memory caches (LowMemoryLimit) up to aggressively terminating user sessions (HardMemoryLimit). A reference to SSAS memory property documentation is included in *See also*.

On-premises data gateway workloads

Scheduled refreshes of imported datasets to Power BI can require significant resources at the time of refresh based on the size of the dataset and whether its M queries can be folded to the data source as SQL statements. For example, if an M function that doesn't have an equivalent expression in the source Oracle database is used, the M engine in the gateway will be used to execute the logic such as filter, sort, and aggregate.

DirectQuery and SSAS live connections are less resource heavy as only queries and query result data are transferred across the gateway. However, these connections generate a high frequency of queries based on the number of concurrent users, their usage or interaction with the published reports, the type and volume of visualizations, and whether **row-level security** (**RLS**) roles have been configured.

 Power BI Premium will support larger Power BI datasets than the current 1 GB limit (for example, 10 GB, then 100 GB+) as well as incremental refresh per the May 2017 Microsoft Power BI Premium Whitepaper. As fully refreshing/importing large Power BI datasets could present a bottleneck for the Gateway server, it will be critical to apply an incremental refresh policy to large datasets once this feature is available. Scalability will also be enhanced via high availability and load balancing features on the On-Premise Data Gateway Roadmap.

There's more...

High availability and load balancing for the on-premises data gateway

Gateway availability and load balancing has been a manual process in which a gateway can be restored to a different machine (perhaps with more resources) and datasets can be split across different gateways. For example, one gateway could be used exclusively by an on-premises SSAS data source while a different gateway server could be used for self-service scheduled refreshes of Power BI datasets. Additionally, the same data source can be defined for multiple gateways and different datasets built with this source can be assigned to different gateways in the Power BI service. Gateways will soon be able to join a "cluster" of gateways such that the cluster will act as a single logical unit of gateway resources. This cluster will initially provide high availability and will later support automatic load balancing.

Reduce network latency via Azure ExpressRoute and Azure Analysis Services

If query performance in Power BI is unsatisfactory despite proper configuration and resources for the on-premises data Gateway and the on-premises SSAS Tabular model (including measures and security), Azure ExpressRoute and Azure Analysis Services are two options to reduce network latency. Azure ExpressRoute creates a private connection between on-premises sources and the Azure data center of the Power BI tenant. Azure Analysis Services avoids the need for an on-premises data gateway and generally eliminates network latency as a performance issue while providing cloud platform-as-a-service benefits, such as the flexibility to scale up or down quickly.

See also

- Guidance for Deploying a Data Gateway for Power BI: http://bit.ly/2t8hk9i
- SQL Server Analysis Services Memory Properties: http://bit.ly/2vuY1I2
- Azure ExpressRoute: https://azure.microsoft.com/en-us/services/expressroute
- Azure Analysis Services: https://azure.microsoft.com/en-us/services/analysis-services

Analyzing Extended Events trace data with Power BI

Extended Events is a highly configurable and lightweight performance monitoring system available to both the SQL Server relational database engine and Analysis Services. A vast library of events are available to specific sessions which can be saved, scheduled and then analyzed to support performance tuning, troubleshooting and general monitoring. However, similar to other monitoring tools such as Windows Performance Monitor and SQL Server Query Store, the Extended Events graphical interface lacks the rich analytical capabilities and flexibility of tools such as Power BI; these are often necessary, or at a minimum helpful, to generate insights from this data.

In this recipe, the output of an Extended Event session containing query execution statistics is retrieved into a dedicated Power BI event analysis report file. The 1.4 million rows of event data from this file are enhanced during the import and report visualizations are developed to call out the most meaningful trends and measures as well as support further self-service analysis.

Getting ready

1. Identify the events associated with the top monitoring and troubleshooting use cases.
2. Create separate extended event sessions tailored to these use cases with filters to exclude irrelevant or redundant data.

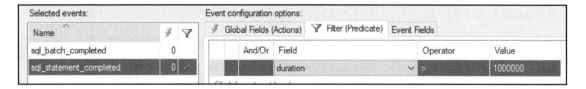

An Extended Events Session with two events and a filter for SQL Statements completed in Over 1 million microseconds

3. Determine the data storage target for the session(s) such as an `event_file` and the location for this file.
4. Optionally, configure settings such as **Event retention mode** and **Max memory size**. Additionally, configure a SQL Agent Job to start and stop the Event Session.

As the primary long-term monitoring tool for SQL Server (see *SQL Server Profiler versus Extended Events* in *There's more...*) the Extended Events architecture of packages, sessions, and targets can be fully managed via scripts. Jonathan Kehayias, Microsoft Data Platform MVP, has written a series of blog posts on utilizing Extended Events at `http://bit.ly/1r5EHXG`.

How to do it...

1. Obtain access to the Extended Events target XEL target file and open it from **SQL Server Management Studio** (**SSMS**) or open it directly from Windows Explorer in a distinct instance of SSMS.
2. With the XEL file open in SSMS, click on the **Extended Events** tab on the toolbar and select **Export to** at the bottom.
3. Choose the **Export to CSV File** option, enter a file name describing the session, and select a network path common to Extended Events and potentially other performance and administrative log files.

Name	Date modified	Type	Size
ExtendedEventsExecutionStats.csv	7/13/2017 1:31 PM	Microsoft Excel Comma Separated Values File	540,241 KB
PowerBI_0_131443571913450000.xel	7/13/2017 1:26 PM	Microsoft SQL Server Extended Event Log File	519,551 KB

An Extended Events Session Target XEL file and its export as a CSV file

By design, Extended Events sessions cannot be written to tables within SQL Server. Additional options for capturing and analyzing event session data are available such as the histogram and `pair_matching` targets. Data can also be viewed live via "Watch Live Data" and the CSV and table export options expose this data to tools like Power BI.

Note that if the events file were exported to a table in SQL Server and no other databases or sources were required for analysis, the Power BI dataset could be configured for DirectQuery mode. Avoiding the import to Power BI via DirectQuery could be a useful or even necessary design choice if large and/or multiple event session files are needed in the same Power BI dataset. The dedicated Admin database described in the first recipe of this chapter could store the Extended Event data and essential Date and Time tables could be imported to this same server and database thus permitting DirectQuery mode.

4. Open a Power BI Desktop file that already contains `Date` and `Time` tables and their database connection parameters.

5. Create a parameter for the directory folder path of the event session files and a parameter for the session filename.

6. Open a blank query that concatenates the two parameters into a full file path. Name this query `XEventsSession`.

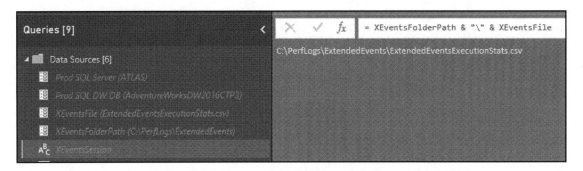

Query Editor View with Data Source Parameters and XEventsSession Query

7. Create a query that uses the text/CSV data connector and replace the file path with the XEventsSession query.

8. Promote the top row as the headers and convert the data types via `Table.TransformColumnTypes()`.

9. Add a `Date` column based on the `Timestamp` column of the source file:

```
Source = Csv.Document(File.Contents(XEventsSession),[Delimiter=",",
Columns=31, Encoding=65001,    QuoteStyle=QuoteStyle.None]),
PromotedHeaders = Table.PromoteHeaders(Source,
[PromoteAllScalars=true]),
ChangeTypes = Table.TransformColumnTypes(PromotedHeaders,
{{"timestamp", type datetime}, {"duration", Int64.Type}}),
DateColumn = Table.AddColumn(RenameColumns, "Timestamp Date", each
DateTime.Date([timestamp]), type date)
```

10. Add a time column and then a `SecondOfDay` column to support a relationship to the `Time` dimension table.

See the *Creating a centralized IT monitoring solution with Power BI* recipe earlier in this chapter for the `SecondOfDay` column logic and syntax. Like the Performance Monitor Counter data in that example, the timestamp from the Extended Events session is not at the seconds grain and thus adding a time column via the `DateTime.Time()` M function, as you could to a `datetime2(0)` column from SQL Server, is not sufficient to support a model relationship to the `Time` dimension table.

11. Name this query `Execution Stats`, disable the load of the XEventsSession query, and click on **Close & Apply**.
12. Create many-to-one, single-direction relationships from `Execution Stats` to the `Date` and `Time` tables.
13. Optionally, create a blank measure group table to organize measures in the **Fields** list (see `Chapter 3`, *Building a Power BI Data Model* for details).
14. Develop and format simple DAX measures to support common aggregations of Extended Events fact columns such as the average, min, and max of query duration, CPU time, logical reads and writes:

    ```
    Average CPU Time = AVERAGE('Execution Stats'[cpu_time])
    Max Duration = MAX('Execution Stats'[duration])
    Minimum Logical Reads = MIN('Execution Stats'[logical_reads])
    ```

If any numeric conversion is applied to the event data within the M query or the DAX measures, such as from milliseconds to seconds, then the measure name should reflect this change (for example, `Max Duration (sec)`). If no conversion has been applied and users are comfortable and familiar with the Extended Events values, then, as this is a dedicated ad hoc analysis tool, this detail can be excluded from the measure names.

15. Finally, create Power BI report visualizations that target the top and most common questions of the event data.

16. Associate hourly slicer filters to support self-service analysis analysis.

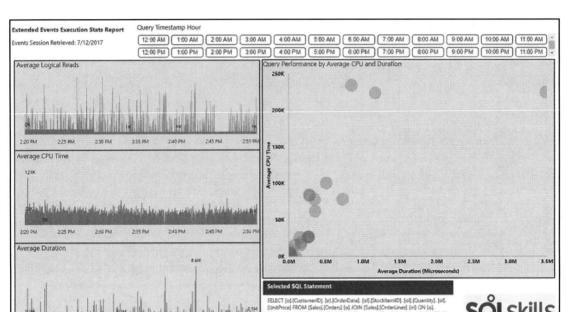

Extended Events Execution Stats Report Page

In this example, three line charts highlight spikes in logical reads, CPU time, and query duration that occurred during the 30 minute Extended Events session. The scatter chart plots individual `query_hash` values by duration and CPU time and uses the Tooltip to expose the individual SQL statement represented. A table visual with word wrapping is used to display the SQL statement associated with the user's selection as well. See *How it works...* for more details on the sample report visual.

How it works...

Self-service Extended Events analysis

The Selected SQL Statement table displays a single DAX measure that retrieves the text value from the SQL statement column if a single scatter chart item (Query Hash) has been selected. The *Displaying the current filter context in Power BI reports* recipe in Chapter 8, *Implementing Dynamic User-Based Visibility in Power BI* provides detailed examples of these expressions. The Edit Interactions feature is configured such that selecting items (Query Hash values) on the scatter chart filters the three line charts to these specific items. See the *Controlling interactive filtering between visuals* recipe in Chapter 4, *Authoring Power BI Reports* for additional details on this feature. The Chiclet Slicer custom visual described in the Configuring custom KPI and Slicer Visuals in Chapter 9, *Applying Advanced Analytics and Custom Visuals* is used with an Hour of Day column of the Time data type. This visual would be useful for future event sessions containing data across multiple hours of a day.

- The owner or team responsible for the Power BI dataset could simply copy the PBIX file and revise the parameters to a separate Extended Events file or export a Power BI Template file (.pbit) and use this to re-load the report.
- Leveraging common dimension tables, parameters, and visuals throughout the solution minimizes complexity.

There's more...

SQL Server Profiler versus Extended Events

SQL Server Profiler is supported in SQL Server 2016 but is now a deprecated feature for the relational database engine, and Extended Events is its long term replacement. Profiler is not a deprecated feature for Analysis Services, although a graphical interface to Extended Events is a new feature in SSAS 2016 and several new SSAS trace events are exclusively available via Extended Events. Regardless of the database engine (relational or analytical) Extended Events is more efficient and flexible than SQL Server Profiler, thus allowing for more nuanced event data collection with less impact on production workloads. Events associated with new SQL Server features are exclusive to Extended Events.

Additional event session integration

Additional standard event sessions such as blocking and deadlocking sessions could be integrated into the Power BI dataset similar to the consolidated dataset and visualization layer described earlier in this chapter. As the solution matures, custom groupings of events and/or bins of numerical columns could be embedded in the dataset to further simplify analysis.

See also

- Extended Events MS Docs: `https://docs.microsoft.com/en-us/sql/relational-databases/extended-events/extended-events`

Visualizing log file data from SQL Server Agent jobs and from Office 365 audit searches

Log files containing SQL Server Agent job history and the Power BI usage activities stored in the Office 365 audit log can also be integrated into the Power BI monitoring solution described earlier in this chapter. For example, SQL Agent job data can reveal important trends such as the performance of a nightly job used to load a data warehouse and the duration and reliability of individual steps within these jobs. Likewise, detailed reporting and, optionally, alerts based on user activities in the Power BI service, such as deleting a dashboard, enable BI and IT administrators to better manage and govern Power BI deployments.

In this recipe, transformations are applied to the structure of the Power BI audit log to convert the audit data stored in JSON and adjust for local time reporting. Additionally, an advanced T-SQL query is used to access the job history data in SQL Server Agent system tables and to prepare this data for visualization in Power BI.

Getting ready

1. In the Power BI admin portal, select **Tenant Settings** and enable audit logging.

Audit and usage settings

◢ Create audit logs for internal activity auditing and compliance
Enabled for the entire organization

Users in the organization can use auditing to monitor actions taken in Power BI by other users in the organization.

 Enabled

Power BI Audit Logging Enabled

- The audit log search can be accessed via the **Go to O365 Admin Center** link in the Power BI admin portal (**Audit logs** tab) or the Office 365 security and compliance portal

An Office 365 license is not required to view the Power BI logs. Global administrators of the Power BI tenant have permission to the Office 365 security and compliance office portal by default. Permissions can be assigned to non-administrators via roles such as the compliance and admin role.

2. As stated in the Microsoft documentation referenced in *How it works...*, create a short PowerShell script that exports Power BI audit log search results to a CSV file on secure network directory.
3. Optionally (though recommended), configure the PowerShell script with dynamic start and end date variables and schedule the script to support recurring Power BI audit reporting.

How to do it...

Power BI Audit Log Integration

1. In Power BI Desktop, create parameters for the file path and name as well as the local time zone offset to UTC.

File path and time zone parameters in the Query Editor

2. Create a blank query that returns the full file path based on the parameters per the image of PBIAuditLog.

3. Create a new query to the CSV file on the network and replace the file path with the query, based on the parameters:

```
let Source =
Csv.Document(File.Contents(PBIAuditLog),[Delimiter=",", Columns=5,
Encoding=65001, QuoteStyle=QuoteStyle.Csv]),
    RemoveTopRows = Table.Skip(Source,2),
    PromoteHeaders = Table.PromoteHeaders(RemoveTopRows,
[PromoteAllScalars=true]),
    ApplyDateType =
Table.TransformColumnTypes(PromoteHeaders,{{"CreationDate", type
datetime}}),
    AddCreationDateColumn = Table.AddColumn(ApplyDateType,
"CreationDateOnly", each DateTime.Date([CreationDate]), type date)
in AddCreationDateColumn
```

4. Remove the top two rows resulting from the PowerShell output and promote the third row as column headers.

5. As an unstructured data source, explicitly apply data types via `Table.TransformColumnTypes()` and add a Date column based on the `CreationDate` log column. Name this query `O365PBIAuditLog`.

The Audit log data is stored in UTC and thus needs to be converted to local time for reporting. A column should be available in the date dimension table that distinguishes **Daylight Savings Time (DST)** dates from Standard time zone dates.

6. Expose the `Date` table view from the SQL Server database as its own query `Date`.

7. In a new query, join the `O365PBIAuditLog` data with the `Date` query based on the `CreationDateOnly` column.

8. Expand the `DST` column from the `Date` query and add a conditional `DateTime` column reflecting local time.

9. Parse the JSON in the `AuditData` column using the `Table.TransformColumns()` function to expose all the fields associated with the event as a `Record` value:

```
let  AuditDateJoin = Table.NestedJoin(O365PBIAuditLog,
"CreationDateOnly",Date,"Date",
"DateTableColumn",JoinKind.LeftOuter),
    DSTFlag = Table.ExpandTableColumn(AuditDateJoin,
"DateTableColumn",{"DST Flag"},{"DST Flag"}),
    LocalCreationDate = Table.AddColumn(DSTFlag,
"LocalCreationDate", each
        if [DST Flag] = "DST" then [CreationDate] +
```

```
#duration(0,USEasternDSTOffset,0,0)
        else if [DST Flag] = "ST" then [CreationDate] +
#duration(0,USEasternSTOffset,0,0) else null,
type datetime),
ParseJSON = Table.TransformColumns(LocalCreationDate,{{"AuditData",
Json.Document}}) in ParseJSON
```

The `CreationDateOnly` column created in the first query
(`O365PBIAuditLog`) is used in the nested outer join to the `Date` table,
thus exposing all `Date` table columns in a nested table value column. With
the `DST` column added to the query from the Date table, the two time zone
parameters are passed to `#duration` values within the `if...else if`
conditional logic. Many of the most valuable audit fields are contained in
the `AuditData` column as JSON.

Power BI Audit Log Query with an adjusted LocalCreationDate column and AuditData parsed into Record values

10. Finally, expand the the parsed `AuditData` column of record values. Name this
    query `Power BI Audit`.

11. Optionally, add `Date` and `Time` columns based on the `LocalCreationDate`
    column (a datetime data type) to support model relationships.

12. Disable the load for all queries except `Power BI Audit`. Click on **Close &**
    Apply.

SQL Server Agent log integration

1. Create a view in the admin SQL Server database (described in the *Creating a*
   centralized IT monitoring solution with Power BI recipe earlier in this chapter) that
   queries the `dbo.sysjobhistory` and `dbo.sysjobs` tables in the `msdb` database:

```
CREATE VIEW BI.vFact_AgentJobHistory AS SELECT
 [h].[server] as [Server], [j].[name] AS [Job Name],
CASE [j].[enabled] WHEN 0 THEN 'Disabled' WHEN 1 THEN 'Enabled' END
AS [Job Status]
, [j].[date_created] as [Date Created], [j].[date_modified] as
[Date Modified]
, [j].[description] as [Job Description], [h].[step_id] AS [Step
ID], [h].[step_name] AS [Step Name]
, CAST(STR([h].[run_date],8, 0) AS date) AS [Run Date]
```

```
, CAST(STUFF(STUFF(RIGHT('000000' + CAST ( [h].[run_time] AS
VARCHAR(6 ) ) ,6),5,0,':'),3,0,':') as time(0)) AS [Run Time]
, ((([run_duration]/10000*3600 + ([run_duration]/100)%100*60 +
[run_duration]%100 + 31 ) / 60)
    AS [Run Duration Minutes]
, CASE [h].[run_status] WHEN 0 THEN 'Failed' WHEN 1 THEN
'Succeeded' WHEN 2 THEN 'Retry'
WHEN 3 THEN 'Cancelled' WHEN 4 THEN 'In Progress' END AS [Execution
Status],
[h].[message] AS [Message Generated]
FROM [msdb].[dbo].[sysjobhistory] [h] INNER JOIN
[msdb].[dbo].[sysjobs] [j] ON [h].[job_id] = [j].[job_id]
```

The `run_date` and `run_time` columns are stored as integers by SQL Server and are thus converted to date and time data types, respectively. The `run_duration` column is stored as an integer in the `HHMMSS` format and is converted to minutes. The `run_status` column is replaced with an `Execution Status` column to display a user-friendly value, such as succeeded, and likewise a `Job Status` column is created from the enabled source column to display disabled versus enabled values.

2. Create or reuse server and database parameters to support the retrieval of the agent data.

SQL Server Agent History View exposed in Query 'AdminProd'; AdminProd passes server and database parameters to Sql.Database()

3. Retrieve the SQL Agent job view into Power BI Desktop:

```
Source = AdminProd,
Agent = Source{[Schema = "BI", Item =
"vFact_AgentJobHistory"]}[Data],
```

SQL Server Agent System Table Data Retrived into Power BI

4. Optionally create a parameter for the number of Agent history days to retrieve, and use this parameter in a `Table.SelectRows()` filter expression like the performance monitor query in the first recipe of this chapter.

5. Create queries to existing `Date` and `Time` dimension tables in a BI or data warehouse database.

6. Disable the load for all queries except the agent job history query and click on **Close & Apply**.

7. Create many-to-one single direction relationships to the `Date` and `Time` tables based on the `Run Date` and `Run Time` columns, respectively.

8. Create DAX measures and report visuals to break out agent jobs by their steps and duration over time.

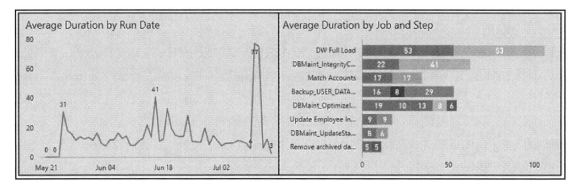

SQL Server Agent History Visuals - average duration by Run Date and Job Step

A stacked bar chart is used to display the individual steps comprising each job; hovering over the bars displays details specific to the job step. User selections on the bar chart filter the line chart enabling easy access to recent performance of any job step. Analyzing SQL Agent job history in Power BI is vastly easier and more flexible than the Job Activity Monitor and Log File Viewer interfaces in SQL Server Management Studio.

How it works...

PowerShell search for Power BI audit log

The `Search-UnifiedAuditLog` cmdlet for PowerShell is used to access Power BI data from the Office 365 Audit Log:

```
Search-UnifiedAuditLog -StartDate $startDt -EndDate $endDt -RecordType
PowerBI | Export-Csv $csvFile
```

Variables for the full CSV file path and start and end date can be defined, evaluated, and passed as parameters to the `Search-UnifiedAuditLog` cmdlet. See the official documentation at `http://bit.ly/2t4LEC0`.

SQL Server agent tables

Over 20 SQL Server Agent system tables are available in the `dbo` schema of the `msdb` database.

There's more...

Power BI usage reporting

The Power BI service provides free usage reporting for dashboards and published reports. These usage reports can be easily extended to analyze activity for all reports and dashboards contained in an app workspace per the following steps:

1. Open the App Workspace and select the 'Usage Metrics Report' icon for a report or dashboard:

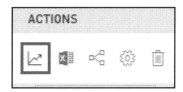

Usage Metrics Report

- Usage metrics can also be accessed with the report or dashboard open via the toolbar icon.

2. With the usage metrics report open, click on **File** ∣ **Save as**:

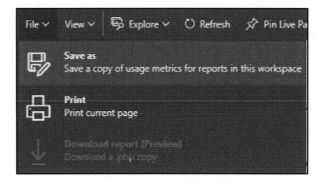

Save as to create a dataset of usage metrics for the workspace

- A new report and a new dataset will be added to the app workspace

3. Open the new report in Edit mode and simply remove the report level filter such that all reports and dashboards are included:

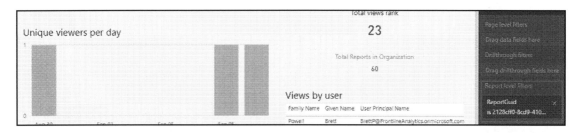

Edit mode of a usage metrics report

- Note that individual users are included in the dataset and default report making it easy to identify who is or isn't accessing content
    - New custom usage reports can be created from scratch by connecting to the usage dataset created in step 2
- Power BI Administrators can access the **Usage metrics for Content Creators** setting in the **Tenant** settings of the Power BI Admin portal to define who has access to usage metrics

See also

- SQL Server Agent Table documentation: `http://bit.ly/2v7kWdc`
- Usage Metrics for Dashboards and Reports: `http://bit.ly/2rUwly4`

11

Enhancing and Optimizing Existing Power BI Solutions

In this chapter, we will cover the following recipes:

- Enhancing the scalability and usability of a data model
- Revising DAX measures to improve performance
- Pushing query processing back to source systems
- Strengthening data import and integration processes
- Isolating and documenting DAX expressions

Introduction

Power BI projects often begin by focusing on specific functional requirements, such as a set of dashboards and reports for a given business area and team. With relatively narrow requirements and small datasets, design and code enhancements to the data retrieval, model, and reporting layers are often unnecessary to deliver sufficient performance and reliability. Additionally, Power BI Premium capacity and tools to migrate a Power BI dataset to **SQL Server Analysis Services** (**SSAS**) provide viable alternatives to enhance the scalability of a dataset.

For larger Power BI projects, and particularly when the options of Power BI Premium and SSAS aren't available, it becomes important to identify opportunities to improve report query performance and to more efficiently use system resources to store and refresh the dataset.

Moreover, the data import process supporting all dependent reports and dashboards can often be strengthened, and standard coding syntax, variables, and comments in both M and DAX expressions further improve the sustainability of Power BI datasets.

This chapter's recipes contain top data modeling, DAX measure, and M query patterns to enhance the performance, scalability, and reliability of Power BI datasets. This includes performance tuning examples of both data models and measures, error handling and query folding examples of M queries, and supporting details on the DAX and M query engines.

Enhancing the scalability and usability of a data model

The performance of all Power BI reports is impacted by the design of the data model. The DAX queries executed upon accessing a report and when dynamically updating report visuals in interactive, self-service user sessions all rely on the relationships defined in the model and optimizations applied to its tables. For in-memory models, the cardinality of the columns imported and the compression of these columns contribute to the size of the dataset and query duration. For DirectQuery data models, the referential integrity of the source tables and optimization of the relational source largely drive query performance.

This recipe includes three optimization processes, all focused on a Reseller Sales fact table with 11.7 million rows. The first example leverages the DMVs and Power BI memory report created in `Chapter 10`, *Developing Solutions for System Monitoring and Administration* to identify and address the most expensive columns. The second example splits a dimension table into two smaller tables, and the final example applies a custom sort order to the imported fact table to optimize the compression of a column commonly used by reports.

Getting ready

1. Obtain a sharp definition of the goal of the optimization or the problem being resolved. For example, is the intent to reduce the size of the overall dataset such that more data can be loaded while remaining under 1 GB? Alternatively, is the goal to make the dataset easier to manage and less error prone during refresh, or is it to improve the query performance experienced with Power BI reports?

2. Document the current state or baseline, such as query duration, to evaluate the effectiveness of the modifications.

Performance optimization is a broad area in Power BI, as many components are involved, including the data sources, data access queries, data models, and DAX measure calculations. Performance is also significantly impacted by the design of reports and dashboards with more dense, unfiltered, and complex report pages and visuals consuming more resources. Additionally, despite efficiency in all of these areas, sufficient hardware must be provisioned to support the given processing and analytical query workloads, such as the server(s) for the on-premises data gateway and Power BI Premium capacity.

The good news is that it's usually not difficult to align a particular issue, such as an excessively large dataset or a slow query, with at least one of its main contributing factors, and there are often simple modifications that can deliver noticeable improvements. Additionally, there are many tools available to analyze and monitor the different components of Power BI as described in Chapter 10, and there are free features in the Power BI service, such as Usage Metrics Reports and View related that can be of further assistance in isolating issues.

3. See the *Migrating a Power BI data model to SSAS tabular* recipe in `Chapter 13`, *Integrating Power BI with Other Applications* for details on this option for enhanced scalability.

How to do it...

Identify expensive columns and quick wins

1. Retrieve and analyze the memory consumed by the columns of the largest fact table or tables:
    - The `DISCOVER_STORAGE_TABLE_COLUMN_SEGMENTS` DMV used in the previous chapter's *Importing and visualizing dynamic management view (DMV) data of SSAS and Power BI data models* recipe will provide this detail.

2. As per the *Choosing columns and column names* recipe of `Chapter 2`, *Accessing and Retrieving Data*, identify expensive columns that may not be needed in the dataset or which can be rounded to lower precision, split as separate columns, or expressed via simple measures.

For import mode models, an expensive column is one with many unique values (high cardinality), such as the Order Number columns used as examples in Chapter 2, *Accessing and Retrieving Data*. Likewise, a DateTime column with multiple time values per date will consume more memory than two separate Date and Time columns. Preferably, only the Date or only the Date and Time columns should be imported rather than the DateTime column.

Also, per the *Choosing columns and column names* recipe (see *There's more... - Fact table column eliminations*), DAX measures which execute simple arithmetic against low cardinality columns, such as Unit Price and Quantity can eliminate the need to import more expensive derived columns such as Sales Amount and Sales Amount with Taxes. Furthermore, though counter-intuitive, the SUMX() measure with arithmetic across multiple columns often outperforms the simple SUM() measure.

3. Identify columns that are stored as decimal number data types with a high scale (number of digits to the right of the decimal point):
    - If this level of precision isn't required, consider rounding off these columns in the SQL view or via the M import query to reduce the cardinality (unique values) and thus improve compression.
    - If a (19,4) column will provide sufficient size and precision, apply the fixed decimal number type in the model.

4. Replace any DAX calculated columns on large fact tables:
    - Calculated columns on fact tables can often be addressed with DAX measures without sacrificing performance.
    - If DAX measures are not an option, move the column's logic to the SQL view or M query of the fact table, or within the data source itself. If the M query is revised, ensure that the logic is folded to the source system.
    - Imported columns achieve much better compression than calculated columns.

5. Secondarily, look to remove or replace DAX calculated columns on any large dimension tables:
    - Like fact table columns, move this logic to the data retrieval process and leverage the source system.

Look for calculated columns with a RELATED() function, which, like an Excel VLOOKUP() function, simply retrieves column values from a table on the one side of a many-to-one relationship with a fact table. Business users often utilize the RELATED() function to flatten or de-normalize a fact table as they would in standard Excel worksheets, but this duplication is rarely necessary in Power BI, and calculated columns are not compressed like standard imported columns. Additionally, look to migrate the logic of calculated column expressions, such as calculated dates, differences in dates, and derived numerical columns, into DAX measures.

- In this example, the current state of the dataset is 334 MB of compressed disk space (the size of the PBIX file converted from KB) and 674 MB of total memory per the memory report introduced in Chapter 10, *Developing Solutions for System Monitoring and Administration*.

Several quick wins are identified on the Reseller Sales fact table (11.7M rows), including the following: only the last four characters of the CarrierTrackingNumber are needed for analysis; the order date, ship date, and due date columns in YYYYMMDD format can be removed, as they are redundant with the date data types for these columns, and only the date data types are used for relationships. Three calculated columns can be removed (Days between Due Date and Order Days, Reseller, and Product Name) as a DATEDIFF() DAX measure and existing dimension columns can be used instead. Finally, Sales Amount, Extended Amount, and Total Product Cost can be removed, as simple DAX measures can compute their values.

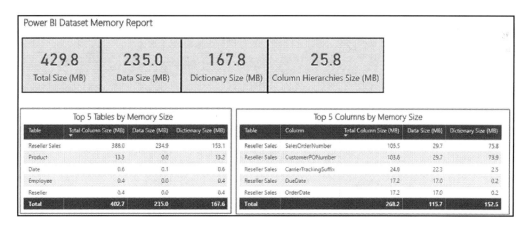

Power BI Memory Report refreshed with a revised SQL View for Reseller Sales

- The revised dataset is 429 MB in memory and the Power BI Desktop file (PBIX) is 221 MB on disk, representing 33%+ savings in memory and disk space.

Normalize large dimensions

Large-dimension tables (approximately one million+ rows), with their high-cardinality relationships to fact tables, are a major performance bottleneck with Power BI and SSAS Tabular import models.

- Consider the following dimension table with attributes describing both resellers and promotions:

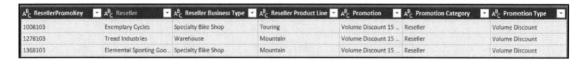

ResellerPromoKey	Reseller	Reseller Business Type	Reseller Product Line	Promotion	Promotion Category	Promotion Type
1008103	Exemplary Cycles	Specialty Bike Shop	Touring	Volume Discount 15 ...	Reseller	Volume Discount
1278103	Tread Industries	Warehouse	Mountain	Volume Discount 15 ...	Reseller	Volume Discount
1368103	Elemental Sporting Goo...	Specialty Bike Shop	Mountain	Volume Discount 15 ...	Reseller	Volume Discount

Reseller promotion dimension table

- The consolidated table contains 10,520 rows and the relationship column on the `Reseller Sales` table is 19.4 MB in size.

Column	Total Column Size (MB)	Data Size (MB)	Dictionary Size (MB)	VERTIPAQ_STATE
CarrierTrackingSuffix	23.9	22.3	1.6	COMPLETED
ResellerPromoKey	19.4	19.2	0.2	COMPLETED
OrderDate	16.7	16.5	0.2	COMPLETED

Reseller Promo Key, approximately 20 MB in size

1. Split (normalize) this table into smaller `Reseller` (701 rows) and `Promotion` (16 rows) dimension tables.

Reseller and Promotion Tables Replace Consolidated Reseller Promo

2. Drop the consolidated `Reseller Promotion` dimension table and the `ResellerPromoKey` column on the fact table.

Although there are more tables and relationships in the model, smaller relationships will improve the performance of queries accessing the `Promotion` and `Reseller` columns. Additionally, the size of the dataset will be reduced by removing the `ResellerPromoKey` relationship column. In this particular example, the row counts are small enough that little impact is observed, but consider splitting large dimension tables over 200K rows into smaller tables (lower granularity) as query workloads increase. For example, a 1M row customer table could possibly be split into two tables for the data model based only on common query patterns such as customer regions or geographies.

Sort imported fact tables

Power BI applies sophisticated algorithms during the import process to determine the sort order that maximizes compression. However, the chosen sort order might not align with the top performance priorities of the model. For example, it may be more important to improve query performance for reports accessing a certain column, such as `Store ID` or `Date` (via relationships to dimension tables), rather than minimizing the size of the overall dataset. Ordering the imported data by these priority columns maximizes their compression while potentially reducing the compression applied to other columns.

1. Identify the column (or columns) to order by and note the current memory. In this example, the `Order Date` column is 16.7 MB.

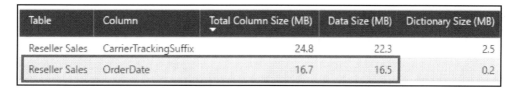

Table	Column	Total Column Size (MB)	Data Size (MB)	Dictionary Size (MB)
Reseller Sales	CarrierTrackingSuffix	24.8	22.3	2.5
Reseller Sales	OrderDate	16.7	16.5	0.2

Order Date Column of 16.5 MB in Data Size (Without Sort)

2. Add an expression to the fact table M query that uses the `Table.Sort()` function to order by the `OrderDate` column:

```
let Source = AdWorksProd,
    ResellerSales = AdWorksProd{[Schema = "BI", Item =
"vFact_ResellerSalesXL_CCI_AllColumns"]}[Data],
        OrderDateSort = Table.Sort(ResellerSales,{{"OrderDate",
Order.Descending}})
in OrderDateSort
```

3. Right-click on the step in the Query Editor and click on **View Native Query** to ensure the sorting was folded to the source.

4. If **View Native Query** is grayed out, consider moving the sort step to the first transformation step per the preceding code.

 Passing the `Order By` operation back to the source (via Query Folding) is generally good for the refresh process and certainly good for the on-premise data gateway but with large fact tables (10 million+ rows) can require large amounts of source system resources. The Power BI Premium Whitepaper from May 2017 identifies incremental refresh as an upcoming feature and this will likely resolve the issue for datasets in dedicated (Premium) capacities.

Table	Column	Total Column Size (MB)	Data Size (MB)	Dictionary Size (MB)
Reseller Sales	CarrierTrackingSuffix	24.8	22.3	2.5
Reseller Sales	ResellerKey	13.4	13.4	0.0
Reseller Sales	ProductKey	12.6	12.6	0.0
Reseller Sales	OrderDate	10.8	10.6	0.2

Improved Compression for the OrderDate Column due to the Sort Order of the Import Query

- Upon refreshing the `Reseller Sales` fact table, the data size of `OrderDate` is reduced by 36% to 10.6 MB.

5. Determine whether any other columns, particularly relationship columns such as `ProductKey` increased in size.

6. Optionally (though it is recommended), evaluate top or common DAX queries for performance changes.

In many scenarios, optimizing the compression on the active relationship date column via sorting offers the best overall performance advantage. However, depending on the structure and distribution of reports and users ordering by a different fact table column such as ProductKey or StoreID could be the best choice. DAX Studio makes it relatively easy to test the performance of queries against many different model designs. Greater detail on the benefits of sorting is included in the *How it works...* section.

How it works...

Columnar database

Remember that DAX queries executed against import mode models access and scan the memory associated with individual columns. Therefore, several very expensive columns with millions of unique values could be present on a fact table but may not negatively impact the performance of a query that doesn't reference these columns. Removing these expensive columns or replacing them with less expensive columns will reduce the overall size of the dataset, but it should not be expected to improve query performance.

Run-length encoding (RLE) compression via Order By

When data is loaded into a Power BI Desktop model (Import mode), the VertiPaq storage engine applies compression algorithms to each column to reduce the memory and thus improve performance. Vertipaq first stores all unique values of a column (either via Value encoding or Hash encoding), and then, more importantly, applies **run-length encoding** (**RLE**) to store a repeated value only once for a set of contiguous rows in which it appears. Therefore, columns with few unique values, such as month names, are highly compressed, while primary key and GUID columns are not compressed at all.

Specifying an `Order By` clause in the import to Power BI exposes the given column to maximum RLE compression given the cardinality of the column.

Segment elimination

The data models in Power BI Desktop (and Power Pivot for Excel) are stored in column segments of one million rows. For example, a 20 million row sales fact table will contain approximately 20 distinct segments. If the data required of report queries is spread across all 20 segments, then more resources (and a longer duration) will be required to access each segment and consolidate these results to resolve the query. However, if the segments are ordered by date or perhaps by a given dimension (for example, store ID) and a report query contains a filter that uses this order, such as fiscal year or store region, then only a subset of the segments will be queried.

As a simple example, assume a 20 million row fact table is ordered by date when importing to Power BI and each calendar year represents one million rows. A report query that is filtered on only 2 years will therefore need to access only two of the 20 column segments-- the other 18 segments will contain dates outside the scope of the query.

There's more...

Minimize loaded and refreshed queries

Avoid loading tables that are only used for data retrieval/transformation logic such as staging queries to a data model. Though hidden from the Fields list, these tables consume processing and storage resources like all other tables of the model and add unnecessary complexity. Right-click on these queries in the Query Editor and disable **Enable load** to remove the table from the data model.

Identify tables that rarely change and consider disabling the default **Include in report refresh** property (by right-clicking in the Query Editor). The table can still be loaded to the data model and thus available for relationships and DAX measures but its source query will no longer be executed with each refresh. Typical candidates for this include an annual budget or plan table that's only updated once a year, a `Currency` table, and possibly a geographic or demographic table.

Data models with many M queries, whether loaded or not, can overwhelm the available threads/resources of the source system during a refresh as all queries will be submitted simultaneously.

Revising DAX measures to improve performance

Just as specific columns and relationships of a data model can be prioritized for performance per the prior recipe, frequently used DAX measures can also be evaluated for potential improvements. Existing DAX measures may contain inefficient data access methods that generate additional, unnecessary queries or which largely execute in a single CPU thread. Revising measures to better leverage the multi-threaded storage engine and to avoid or reduce unnecessary queries and iterations can deliver significant performance improvements without invasive, structural modifications to the model.

In this recipe, the DAX queries executed by Power BI visuals are captured in SQL Server Profiler and then analyzed in DAX Studio. The first example highlights a common misuse of the FILTER() function for basic measures. In the second example, two alternative approaches to implementing an OR filter condition across separate tables are described relative to a common but less efficient approach. Additional details of the DAX Query Engine, using DAX Variables to improve performance, and DAX as as query language, are included in the *How it works...* and *There's more...* sections.

Getting ready

1. Open DAX Studio and the Power BI Desktop file containing the data model and measures to be analyzed.
2. If necessary, build a sample report page that aligns with a poorly performing report or a common report layout.
3. Open SQL Server Profiler and connect to the SSAS instance within the Power BI Desktop file.

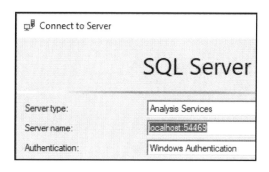

Creating an SSAS Trace against a Power BI Desktop Dataset via SQL Server Profiler (v17.2)

The server name for the local Power BI Desktop file is the local port used by the SSAS instance of the open PBIX file. As per Chapter 10's recipes, this value is visible in the lower-right corner of DAX Studio's status bar once you've connected to the running Power BI Desktop file from DAX Studio. SQL Server Profiler is part of the **SQL Server Management Studio (SSMS)** download (`http://bit.ly/2kDEQrk`). The latest version (17.2+) is recommended for connecting to PBIX and SSAS 2017 models.

4. The only event needed from Profiler in this exercise is the `Query End` event. DAX Studio will provide other event data.
    - The DAX queries created by Power BI Desktop will be displayed in the lower pane and the `TextData` column

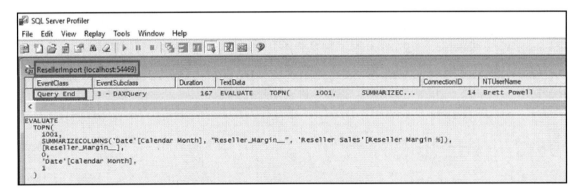

SQL Server Profiler trace running against a Power BI Desktop file ('ResellerImport') and retrieving Query End Events

- With these three applications open, you're able to quickly capture, analyze, revise, and test alternative DAX expressions

How to do it...

Improper use of FILTER()

1. Make a selection on one of the Power BI Desktop report visuals and observe the DAX queries in SQL Profiler.

2. Choose a DAX query statement as the sample or baseline and paste the query into DAX Studio:

```
DEFINE
VAR __DS0FilterTable = FILTER(KEEPFILTERS(VALUES('Date'[Calendar
Year])),
    OR('Date'[Calendar Year] = 2016, 'Date'[Calendar Year] =
2017))
VAR __DS0FilterTable2 =
FILTER(KEEPFILTERS(VALUES('Product'[Product Category])),
    'Product'[Product Category] = "Bikes")
VAR __DS0FilterTable3 =
FILTER(KEEPFILTERS(VALUES('Promotion'[Promotion Type])),
    OR(OR(OR('Promotion'[Promotion Type] = "Excess Inventory",
    'Promotion'[Promotion Type] = "New
Product"),'Promotion'[Promotion Type] = "No Discount"),
    'Promotion'[Promotion Type] = "Volume Discount"))
EVALUATE
TOPN(1001,SUMMARIZECOLUMNS('Reseller'[Reseller],__DS0FilterTable,__
DS0FilterTable2,__DS0FilterTable3,
    "Gross_Sales_Warehouse", 'Reseller Sales'[Gross Sales
Warehouse]),
    [Gross_Sales_Warehouse],0,'Reseller'[Reseller],1)
```

In this example, the `Gross_Sales_Warehouse` measure is currently defined as follows:

```
= CALCULATE([Reseller Gross
Sales],FILTER('Reseller','Reseller'[Business Type] =
"Warehouse"))
```

In this case, the `FILTER()` function does not operate on the results of an `ALL()` function like with Date Intelligence patterns. The `TOPN()` function accepts the table from `SUMMARIZECOLUMNS()`, which groups by individual Reseller companies and their associated gross sales warehouse values.

3. In DAX Studio, enable **Server Timings** and **Query Plan** on the top toolbar.
4. With the DAX Studio trace running, click on **Run** or the *F5* key and note the performance in the **Server Timings** window.
5. Click on **Clear Cache** and execute the query again to obtain a baseline average for duration, SE queries, and SE %.

6. In Power BI Desktop, create a new measure which avoids the `FILTER()` function:

   Gross Sales Warehouse Rev = CALCULATE([Reseller Gross Sales],'Reseller'[Business Type] = "Warehouse")

   Within the DAX query engine, the Gross Sales Warehouse Rev measure is expressed as the following:

   CALCULATE([Reseller Gross Sales],FILTER(ALL('Reseller'[Business Type]),'Reseller'[Business Type] = "Warehouse"))

   Some BI organizations may adopt standards that require the longer, more explicit version and avoid "syntax sugar".

7. Return to DAX Studio and replace the existing references to the current measure with the name of the measure:

   ```
   EVALUATE
   TOPN(1001,SUMMARIZECOLUMNS('Reseller'[Reseller],__DS0FilterTable,__
   DS0FilterTable2,__DS0FilterTable3,
    "Gross Sales Warehouse Rev", [Gross Sales Warehouse Rev]),[Gross
   Sales Warehouse Rev],0,
   'Reseller'[Reseller],1)
   ```

8. With the cache cleared, execute the query with the revised measure. Create a revised average based on 4-5 separate query executions.

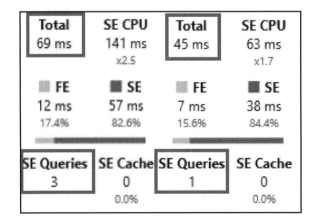

Server Timings of the baseline query with the original measure versus the revised measure in DAX Studio

- The baseline query executed 35% faster (69 ms to 45 ms) with the revised measure and only needed 1 SE query.

The reason the first measure is slower is because with the `FILTER()` on Reseller, the filter selections on slicer visuals of the report (`Date`, `Product`, and `Promotion`) have to be respected before the filter on warehouse is executed. For example, the `Reseller` dimension table will be filtered to only include resellers with bike category sales in 2016-2017 and of certain promotions before the Warehouse filter is applied. This requires additional scans of the fact table and is thus less efficient.

Optimizing OR condition measures

In this example a measure must be filtered by an OR condition on two columns from separate tables.

A `FILTER()` function cannot be avoided in this scenario like in the prior example, since multiple columns must be referenced in the same expression (the OR condition). For example, the following expression is not allowed:

```
CALCULATE([Reseller Gross Sales],
'Product'[Product Subcategory] = "Mountain Bikes" ||
'Reseller'[Reseller Country] IN {"United States",
"Australia"})
```

The current measure is defined as follows:

```
Reseller Gross Sales (Filter OR) =
CALCULATE([Reseller Gross Sales], FILTER('Reseller Sales',
RELATED('Product'[Product Subcategory]) = "Mountain Bikes" ||
RELATED('Reseller'[Reseller Country]) IN {"United States", "Australia"}))
```

- A `FILTER()` is applied on the fact table and separate `RELATED()` functions are used to implement the required OR logic.

1. Just like in the previous example, capture a sample DAX query generated in Power BI Desktop from a Profiler trace.
2. Test and analyze the query in DAX Studio to establish a baseline for the current measure.

3. Now create two separate alternative measures--one with SUMMARIZE() and another with CROSSJOIN():

```
Reseller Gross Sales (Summarize OR) =
CALCULATE([Reseller Gross Sales], FILTER(
SUMMARIZE('Reseller Sales','Product'[Product
Subcategory],'Reseller'[Reseller Country]),    'Product'[Product
Subcategory] = "Mountain Bikes" || 'Reseller'[Reseller Country] IN
{"United States", "Australia"}))
```

```
Reseller Gross Sales (Crossjoin OR) =
CALCULATE([Reseller Gross Sales], FILTER(
CROSSJOIN(ALL('Product'[Product Subcategory]),ALL(Reseller[Reseller
Country])), 'Product'[Product Subcategory] = "Mountain Bikes" ||
'Reseller'[Reseller Country] IN {"United States", "Australia"}))
```

4. In Power BI Desktop, confirm that the new measures produce the same results as the current measure.

5. In DAX Studio, replace the references to the (filter OR) measure with references to the new measures.

6. Repeat the process of executing multiple queries with the cache cleared and documenting the performance to establish baselines for all three versions of the measure.

Total	SE CPU	Total	SE CPU	Total	SE CPU
2,844 ms	7,484 ms	171 ms	453 ms	164 ms	657 ms
	x4.0		x2.8		x4.4
FE	SE	FE	SE	FE	SE
993 ms	1,851 ms	11 ms	160 ms	14 ms	150 ms
34.9%	65.1%	6.4%	93.6%	8.5%	91.5%
SE Queries	SE Cache	SE Queries	SE Cache	SE Queries	SE Cache
6	0	2	0	4	0
	0.0%		0.0%		0.0%

Server Timings of the baseline query with the original measure (Filter OR) versus the two new measures in DAX Studio

- Both new measures were 16.7X faster than the current state (2,844 to 170 ms) and were over 90% executed in the SE.

In this scenario, the CROSSJOIN() approach was slightly faster than SUMMARIZE() but this comparison would vary based on the cardinality of the columns involved. The larger point from this example is the danger with implementing logic not supported by the storage engine within the expression parameter of iterating functions like FILTER() and SUMX(). This is especially true when the table parameter to these functions has many rows such as the 11.7M row Reseller Sales fact table used in this recipe.

Note that the ALL() function can be used to produce the table parameter if both columns are from the same table such as ALL('Product'[Product Category],'Product'[Product Color]). ALL() cannot directly access columns from separate tables.

At a high level, always think about the size of the table being filtered and look for simple filter conditions and single columns that can be used to reduce the size of this table. For example, replace the table parameter of functions like SUMX() and FILTER() with a CALCULATETABLE() function that implements simple, efficient filter conditions. More complex expressions that can't be handled by the storage engine can then operate against this smaller table. Similarly, consider (and test) nesting filter conditions such that the most selective, efficient filter condition is applied first (the inner FILTER(), the outer CALCULATE()).

How it works...

DAX query engine - formula and storage

DAX queries from Power BI report visuals are resolved by the DAX formula engine and the DAX storage engine. The storage engine is the in-memory columnar compressed database for import mode models (also known as VertiPaq) and is the relational database for DirectQuery models. In either mode, the formula engine is responsible for generating query plans and can execute all DAX functions, including complex expression logic, though it is limited to a single thread and no cache.

The formula engine sends requests to the storage engine and the storage engine, if it does not have the requested data in an existing data cache, utilizes multiple threads to access segments of data (1 thread per segment, 1M rows per segment) from the data model. The storage engine executes simple join, grouping, filter, and aggregations, including distinct count to make requested data caches available to the formula engine. Given this architecture a fundamental DAX and Power BI model design practice is to maximize the allocation of queries to the storage engine and minimize the size of data caches operated on by the formula engine.

There's more...

DAX variables for performance

- The primary benefit of DAX variables is improved readability. However, variables can also reduce the number of queries associated with a measure (and hence its execution duration) since variables are evaluated only once and can be reused multiple times in an expression.

> Look for DAX measures with multiple branches of IF or SWITCH conditions that reference the same measure multiple times. For these measures, consider declaring a variable that simply references the existing measure (VAR MyVariable = [Sales Amount] RETURN) and then reference this variable in each logical condition, rather than the measure.

DAX as a query language

- The DAX queries generated by Power BI cannot be edited but DAX queries can be completely authored from scratch for other tools such as the datasets in **SQL Server Reporting Services (SSRS)** reports
- Many of the newer DAX functions are particularly helpful with queries and generally the same performance considerations apply to both measures and queries
- Studying Power BI-generated DAX queries is a great way to learn how to write efficient DAX queries and DAX in general

Pushing query processing back to source systems

During the scheduled refresh of datasets retrieving from on-premises sources, any query transformations not executed by the source system will require local resources of the **M** (**Mashup**) engine of the on-premises data gateway server. With larger datasets, and potentially with other scheduled refreshes occurring on the same gateway server at the same time, it becomes important to design M queries that take full advantage of source system resources via query folding. Although transformations against some sources such as files will always require local resources, in many scenarios M queries can be modified to help the engine generate an equivalent SQL statement and thus minimize local resource consumption.

In this recipe, a process and list of items is provided to identify queries not currently folding and the potential causes. Additionally, a query based on an existing SQL statement is redesigned with M expressions to allow query folding.

Getting ready

1. Identify the dataset to evaluate for query folding.

 This will generally have large PBIX files (100 MB+) published to the Power BI service with a scheduled refresh configured to use an on-premises data gateway and which queries a relational database as the primary source. If the large PBIX file is retrieving from a file or a collection of files within a folder, revisions are certainly possible, such as filtering out files based on their modified date relative to the current date as per `Chapter 10`, *Developing Solutions for System Monitoring and Administration*. However, query folding is not an option for file sources, while maximum query folding is available for common relational database sources such as SQL Server and Oracle.

2. Use performance counter data to establish a baseline of the resources currently used to perform refreshes.
    * Counters for the gateway server memory and **M** (**Mashup**) queries should be impacted by the changes

How to do it...

Query folding analysis process

1. Open the Power BI Desktop file used as the published dataset with scheduled refreshes of on-premises data.
2. Click on **Edit Queries** from the **Home** tab to open Query Editor.
3. Starting with the largest queries (the fact tables), right-click on the final step exposed in the **Query Settings** window.

View Native Query Disabled for Final Query Step

- If the **View Native Query** option is disabled, then the local M engine is performing at least this final step.

4. Check the previous steps to determine which steps, if any, were folded, and thus the step which caused the query to use local resources. Once a step (M variable expression) in a query uses local resources all subsequent steps in the query will also use local resources.

If there are required transformations or logic that aren't supported by the source system for query folding the recommendation is to move these steps to the very end of the query. For example, allow SQL Server to execute the filter, the derived columns, and other simple steps via Query Folding and only then apply the complex steps locally on top of the SQL query result set.

- If **View Native Query** is not disabled, you can optionally view the SQL statement per prior recipes.

5. Identify the cause of the local operation, such as a specific M function not supported by the source system.
6. Consider revising the source database object, the M expressions, and data source privacy levels to enable query folding.

Several common M functions are not supported by most relational database sources, such as `Table.Distinct()`, which removes duplicate rows from tables, and `Table.RemoveRowsWithErrors()`, which removes rows with errors from tables. If data sources are merged in the query, check their privacy level settings (**Data source settings** | **Edit Permissions...**) to ensure that privacy is configured to allow folding, such as from an Organizational source to a different Organizational source.

As per the query folding redesign example in this recipe, if the first step or **Source** step of the query is a native SQL statement, consider revising the M query steps to help the M engine form a SQL query (fold the M query).

Query folding redesign

In this example, a business analyst has used a SQL statement and the Query Editor to construct a customer query.

```
let
    Source = Sql.Database("ATLAS", "AdventureWorksDW2016CTP3",
[Query="Select CustomerKey,FirstName,LastName,BirthDate,MaritalStatus,YearlyIncome From dbo.DimCustomer"]),
    ChangedType = Table.TransformColumnTypes(Source,{{"BirthDate", type date}, {"YearlyIncome", Int64.Type}}),
    ReplacedValue = Table.ReplaceValue(ChangedType,"M","Married",Replacer.ReplaceText,{"MaritalStatus"}),
    ReplacedValue1 = Table.ReplaceValue(ReplacedValue,"S","Single",Replacer.ReplaceText,{"MaritalStatus"}),
    MergedColumns = Table.CombineColumns(ReplacedValue1,{"FirstName", "LastName"},Combiner.CombineTextByDelimiter(" ", QuoteStyle.None),"Customer Name"),
    RenamedColumns = Table.RenameColumns(MergedColumns,{{"MaritalStatus", "Marital Status"}, {"YearlyIncome", "Yearly Income"}, {"BirthDate", "Date of Birth"}}})
in RenamedColumns
```

Customer Query based on Native SQL Statement and M Transformations

In this scenario, the SQL statement is against the base customer table in the data warehouse (not the view) and the transformations applied against the query results all use local gateway server resources during each refresh process given the native SQL query. The existing SQL view (`vDim_Customer`) contains the `Customer Name` column, eliminating the need for the merge operation, though the `Marital Status` column is not transformed into the longer `Married` or `Single` string per the analyst's transformations.

1. Create a new M query that uses parameters for the server and database and which uses the customer SQL view:

```
let Source = AdWorksProd,
Customer = AdWorksProd{[Schema = "BI", Item =
"vDim_Customer"]}[Data],
SelectColumns = Table.SelectColumns(Customer,{"Customer Key",
"Customer Name", "Date of Birth",
"Marital Status", "Annual Income"}),
MarriageStatus = Table.AddColumn(SelectColumns, "M Status", each if
[Marital Status] = "M" then "Married" else "Single", type text),
RemovedColumns = Table.RemoveColumns(MarriageStatus,{"Marital
Status"}),
RenamedColumns = Table.RenameColumns(RemovedColumns,{{"M Status",
"Marital Status"},
{"Annual Income", "Yearly Income"}})
in RenamedColumns
```

The `AdWorksProd` source query used in other recipes references the server (Atlas) and database (`AdventureWorksDW2016CTP3`) parameters. The existing SQL view, `vDim_Customer`, is leveraged and the Marital Status conditional logic is built within a `Table.AddColumn()` expression. The few remaining steps simply select, remove, and rename columns-- transformations that can be folded back to SQL Server.

2. Right-click on the final step of the new, revised query and ensure that **View Native Query** is enabled.

```
Native Query

select [_].[Customer Key] as [Customer Key],
    [_].[Customer Name] as [Customer Name],
    [_].[Date of Birth] as [Date of Birth],
    [_].[Annual Income] as [Yearly Income],
    case
        when [_].[Marital Status] = 'M' and [_].[Marital Status] is not null
        then 'Married'
        else 'Single'
    end as [Marital Status]
from
(
    select [Customer Key],
        [Customer Name],
        [Date of Birth],
        [Marital Status],
        [Annual Income]
    from [BI].[vDim_Customer] as [$Table]
) as [_]
```

Native Query (Folded) Based on Revised M Query for Customers

- The new query returns the same results but is now folded back to SQL Server rather than using local resources
- The `if...then...else` M expression was folded into a `CASE` expression for SQL Server to execute

How it works...

Query folding factors

Query folding is impacted by the transformations supported by the source system, internal proprietary M engine logic, privacy levels assigned to data sources, the use of native database queries (SQL statements), and the use of custom M functions and logic

For example, even if query folding is appropriate from a performance standpoint such as using a server in a join operation with a local file, folding will not occur if the local file is configured as a private data source

Native SQL queries

Any M transformation applied on top of a native SQL database query (via `Value.NativeQuery()`) will not be folded to the source system

If native SQL queries are used, such as the stored procedure examples in previous recipes, the recommendation is to embed all query steps and transformations in the native SQL query itself. If this is not possible, embed the most resource intensive operations in the stored procedure and pass filtering parameters from Power BI to the stored procedure to reduce the workload on the local M engine.

There's more...

Parallel loading of tables

For large models with many queries and large tables, consider disabling the default parallel loading of tables

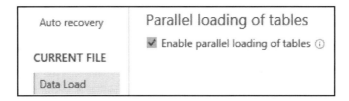

Parallel loading of tables - current file setting

Many queries executed at once may overwhelm source system resources and cause the refresh process to fail

Improving folded queries

Just because a query is folded into a SQL statement, it doesn't mean there are no possible performance issues. For example, the query might be selecting more columns than needed by the data model or might be executing outer join queries when the database schema supports inner joins. Visibility of these queries can inform changes to the BI architecture and M queries.

Owners of the relational database system or data warehouse can take note of Power BI's folded SQL queries via tools like Extended Events (see `Chapter 10`, *Developing Solutions for System Monitoring and Administration*). For example, database administrators or BI team members could revise existing SQL views, table indexes, and more. Likewise, the Power BI query author could be informed of better or preferred methods of accessing the same data such as joining on different columns.

Strengthening data import and integration processes

Many Power BI datasets must be created without the benefit of a data warehouse or even a relational database source system. These datasets, which often transform and merge less structured and governed data sources such as text and Excel files generally require more complex M queries to prepare the data for analysis. The combination of greater M query complexity and periodic structural changes and data quality issues in these sources can lead to refresh failures and challenges in supporting the dataset. Additionally, as M queries are sometimes initially created exclusively via the Query Editor interface, the actual M code generated may contain unexpected logic that can lead to incorrect results and unnecessary dependencies on source data.

This recipe includes three practical examples of increasing the reliability of data import processes and making these processes easier to manage. This includes data source consolidation, error handling and comments, and accounting for missing or changed source columns.

How to do it...

Data source consolidation

1. Open the Power BI Desktop file and identify the data sources being accessed by all queries.
2. The **Data source settings** dialog from the **Edit Queries** dropdown in Report view will expose current file sources.

3. For greater detail, open the Query Editor and click on **Query Dependencies** from the **View** tab of the toolbar.

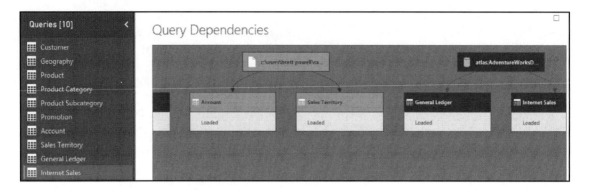

Query Dependencies View of 10 Queries

- In this example, 10 queries use three separate sources (SQL Server, an Excel file, and an MS Access database file)

4. Create the following folder groups in the queries window: `Parameters`, `Data Source Queries`, `Dimensions`, and `Facts`.

5. Create six text parameters to abstract the file name, file path, server, and database names from the three sources.

6. Develop three data source queries from individual blank queries which reference these parameters:

```
= Sql.Database(#"SQL Server AdWorks Server", #"SQL Server AdWorks
DB")
= #"MS Access AdWorks Path" & "\" & #"MS Access AdWorks DB" &
".accdb"
= #"MS Excel Ad Works Path" & "\" & #"MS Excel Ad Works File" &
".xlsx"
```

7. Assign names to these queries such as `MS Access Ad Works Connection` and disable their load to the data model.

8. Finally, modify each of the 10 queries to reference one of the three data source queries such as the following:

```
let Source = Access.Database(File.Contents(#"MS Access Ad Works
Connection"), [CreateNavigationProperties=true]),
Customer = Source{[Schema="",Item="DimCustomer"]}[Data]
in Customer
```

- The pound sign and double quotes are required when referencing queries, parameters and variables that contain spaces

Consolidated and parameterized data sources organized in the Query Editor

- The folder groups, parameters, and data source queries make it easier to understand and manage the retrieval process

Error handling, comments, and variable names

In this example, the `Product` query is joined to the `Product Subcategory` query to add a column from `Product Subcategory`. The query includes error handling by wrapping both expressions with a `try` expression and an `otherwise` clause. If an error occurs, such as if the `Product Subcategory` query changes, the `Product` query is used for loading to the data model.

```
/* This query joins the Product query to the Product Subcategory query.
   The product subcategory column 'EnglishProductSubcategoryName' is
renamed 'Product Subcategory' */
let ProductToProductSubCatJoin =
try
// Nested outer join based on Subcategory Surrogate Key
Table.NestedJoin(Product,{"ProductSubcategoryKey"},#"Product
```

```
Subcategory",{"ProductSubcategoryKey"},"ProductSubCatColumns",JoinKind.Left
Outer) otherwise Product,
AddProductSubCatColumn =
try
// Will return nulls if EnglishProductSubcategoryName is renamed or missing
in Product Subcategory query
Table.ExpandTableColumn(ProductToProductSubCatJoin,
"ProductSubCatColumns",{"EnglishProductSubcategoryName"}, {"Product
Subcategory"}) otherwise Product
in AddProductSubCatColumn
```

Comments are used in both multi-line and single-line formats to help explain the logic. Multi-line comments begin with /* and end with */ while single-line comments are preceded by the // characters.

Variable names (that is, AddProductSubCatColumn) are in proper casing with no spaces so as to avoid unnecessary double quotes and to further describe the process.

Handling missing fields

The objective of this example is to retrieve four columns from a text file containing 30 columns describing customers.

1. Connect to the file with the text/CSV connector and replace the hardcoded path with a query created from parameters:

```
let Source =
Csv.Document(File.Contents(CustomerTextFile),[Delimiter=" ",
Columns=30, Encoding=1252, QuoteStyle=QuoteStyle.None]),
PromotedHeaders = Table.PromoteHeaders(Source,
[PromoteAllScalars=true])
in PromotedHeaders
```

2. Delete the default Columns parameter of the Csv.Document() function (Columns=30).

3. Use a Table.SelectColumns() function to select the four columns needed and specify the optional MissingField.UseNull parameter.

4. Finally, set the data types for each of the four columns:

```
let Source = Csv.Document(File.Contents(CustomerTextFile),
        [Delimiter=" ", Encoding=1252, QuoteStyle=QuoteStyle.None]),
PromoteHeaders = Table.PromoteHeaders(Source,
[PromoteAllScalars=true]),
SelectColumns = Table.SelectColumns(PromoteHeaders,
        {"CustomerKey", "CustomerAlternateKey", "EmailAddress",
"BirthDate"},  MissingField.UseNull),
TypeChanges = Table.TransformColumnTypes(SelectColumns,
        {{"CustomerKey", Int64.Type}, {"CustomerAlternateKey", type
text}, {"BirthDate", type date}})
in TypeChanges
```

With these changes, the query has access to all columns of the source file (not just 30) but only creates dependencies on the the four columns needed. Most importantly, the `MissingField.UseNull` option protects the query from failing if one of the four columns is renamed or removed from the source file. The data type change expression is necessary since the automatic type selection behavior was disabled as recommended.

Be sure to avoid the automatic data type changes applied by default to unstructured sources. If enabled, this will effectively create a hard coded dependency to each of the 30 columns in the source. Likewise, for all other transformations try to limit or avoid explicitly referencing column names and always favor selecting required columns rather than removing unnecessary columns. The columns explicitly selected are less likely to be changed or removed in the future and removing columns creates a risk that new columns added to the source will be loaded to the data model.

How it works...

MissingField.UseNull

If one of the four columns selected is removed or renamed, a null value is substituted thus avoiding query failure:

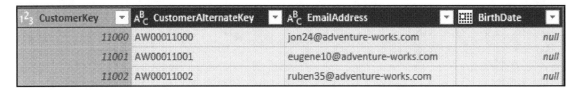

1²₃ CustomerKey	A^BC CustomerAlternateKey	A^BC EmailAddress	BirthDate
11000	AW00011000	jon24@adventure-works.com	null
11001	AW00011001	eugene10@adventure-works.com	null
11002	AW00011002	ruben35@adventure-works.com	null

Four columns selected from the text file despite the BirthDate column removed from the source

A `MissingField.Ignore` option is also available to retrieve only the columns found in `Table.SelectColumns()`.

See also

- *10 Common Mistakes in Power Query and How to Avoid Pitfalls* by Gil Raviv: `http:/ /bit.ly/2uW6c33`

Isolating and documenting DAX expressions

Isolating expressions into independent and interchangeable DAX measures or as variables within measures is recommended to simplify development and to maintain version control. Independent measures can be hidden from the **Fields** list yet contain core business definitions and efficient filtering logic to drive the results and performance of many other measures in the model. Although scoped to each measure, DAX variables provide a self-documenting coding style and, unlike scalar-valued measures, also support table values thus allowing for even greater modularity.

In this recipe, DAX variables, measures, and comments are used in two separate examples. The first example provides a variable-driven approach to the Reseller Margin % measure described in `Chapter 3`, *Building a Power BI Data Model*. The second example leverages three table-valued variables in defining a filter context for a measure.

Getting ready

Briefly review the sales and margin measures in the *Embedding Business Definitions into DAX Measures* recipe of `Chapter 3`, *Building a Power BI Data Model*.

How to do it...

Reseller Margin % with variables

The purpose of this example is to develop a new `Reseller Margin %` measure that uses variables and comments to explicitly identify the logic and source columns of the net sales and product cost calculations:

```
Reseller Margin % =
/*
Net Sales = Gross sales net of discounts that have shipped
Product Cost = Product standard cost of all ordered products (including not
shipped)
Date of 12/31/2099 used for unshipped sales order lines since 1/1/2015
*/
VAR ShippedSales = CALCULATETABLE('Reseller Sales','Reseller
Sales'[ShipDate] <> DATEVALUE("12/31/2099"))
VAR NetSalesShipped = CALCULATE([Reseller Gross Sales] – [Reseller Discount
Amount],ShippedSales)
VAR ProductCost = SUMX('Reseller Sales',
'Reseller Sales'[OrderQuantity]*'Reseller Sales'[ProductStandardCost])
RETURN
DIVIDE(NetSalesShipped – ProductCost,NetSalesShipped)
```

 The new measure includes three lines of comments to describe the business definitions of the measure's components. Comments can also be added per line via the -- and // characters and Power BI applies green color coding to this text. Embedding comments is recommended for both complex measures with multiple components and simple measures, which form the foundation for many other measures.

Variable table filters

The purpose of this measure is to isolate the filter requirements of a measure into its three separate dimension tables:

```
Reseller Gross Sales (Custom) =
VAR ResellerTypes = CALCULATETABLE('Reseller',Reseller[Business Type] =
"Warehouse")
VAR PromotionTypes = CALCULATETABLE('Promotion',
'Promotion'[Promotion Type] IN {"New Product","Excess Inventory"})
VAR DateHistory = --Trailing 10 Days
FILTER(ALL('Date'),'Date'[Date] <= MAX('Date'[Date]) && 'Date'[Date] >=
MAX('Date'[Date]) - 10)
RETURN
CALCULATE([Reseller Gross Sales],ResellerTypes,PromotionTypes,DateHistory)
```

 Variables are declared for each of the three tables to be filtered and a comment (`Trailing 10 Days`) is inserted to help explain the `DateHistory` variable. The variables are invoked as filter parameters to `CALCULATE()`, and so the `Reseller Gross Sales` measure reflects this modified filter context. The same functional result can be achieved by defining all the filtering logic within `CALCULATE()` but this would make the expression less readable and more difficult to support.

How it works...

Reseller Margin % with variables

The `ShippedSales` variable filters the sales fact table to exclude the unshipped sales order lines and this table is used as a filter parameter to the `NetSalesShipped` variable. The existing `Reseller Gross Sales` and `Reseller Discount Amount` measures are referenced, but the `ProductCost` variable, which was a distinct measure in Chapter 3, *Building a Power BI Data Model*, is explicitly defined against the `Reseller Sales` fact table (shipped or not).

Though significantly longer than the `Reseller Margin %` measure in Chapter 3, *Building a Power BI Data Model*, the use of variables and comments eliminates (or reduces) the need to review other measures to understand the logic and source columns.

There's more...

DAX Formatter in DAX Studio

DAX Formatter can be used within DAX Studio to align parentheses with their associated functions.

DAX Formatter in DAX Studio used to format a Year-to-Date Measure

Long, complex DAX measures can be copied from Power BI Desktop into DAX Studio to be formatted.

Click on **Format Query** in DAX Studio and replace the expression in Power BI Desktop with the formatted expression.

> DAX authoring in Power BI Desktop also supports parentheses highlighting, but DAX Formatter isolates functions to individual lines and indents inner function calls such as the ALL() function used as a parameter within the FILTER() function per the image. Without the function isolation and indentation provided by DAX Formatter, complex expressions are often wide and difficult to interpret or troubleshoot.

12
Deploying and Distributing Power BI Content

In this chapter, we will cover the following recipes:

- Preparing a content creation and collaboration environment in Power BI
- Managing migration of Power BI content between development, testing, and production environments
- Sharing Power BI dashboards with colleagues
- Configuring Power BI app workspaces
- Configuring refresh schedules and DirectQuery connections with the on-premises data gateway
- Creating and managing Power BI apps
- Building email subscriptions into Power BI deployments
- Publishing Power BI reports to the public internet
- Enabling the mobile BI experience

Introduction

On May 3rd of 2017, Power BI premium and Power BI apps were introduced as services to support the deployment and distribution of Power BI content to large groups of users. Power BI premium is, at its core, a dedicated hardware resource for organizations to provision and utilize according to their distinct deployment needs. With Power BI premium, new deployment options are supported, including on-premises solutions with the Power BI report server, embedding Power BI in business applications, and publishing Power BI apps to large groups of users for access via the Power BI service and mobile applications. Additionally, premium dedicated capacities can be used in hybrid deployment scenarios such as limiting certain reports and dashboards to the on-premises Power BI Report Server or using one dedicated capacity for embedding Power BI analytics into an application and another capacity for Power BI apps in the Power BI service.

Most importantly, for larger scale deployments Power BI premium avoids the need to purchase licenses for all users--read only users can access Power BI premium content without a pro license. Additionally, as a managed cloud service, resources can be aligned with the changing needs of an organization via simple scale up and scale out options.

> *"In many cases Power BI Premium was built to address the challenges of deploying Power BI at scale where you have larger data models that have grown over time and when you have more users that are accessing the content."*
> *- Adam Wilson, Power BI group program manager*

This chapter contains detailed examples and considerations for deploying and distributing Power BI content via the Power BI service and Power BI mobile applications. This includes the creation and configuration of app workspaces and apps, procuring and assigning Power BI premium capacities, configuring data sources and refresh schedules, and deriving greater value from the Power BI mobile applications. Additionally, processes and sample architectures are shared, describing staged deployments across development and production environments and multi-node premium capacity deployments.

Preparing a content creation and collaboration environment in Power BI

Power BI collaboration environments can take many forms ranging from a small group of Power BI Pro users creating and sharing content with each other in a single app workspace to large scale corporate BI scenarios characterized by many read-only users accessing Power BI premium capacity resources via Power BI apps. Given the cost advantages of the capacity-based pricing model Power BI Premium provides, as well as the enhanced performance and scalability features it delivers, it's important to properly provision and manage these resources.

This recipe provides two processes fundamental to the overall purpose of this chapter: deploying and distributing Power BI content. The first process highlights several critical questions and issues in planning and managing a Power BI deployment. The second process details the provisioning of Power BI premium dedicated capacity resources and the allocation of those resources to specific deployment workloads via app workspaces. See the *How it works...* and *There's more...* sections following this recipe for details on the Power BI premium capacity nodes and scenarios for scaling up and out with Power BI premium capacity.

How to do it...

Evaluate and plan for Power BI deployment

1. Determine how Power BI content (datasets, reports and dashboards) will be deployed and consumed by users.
    - Will content by deployed to the Power BI Service and accessed via apps and Power BI mobile apps?
    - Will content be deployed to the Power BI Service but embedded into business applications?
    - Will content be deployed to the Power BI report server on-premises and accessed via the reporting services web portal as well as the Power BI mobile app?

It's essential to carefully review the licensing and features associated with each deployment option. For example, many of the features in the Power BI Service such as dashboards and Q & A (natural language queries) are not available in the on-premises Power BI Report Server. Likewise, certain Power BI Premium SKUs are exclusive to embedding Power BI into applications and do make features such as analyze in Excel.

For hybrid deployments, such as using both the Power BI service and embedding or the Power BI service and the Power BI report server, estimate the resources required for each of these workloads and evaluate either a consolidated licensing model or separate, dedicated licenses. For example, if 16 virtual cores are provisioned with a Power BI premium P2 SKU, 16 separate cores are also available for licensing the Power BI report server on-premises.

2. Identify or estimate the Power BI Pro and Power BI Free users based on their roles and needs in the organization.
    - Will the user create and publish content (Power BI Pro)?
    - Will the user only consume content and optionally create content for their personal use (Power BI Free)?

Connecting to published datasets via analyze in Excel and Power BI Service Live Connections are Power BI Pro features and are not available to Power BI Free users even if the dataset is assigned to a Power BI Premium capacity. However, a Power BI Free user, can still get subscriptions to reports and dashboards to the apps they access from Premium capacity, and can export content to CSVs and PowerPoint. This is all in addition to the rich consumption capabilities of the Power BI Service and Power BI mobile apps.

3. For larger deployments with many read-only users, estimate the Power BI Premium resources required.
    - Use the Power BI Premium Pricing Calculator as a starting point referenced in the *See also* section.
    - Plan for how deployment workloads will be allocated across premium capacity nodes.
    - Will a given workload (or perhaps a business function) have its own capacity, or will a single, larger capacity support multiple or all workloads or teams?

If Power BI datasets in import mode will serve as the primary data storage option supporting reports and dashboards, consider their memory usage relative to the memory available per Power BI Premium SKU. For example, 25 GB of RAM is currently available in a P1 capacity node, and this would thus be insufficient for larger dataset (model) sizes stored in the service with scheduled refresh. Like SSAS tabular models, 2.5X of memory should be provisioned to support both processing and refresh, queries, and temporary the memory structures created during queries.

4. Evaluate and plan for data storage options (datasets).
    - Will Power BI Desktop be exclusively used for datasets, or will **SQL Server Analysis Services (SSAS)** be used?
    - Will either or both of these tools be in import mode or use DirectQuery?
    - Are changes to a relational data source, or infrastructure necessary to support performance?

In some scenarios, the relational data source must be revised or enhanced to support sufficient DirectQuery performance. These enhancements vary based on the source but may include indexes (such as Columnstore indexes in SQL Server), greater compute and memory resources, denormalization, and referential integrity. If SSAS is being used on-premises as the source for Power BI (via the on-premises data gateway), it may be beneficial to utilize Azure ExpressRoute to create a private connection to the Azure data center of the Power BI tenant.

5. Plan for scaling and migrating Power BI projects as adoption and needs change.
   - Identify key points of the project life cycle and the capabilities needed to migrate and scale as needs change.

Examples of this include adding separate Power BI Premium capacity nodes (scale out), larger capacity nodes (scale up), migrating a Power BI Desktop Dataset to SSAS or Azure Analysis Services, staging deployments across Dev, Test, and Production Power BI workspaces and apps, moving workspaces into and out of premium capacities, and transferring ownership of content across team such as from a business teams, to a corporate BI team.

6. Assign roles and responsibilities to Power BI team members.
   - Dataset authors including source connectivity, retrieval queries, data modeling, and measure development
   - Report authors including dashboards, mobile optimized reports and dashboards, and apps
   - Administrators including the on-premise data gateway, premium capacities, and tenant settings

7. Target skills and knowledge specific to these team roles.
   - Dataset authors, should learn the fundamentals of DAX, M, and Data Modeling for Power BI and SSAS
   - Report authors, should know or learn visualization standards, interactivity and filtering, and custom visuals
   - Administrators, should study monitoring tools and data available for the on-premises gateway monitoring, app workspaces, premium capacities, and the Office 365 Audit Log

Dataset authors may learn the process of migrating a Power BI Dataset to SSAS Tabular and working with Analysis Services projects in Visual Studio. See `Chapter 13`, *Integrating Power BI with Other Applications*, recipe *Migrating a Power BI data model to SSAS tabular* for additional details on this process. Report authors, who are often business analysts outside of the IT or BI organizations, should regularly review new and recent report features released in the Power BI monthly updates.

8. Build collaboration processes across teams.
- Dataset authors should collaborate with the owners and subject matter experts of data sources.
  - For example, any changes to data source schemas or resources should be communicated.
- Report authors should have access to dataset documentation and collaborate with dataset authors.
  - For example, metrics or dimensions not available for new reports should be communicated.
  - Any standards such as a corporate Power BI report theme or fonts should be documented.
  - See `Chapter 4`, *Authoring Power BI Reports*, recipe *Enhancing exploration of reports* for details on report themes.
- Administrators should collaborate with the Office 365 global admin, data governance, and security teams.
  - For example, administrators should confirm that Power BI tenant settings align with organizational policies. Additionally, administrators can request or procure security groups to manage Power BI.
- Plan for common support scenarios, new project requests, and requests for enhancements.
  - For example, create a process for automatically assigning Power BI licenses and security group memberships. Additionally, plan for questions or issues from consumers of Power BI content.

Successful Power BI deployments of any significant scale require planning, team and cross-team collaboration, business processes, active management, and targeted skills and resources. The steps in this recipe only identify several of the fundamental topics--the actual process is always specific to an organization and its deployment goals, policies, and available skills and resources.

Set up a Power BI service deployment

In this example, app workspaces specific to functional areas in an organization are associated with two separate Power BI Premium capacity nodes. An additional workspace and the my workspace associated with all accounts (Power BI Free and Pro) are included in a shared capacity--the multi-tenancy environment of the Power BI Service.

1. An Office 365 global admin or billing admin purchases Pro and Free licenses required in the Office 365 Admin center
2. These licenses are assigned to users according to the roles determined in the planning stage earlier

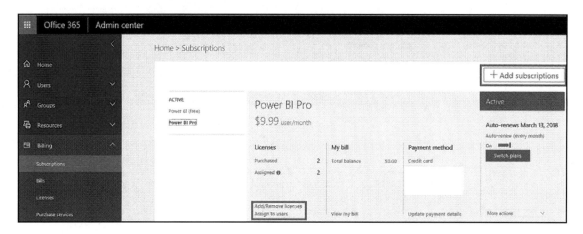

Office 365 Admin center: subscriptions

- The **Add subscriptions** button and the **Purchase services** menu item both expose Power BI Premium subscriptions
- Office 365 Powershell can be used to assign purchased licenses to users as well. Click on **Add subscriptions**

3. Purchase a P2 Power BI Premium capacity node.

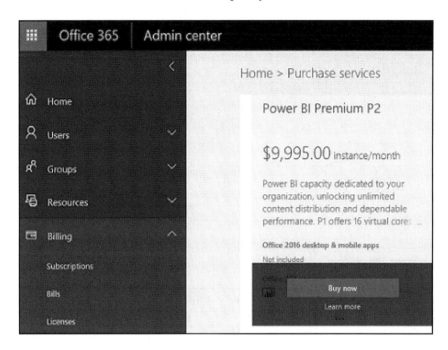

The Purchase services menu: Power BI Premium P2 capacity instance (node)

4. Purchase a P3 Power BI Premium capacity node.

As of this writing, the P2 and P3 SKUs both require an annual commitment while the P1 SKU is available on a month-to-month basis. Of the Power BI Premium SKUs specific to embedding, only the EM3 SKU is listed and available on a month-to-month basis. Payments can be made annually or monthly.

Currently, each instance or capacity purchased is associated with one node and these capacities operate independently. Per the roadmap for Power BI Premium, multi-node capacities will be available, such as having three P3 nodes in a single capacity. Multi-node capacities will likely also support other roadmap features, such as read-only replicas and dedicated data refresh nodes.

5. Confirm that the new Power BI Premium subscriptions appear in the subscriptions window along with the existing Power BI Pro and Power BI Free licenses from step 1.

6. The Office 365 Global Admin or Power BI Service Administrator opens the Power BI Admin Portal.
    - In the Power BI Service, click on the Gear icon in the top right and select Admin Portal

7. Select the **Premium** settings from the admin portal and then click on **Set up new capacity**.

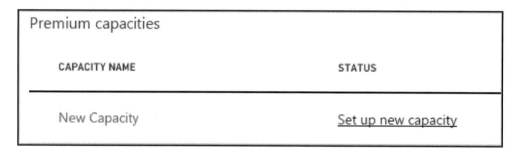

Setting up a new capacity in the Power BI Admin Portal

- Existing capacities will be marked as active and identify the associated capacity administrators.

8. Give the capacity a descriptive name and assign the capacity admin role to a user or users.

 Global Admins and Power BI Service Admins are capacity admins by default, but the capacity admin role can be assigned to users that are not Power BI Service Admins. Capacity admin role privileges are specific to the given capacity.

9. Grant workspace assignment permissions to specific Power BI Pro users or groups for this capacity.

User permissions in premium settings

9. Setup the other capacity purchased, assign its capacity admins, and grant its workspace assignment permissions.

10. Power BI Pro users with workspace assignment permissions can create app workspaces in the Power BI Service.

    - Power BI Pro users with edit rights are added as members and the workspace is assigned to premium capacity.
    - See the recipes later in this chapter for details on App Workspaces and apps.

 Alternatively, in the Power BI admin portal, capacity admins can assign or remove workspaces from premium capacity, as well as whitelist users such that all of a given user's app workspaces are assigned to premium capacity.

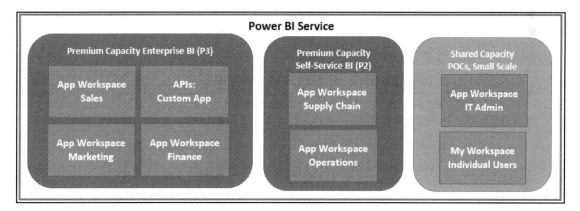

Power BI Premium capacity assigned to workspaces

In this example, three App Workspaces (sales, marketing, and finance) are assigned to a Power BI Premium Capacity named Enterprise BI (P3). Additionally, this capacity also supports the embedded reporting needs of a custom application. The larger P3 (32 cores, 100 GB RAM) capacity was chosen given the higher volume of query traffic for these workspaces, as well as the need for larger dataset sizes.

Supply chain and operations workspaces were assigned to a P2 capacity. In this case, though less of a workload than the P3 capacity, these groups still need to share content with many Free Users. Finally, an App Workspace for a small group of IT users (IT Admin) with Power BI Pro licenses is maintained in Shared Capacity. This workspace didn't require Power BI Premium, given minimal needs for distribution to Free Users and given smaller datasets with relatively infrequent refresh schedules.

How it works...

Premium capacity nodes - frontend cores and backend cores

- The virtual cores of the capacity nodes purchased are split evenly between frontend and backend processes.

CAPACITY NODE	CORES	BACKEND CORES	FRONTEND CORES
P1	8 v-Cores	4 cores, 25 GB RAM	4 cores
P2	16 v-Cores	8 cores, 50 GB RAM	8 cores
P3	32 v-Cores	16 cores, 100 GB RAM	16 cores

Power BI capacity nodes as of GA

- Only the backend cores are fully dedicated to the organization and the back.

The backend cores which handle query processing, data refresh, and the rendering of reports and images. If import mode datasets will be stored in Power BI Premium capacity, it's important to avoid or minimize the duplication of datasets and to review datasets for opportunities to reduce memory usage.

There's more...

Scaling up and scaling out with Power BI Premium

- Scaling out Power BI Premium involves distributing provisioned capacity (v-cores) across multiple capacities.

  For example, the 32 v-cores purchased as part of a P3 capacity node could optionally be split into three separate capacities: two P1 capacities of 8 v-cores each and one P2 capacity of 16 v-cores (*8 + 8 + 16 = 32*). This ability to distribute v-cores across distinct premium capacities is referred to as *v-core pooling*.

- Scaling up power premium or in-place scale up involves purchasing an additional capacity node in the Office 365 Admin center per the recipe then adjusting the capacity size of a given premium capacity to reflect the additional cores:

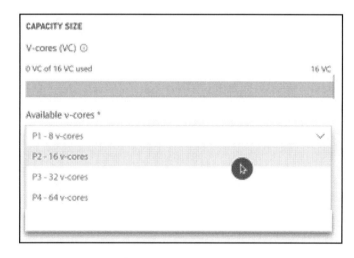

Available v-cores for a capacity in the Power BI Admin Portal

For example, if a P1 capacity is determined to be insufficient for desired performance or scalability, an additional P1 capacity can be purchased. At this point, with two P1 capacities purchased at 8 v-cores each, a P2 capacity size (16 v-cores) can be set for the original capacity in the Power BI Admin portal. This makes it quick and easy to incrementally scale up as requirements change.

See also

- Power BI Premium cost calculator: `https://powerbi.microsoft.com/en-us/calculator/`
- Planning a Power BI enterprise deployment whitepaper: `http://bit.ly/2wBGPRJ`

Managing migration of Power BI content between development, testing, and production environments

Corporate BI and IT teams familiar with project lifecycles, source control systems, and managing development, testing, and production environments should look to apply these processes to Power BI deployments as well. Power BI Desktop does not interface with standard source control systems such as **Team Foundation Server** (**TFS**), but PBIX files can be stored in OneDrive for business to provide visibility of version history, restore capabilities, and group access. In the Power BI Service, separate development, test, and production App Workspaces and their corresponding apps can be created to support a staged deployment. Utilizing these tools and features enables Power BI teams to efficiently manage their workflows and to deliver consistent, quality content to users.

This recipe contains both a high level overview of a staged deployment of Power BI as well as the detailed steps required to execute this process. Additional details regarding OneDrive for Business and the Power BI Rest APIs are included in the *How it works...* section.

Getting ready

- Users must be assigned Power BI Pro licenses to create App Workspaces in the Power BI Service.
- Add any new data sources to on-premise data gateway in Power BI Service.

- Also ensure that users publishing the dataset are authorized to use the gateway for these sources.
- Obtain access to OneDrive for business for storing and managing Power BI Desktop files.

If OneDrive for business is not available, consider storing the PBIX files and optionally, PBIT template files in an alternative version control system. For example, if TFS is being used, Power BI Desktop files can be added to a folder in a Visual Studio solution and checked in and out as changes are implemented. The file size limit in OneDrive for business is currently 10 GB, which should be sufficient for almost all datasets, and PBIT template files can be used if file size is a constraint. See the *Preserving report metadata with Power BI templates* recipe in `Chapter 7`, *Parameterizing Power BI Solutions* for more details.

How to do it...

Staged deployment overview

The process in this recipe reflects the following five step staged deployment model:

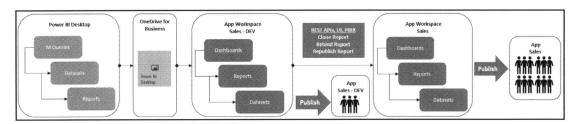

Staged deployment via App Workspaces

1. Power BI Desktop is used to create datasets and reports.
2. Power BI Desktop files (PBIX) are stored in OneDrive for business to maintain version history.
3. A development App Workspace is used to publish a development app to a small group of test or QA users.
4. The Power BI REST APIs or an interface in the Power BI Service is used to clone and rebind reports to the Production App Workspace. Additionally, development or QA Power BI reports can be revised to retrieve from a production dataset and publish to a production App Workspace.

Once approved or validated, a Power BI Desktop report based on a Power BI Service Live Connection to a development App Workspace can be revised to reference a separate dataset from a production App Workspace. Provided the production dataset follows the same schema, the revised report can then be published to production. Switching Power BI Service datasets is accomplished by selecting **Data source** settings from the **Edit Queries** menu on the **Home** tab of Power BI Desktop.

5. The production App Workspace is used to publish an app to a large group of users.

Development environment

1. Create an App Workspace for development in the Power BI Service and add members who will create and edit content.

As the workspace (Sales-DEV) will only be used for development, it may not be necessary to assign the workspace to a Premium capacity, or perhaps the workspace could be assigned to a smaller premium capacity (that is, P1). The production workspace (sales) will of course be accessed by many more users and may also contain a larger dataset and more frequent data refresh requirements, which can only be supported by Power BI Premium.

2. Import a Power BI Desktop file (PBIX) containing a development dataset to OneDrive for business.

	Name ↑		Modified	Modified By	File Size	Sharing
⊘		AdWorksEnterpriseDev.pbix	44 minutes ago	Brett Powell	4.38 MB	🔒 Only you

Files > Power BI > Power BI Dev D... > Sales - DEV

Power BI Desktop file uploaded to OneDrive for business

Clicking on the ellipsis of the file in OneDrive for Business exposes a menu of file management options including version history, download, share, and more. Version history identifies the user, time, and any comments associated with the modification of a given version. The file or folder of files can be shared with other users or Office 365 groups.

3. Connect to the PBIX file on OneDrive for business from the development App Workspace.

   Open the App Workspace in the Power BI Service and click on the **Get Data** menu item below **Datasets**.

   Click on **Get** from the **Files** option under **Import or Connect to Data** and select the OneDrive for business icon.

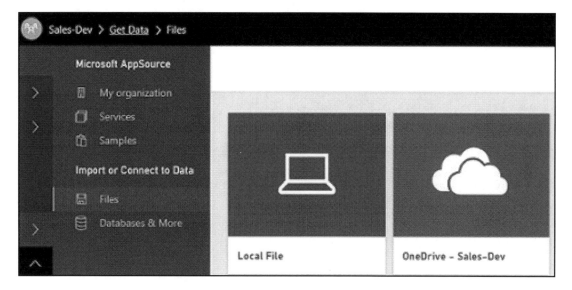

Creating a connction from the Dev App Workspace to the PBIX file on OneDrive for business

Navigate to the PBIX file, select it, and click on the **Connect** button in the top right.

The dataset will be imported to the App Workspace, and by default an hourly synchronization will be scheduled such that changes in the PBIX file will be reflected in the Power BI Service. See *How it works...* for more details on this process.

4. In Power BI Desktop, create reports based on live connections to the dataset in the development App Workspace.

Power BI Service live connection to the development App Workspace dataset

- Publish the reports, save the PBIX files, and then upload the report files to OneDrive for business (or an alternative).

5. In the Power BI Service, configure a scheduled refresh if the dataset is not in DirectQuery mode.
6. Create and format dashboards based on the published reports.
7. Publish an App from the development App Workspace to a small security group of QA or test users.

Production environment

1. Create an App Workspace for Production in the Power BI Service and add members who will create and edit content.
    - For large deployments, assign the production workspace to a Power BI Premium capacity.
2. Import a Power BI Desktop file (PBIX) containing a production dataset to OneDrive for business.

The production dataset should follow the same schema of the development dataset but may contain sensitive data and corresponding row-level security roles. Additionally, development and production datasets often have their own development and production data sources, such as a Dev and Prod SQL Server. Any variance between these source systems should be known and tested to isolate this issue from any version control issues with Power BI content.

3. Connect to the Production PBIX file on OneDrive for business from the development App Workspace.

4. Configure a scheduled refresh for the dataset if in import mode.
   - If DirectQuery or a live connection is used, configure the dashboard tile cache refresh frequency based on requirements.

5. Add users or security groups to RLS roles configured in Power BI Desktop for the dataset.

6. Clone existing reports from the development workspace to the production workspace.

7. Rebind the cloned reports to the production dataset.
   - Alternatively, open the development reports in Power BI Desktop, switch their data source to the production App Workspace dataset (see **Data Source Settings** under **Edit Queries**), and publish these reports to the production App Workspace.

 At the time of this writing, only the Power BI REST APIs are available to execute the clone and rebind report operations. A user interface in the Power BI Service (for App Workspaces) for cloning and rebinding reports is expected soon, and other lifecycle features such as cloning dashboards will likely follow this release. See the *How it works...* section for details on the two Power BI REST APIs.

8. Publish an app from the production App Workspace to a security group.

How it works...

Automated report lifecycle - clone and rebind report APIs

- The clone report and rebind report Power BI REST APIs can be used to deploy reports from a development App Workspace to a Production App Workspace
- Clone report allows you to clone a report to a new App Workspace
  - `https://api.powerbi.com/v1.0/myorg/reports/{report_id}/Clone`
- Rebind report allows you to clone a report and map it to a different dataset
  - `https://api.powerbi.com/v1.0/myorg/reports/{report_id}/Rebind`

OneDrive for business synchronization

- Power BI Desktop (PBIX) and Excel (XLSX) files stored in OneDrive or SharePoint Online are synchronized with their corresponding datasets and reports in the Power BI Service approximately every one hour.

 The synchronization process (technically a file level package refresh) is managed by the Power BI Service and copies the dataset out of the PBIX file and into Power BI. The process also reflects any changes made to report pages. This process does not, however, run a data refresh from the underlying source data. See the *Configuring live connections and refresh schedules with the on-premises data gateway* recipe later in this chapter for details on this process.

Version restore in OneDrive for business

- Prior versions of Power BI Desktop files can be restored via OneDrive for business version history

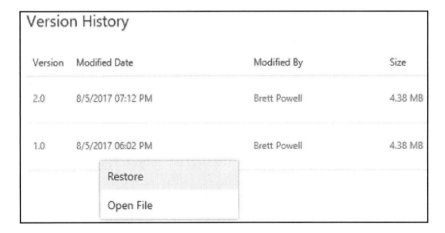

Version history in OneDrive for business

- Select the ellipsis of a specific version and click on **Restore** to replace the current version with this version

See also

- Power BI REST API reference for Report operations: `http://bit.ly/2v8ifKg`

Sharing Power BI dashboards with colleagues

Power BI apps are the recommended content distribution method for large corporate BI deployments, but for small teams and informal collaboration scenarios, sharing dashboards provides a simple alternative. By sharing a dashboard, the recipient obtains read access to the dashboard, the reports supporting its tiles, and immediate visibility to any changes in the dashboard. Additionally, dashboards can be shared with Power BI Pro users external to an organization via security groups and distribution lists, and Power BI Pro users can leverage analyze in Excel as well as the Power BI mobile apps to access the shared data. Moreover, Power BI Free users can consume dashboards shared with them from Power BI Premium capacity.

In this recipe, a Power BI dashboard is shared with a colleague as well as a contact in an external organization. Guidance on configuring and managing shared dashboards and additional considerations are included throughout the recipe and the *How it works...* and *There's more...* sections.

Getting ready

- Confirm that both the owner of the dashboard and the recipient(s) or consumers have Power BI Pro licenses.
- If the recipient(s) does not have a Power BI Pro license, check if the dashboard is contained in an App Workspace that has been assigned to premium capacity.
  - Either Pro licenses or Premium capacity are required to share the dashboard. A Power BI Pro user cannot share a dashboard hosted in Power BI shared capacity with a Power BI Free user.
- Enable the external sharing feature in the Power BI Admin Portal, either for the organization or specific security groups.

The owner of a shared dashboard can allow recipients to reshare a dashboard but any dashboards shared with external users cannot be shared. Additionally, user access to the dashboard, and the ability to reshare can be removed by the dashboard owner. Unlike the publish to web feature described later in this chapter, external sharing can be limited to specific security groups or excluded from specific security groups.

How to do it...

In this example, Jennifer from the BI team is responsible for sharing a dashboard with Brett from the Canada sales team and another X from outside the organization. Brett will need the ability to share the dashboard with a few members of his team.

1. Create a dedicated App Workspace in the Power BI Service.

Content should always be distributed from App Workspaces and not My Workspace. Even in relatively informal scenarios such as sharing a dashboard with one user, sharing a dashboard from My Workspace creates a dependency on the single user (Jennifer in this case) to maintain the content. Sharing the content from an App Workspace with multiple members of the BI team addresses the risk of Jennifer not being available to maintain the content and benefits from Microsoft's ongoing investments in administration and governance features for App Workspaces.

2. Set the privacy level of the workspace to allow members to edit content and add team members to the workspace.
3. Create a security role in Power BI Desktop for the Canada sales team.

4. Publish the Power BI Desktop file to the workspace and add members or security groups to the Canada security role.

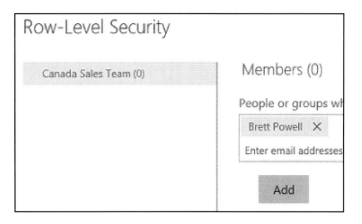

Adding dashboard recipients to members of a row-level security role

By using security roles, an existing Power BI Sales dataset containing sales for other countries can be used for the dashboard. Brett will be allowed to share the dashboard, but RLS will prevent him and those mapped to the security role via security groups from viewing sales data for other countries. See Chapter 8, *Implementing Dynamic User-Based Visibility in Power BI* for details on configuring RLS.

5. Create new Power BI Desktop report files with live connections to the published dataset in the app workspace.
6. Build essential visualizations in each file and publish these reports.

Per other recipes, reports should be developed locally in Power BI Desktop rather than the Power BI Service and OneDrive for Business is recommended to maintain version control.

7. In the Power BI Service, create a new dashboard, pin visuals from reports, and adjust the layout.

8. Click on **Share** from the Canada Sales Dashboard in the App Workspace of the Power BI Service.

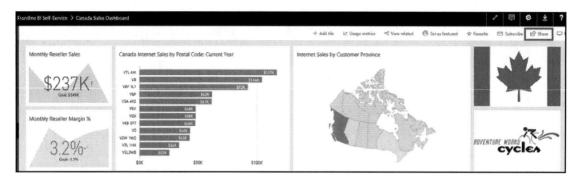

Sharing the Canada Sales dashboard from the frontline BI self-service App Workspace

9. Add Brett, the external user, and optionally a message in the share dashboard form.

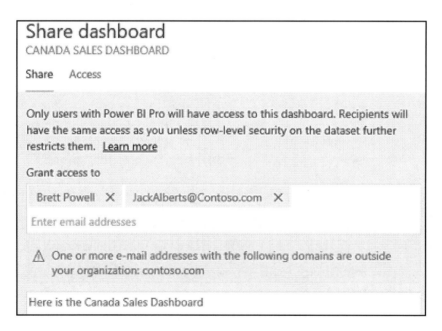

Share dashboard in the Power BI Service

Power BI will detect and attempt to auto-complete as email addresses are entered in the **Grant access to** input box. Additionally, though sharing dashboards is sometimes referred to as peer-to-peer sharing, a list of email addresses can be pasted in, and all common group entities are supported, including distribution lists, security groups, and Office 365 groups. Per the image, a warning will appear if a user external to the organization is entered.

10. In this example, leave the **Allow recipients to share your dashboard** option enabled below the message. Click on **Share**.

    If left enabled on the share form, recipients will receive an email notification as well as a notification in Power BI.

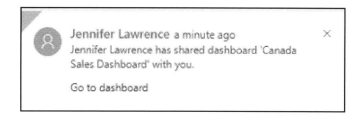

Notification center in the Power BI Service of the dashboard recipient

- A URL to the dashboard is also provided at the bottom of the share dashboard form for facilitating access.

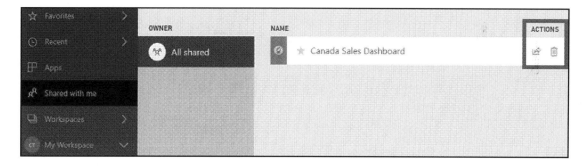

The Canada Sales dashboard in the Shared with Me tab of the Power BI Service

For the recipient, the dashboard appears in the **Shared with me** tab. If enabled by the dashboard owner (and if the user is internal to the organization), the option to reshare the dashboard with others will be visible. The user will be able to favorite the dashboard, access it from the Power BI mobile apps, and interact with the content such as filter selections but cannot edit the report or dashboard. The user can, however, create Excel reports against the underlying dataset per the *There's more...* section.

How it works...

Managing shared dashboards

- Members of the App Workspace with edit rights can disable reshares of the dashboard and stop sharing altogether.

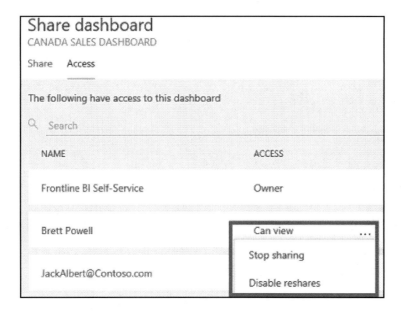

Share dashboard form: access tab

- Open the dashboard, click on **Share**, and then select the **Access** tab to identify and optionally revise the current access.

There's more...

Analyze shared content from Excel

- The recipient of the shared dashboard can use the Power BI Publisher for Excel to build ad hoc pivot table reports.
- Click on **Connect to Data** from Power BI Publisher and identify the shared dataset icon (visible under My Workspace).
- This is a powerful feature, as the entire dataset is available (that is, all measures and columns) unlike in the Power BI Service.

 In the Power BI Service, only the shared dashboard and reports are available--not the dataset. Additionally, the queries sent from the local Excel workbook to the dataset in the Power BI Service will respect the RLS definitions.

Sharing dashboards from Power BI mobile apps

- Dashboards can also be shared from the Power BI mobile applications for all platforms (iOS, Android, and Windows).
- Additionally, the same unsharing and edit rights available in the Power BI Service are available in the mobile apps.

Configuring Power BI app workspaces

App workspaces are shared workspaces in the Power BI Service for Power BI Pro users to develop content. The datasets, reports, and dashboards contained within App Workspaces can be published as a Power BI app for distribution to groups of users. Additionally, App Workspaces can be assigned to Power BI Premium capacities of dedicated hardware to enable all users, regardless of license, to consume the published app and to provide consistent performance and greater scalability. Furthermore, App Workspaces retain a one-to-one mapping to published apps, enabling members and administrators of App Workspaces to stage and test iterations prior to publishing updates to apps.

In this recipe, an App Workspace is created and configured for Power BI Premium capacity. Within the recipe and in the supporting sections, all primary considerations are identified, including the scope or contents of App Workspaces and the assignment of App Workspaces to premium capacity.

Getting ready

1. Confirm that Power BI Pro licenses are available to administrators and members of the app workspace.
2. Ensure that the workspace aligns with the policy or standard of the organization for Power BI content distribution.

> Per the *Preparing a content creation and collaboration environment in Power BI* recipe earlier in this chapter, workspaces have a one-to-one mapping to apps and can have a wide scope (for example, sales), a narrow scope such as a specific dashboard, or a balance between these two extremes, such as European sales. If broad workspaces are used, then it may not be necessary to create a new workspace for a particular project or dashboard--this new content should be added to an existing workspace. However, as an increasing volume of reports and dashboards is added to workspaces it may be beneficial to consider new, more focused workspaces and revisions to the policy.

3. If premium capacity has been provisioned but not bulk assigned to all workspaces of an organization, determine if the new app workspace will be hosted in a premium capacity.
    *   Premium capacity is required to share the content with users who do not have Power BI Pro licenses.
    *   See the first recipe of this chapter for details on other features, benefits, and use cases of Power BI Premium.
4. If Premium capacity has been provisioned and authorized for the new workspace.
    *   Evaluate the current utilization of premium capacity and determine if the expected workload of datasets and user queries from the new app deployment will require a larger or separate capacity.
    *   Confirm that the app workspace administrator has workspace assignment permission, or assign this permission in the Power BI Admin Portal per the first step in *How to do it...*

How to do it...

1. Open the Power BI Admin Portal and select the provisioned capacity under **Premium Settings**.

Premium capacities in Power BI Admin Portal

2. View the recent performance of the capacity via the usage measurements for CPU, memory, and DirectQuery.
3. Ensure that the Power BI Pro user who will be the workspace administrator has assignment permissions to the capacity.

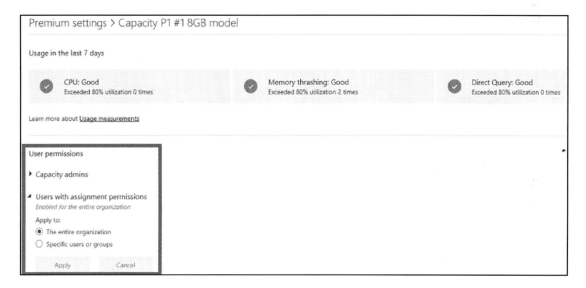

Settings for the Power BI Premium Capacity: capacity P1 #1 8 GB model

In this example, the premium capacity hasn't experienced performance degradations in the past 7 days--otherwise the usage tiles would be yellow or red. Additionally, the capacity has been bulk assigned to all workspaces for the organization per the highlighted user permissions setting. If the capacity was not bulk assigned, the workspace administrator would need to be included as either an individual user or via a security group in the **Apply to specific users or groups** setting.

Note that the workspaces assigned to the capacity are listed at the bottom and can be individually removed (and thus migrated to shared (non-dedicated) capacity). For example, it may be determined that a workspace does not require dedicated resources or that a new app workspace is a higher priority for the performance and scalability benefits of Power BI Premium. Analyzing the Office 365 Audit Log data per `Chapter 10`, *Developing Solutions for System Monitoring and Administration* and Power BI's usage metrics can help determine which workspaces are consuming the most resources.

4. The Power BI Pro user with workspace assignment permissions logs into the Power BI Service.
5. Click on the arrow next to Workspaces and then click on **Create app Workspace**.

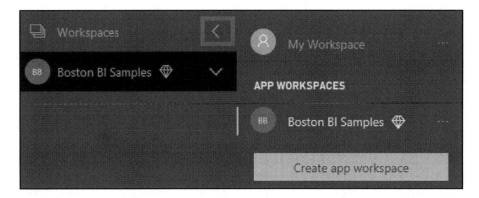

App Workspaces in the Power BI Service

App Workspaces assigned to premium capacity are identified with a diamond icon in the Power BI Service.

6. Name the workspace, define the workspace as private, and allow workspace members to edit content.

Technically it's possible to add members to a view only group and assign developers to the role of workspace admin such that they can edit content. This method of collaboration is not recommended, as the view only members will have immediate visibility to all changes, as with sharing dashboards. Published apps from App Workspaces provide for staging deployments and are the recommended solution for distributing content to read only members.

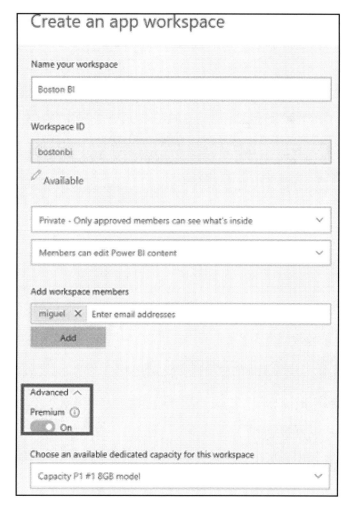

Creating a private App Workspace assigned to premium capacity

7. Add workspace members and associate the workspace with a Power BI Premium capacity via the advanced slider.

Workspace members can now publish datasets and reports and create dashboards to distribute via an app.

Currently, only individual users can be added as members and admins of App Workspaces. In a near future iteration, AD security groups and Office 365 modern groups will be supported as well.

 In small Power BI deployments such as a team of approximately 10 users within a department, it may be unnecessary to publish an app from an App Workspace. In this scenario, in which flexibility and self-service BI is a top priority, all team members could be added to an App Workspace with edit rights. Members would need Power BI Pro licenses but could view and interact with the content via the App Workspace itself, Excel, or the mobile apps, and could simply share dashboards and reports with other Power BI Pro users.

How it works...

App workspaces and apps

- Apps are simply the published versions of App Workspaces.

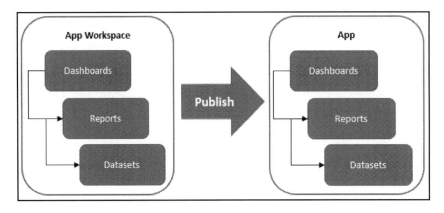

App Workspaces: one to one relationship with published apps

- Users consume and interact with apps. Content is created and managed in App Workspaces.
- Consumers of Apps only have visibility to published versions of Apps, not the Workspace content.
- Per the creating and managing Power BI Apps recipe in this chapter, not all content from an App Workspace has to be included in the published App.

App workspaces replace group workspaces

- Existing Power BI group workspaces were renamed App Workspaces, and all new workspaces are App Workspaces.
- All App Workspaces, including those converted from group workspaces, can be used to publish apps.
- All content within App Workspaces is included when the workspace is published as an app for distribution.

 As App Workspaces are intended for creation, Microsoft intends to provide new features and configurations around the administration and governance of their content. The added complexity of these features within App Workspaces will not be visible to consumers of published apps. The other workspace, My Workspace, is available to all users (including Power BI Free users) as a personal scratchpad and will not receive these enhancements.

There's more...

Power BI premium capacity admins

- Office 365 Global Admins and Power BI Admins are Capacity Admins of Power BI Premium capacities by default.
- These admins can assign users as Capacity Admins per capacity during initial setup of the capacity and later via User Permissions within the Premium settings of a capacity in the Power BI Admin Portal.

- Capacity Admins have administrative control over the given capacity but must also be granted assignment permissions in the **Users with assignment permissions** setting to assign workspaces to premium capacities if the capacity admin will be responsible for associating an app workspace to premium capacity.
- Power BI Admins are expected to have the ability to assign individual workspaces to premium capacity from the admin portal by Q4 of 2017.

See also

- Manage Power BI Premium: `http://bit.ly/2vq8WHe`

Configuring refresh schedules and DirectQuery connections with the on-premises data gateway

The promise of leveraging the Power BI Service and mobile applications to provide access to a rich set of integrated dashboards and reports across all devices requires thoughtful configuration of both the data sources and the datasets which use those sources. For most organizations, the primary business intelligence data sources are hosted on-premises, and thus, unless Power BI reports are exclusively deployed to the on-premises Power BI Report Server, the on-premises data gateway is needed to securely facilitate the transfer of queries and data between the Power BI Service and on-premises systems. Additionally, the datasets which typically support many reports and dashboards must be configured to utilize an on-premises data gateway for either a scheduled refresh to import data into Power BI or to support DirectQuery and SSAS Live Connection queries generated from Power BI.

This recipe contains two examples of configuring data sources and scheduled refreshes for published datasets. The first example configures two on-premises data sources (SQL Server and Excel) for an import mode Power BI dataset and schedules a daily refresh. The second example configures a separate on-premise SQL Server database for a DirectQuery Power BI dataset and sets a 15 minute dashboard tile refresh schedule.

Getting ready

1. Download and install the on-premises data gateway per `Chapter 1`, *Configuring Power BI Development Tools*, if necessary.
2. Become an administrator of the on-premises data gateway.

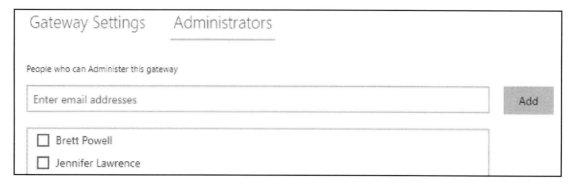

Administrators of a on-premises data gateway

- It's strongly recommended to have at least two administrators for each gateway installed.

How to do it...

Scheduled refresh for import mode dataset

In this example, an import mode dataset has been created with Power BI Desktop to retrieve from two on-premises data sources--a SQL Server database and an Excel file.

Configure data sources for the on-premises data gateway

1. Identify the server name and database name used in the Power BI Desktop file.
2. Identify the full path of the Excel file.
3. In the Power BI Service, click on the Gear icon in the top right corner and select **Manage Gateways**.

4. From the **Manage Gateways** interface, click on **Add Data Source** and choose SQL Server.

5. Provide an intuitive source name that won't conflict with other sources and enter the server and database names.

Adding a SQL Server database as a source for an on-premises data gateway

The server and database names for the gateway must exactly match the names used in the Power BI dataset.

If configuring an SSAS data source (data source type = analysis services) for a gateway, ensure that the credentials used are also an SSAS server administrator for the given SSAS instance. The server administrator credential is used in establishing the connection but each time a user interacts with the SSAS data source from Power BI their UPN (user principal name) is passed to the server via the `EffectiveUserName` connection property. This allows for RLS roles defined in the SSAS database to be applied to Power BI users.

6. Under **Advanced Settings**, check that the source uses the appropriate privacy level such as organizational or private.
7. Click on **Add** and then, via the **Users** tab, add users authorized to use this gateway for this data source.

Successful setup of a data source for the on-premises data gateway

8. Add an additional data source for the Excel file using the file data source type.

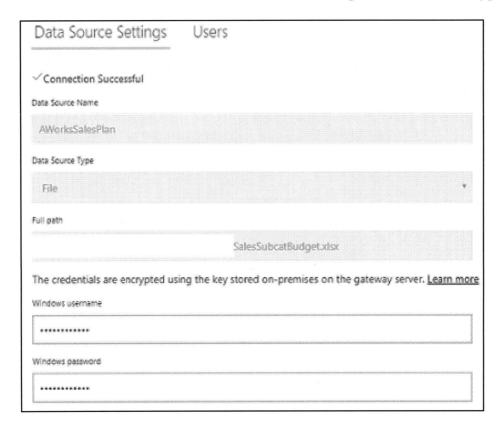

Excel file data source configured for the on-premises data gateway

9. Like the SQL Server data source in step 7, authorize users for this gateway and this data source via the users page.

The gateway will appear as an option for data refresh if the following three criteria are met:

- The user is listed on the Users page of the data source(s) within the gateway
- The server and database names configured in the Power BI Service for the gateway match the names used in the Power BI Desktop file
- Each data source used by the dataset is configured as a data source for the gateway

Note that only a single gateway can be used to support the refresh or queries of a given dataset.

 As of this writing, only certain online sources are supported by the on-premises data gateway. Therefore, given the single gateway per dataset requirement, if an online data source used by the dataset isn't yet available to the on-premises gateway, a current workaround is to temporarily install and configure the personal gateway.

Schedule a refresh

The following process could be carried out by a Power BI Pro user authorized to use the gateway for the two data sources:

1. Publish the import mode Power BI Desktop file (dataset) to an App Workspace in the Power BI Service.
2. Access this App Workspace from the datasets list and click on the **Schedule refresh** icon.

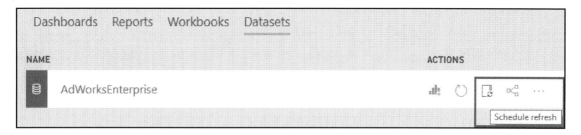

Actions available to a published dataset in the Power BI Service

- Alternatively, click on the ellipsis and then select **Settings**. Both options open the settings for the dataset.

3. From settings for the dataset (`AdWorksEnterprise`), associate the dataset with the gateway.

Associating the AdWorksEnterprise dataset with the Power BI cookbook gateway

4. Click on **Apply** on the **Gateway** connection menu; a successful connection message will appear.

   The gateway appeared because both the Excel file and the database were added as sources for this gateway.

5. In the **Scheduled refresh** menu below gateway connection, configure a daily refresh with email notification of failures.

Scheduled refresh of dataset

 There is no guarantee that scheduled refreshes will occur at the exact time they are scheduled, such as 5:00 AM in this example. The actual refresh may take place as long as 20-30 minutes after the time scheduled in the Power BI Service.

DirectQuery dataset

In this example, a Power BI Desktop file (dataset) in DirectQuery mode based on a separate on-premise SQL Server database must be deployed to the Power BI Service. The intent is for the dashboards based on this dataset to be as current as possible.

Configure data sources for the on-premises data gateway

1. Like the import mode dataset, add the SQL Server database as a data source to the gateway.
2. Assign user(s) to this data source and gateway.

Configure the DirectQuery dataset

The following process could be carried out by a Power BI Pro user authorized to use the gateway for the SQL Server database:

1. Publish the DirectQuery Power BI Desktop file (dataset) to an App Workspace in the Power BI Service.

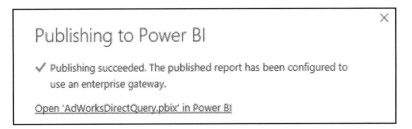

Publishing a DirectQuery dataset from Power BI Desktop

- Power BI automatically configures the dataset to use a gateway by matching the data sources configured in the PBIX file and the sources configured in the Power BI Service for the gateway. The user must also be listed for the gateway.

2. Access this App Workspace in the Power BI Service and from the datasets list click on **Settings** via the ellipsis (**...**).
3. Modify the scheduled cache refresh frequency from 1 hour to 15 minutes.

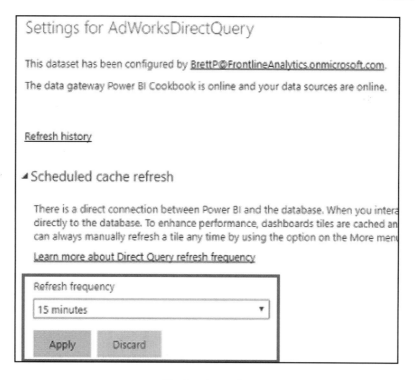

DirectQuery dataset settings

By default, the dashboard tiles are refreshed each hour for DirectQuery and Live Connection datasets. In this process, queries are sent by the Power BI Service through the gateway to the dataset sources. In this scenario, the organization is comfortable with the more frequent queries but in other scenarios simply a daily or even a weekly dashboard refresh would be sufficient to avoid adding workload to the data source.

How it works...

Dataset refreshes

- Import mode datasets can be refreshed via the schedule manually in the Power BI Service or via REST API
- Only the metadata is refreshed for DirectQuery and SSAS datasets

Dashboard and report cache refreshes

- Data caches used by dashboard tiles are updated after refresh operations for import mode datasets (or manually).
- For DirectQuery and SSAS live connection datasets, dashboard tiles are updated hourly (default) or as configured in the settings for the dataset.
- The Power BI Service also caches data for report visuals and updates these caches as datasets are refreshed.

 Dashboard tiles can also be refreshed manually in the Power BI Service via the **Refresh Dashboard Tiles** menu item (top right, via ellipsis). Likewise, reports can be manually refreshed from the Power BI Service, but this is only relevant for DirectQuery and SSAS live connections--this does not initiate a refresh for an import mode dataset.

There's more...

Refresh limits: Power BI premium versus shared capacity

 If an import mode dataset is hosted in an App Workspace assigned to Power BI Premium capacity, up to 48 refreshes can be scheduled per day. Additionally, an incremental refresh will be available to datasets in Power BI Premium workspaces, such that only changed or new data will be loaded to the Power BI Service. If the dataset is in a shared capacity workspace, a max of eight refreshes per day can be scheduled and the entire dataset must be refreshed (incremental refresh will not be available).

Currently scheduled refreshes must be separated by a minimum of 30 minutes.

Trigger refreshes via data refresh APIs in the Power BI Service

- Power BI data refresh APIs allow BI teams to trigger refresh operations in the Power BI Service programmatically.

For example, a step can be added to an existing nightly (or more frequently) data warehouse or ETL process that initiates the refresh of a Power BI dataset which uses this data source. This allows dashboards and Reports in the Power BI Service to reflect the latest successful refresh of the data source(s) as soon as possible. In other words, the gap or lag between the source system refresh and the Power BI dataset scheduled refresh can be reduced to the amount of time needed to refresh the dataset in the Power BI service. Note that the dataset refresh process itself will soon be more efficient via incremental refreshes for workspaces assigned to Power BI Premium capacities.

To trigger refresh for a dataset in the Power BI Service, simply make the following HTTP request:

```
POST
https://api.powerbi.com/v1.0/myorg/groups/{group_id}/datasets/{dataset_id}/
refreshes
```

- See documentation on Power BI REST API authentication and the Power BI REST API reference in *See also*

See also

- Power BI REST API reference: `https://msdn.microsoft.com/en-us/library/mt203551.aspx`
- Power BI REST API authentication: `http://bit.ly/2hsJMBr`

Creating and managing Power BI apps

The datasets, reports, and dashboards contained in the App Workspaces described earlier in this chapter can be published as apps to make this content accessible to users. Apps can be configured for an entire organization or specific users or groups and published and optionally updated from their corresponding App Workspaces. Users can easily access and install published apps and they obtain read access to view and interact with apps in both the Power BI Service and Power BI mobile applications. Additionally, if the App Workspace for the app has been assigned to a Power BI Premium capacity, the app will be available to all users, including those without Power BI Pro licenses and users will also benefit from the improved performance, scale, and other features of Power BI Premium.

> *"Apps are our solution to enterprise-scale distribution of content in Power BI."*
> *- Ajay Anandan, senior program manager, Microsoft*

In this recipe, an App Workspace (Canada Sales) is published as an App and installed by a user. Additional details on the comparison of Apps with content packs, which Apps will soon replace, is included in the *There's more...* section.

Getting ready

1. Determine if consumers of the app will have access via individual Power BI Pro licenses or if the App Workspace will be assigned to a Power BI Premium capacity.
2. Either assign Power BI Pro licenses to consumers or assign the App Workspace to a Power BI Premium capacity per the *Configuring Power BI app workspaces* recipe earlier in this chapter.

   With smaller and relatively simple deployments in terms of data size, refresh requirements, and the volume of users, it may be more cost effective to simply publish the app to the shared capacity and assign Power BI Pro licenses to users. Apps and Power BI Premium capacities are particularly well suited for wider distribution, with many read only users and more demanding requirements that leverage Premium features such as incremental refreshes and larger datasets.

3. Identify any content in the App Workspace which should be excluded from the published app, such as test or sample reports used by the App Workspace team but not of any value to the consumers of the App.

4. Optionally, determine whether the App should use a landing page such as a dashboard or just the list of content.

How to do it...

In this example, the BI team has created an App Workspace (Canada Sales) containing three dashboards and five reports for distribution to the Canada Sales organization. All of this content is based on one dataset, a published Power BI Desktop file (PBIX) and with Row-level security has been applied.

Publishing an app

1. Open the Canada Sales App Workspace in the Power BI Service.

2. Set the **INCLUDED IN APP** property for each item in the workspace (that is reports and dashboards) to **Included** or **Not included**.

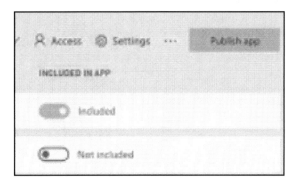

Selective publish in App Workspaces

When Apps were first released, all content from the source App Workspace was included in the App. The selective publish feature reflected in the preceding screenshot allows the owners or administrators of the App Workspace to optionally utilize additional dashboards, reports, and datasets within the workspace without exposing this content to consumers of the App.

3. Click on the **Publish app** button in the top right menu.
   - If the app has already been published, an update app icon will appear but link to the same menus.

4. Enter a brief description on the **Details** menu. This is required to publish the app.

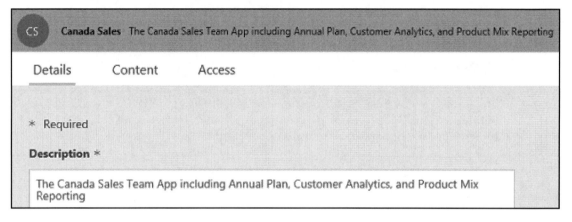

App creation menus for an App Workspace in the Power BI Service

5. On the **Content** menu, choose whether users will be defaulted to a specific dashboard, report, or a basic list of the content (report, dashboards and datasets) in the app.

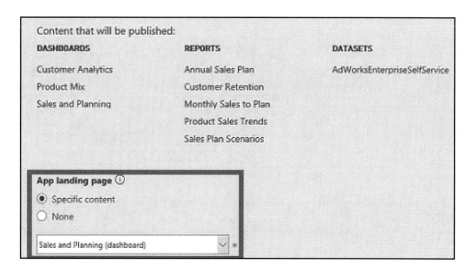

Default landing page setting for app users

6. On the **Access** menu, choose the specific individuals or security groups to distribute the app to.

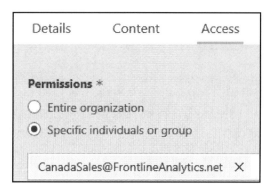

Granting access to the app to members of a security group

7. Click on **Finish** at the top right, then select **Publish**.

SUCCESSFULLY PUBLISHED

Canada Sales

You can now share this link with everyone you have given access to. Users that were given access can also install the app by visiting Get Apps.

| https://app.powerbi.com/Redirect?action=OpenApp&appId=4c3 | Copy |

Successful publishing message with URL to the app

8. Power BI Service will check that the access email addresses are valid and provide a URL to the app.

The app icon can be set to an image if an exchange online license is available to an App Workspace member. A members option will appear when clicking on the ellipsis next to the App Workspace, and this links to the Office 365 Outlook account associated with the workspace. Hover over the workspace icon in Outlook Online, select the pencil icon, and navigate to the image you'd like to use for the workspace.

Distributing and installing the app

- The URL to the app, as well as URLs to dashboards within the app, will be available on the Access menu in the App Workspace via the **Update app** button.
- URLs to the app can be added to portals or sent via email or instant message (IM).
- Alternatively, users can select the **Apps** menu in the Power BI Service and find the app in the AppSource gallery.

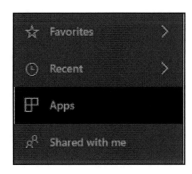

Apps menu in the Power BI Service

All content consumption options, including apps are listed above
Workspaces. Users can add apps, to their list of **Favorites** like dashboards
and Apps accessed also appear in the **Recent** menu. In the near future, it
will be possible to push apps directly to users without the need to share
the link or to find and install the app in AppSource.

- Click **Get Apps** or **Get More Apps** and find the published app for installation.

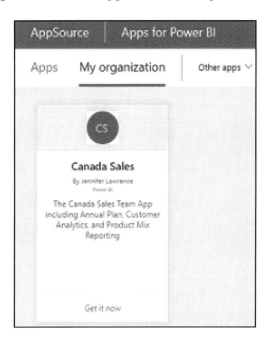

Published App available for install via AppSource

- Users can click on **View content list** at the the the top right to see all dashboards, reports, and datasets in the app

The content list menu provides links to directly open each dashboard or report. Additionally, the **View Related** items feature exposes dependencies between the content and, for Power BI Pro users, an analyze in Excel option allows the user to download the ODC file for connecting from a local Excel workbook.

Folders have been a highly requested feature and are expected to be available to apps relatively soon. As an additional organizational or grouping layer, apps could more easily support broadly scoped App Workspaces (for example, Finance) that contain many dashboards and reports.

How it works...

App workspaces to apps

- Apps are exclusively the published version of all content contained within App Workspaces
    - Per step 2 of the *Publishing an app* section, not all content in the App Workspace has to be included in the published app
- Both App Workspace admins and members of App Workspaces with edit rights can publish and update apps
- The dashboards and reports of apps retain their identity as part of the app and thus simplify user navigation
- Other distribution methods (that is, sharing and content packs) can lead to a cluttered, more complex user experience

There's more...

Apps replacing content packs

- Organizational content packs in which specific dashboards and reports of a workspace can be defined and which allow recipients to personalize a copy of the content received will soon be replaced by Apps
- Content packs are currently supported from App Workspaces but should only be used if both user customization is required and if the new customization feature of Apps is not yet available

Building email subscriptions into Power BI deployments

Power BI reports and dashboards can be scheduled for delivery to user email accounts via subscriptions. Once a subscription is configured in the Power BI Service, Power BI will send an updated snapshot of the dashboard or report page to the user email account, along with a link to access this content in Power BI. Subscription emails are generated based on changes to the source dataset, such as daily scheduled refreshes and depending on the type of connection method used by the source dataset, the frequency of email deliveries can be defined for the subscription.

This recipe walks through the process of configuring and managing report and dashboard subscriptions. Additional details on current limitations such as custom visuals, published Power BI Apps, and alternative email addresses are included within the recipe and the *There's more...* section.

Getting ready

Determine feasibility - recipient, distribution method, and content

As of July 31, 2017, subscriptions are created and managed by individual Power BI users on their own behalf. The user must either have a Power BI Pro license or the reports and dashboards to be subscribed to must be published from an App Workspace in Power Premium capacity. Additionally, subscription emails are exclusive to the **User Principal Name (UPN)** and only custom visuals that have been certified by Microsoft for security are supported.

The abilities to configure email subscriptions for other users or security groups and to receive emails at non-UPN email accounts are both planned enhancements to subscriptions.

1. Identify the users requiring email subscriptions and either assign Power BI Pro licenses or ensure that the Apps these users will access are published from an App Workspace assigned to a Power BI Premium capacity.
2. In a Power BI Pro license only scenario, add the user to an app workspace containing these reports and dashboards.
3. An app workspace administrator can set member privacy to view only and add the users as members.
    * Content creators or BI/IT professionals could be defined as workspace admins to retain edit rights.

How to do it...

In this scenario an App has been published from an App Workspace in Power BI Premium Capacity to a security group of USA Sales users. The USA Sales user, who doesn't have a Power BI Pro license, can create and manage subscriptions as follows.

Create dashboard and report subscriptions

1. Log into the Power BI Service and install the published app (USA Sales Analysis).

Published USA Sales Analysis App available in AppSource

- In this example, the user opened the **Apps** menu item (under **Recent**) and clicked **Get it now** for **USA Sales Analysis**
- Apps that the user has access to will be visible, and alternatively, a URL to the App can be shared with users

2. Open the dashboard and select **Subscribe** in the top menu (envelope icon).

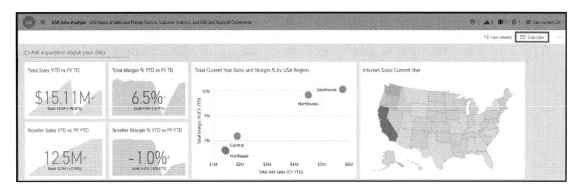

Subscribe option (top right) for a dashboard from the app

3. A slider bar for the dashboard will be enabled--click on **Save and Close**.

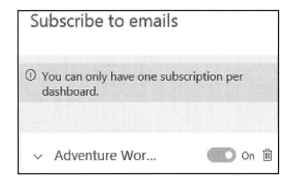

Dashboard email subscription

4. Open a report in the app, navigate to the specific report page, and click on **Subscribe** in the top menu (envelope icon).

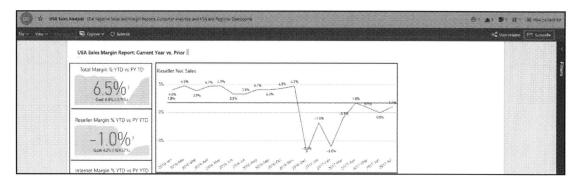

Subscribe to a report page

5. Choose the report page to subscribe to via the report page dropdown. Click on **Save and Close**.

6. Repeat this process for other pages in the same report or for other report pages.

Given that links to the dashboards and reports will be included in the emails, and given the data alerts and email notifications capability described in `Chapter 5`, *Creating Power BI Dashboards*, it may not be necessary to configure more than a few subscriptions. To minimize emails received and subscriptions to manage, try to consolidate critical measures in dashboards and onto summary level report pages per report. The user will be able to quickly access the reports supporting the dashboard, as well as the other report pages of a report subscription.

Manage subscriptions

To manage subscriptions, such as disabling, deleting, or changing the frequency of emails, a user has two options:

1. Access the app and open any dashboard or report.
2. Click on **Subscribe** and then **Manage all Subscriptions** at the bottom of the subscriptions menu.
   - Alternatively, with the app open, the user can click on **Settings** from the Gear icon and navigate to **Subscriptions**.

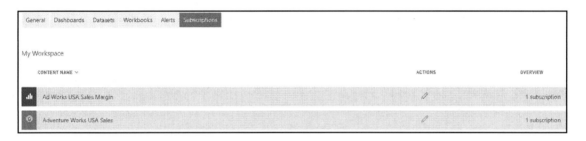

Subscriptions in App Workspace settings

Each dashboard and report with a subscription is identified along with the number of subscriptions per report.

With Power BI's increased focus on supporting large scale deployments (that is, Power BI Premium, apps) in which many users only need minimal read access (such as a daily email), more robust subscription features and controls are expected. For example, if an app workspace is assigned to a Premium capacity, then workspace administrators may be able to configure subscriptions for recipients who have not been assigned Power BI Pro licenses.

There's more...

- Users cannot create subscriptions to dashboards that have been shared with them if the dashboard was shared from a separate Power BI tenant
- For dashboard subscriptions, streaming, video, and custom web content tiles are not yet supported

See also

- Certified custom visuals: `https://powerbi.microsoft.com/en-us/documentation/powerbi-custom-visuals-certified/`
- Power BI email subscriptions: `https://powerbi.microsoft.com/en-us/documentation/powerbi-service-subscribe-to-report/`

Publishing Power BI reports to the public internet

The publish to web feature in the Power BI Service allows for Power BI reports to be shared with the general public by embedding the report within websites, blog posts, and sharing URL links. If the publish to web tenant setting is enabled and if a user has edit rights to a report an embed code can be generated containing both the HTML code for embedding the report and a URL to the report. All pages of the report including any custom visuals and standard interactive functionalities such as filtering and cross highlighting, are available to consumers of the report. Additionally, the report is automatically updated to reflect refreshes of its source dataset and embed codes can be managed and optionally deleted if necessary to eliminate access to the report via the embed code and URL.

This recipe walks through the fundamental steps and considerations in utilizing the publish to web feature.

Getting ready

The publish to web feature is enabled for organizations by default. However, given the clear security risk of confidential information being exposed to the public, administrators may choose to disable this feature until a business case or project requiring the functionality has been formally approved. Additionally, some organizations may choose to disable this feature until it can be enabled for only specific security groups, like with other Power BI features.

1. In the Power BI Service, click on the gear icon and select admin portal to open the Power BI admin portal.
2. Find **Publish to web** in the list of tenant settings and enable the feature if disabled.

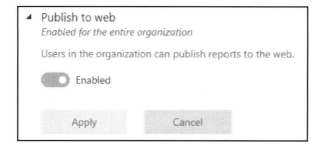

Publish to web setting within tenant settings of the Power BI Admin Portal

The publish to web feature can be either enabled or disabled for all users in the organization. Some tenant settings, such as export data and print dashboards and reports offer more granular administrative controls. For example, the **Print dashboards and reports** feature can be enabled for only a specific security group or groups within an organization or it can be enabled for the entire organization, except for a specific security group or groups.

How to do it...

1. Create a private app workspace in the Power BI Service to host publish to web reports and datasets.
2. Assign a descriptive name to the workspace that associates it to publish to web content or publicly available data.
3. Allow members to edit content and only add the individual users that require edit rights to the content.
4. Optionally, assign the app workspace to a Power BI Premium capacity.

A separate workspace isn't technically necessary for publish to web, but this isolation is recommended for manageability and limiting the risk of publishing confidential or proprietary information. Likewise, Premium capacity isn't required in all **Publish to web** scenarios but could be appropriate for larger datasets or when more frequent data refreshes and consistent performance are important.

5. Create a new Power BI Desktop file that will serve as the dataset for the publish to web report.
6. Develop essential data connections, queries, model relationships, and measures to support the report.
7. Save the file and publish it to the app workspace created earlier.

The sources, query transformations, and modeling of the dataset should be minimal to the needs of the publish to web report. Per Chapter 3, *Building a Power BI Data Model*, usually import mode models (rather than DirectQuery) are appropriate and, also like other models, a centralized and managed data source is preferred over M query transformations embedded in the dataset.

SSAS tabular databases hosted on premises cannot be used as datasets for publish to web reports and RLS cannot be applied to the dataset.

8. Open a new Power BI Desktop file that will serve as the publish to web report.
9. Click on **Get Data** and connect to the published dataset via the Power BI Service data connector available in the online services category of data sources.

10. Develop the report including all visuals, layout, and formatting options, including page size (16:9 or 4:3).

11. Name the file, save, and click on **Publish**. The report will be published to the workspace of the source dataset.

OneDrive for business can be used to maintain version control of the Power BI Desktop files published as datasets and reports. Click on the ellipsis next to the file in OneDrive for business and select **Version History** to access prior versions. Other forms of source control common to BI projects, such as Team Foundation Server, are not available to Power BI Desktop files.

12. Access the app workspace in the Power BI Service.

13. Add any new on-premises data sources to the on-premises data gateway in the manage gateways portal.

14. Open the settings for the dataset, assign a gateway (if applicable), and configure a scheduled refresh.

15. Open the report, click on **File** and select **Publish to web**.

Publish to web Option for a Report in the Power BI Service

16. Click on **Create embed code** and then select **Publish** in the following message box that warns about public access.
    - A **Success** message box will appear with the URL to the report and the HTML code for embedding the iFrame.

17. Click on the Gear icon again and select **Manage embed codes**.

AdventureWorks Publish to Web

Associated Report	Status	Date Created	
Boston Property Assessment	Active	7/30/2017, 5:56:39 PM	··· </> Get code 🗑 Delete

Manage embed codes interface for the AdventureWorks Publish to Web App Workspace

- All embed codes for the given workspace will be exposed as either **Active**, **Blocked**, or **Not Supported**.

 A **Not Supported** status indicates that one of the few unsupported features has been used by the report, such as RLS, SSAS tabular on premises, or R visuals. As of July 30, 2017, ArcGIS Maps for Power BI are also not supported in Publish to web reports.

18. Click on the ellipsis per the image and select **Get code**.

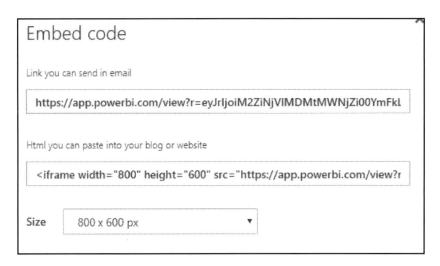

Embed Code for Publish to web Report

The html code provided can be edited manually to improve the fit of the report on the destination for embedding. Adding 56 pixels to the height dimension can adjust for the size of the bottom bar. Setting the page size in Power BI Desktop, the view mode in the Power BI Service (**View** button next to **File**), and manually adjusting the iFrame height and width values may be necessary for a perfect fit.

How it works...

Publish to web report cache

- Power BI caches the report definition and the results of the queries required to view the report as users view the report
- Given the cache, it can take approximately one hour before changes to the report definition or the impact of dataset refreshes are reflected in the version of the report viewed by users

There's more...

Embed in SharePoint online

- Per the image of the report **File** menu, Power BI reports can also be embedded in SharePoint online
- Clicking on **Embed in SharePoint Online** provides a URL that can be used with a Power BI web part in SharePoint online
- Users accessing the SharePoint online page must also have access to the report in the Power BI Service

See also

- Publish to web from Power BI: `https://powerbi.microsoft.com/en-us/documentation/powerbi-service-publish-to-web`

Enabling the mobile BI experience

The Power BI mobile apps have been designed to align closely with the user experience and feature set available in the Power BI Service. This provides a simple, familiar navigation experience for users and allows BI and IT teams to leverage existing Power BI assets and knowledge to enhance the mobile experience in their organization. In relatively new or less mature Power BI deployments, core functionalities such as mobile optimized reports and dashboards, data driven alerts, and annotate and share can deliver significant value. For more advanced and specific use cases, conversational BI with Q & A, interactive meetings with the Power BI Windows 10 universal app, geo-filtering, and more, provide mobile solutions to mobile business scenarios.

This recipe contains two processes to take advantage of Power BI's mobile capabilities. The first process helps identify 'quick win' opportunities that require limited BI/IT investment to better utilize basic Power BI mobile features. The second process identifies somewhat less common yet powerful and emerging uses cases for Power BI mobile applications.

How to do it...

Enhance basic mobile exploration and collaboration

1. Identify the most highly used dashboards and reports.
    *   Open the Power BI admin portal (Gear icon: admin portal) and select the usage metrics menu

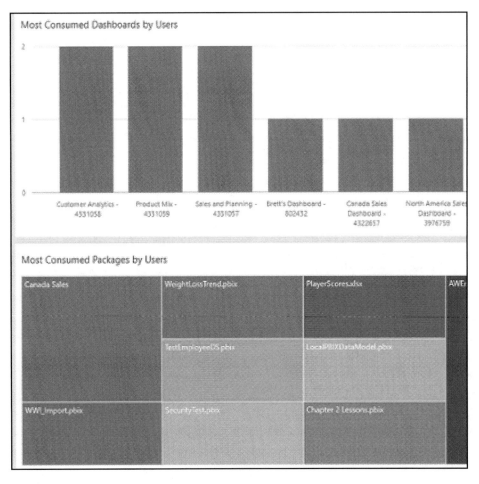

Usage Metrics in the Power BI Admin Portal

The most consumed dashboards and packages visuals provide a summary of consumption or usage by count of users

For much more granular analysis of usage, the Office 365 Audit Log for Power BI events can be imported and analyzed per Chapter 10, *Developing Solutions for System Monitoring and Administration*, recipe *Visualizing log file data from SQL server agent jobs and from Office 365 audit searches.* Additionally, usage metrics reports specific to individual dashboards and reports are now available in the Power Bi Service in the Actions menu. Though scoped to a specific item, these reports also indicate the split between web and mobile usage.

2. Decide which dashboards and reports from step 1 to target for mobile enhancements.
3. Optimize Power BI dashboards for mobile consumption.

Open the dashboard and switch to **Phone View**.

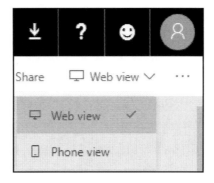

Switching from Web view to Phone View for a Dashboard in the Power BI Service

Unpin image, text, and less mobile-friendly or relevant tiles from the phone view.

Resize and organize KPIs and essential visuals at the top of the **Phone View**.

Customizing Phone View of a Dashboard in the Power BI Service

Only the owner of the dashboard will have the option to customize the Phone view in the Power BI Service. As per Chapter 4, *Authoring Power BI Reports*, the Phone layout for report pages is implemented within Power BI Desktop files. Therefore, any Power BI Pro User with access to the App Workspace of the report in the Power BI Service and the source PBIX file(s) could optimize these reports for mobile consumption.

4. Open the reports (PBIX files) from step 2 locally and enable the responsive formatting property for visuals.

Responsive Visuals (Preview) in Power BI Desktop

By enabling the Responsive Visuals property for Cartesian visuals such as the column, bar, and line charts, these visuals will be optimized to display their most important elements as their size is reduced. This effectively makes it realistic to use these more dense visuals in the phone layout for reports and phone view for dashboards. However, it still may make sense to prioritize KPI, card, and gauge visuals in mobile layouts, given the limited space.

5. On the **View** tab of the most important report pages, click on **Phone Layout** and design a custom mobile view of the page.
   - See `Chapter 4`, *Authoring Power BI Reports*, recipe *Designing mobile report layouts* for details on this process.
6. Publish the updated Power BI reports to their App Workspaces in the Power BI Service and repin any dashboard tiles.
7. Test the mobile optimized dashboards and reports from mobile devices.
8. Publish updates from Power BI App Workspaces to Power BI apps containing these mobile enhancements.
9. Check that Favorites are being used for dashboards and for apps by mobile users.
10. Demonstrate the process of configuring a data alert with notification on a dashboard tile in the Power BI mobile app.

Notifications of Data Alerts Appear Outside the Mobile App

Data alerts configured by users are only visible to those users, and there are not limits on the volume of alerts that can be configured. For example, a user may want to set two alerts for the same dashboard tile to advise of both a high and a low value. Currently, data alert and favorite activity is not stored in the Office 365 audit logs, so it's necessary to engage mobile users on these features to understand adoption levels.

11. Demonstrate the annotate and share feature and related scenarios to mobile users.

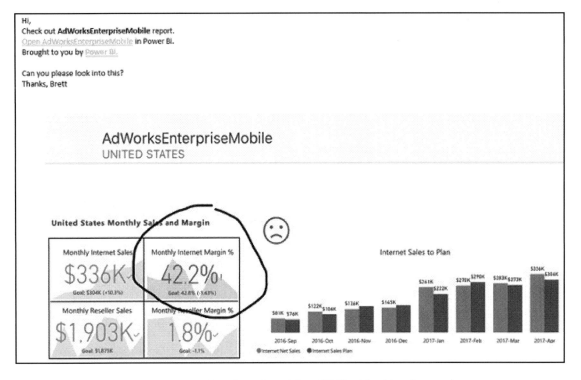

Annotation Added to a Power BI Report in Power BI Mobile and Shared via email

In this example, a report accessed in Power BI mobile is lightly annotated, and a short message is shared with a colleague, requesting further analysis. A link to the report annotated is built into the shared email enabling the recipient to immediately act on the message and optionally share an annotated response that addresses the request.

Enable advanced mobile BI experiences

1. Use the Power BI Windows 10 universal App in meetings and presentations.

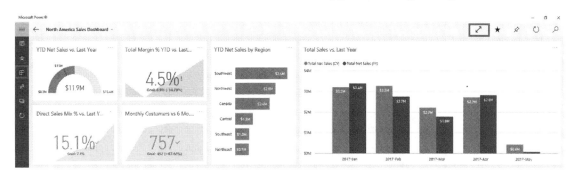

Power BI Windows 10 Universal App

> The Windows 10 universal app supports touch-enabled devices, annotations, and easy navigation controls.

2. Optimize datasets conversational BI with Q & A.

> See the recipe *Preparing your datasets and reports for Q & A Natural Language Queries* in `Chapter 5`, *Creating Power BI Dashboards*, for more details.

> Test common questions and provide users with examples and keywords to better use the feature.

3. Leverage operational features such as scanning barcodes and geo-filtering.

> Integrate a product column containing barcodes into a dataset and set the data category to Barcode.

> Collaborate with frequently traveling stakeholders on the reports they need to reflect their current location.

How it works...

Responsive visualizations

- In this example, the responsive visuals formatting property has been enabled for a clustered column chart.

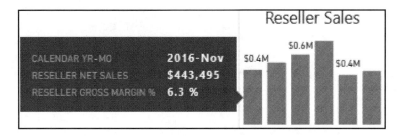

Responsive Formatting Enabled: Clustered Column Chart Dynamically Resizes

- Despite its very small size (148 x 120), the essential data from the visual is still displayed and tooltips provide details.

There's more...

Apple watch synchronization

- Power BI dashboards can be synchronized with the Apple Watch via the Power BI for iOS application.
- The Power BI Apple Watch app comes with the Power BI app for iOS--no extra downloads are required.

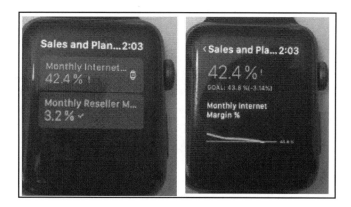

Index Screen (left) and the In-Focus Tile (right) of the Power BI Mobile App on the Apple Watch

- Simply open a dashboard in Power BI for iOS, click on the ellipsis (...) and then click on **Sync with watch**.
- Only card and KPI tiles are supported, but Apple Watch faces can be configured to display one of the Power BI tiles.

SSRS 2016 on-premises via Power BI mobile apps

- SSRS Reports can be accessed and viewed from the Power BI mobile apps.

Navigation Menu in Power BI Mobile with Connection to an SSRS Server

- Tap the global navigation button (three lines next to **Favorites**) and then select the gear icon highlighted in the image.
- The **Settings** menu will then expose a **Connect to Server** option for a report server.
  - Up to five SSRS report server connections can be configured for all devices.

As of this writing, Power BI Report Server supports on-premises Power BI reports in addition to all other report types included in SSRS 2016 and is available as a preview for iOS and Android devices.

Filters on phone reports

- Filters applied to the report, page, and visual level will soon be available in Power BI mobile applications
- This will include the same filtering options available in Power BI, including top N and advanced filtering conditions

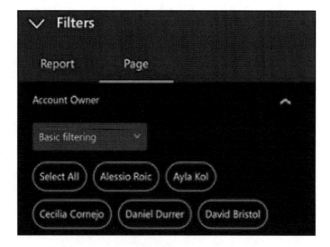

Report Filters in Power BI Mobile

- Reports with filters that are applied at any scope (report, page, or visual) and which use phone layout will be able to interact with filters as they can in Power BI Desktop and the Power BI Service

See also

- SSRS 2016 in the Power BI mobile apps: `http://bit.ly/2noIloX`

13
Integrating Power BI with Other Applications

In this chapter, we will cover the following recipes:

- Integrating Excel and SSRS objects into Power BI solutions
- Migrating a Power Pivot for Excel Data Model to Power BI
- Accessing and analyzing Power BI datasets from Excel
- Building Power BI reports into PowerPoint presentations
- Migrating a Power BI Data Model to SSAS tabular
- Accessing MS Azure hosted services such as Azure Analysis Services from Power BI
- Using Power BI with Microsoft Flow and PowerApps

Introduction

Power BI tools and services--including Power BI Desktop, the Power BI Service, and Power BI Mobile applications--form a modern, robust business intelligence and analytics platform by themselves. Power BI Premium further extends the scalability and deployment options of Power BI, enabling organizations to deliver Power BI content to large groups of users via apps in the Power BI Service, the on-premises Power BI Report Server, embeds within custom applications, or some combination of these distribution methods.

However, many organizations either already have extensive self-service and corporate BI assets and skills in other applications such as Excel, **SQL Server Analysis Services** (**SSAS**), and **SQL Server Reporting Services** (**SSRS**), or are interested in utilizing the unique features of these tools as part of their Power BI solutions. As one example, an organization may choose to migrate all or part of a Power BI dataset built with Power BI Desktop to an IT-managed SSAS model in Visual Studio, develop both SSRS reports and Power BI reports against this model, and consume these different report types from the same Power BI dashboard. Additionally, organizations must evaluate current and future use cases for Excel, such as whether Excel-based queries and data models should be migrated to Power BI datasets and how the Analyze in Excel feature can be best utilized to further augment Power BI and other reporting tools.

The recipes in this chapter highlight new and powerful integration points between Power BI and SSAS, SSRS, Excel, PowerPoint, PowerApps, and Microsoft Flow. This includes migrating a Power BI Desktop file to SQL Server Analysis Services, leveraging DAX as a query language to support custom reports in both SSRS and Excel, and utilizing cube formulas to build template or scorecard report layouts. Additionally, an example is provided of designing an automated workflow with Microsoft Flow to push data from a relational database to a streaming dataset in the Power BI Service, thus delivering real-time visibility to source data changes via common Power BI visualization and data alert capabilities.

Integrating Excel and SSRS objects into Power BI Solutions

Power BI Desktop is the primary report authoring tool for content published to the Power BI Service as well as for Power BI report visuals embedded in custom applications. However, for many organizations a significant portion of existing BI workloads with SSRS and data analysis in Excel must be maintained. In many cases, existing SSRS reports and Excel-based data analysis processes can be migrated to Power BI but Power BI is not intended as a full replacement for all the features and use cases these tools support. The Power BI Service accounts for the need of integrated visibility across Power BI, Excel, and SSRS-based content via scheduled refresh of Excel workbooks and SSRS subscriptions of pinned report items. Additionally, given the common database engine and DAX language of Power BI, Power Pivot for Excel, and SSAS Tabular, BI teams can take full control of reports rendered in SSRS and Excel by authoring custom DAX queries.

This recipe contains two examples of authoring and publishing content from SSRS and Excel to Power BI. In the SSRS report, an existing SSAS Tabular database is used as the data source and a custom DAX query is utilized as the dataset. In the Excel report, an additional custom DAX query is used against the workbook's internal Data Model (formerly Power Pivot). Using DAX as a query language is of course not required to integrate Excel and SSRS objects into Power BI but this approach does have advantages in supporting dashboard tiles and in utilizing a common query language across all three Microsoft BI tools.

Getting ready

1. Confirm that the Excel reporting content uses the Excel Data Model as its data source:
   - Only workbooks with data models can be configured for scheduled refresh in the Power BI Service

2. Identify the data source used by the Excel Data Model and add this source to the on-premise Data Gateway if necessary.

3. Develop and test DAX queries in DAX Studio to be used as the datasets and tables in SSRS and Excel, respectively.

4. Ensure that SSRS is configured for Power BI integration:

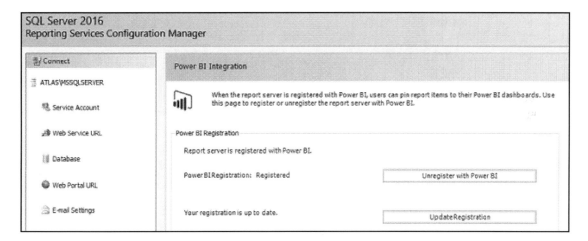

SSRS 2016 Configuration Manager—Power BI Integration

5. The Power BI Integration menu item is at the bottom of the list and includes the Power BI tenant name (ID).

How to do it...

1. Create or identify the App Workspace in the Power BI Service to host the Excel and SSRS report content.
2. Create or identify the dashboards in this App Workspace that will display the Excel and SSRS report content.

SSRS

In this example, a DAX query is used to retrieve 100 customers based on current year sales and to group their purchase activity by calendar month:

1. Create a new Report Server project in Visual Studio or open an existing one.
2. Configure a SSAS Tabular Database as a Shared Data Source for the project:

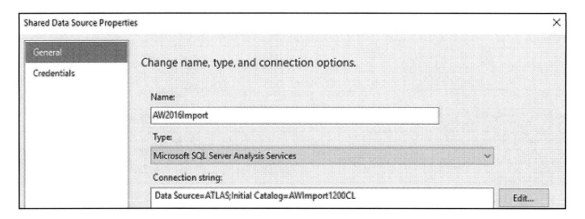

Report Server Project —shared data source Configuration for an SSAS database

3. Right-click on the reports folder, choose to add a new item, select report, and click on **Add**.
4. Rename the new SSRS report and configure its data sources to use the shared SSAS source from step 2.
5. Right-click on the datasets folder for the report and select **Add Dataset**.

6. Choose to embed the data source from step 4 and give the dataset a name:

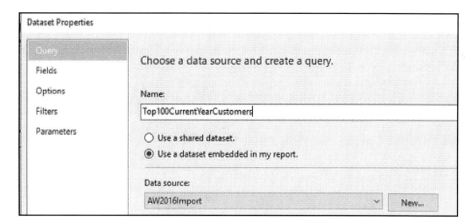

Dataset Configuration for SSRS Reports

7. Click on the **Query Designer** button below the Query window.

8. In **Query Designer**, click on the Command Type DMX icon (data mining symbol) and then select the Design Mode icon:

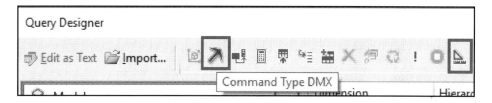

Dataset Query Designer - Switching to DMX Query Designer in Design Mode

A graphical interface with the Fields List, measures, and KPIs is exposed when first opening Query Designer and this can be useful for basic DAX queries. The DMX Design Mode, however, offers the full flexibility of DAX queries including report scoped variables and measures.

9. Paste in the DAX query that was developed and tested in DAX Studio in step 3 of the *Getting ready* section.

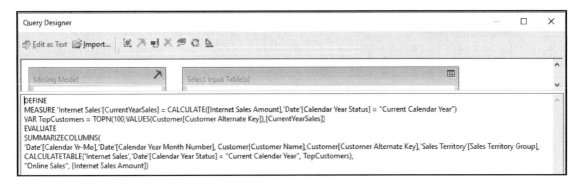

SSRS Dataset DAX Query

In this query, a `CurrentYearSales` measure is defined and then referenced in the `TopCustomers` variable. This variable returns the top 100 customers (based on current year sales) via the `TOPN()` function as a table. The Internet Sales fact table is filtered by both the `TopCustomers` table and the `Current Calendar Year` rows of the date dimension table in `CALCULATETABLE()`. `SUMMARIZECOLUMNS()` selects and groups columns based on this filtered table and applies a single aggregation column (`online sales`) using the Internet Sales Amount measure.

10. Use the dataset to create the SSRS report visuals for pinning. Charts, gauge panels, maps, and images can be pinned from SSRS to Power BI Dashboards.

11. Deploy the SSRS report to a report folder in the SSRS portal and confirm that it renders properly:

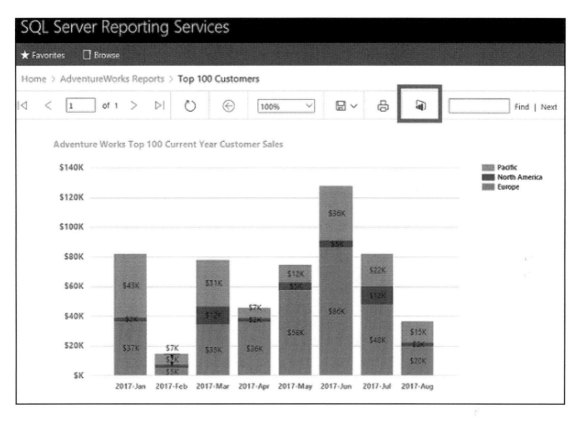

Stacked Column Visual in SSRS 2016 Report based on DAX Query

12. Click on the Power BI Icon and then on the Report chart.

13. Choose the app workspace, the dashboards, and the frequency of updates. Click on **Pin**.

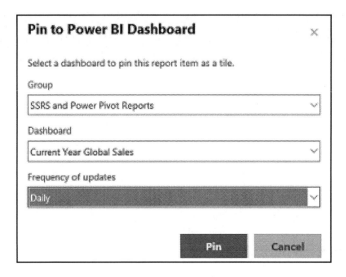

Pin to Power BI from SSRS 2016 Dialog

A **Pin Successful** message will appear, with a link to the dashboard in the Power BI Service.

14. In the SSRS portal, click on the Gear icon and select my subscriptions to confirm the Power BI Dashboard subscription:

	Edit	Report ∧	Description	Status	Type	Folder	Delivery
☐	Edit	Top 100 Customers		Enabled	Standard	/AdventureWorks Reports	Power BI Dashboard

15. In the Power BI service, adjust the size, position, and optionally the title and subtitle of the dashboard tile.
16. Click on the dashboard tile to test that the URL opens the report in the SSRS portal. Set the link to open in a separate tab.

Excel

In this example, two tables containing the top 15 products based on year-to-date and prior year-to-date sales are retrieved into Excel via DAX queries:

1. Open the Excel workbook containing the Data Model.
2. From the **Data** tab, click on **Existing Connections** and select one of the queries used to load the data model. Choose one of the smaller dimension table queries, such as `Currency`.

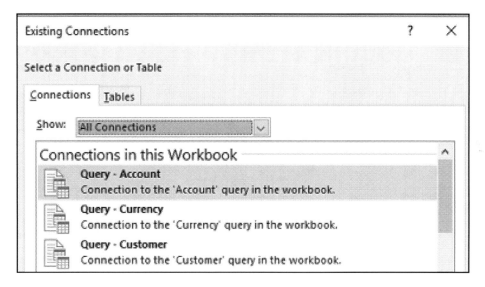

Existing Connections - M Queries used to load the Data Model

3. Click on **Open** in the Existing Connections menu and then select **Table** from the **Import Data** dialog.

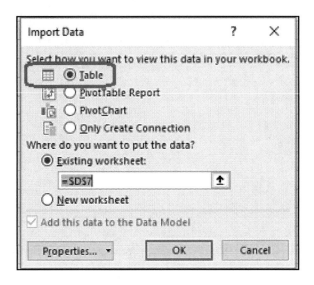

Import Data: The Table option

4. An Excel table reflecting the chosen query will be loaded to a worksheet.

5. Right-click on any cell inside the imported table, and from the **Table** options, select **Edit DAX**:

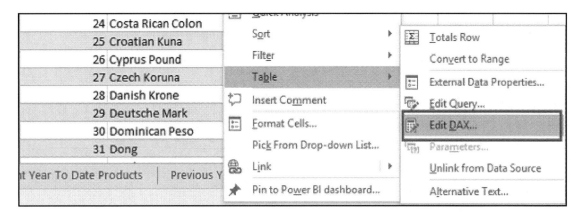

Excel table options - Edit DAX

6. From the **Edit DAX** window, change the **Command Type** drop-down from **Table** to **DAX** and paste in the DAX query:

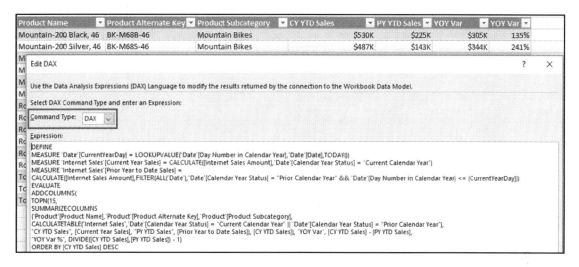

DAX Query to Retrieve the Top 15 Products Based on Current Year to Date Sales

A measure is defined to retrieve the day number of the current year and this is used as a filtering parameter in the definition of the 'Prior Year to Date Sales' local measure. The Internet Sales fact table within the SUMMARIZECOLUMNS() function is filtered to only include the Current Calendar Year and Prior Calendar Year rows. A TOPN() function retrieves 15 product values from this product grouping based on the CY YTD Sales column, which reflects the locally defined Current Year Sales measure. Finally, two additional columns are added via ADDCOLUMNS() to display the variance and variance percentages between the current year-to-date sales and the prior year-to-date sales columns.

7. Copy the Excel table and edit the copied table's query to retrieve the top 15 products based on Prior Year to Date Sales. Revise the second parameter of the TOPN() function to use the PY YTD Sales column.

8. Make any formatting adjustments to the tables such as a custom number format to display sales in thousands.

9. Save the workbook. If available, save a copy to OneDrive for Business or an alternative version history system.

10. In Excel 2016, click on **File**, and from the **Publish** menu, choose the App Workspace in Power BI.

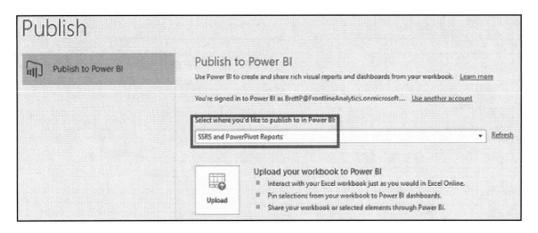

Uploading the Excel Data Model to the Power BI App Workspace

11. Click on **Upload**. An information bar will appear, indicating a successful upload, with a link to the Power BI Service.
12. Open the Power BI Service; navigate to the app workspace containing the published Excel workbook.
13. From the Workbooks menu of the app workspace, select the Schedule Refresh icon under Actions. This will open the settings interface for Workbooks.
14. Associate the workbook with a data gateway, click on **Apply**, and then schedule a data refresh:

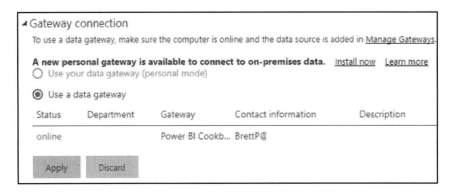

Workbook settings - Gateway connection

15. Select the Workbook to open the report. Select the entire table and then click on **Pin**.

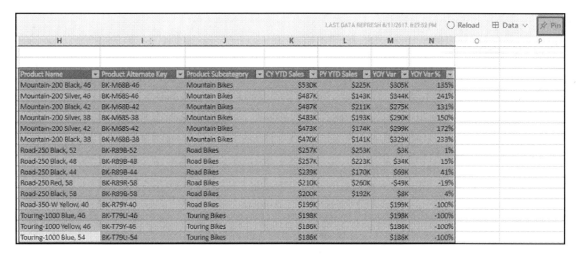

Excel Table in the Published Workbook Selected - Pin to Dashboard is in the top right

16. On the Pin to Dashboard interface, choose the dashboard and click on **Pin**. Pin both Excel tables to the dashboard.

The preview of the tile should include the Excel table name. This is the same table name that's visible within the **Table Tools Design** tab in Excel when the table is selected. Using defined Excel tables is always recommended over ranges of cells.

17. Optionally adjust the title, subtitle, size, and positioning of the Excel tiles relative to the SSRS tile(s):

Power BI Dashboard with SSRS and Excel-based tiles

Very rarely would a plain table of data be used in a dashboard. In most cases, formatted Excel charts and pivot charts would be pinned to the dashboard. The purpose of these examples is not the visualization choices but rather the data retrieval methods with DAX queries. Note that custom DAX queries can be reused across Power BI datasets, Excel Data Models, and SSAS Tabular databases provided these three tools align to a common schema.

There's more...

Power BI, Excel, and SQL Server Reporting Services (SSRS) all offer extensive report authoring capabilities and organizations often already have significant investments with Excel and SSRS. Therefore, common questions are "Should we stop using Excel and SSRS?" and/or "Should we migrate existing Excel and SSRS reports to Power BI?"

Microsoft has been clear that each of these three tools is designed for unique BI workloads and scenarios such that organizations can choose the tool that's best suited for their given projects as well as use multiple report authoring tools within the same solution and overall BI deployment. Power BI is designed for a modern, interactive and rich data exploration experience. Microsoft Excel provides great ad hoc analytical flexibility for small scale, business maintained applications. SQL Server Reporting Services (SSRS), now included with the Power BI Report Server, continues to deliver robust enterprise reporting capabilities with updated paginated report objects suited for operational reporting and distribution features such as subscriptions.

SSRS and Excel use cases

In certain reporting scenarios, a paginated or 'classic' report with a fully configured page and report layout defined in a Visual Studio SSRS project is appropriate. Additionally, for organizations which can only deploy BI on-premises or if certain BI content such as highly sensitive reports must remain on-premises, Power BI Report Server provides a single on-premises solution and portal to include both traditional SSRS reports and optionally Power BI reports as well.

Similarly, although Power BI Desktop supports many of the most commonly used Excel features in addition to many other advantages, the free-form flexibility of spreadsheet formulas for complex 'what-if' scenario modeling across many variables and granular (cell specific) formatting controls makes Excel the proper tool in certain small scale self-service BI scenarios.

SSRS

- Operational reporting workloads in which relatively simple, tabular report documents need to be distributed or made available across groups or teams in a specific file format such as PDF or Excel align well with SSRS.

- Paginated SSRS reports can provide a basic level of user interaction and data visualization via report parameters and charts, but this is not its strength or core use case. Note that SSRS also has a mobile report type and mobile report authoring tool in the Microsoft SQL Server Mobile Report Publisher.

- Power BI supports individual user email subscriptions to reports, but SSRS supports data-driven report subscriptions that apply parameters to a report based on subscriber information, such as Eastern Region or Sales Managers.

 Future improvements to Power BI's report and dashboard subscription capabilities along with greater control over tabular and matrix visuals and Power BI Premium dedicated hardware may position Power BI to assume a greater share of reporting workloads traditionally handled by SSRS.

Microsoft Excel

- Small scale analytical modeling or what if reporting involving variable inputs and changing business logic is generally best performed by Microsoft Excel and the business analysts closest to these needs:
    - Examples of this include budgeting or planning scenario tools and break even or price sensitivity analyses
    - Legacy data processes driven by Excel VBA macros.

- Power BI Desktop supports parameters inputs and combined with DAX and M functions it can be customized to deliver these report types. However, parameters are not supported in the Power BI Service and Power BI Desktop lacks the inherent flexibility of spreadsheet formulas and custom cell-level formatting and conditional logic.

 Power BI's table and matrix visuals now support the most commonly used Excel pivot table features such as showing values (ie metrics) on rows, three separate conditional formatting options (Data Bars, Font Colors, Background Colors), as well as a What if parameter interface. These improvements, combined with training or experience with Power BI Desktop and the many other advantages of Power BI over Excel per Chapter 1, *Configuring Power BI Development Tools*, will likely reduce existing dependencies and user preferences for Excel.

Migrating a Power Pivot for Excel Data Model to Power BI

As Power BI has become more mature as a product and as business users become more comfortable with the platform it's often beneficial to migrate data models (formerly Power Pivot) and M queries from Excel to Power BI. A table of 14 distinct advantages of Power BI over Excel is provided in the *See also* section of the *Configuring Power BI Desktop options and settings* recipe in the first chapter, and includes things like greater capacity (1 GB versus 250 MB) and support for **Row-level Security** (**RLS**). Additionally, from a data management and governance standpoint, it's preferable to consolidate data models to either Power BI and/or SSAS datasets and to limit Excel's role to ad hoc analysis such as pivot tables connected to datasets in the Power BI Service via Analyze in Excel.

In this brief recipe a data model and its source M queries contained in an Excel workbook is migrated to a Power BI dataset via the Import Excel Workbook to Power BI Desktop migration feature. Additional details on the workbook content imported and other options and considerations for Excel to Power BI migrations are included in the *How it works...* and *There's more...* sections.

Getting ready

Analyze the Excel workbook to identify the components that can be imported to Power BI Desktop. For example, a table or range of data in an Excel worksheet will not be imported but tables in the Excel data model will be imported. Similarly, Power View report sheets in Excel and their visuals will be migrated but standard Excel charts, pivot tables, and worksheet formulas and formatting will not be migrated.

In some scenarios it may be necessary to revise the Excel workbook to establish a data source connection and query that will be migrated. Additionally, it may be necessary to re-create Excel-specific report visualizations such as pivot tables and charts with Power BI Desktop report authoring visuals. Excel workbooks which contain a high level of customization such as VBA macros and complex Excel formula logic may require significant modifications to the Excel workbook or to the Power BI Desktop model or some combination of both to support a migration.

How to do it...

1. Save or download the latest Excel Workbook to a secure, accessible network directory.
2. Open a new Power BI Desktop (PBIX) file.
3. From Report View, click **File** and navigate to the Import Excel workbook contents menu item.

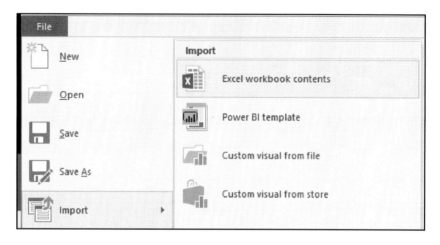

Import Excel Workbook Option in Power BI Desktop

4. Select the Excel file and click **Open** to initiate the Import process. A warning message will appear advising that not all contents of the workbook are included in the import.
5. A migration completion message will appear that breaks out the different items completed. Click **Close**.

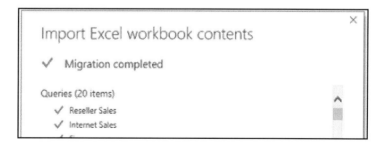

Import Excel Model to Power BI Desktop Migration Poroc

The migration may take a few minutes depending on the size of the data model imported. In this example, a complex data model with 20 queries and over 100 measures was imported from Excel.

6. Save the Power BI Desktop file and use the **Relationships** window to confirm all relationships were imported successfully.
7. Click **Refresh** from the **Home** tab to test that all *M* queries were imported successfully.
8. With essential testing complete, click **Publish** from the **Home** tab and choose an App Workspace for the new dataset.

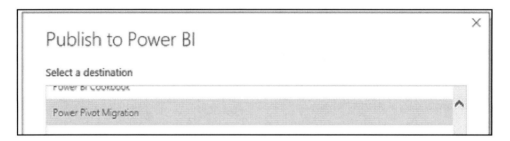

Publishing the Power BI Dataset to an App Workspace from Power BI Desktop

9. Save the PBIX file to OneDrive for Business or an alternative version history system.
10. In the Power BI Service, configure a scheduled refresh on the Power BI dataset.
11. If necessary, create new Power BI reports via Power BI Service Live Connections to the published dataset.

For example, if the Power Pivot for Excel workbook contained several worksheets of pivot tables, pivot charts, and standard Excel charts new Power BI reports containing the same metrics and attributes can be developed as alternatives. With both the data model and the reports completely migrated to Power BI, the Excel workbook can be removed from the Power BI Service or any other refresh and distribution process.

Power BI has now built into its table and matrix visuals the most important features of Excel pivot tables such as rich conditional formatting options, displaying multiple measures on rows, drill up/down hierarchies on rows and columns, controls for subtotals visibility, a stepped or staggered layout, percentage of row/column/totals, and more. These enhancements, along with the powerful cross highlighting capabilities exclusive to Power BI reports, make it feasible and advantageous to migrate most Excel pivot table-based reports to Power BI.

How it works...

Excel items imported

Power BI Desktop imports M queries, data model tables, DAX measures and KPIs, and any power view for Excel sheets.

Workbooks with significant dependencies on items not imported such as Excel formulas, standard Excel tables (not model tables), worksheet range data, standard Excel charts and conditional formatting may need to remain supported in some capacity. For example, a minimum amount of data could be imported to Excel's data model to continue to drive Excel-based reports and this workbook could be uploaded to the Power BI Service and refreshed.

There's more...

Export or upload to Power BI from Excel 2016

Upload Excel Workbook to Power BI

If certain Excel-specific content is needed despite the migration, the Power Pivot for Excel data model can be uploaded to the same App Workspace and a refresh schedule can be configured on this workbook in the Power BI Service.

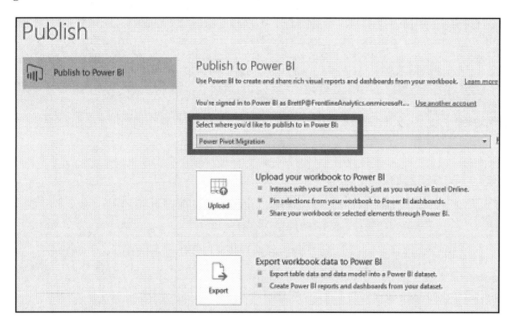

Publish Excel 2016 Workbook with Data Model to Power BI - Upload Option to Maintain Excel Contents

Earlier versions of Excel can be accessed within the Power BI Service via the get data from **File** menu.

An Excel Data Model and its imported Power BI Dataset in the same App Workspace in the Power BI Service

Export Excel Workbook to Power BI

The Export option in Excel 2016 is equivalent to the import migration process to Power BI Desktop from this recipe except that the new dataset is already published to an App Workspace in the Power BI Service.

This approach to migration isn't recommended, however, as you lose the ability to download the PBIX file of the created dataset from the Power BI Service. Importing to Power BI Desktop first, per this recipe, maintains this option.

Accessing and analyzing Power BI datasets from Excel

With a centralized Power BI dataset in the Power BI Service, Power BI Pro users can take full advantage of Excel's familiar user interface as well as advanced data connection methods such as cube formulas and DAX queries to support custom paginated report layouts. Although these Excel reports, like SSRS paginated reports, are only a supplement to the Power BI reports and dashboards in the Power BI Service, they are often useful for scorecard layouts with custom formatting and many measures and columns. In this scenario, an experienced Excel user with deep business knowledge can leverage the performance, scale, and automatic refresh of the published Power BI dataset to create custom, fully formatted Excel reports. Additionally, the Excel report author has the flexibility to apply report-scoped logic on top of the dataset using familiar techniques and these customizations can inform BI teams or dataset owners of existing gaps or needed enhancements.

This recipe contains two examples of accessing and analyzing Power BI datasets in Excel. The first example uses cube formulas and Excel slicers to produce an interactive template report. The second example passes a custom DAX query to the Power BI dataset to support an Excel map. Additional details on cube functions in Excel and new Excel 2016 visuals are included in the supporting sections.

Getting ready

1. Ensure that Power BI Publisher for Excel is installed and that the user has a Power BI Pro license.
2. Confirm that the Power BI Pro user has access to the App Workspace containing the dataset.

How to do it...

Cube formulas

The purpose of this report is to follow a standard, paginated template layout reflecting top metrics by quarter and half year:

1. Open Excel and from the **Power BI Publisher for Excel** tab click on **Connect to Data**.

2. Select the dataset and click on **Connect**:

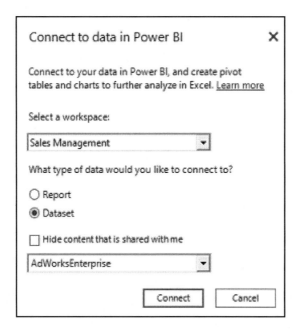

Power BI Publisher for the Excel Connect to Power BI dialog

3. Create a pivot table containing the essential measures, attributes, and filters needed for the report.

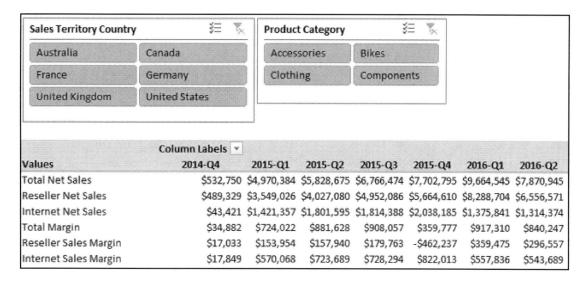

Sales Territory Country		Product Category	
Australia	Canada	Accessories	Bikes
France	Germany	Clothing	Components
United Kingdom	United States		

Values	Column Labels						
	2014-Q4	2015-Q1	2015-Q2	2015-Q3	2015-Q4	2016-Q1	2016-Q2
Total Net Sales	$532,750	$4,970,384	$5,828,675	$6,766,474	$7,702,795	$9,664,545	$7,870,945
Reseller Net Sales	$489,329	$3,549,026	$4,027,080	$4,952,086	$5,664,610	$8,288,704	$6,556,571
Internet Net Sales	$43,421	$1,421,357	$1,801,595	$1,814,388	$2,038,185	$1,375,841	$1,314,374
Total Margin	$34,882	$724,022	$881,628	$908,057	$359,777	$917,310	$840,247
Reseller Sales Margin	$17,033	$153,954	$157,940	$179,763	-$462,237	$359,475	$296,557
Internet Sales Margin	$17,849	$570,068	$723,689	$728,294	$822,013	$557,836	$543,689

Excel Pivot Table with two Slicers based on the Power BI dataset

4. Select the **OLAP Tools** drop-down from the **Analyze** tab and click on **Convert to Formulas**.

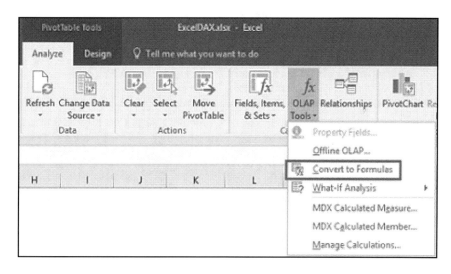

Convert to Cube Formulas Option in the Analyze Tab of Excel 2016

The pivot table will need to be active or selected for the **Analyze** tab to be visible on the toolbar. The pivot table will be converted to Excel formulas such as the following:

```
=CUBEVALUE("Power BI-
AdWorksEnterprise",$C11,H$10,Slicer_Product_Category,Slicer_Sales_T
erritory_Country)
```

In this example, the workbook cell H11 ($9,231,893) references the Total Net Sales measure in cell C11 and the 2016-Q4 dimension value in cell H10 per the preceding code snippet. Note that the two Excel slicer visuals remain connected to each CUBEVALUE() formula cell and thus can be used for filtering the report. The calendar quarters (e.g. '2016-Q4') are converted to CUBEMEMBER() functions with a hard coded reference to a specific value. These formulas must be maintained and/or updated by the Excel report author.

```
=CUBEMEMBER("Power BI - AdWorksEnterprise","[Date].[Calendar Yr-
Qtr].&[2016-Q4]")
```

5. Apply a custom report layout with borders, background colors, titles, spacing, and more as needed for the report. The cube formula cells can be formatted and referenced in standard Excel formulas if necessary.

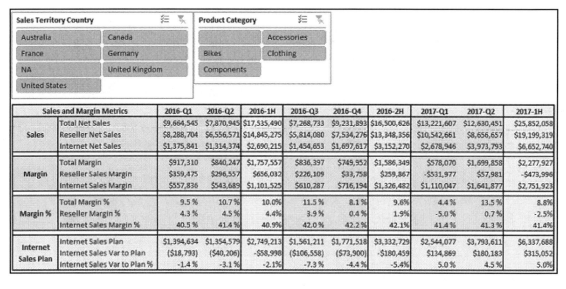

Template Excel Report via Cube Formulas in the Power BI Service Dataset

Standard Excel slicers can be used for filtering, moved to a separate worksheet, or deleted.

In this example, the layout groups four different sets of metrics (Sales, Margin, Margin %, and Internet Sales Plan) and groups quarters into their own half-years. The half-year date attribute is not currently in the dataset and so Excel formulas are used, but even if it were, a cube formula or an Excel formula summing the two quarters would be needed to support the flat table layout. In many scenarios, business users may also need to add columns to the report for certain variance calculations (such as quarter over quarter) not currently available in the dataset.

The Excel report author(s) can quickly learn to further customize the cube formulas such as applying different filters and to support changes to the report including new metrics (rows) and attribute values (columns). Similar to the customization applied to Power BI reports exported as PowerPoint presentations, any significant level of repetitive manual effort or 'alternative definition' implemented locally in Excel should be communicated back to the BI team and dataset owner.

DAX query to Power BI

In this example, a DAX query is passed from an Excel data connection to a dataset in the Power BI Service to support an Excel map visual of Year-to-Date sales by US State:

1. Open Excel and from the Power BI Publisher for **Excel** tab; click on **Connect to Data**.
2. Select the dataset and click on **Connect** as per the previous example for cube formulas. A blank pivot table will be created by default with the dataset fields list on the right.
3. Create a simple pivot table report with one measure and one attribute such as Sales by Product Category.

Row Labels ▾	Internet Net Sales
Accessories	$224,586
Bikes	$17,446,201
Clothing	$105,583
Grand Total	$17,776,370

Excel Pivot Table Based on Power BI Service Dataset

4. Double-click on one the measure cells such as $105,583 to execute a 'drill through' query.

    All columns of the underlying Internet Sales fact table will be retrieved filtered by the Clothing category.

    The number of rows to retrieve can be adjusted in the OLAP Drill Through property in Connection Properties.

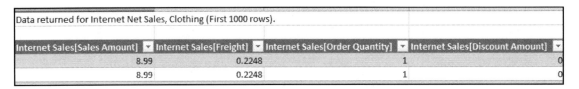

Internet Sales[Sales Amount]	Internet Sales[Freight]	Internet Sales[Order Quantity]	Internet Sales[Discount Amount]
8.99	0.2248	1	0
8.99	0.2248	1	0

Data returned for Internet Net Sales, Clothing (First 1000 rows).

Excel Table Result from Drill Through

Most importantly, Excel creates a separate data connection to the dataset specifically for this table.

5. Select a cell in the Excel table and right-click to expose the **Table** options. Click on **Edit Query...**.

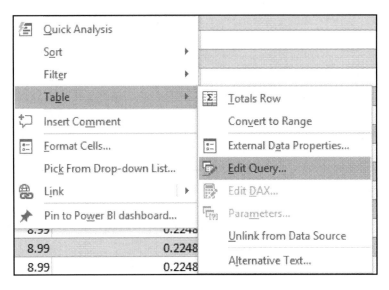

Excel Table Options

6. In the **Command Text** window, enter (or paste) the custom DAX query and click on **OK**.

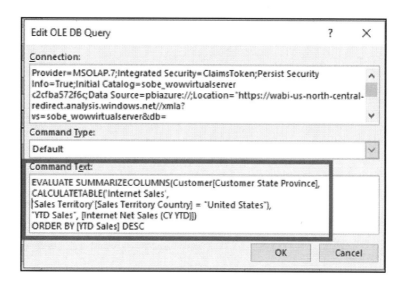

Edit OLE DB Query

Connection:

Provider=MSOLAP.7;Integrated Security=ClaimsToken;Persist Security
Info=True;Initial Catalog=sobe_wowvirtualserver
c2cfba572f6c;Data Source=pbiazure://;Location="https://wabi-us-north-central-
redirect.analysis.windows.net/xmla?
vs=sobe_wowvirtualserver&db=

Command Type:

Default

Command Text:

EVALUATE SUMMARIZECOLUMNS(Customer[Customer State Province],
CALCULATETABLE('Internet Sales',
'Sales Territory'[Sales Territory Country] = "United States"),
"YTD Sales", [Internet Net Sales (CY YTD)])
ORDER BY [YTD Sales] DESC

OK   Cancel

DAX Query pasted from DAX Studio into the Command Text window of the Edit Query dialog

7. If the query is valid, the Excel table will update to return the columns specified in the query.
8. Create an Excel map visual using this table (DAX query) as its data source.

Customer[Customer State Province]	[YTD Sales]
California	$1,686,426
Washington	$715,031
Oregon	$344,105
Florida	$2,398
Wyoming	$2,322
Massachusetts	$2,049
New York	$1,736
Utah	$841
Illinois	$637
Ohio	$182
Kentucky	$120
Texas	$94
Montana	$92
Missouri	$81
Arizona	$33
Georgia	$29
North Carolina	$7
Alabama	$2

Excel table results from the DAX query (left) and Excel maps visual (right)

A custom data label format is applied to the visual to express the values in thousands with one decimal place.

Note that the default pivot table could not be used as the source for this visual or several other new Excel visuals.

How it works...

Cube Formulas

- The CUBEVALUE() and CUBEMEMBER() are the most common cube functions but several others can be used as well.

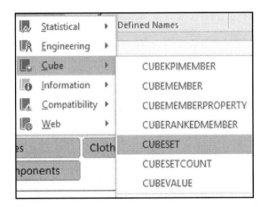

Cube formulas category in formulas tab of Excel 2016

- The Formulas interface in Excel provides information on the arguments for each function.
- In more advanced scenarios, Named Ranges can be assigned to Cube Formulas and optionally other formulas in the report, and then passed into cube formulas as parameters:

```
=CUBEMEMBER(strConn,"[PeriodStart].[Period Start].["&SPUser&"]")
```

In this example, `strConn` is a Named Range in Excel containing the name of the data connection to the Power BI dataset. `PeriodStart` is a column in a disconnected and hidden `PeriodStart` table in the data model and `SPUser` is a named range reflecting a business user's selection on a classic combo box form control in Excel. A separate `CUBEVALUE()` function can reference this `CUBEMEMBER()` function such that user selections in simple Excel controls can be passed via cube functions to the source dataset and reflected in the report.

DAX query data connection

- The initial connection to the Power BI Service dataset creates a cube command type connection

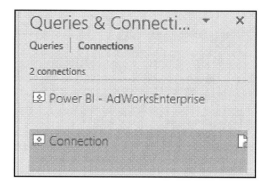

Separate data connection created for query

- The drill-through action creates a separate data connection with a default command type
- By default, the `command text` property for this connection uses an MDX `DRILLTHROUGH` statement, but per the recipe this command text can be easily revised to a DAX query
- As separate data connections they can be refreshed independently or simultaneously via the `Refresh All` command

Although Power BI and SSAS Tabular data models support MDX client queries such as Excel pivot tables, DAX queries and particularly the DAX queries generated by Power BI have a performance advantage. For example, DAX queries can take advantage of variables and "measure fusion" can be used internally by the engine to consolidate the number of queries required when multiple measures are used from the same source table.

There's more...

Sharing and distribution limitations

- Given the external data connection, the uploaded workbook cannot be refreshed in the Power BI Service. Workbooks with data models (Power Pivot) are currently required to schedule refresh in Power BI
- Additionally, several new Excel visuals are not supported in the Power BI Service

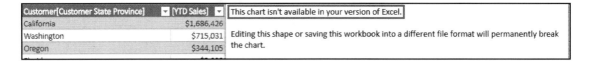

USA Sales Year-to-Date map visual not rendered in the Power BI Service

New Excel visual types table requirement

- Excel 2016 supports several modern visuals such as Treemap, Sunburst, Waterfall and the Map visual used in this recipe

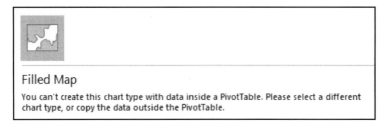

Non-Standard Visual Type not supported via Pivot Table

- However, as per the message in the preceding image for the **Filled Map** visual, pivot tables cannot be used as sources for these new visualizations.
- This implies that DAX queries, either against a published dataset in the Power BI Service or against a local Excel data model, or an alternative data table source such as M queries will be needed to support these visuals.

Building Power BI reports into PowerPoint presentations

Microsoft PowerPoint remains a standard slide presentation application and the integration of data analyses and visualizations from external tools is very commonly an essential component to effective presentation decks. In response to the volume of customer requests, the ability to export Power BI reports as PowerPoint files is currently available as a preview feature. Each page of the Power BI report is converted into an independent PowerPoint slide and the Power BI Service creates a title page based on the report and relevant metadata, such as the last refreshed date. Like most preview features, there are certain current limitations, such as the static nature of the exported file and the visuals supported, but the feature is available to all Power BI users to streamline the creation of presentation slides.

This recipe contains a preparation process to better leverage the Export to PowerPoint feature and to avoid current limitations. Additionally, a sample process is described of a user exporting a Power BI report from a published app and accessing the content in PowerPoint.

Getting ready

- Enable the Export to PowerPoint feature in the Power BI admin portal:

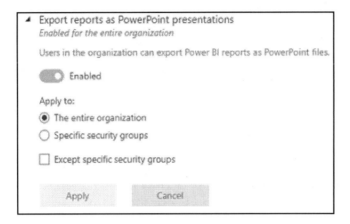

Tenant settings in the Power BI admin portal

- As per the preceding screenshot, the Power BI admin or Office 365 global admin can also limit the feature to specific security groups.

How to do it...

Prepare a report for PowerPoint

1. Identify the Power BI report that will serve as the source of the PowerPoint to be created and its dataset.

Similar to other planning and precautions with highly visible content such as executive dashboards, it's important to obtain knowledge and confidence in the data sources, refresh process, data quality, and ownership. For example, if the source dataset retrieves from multiple sources including ad hoc Excel files and has a history of refresh failures then the report might not be a good candidate for the PowerPoint presentation. A report based on an IT-managed SSAS model that's already been validated and has a clear owner would be a much better choice.

2. If the report contains many pages, count the number of report pages. Currently reports with over 15 pages cannot be exported.

3. Determine whether any report visuals are not supported, including R visuals and custom visuals that have not been certified.

4. Check whether any background images are used in the report visuals or if any custom page sizes have been set.

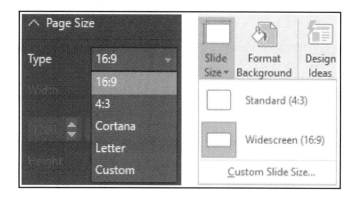

Power BI page size card in the format menu (left) and slide size options in the PowerPoint design menu (right)

 Background images will be cropped with a chart's bounding area and thus it's recommended to remove or avoid background images. Additionally, the exported report pages always result in standard 16:9 PowerPoint slide sizes; they don't reflect custom or non-standard page sizes in the report. Shapes such as rectangles and lines to provide custom groupings, borders, and background colors for visuals may also need to be removed for proper PowerPoint rendering.

5. Based on steps 1 through 4 and initial tests of the export, either apply revisions to the existing report or create a separate report (using the current report as a starting point) that will be dedicated to PowerPoint.

 If an alternative source dataset is needed (from step 1) it may be possible to clone and rebind the report to a separate app workspace either via REST APIs or a new user interface in the Power BI Service. Additionally, and particularly for the purpose of the PowerPoint presentation or meeting, standard and certified custom visuals are usually available as supported alternatives to non-certified custom visuals and R visuals.

Export report to PowerPoint

In this example, the Power BI report is included in a published app that a business user has added as a favorite:

1. The business user accesses the Canada sales app from the list of favorites. Alternatively, the user can also open the app via **Recent** or the **Apps** menu item itself.

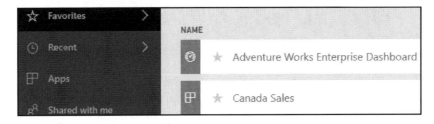

An app containing a report to export in favorites

2. The user opens the report monthly sales to plan, and from the **File** menu, he selects **Export to PowerPoint**.

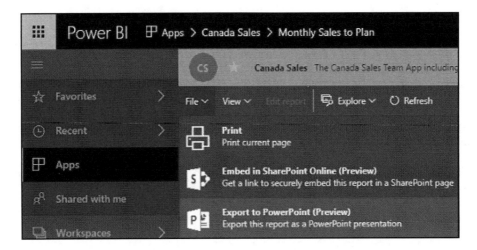

Export to PowerPoint (preview) from the file menu of the monthly sales to plan report

A message will indicate that the export is in progress and may take a few minutes.

Depending on the browser and its download settings, either the file is downloaded to a specific path or the browser displays a message for saving or opening the PowerPoint file.

3. Save the file to a secure network directory path.
4. Open the PowerPoint file and make additional adjustments as needed in PowerPoint.

An exported Power BI report in slide sorter view of Microsoft PowerPoint

A title page is generated automatically by the export process, containing the name of the report and a link to the report in the Power BI Service. The title page also includes a last data refresh and a downloaded at date and time value. Each report page is converted into a slide and the visuals reflect their state when last saved. For example, the user accessing the report via the app will be able to interact with the report in the Power BI Service and apply filter selections but these selections will not be reflected in the exported file.

How it works...

High resolution images and textboxes

- Visuals are converted into high-resolution images but textboxes from the report are retained for editing in PowerPoint.

PowerPoint slide objects—visuals converted to images and textboxes from Power BI report

- The ability to interact with exported report visuals such as filtering and cross-highlighting may be added in the future.

There's more...

Embed Power BI tiles in MS Office

- A third-party add-in is available for integrating Power BI tiles from the Power BI Service into Microsoft Office documents.

Power BI tiles add-in from Devscope

- The offering from Devscope includes an automated Office to Power BI refresh process and supports Word, Outlook, and PowerPoint. Currently the online version is free and a trial version is available for desktop.

See also

- Power BI tiles: `http://www.powerbitiles.com/`

Migrating a Power BI Data Model to SSAS Tabular

Despite the efficient design of a Power BI dataset as well as new and future features of Power BI Premium that support larger datasets and greater performance, many organizations may choose SSAS for its rich and mature corporate BI features, such as source control integration, programmability, and partitions. With the Azure Analysis Services Web Designer, a Power BI dataset (PBIX file) can be migrated to a new SSAS Tabular project and deployed to either an on-premises SSAS server or to an Azure Analysis Services server. Additionally, via tools such as the BISM Normalizer, specific components of a Power BI Desktop model can be added to an existing SSAS Tabular project to promote reusability and consistency.

> *"I think it's fair to say that we're the only vendor that can claim a strong presence in self-service business intelligence with Power BI and corporate business intelligence, which is typically owned and managed by IT, with Analysis Services." - Christian Wade, Senior Program Manager*

In this recipe, an Azure Analysis Services server is created and a Power BI Desktop file is imported to this server. The migrated model is then opened in SQL Server Data Tools for Visual Studio as an analysis services project.

Getting ready

1. Install **SQL Server Data Tools** (**SSDT**) for Visual Studio to create analysis services Project types (`http://bit.ly/2tfN4c5`).
2. Obtain an MS Azure subscription.
3. Confirm that the data source and storage mode of the Power BI Desktop model is supported by the Azure Analysis Services Web Designer.

Currently only import mode models (not `DirectQuery`) can be migrated to Azure Analysis Services. Additionally, only the following four data sources are currently supported: Azure SQL Database, Azure SQL Data Warehouse, Oracle, and Teradata. Similar to Power BI monthly updates, new connectivity options and supported data sources for import from Power BI Desktop will be added to Azure Analysis Services every month.

4. Identify the location of your Power BI Service tenant.

Power BI service tenant location

In the Power BI Service, click on the question mark in the top-right menu and select **About Power BI**.

How to do it...

1. Log in to the the Microsoft Azure Portal and click on **New**.
2. From the list of marketplace categories, choose **Data + Analytics** and then select **Analysis Services**.

3. Create an Azure Analysis Services server by filling in the following required fields of the analysis services blade:

Create Azure Analysis Services Server

For minimal latency, the location selected should match the location of your Power BI tenant from *Getting ready*.

A standard or developer tier Azure Analysis Services instance is required for the import from Power BI Desktop.

4. Click on **Create** and wait for the server to be visible in the Azure portal (usually less than one minute). If pin to dashboard is selected, a Deploying Analysis Services tile will appear.

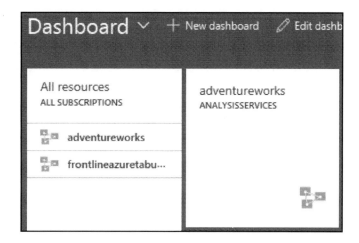

MS Azure Dashboard with Azure Analysis Services Server

 The new server can also be accessed via the analysis services, all resources, and resource groups menu items in the Azure portal. The Azure portal dashboard provides direct access to the server via the server-specific tile and Azure portal dashboards can be customized for different tile sizes and positioning.

5. Open the server created (adventureworks) and then click on **Open** on the Azure Analysis Services Web Designer.

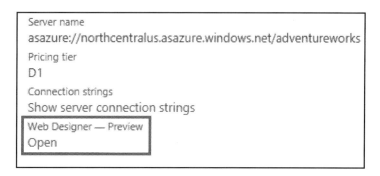

Azure Analysis Services in Azure Portal - Web Designer

Note the server name for accessing this Azure Analysis Services server from other tools, such as Power BI Desktop, Excel, and **SQL Server Management Studio** (**SSMS**).

6. With the server selected, click on **Add** under **Models**.

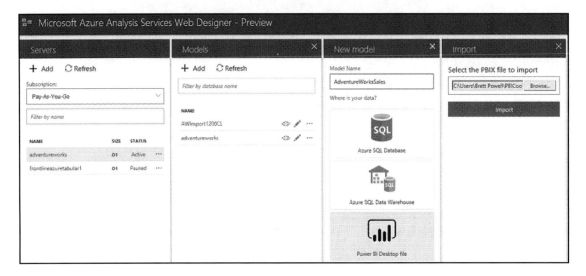

Importing Power BI Desktop Model to Azure Analysis Services Server

7. In the new model menu, select the Power BI Desktop icon and enter a model name (AdventureWorksSales).

8. In the **Import** menu, browse to the source PBIX file and click on **Import** to create an Azure Analysis Services model.

9. Under **Models**, click on the ellipsis (**...**) to expose options to open the model with Visual Studio, Power BI Desktop, or Excel.

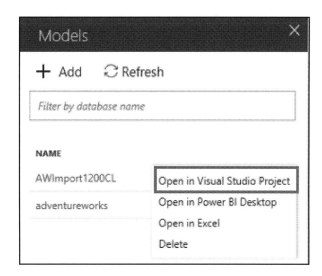

The Analysis Services Web Designer Context Menu

10. Click on **Open in Visual Studio Project** to download a ZIP file named after the model name in Azure Analysis Services. The ZIP file contains a Visual Studio tabular project file (`.smproj`) and the `Model.bim` SSAS Tabular Model file.

11. Open a Visual Studio solution file (`.sln`), and from the **File** menu, click to **Add an Existing Project.** Alternatively, a new solution file can be created by opening the project file (`.smproj`).

12. Navigate to the downloaded tabular project file (`.smproj`) and click on **Open**.

13. Choose the workspace server (either integrated in SSDT or an SSAS instance) and click on **OK**.

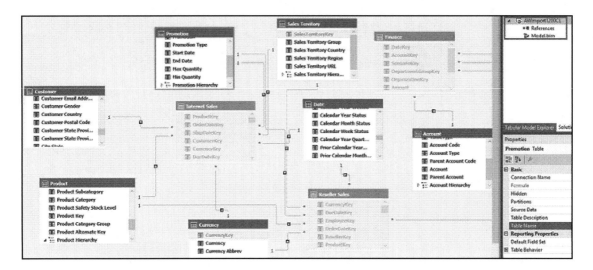

Visual Studio—SSAS tabular project File with Model.bim file open in diagram view

With the project open in Visual Studio, the deployment server project property can be revised just like other SSAS projects. Therefore, the migrated PBIX model can be deployed to an on-premises SSAS server rather than the Azure Analysis Services server and the Azure Analysis Services server could then be paused or deleted. Likewise, existing on-premises SSAS databases could be migrated to the Azure Analysis Services server provided sufficient Azure Analysis Services resources have been provisioned.

How it works...

Azure analysis services pricing and performance

- Azure analysis services instances are priced per hour according to **QPUs** (**Query Processing Units**) and memory. One virtual core is approximately equal to 20 QPUs.
- For example, an S4 instance with 400 QPUs has roughly 20 virtual cores and 100 GB of RAM.

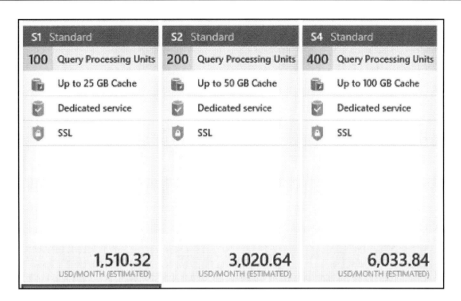

Azure analysis services instance pricing (as of 8/12/2017)

- Currently only SSAS tabular models are supported, not SSAS multidimensional models.
- The largest instance currently available (S9) has 640 QPUs (32 cores) and 400 GB of RAM (after compressed).

Azure Analysis Services servers can be paused and no charges are incurred while servers are paused. Additionally, the pricing tier of a server can be moved up or down a service tier such as from S1 to S3 or vice versa. A server can also be upgraded from lower service tiers such as from development to standard, but servers cannot be downgraded from higher service tiers. Additionally, the ability to scale out Azure Analysis Services servers to support large volumes of concurrent users/queries is planned.

There's more...

Direct import to SQL server data tools

- In addition to the Azure Analysis Services Web Designer approach described in this recipe, it may soon be possible to import a PBIX model directly to SSDT, similar to the **Import from PowerPivot** feature.

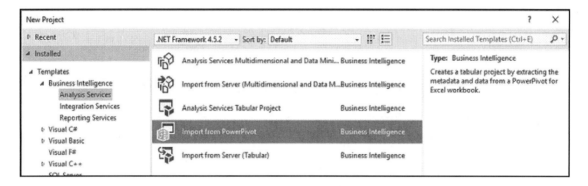

New SSAS project based on PowerPivot for the Excel data model

SSDT and SSMS are still the primary tools for developing and managing SSAS projects, respectively. The Azure Analysis Services Web Designer is intended to enable SSAS developers and managers to quickly and easily get started with Azure AS models, review models, and implementing simple modifications.

See also

- Azure Analysis Services: `https://azure.microsoft.com/en-us/services/analysis-services/`

Accessing MS Azure hosted services such as Azure Analysis Services from Power BI

Given that Power BI and Analysis Services tabular share the same database engine and because Azure Analysis Services eliminates the query latency and infrastructure costs of communication between the Power BI Service and on-premises servers via the on-premises data gateway, organizations may consider migrating their Power BI and SSAS models to Azure Analysis Services per the previous recipe. As one example, the data source for a model such as teradata can remain on-premises but the scheduled or triggered model refresh process of model tables and table partitions would update the Azure-hosted model through the on-premises data gateway. In addition to the other cost and flexibility advantages of the Azure Analysis Services **Platform-as-a-Service (PaaS)** offering, Power BI premium capacities can enable all business users to access the Power BI reports and dashboards built on top of Azure Analysis Services models.

In this brief recipe, an Azure Analysis Services model is accessed as the source for a Power BI report. Additional connectivity details of the Azure Activity Directory and Excel are included in the *There's more...* section.

Getting ready

1. Obtain the Azure Analysis Services server name from the Azure portal.

Resource group (change)	Server name
fronlineazureasresourcegroup	asazure://southcentralus.asazure.windows.net/frontlineazuretabular1
Status	Pricing tier
Active	D1
Location	Connection strings
South Central US	Show server connection strings
Subscription name (change)	Web Designer — Preview
Pay-As-You-Go	Open

Azure Analysis Services resource in the Azure portal

2. If multiple models are on the server, confirm the model name and optionally the perspective to connect to. All models on the Azure Analysis Services Server are also listed in the Azure Portal.

3. Ensure that client libraries (MSOLAP and ADOMD) are updated to the latest version. Azure Analysis Services requires the latest version. See *How it works...* for more details.

How to do it...

1. Open a new Power BI Desktop file and click on **Get Data**.
2. From the **Database** category, select the **SQL Server Analysis Services database**. Click on **Connect**.

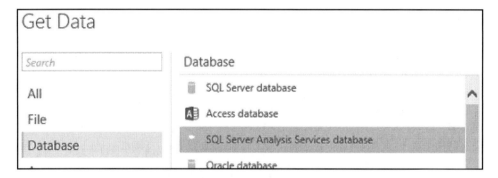

The SSAS data source used both Azure Analysis Services and on-premises analysis services

3. Enter or paste the server name and the database (name of the model).

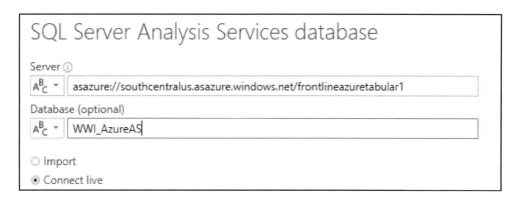

SQL Server Analysis Services database

Server ⓘ

A^B_C ▾ | asazure://southcentralus.asazure.windows.net/frontlineazuretabular1

Database (optional)

A^B_C ▾ | WWI_AzureAS

○ Import

◉ Connect live

Azure SSAS data source configuration in Power BI Desktop

Connect live is the default option and this should represent the vast majority if not all connections as data has already been imported to (or connected from, in the case of SSAS DirectQuery models) the Azure Analysis Services database. Importing data to Power BI Desktop would require its own refresh process, but in certain rare scenarios, a DAX query can retrieve from the Azure AS database and then optionally merge or integrate this data with other data sources in Power BI Desktop.

4. Click on **OK** from the SSAS data source configuration menu.

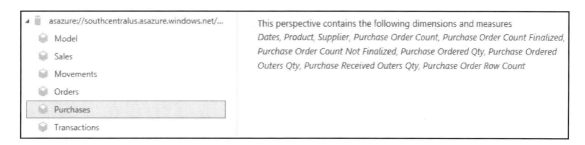

Navigator for SSAS database—perspectives

In this example, the `WWI_AzureAS` model contains five perspectives. Perspectives are effectively views of the data model that make larger models with many fact tables and dimensions more user friendly. For example, a business user could access the purchases perspective and not have to navigate through other measures and tables associated with sales, transactions, and other entities. Power BI Desktop does not currently support Perspectives.

5. In this example, the model is accessed exposing all measures and dimensions that the user has security access to.

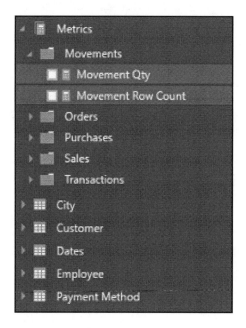

Azure SSAS model field list exposed in Power BI Desktop

Display folders for a dedicated metrics measure group table are used to further simplify and streamline the report authoring experience for business users. Like Perspectives, display folders are currently not supported in Power BI Desktop.

6. Create a Power BI report and publish it to an app workspace in the Power BI Service.

Ensure the app workspace is assigned to a Power BI Premium capacity to allow Power BI free users access the content.

How it works...

Report level measures for live connections to SSAS

- Just like Power BI Desktop reports with live connections to datasets in the Power BI Service, the report author can also create DAX measures specific to the given report with live connections to analysis services.

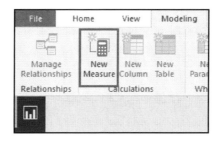

Report level measure icon enabled

This feature enables report authors familiar with DAX to address the unique metric requirements of a report. If the same report level measures are being remade across multiple reports, the BI/IT team responsible for the SSAS model can consider implementing this logic into the model.

Client libraries for Azure Analysis Services

Client applications use MSOLAP, AMO, or ADOMD client libraries to connect to SSAS servers and Azure Analysis Services requires the latest versions of these libraries. Power BI Desktop and Excel install all three client libraries, but depending on the version or frequency of updates, these libraries may not be the latest versions required by Azure Analysis Services. The latest client libraries are also included with SSDT and SSMS installations and can be downloaded from MS Azure documentation per the *See also...* link.

There's more...

Power BI premium DirectQuery and SSAS live connection query limits

- Power BI premium capacities are limited by query per second values for both DirectQuery and SSAS live connections. This applies to both on-premises and cloud connections.
- The current limits are 30, 60, and 120 queries per second for P1, P2, and P3 Power BI premium capacities, respectively.

For Azure Analysis Services connections, the CPU and memory resources would be provisioned through the Azure AS instance (that is, QPUs) but a larger Power BI Premium capacity may still be required in large deployments to avoid the query per second throttle or limit. The Power BI Admin portal's DirectQuery usage metric for Power BI premium capacities will advise how frequently utilization approached its limit for this value in the past week.

See also

- Client libraries for connection to Azure Analysis Services: http://bit.ly/ 2vzLAvO

Using Power BI with Microsoft Flow and PowerApps

Power BI's tools and services are built to derive meaning and insights from data as well as to make those insights accessible to others. While these are both essential functions, Power BI itself doesn't execute business decisions or business user actions based on the data it represents. Additionally, information workers regularly interface with many applications or services and thus to remain productive there's a need to automate workflows and embed logic between Power BI and these applications to streamline business processes. PowerApps and Microsoft Flow, both Office 365 applications and part of the Business Application Platform along with Power BI, serve to address these needs by enabling business users to create custom business applications and workflow processes via graphical user interface tools.

In this recipe an MS Flow is created to support a streaming dataset in the Power BI Service. Specifically, the MS Flow is configured to read from an on-premises SQL Server table every two minutes and push this data into Power BI to provide near real-time visibility and support for data driven alerts and notifications.

Getting ready

- Open PowerApps in Office 365 and configure connections to the Power BI service, data sources, and other services.

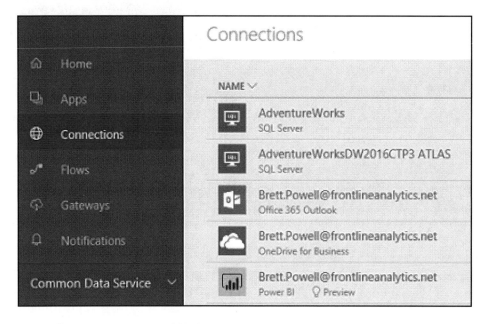

Office 365 PowerApps Menu - Connections

- On the **Gateways** tab confirm that an on-premises data gateway is available.

In this recipe, an on-premises data gateway is used to support a Power BI streaming dataset from an on-premises SQL Server database table via Microsoft Flow. Per previous chapters the same gateway that supports Power BI refresh processes and live connections or DirectQuery models can also be used for PowerApps and MS Flow. Depending on the workloads generated by these different activities and applications, and based on gateway resource monitoring, it may be necessary to isolate PowerApps and MS Flow to a dedicated on-premises gateway or, in the future, add a server to a high availability gateway cluster.

How to do it...

Streaming Power BI dataset via MS Flow

1. Open an app workspace in the Power BI Service and click on the **Create** button in the top menu bar.

Create Options in the Power BI Service

2. Select **Streaming dataset** and choose the API source icon. Click on **Next**.

3. Configure the streaming dataset to align with the columns and data types of the source table.

Streaming dataset configuration—customer service calls

4. Give the dataset a name and enable the **Historic data analysis** setting. Click on **Create**. A Push URL will be provided, as well as a message advising that the dataset schema has been created.

When historical data analysis is enabled, the dataset created is both a streaming dataset and a push dataset. As a push dataset, a database and table for the dataset is created in the Power BI Service allowing Power BI report visuals and functionality to be created from this table. Without historical data analysis enabled (the default), the dataset is only a streaming dataset. Power BI temporarily caches the data but there is no underlying database, and thus the only method for visualizing this data is via the real-time streaming dashboard tile.

5. Click on **Done** in the Power BI Service and then open Microsoft Flow in Office 365.

   All MS Flows are configured either in the Office 365 web application or the MS Flow mobile application.

   See the *There's more...* section for details on PowerApps Studio and the mobile applications for PowerApps and MS Flow.

6. Click on **Create from Blank** in MS Flow and choose the schedule connector as the trigger for the flow. Set a frequency and interval for this connector, such as every 2 minutes, and click on **New Step**.

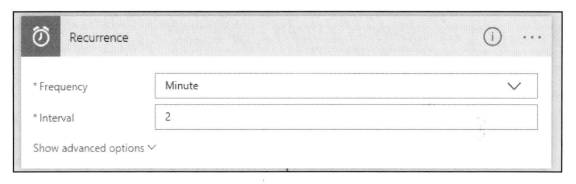

Schedule—recurrence trigger configured to initiate the Ffow

7. Click on **Add an Action** in the **New Step** and search for SQL server. Choose the **SQL Server - Get rows** action.

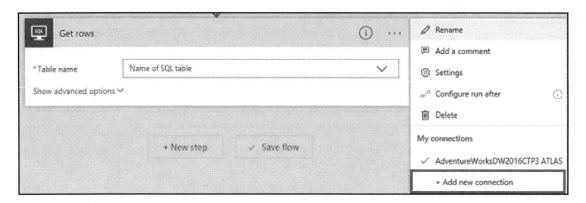

Add a Connection to a SQL Server Database in MS Flow

An existing database connection can be selected if there are multiple or a new connection can be configured

8. Choose the SQL Server table, and then click on **New Step** and add an action.
9. Search for Power BI and select the **Add rows to a dataset** action.

   Specify the Power BI App Workspace and Dataset; a `RealTimeData` table name will be applied automatically.

   Associate the SQL Server table columns with the columns of the Power BI streaming dataset table.

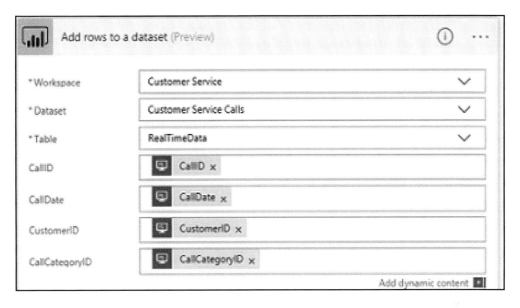

Power BI add rows to a dataset action in MS Flow

10. Click on **Save Flow** and then update the flow with a descriptive name.

Configured and Active MS Flow

The run history of the flow, including successful and unsuccessful executions, is available by clicking on the Flow name from **My Flows**. Additionally, the **My Flows** page specific to the given flow allows for adding owners, viewing connections, opening the Flow in Edit mode, and turning the Flow off.

11. Open a new Power BI Desktop file and click to **Get Data** from the Power BI service. Navigate to the app workspace of the streaming dataset, select the dataset, and click on **Load**.

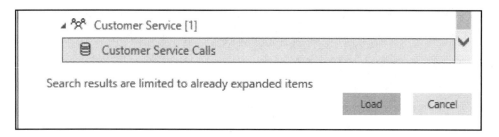

Streaming Dataset Accessed via Live Connection from Power BI Desktop

12. From the **Modeling** tab, click on New **Measure** to add report-level measures to support report visualizations.

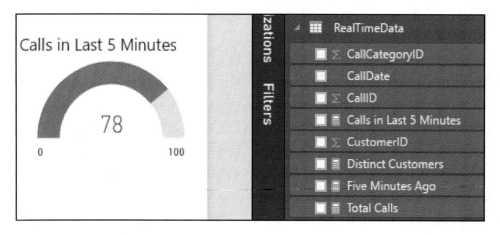

Fields List in Power BI Desktop of the Streaming Dataset in the Power BI Service

Distinct customers, total calls, and the calls in last 5 minutes measure are added to the report:

```
Calls in Last 5 Minutes =
VAR Prior5Mins = NOW() - .003472  Return
CALCULATE(COUNTROWS('RealTimeData'),FILTER(ALL('RealTimeData'),Real
TimeData[CallDate] >= Prior5Mins))
```

For a streaming dataset, it's likely necessary to configure data alerts and notifications in the Power BI Service. Therefore, use card, gauge, or the standard KPI visual in building the report and pin these items to a dashboard to configure the alerts. In this example, rows with date/time values greater than 5 minutes prior to the current date/time are used for a gauge visual (1,440 minutes per day, 5 /1440 = .003472).

13. Publish the report to the Power BI Service and optionally pin the visual(s) to a dashboard and configure alerts.

How it works...

Microsoft Flow

- MS Flows are conceptually similar to the control flow interface for SSIS packages

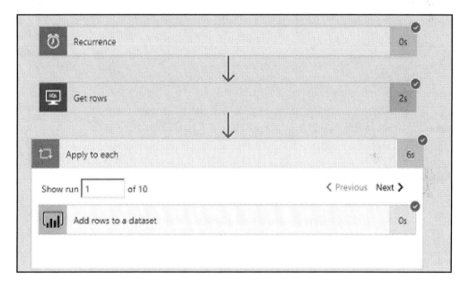

MS Flow in Design Mode - Successful Execution

- MS Flow automatically added an apply to each container for the Power BI action and advises of success per step.

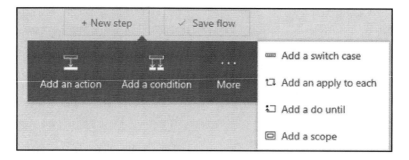

MS Flow in design mode—The more' context menu selected

 Complex logic can be added to MS flows via branching conditions, scopes, and looping constructs. MS Flow is intended for self-service scenarios and business power users. Logic apps is also a cloud-based integration service that can be supported by the on-premises data gateway, but it's more oriented toward developers and enterprise integration scenarios.

There's more...

Write capabilities and MS Flow premium

- Unlike Power BI, which only reads source data, PowerApps and MS Flow can both write or edit source data

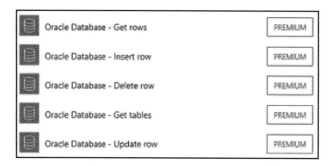

MS Flow actions for Oracle, including insert, delete, and update

- Certain connectors such as Oracle and IBM DB2 are only available in MS Flow premium pricing plans and are not included in MS Flow for Office 365 licenses
- Currently two premium flow plans are available at $5 and $15 per user per month.
- See the linked plan feature table in *See also* for more details

PowerApps Studio and mobile applications

- PowerApps Studio is a dedicated authoring application for Windows devices (version 8.1 or higher)

PowerApps Studio in the Windows Store

- PowerApps can also be developed in the Office 365 web application like Microsoft Flow
- PowerApps Mobile and the MS Flow mobile app are both available for iOS and Android devices

 The MS Flow mobile app supports the same create and edit functionality and activity history details available in the Office 365 web application. PowerApps can be designed for tablet and mobile form factors but will render on desktop as well. The PowerApps mobile application can access and utilize PowerApps but does not create or edit PowerApps.

See also

- MS Flow plan feature matrix: http://bit.ly/2w5oeS7

Index

SQL Server Data Tools (SSDT) 726
SQL Server DBA productivity
    increasing, with Power BI 538, 539, 540, 541,
        542, 543, 544
SQL Server Management Studio (SSMS) 590, 730
SQL Server Reporting Services (SSRS)
    about 27, 52, 219, 287, 596, 690, 703
    integrating 692, 693, 694, 695, 696
    uses cases 702
SQL
    date intelligence columns, adding via 330, 331,
        332
SSAS, dynamic management view (DMV)
    importing 533
SSRS 2016 on-premises
    via Power BI mobile apps 685, 686
SSRS 2016, in Power BI mobile apps
    reference 687
SSRS report items
    pinning 319, 320
staged deployment model
    about 627
    development environment 628, 629, 630
    production environment 630, 631
staging queries
    versus inline queries 120, 121
staging query approach 68
static queries
    converting, into dynamic functions 373, 374,
        375, 376
    local resource usage 377
statistical analysis
    about 481
    DAX calculated tables 488
    embedding, into model 481
    regression report 485, 486
    regression table and measures 482
    residuals table and measures 484
    statistical formulas 487, 488
storage engine 143
subject matter experts (SMEs) 526
subscriptions
    managing 670
SUMMARIZECOLUMNS() function 193
summary to detail example 202

surrogate key date conversion 334

T

table and matrix visuals
    about 227
    blanks, identifying 229, 230
    creating 227
    data bar conditional formatting 234
    matrix visual hierarchies 230
    measures on matrix rows 233
    percent of total formatting 232
    table visual exceptions 227, 228, 229
    URL and mail to email support 232
    working 231
tables
    measures, isolating from 171, 172
    visibility, setting 171
Team Foundation Server (TFS) 626
text columns
    numeric columns, adding from 124
tooltip measures 305

U

United States online Bike Sales Role 414
unnatural hierarchies
    versus natural hierarchies 212
usability
    enhancing, of data model 580
User Acceptance Testing (UAT) 53
user principal name (UPN) 408
user selections
    capturing, with parameter tables 388
    sales plan growth scenarios 389, 390, 391
    scenario-specific measures, creating 392
user-based filtering logic
    manual user clicks, avoiding with 438, 439, 441,
        443
USERNAME()
    versus USERPRINCIPALNAME() 411

V

variable names 605
variable table filters 610
version restore
    in OneDrive for business 632

Made in United States
Orlando, FL
10 May 2023